4th Edition

Business Mathematics

A College Course

Loyce C. Gossage, Ed. D.

Faculty Emeritus
Mt. San Antonio College
Walnut, California

MB65DA
PUBLISHED BY
SOUTH-WESTERN PUBLISHING CO.
CINCINNATI   WEST CHICAGO, IL   CARROLLTON, TX   LIVERMORE, CA

ISBN: 0-538-80034-8

Library of Congress Catalog Card Number: 87-72807

4 5 6 K 3
Printed in the United States of America

Cover Photo: COMSTOCK INC./Mike and Carol Werner

Preface

Business Mathematics—A College Course is designed to provide students with the mathematical skills and concepts that are beneficial in three ways: (1) in the study of other courses, (2) in the pursuit of a successful business career, and (3) in the everyday activity of being a consumer.

A primary objective of this book is to provide students with a firm foundation in mathematical abilities that will enhance their success in the study of principles of accounting. Students who have studied business mathematics enjoy a greater degree of success in the study of principles of accounting because they can transfer the knowledge of how and why certain business computations are made. They are thus able to concentrate on learning the principles underlying accounting entries without undue consideration to the calculations involved. For example, after having learned in business mathematics how to calculate discounting of promissory notes, the student in accounting can concentrate on learning the principles pertaining to the recording of notes and interest. After studying business mathematics, students are better prepared for success in a number of courses in addition to accounting—courses such as data processing, retailing, finance, real estate, insurance, and statistics.

There is no escape from mathematics! Computations such as those illustrated in this text permeate business and consumer activities. The business employee who understands well and can use expertly the subject matter of this text is likely to be promoted much sooner than less knowledgeable fellow employees. Furthermore, any college student, whether employed or not, can become a more intelligent consumer and investor by mastering the topics presented. From a personal-use perspective, this book is more practical and advantageous than a text in mathematics of finance or mathematical analysis.

The textbook and student workbook contain a wealth of problems. There is more than a sufficient quantity of problems in the textbook alone for a two-semester or three-quarter course in business mathematics. For a shorter course of one semester or one or two quarters, the instructor may select those topics needed to meet the objectives of the course. For a short course, almost all of the topics contained in Chapters 7, 8, 12 and 14 should serve as the core around which the course is constructed. Topics from the other chapters should be selected in accordance with the needs of the students to be served.

The sequence of topics is such that knowledge of a subsequent topic is not needed to solve any specific problem. In each section of work, the topic is presented through explanations, illustrations, and examples followed by exercise problems. Any basic term used in the explanation is clearly defined when initially presented. The problems in each exercise are arranged in order of difficulty. Drill problems designed to promote understanding of the topic at hand usually precede the word problems in an exercise. To reinforce learning, review problems are provided at the end of each chapter and answers to odd-numbered problems and all review problems are provided at the back of the book.

The numbers of the review problems at the end of each chapter are keyed to the exercise numbers within the chapter. More specifically, all review problems numbered **1** are similar to the problems found in the first exercise of the chapter, those numbered **2** are similar to those in the second exercise, and so on. If a specific review problem seems quite difficult to solve, the presentation preceding the exercise with the same number as the problem should be restudied.

The first few chapters provide a review of the fundamental operations in mathematics and algebra without presuming that the student has prior knowledge of the topics. Therefore, these chapters may be completely or selectively omitted in advanced classes. The review problems at the end of each of the first few chapters may be used for testing purposes to determine which, if any, of the fundamental topics need to be reviewed.

In this edition, the basic structure of the text remains the same as in the last edition; however, some topics are expanded to reflect current business practices. All word problems have been modernized as needed to make the text more meaningful to students. Instruction in the use of the pocket calculator and detailed explanations for its use in alternate solutions to example problems, both popular additions to the third edition, have been retained. The units of study have been rearranged into eighteen chapters. The chapters are grouped into five logical parts starting with the mathematics applications in preparing a basic foundation for success in the study of business mathematics and progressing through those in starting, operating, analyzing, and investing in a business enterprise. In addition, the chapter on insurance has been expanded to include the topics of life and automobile insurance, and the modified accelerated cost recovery system (MACRS) is presented.

A challenge problem, which is longer and/or more difficult than those in the regular exercises, has been added to each chapter following the review problems. The challenge problems are designed to make the student more aware of the usefulness and importance of business mathematics. The student is placed in a practical personal or business situation that challenges her or him to reach a decision based on computations that apply the concepts studied in the chapter.

Abbreviations and symbols commonly used in business and in mathematics are contained in Appendices A and B respectively. Appendix C lists the tables used in the textbook and the page numbers where they are located.

The workbook consists of problems similar to those in the textbook. As the workbook does not contain any explanations, illustrations, or examples, it should be used only in conjunction with the textbook. Each unit in the workbook is numbered to correspond to the exercise in the textbook that contains similar problems. Each two-page sheet in the workbook may be treated as an individual assignment worth 100 points. Removal of an assignment sheet from the workbook does not jeopardize the solution to any preceding or following problem. To provide a comprehensive review of each chapter, a study guide of objective questions, as well as appropriate problems, follows the chapter problems in the workbook.

The key includes solutions to text problems which not only show the answers to simple drill problems but also the detailed solutions to all word problems. The solutions are set in large type so they may be used to make transparencies. The key also includes solutions to the worksheets in the student workbook and two photo-ready tests (Tests A and B) for each chapter. The test solutions are also included in the key.

The supplemental teaching aids have been expanded in this edition to include over 150 transparency masters, an IBM®[1] computerized test bank, and a computerized version of the study guides. The test bank, *MicroSWAT II*, contains true/false and objective questions and allows instructors to create their own individualized test banks. The questions can be randomly selected or specifically chosen by the instructor. The computerized version of the study guide, *Microcomputer Study Guide,* presents text reinforcement in a flexible format. The student has complete control over the types and order of problems to be solved. The program also has a "pop-up" calculator and on-screen help windows tailored to each problem. The *Microcomputer Study Guide* may be packaged with each student text at your option.

The key, the instructional transparency masters, and *MicroSWAT II* are free to adopters of this textbook.

The author hereby acknowledges the constructive suggestions made by numerous instructors who used previous editions in their classes. Special gratitude is given to Wilford Rosener and Russell Gentry of Mt. San Antonio College.

---

[1]IBM® is a registered trademark of the International Business Machines Corporation. Any reference to the IBM Personal Computer refers to this footnote.

Contents

Contents   vii

Part One

Mathematics Applications in Preparing a Basic Foundation

At the beginning of the twentieth century, having a college degree was not as important for success in business as it is today. At that time, an education in business was usually acquired on the job. Only in the past few decades has the MBA (Master of Business Administration) degree grown to such importance. Having a college degree, even today, is not essential for success in business. Steve Wozniak, cofounder of Apple Computer, Inc., acquired his degree years after earning a fortune. For most people, however, a college degree is the "admission ticket" to management and administrative positions in large businesses.

With or without a college degree, successful business people possess the business mathematical skills presented in this book. As one of the Rothschilds said: "Compound interest is the eighth wonder of the world." To successfully utilize business mathematical calculations, such as for compound interest, one must also understand the basic applications of arithmetic. Therefore, Part One presents a review of the basic mathematical concepts that are the foundation for success in the study of business mathematics.

Chapter 1

Numbers and Fundamental Operations

Objectives

After mastering the material in Chapter 1, you will be able to:

- Understand the meaning of *addend, sum, total, subtrahend, minuend, remainder, multiplier, multiplicand, factors, product, dividend, divisor, quotient, average,* and *arithmetic mean.*
- Read, write, and round whole numbers.
- Add, subtract, multiply, and divide whole numbers.
- Check the accuracy of addition, subtraction, multiplication, and division.
- Calculate arithmetic averages.

Modern information systems, automation, and other technological innovations have contributed greatly to the increasingly complex techniques employed in business and industry. Mathematics plays an important role in these complex procedures. Mathematics is not only a useful tool, it is also a system of thinking. The employee in business who is able to understand symbols and formulas; to interpret significant reports, graphs, and statistics; and, in general, to think in mathematical terms, has a distinct advantage over less capable employees. Mathematics, then, is a very important part of education for employment success.

2

NOTATION AND NUMERATION: HINDU-ARABIC SYSTEM

The writing of numbers is called **notation.** The naming or reading of numbers is called **numeration.** There are many systems of notation and numeration. The two systems most commonly encountered in business situations are the Hindu-Arabic (or decimal system) and the binary system. Some of the basic concepts and operations in the Hindu-Arabic system are considered in this chapter. The binary system is considered in Chapter 6.

The common number system that is most widely used today is the **decimal system.** It is based on the number ten. The word "decimal" is derived from the Latin word *decimus* which means tenth.

The symbols used to represent numbers are called numerals. A **numeral** is a name for a number. Many symbols may be used to represent a particular number. For example, VI, 0110, 4 + 2, 7 − 1, 2 × 3, $\frac{18}{3}$, and 6 are but a few of the ways in which the name or numeral for the number six may be written. The numeral 6, however, is the most common expression for the number six. In the Hindu-Arabic system, the numerals used to write numbers are known as **digits.**

Consider the numeral 333. The digit 3 in the first position on the right indicates three ones; that is, three of whatever is being counted or considered. The digit 3 in the second place from the right designates three groups of ten. In the third place from the right, the digit 3 designates three groups of "ten 10s." In this manner, the **place** the digit occupies determines the value it represents. The value of each place is ten times the value of the place to its right. Any one of the digits can occupy any one of the positions.

The number represented by the digit 4 in 457 is a product. It is the product of four and the place value assigned to the third position on the left, which is one hundred. The number represented by the digit 5 is the product of five and the place value assigned to the second position, which is ten. The 7 represents the product of seven and the place value assigned to the first position, which is one. The complete numeral represents the sum of the three products:

$$457 = (4 \times 100) + (5 \times 10) + (7 \times 1)$$
$$= \quad 400 \quad + \quad 50 \quad + \quad 7$$
$$= \qquad\qquad 457$$

In a whole number, the digit farthest to the right indicates the ones place. In a numeral such as 516.8, the decimal point indicates the starting place. The first digit to the left of the decimal point designates the ones place. The decimal point makes it possible to determine the agreed-on starting place.

In summary, the five basic characteristics of the decimal system are:

1. *Symbols or Digits.* The symbols in use have evolved historically. There are symbols for the numbers one through nine, plus a symbol for the placeholder zero.
2. *Base of Ten.* A finite group of ten symbols is used.
3. *Place Value.* When a digit is shifted one place to the left, its value is increased tenfold. Conversely, when a digit is shifted one place to the right, its value becomes one-tenth of its former value.

4. *Values Designated by the Various Digits are Added.* For example, 368 means $(3 \times 100) + (6 \times 10) + (8 \times 1)$.
5. *Agreed-on Starting Place.* There must be a means of determining which digit occupies the ones place. The digit farthest on the right is understood to be in the ones place in a whole number. The decimal point is used to indicate the ones place when digits are used to show a decimal value smaller than one.

Reading and Writing Numbers

Many companies sell billions of dollars worth of goods and earn millions of dollars annually. A few state governments and the federal government have annual budgets of billions of dollars. The national debt of the United States amounts to trillions of dollars. Thus, as the use of large numbers is becoming increasingly common, people must be able to read, write, and understand them.

To facilitate reading a number, commas are inserted (starting from the right) to separate each group of three digits. Each three-digit group is called a **period;** each period has a name, such as thousands, millions, billions, etc. The ones, tens, and hundreds in each three-digit period, other than units, are read as an individual number followed by the period name. Study the decimal place-value names of each period in Table 1–1.

	trillions			billions			millions			thousands			units		
	hundred trillions	ten trillions	trillions	hundred billions	ten billions	billions	hundred millions	ten millions	millions	hundred thousands	ten thousands	thousands	hundreds	tens	units
A.													1	5	8
B.										3	3	9,	2	4	7
C.								3	1,	5	7	1,	1	1	9
D.				1	0	4,	8	0	1,	0	0	6,	0	2	0
E.		6	0,	0	5	3,	0	0	6,	0	0	0,	8	1	0

Table 1–1 Decimal Place-Value Names

The numerals in Table 1–1 are read as follows:

A. One hundred fifty-eight.
B. Three hundred thirty-nine *thousand,* two hundred forty-seven.

C. Thirty-one *million,* five hundred seventy-one *thousand,* one hundred nineteen.

D. One hundred four *billion,* eight hundred one *million,* six *thousand,* twenty.

E. Sixty *trillion,* fifty-three *billion,* six *million,* eight hundred ten.

Notice in the preceding examples that the hyphen (-) is used for compound numbers, such as fifty-eight. The hyphen is used when the numbers twenty-one through ninety-nine are expressed in compound words.

● Exercise 1–1

A. Read or write the following numbers.

1. 48	**11.** 22,003,060
2. 223	**12.** 800,004,006,005
3. 2,413	**13.** 73,000,025,590,058
4. 42,167	**14.** 30,000,003,000,530
5. 930,930	**15.** 9,000,033,000
6. 6,243,616	**16.** 995,891,000,000,008
7. 80,078,651	**17.** 17,004,046,069
8. 637,639,440	**18.** 9,141,940,625
9. 86,027,065,009	**19.** 7,209,069,961,000
10. 10,053,537,100,400	**20.** 610,024,132

B. Express the following as numerals with commas inserted where applicable.

1. Forty-three

2. Eight hundred twenty-nine

3. Seven thousand, three hundred eighty-three

4. Eighteen thousand, seven hundred thirty-two

5. Eighty thousand, six hundred seventy-four

6. Two hundred forty-five thousand, two hundred one

7. One million, eight hundred twenty-two thousand, two hundred ten

8. One hundred six million, one hundred thousand, five

9. Seven billion, nine million, four thousand, three

10. Thirty-seven trillion, five hundred fifteen million, forty-eight thousand

Rounding Numbers

A number must sometimes be rounded because either the exact number desired cannot be determined or an exact number should not be used.

Follow these rules* to round a whole number:

---

1. Underline the digit in the specified place. This is the place digit.
2. The digit to the immediate right of the place digit is the test digit.
3. If the test digit is 5 or larger, add 1 to the place digit and substitute zeros for all digits to its right.
4. If the test digit is 4 or smaller, substitute zeros for it and all digits to the right.

In rounding 738,620 to the nearest thousand (Example A), the place digit, which occupies the thousands place, is 8. The digit to its right, the test digit, is 6.

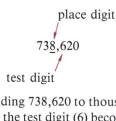

place digit

738,620

test digit

Because the test digit in rounding 738,620 to thousands is 5 or larger, the place digit (8) is increased by 1 and the test digit (6) becomes 0. The 2 also becomes 0, making the rounded number 739,000.

Example A: Round 738,620 to the nearest thousand.

Solution:
738,620   Test digit (6) is 5 or larger.
+1   Place digit (8) is increased by 1,
739,000   and zeros are substituted to its right.

Example B: Round 486,352 to the nearest thousand.

Solution:
486,352   Test digit (3) is 4 or smaller.
   0   Place digit (6) remains unchanged,
486,000   and zeros are substituted to its right.

Example C: Round 56,973,280 to the nearest hundred thousand.

Solution:
56,973,280   Test digit (7) is 5 or larger.
+ 1   Place digit (9) is increased by 1,
57,000,000   and zeros are substituted to its right.

---

*These rules are the ones commonly used in business. There are, however, other more technical rules used by scientists, actuaries, and statisticians for rounding when the part omitted is exactly 5.

Round each of the following to the place indicated.

1. 6,433 to the nearest thousand

2. 80,674 to the nearest thousand

3. 24,520 to the nearest ten thousand

4. 18,222 to the nearest ten thousand

5. 10,610,057 to the nearest hundred thousand

6. 943,751,548 to the nearest ten million

7. 619,628,663 to the nearest million

8. 39,631,404,510 to the nearest ten billion

9. 493,445,576,392,984 to the nearest million

10. 78,299,726,483,741 to the nearest trillion

11. 4,757,550,471,729,899 to the nearest hundred billion

12. 788,170,350,978,673 to the nearest ten trillion

13. 73,181,299,731,866 to the nearest hundred million

14. 404,555,898,845 to the nearest hundred billion

15. 9,651,675,336,812 to the nearest trillion

16. 317,730,958,620,080 to the nearest billion

ADDITION OF WHOLE NUMBERS

Addition is the arithmetic operation of combining numbers to obtain a single expression that is an equivalent quantity. Numbers that are added together are **addends.** The single expression that represents an equivalent quantity is the **sum** or **total.**

Example A: Add the following problem.

Solution:

$$
\begin{array}{r}
7 \\
+\,8 \\
\hline
15 \\
\end{array}
\quad
\begin{array}{l}
\text{addend} \\
\text{addend} \\
\text{total}
\end{array}
$$

As a general rule, only like items (chairs and chairs, ones and ones) should be added together. In the addition of long numerals using pencil and paper, ones are added to ones, tens to tens, hundreds to hundreds, etc., until the total is obtained.

Example B: Add the numerals in this problem.

Solution:
$$\begin{array}{r} \scriptstyle 31 \\ 253 \\ 92 \\ 370 \\ 87 \\ \underline{146} \\ 948 \end{array}$$

Notice in Example B that the sum of the ones column is 18, which means 8 ones and 1 ten. Therefore, the 8 is written in the ones column and the 1 is carried to the tens column. After the 1 is carried, the sum of the tens column is 34, which means 4 tens and 3 hundreds. When the 3 is carried and added to the hundreds column, the total of 948 is obtained and the problem is solved.

Learn to add down a column of digits without hesitation to improve speed and accuracy.

Checking Accuracy

Once the answer to any mathematical problem has been obtained, it should always be checked for accuracy.

The most frequently used method of proving the accuracy of an addition answer is the *reverse-order check*. Changing the order of a set of addends does not change the sum of the addends. For this reason, the accuracy of the sum of a set of numbers may be checked by reversing the order in which the numbers are added. If the digits were added down the first time, add them up the second time. This probably is the best method when using a nonprinting calculator.

Example: Add the following problem. Prove your answer by using the reverse-order check.

Solution:
$$\begin{array}{r} 1,847 \\ 256 \\ 381 \\ 748 \\ \underline{462} \\ 1,847 \end{array}$$

↑ Add up to check accuracy.

▼ Add down to obtain sum.

● Exercise 1–3

Add. Check each answer by adding in reverse order.

1. 882	**2.** 269	**3.** 321	**4.** 287	**5.** 792
285	877	728	149	903
263	542	861	648	488
198	55	287	773	764

Part 1.   Mathematics Applications in Preparing a Basic Foundation

6. 2,198	7. 4,475	8. 2,876	9. 1,689	10. 3,764
8,146	2,342	4,728	846	4,598
3,588	3,215	193	4,478	956
2,175	1,399	1,690	773	3,987
4,600	7,252	785	8,129	708

11. 13,237	12. 52,112	13. 88,441	14. 479,314	15. 4,134,795
37,470	8,158	7,783	88,137	531,885
9,094	66,914	78,613	139,172	2,173,916
18,899	7,019	66,561	83,034	34,083
3,923	96,779	3,617	4,163	361,409
43,776	4,867	93,585	494,173	3,178,442
5,802	5,690	86,123	55,467	67,455

Subtotaling

A method that can be used to simplify a long addition problem consists of obtaining subtotals for portions of the problem and of adding the subtotals together.

Example: Add the following problem by first finding the subtotals.

Solution:

```
749  │
253  │
492  ▼
635   2,129   subtotal
842  │
476  │
548  ▼
728   2,594   subtotal
687  │
282  │
855  ▼
765   2,589   subtotal
      7,312   total
```

● Exercise 1–4

Add these problems by first finding the subtotals.

1. 944	2. 701	3. 8,123	4. 3,175
775	437	7,510	5,952
753	461	1,085	8,106
107	441	6,534	3,843
779	849	9,469	5,495
811	519	3,638	1,745

5. 704	6. 381	7. 8,275	8. 7,036
249	632	2,618	9,849
729	816	1,034	5,075
879	489	6,345	8,732
525	281	9,135	8,147
603	536	1,358	6,153
349	669	6,948	8,373
697	753	4,163	9,257
369	373	9,451	8,093
547	877	4,349	8,307

9. 939	10. 565	11. 8,451	12. 1,972
672	185	2,194	6,766
869	907	3,175	2,139
794	318	1,513	7,157
978	550	4,162	1,924
847	885	4,839	7,302
586	187	7,396	7,670
848	614	4,151	9,937
947	947	9,215	1,926
461	738	4,912	9,150
807	542	1,468	3,941
378	282	1,954	5,706

Horizontal Addition

On business records and reports, numerals are often arranged horizontally. Much time can be saved by adding such numbers horizontally rather than rewriting them vertically and then adding.

Example:

Solution:

Add the numerals in the following problem.

$$7 + 6 + 5 + 8 + 9 + 4 =$$

13 18 26 35 39

If the horizontally arranged numerals to be added contain more than one digit, add like digits to like digits. In other words, add ones to ones, tens to tens, etc., until the addition is complete.

● Exercise 1–5

Add the following problems without taking time to copy the numerals vertically.

1. $7 + 3 + 7 + 9 + 7 + 4 + 8 + 7 + 4 + 8 =$

2. $9 + 6 + 7 + 8 + 6 + 8 + 4 + 9 + 3 + 5 =$

3. $9 + 3 + 5 + 7 + 9 + 8 + 6 + 8 + 4 + 9 =$

4. $8 + 6 + 7 + 4 + 8 + 7 + 9 + 5 + 8 + 6 =$

5. $9 + 8 + 7 + 8 + 9 + 7 + 8 + 9 + 9 + 7 =$

6. $12 + 19 + 27 + 21 + 18 + 29 =$

7. $34 + 35 + 43 + 62 + 37 + 56 =$

8. $309 + 123 + 508 + 671 + 690 + 615 =$

9. $432 + 513 + 726 + 631 + 770 + 349 =$

10. $842 + 6,658 + 4,753 + 728 + 3,627 + 816 =$

Horizontal and Vertical Addition

Many reports in business, such as inventory and production reports, require horizontal and vertical addition. The vertically arranged numbers are added together and the horizontally arranged numbers are added together. Usually the sums of the horizontal rows are added to obtain the **grand total.** The same grand total must be obtained when the sums of the vertical columns are added together.

Example:

Add vertically and horizontally and find the grand total.

Solution:

```
 5 +  7 +  6 = 18
 8 +  4 +  9 = 21
 7 +  3 +  7 = 17
20    14    22 = 56   grand total
```

● Exercise 1-6

Add vertically and horizontally and find the grand total.

A.
  1. $83 + 91 + 80 + 62 + 71 = $ ____
  2. $42 + 11 + 86 + 19 + 61 = $ ____
  3. $46 + 25 + 88 + 59 + 10 = $ ____
  4. $30 + 37 + 52 + 48 + 39 = $ ____
  5. $28 + 89 + 25 + 54 + 15 = $ ____
  6. $69 + 41 + 88 + 41 + 84 = $ ____
  7. $77 + 79 + 86 + 93 + 87$ ____

   (8) (9) (10) (11) (12)   (13)

B.
  1. $92 + 18 + 19 + 81 + 11 = $ ____
  2. $99 + 82 + 81 + 71 + 84 = $ ____
  3. $88 + 97 + 86 + 76 + 51 = $ ____
  4. $84 + 61 + 79 + 92 + 94 = $ ____
  5. $44 + 30 + 78 + 13 + 65 = $ ____
  6. $28 + 17 + 30 + 26 + 85 = $ ____
  7. $15 + 10 + 80 + 52 + 40$ ____

   (8) (9) (10) (11) (12)   (13)

Chapter 1. Numbers and Fundamental Operations

C.

Items Manufactured

	Monday	Tuesday	Wednesday	Thursday	Friday	Saturday	Totals
1.	162	176	169	174	180	–0–	____
2.	147	–0–	150	153	158	149	____
3.	189	178	–0–	182	187	190	____
4.	201	197	198	–0–	195	186	____
5.	–0–	191	186	195	189	193	____
6.	198	203	187	199	–0–	202	____
7.	–0–	187	194	201	196	200	____
8.	153	167	165	157	154	–0–	____
	(9)	(10)	(11)	(12)	(13)	(14)	(15)

SUBTRACTION OF WHOLE NUMBERS

Subtraction is the arithmetic operation of deducting one number from another. The number that is deducted is the **subtrahend.** The number from which the subtrahend is deducted is the **minuend.** The number obtained when the subtrahend is deducted from the minuend is the **difference** or **remainder.**

When subtracting, ones are deducted from ones, tens from tens, hundreds from hundreds, etc. If any digit in the subtrahend is larger than the digit occupying the same place in the minuend, the digit in the minuend is increased by 10. This is accomplished by "borrowing" 1 from the first nonzero digit on the left. In the example below, the 8 is not subtracted from the 7 until 1 is borrowed from the 6 and the 0 is changed to 9. (Notice that $590 + 17 = 607$.) The subtraction is then completed by taking the 8 from the 17 (ones), the 4 from the 9 (tens), and the 2 from the 5 (hundreds).

Example: Subtract 248 from 607.

Solution:

$$
\begin{array}{r}
\overset{5\,9}{\underset{1}{6}}07 \\
\underline{248} \\
359
\end{array}
$$
  | minuend
  | subtrahend
  | difference (or remainder)

Checking Accuracy

The most popular method of checking the accuracy of the difference obtained in a subtraction problem is simply to add the difference to the subtrahend. The sum thus obtained will equal the minuend if the answer is correct.

Example: Subtract and check the accuracy of the difference by adding.

Solution:

Add:
$$
\begin{array}{r}
598 \\
247 \\
\underline{351}
\end{array}
$$
  minuend
  subtrahend
  difference

Check: $598 =$ minuend

Part 1. Mathematics Applications in Preparing a Basic Foundation

There is actually no need to write the check numeral. The easiest way to use this method is merely to "add up." The difference added to the subtrahend must equal the minuend.

Subtract and check the differences by adding.

1. 743	**2.** 6,838	**3.** 58,355	**4.** 637,859	**5.** 9,251,817
615	3,201	36,876	218,147	6,256,267
6. 907	**7.** 3,982	**8.** 90,548	**9.** 958,627	**10.** 3,138,743
634	1,014	57,080	725,191	121,965
11. 735	**12.** 8,753	**13.** 70,357	**14.** 280,786	**15.** 4,498,826
265	6,937	40,456	97,617	3,200,131
16. 767	**17.** 9,151	**18.** 82,103	**19.** 309,085	**20.** 9,745,387
289	7,596	76,590	89,048	9,102,303

Horizontal Subtraction

At times horizontally arranged numerals on business forms and records must be subtracted. If a calculator is not available, don't take time to rearrange the numerals. Subtract ones from ones, tens from tens, and so forth, until the problem is solved.

When the differences are found between the numerals in two vertical columns, accuracy can be checked by adding the columns vertically and then subtracting the total of the subtrahend column from the total of the minuend column. The difference in the sums of these two columns should equal the total of the differences. The example below illustrates horizontal subtraction.

Example:

Solution:

Subtract the numerals in the columns horizontally and then add the columns vertically.

Minuends		Subtrahends		Differences
67	—	51	=	16
79	—	36	=	43
86	—	51	=	35
45	—	24	=	21
98	—	62	=	36
375		224		151

Chapter 1. Numbers and Fundamental Operations

- Exercise 1–8

Subtract the numerals in the columns horizontally and then add the columns vertically.

A.
1. $8,547 - 6,231 =$ _____
2. $4,768 - 3,892 =$ _____
3. $6,287 - 5,375 =$ _____
4. $3,456 - 1,082 =$ _____
5. $9,878 - 4,259 =$ _____
6. $7,045 - 2,089 =$ _____
7. $\underline{5,272} - \underline{\ \ 975} =$ _____

    (8)   (9)   (10)

B.
1. $4,356 - 2,026 =$ _____
2. $7,923 - 5,709 =$ _____
3. $9,735 - 3,456 =$ _____
4. $8,639 - 2,756 =$ _____
5. $6,985 - 5,439 =$ _____
6. $5,667 - 4,357 =$ _____
7. $\underline{9,080} - \underline{3,489} =$ _____

    (8)   (9)   (10)

C. Determine the amount of increase or decrease in units produced by the employees listed. The total of the Month Before Last column, plus the total of the Increase column, minus the total of the Decrease column must equal the total of the Last Month column.

		Units Produced		Amount of Increase	Amount of Decrease
Employees	Month Before Last	Last Month			
1. Anderson, J.	10,105	9,613		_____	_____
2. Crisp, M.	8,872	9,859		_____	_____
3. Duncan, W.	9,269	11,243		_____	_____
4. Hicks, A.	11,788	12,752		_____	_____
5. Jensen, J.	9,846	8,926		_____	_____
6. Kelley, B.	10,100	8,138		_____	_____
7. Miller, E.	8,986	10,451		_____	_____
8. Olson, G.	12,572	12,364		_____	_____
9. Schwartz, A.	9,873	9,278		_____	_____
10. Vasquez, J.	9,325	11,125		_____	_____
Totals	_____	_____		_____	_____
	(11)	(12)		(13)	(14)

MULTIPLICATION OF WHOLE NUMBERS

Multiplication is the mathematical operation that is a shortcut method of adding a number to itself a specific number of times. For example, in the multiplication of $4 \times 5 = 20$, the correct answer can be obtained by thinking $5 + 5 + 5 + 5 = 20$. Thus, multiplication is based on addition, which is based on counting. Multiplying is generally much faster than adding a group of equal addends.

The number by which another number is multiplied is the **multiplier.** The number that is multiplied by the multiplier is the **multiplicand.** The number resulting from the multiplication is the **product.** The numbers or symbols in a mathematics problem that are multiplied together are **factors.** The number obtained when the multiplicand is multiplied by one of the digits in a multidigit multiplier is a **partial product.**

Example:

Multiply 56 × 32.

Solution:

56	multiplicand	
32	multiplier	} factors
112	partial product	
168	partial product	
1,792	product	

Checking Accuracy

The most popular methods of checking the accuracy of a product are (1) reversing the factors, and (2) dividing the product by a factor. Learn to use both of these methods. One of these methods should be used to check accuracy when a display calculator is being used.

Reversing the Factors. Reversing the order of the multiplicand and the multiplier is the most popular method of checking the accuracy of a product. The product obtained when the factors are reversed and multiplied should be equal to the product obtained in the original problem.

Example:

Multiply 56 × 32 and check.

Solution:

Problem:	**Check:**
56	32
32	56
112	192
168	160
1,792	1,792

● Exercise 1–9

Multiply and check each product by reversing the factors.

1. 381	**2.** 275	**3.** 698	**4.** 457	**5.** 827
43	65	71	28	109
6. 403	**7.** 322	**8.** 7,500	**9.** 7,809	**10.** 2,134
87	406	7,040	9,060	698
11. 2,152	**12.** 3,983	**13.** 5,436	**14.** 7,304	**15.** 6,385
427	289	608	503	1,437

Dividing the Product by a Factor. When the product of a multiplication is divided by one of the factors, the resulting answer, the quotient, should equal the other factor. The multiplier should be used as the divisor because while dividing in the conventional manner, you multiply by the digits in the multiplicand.

Example: Multiply 75 × 43 and check.

Solution:

Problem:	**Check:**
75	75
43	43)3,225
225	3 01
3 00	215
3,225	215

● Exercise 1–10

Multiply and check each product by dividing it by the multiplier.

1. 987	**2.** 465	**3.** 621	**4.** 846	**5.** 462
54	96	37	79	143

6. 389	**7.** 2,389	**8.** 7,292	**9.** 5,469	**10.** 9,829
407	375	524	697	468

11. 65,251	**12.** 46,264	**13.** 99,099	**14.** 52,769	**15.** 84,605
569	427	5,032	3,681	8,506

Multiplication by 10 and by Multiples of 10

When a digit in a number is moved one place to the left, its value is increased tenfold. For this reason, multiplying by 10 and by multiples of 10 may be accomplished simply by appending the appropriate number of zeros to the right of the number. For example, 8 × 10 becomes 80; 8 × 100 becomes 800; and 8 × 1,000 becomes 8,000.

As an extension of this, an easy way to multiply when either or both factors end in one or more zeros is to multiply the two factors while ignoring the ending zeros and then to append the total number of zeros to the right.

Example: Multiply 250 by 300.

Solution: **Think:** 25 × 3 = 75; append three zeros.

$$250 \times 300 = 75,000$$

● Exercise 1–11

Multiply by using short methods to find the product in each of the following problems.

1. 213 × 30   **3.** 648 × 3,000   **5.** 260 × 600

2. 302 × 700   **4.** 130 × 80   **6.** 3,200 × 500

7. 3,710 × 9,000	**12.** 4,800 × 60	**17.** 5,680 × 4,000
8. 5,200 × 70	**13.** 4,830 × 5,000	**18.** 6,500 × 50
9. 6,500 × 6,000	**14.** 3,440 × 400	**19.** 89,100 × 8,000
10. 6,405 × 800	**15.** 3,812 × 7,000	**20.** 96,000 × 900
11. 9,000 × 90	**16.** 7,560 × 300	

DIVISION OF WHOLE NUMBERS

Division is the basic arithmetic operation that is used to determine how many times one number is contained in another number. Thus, division is just the reverse of multiplication.

The number by which another number is divided is the **divisor.** The number into which the divisor is divided is the **dividend.** The number resulting from the division of the dividend by the divisor is the **quotient.** The final undivided amount after dividing is the **remainder.** Of course, when the division is completed correctly, the remainder must be smaller than the divisor.

Example: Divide 437 by 7.

Solution:

$$
\begin{array}{r}
62 \\
7{\overline{\smash{\big)}\,437}} \\
\underline{42} \\
17 \\
\underline{14} \\
3
\end{array}
$$

quotient
dividend

remainder

divisor

Checking Accuracy

In division, as in the other fundamental operations, the accuracy of the solution should be checked. This may be done by multiplying the factors.

We have said that division is the inverse of multiplication. This is the basis for checking the accuracy of a quotient by multiplying the factors. The quotient is used as one factor and the divisor is used as the other. If there is no remainder in the division problem, the product of these two factors must equal the dividend. When there is a remainder, the remainder is added to the product. The result must equal the dividend. This procedure is recommended when a display calculator is being used. It is summarized in the following equation:

$$Quotient \times Divisor + Remainder = Dividend$$

Example: Divide 31,625 by 75 and check by multiplying the factors.

Solution:

Problem:	Check:	
421	421	quotient
75)31,625	× 75	divisor
30 0	2,105	
1 62	2,9 47	
1 50	3 1,575	
125	+ 50	remainder
75	3 1,625	
50		

● Exercise 1–12

Divide and check each quotient by multiplying the factors.

1. 18)66,378
2. 27)75,816
3. 36)181,445
4. 49)279,496
5. 54)580,354

6. 65)758,729
7. 271)2,729,401
8. 71)761,065
9. 83)849,479
10. 362)4,636,894

11. 453)7,805,279
12. 1,294)9,537,977
13. 492)1,064,448
14. 374)8,253,806
15. 1,605)98,813,478

Averages

An **average** is the numerical result obtained by dividing the sum of two or more values by the number of values in the set. It is commonly called the **arithmetic mean**. An average, then, is a single number that represents each of the numbers in a set of numbers. The use of averages has wide application in business affairs, such as in the computation of average prices, average sales, average costs, average inventories and the like.

Example: Find the average of these numbers: 9, 11, 8, 12, 7.

Solution: Find the sum of the numbers.

$$
\left.\begin{array}{c} 9 \\ 11 \\ 8 \\ 12 \\ 7 \\ \hline 47 \end{array}\right\} \text{5 values in the set}
$$

Divide by the number of values in the set.

$$47 \div 5 = 9\tfrac{2}{5} \text{ average}$$

● Exercise 1–13

Find the average for each of the following sets of numbers.

1. 89, 67, 54, 87, 84, 79, 93

2. 874, 732, 416, 804, 728

3. 837, 724, 632, 806, 849, 784, 951

4. 7,873; 9,272; 8,730; 9,008; 5,584; 8,253

5. 13,538; 12,458; 11,826; 14,658; 10,989

6. A machine operator produced 542 parts on Monday, 567 on Tuesday, 639 on Wednesday, 659 on Thursday, and 683 on Friday. How many parts were produced on the average each day?

7. Maintenance costs in a certain factory over a period of years were as follows: $195,817; $238,427; $256,115; $298,382; $278,322; $311,782. What was the average yearly maintenance cost?

8. One machine can produce 4,000 parts in an eight-hour working day. How many similar machines will be needed to produce 240,000 parts in five days?

9. A manufacturer sold 38,564 electric motors during the first quarter of the year, 46,835 during the second quarter, 37,417 during the third quarter, and 52,956 during the fourth quarter. What is the average number of electric motors the manufacturer sold each month during this period?

10. A local dairy sold 241,479 gallons of milk during a seven-day period last year. During the corresponding period this year, the dairy sold 317,499 gallons of milk. How much is the average daily gain in sales?

REVIEW PROBLEMS

Solve these problems. The problems under a specific number are similar to those contained in the exercise in this chapter with the same last number. Thus, problems 2a and 2b are similar to those in Exercise 1–2; 6a and 6b, to those in Exercise 1–6. If you have difficulty solving any problem, study the appropriate section in this chapter. This numbering sequence for review problems is followed throughout the book.

1. Express the following as numerals with commas inserted.

   a. Seventy-one billion, four hundred thousand, nine hundred thirty-five

   b. Forty-three million, two hundred ninety-two thousand

2. Round each of the following to the place indicated.

   a. 27,809 to the nearest thousand

   b. 93,544,932 to the nearest hundred thousand

3. Add. Check each answer by adding in reverse order.

a. 24,348	**b.** 48,781	**c.** 749,143	**d.** 4,341,957
48,581	8,773	74,837	315,568
10,105	67,813	319,712	3,713,196
99,900	87,615	37,804	47,305
4,034	39,858	7,706	176,049
54,887	78,213	584,389	5,781,242
6,913	6,731	46,575	76,567

4. Add these problems by first finding the subtotals.

a. 815	**b.** 492
350	743
830	927
980	590
636	392
714	647
450	770
708	864
470	484
658	988

5. Add the following problems without taking time to copy the numerals vertically.

a. $9 + 5 + 7 + 8 + 6 + 4 + 7 =$

b. $8 + 9 + 6 + 5 + 9 + 7 + 8 =$

c. $23 + 36 + 54 + 73 + 47 + 65 =$

d. $753 + 625 + 538 + 852 + 790 =$

6. Add vertically and horizontally and find the grand total.

a. $21 + 39 + 18 + 47 + 54 =$ _____ **l.** $87 + 53 + 66 + 76 + 55 =$ _____

b. $38 + 22 + 69 + 71 + 53 =$ _____ **m.** $43 + 16 + 12 + 10 + 61 =$ _____

c. $64 + 52 + 77 + 95 + 17 =$ _____ **n.** $43 + 82 + 29 + 73 + 83 =$ _____

d. $40 + 73 + 25 + 45 + 51 =$ _____ **o.** $21 + 37 + 99 + 12 + 51 =$ _____

e. $\underline{96} + \underline{79} + \underline{75} + \underline{69} + \underline{36} =$ _____ **p.** $\underline{34} + \underline{10} + \underline{50} + \underline{11} + \underline{34} =$ _____
   $\_ + \_ + \_ + \_ + \_ =$ ___ $\_ + \_ + \_ + \_ + \_ =$ ___
   (f) (g) (h) (i) (j) (k)   (q) (r) (s) (t) (u) (v)

7. Subtract and check the differences by adding.

a. 67,055	**b.** 61,517	**c.** 57,383	**d.** 96,005
27,393	39,024	23,002	44,424

8. Subtract the numerals in the columns horizontally and then add the columns vertically.

a. $6,020 - 1,826 =$ _____

b. $7,212 - 2,928 =$ _____

c. $9,405 - 7,293 =$ _____
d. $6,638 - 2,936 =$ _____
e. $8,385 - 6,198 =$ _____
f. $19,680 - 9,839 =$ _____
g. $3,789 - 2,850 =$ _____

_____ − _____ = _____
(h)   (i)   (j)

9. Multiply and check each product by reversing the factors.

a. 709	b. 568	c. 938	d. 8,910
82	39	210	745

10. Multiply and check each product by dividing it by the multiplier.

a. 732	b. 957	c. 573	d. 8,303
48	79	256	635

11. Multiply by using short methods to find the product in each of the following problems.

a. 324×40 c. $4,820 \times 8,000$ e. $8,670 \times 6,000$

b. $4,300 \times 600$ d. $6,300 \times 900$ f. $90,200 \times 70$

12. Divide and check each quotient by multiplying the factors.

a. $65\overline{)690,465}$ c. $84\overline{)916,380}$

b. $397\overline{)9,648,088}$ d. $182\overline{)7,335,510}$

13. Find the average for each of the following sets of numbers.

a. 90, 78, 65, 98, 95, 80, 104

b. 948; 835; 743; 917; 1,062

c. 9,884; 10,383; 9,841; 10,119; 6,695; 9,364

d. 24,649; 23,569; 22,937; 25,769

CHALLENGE PROBLEM

The treasurer of a local union reported the local's treasury balance on January 1 was $50,168. During the year, monthly dues of $25 were collected from 1,492 members. Each month, the local forwards $5 of each member's dues to the union's national headquarters and keeps the balance. From the treasury, the local paid $80,000 to its business manager, $60,000 to its economist, $50,000 to its office manager, $9,000 a month to other employees, and $3,000 a month for office rent. Miscellaneous expenses totaled $12,144. **(a)** What balance should be in the treasury at the end of the year? **(b)** The increase in the treasury's balance amounted to how much per member?

Chapter 2

Introduction to Algebra and the Pocket Calculator

Objectives

After mastering the material in Chapter 2, you will be able to:

- Add, subtract, multiply, and divide signed numbers.
- Understand the commutative, associative, and distributive laws of mathematics.
- Solve equations that contain one unknown.
- Use a pocket calculator to add, subtract, multiply, and divide.
- Use equations to solve word problems.

The study of mathematics beyond arithmetic usually requires studying elements of algebra. Algebraic principles and procedures are not essential to solve correctly all of the mathematical problems that arise in business. However, many solutions to business problems are based on equations and formulas derived from algebra and higher mathematics. The popular formula for computing simple interest *(I=PRT)* is a good example of how algebra is used in business.

Although the symbols used in algebra to indicate the four fundamental operations are identical to those used in arithmetic, algebra differs from arithmetic in many ways. One basic difference is that algebra uses letters and other symbols as well as numerals to represent numbers. Often the letters used in formulas to represent numbers will consist of the first letter of key words. In the simple interest formula, for example, *I* stands for *interest, P* for *principal,*

R for *rate,* and *T* for *time.* Another difference between algebra and arithmetic is that the signs for addition and subtraction may also be used in algebra to express negative and positive relationships.

SIGNED NUMBERS

In dealing with numbers, there are many instances in which results are expressed with negative numbers. A business may make a profit of $1,000 one month but have a loss of $1,200 the following month. The actual net loss for this two-month period is $1,000 − $1,200 = − $200. Weather temperatures in Fahrenheit degrees are frequently expressed as +23° for 23 degrees above zero and −8° for 8 degrees below zero. On occasion, then, negative numbers are used for convenient interpretations.

Positive and negative numbers can be represented by equidistant points on a number line, as illustrated in Figure 2–1.

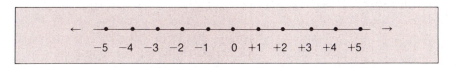

Figure 2–1 Positive and Negative Numbers on a Number Line

The arrows illustrate that a straight line is endless and that the set of positive numbers and the set of negative numbers are both infinite. Any point on a number line may be selected as the starting point, called the **origin,** and labeled 0. Equidistant points to the right of the origin are labeled +1, +2, +3, etc., and points to the left are labeled −1, −2, −3, etc. Fractions, both negative and positive, may be represented by positions between the points shown. A representation of the number $+2\frac{1}{2}$ would fall halfway between +2 and +3; the number $-3\frac{1}{2}$ would fall halfway between −3 and −4. Positive and negative numbers are called **signed numbers** or **directed numbers.**

The signs + and − are used to indicate the fundamental operations of addition and subtraction. The same signs, however, are also used to indicate whether certain numbers are positive or negative. The + sign before a number shows that the number is positive, and the − sign before a number shows that the number is negative. The + sign may be omitted before a positive number, but the − sign must be used to indicate that a number is negative. If no sign is used, the number is assumed to be positive.

Signed numbers are called directed numbers because the + and − signs indicate direction of movement along a number line. In this scheme, + means move to the right, and − means move to the left. The following six figures illustrate this concept. In each figure, the first number is represented by the arrow labeled A; the second number, by the arrow labeled B.

Figure 2–2 shows that (+5) + (+2) = +7 means move 5 units to the right and then 2 more to the right, making 7 units to the right.

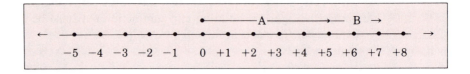

Figure 2-2 Addition of +5 and +2 Diagramed on a Number Line

In Figure 2-3, we see that $(-5) + (-2) = -7$ means move 5 units to the left and then 2 more units to the left, making 7 units to the left.

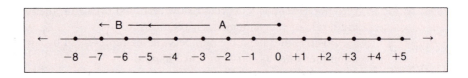

Figure 2-3 Addition of −5 and −2 Diagramed on a Number Line

Figure 2-4 illustrates that $(+5) + (-2) = +3$ means move 5 units to the right and then back 2 units to the left, making 3 units to the right.

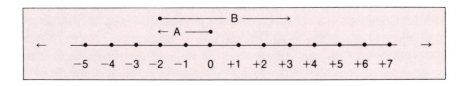

Figure 2-4 Addition of +5 and −2 Diagramed on a Number Line

When the two addition numerals in Figure 2-4 are reversed, giving $(-2) + (+5) = +3$, the same answer and the same interpretation of movement are justified, as Figure 2-5 illustrates.

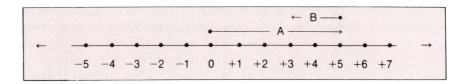

Figure 2-5 Addition of −2 and +5 Diagramed on a Number Line

Figure 2-6 shows that $(-5) + (+2) = -3$ means move 5 units to the left and then back 2 units to the right, making 3 units to the left.

Part 1.   Mathematics Applications in Preparing a Basic Foundation

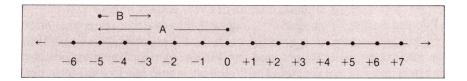

Figure 2-6 Addition of -5 and $+2$ Diagramed on a Number Line

If the numerals are simply reversed, giving $(+2) + (-5) = -3$, the preceding rationale, illustrated in Figure 2-7, is still justified.

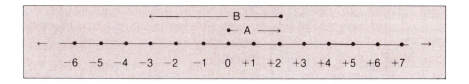

Figure 2-7 Addition of $+2$ and -5 Diagramed on a Number Line

A negative number does not always mean less than zero, nor does it necessarily mean a number to be subtracted. A negative number, depending on its use in each case, may be thought of as having only one or both of these meanings. These interpretations depend on the circumstances under which the negative number is used. In all cases, however, a negative number may be interpreted to represent something that is measured in a certain direction.

The value of a signed number when its sign is ignored is called its **absolute value** or its **numerical value.** That is, the numerical value of $+4$ and also of -4 is 4. On a number line, the numerical value or absolute value of a number is the distance, without regard to direction, from zero to the point representing the number.

When signed numbers are used to represent change, the numerical value represents the amount of change and the sign represents the direction. Thus, when a gain of \$1,000 is represented by $+\$1,000$ and a loss of \$1,200 is represented by $-\$1,200$, the 1,000 and 1,200 indicate the amount of the gain or loss and the positive and the negative signs indicate the direction of the change.

Addition of Signed Numbers

An examination of Figure 2-2 reveals that the addition of signed numbers is the same as the addition of arithmetic numbers if all the numbers are positive. In the presentation of $(+5) + (+2) = +7$, two interpretations of the $+$ sign are employed. When used within the parentheses, the $+$ sign indicates that the number is positive. When used outside the parentheses, the $+$ sign indicates that the operation of addition is to be performed. In mathematics the $+$ sign is not ordinarily used within parentheses in this manner because the absence of any sign indicates that a number is positive. This problem, therefore, would commonly be written as $5 + 2 = 7$.

Figures 2–4 through 2–7 illustrate that if one number is positive and one number is negative, the sum of the two numbers equals their numerical difference. These figures further illustrate that the numerical difference is negative when the number with the larger numerical value is negative and the numerical difference is positive when the number with the larger numerical value is positive. Based on these considerations, the following rules may be stated:

> 1. To add numbers having like signs, add their numerical values and prefix the common sign.

Example A: Add $+5$, $+3$, and $+4$.

Solution:
```
 +5
 +3
 +4
+12
```

Example B: Add -8, -5, and -6.

Solution:
```
 -8
 -5
 -6
-19
```

> 2. To add two numbers with unlike signs, determine the difference in the numerical values of the numbers and prefix the sign of the one having the larger numerical value.

Example C: Add $+32$ and -17.

Solution:
```
+32
-17
+15
```

Example D: Add -43 and $+22$.

Solution:
```
-43
+22
-21
```

When several numbers with unlike signs are contained in the same problem, as in Example E, the sum may be found in two different ways.

Example E: Add -5, 2, -8, 9, -4.

Solution:

```
-5
 2  ----> -3
-8  ----> -11
 9  ----> -2
-4
-6
```

Or

```
  2   -5   +11
  9   -8   -17
+11   -4    -6
      -17
```

Explanation:
1. The terms may be added as they stand by thinking -3, -11, -2, and -6.
2. All of the positive numbers may be added, giving the sum of $+11$; then all of the negative numbers may be added, giving the sum of -17. The total of these two sums is -6.

When the numerals to be added are small, the first method is more convenient. Actually the small numerals shown in Example E could be easily added horizontally. When the numerals are large, or for some other reason the problem is complicated, the second method may be preferable.

Any symbol or combination of symbols that represent a number may be called an **expression.** An expression may be composed of numerals, other symbols, and one or more of the fundamental operations signs. For example, $3x + 5y - 7xy$ is an **algebraic expression.** Each of the parts of an expression, together with the sign preceding it, is called a **term.** The terms of this algebraic expression are $3x$, $+5y$, and $-7xy$. **Like terms** are terms that contain the same letter or letters. Thus, $8ab$ and $9ab$ are like terms. Like terms may be added or subtracted. For example, $4xy + 3xy = 7xy$. Unlike terms cannot be added or subtracted.

The term $7xy$ is a product of the factors 7, x, and y. Any factor of a term is called the **coefficient** of the remaining factors. When a factor is a specific numeral, it is called the **numerical coefficient** of the term; other factors are called **literal coefficients.** The numerical coefficient in the term $7xy$ is 7; the literal coefficient is xy. If no numerical coefficient is shown in the term, the numerical coefficient is understood to be 1.

● Exercise 2-1

Add these signed numbers.

1. $+8$ $\underline{+4}$	**2.** -9 $\underline{-6}$	**3.** -10 $\underline{-6}$	**4.** $+7$ $\underline{+3}$	**5.** $+9$ $\underline{-5}$
6. -10 $\underline{+4}$	**7.** -3 $\underline{+7}$	**8.** 10 $\underline{-4}$	**9.** -3 $\underline{8}$	**10.** 9 $\underline{3}$
11. $+3$ $+4$ $\underline{-8}$	**12.** -9 -3 $\underline{6}$	**13.** -3 -4 $\underline{-2}$	**14.** -6 $+6$ $\underline{-3}$	**15.** -5 3 $\underline{-4}$
16. $5x$ $-8x$ $3x$ $\underline{6x}$	**17.** $6ab$ $-4ab$ $-9ab$ $\underline{5ab}$	**18.** $10xy$ $4xy$ $-15xy$ $\underline{-3xy}$	**19.** $-92x$ $48x$ $90x$ $-27x$ $\underline{-32x}$	**20.** $65abc$ $26abc$ $-44abc$ $-13abc$ $\underline{abc}$

Multiplication of Signed Numbers

Multiplication is a shortcut method of adding. The multiplication of $3 \times 5 = 15$ may be interpreted to mean $5 + 5 + 5 = 15$. As the sum of positive numbers is positive, the product of positive numbers is positive. Thus, $(+3) \times (+5) = +15$.

Suppose that one of the numbers is negative and the problem becomes $(+3) \times (-5)$. This problem may be considered to mean $(-5) + (-5) + (-5) = -15$. As the sum of negative numbers is negative, the product of a negative number and a positive number is negative. Therefore, $3 \times (-5) = -15$ and $-3 \times 5 = -15$.

There is a general rule in mathematics that when a negative number is multiplied by a negative number, the product is positive. Therefore, $(-3) \times (-5)$ means $5 + 5 + 5 = 15$.

The procedures for the multiplication of signed numbers may be summarized in the following two rules:

---

1. To multiply two signed numbers, find the product of their numerical values. If the factors have like signs, the product is positive; if they have unlike signs, the product is negative.

Example A: Multiply $(+9) \times (+6)$.

Solution:
$$\begin{array}{r} +9 \\ \times\ +6 \\ \hline +54 \end{array}$$

Example B: Multiply $(-9) \times (-6)$.

Solution:
$$\begin{array}{r} -9 \\ \times\ -6 \\ \hline +54 \end{array}$$

Example C: Multiply $(-6) \times (+9)$.

Solution:
$$\begin{array}{r} 9 \\ \times\ -6 \\ \hline -54 \end{array}$$

Example D: Multiply $(+6) \times (-9)$.

Solution:
$$\begin{array}{r} -9 \\ \times\ 6 \\ \hline -54 \end{array}$$

---

2. When more than two signed numbers are multiplied together, the product is positive if there is an even number of negative factors; the product is negative if there is an odd number of negative factors.

Example E: Multiply $(-6) \times (-4) \times (+7)$.

Solution:
$$\begin{array}{r} -6 \\ \times\ -4 \\ \hline +24 \\ \times\ 7 \\ \hline +168 \end{array}$$

Example F: Multiply $(-6) \times (-4) \times (+7) \times (-2)$.

Solution: $(-6) \times (-4) \times (+7) = +168$ from Example E.
$$\begin{array}{r} 168 \\ \times\ -2 \\ \hline -336 \end{array}$$

Remember:

1. A positive times a positive yields a positive.
2. A negative times a positive yields a negative.
3. A negative times a negative yields a positive.

● Exercise 2–2

Multiply these signed numbers.

| 1. | 8 | 2. | 8 | 3. | −8 | 4. | −8 | 5. | −7 |
| | 7 | | −7 | | 7 | | −7 | | +9 |

| 6. | 12 | 7. | −4 | 8. | −17 | 9. | −15 | 10. | −24 |
| | −4 | | 11 | | −9 | | 8 | | 4 |

| 11. | −34a | 12. | 8ab | 13. | −36x | 14. | −125xy | 15. | −83abc |
| | −5 | | −16 | | 6 | | 3 | | −5 |

16. $(-4) \times (-3) \times (+6)$ 17. $(+6) \times (-5) \times (+7)$

18. $(-9) \times (+4) \times (-8)$ 19. $(-3) \times (-4) \times (+6) \times (-9) \times (-8)$

20. $(-6) \times (+4) \times (-5) \times (+3) \times (+8) \times (-7)$

Subtraction of Signed Numbers

Subtraction may be defined as the operation that undoes the operation of addition. For example, $8 - 5$ may be interpreted to mean: What number added to 5 equals 8? Of course, $8 - 5 = 3$ and $5 + 3 = 8$. The rule is:

To subtract signed numbers, change the sign of the subtrahend and add.

Example A:

If a small business has a loss of $10 one day, how much profit must it earn the next day in order to have a net profit of $15 for the two days? That is, what profit when added to a loss of $10 will give a profit of $15?

Solution:

$$\begin{array}{r} \$15 \\ -(-10) \\ \hline \$25 \end{array}$$

Explanation:

$\$15 - (-\$10) = \$15 + \$10 = \$25$

The following examples support the rule of subtraction of signed numbers by changing the sign of the subtrahend and adding. In practice, the sign of the subtrahend should be changed mentally prior to proceeding with the calculation.

Example B: Subtract +9 from +17.   Example C: Subtract −9 from −17.

Solution: +17   Solution: −17
                  −(+9)   −(−9)
                  ─────   ─────
                   +8   −8

Example D: Subtract −9 from +17.   Example E: Subtract +9 from −17.

Solution: +17   Solution: −17
                  −(−9)   −(+9)
                  ─────   ─────
                  +26   −26

In order to check the result of a subtraction, add the difference to the subtrahend; the result should equal the minuend.

Example F: +17   **Check:** This can be shown to be correct by the adding-up
                  −(−9)   check:
Solution: +26   +26 + (−9) = +17

● Exercise 2–3

Subtract these signed numbers. Check the accuracy of each answer.

1.	+9	**2.**	+9	**3.**	−9	**4.**	−9	**5.**	+4
	+5		−5		+5		−5		+5
6.	+9	**7.**	−3	**8.**	−4	**9.**	−5	**10.**	+17
	−7		+7		−9		−6		−28
11.	−37	**12.**	84	**13.**	18	**14.**	−28	**15.**	−59
	+73		−18		−40		36		−65
16.	−6a	**17.**	−18ab	**18.**	−88x	**19.**	76xy	**20.**	260abc
	4a		18ab		−97x		94xy		−235abc

Division of Signed Numbers

As division is the inverse of multiplication, the rule for dividing signed numbers is derived from the rules for multiplying signed numbers.

> In division, like signs give a positive answer and unlike signs give a negative answer.

The problem $8 \div 2$, or $\frac{8}{2}$, may be interpreted as if it asks the question: What number when multiplied by 2 gives 8? That is, $\frac{8}{2} = 4$ also means $2 \times 4 = 8$. The dividend is the product of the divisor and the quotient.

Example A: $8 \div 2$

Solution:

$$2\overline{)8}^{\,4} \quad \text{because} \quad \begin{array}{r} 2 \\ \times\ 4 \\ \hline 8 \end{array}$$

Example B: $8 \div (-2)$

Solution:

$$-2\overline{)\ 8}^{\,-4} \quad \text{because} \quad \begin{array}{r} -2 \\ \times\ -4 \\ \hline 8 \end{array}$$

Example C: $(-8) \div 2$

Solution:

$$2\overline{)-8}^{\,-4} \quad \text{because} \quad \begin{array}{r} 2 \\ \times\ -4 \\ \hline -8 \end{array}$$

Example D: $(-8) \div (-2)$

Solution:

$$-2\overline{)-8}^{\,4} \quad \text{because} \quad \begin{array}{r} -2 \\ \times\ 4 \\ \hline -8 \end{array}$$

Based on these considerations, the rule for dividing signed numbers may be written as follows:

> To divide signed numbers, find the quotient of their numerical values; if the numbers have like signs, the quotient is positive; if they have unlike signs, the quotient is negative.

Exercise 2–4

Divide these signed numbers. Check each answer by multiplying the quotient by the divisor.

1. $\frac{+9}{+3}$ **2.** $\frac{-8}{-4}$ **3.** $\frac{+9}{-3}$ **4.** $\frac{-9}{+3}$ **5.** $\frac{-9}{-3}$

6. $\frac{-24}{-6}$ **7.** $\frac{-36}{6}$ **8.** $\frac{-48}{8}$ **9.** $\frac{28}{7}$ **10.** $\frac{63}{-9}$

11. $\frac{-72}{8}$ **12.** $\frac{72}{-9}$ **13.** $\frac{-75}{+15}$ **14.** $\frac{-96}{-16}$ **15.** $\frac{108}{-6}$

16. $\frac{-525}{-25}$ **17.** $\frac{-144x}{-8}$ **18.** $\frac{154a}{-7}$ **19.** $\frac{69ab}{-3ab}$ **20.** $\frac{-9xy}{-x}$

EQUATIONS

A complete statement of the equality or equivalence of mathematical expressions is a **number sentence** or **equation.** For example, $2 + 6 = 8$ is a complete statement that shows equality in mathematical terms.

Each side of an equation may be referred to as an expression, and each expression may be composed of one or more terms. The left and right sides of an equation, however, are more commonly called the **members** of the equation. In the equation $2 + 6 = 8$, the expression $2 + 6$ is the left member and 8 is the right member.

The letters of the alphabet are commonly used to represent quantities in equations. For example, in the equation $x + 2 = 8$, the letter x represents the numeral 6. The symbol used in a mathematical equation to represent the quantity being sought is called the **unknown.** The equation is said to be solved when the value of the unknown is discovered. Such a value is said to satisfy the equation and is called a **root** of the equation.

The equation is one of the most powerful means ever invented for the solution of problems. It is used systematically in practically all mathematics beyond elementary arithmetic. The original rules pertaining to equations were set forth by the Hindus and have since been expanded by many mathematicians through the centuries. The proper usage of equations rests on logic and certain explicit rules or properties. Three important properties follow.

Commutative Property

Changing the order of a set of addends does not change the sum of those addends. Notice that $6 + 2 = 8$; when the order of the 6 and 2 is changed, the result is $2 + 6 = 8$. Likewise, changing the order of a set of factors does not change the product of those factors. For example, $4 \times 5 = 20$; when the order of the factors is changed, the result is $5 \times 4 = 20$. Thus, addition and multiplication are **commutative** because the result obtained is independent of the order in which the elements are taken.

In subtraction and division, however, the order of the numerals is quite important. Completely different answers result when the order of the numerals in these operations is changed. Notice that $8 - 2 = 6$, whereas $2 - 8 = -6$, and that $15 \div 5 = 3$, but $5 \div 15 = \frac{1}{3}$.

$$8 - 2 = 6 \qquad\qquad 15 \div 5 = 3$$
$$2 - 8 = -6 \qquad\qquad 5 \div 15 = \tfrac{1}{3}$$

Therefore, the operations of subtraction and division are not commutative.

Associative Property

If the elements in an arithmetic operation may be combined in such a way that the result is independent of the grouping of those elements, the operation is said to be **associative.** In the addition problem $6 + 4 + 5$, if the 4 is grouped with the 6, as in $(6 + 4) + 5$, the solution is $10 + 5 = 15$. On the other hand, if the 4 is grouped with the 5, as in $6 + (4 + 5)$, the solution becomes $6 + 9 = 15$. In either case the sum is 15.

$$(6 + 4) + 5 = 15 \qquad\qquad 6 + (4 + 5) = 15$$
$$10 \;+ 5 = 15 \qquad\qquad 6 + \quad 9 \quad = 15$$

Moreover, in the multiplication problem $4 \times 5 \times 2$, notice that $(4 \times 5) \times 2$ gives $20 \times 2 = 40$ and that $4 \times (5 \times 2)$ gives $4 \times 10 = 40$.

$$(4 \times 5) \times 2 = 40 \qquad\qquad 4 \times (5 \times 2) = 40$$
$$20 \quad \times 2 = 40 \qquad\qquad 4 \times \quad 10 \quad = 40$$

Addition and multiplication, then, are associative operations.

Subtraction and division are not associative operations. The grouping of the terms in subtraction and division cannot be changed if equality is to be maintained. In the subtraction problem $14 - 4 - 3$, the grouping (i.e., association) of the numerals does affect the end result. If the grouping is $(14 - 4) - 3$, the solution is $10 - 3 = 7$. However, in the grouping $14 - (4 - 3)$, the solution is $14 - 1 = 13$. In the division problem $32 \div 4 \div 2$, the grouping $(32 \div 4) \div 2$ gives $8 \div 2 = 4$; but the grouping $32 \div (4 \div 2)$ gives $32 \div 2 = 16$.

$$(14 - 4) - 3 = 7 \qquad\qquad (32 \div 4) \div 2 = 4$$
$$10 \quad - 3 = 7 \qquad\qquad 8 \quad\quad \div 2 = 4$$

$$14 - (4 - 3) = 13 \qquad\qquad 32 \div (4 \div 2) = 16$$
$$14 - \quad 1 \quad = 13 \qquad\qquad 32 \div \quad\quad 2 = 16$$

Based on these considerations, we must conclude that subtraction and division are not associative.

Distributive Property

When we write an expression in which the sum of two numbers is multiplied by another number, parentheses are used to insure that the expression is interpreted properly. Generally the symbols within parentheses are treated as an individual number. For example, $3 \times (4 + 2)$ means $3 \times (6) = 18$. The parentheses indicate that the 3 is to be multiplied by the sum of 4 and 2 rather than 3 times the 4 and then plus 2.

In general, if a, b, and c are whole numbers, then:

> 1. $a \times (b + c) = (a \times b) + (a \times c)$ and
> 2. $(b + c) \times a = (b \times a) + (c \times a)$

This is called the **distributive property of multiplication over addition.** The distribution can be made from left to right, as in the first statement, and from right to left, as in the second statement. The first statement is equivalent to the second statement because of the commutative property of multiplication.

You should be able to distribute multiplication over addition, that is, go from the left side to the right side in a statement, such as

$$3 \times (4 + 2) = (3 \times 4) + (3 \times 2),$$

and also be able to **undistribute,** that is, go from the right to the left.

As justification of the distributive property, the preceding statement may be evaluated in the following manner:

$$3 \times (4 + 2) = (3 \times 4) + (3 \times 2)$$
$$3 \times \quad 6 \quad = \quad 12 \quad + \quad 6$$
$$18 = 18$$

Multiplication also may be distributed over subtraction, as in the following problem.

$$3 \times (4 - 2) = (3 \times 4) - (3 \times 2)$$
$$3 \times \quad 2 \quad = \quad 12 \quad - \quad 6$$
$$6 = 6$$

The distributive rule may be used in rewriting two factors as the sum of two products.

$$6 \times 78 = 6 \times (70 + 8) = (6 \times 70) + (6 \times 8)$$

● Exercise 2–5

A. Name the mathematical property illustrated by each of the following.

1. $4 + 7 = 7 + 4$

2. $(3 + 5) + 6 = 3 + (5 + 6)$

3. $2 \times (4 \times 6) = (2 \times 4) \times 6$

4. $7 \times (5 + 6) = (7 \times 5) + (7 \times 6)$

5. $9 \times 5 = 5 \times 9$

6. $(5 \times 9) + (5 \times 7) = 5 \times (9 + 7)$

7. $6 \times 9 = (6 \times 5) + (6 \times 4)$

8. $9 \times 10 \times 11 = 10 \times 9 \times 11$

9. $(7 \times 15) - (7 \times 10) = 7 \times (15 - 10)$

10. $8 \times (10 \times 12) = (8 \times 10) \times 12$

B. Use the distributive property to rewrite each of the following as the sum of two products.

1. $5 \times (70 + 30)$

2. $(40 + 6) \times 4$

3. $(20 + 7) \times 8$

4. $(30 + 8) \times 9$

5. $6 \times (50 + 9)$

6. $8 \times (25 + 10)$

C. Use the distributive property to rewrite each of the following as a multiplier times two addends.

1. $(9 \times 3) + (9 \times 5)$

2. $(4 \times 6) + (4 \times 7)$

3. $(7 \times 10) + (7 \times 14)$

4. $(8 \times 12) + (8 \times 20)$

5. $(15 \times 10) + (23 \times 10)$

6. $(25 \times 5) + (30 \times 5)$

D. Use the distributive property to rewrite each of the following as the sum of two or more products.

1. 5 × 12   **3.** 3 × 35   **5.** 7 × 376

2. 7 × 36   **4.** 5 × 24   **6.** 3 × 735

E. Use the distributive property to rewrite each of the following.

1. 4 × (5 − 2)   **3.** (27 − 12) × 5   **5.** (3 × 38) − (3 × 20)

2. 6 × (35 − 8)   **4.** (19 − 5) × 9   **6.** (45 × 7) − (26 × 7)

Addition and Subtraction Equations

An **axiom** is an assumption so basic that its truth is accepted without proof. The statement, "things equal to the same thing are equal," is an example of an axiom.

Solving a simple addition and subtraction equation containing only one unknown rests on the following axiom.

Axiom 1. If the same quantities are added to (or subtracted from) both sides of an equation, the result is a valid equation.

Example A: If 5 + 6 = 11, then 5 + 6 + 4 = 11 + 4

Solution: 15 = 15

Example B: If 5 + 6 = 11, then 5 + 6 − 3 = 11 − 3

Solution: 8 = 8

In solving an equation, the terms are rearranged so that the term or terms representing the unknown appear on one side of the equals sign and the other symbols appear on the other side. The value of the root should be determined through a series of logical steps.

When the value of the unknown has been determined, the accuracy of the value should be checked. This is accomplished by substituting in the equation the value obtained for the symbol representing the unknown. For the answer to be correct, a true equation must result.

Examples C and D illustrate how Axiom 1 may be applied to the solution of equations.

Example C: What number decreased by 12 becomes 27?

Solution:
$$N - 12 = 27$$
$$N - 12 + 12 = 27 + 12 \quad \text{(12 added to each member)}$$
$$N = 39$$

Check: 39 − 12 = 27
           27 = 27

Example D: What number increased by 25 becomes 65?

Solution:
$$N + 25 = 65$$
$$N + 25 - 25 = 65 - 25 \quad \text{(25 subtracted from each side)}$$
$$N = 40$$

Check: $40 + 25 = 65$
$$65 = 65$$

The procedure used to solve these equations is called **cancellation** because the term added to or subtracted from each side cancels another term. Notice in Example C that the positive 12 on the left side cancels the negative 12. In Example D, the negative 25 in the left member cancels the positive 25.

Another popular method of solving equations is based on **transposition**. To **transpose** means to transfer a term from one side of the equals sign to the other. This method is based on the following principle:

When an addend or subtrahend is transferred from one side of an equation to the other, its sign is changed from positive to negative or from negative to positive.

Example E: Find the value of x in the following equation.

Solution:
$$x + 8 = 26$$
$$x = 26 - 8$$
$$x = 18$$

Check: $18 + 8 = 26$
$$26 = 26$$

Example F: Solve the following equation.

Solution:
$$y - 7 = 32$$
$$y = 32 + 7$$
$$y = 39$$

Check: $39 - 7 = 32$
$$32 = 32$$

Because the order of numerals can be important, the term being transposed is usually written to the right of the terms that were already on the side to which the transfer is being made.

● Exercise 2-6

Solve these equations and check each answer.

1. $x - 48 = 22$	**5.** $57 - X = 37$	**9.** $89 = X - 57$
2. $y + 10 = 36$	**6.** $77 + Y = 92$	**10.** $85 = Y + 47$
3. $z + 13 = 24$	**7.** $56 + Z = 99$	**11.** $91 = 28 + Z$
4. $N - 16 = 42$	**8.** $96 - N = 30$	**12.** $55 = 63 - N$

Multiplication and Division Equations

A dot written slightly above the writing line is sometimes used to indicate multiplication because the sign $\times$ could be interpreted to represent an unknown. For example, $5 \cdot 6 = 30$. Another means of indicating multiplication is to closely join the symbols representing factors. That is, PRT means $P \cdot R \cdot T$; $5x$ means $5 \cdot x$; and $6(n + 1)$ means $6 \times (n + 1)$.

Use of the division sign ($\div$) may be avoided in equations. If the sign is read hastily or is poorly written, it may be mistaken for the plus sign ($+$). Many people prefer to use the common fraction form to indicate division, such as $\frac{8}{2}$ rather than $8 \div 2$.

The procedures used to solve for the unknown in equations that require multiplication or division depend on the following axiom.

> **Axiom 2.** If both sides of an equation are multiplied (or divided) by the same quantity, the result is a valid equation.

Example A: Since $7 + 8 = 15$, show that $6 \times (7 + 8) = 6 \times 15$.

Solution:
$$6 \times (7 + 8) = 6 \times 15$$
$$6 \times \quad 15 \quad = 6 \times 15$$
$$90 = 90$$

Example B: Since $7 + 8 = 15$, show that $(7 + 8) \div 3 = 15 \div 3$

Solution:
$$(7 + 8) \div 3 = 15 \div 3$$
$$15 \quad \div 3 = 15 \div 3$$
$$5 = 5$$

Notice in the second step of the solution in Example C, below, that the divisor 47 on the left side is in effect canceled by the multiplier 47 in the left member.

Example C: What number divided by 47 gives 5?

Solution:
$$N \div 47 = 5$$
$$(N \div 47) \times 47 = 5 \times 47 \quad \text{(Each side multiplied by 47.)}$$
$$N = 5 \times 47$$
$$N = 235$$

Check: $235 \div 47 = 5$
$$5 = 5$$

The correct answer may be obtained more quickly by using the transposition method. The solution may be arranged like this:

Solution:
$$\frac{N}{47} = 5$$
$$N = 5 \times 47$$
$$N = 235$$

In Example D, the multiplier in the left member is canceled by the divisor on the left side. The multiplier 25 is canceled by the divisor 25.

Example D: What number multiplied by 25 yields 175?

Solution:
$$25N = 175$$
$$25N \div 25 = 175 \div 25$$
$$N = 7$$

Check: $25 \cdot 7 = 175$
$$175 = 175$$

When the transposition method is used to find the root to the problem in Example D, the solution may look like this:

Solution:
$$25N = 175$$
$$N = \frac{175}{25}$$
$$N = 7$$

Notice that when a multiplier is transferred to the other side of the equals sign it becomes a divisor, and a transferred divisor becomes a multiplier. These considerations may be summarized in another principle of algebra:

> When a multiplier or divisor is transferred from one side of an equation to the other, its sign is changed from × to ÷ or from ÷ to ×.

● Exercise 2–7

Solve these equations. Check each answer.

1. $9x = 378$
2. $Y \div 7 = 315$
3. $z \div 11 = 99$
4. $20N = 480$
5. $760 = 95x$
6. $102 = N \div 51$
7. $36 = 540 \div Y$
8. $52Z = 832$
9. $3{,}525 \div N = 705$

10. $66 = X \div 48$
11. $3x + 5 = 17$
12. $5x + 2 = 37$
13. $2x - 7 = 25$
14. $6x - 6 = 42$
15. $92 + 4N = 308$
16. $58 + 8N = 314$
17. $72 + 7N = 275$
18. $274 - 5N = 139$

Part 1.   Mathematics Applications in Preparing a Basic Foundation

19. $361 + 368 = 9x$

20. $197 + 272 = 7Y$

21. $469 - 25 = 6Z$

22. $385 - 97 = 8N$

23. $9x + 46 = x + 86$

24. $4Y + 56 = 3Y + 147$

25. $3Z + 17 = 5Z - 75$

26. $10N + 92 = 14N - 108$

27. $2x + x + 3x - x = 105$

28. $3y + 2 - y + 3y - 4 = 403$

29. $3Z - 2 = 5Z - 3Z + 40$

30. $7N + 12 = 5N + 4N - 56$

Signs of Aggregation in Equations

If an equation contains parentheses or other **signs of aggregation,** such as brackets, [ ], or braces, { }, they must be removed before the equation can be solved.

Example A:

$(5x + 9) - 25 = 124$

Solution:

$5x + 9 = 124 + 25$
$5x = 149 - 9$
$x = 140 \div 5$
$x = 28$

Check: $[5(28) + 9] - 25 = 124$
$[140 + 9] - 25 = 124$
$149 - 25 = 124$
$124 = 124$

The equation in Example B is read as "two times the *quantity of x plus three* equals ninety-six." The procedure in the solution on the left rests on the distributive property: the operation of multiplication is to be performed on each addend or subtrahend enclosed by the parentheses. The procedure shown in the solution on the right is based on the principle of transposition: a factor transferred to the opposite member of an equation becomes a divisor.

Example B:

$2(x + 3) = 96$

Solution:

$2x + 6 = 96$ **Or** $x + 3 = \dfrac{96}{2}$
$2x = 96 - 6$ $x = 48 - 3$
$x = 90 \div 2$ $x = 45$
$x = 45$

Check: $2(45 + 3) = 96$
$2 \cdot 48 = 96$
$96 = 96$

Although parentheses are mentioned most frequently in the following rules, these rules apply to all signs of aggregation. If the mathematical operation is indicated by a plus or minus sign before the parentheses, the parentheses may be removed by following these rules:

> 1. When the parentheses are preceded by a positive sign (+), the parentheses may be removed without any change in the signs of the previously enclosed terms.

Example C: $3x + (2x - 4) =$

Solution: $3x + 2x - 4 = 5x - 4$

> 2. If the parentheses are preceded by a negative sign (−), when the parentheses are removed, the sign of each of the formerly enclosed terms must be changed.

Example D: $8N - (2N + N - 7) =$

Solution: $8N - 2N - N + 7 = 5N + 7$

> 3. When parentheses that enclose addends or subtrahends are preceded by a factor, the distributive property may be applied to eliminate the parentheses.

Example E: $3(n - 2) + 2(n + 4) = 267$

Solution:
$$3n - 6 + 2n + 8 = 267$$
$$3n + 2n = 267 + 6 - 8$$
$$5n = 273 - 8$$
$$5n = 265$$
$$n = 265 \div 5$$
$$n = 53$$

Check: $3(53 - 2) + 2(53 + 4) = 267$
$$3 \cdot 51 + 2 \cdot 57 = 267$$
$$153 + 114 = 267$$
$$267 = 267$$

> 4. If several algebraic expressions are enclosed one within the other by signs of aggregation, such as parentheses within brackets, remove the innermost pair of signs first and collect terms; then remove the next pair of signs and collect terms; and so on until each pair of signs is removed.

Example F: $(5a - a) - [30 + (4 + a) - (7 - a)] = 19$

Solution:

$$4a - [30 + 4 + a - 7 + a] = 19$$
$$4a - 30 - 4 - a + 7 - a = 19$$
$$2a - 27 = 19$$
$$2a = 19 + 27$$
$$2a = 46$$
$$a = 23$$

Check: $(5 \cdot 23 - 23) - [30 + (4 + 23) - (7 - 23)] = 19$
$$(115 - 23) - [30 + (27) - (-16)] = 19$$
$$92 - [30 + 27 + 16] = 19$$
$$92 - [73] = 19$$
$$19 = 19$$

● Exercise 2–8

Solve these equations and check each answer.

1. $(x \cdot 6) + 70 = 112$

2. $(M \cdot 7) - 91 = 539$

3. $N(530 \div 5) = 10{,}282$

4. $(90Y \div Y) - 2Y = 5Y - 36$

5. $8(x - 6) = 464$

6. $30(Y - 5) = 10Y + 10$

7. $4(40 - 3Z) = Z + 30$

8. $14 + 7(N + 6) = 5 + 3(3N + 7)$

9. $12 - 4(a - 4) = a - 122$

10. $9x + (5 - x) = 3x + 85$

11. $200Y = 50(20 - Y)$

12. $10 + 4(z + 6) = 5(z + 3) + 8$

13. $12 = 150 - 3(a - 4)$

14. $2(x - 3) + 3(x - 6) = 361$

15. $3(Y + 4) - 2(Y - 3) = 49$

16. $4(Z - 6) - 3(Z - 2) = 165$

17. $3(5N - 9) = 201 - 3(N + 4)$

18. $5(3a - 1) = 3(2a + 5) + 871$

19. $2(4x - 3) = 664 - 3(x - 4)$

20. $9(Y + 3) - (4Y - 9) = 121$

21. $\dfrac{2(x + 3)}{3} = x - 1$

22. $\dfrac{3(z - 2)}{2} = z + 17$

23. $\dfrac{170}{5(a - 3)} = \dfrac{44}{a + 2}$

24. $\dfrac{9}{x - 1} = \dfrac{189}{7(x + 5)}$

25. $2[3b + 4(b - 1)] = 13b + 5$

26. $5[3a - 2(a + 4)] = 4(a + 9) - 2$

27. $3(c - 2) + 30 = 2[c - (5 - c)]$

28. $4[x - (10 - x)] = 186 - 2(x - 2)$

29. $2[3N - 2(N - 7)] = 3N - 9$

30. $5[3Y - 2(Y + 3)]$
$$= 2(Y - 40) + 4(Y - 25)$$

USING A POCKET CALCULATOR

Pocket calculators are now so inexpensive that they have become very popular. Some are as small as a credit card or wristwatch. Thus, they are convenient to carry and to use. Small calculators are tools that can be used for personal calculations just as larger calculators and computers are used for business calculations.

The problems considered thus far have been presented with pencil and paper solutions primarily in mind. However, reversing the order of the addends is a good way to check accuracy in addition when a nonprinting calculator is used. Reversing the order of the factors is a recommended way to check accuracy in multiplication. Understanding the concepts, therefore, can be beneficial whether or not a calculator is being used.

If you plan to buy a calculator, get one with at least eight digits, a floating decimal point, and a fully-addressable memory. A calculator with a fully-addressable memory has M+ and M− keys. Some of the least expensive calculators contain these recommended features. A simple calculator of this type is adequate to solve the problems in this book. A more versatile machine may be advisable for advanced courses in mathematics or statistics.

Simple calculators usually fall into one of two major types: arithmetic or algebraic. Machines having arithmetic logic generally have a ± key and perhaps a ⊟ key also. Algebraic machines have a separate = key. Because algebraic logic is the more common, instructions for algebraic machines are given in appropriate sections of this book. Numbers are entered into an algebraic machine as they would be written in an algebraic equation.

Addition and Subtraction

Before starting any problem, press the C key twice. Pressing this key **clears** the machine of any prior computations. Many calculators also have a **clear-entry** feature. This may be controlled by a separate key labeled CE or it may be controlled by the clear key, labeled C/CE or just C . Pressing the CE key clears the number displayed so that a number entered in error may be erased without starting over. If there is just one key for clear and clear-entry, one press clears the entry and two presses clear the machine.

To add 7 + 15 + 23 + 46 on an algebraic calculator, enter the numbers and signs as you read them from left to right:

and 91 will appear as the answer.

When finding sums on a nonprinting calculator for a group of problems, find the sums for all of them and then check accuracy by re-adding each problem in reverse order.

To find the difference for 843 − 479, enter the numbers as they are written:

and 364 will appear as the difference.

Place the difference in the answer space (or in memory). Then while 364 is still displayed, add the subtrahend of 479 to it and the minuend of 843 will appear. As in addition, however, accuracy in subtraction may be checked with a calculator by entering the numbers in reverse order *if* the signs are entered. Notice:

 gives 364.

The foregoing illustrates that *signed* numbers may be added (but not subtracted, multiplied, or divided) with a pocket calculator. The problem

is the same as

There is no need to press the ⬜= key after each new number. For example, in 23 + 45 − 67 + 98 − 10, the numbers are entered as written:

and the answer 89 appears.

• Exercise 2–9

A. Find each total and check accuracy by adding in reverse order.

1. 546 + 867 + 923 + 876   **3.** 5,906 + 4,558 + 3,987 + 4,735

2. 562 + 728 + 806 + 539   **4.** 6,569 + 6,097 + 4,365 + 9,750

5. 85,987 + 98,725 + 23,697 + 72,678

6. 70,792 + 37,448 + 94,360 + 63,715

7. 80,635 + 8,374 + 67,852 + 9,254 + 94,983

8. 26,587 + 52,977 + 8,794 + 48,087 + 9,671

B. Find the difference and check the accuracy of each answer.

1. 6,800 − 6,561   **5.** 87,757 − 83,074

2. 4,840 − 3,482   **6.** 64,065 − 29,163

3. 58,700 − 35,748   **7.** 379,197 − 429,760

4. 91,346 − 58,879   **8.** 417,714 − 869,468

C. Solve each problem.

1. 578 + 798 − 350 − 985

2. 1,076 − 483 + 679 − 983

3. 59,706 − 8,935 − 102,784 + 9,055

4. 74,260 + 7,105 − 24,830 − 47,967

5. $98,344 - 35,286 - 27,329 - 45,702 - 21,576$

6. $35,806 - 98,750 + 85,043 - 4,734 - 100,530$

D. Add these signed numbers.

1. $+8 + (-5)$

2. $+9 + (-3)$

3. $29 + (-23) + (-24) + 25$

4. $39 + (-34) + (-35) + 38$

5. $-453 + 734 + (-478) + 437$

6. $-867 + 800 + (-734) + 705$

7. $-354 + 607 + (-748) + (-822) + 945$

8. $-500 + 935 + (-237) + (-789) + 452$

E. King Company operates four shops in an urban area. The gains and losses of each shop for the third quarter are shown below. Losses are shown in parentheses. Find the total gains (or losses) for each shop (A, B, C, D), for each month, and for the company.

	Month	A	B	C	D	Totals
1.	July	$5,356	$4,683	$ 978	($ 846)	$_____
2.	August	3,859	1,219	(302)	1,047	$_____
3.	September	4,281	(274)	1,459	(2,354)	$_____
	Totals	$_____	$_____	$_____	$_____	
		(4)	(5)	(6)	(7)	(8)

Multiplication and Division

Problems involving multiplication and division are also entered as the numbers and symbols are read from left to right.

Example A: Multiply 53×47

Solution: 53 ⬚×⬚ 47 ⬚=⬚ → 2491

Example B: Divide $2,170 \div 35$.

Solution: 2170 ⬚÷⬚ 35 ⬚=⬚ → 62

Multiplication and division in the same problem may be linked together from left to right without using the ⬚=⬚ key for each operation.

Example C: Solve this problem: $52 \times 34 \div 13$.

Solution: 52 ⬚×⬚ 34 ⬚÷⬚ 13 ⬚=⬚ → 136

When division is shown in common fraction form as $\frac{36}{4}$, rewriting the division in on-line form, $36 \div 4$, may be useful as a reminder to use the ⬚÷⬚ key.

Example D: $\dfrac{76 \times 23}{19}$

Solution: 76 ⬚×⬚ 23 ⬚÷⬚ 19 ⬚=⬚ → 92

A. Multiply. Check accuracy by multiplying the factors in reverse order.

1. 467 × 83
2. 842 × 45
3. 144 × 997
4. 489 × 675
5. 676 × 34 × 26

6. 529 × 53 × 46
7. 488 × 25 × 61
8. 828 × 113 × 43
9. 5,929 × 92 × 67
10. 4,624 × 95 × 49

B. Divide. Check accuracy by multiplying the quotient by the divisor.

1. 848,511 ÷ 9,753
2. 590,625 ÷ 9,375
3. 6,715,310 ÷ 78,085
4. 8,372,808 ÷ 57,348

5. $\dfrac{71,918}{467}$

6. $\dfrac{657,804}{382}$

7. $\dfrac{2,459,331}{2,653}$

8. $\dfrac{4,580,526}{1,739}$

C. Solve these problems.

1. 232 × 352 ÷ 22
2. 144 ÷ 8 × 53
3. 3,648 ÷ 57 × 68

4. 259,192 × 19 ÷ 179
5. 340,575 × 47 ÷ 95
6. 3,517,394 ÷ 613 × 87

7. $\dfrac{2,035 \times 579}{37}$

8. $\dfrac{37,362 \times 354}{479}$

Order of Operations

Regardless of whether or not a calculator is being used to solve an equation, there are certain rules pertaining to the order in which the arithmetic operations are performed. To solve equations, the operations are done in the following order:

1. Do all operations that are in parentheses first.
2. Do all multiplications and divisions as they occur from left to right.
3. Do all additions and subtractions as they occur from left to right.

Example A: Solve this equation: $n = 3 - (8 + 2)$

Solution: $n = 3 - 10$
              $n = -7$

Explanation: The parentheses tell us that the 8 and 2 are associated, so the addition should be done first and the subtraction second.

The fraction bar may also be used to group symbols together. Rewriting the equation in on-line form may be beneficial.

Example B:	Solve this equation: $n = \dfrac{245 - 50}{40 + 25}$
Solution:	$n = (245 - 50) \div (40 + 25)$ $n = 195 \div 65$ $n = 3$
Explanation:	The fraction bar tells us that the 245 and 50 are associated and that the 40 and 25 are associated. The on-line form shows that the subtraction and addition should be done before the division.
Example C:	Rewrite in on-line form: $n = \dfrac{2 \times 12 \times 195}{13 \times 5}$
Solution:	$n = (2 \times 12 \times 195) \div (13 \times 5)$
Explanation:	The fraction bar tells us that the 2, 12, and 195 are associated, so the multiplication should be done first and the division second.
	The equation in Example C may also be written in on-line form without using parentheses as follows.
Solution:	$n = 2 \times 12 \times 195 \div 13 \div 5$
Explanation:	Multiply and divide from left to right. Dividing by 13 and then by 5 gives the same answer as dividing by their product of 65.
	Of course, more than one set of signs of aggregation may be needed to rewrite an equation in on-line form.
Example D:	Rewrite in on-line form: $n = \dfrac{3(8 + 6)}{7}$
Solution:	$n = [3(8 + 6)] \div 7$
	Multiplication and division take precedence over addition and subtraction.
Example E:	Solve this equation: $n = 4 + 5 \times 7$
Solution:	$n = 4 + 35$ $n = 39$
Explanation:	As there are no parentheses, the multiplication is done first and the addition second.
	The following example illustrates all of the above rules for the order of operations.
Example F:	Solve this equation: $n = 8 - 6 \times 5 \div (4 - 1) + 7$
Solution	$n = 8 - 6 \times 5 \div 3 + 7$ $n = 8 - 30 \div 3 + 7$ $n = 8 - 10 + 7$ $n = -2 + 7$ $n = 5$
Explanation:	First, eliminate parentheses; second, multiply and divide from left to right; third, add and subtract from left to right.

Exercise 2-11

A. For each of the following, indicate which operation should be done first.

1. $(30 - 6) \times 3$
2. $30 - (6 \times 3)$
3. $(30 + 6) \div 3$
4. $30 + (6 \div 3)$

5. $25 + 7 \times 4$
6. $18 - 5 + 9$
7. $12 + 18 \div 2$

8. $32 - 2 \times 4$
9. $(14 + 7) \div 3$
10. $16 \div 5 \times 3$

B. Write the on-line form for each of the following.

1. $\dfrac{15 + 7}{11}$

2. $\dfrac{37 - 2}{7}$

3. $\dfrac{24}{6 + 2}$

4. $\dfrac{36}{12 - 3}$

5. $\dfrac{18 + 4}{15 - 3}$

6. $\dfrac{29 - 3}{8 + 5}$

7. $\dfrac{3 \times 7 \times 108}{6 \times 9}$

8. $\dfrac{425 \times 4 \times 9}{17 \times 12}$

9. $\dfrac{8 \times (16 - 4)}{24}$

10. $\dfrac{(45 + 9) \times 3}{27}$

11. $\dfrac{1{,}600 \div (14 + 6)}{36 + 4}$

12. $\dfrac{(840 - 140) \div 7}{34 - 9}$

C. Solve each of the following equations.

1. $n = 324 \div 36 \times 3$
2. $n = 720 \div 45 \times 2$
3. $x = 720 \div (45 \times 2)$
4. $x = 324 \div (36 \times 3)$
5. $y = 28 \times 14 + 35 \times 21$
6. $y = 18 \times 30 + 24 \times 12$
7. $z = 32 \times 16 - 16 + 56$
8. $z = 25 \times 15 + 30 - 10$
9. $a = 35 + 28 \times 21 - 14$
10. $a = 36 + 12 \times 24 - 30$
11. $b = 48 \times 36 + 72 \div 24$
12. $b = 72 \times 40 - 48 \div 24$

13. $c = 208 - \dfrac{117}{13}$

14. $c = 224 - \dfrac{140}{35}$

15. $n = \dfrac{450 + 30 \times 75}{150}$

16. $n = \dfrac{104 \times 130 - 26}{78}$

17. $x = \dfrac{81 \times 54 + 261 \times 108}{243}$

18. $x = \dfrac{224 \times 140 - 112 \times 168}{196}$

19. $y = \dfrac{392 \div 8 + 35 \times 14}{63 - 52}$

20. $y = \dfrac{160 \div 40 + 32 \times 16}{27 + 16}$

Calculator Memory

Keyboards of pocket calculators are not standardized, but the least expensive models are becoming more similar in their operations. Some have a storage-recall type of memory in which a number may be simply stored and recalled when needed. Most recent models, however, have a fully-addressable memory in which a number may be stored, increased or decreased (perhaps multiplied or divided) by the number in display, and recalled. The following keys are usual on calculators with fully-addressable memory:

$\boxed{\text{M}+}$ Adds the number in display to the invisible memory register.

$\boxed{\text{M}-}$ Subtracts the number in display from the memory register.

$\boxed{\text{MR}}$ Recalls and displays the current balance that is in the memory. Does not clear the memory register.

$\boxed{\text{MC}}$ Clears the memory register to zero balance.

In finding the sum of two products, both products may be added to memory and then recalled.

Example A: Solve this equation: $x = (26 \times 53) + (12 \times 64)$

Solution: $\boxed{\text{MC}}$ 26 $\boxed{\times}$ 53 $\boxed{\text{M}+}$ 12 $\boxed{\times}$ 64 $\boxed{\text{M}+}$ $\boxed{\text{MR}}$ → 2,146.

When finding the difference of two products, a similar procedure may be followed.

Example B: Solve this equation: $y = (18 \times 45) - (6 \times 37)$

Solution: $\boxed{\text{MC}}$ 18 $\boxed{\times}$ 45 $\boxed{\text{M}+}$ 6 $\boxed{\times}$ 37 $\boxed{\text{M}-}$ $\boxed{\text{MR}}$ → 588.

When the memory register does not include division, first computing the divisor and storing it in memory may be more efficient for finding a quotient.

Example C: Solve this equation: $x = (45 \times 600) \div (15 \times 75)$

Solution: $\boxed{\text{MC}}$ 15 $\boxed{\times}$ 75 $\boxed{\text{M}+}$ 45 $\boxed{\times}$ 600 $\boxed{\div}$ $\boxed{\text{MR}}$ $\boxed{=}$ → 24.

● **Exercise 2–12**

Use the memory register of your calculator to solve these equations.

1. $n = (35 \times 52) + (48 \times 34)$

2. $n = (38 \times 67) + (64 \times 73)$

3. $x = (28 \times 63) + (39 \times 57)$

4. $x = (46 \times 82) + (93 \times 58)$

5. $y = (98 \times 45) - (38 \times 26)$

6. $y = (81 \times 53) - (46 \times 39)$

7. $z = (76 \times 34) - (42 \times 25)$

8. $z = (103 \times 47) - (61 \times 58)$

9. $n = (57 \times 152) \div (19 \times 38)$

10. $n = (126 \times 84) \div (21 \times 14)$

11. $x = (153 \times 34) \div (51 \times 17)$

12. $x = (192 \times 96) \div (64 \times 32)$

WORD PROBLEMS

Some students who can perform the basic arithmetic operations skillfully often experience difficulty when solving word problems. But by becoming adept at using equations to solve word problems, students discover that they can solve word problems with much less difficulty. Keep in mind, too, that all problems in business and industry start out as word problems. Through earnest study and diligent practice, the student can learn to use equations to solve word problems.

Translation into Algebraic Terms

In the following chapters, there are many occasions when ideas are conveniently and concisely expressed by symbols and formulas. One should be able to (1) express ideas with algebraic symbols and (2) interpret algebraic expressions — that is, translate algebraic expressions into words. The first of these requirements gives students the greater difficulty because the process of changing from words to mathematical symbols can seem complicated, even when the arithmetic operations to be performed are quite simple.

The process of translating from written words to algebraic terms rests on two primary rules:

> 1. Let a symbol such as x represent one of the unknown quantities.
> 2. Express the other unknown quantities in terms of the same symbol.

Example A: Joe is x years old.

Solution:

His age 3 years ago:	$x - 3$ years
His age y years ago:	$x - y$ years
His age 5 years from now:	$x + 5$ years
His age n years from now:	$x + n$ years
Twice his present age:	$2x$ years
Half his present age:	$\dfrac{x}{2}$ years
Half his age 2 years ago:	$\dfrac{x - 2}{2}$ years

Example B: John and Jane together earn $2,000 a month; John's monthly salary is x.

Solution:

The amount Jane earns a month:	$2,000 - x$
The amount Jane earns a year:	$12(2,000 - x)$
The amount John earns a year:	$12x$
John's salary increased by $50 a month:	$x + 50$
Jane's salary decreased by $25 a month:	$(2,000 - x) - 25$
The amount John earns in n months:	nx

Example C: Candy costs *n* cents a pound.

Solution: The cost of 7 pounds: $7n$ cents
                The cost of *m* pounds: mn cents

                The quantity 75 cents will buy: $\dfrac{75}{n}$ pounds

                The quantity \$3 will buy: $\dfrac{300}{n}$ pounds

                The cost of 2 pounds if the price is
                reduced 3 cents a pound $2(n - 3)$ cents

● Exercise 2–13

Use algebraic symbols to write each of the following.

1. 5 added to *n*	**11.** One-half of *t*
2. *x* plus *y*	**12.** $\frac{2}{3}$ of *t*
3. 7 more than *n*	**13.** 2.5 times *x*
4. *a* minus *b*	**14.** 0.5 times *y*
5. 8 less than *y*	**15.** 0.25 of *z*
6. 5 times *y*	**16.** 3 times the sum of *b* and *c*
7. *p* times *r*	**17.** Four times the sum of *x* and *y*
8. *t* times 7	**18.** *a* decreased by *b*
9. *r* divided by *b*	**19.** *x* decreased by $\frac{1}{2}$ of *x*
10. *p* divided by 4	**20.** *y* increased by $\frac{1}{4}$ of itself

21. If *n* represents Joan's present age in years, what algebraic symbols should be used to represent her age in each of the following?
   a. Five years from now   **c.** Five years ago
   b. *x* years from now   **d.** *y* years ago

22. Using *n* to represent the unknown number, write each of the following in algebraic form.
   a. Seven more than a number   **c.** A number divided by twelve
   b. Four times a number   **d.** A number increased by half itself

23. Let *x* represent the number of inches in a certain piece of copper tubing. Write the expression that represents a length of tubing that is:
   a. 3 inches longer   **c.** Twice as long
   b. 3 inches shorter   **d.** Half as long

24. Use algebraic symbols to represent each of the following.
   a. 7 more than 5 times *x*
   b. 5 more than half of *n*
   c. 4 less than half of *y*
   d. The amount by which 78 exceeds twice an unknown number *z*

25. In his coin collection, Frank has 245 fewer dimes than Jim. Select a letter to represent the number of dimes in Jim's collection, and write the expression that represents the number of dimes in Frank's collection.

26. The difference in two numbers is 9. If x represents the smaller number, what expression represents the larger number?

27. If the sum of two numbers is s and one of the numbers is 28, what expression represents the other number?

28. Use algebraic symbols to express the cost of x number of oranges if one dozen oranges cost n cents.

29. If $2n-1$ represents an odd number, what expression represents the next larger odd number?

30. A bank pays i dollars interest per dollar per year. What expression represents the amount of interest the bank would pay for x dollars for four months?

Solution of Word Problems

The equation can be used to solve word problems quickly and accurately. Some word problems can be solved by trial and error, without resorting to the use of equations. The use of algebraic symbols and equations, however, reduces the solution of such problems to an orderly, logical process. The process of trial and error is completely eliminated. Furthermore, the algebraic form makes it easier to check the accuracy of completed work.

There is no set of rules to insure the correct solution to every word problem. There are some general guidelines, however, that can be used to solve word problems:

1. Read the problem all the way through.
2. Determine what the problem asks.
3. Let a symbol such as x represent one of the unknown quantities.
4. Express the other unknown quantities in relation to this symbol.
5. Write an equation expressing the relationship between the given and the unknown quantities.
6. Solve the equation to find the value of the unknown.
7. Check the solution.

A careful reading of the problem is essential. Several readings of the problem may be required before setting up the equation. Once the equation has been set up, the solution is relatively simple, depending only on the routine procedures for solving equations that you have learned.

The following examples illustrate how equations can be used to solve word problems. Carefully study each example.

Example A: The sum of two numbers is 27. One of the numbers is 3 more than the other number. Find the numbers.

Solution: Let x = the smaller number, and $x + 3$ = the larger number

$$x + x + 3 = 27$$
$$2x = 24$$
$$x = 12 \quad \text{the smaller number}$$
$$x + 3 = 15 \quad \text{the larger number}$$

Check: $12 + 12 + 3 = 27$
$$27 = 27$$

Example B: The sum of two consecutive numbers is 59. Find the numbers.

Solution: Let n = the first number, and $n + 1$ = the second number.

$$n + n + 1 = 59$$
$$2n = 58$$
$$n = 29 \quad \text{the first number}$$
$$n + 1 = 30 \quad \text{the second number}$$

Check: $29 + 29 + 1 = 59$
$$59 = 59$$

Example C: The sum of two consecutive even numbers is 74. Find the numbers.

Solution: Let x = the first number, and $x + 2$ = the second number.

$$x + x + 2 = 74$$
$$2x = 72$$
$$x = 36 \quad \text{the first even number}$$
$$x + 2 = 38 \quad \text{the second even number}$$

Check: $36 + 36 + 2 = 74$
$$74 = 74$$

Example D: A dealer bought 50 machines at a cost of $1,000 each. The dealer sold some of the machines at $1,500 each and the remainder at $900 each. The total gain amounted to $7,000. How many machines were sold at each price?

Solution: Let n = number of machines sold at $1,500 each, and $50 - n$ = number of machines sold at $900 each.

$$\$1,500n + \$900(50 - n) = (50 \times \$1,000) + \$7,000$$
$$\$1,500n + \$45,000 - \$900n = \$50,000 + \$7,000$$
$$\$1,500n - \$900n = \$57,000 - \$45,000$$
$$\$600n = \$12,000$$
$$n = 20 \quad \text{at } \$1,500 \text{ each}$$
$$50 - n = 30 \quad \text{at } \$900 \text{ each}$$

Check: $(20 \cdot \$1,500) + (30 \cdot \$900) = \$50,000 + \$7,000$
$$\$30,000 + \$27,000 = \$57,000$$
$$\$57,000 = \$57,000$$

In the problem in Example D, notice that:

1. One of the unknown quantities is "some of the machines," and the symbol n is used to represent this quantity.
2. The other unknown is "the remainder," and this quantity is represented by $50 - n$.
3. The total profit is $7,000. This statement supplies a clue to be used in the equation.
4. The equation represents the conclusion that after all of the machines had been sold, the total income had to be sufficient to return the original investment plus a gain of $7,000.

● Exercise 2–14

Use an equation to solve each of the following problems. Check each answer.

1. The sum of two numbers is 283. One of the numbers is 7 more than the other number. Find the numbers.

2. The sum of two numbers is 99. One of the numbers is 5 less than the other number. Find the numbers.

3. The sum of two numbers is 84, and the difference of these same numbers is 24. What are the two numbers?

4. The sum of two numbers is 75. One number is 21 larger than the other number. What is the smaller number?

5. The sum of two numbers is 79. The smaller number is 13 less than the larger number. What is the larger number?

6. Find three consecutive numbers whose sum is 348.

7. The sum of four consecutive even numbers is 284. Find the numbers.

8. The sum of three numbers is 396. The second number is twice the size of the first number, and the third number is three times the second number. Find the numbers.

9. The sum of two numbers is 595. One of the numbers is 39 more than the other number. Find the numbers.

10. The sum of three consecutive numbers is 237. Find the numbers.

11. The sum of three numbers is 206. The second number is twice the first number, and the third number is 6 more than the first number. Find the numbers.

12. The sum of two numbers is 64. One of the numbers is three times the other number. Find the numbers.

13. One number is twice the size of another number. Their sum is 87. Find the numbers.

14. The sum of two consecutive numbers is 341. Find the numbers.

15. The sum of two consecutive even numbers is 266. Find the numbers.

16. Find three consecutive odd numbers whose sum is 681.

17. The sum of three consecutive odd numbers is 219. Find the numbers.

18. If a certain number is added to 72, the result is the same as 4 more than three times the number. Find the number.

19. If twice a certain number is increased by 50, the result is the same as when three times the number is increased by 2. Find the number.

20. The difference between two numbers is 29. The sum of the two numbers is 209. Find the numbers.

21. A woman is four times as old as her daughter. In 4 years she will be only three times as old as her daughter will be then. How old are **(a)** the daughter and **(b)** the mother?

22. A father is five times as old as his son. Nine years from now he will be only three times as old as his son will be then. How old are **(a)** the son and **(b)** the father?

23. When 197 is subtracted from three times a certain number, the result is the same as when 35 is subtracted from twice the number. Find the number.

24. At a theater, the charge was $12 for each reserved seat ticket and $7 for each general admission ticket. A total of 750 tickets were sold for a total of $6,390. **(a)** How many general admission tickets were sold? **(b)** How many reserved seat tickets were sold?

25. Partners Abbott and Barstow earned $356 in a certain business transaction. By agreement, Abbott received three times as much as Barstow. How much did each partner receive?

26. How much will 8 boxes of apples cost if 3 boxes cost $27?

27. Susan drove 797 miles in two days. On the second day she drove 75 miles farther than she drove on the first day. How many miles did she drive the second day?

28. Barton and Carter invested $54,000 in a business. Barton invested $2,500 more than Carter. How much did Carter invest in the business?

29. Twenty bills of currency consisting of $5 bills and $10 bills amount to a total of $160. **(a)** How many $5 bills are there? **(b)** How many $10 bills are there?

30. Mary Scuhler bought 200 shares of a certain stock for $30 a share. She sold part of them for $40 each and the remainder for $25 each. Her gross profit amounted to $950. **(a)** How many shares of this stock did she sell for $40 each? **(b)** How many shares did she sell at $25 each?

Solve these problems. If you have difficulty solving any problem, restudy the appropriate section in this chapter. The problems under a specific number are related to those contained in the exercise with the same last number.

1. Add these signed numbers.

a. $+7$
$\underline{+6}$

b. -9
$\underline{-7}$

c. $+7$
$\underline{-5}$

d. $-7x$
$\underline{+4x}$

e. -60
-11
$\underline{-30}$

f. $+69$
-29
$\underline{+43}$

g. -91
$+19$
$\underline{+52}$

h. $-86ab$
$+99ab$
$\underline{-34ab}$

2. Multiply these signed numbers.

a. 9
$\underline{6}$

b. 9
$\underline{-6}$

c. -9
$\underline{6}$

d. -9
$\underline{-6}$

e. $-807ab$
$\underline{5}$

f. $(-7)(+6)(-9)$

g. $(-7)(+7)(+4)(-5)$

h. $(-4)(+3)(-4)(+2)(-8)$

3. Subtract these signed numbers. Check the accuracy of each answer.

a. $+63$
$\underline{+42}$

c. -67
$\underline{-51}$

e. -58
$\underline{32}$

g. $+628$
$\underline{+409}$

b. $+50$
$\underline{-39}$

d. $-56n$
$\underline{+47n}$

f. -140
$\underline{-95}$

h. $+410xy$
$\underline{-268xy}$

4. Divide these signed numbers. Check each answer by multiplying the quotient by the divisor.

a. $\dfrac{+52}{+4}$

c. $\dfrac{-95}{+5}$

e. $\dfrac{-72}{-8}$

g. $\dfrac{351}{-9}$

b. $\dfrac{-54}{-3}$

d. $\dfrac{+96}{-6}$

f. $\dfrac{-68}{4}$

h. $\dfrac{-448}{-7}$

5. Use the distributive property to rewrite each of the following.

a. $6(20 + 9)$

c. $(7 \times 6) + (6 \times 8)$

e. $8(27 - 4)$

b. $(40 + 7) \times 5$

d. $(4 \times 23) - (4 \times 15)$

f. 5×45

6. Solve these equations and check each answer.

a. $n + 58 = 73$

c. $x - 25 = 81$

b. $121 = Y - 64$

d. $65 = 29 + Z$

7. Solve these equations. Check each answer.

a. $7n = 266$

d. $3n + 3 + 8n = 4n + 24$

b. $237 - 6Z = 75$

e. $4y + 3 = 75$

c. $x \div 13 = 15$

f. $6x + 16 = 5x + 3x - 62$

8. Solve these equations and check each answer.

a. $n(270 \div 9) = 60$

b. $4(x - 3) + 2(x - 1) = 106$

Chapter 2. Introduction to Algebra and the Pocket Calculator

c. $6y + 3(y - 5) = 7y + 3$
d. $5(z + 4) - 3(z - 3) = 39$
e. $3[4z - 2(z + 5)] = 4(z + 7) - 28$
f. $3[7n - 3(n + 2)] = 5(n - 2) + 6(n + 1) - 2$

9. Solve each problem.
    a. $93,452 + 10,854 - 43,059 - 66,159$
    b. $54,725 - 97,942 + 84,235 - 6,853 - 92,452$
    c. $-645 + 926 + (-660) + 629$
    d. $-546 + 899 + (-930) + (-914) + 837$

10. Solve these problems.

    a. $868 \times 53 \times 45$

    b. $7,848 \times 84 \times 86$

    c. $9,566,250 \div 76,530$

    d. $\dfrac{10,030,236}{3,658}$

    e. $441,558 \times 38 \div 481$

    f. $\dfrac{57,021 \times 354}{687}$

11. Solve these problems.

    a. Write the on-line form for $\dfrac{1,288 \times 5 \times 6}{8 \times 7}$.

    b. Write the on-line form for $\dfrac{(34 + 8) \times 4}{14}$.

    c. $n = 57 + 31 \times 45 \div 15$

    d. $n = \dfrac{336 \div 4 + 51 \times 35}{15 + 6}$

12. Use the memory register of your calculator to solve these equations.
    a. $n = (54 \times 71) + (67 \times 53)$ **c.** $y = (207 \times 92) \div (69 \times 23)$
    b. $x = (47 \times 82) - (58 \times 45)$ **d.** $z = (675 \times 162) \div (135 \times 54)$

13. Use algebraic symbols to write each of the following.
    a. 3 times the sum of x and y **c.** One-half of n
    b. 7 less than x **d.** y decreased by half itself

14. Use an equation in good form to solve each of the following problems. Check each answer.
    a. The sum of two numbers is 326. One of the numbers is 48 larger than the other number. Find the numbers.
    b. The sum of three consecutive numbers is 384. Find the numbers.
    c. The sum of three consecutive odd numbers is 291. Find the numbers.
    d. The sum of three numbers is 321. The second number is twice the first number, and the third number is 6 more than the second number. Find the numbers.
    e. The sum of two numbers is 34. Four times the larger number is 4 more than seven times the smaller number. Find the numbers.
    f. Pedro traveled 859 miles in two days. On the second day he traveled 63 miles farther than on the first day. How many miles did he travel the first day?

g. If 5 employees are paid a total of $400 a day, how much would be paid to 9 employees earning the same daily wages?

h. Long and Martin invested a total of $134,500 in a business. Long invested $14,500 more than Martin. How much did Long invest?

i. Nan is four times as old as her younger brother Mike. In 6 years she will be only twice as old as her brother will be then. How old are **(1)** Mike and **(2)** Nan?

j. After the taxes, legal fees, and other claims had been paid, $662,400 remaining of an estate was divided among the wife, two sons, and two grandchildren of the deceased. The wife received three times as much as each son, and each son received twice as much as each grandchild. How much was received by **(1)** each grandchild, **(2)** each son, and **(3)** the wife?

CHALLENGE PROBLEM

Wendy Cretty borrowed $480 from her mother for a business venture. She paid the city $50 for a vending permit to sell large, individually-wrapped cookies to spectators at the local college's homecoming parade on Main Street. She rented four vending cases with shoulder straps. The cases rented for $15 each, which could be paid on their return, but the deposit of $35 each had to be paid in advance. She spent $30 for paper napkins. The baker knew her and agreed to let her have $460 of cookies with a down payment of $260 and the right to return any wrapped and unbroken cookies for full credit. During the parade she and three helpers (at $20 each) sold $785 of cookies. After she returned $50 worth of cookies and paid the baker, she returned the vending cases. How much did she earn if she insisted that her mother take $25 for the use of the venture capital?

Chapter 3

Common Fractions

Objectives

After mastering the material in Chapter 3, you will be able to:

- Understand the meaning of *numerator, denominator, improper fraction, complex fraction, mixed number, greatest common divisor, lowest common denominator, reciprocal, ratio,* and *proportion.*
- Change common fractions to higher and lower terms.
- Understand the rules regarding divisibility of numbers.
- Find the greatest common divisor and the lowest common denominator.
- Change improper fractions to mixed numbers and vice versa.
- Add, subtract, multiply, and divide common fractions and mixed numbers.
- Simplify complex fractions.
- Solve ratio and proportion problems.
- Solve equations and word problems that contain common fractions.

> **COUNTRY SETTING**
>
> This sparkling 3,250 sq ft home will delight you with its four bedrooms, 3-1/2 baths, convenient built-ins, new draperies, and quality carpeting. It is located near the foothills on 1/3 acre that is attractively landscaped. Call now to see this excellent buy at only $259,500 with 1/5 down.

58

The preceding advertisement of a house for sale is just one example of how fractions are found in personal and business mathematics. Every day, via newspapers, radio, and television, one can see and hear similar uses of fractions. Here are just a few examples: "Save $\frac{1}{4}$ on this automobile that is powered by a gas-saving engine"; "Cascade Corporation shares, $67\frac{3}{8}$"; "driving time, $3\frac{1}{2}$ hours"; "$\frac{3}{4}$ horsepower motor." Such numbers are so prevalent that the business employee needs a solid foundation in the use of fractions.

PROPERTIES OF COMMON FRACTIONS

Numbers such as $\frac{1}{2}$, $\frac{2}{3}$, and $\frac{3}{4}$ are **common fractions.** Each of these numbers is composed of a **numerator** (the top digit) and a **denominator** (the bottom digit). The denominator indicates the name of the fraction, as half, third, fourth, etc. The numerator of a fraction indicates the number of parts contained in the fraction, as "one" half, "two" thirds, and "three" fourths. The numerator and denominator are the **terms** of the fraction.

$$\frac{2}{3} \quad \begin{array}{l} \text{numerator} \\ \text{denominator} \end{array}$$

A **proper fraction** is one in which the numerator is smaller than the denominator, such as $\frac{2}{3}$. An **improper fraction** is one in which the numerator is equal to or larger than the denominator, such as $\frac{3}{3}$ or $\frac{4}{3}$. A **mixed number** is a number composed of both a whole number and a common fraction, such as $3\frac{1}{4}$. Fractions in which the numerator or the denominator or both are fractions or mixed numbers are **complex fractions.** The following are examples of complex fractions:

$$\frac{\frac{1}{4}}{\frac{1}{2}} \qquad \frac{\frac{1}{4}}{3} \qquad \frac{4}{\frac{1}{2}} \qquad \frac{3}{4\frac{1}{2}} \qquad \frac{3\frac{1}{4}}{5} \qquad \frac{5\frac{1}{2}}{4\frac{1}{4}}$$

Equivalent Fractions

Two twenty-five cent pieces may be thought of as two quarters or one-half dollar or fifty cents. In other words, two quarters may be thought of as $\frac{2}{4}$, $\frac{1}{2}$, or $\frac{50}{100}$ of a dollar. Any common fraction is simply one member of an infinite set of equal fractions. For example, $\frac{1}{2}$, $\frac{2}{4}$, $\frac{4}{8}$, $\frac{8}{16}$, and $\frac{16}{32}$ are some of the fractions contained in the infinite set of fractions that equal $\frac{1}{2}$. Similarly, $\frac{1}{3}$, $\frac{2}{6}$, $\frac{3}{9}$, $\frac{4}{12}$, and $\frac{7}{21}$ are some of the fractions contained in the set of equal fractions that may be represented by $\frac{1}{3}$ in lowest terms.

The procedures involved in changing a fraction from one denominator to another rest on two fundamental principles:

> 1. Multiplying both the numerator and the denominator of a fraction by the same number, except zero, gives another fraction of equal value.
> 2. Dividing both the numerator and the denominator of a fraction by the same number, except zero, gives another fraction of equal value.

Changing Fractions to Higher Terms. To change a fraction to an equivalent fraction in higher terms, multiply both the numerator and the denominator by the single number that will produce the desired denominator. The factor to be used is found by dividing the desired denominator by the given denominator. In the following example, notice that the desired denominator 15 divided by the given denominator 3 reveals the factor 5. The solution to changing the form of the fraction to fifteenths, therefore, rests on multiplying both the denominator 3 and the numerator 2 by the same number, which is 5. The procedure gives $\frac{10}{15}$ as the equivalent fraction.

Example: $\frac{2}{3} = \frac{?}{15}$

Solution: $\frac{2 \times 5 = 10}{3 \times 5 = 15}$ The numerator and denominator must be multiplied by the same number.

Another analysis for solving the problem in the example is this:

$$\frac{2}{3} = \frac{n}{15}$$

$$\frac{2}{3} \times 15 = n$$

$$10 = n$$

Changing Fractions to Lower Terms. When both the numerator and denominator of a fraction are divided by the same number, other than zero, an equivalent fraction in lower terms is obtained. The divisor used to obtain a desired denominator is found by dividing the given denominator by the desired denominator. In the example below, the given denominator 18 is divided by the desired denominator 3 to reveal the common divisor 6. The problem is then solved by dividing the numerator by 6.

Example: $\frac{12}{18} = \frac{?}{3}$

Solution: $\frac{12 \div 6}{18 \div 6} = \frac{2}{3}$ The numerator must be divided by the same number as the denominator.

Part 1.   Mathematics Applications in Preparing a Basic Foundation

Another analysis for solving this equation is this:

$$\frac{12}{18} = \frac{n}{3}$$

$$\frac{12}{18} \times 3 = n$$

$$2 = n$$

● Exercise 3–1

Change these fractions to the higher or lower terms indicated.

1. $\frac{1}{4} = \frac{}{24}$ 7. $\frac{5}{8} = \frac{}{120}$ 13. $\frac{9}{36} = \frac{}{4}$ 19. $\frac{60}{100} = \frac{}{5}$

2. $\frac{3}{4} = \frac{}{24}$ 8. $\frac{7}{9} = \frac{}{108}$ 14. $\frac{3}{18} = \frac{}{6}$ 20. $\frac{12}{32} = \frac{}{8}$

3. $\frac{1}{3} = \frac{}{24}$ 9. $\frac{8}{11} = \frac{}{154}$ 15. $\frac{14}{21} = \frac{}{3}$ 21. $\frac{63}{77} = \frac{}{11}$

4. $\frac{2}{3} = \frac{}{24}$ 10. $\frac{5}{12} = \frac{}{156}$ 16. $\frac{54}{72} = \frac{}{4}$ 22. $\frac{35}{75} = \frac{}{15}$

5. $\frac{3}{5} = \frac{}{60}$ 11. $\frac{9}{16} = \frac{}{144}$ 17. $\frac{45}{72} = \frac{}{8}$ 23. $\frac{12}{56} = \frac{}{14}$

6. $\frac{4}{7} = \frac{}{42}$ 12. $\frac{5}{24} = \frac{}{120}$ 18. $\frac{5}{60} = \frac{}{12}$ 24. $\frac{84}{144} = \frac{}{12}$

Finding the Greatest Common Divisor

A common fraction in an answer to a problem should be expressed in lowest terms. When the numerator and the denominator of a common fraction have no common divisor except 1, the fraction is in lowest terms. One means of reducing a fraction to lowest terms is to use successive divisors until the number 1 is the only common divisor.

Example A: Reduce $\frac{24}{36}$ to lowest terms.

Solution: $\frac{24}{36} = \frac{24 \div 4}{36 \div 4} = \frac{6}{9} = \frac{6 \div 3}{9 \div 3} = \frac{2}{3}$

Another method of reducing a common fraction to lowest terms is to use the **greatest common divisor** (GCD). The GCD is the largest number that will divide without remainder into both the numerator and the denominator. Because fewer reduction steps are taken, using the GCD is usually faster than using successive divisors. Notice that in Example B only one step is used to reduce the fraction $\frac{24}{36}$, whereas two steps are used in Example A for the same fraction.

Chapter 3. Common Fractions

Example B: Reduce $\frac{24}{36}$ by using the greatest common divisor.

Solution: $\frac{24}{36} = \frac{24 \div 12}{36 \div 12} = \frac{2}{3}$

Finding the GCD through an arithmetic process may be desirable when a common divisor to reduce a fraction cannot be discovered by observation. To find the greatest common divisor of the numerator and denominator in a common fraction:

1. Divide the smaller number into the larger number.
2. Divide the remainder, if any, into the divisor used in the preceding step.
3. Repeat Step 2 until there is no remainder. The last divisor used is the GCD.

Example C: Change $\frac{91}{208}$ to lowest terms using the GCD.

Solution:

To find the GCD:

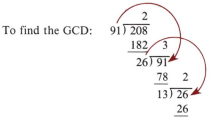

The last divisor (13) is the GCD.

To reduce: $\frac{91}{208} = \frac{91 \div 13}{208 \div 13} = \frac{7}{16}$

If the GCD is 1, the fraction is already in lowest terms.

● **Exercise 3–2**

Find the GCD and reduce the fraction to lowest terms.

1. GCD _____ $\frac{153}{180} =$ _____   **9.** GCD _____ $\frac{345}{420} =$ _____

2. GCD _____ $\frac{66}{143} =$ _____   **10.** GCD _____ $\frac{532}{635} =$ _____

3. GCD _____ $\frac{35}{84} =$ _____   **11.** GCD _____ $\frac{132}{372} =$ _____

4. GCD _____ $\frac{56}{128} =$ _____   **12.** GCD _____ $\frac{147}{378} =$ _____

5. GCD _____ $\frac{104}{265} =$ _____   **13.** GCD _____ $\frac{209}{266} =$ _____

6. GCD _____ $\frac{845}{923} =$ _____   **14.** GCD _____ $\frac{540}{837} =$ _____

7. GCD _____ $\frac{324}{390} =$ _____   **15.** GCD _____ $\frac{496}{640} =$ _____

8. GCD _____ $\frac{96}{2,252} =$ _____   **16.** GCD _____ $\frac{211}{712} =$ _____

17. GCD _____ $\dfrac{299}{345} =$ _____   **19.** GCD _____ $\dfrac{1,625}{1,716} =$ _____

18. GCD _____ $\dfrac{1,064}{1,925} =$ _____   **20.** GCD _____ $\dfrac{3,763}{4,240} =$ _____

Divisibility of Numbers

Whether one should attempt to reduce a common fraction by using a series of divisors common to the numerator and denominator or by finding the greatest common divisor is a decision that must be based on experience and familiarity with number relationships. Finding the greatest common divisor can be time-consuming. On the other hand, attempting to reduce a fraction by trial and error can be even more time-consuming unless certain rules regarding the divisibility of numbers are known. The skill acquired through a knowledge of these rules can be very helpful in reducing fractions to lowest terms and in solving problems in which canceling may be used. For example, reducing by canceling greatly facilitates the solving of problems in multiplication of common fractions.

Memorize these rules of divisibility for greater problem-solving skill.

1. A number is divisible by 2 without remainder if it is an even number. Thus, any number ending with 0, 2, 4, 6, or 8 is divisible by 2.
2. A number is divisible by 3 without remainder if the sum of its digits is divisible by 3. Thus, 267 is divisible by 3 because the sum of its digits (2 + 6 + 7), which is 15, is divisible by 3.
3. A number is divisible by 4 without remainder if its last two digits, considered as an individual number, are divisible by 4 or are zeros. Thus, 732 and 300 are divisible by 4.
4. A number is divisible by 5 without remainder if it ends in 0 or 5. Thus, 46,780 and 98,765 are divisible by 5.
5. A number is divisible by 6 without remainder if it is an even number and if the sum of its digits is divisible by 3. Thus, 2,574 is divisible by 6 because it is an even number and because the sum of its digits (18) is divisible by 3.
6. There is no simple method of testing divisibility by 7.
7. A number is divisible by 8 without remainder if its last three digits, considered as an individual number, are divisible by 8 or are zeros. Thus, 26,752 is divisible by 8 because its last three digits (752) are divisible by 8, and 21,000 is divisible by 8 because its last three digits are zeros.
8. A number is divisible by 9 without remainder if the sum of its digits is divisible by 9. Thus, 2,574 is divisible by 9 because the sum of its digits (18) is divisible by 9.
9. A number is divisible by 10 without remainder if its last digit is zero.

Determine which of the following numbers are exactly divisible by 2, 3, 4, 5, 6, 8, 9, and 10.

1. 37,256	11. 35,471	21. 78,295	31. 48,297	41. 8,325
2. 37,140	12. 57,692	22. 52,013	32. 68,427	42. 57,496
3. 28,769	13. 73,260	23. 51,023	33. 62,000	43. 54,386
4. 32,109	14. 82,419	24. 74,688	34. 36,985	44. 27,324
5. 54,768	15. 72,108	25. 21,350	35. 74,859	45. 24,684
6. 23,718	16. 31,027	26. 28,346	36. 47,281	46. 37,648
7. 70,920	17. 78,564	27. 27,652	37. 39,254	47. 92,768
8. 39,815	18. 84,233	28. 60,247	38. 48,357	48. 32,104
9. 58,680	19. 96,272	29. 30,219	39. 84,678	49. 83,245
10. 24,765	20. 59,036	30. 53,671	40. 6,702	50. 97,837

Converting Improper Fractions and Mixed Numbers

Changing Improper Fractions to Mixed Numbers. Answers that contain improper fractions should be changed to whole or mixed numbers. To change an improper fraction to a mixed number:

1. Divide the numerator by the denominator.
2. Show any remainder over the denominator.
3. If necessary, reduce the fractional portion of the mixed number to lowest terms.

Example: Change $\frac{108}{8}$ to a mixed number.

Solution: $\frac{108}{8} = 108 \div 8 = 13\frac{4}{8} = 13\frac{1}{2}$

Changing Mixed Numbers to Improper Fractions. Mixed numbers may be changed to improper fractions in the following manner:

1. Multiply the whole number by the denominator of the fraction.
2. Add the numerator of the fraction to the product obtained in Step 1.
3. Write the sum obtained in Step 2 over the denominator.

Example: Change $21\frac{3}{4}$ to an improper fraction.

Solution: $21\frac{3}{4} = 21 + \frac{3}{4} = \frac{84}{4} + \frac{3}{4} = \frac{87}{4}$

- Exercise 3–4

A. Change each improper fraction to a whole or mixed number in lowest terms.

1. $\frac{40}{3}$ 6. $\frac{207}{9}$ 11. $\frac{103}{8}$ 16. $\frac{286}{13}$ 21. $\frac{259}{24}$

2. $\frac{67}{5}$ 7. $\frac{25}{4}$ 12. $\frac{166}{9}$ 17. $\frac{1,052}{14}$ 22. $\frac{2,488}{30}$

3. $\frac{145}{2}$ 8. $\frac{179}{6}$ 13. $\frac{249}{12}$ 18. $\frac{488}{21}$ 23. $\frac{3,755}{48}$

4. $\frac{68}{7}$ 9. $\frac{379}{9}$ 14. $\frac{165}{11}$ 19. $\frac{260}{12}$ 24. $\frac{8,961}{60}$

5. $\frac{217}{8}$ 10. $\frac{421}{5}$ 15. $\frac{133}{16}$ 20. $\frac{989}{20}$ 25. $\frac{5,551}{75}$

B. Change these mixed numbers to improper fractions.

1. $14\frac{1}{5}$ 6. $62\frac{1}{6}$ 11. $39\frac{5}{9}$ 16. $87\frac{1}{12}$ 21. $896\frac{3}{10}$

2. $32\frac{1}{4}$ 7. $321\frac{5}{8}$ 12. $67\frac{3}{4}$ 17. $541\frac{9}{10}$ 22. $41\frac{13}{24}$

3. $27\frac{1}{2}$ 8. $18\frac{7}{9}$ 13. $56\frac{2}{3}$ 18. $122\frac{5}{12}$ 23. $137\frac{9}{16}$

4. $23\frac{1}{3}$ 9. $34\frac{3}{5}$ 14. $171\frac{3}{8}$ 19. $120\frac{11}{20}$ 24. $214\frac{28}{30}$

5. $19\frac{1}{8}$ 10. $90\frac{2}{7}$ 15. $240\frac{4}{9}$ 20. $123\frac{4}{15}$ 25. $34\frac{35}{48}$

Finding the Lowest Common Denominator

The number 1 is called the **identity element** for multiplication and division because multiplying or dividing a number by 1 does not change the value, or identity, of the number. Any number larger than 1 that is divisible only by 1 and by itself is a **prime number.** For example, 5 can be divided without remainder only by 1 and by 5. This rule of divisibility also applies to 2, 3, 7, 11, 13, and many other numbers. The number 1 is not prime.

Any number that is divisible by some number other than 1 and itself is a **composite number.** For example, the number 4 is divisible not only by 1 and by 4 but also by 2. In other words, the number 4 is "composed" of 2 × 2. Other examples of composite numbers are 6, 8, 9, 10, and 12.

Common fractions should not be added or subtracted unless they are in a common denomination. Thus, when unlike fractions are to be added or subtracted, a common denominator must be found so that they may be changed to like fractions. In many cases, a common denominator may be obtained through inspection; in others, the lowest common denominator should be found through an arithmetic process. The **lowest common denominator** (LCD) is the smallest number into which each denominator in a set of fractions will divide without remainder.

A common denominator of a set of fractions may be found by multiplying the several denominators. The product obtained will be a common denominator, but it may be too large to facilitate accurate computation. To eliminate this possibility, the lowest common denominator should be found. To find the LCD:

1. Arrange the set of denominators in a row.
2. Divide a prime number into two or more of the denominators.
3. Write the quotients obtained and any numbers not divisible by the prime number below the dividends.
4. Continue dividing by prime numbers until no pair of numbers in a row is divisible by a prime number.
5. Multiply all of the divisors and final quotients together to obtain the lowest common denominator.

Example A:

Find the LCD of $\frac{3}{4}$, $\frac{5}{8}$, $\frac{7}{12}$, and $\frac{2}{15}$.

Solution:

```
2) 4    8    12    15
2) 2    4     6    15
3) 1    2     3    15
   1    2     1     5     LCD = 2 × 2 × 3 × 1 × 2 × 1 × 5 = 120
```

The process of finding the LCD may be shortened by canceling in this manner:

1. Cancel any denominator that will divide without remainder into any other denominator in the set.
2. Cancel any quotient that will divide without remainder into any number in its row.

Example B:

Find the LCD of $\frac{3}{4}$, $\frac{5}{8}$, $\frac{7}{12}$, and $\frac{2}{15}$.

Solution:

```
2) 4    8    12    15
2)       4     6    15
         2     3    15     LCD = 2 × 2 × 2 × 15 = 120
```

● Exercise 3–5

A. Find the lowest common denominator for each set of fractions.

1. $\frac{5}{6}$, $\frac{5}{12}$, $\frac{7}{18}$, $\frac{13}{30}$

2. $\frac{3}{8}$, $\frac{11}{12}$, $\frac{5}{9}$, $\frac{7}{15}$

3. $\frac{1}{2}$, $\frac{2}{3}$, $\frac{3}{4}$, $\frac{4}{5}$

4. $\frac{2}{7}$, $\frac{5}{14}$, $\frac{9}{10}$, $\frac{8}{21}$

5. $\dfrac{3}{5}, \dfrac{7}{9}, \dfrac{11}{42}, \dfrac{13}{24}$

6. $\dfrac{6}{11}, \dfrac{13}{45}, \dfrac{29}{54}, \dfrac{5}{66}$

7. $\dfrac{8}{9}, \dfrac{7}{12}, \dfrac{3}{8}, \dfrac{5}{36}$

8. $\dfrac{14}{27}, \dfrac{22}{75}, \dfrac{18}{35}, \dfrac{20}{90}$

9. $\dfrac{24}{49}, \dfrac{26}{63}, \dfrac{11}{18}, \dfrac{20}{45}$

10. $\dfrac{4}{13}, \dfrac{31}{84}, \dfrac{47}{60}, \dfrac{42}{65}$

B. For each problem, find the lowest common denominator for the set of fractions and then convert each fraction in that set to an equivalent fraction with the lowest common denominator.

1. $\dfrac{5}{6}, \dfrac{1}{4}, \dfrac{3}{8}, \dfrac{4}{9}$

2. $\dfrac{5}{8}, \dfrac{3}{4}, \dfrac{7}{12}, \dfrac{3}{5}$

3. $\dfrac{2}{5}, \dfrac{5}{6}, \dfrac{2}{3}, \dfrac{7}{9}$

4. $\dfrac{3}{7}, \dfrac{4}{5}, \dfrac{2}{3}, \dfrac{1}{2}$

5. $\dfrac{13}{15}, \dfrac{17}{20}, \dfrac{7}{12}, \dfrac{9}{10}$

6. $\dfrac{11}{15}, \dfrac{51}{63}, \dfrac{23}{45}, \dfrac{8}{9}$

OPERATIONS WITH COMMON FRACTIONS

Addition of Common Fractions and Mixed Numbers

Addition of Common Fractions. When common fractions are in the same denomination, addition is easy. Notice that 3 eighths plus 4 eighths equals 7 eighths, which may be expressed as $\dfrac{3}{8} + \dfrac{4}{8} = \dfrac{7}{8}$. Like fractions, those expressed with a common denominator, may be added by placing the sum of their numerators over the common denominator.

Only like items, chairs and chairs, dollars and dollars, eighths and eighths, should be added together. Therefore, to obtain a correct sum, unlike fractions should be changed to equivalent fractions expressed with a common denominator. To add unlike fractions:

1. Change the fractions to equivalent fractions expressed with a common denominator.
2. Add the numerators of the equivalent fractions and write the sum over the common denominator.
3. If applicable, reduce the answer to a common fraction or mixed number in lowest terms.

Example:

$$\dfrac{3}{5} + \dfrac{7}{10} + \dfrac{19}{20} + \dfrac{7}{16} =$$

Solution:

$$\dfrac{48}{80} + \dfrac{56}{80} + \dfrac{76}{80} + \dfrac{35}{80} = \dfrac{215}{80} = 2\dfrac{55}{80} = 2\dfrac{11}{16}$$

Addition of Mixed Numbers. Finding the sum of a set of mixed numbers may be accomplished in two steps:

1. Add the fractional parts of the mixed numbers.
2. Add the sum of the fractional parts to the whole-number parts of the addends.

Of course, the fractional parts should be expressed with a common denominator before their numerators are added, and the final sum should be expressed in lowest terms.

Example:

Add $23\frac{1}{4}$, $48\frac{2}{3}$, and $69\frac{1}{2}$.

Solution:

$$23\frac{1}{4} = 23\frac{3}{12}$$
$$48\frac{2}{3} = 48\frac{8}{12}$$
$$69\frac{1}{2} = 69\frac{6}{12}$$
$$140\frac{17}{12} = 141\frac{5}{12}$$

● Exercise 3-6

A. Add and show each sum in lowest terms as a common fraction or mixed number.

1. $\frac{2}{9} + \frac{5}{9}$ 2. $\frac{1}{3} + \frac{5}{6}$ 3. $\frac{3}{4} + \frac{7}{8}$ 4. $\frac{5}{12} + \frac{5}{6}$ 5. $\frac{8}{15} + \frac{4}{5}$

6. $7\frac{1}{2} + 13\frac{5}{8}$ 7. $3\frac{2}{9} + 5\frac{5}{6}$ 8. $9\frac{3}{7} + 6\frac{11}{14}$ 9. $8\frac{5}{16} + 7\frac{1}{4}$ 10. $6\frac{5}{21} + 8\frac{5}{7}$

11. $\frac{2}{3}$ 12. $\frac{3}{5}$ 13. $\frac{3}{4}$ 14. $\frac{3}{8}$ 15. $\frac{7}{10}$
$\frac{5}{8}$ $\frac{7}{8}$ $\frac{5}{9}$ $\frac{7}{12}$ $\frac{5}{8}$
$\frac{7}{12}$ $\frac{11}{12}$ $\frac{5}{6}$ $\frac{5}{6}$ $\frac{5}{16}$

16. $12\frac{7}{8}$ 17. $18\frac{4}{9}$ 18. $13\frac{2}{5}$ 19. $32\frac{3}{4}$ 20. $58\frac{5}{16}$
$7\frac{1}{4}$ $42\frac{5}{6}$ $19\frac{9}{10}$ $36\frac{5}{9}$ $77\frac{11}{24}$
$10\frac{1}{2}$ $13\frac{1}{3}$ $27\frac{7}{15}$ $47\frac{2}{3}$ $65\frac{3}{8}$

21. $9\frac{4}{7}$ 22. $7\frac{3}{5}$ 23. $19\frac{1}{7}$ 24. $23\frac{5}{16}$ 25. $54\frac{3}{4}$
$3\frac{1}{2}$ $4\frac{7}{10}$ $12\frac{5}{21}$ $19\frac{5}{24}$ $76\frac{1}{12}$
$6\frac{7}{10}$ $8\frac{5}{6}$ $4\frac{9}{14}$ $42\frac{3}{8}$ $32\frac{5}{18}$
$20\frac{3}{14}$ $5\frac{7}{15}$ $17\frac{3}{28}$ $37\frac{13}{32}$ $89\frac{7}{16}$

26. $4\frac{3}{7}$ 27. $39\frac{3}{32}$ 28. $42\frac{2}{5}$ 29. $152\frac{2}{5}$ 30. $422\frac{1}{2}$
$6\frac{5}{8}$ $8\frac{7}{16}$ $37\frac{7}{8}$ $685\frac{5}{9}$ $734\frac{4}{5}$
$7\frac{5}{21}$ $23\frac{5}{64}$ $68\frac{8}{15}$ $360\frac{14}{15}$ $276\frac{6}{7}$
$9\frac{3}{14}$ $17\frac{9}{20}$ $51\frac{2}{3}$ $834\frac{13}{18}$ $535\frac{24}{35}$

Part 1.   Mathematics Applications in Preparing a Basic Foundation

B. In the writing of the yardages of some kinds of cloth, eighths of a yard are indicated with a small numeral written at the upper right side of the whole number. In this case, 24^1 means $24\frac{1}{8}$ yards; 17^5 means $17\frac{5}{8}$ yards. To add a set of these yardages, (1) add the fractions; (2) divide the sum of the fractions by 8; (3) express the result as a mixed number in lowest terms; and (4) add the mixed number to the whole numbers.

Add each of the following sets of yardages.

1. $23^2 + 24^1 + 45^3 + 37^2 + 22^7 + 48^6 + 56^5$

2. $34^3 + 22^5 + 19^2 + 46^4 + 35^2 + 51^4 + 42^3$

3. $13^5 + 23^6 + 29^5 + 14^3 + 31^7 + 38^2 + 27^4 + 17^1 + 12^7 + 16^2$

4. $54^2 + 30^1 + 28^1 + 23^7 + 42^5 + 28^1 + 24^5 + 15^4 + 18^3 + 20^6$

Subtraction of Common Fractions and Mixed Numbers

Subtraction of Common Fractions. Only like items should be subtracted. Common fractions with different denominators, therefore, should be changed to equivalent fractions with a common denominator before subtracting. To subtract $\frac{1}{2}$ from $\frac{5}{6}$, the fractions should be expressed with a common denominator. Changing the $\frac{1}{2}$ to $\frac{3}{6}$ makes the subtraction easy; that is, $\frac{3}{6}$ from $\frac{5}{6}$ leaves $\frac{2}{6}$, which is $\frac{1}{3}$. The subtraction may be expressed as $\frac{5}{6} - \frac{3}{6} = \frac{2}{6} = \frac{1}{3}$. Notice that the difference between the numerators is found and the answer is expressed in lowest terms.

To subtract fractions having unlike denominators:

1. Change the fractions to equivalent fractions having a common denominator.
2. Find the difference of the numerators in the fractions having the common denominator.
3. Write the difference over the common denominator.
4. If applicable, reduce the answer to lowest terms.

Example: Subtract $\frac{1}{4}$ from $\frac{11}{12}$.

Solution: $\frac{11}{12} - \frac{1}{4} = \frac{11}{12} - \frac{3}{12} = \frac{8}{12} = \frac{2}{3}$

Subtraction of Mixed Numbers. The subtraction of a mixed number may be accomplished in two steps: (1) subtract the fractional portion of the subtrahend and (2) subtract the whole-number portion of the subtrahend. Of course, the fractional portions of two mixed numbers should be expressed with a common denominator before the operation of subtraction is performed.

Example A: Subtract $8\frac{1}{2}$ from $17\frac{2}{3}$.

Solution:

$$17\frac{2}{3} = 17\frac{4}{6}$$
$$8\frac{1}{2} = 8\frac{3}{6}$$
$$\overline{9\frac{1}{6}}$$

Chapter 3. Common Fractions

Frequently in the subtraction of mixed numbers, as in the subtraction of whole numbers, one whole unit should be "borrowed" from the next digit on the left. When the fractional part of the subtrahend is larger than the fractional part of the minuend, borrowing one whole unit simplifies the operation. The number of fractional parts contained in the whole unit is always equal to the denominator of the minuend. Observe in Example B, below, that the borrowed 1 is equal to $\frac{12}{12}$.

Example B: Subtract $15\frac{2}{3}$ from $36\frac{1}{4}$.

Solution:

$$36\frac{1}{4} = 36\frac{3}{12} = 35\frac{15}{12}$$
$$15\frac{2}{3} = 15\frac{8}{12} = 15\frac{8}{12}$$
$$\overline{\qquad 20\frac{7}{12}}$$

As $\frac{8}{12}$ is larger than $\frac{3}{12}$, borrow 1 whole unit, or $\frac{12}{12}$, from the whole number 36. This changes $36\frac{3}{12}$ to $35\frac{15}{12}$.

● ### Exercise 3–7

Subtract and show the differences in lowest terms.

1. $\frac{7}{8} - \frac{5}{8}$ 2. $\frac{7}{8} - \frac{1}{2}$ 3. $\frac{1}{2} - \frac{3}{8}$ 4. $\frac{13}{16} - \frac{5}{8}$ 5. $\frac{2}{3} - \frac{1}{8}$

6. $\frac{3}{4} - \frac{2}{9}$ 7. $\frac{5}{6} - \frac{3}{20}$ 8. $\frac{7}{10} - \frac{1}{4}$ 9. $\frac{11}{12} - \frac{3}{5}$ 10. $\frac{5}{7} - \frac{2}{9}$

11. $27\frac{1}{2}$	12. $39\frac{1}{4}$	13. $42\frac{1}{3}$	14. $68\frac{1}{5}$	15. $890\frac{1}{8}$
$\underline{8}$	$\underline{23}$	$\underline{27}$	$\underline{41}$	$\underline{671}$

16. 19	17. 16	18. 23	19. 42	20. 54
$\underline{12\frac{1}{3}}$	$\underline{4\frac{1}{4}}$	$\underline{19\frac{1}{2}}$	$\underline{27\frac{1}{6}}$	$\underline{38\frac{3}{7}}$

21. $85\frac{5}{9}$	22. $42\frac{3}{4}$	23. $74\frac{5}{6}$	24. $37\frac{7}{8}$	25. $34\frac{3}{5}$
$\underline{78\frac{2}{9}}$	$\underline{26\frac{1}{4}}$	$\underline{62\frac{5}{6}}$	$\underline{22\frac{1}{4}}$	$\underline{16\frac{3}{10}}$

26. $93\frac{3}{8}$	27. $78\frac{2}{3}$	28. $57\frac{5}{6}$	29. $72\frac{5}{7}$	30. $70\frac{3}{4}$
$\underline{34\frac{5}{16}}$	$\underline{42\frac{1}{9}}$	$\underline{48\frac{2}{5}}$	$\underline{29\frac{1}{4}}$	$\underline{24\frac{5}{14}}$

31. $28\frac{7}{9}$	32. $94\frac{1}{2}$	33. $176\frac{7}{10}$	34. $54\frac{2}{3}$	35. $63\frac{5}{6}$
$\underline{21\frac{1}{6}}$	$\underline{41\frac{1}{3}}$	$\underline{42\frac{2}{3}}$	$\underline{21\frac{1}{7}}$	$\underline{34\frac{4}{5}}$

36. $45\frac{3}{16}$	37. $64\frac{1}{4}$	38. $83\frac{3}{8}$	39. $92\frac{1}{16}$	40. $70\frac{1}{8}$
$\underline{21\frac{3}{4}}$	$\underline{29\frac{1}{2}}$	$\underline{44\frac{3}{4}}$	$\underline{45\frac{3}{8}}$	$\underline{52\frac{7}{8}}$

41. $57\frac{1}{2}$	42. $76\frac{2}{3}$	43. $79\frac{7}{15}$	44. $47\frac{5}{9}$	45. $192\frac{1}{6}$
$\underline{32\frac{4}{9}}$	$\underline{53\frac{7}{8}}$	$\underline{38\frac{4}{5}}$	$\underline{29\frac{5}{6}}$	$\underline{87\frac{3}{5}}$

Part 1.   Mathematics Applications in Preparing a Basic Foundation

46. $924\frac{7}{9}$	**47.** $862\frac{5}{14}$	**48.** $753\frac{5}{11}$	**49.** $627\frac{3}{8}$	**50.** $568\frac{5}{6}$
$637\frac{5}{6}$	$383\frac{3}{5}$	$709\frac{2}{3}$	$254\frac{5}{12}$	$375\frac{25}{36}$

Multiplication of Common Fractions and Mixed Numbers

Multiplication of Common Fractions. All problems requiring multiplication with common fractions can be summarized in this manner:

$$\frac{numerator \times numerator}{denominator \times denominator}$$

If any factor in a problem involving the multiplication of fractions is a whole number, it can be expressed as a numerator over the denominator 1. The numerical value of $\frac{13}{1}$ is the same as the numerical value of 13.

Example A: Multiply 13 by $\frac{2}{3}$.

Solution: $13 \times \frac{2}{3} = \frac{13 \times 2}{1 \times 3} = \frac{26}{3} = 8\frac{2}{3}$

When a whole number is multiplied by a common fraction, the product shows the value of the corresponding fractional part of the whole number. In Example A, $8\frac{2}{3}$ is the value of $\frac{2}{3}$ of 13.

Multiplying a fraction by a fraction shows the value of a fractional part of a fraction. For example, $\frac{5}{6}$ of $\frac{3}{10}$ is $\frac{1}{4}$. Or conversely, in accordance with the commutative law, $\frac{3}{10}$ of $\frac{5}{6}$ is $\frac{1}{4}$.

Example B: Multiply $\frac{5}{6}$ by $\frac{3}{10}$.

Solution: $\frac{5}{6} \times \frac{3}{10} = \frac{5 \times 3}{6 \times 10} = \frac{15}{60} = \frac{1}{4}$

Common fractions in a multiplication problem may be reduced before the numerators and denominators are multiplied. The process of dividing the same number into a numerator and a denominator is called **cancellation.** The divisor used must divide without remainder into both a numerator and a denominator. The numerator and denominator need not be members of the same fraction; but if a numerator is divided, a denominator must be divided by the same number.

Example C: Use cancellation to multiply $\frac{4}{9}$ by $\frac{3}{10}$.

Solution:
$$\overset{2}{\underset{3}{\cancel{\frac{4}{9}}}} \times \overset{1}{\underset{5}{\cancel{\frac{3}{10}}}} = \frac{2 \times 1}{3 \times 5} = \frac{2}{15}$$

Before multiplying, the numerator 4 and the denominator 10 are divided by 2; the denominator 9 and the numerator 3 are divided by 3.

Chapter 3.   Common Fractions

Multiplication of Mixed Numbers. Multiplying a mixed number by a fraction determines the value of a fractional part of the mixed number. Problems in which a mixed number is multiplied by a fraction can be summarized in the following manner:

$$\frac{numerator \times numerator}{denominator \times denominator}$$

The mixed number may be converted to an improper fraction.

Example A: Multiply $7\frac{1}{2}$ by $\frac{1}{3}$.

Solution: $7\frac{1}{2} \times \frac{1}{3} = \frac{\overset{5}{\cancel{15}}}{2} \times \frac{1}{\underset{1}{\cancel{3}}} = \frac{5 \times 1}{2 \times 1} = \frac{5}{2} = 2\frac{1}{2}$

When the mixed numbers are small, converting them to improper fractions and proceeding as in the multiplication of common fractions is quite satisfactory. To save time when the mixed numbers to be multiplied are relatively large, however, follow the procedure illustrated and summarized in Example B.

Example B: Multiply $45\frac{2}{3}$ by $32\frac{1}{2}$.

Solution:

$$45\frac{2}{3}$$
$$32\frac{1}{2}$$

$\frac{2}{3} \times \frac{1}{2} = \frac{1}{3} = \qquad \frac{2}{6}$ 1. Multiply fraction in multiplicand by fraction in multiplier.

$45 \times \frac{1}{2} = 22\frac{1}{2} = \qquad 22\frac{3}{6}$ 2. Multiply whole number in multiplicand by fraction in multiplier.

$\frac{2}{3} \times 32 = 21\frac{1}{3} = \qquad 21\frac{2}{6}$ 3. Multiply fraction in multiplicand by whole number in multiplier.

$45 \times 32 = \underline{1,440}$ 4. Multiply whole number in multiplicand by whole number in multiplier.

$1,483\frac{7}{6} = 1,484\frac{1}{6}$ 5. Add the properly aligned products.

Notice in Example B that the fractions in the partial products are converted to a common denomination and aligned properly before they are added together. Proper alignment, so that ones will be added to ones and tens will be added to tens, can be accomplished by placing the fractions in the partial products directly below the fraction in the multiplier.

Part 1. Mathematics Applications in Preparing a Basic Foundation

A. Show the value of each of the following in lowest terms.

1. $\frac{2}{3}$ of 18   **5.** $\frac{2}{3}$ of $\frac{3}{4}$ **9.** $\frac{4}{5}$ of $\frac{2}{3}$ **13.** $\frac{3}{5}$ of 72

2. $\frac{4}{7}$ of 35   **6.** $\frac{1}{4}$ of $\frac{2}{3}$ **10.** $\frac{5}{8}$ of $\frac{7}{10}$ **14.** $\frac{2}{3}$ of 42

3. $\frac{7}{8}$ of 48   **7.** $\frac{3}{5}$ of $\frac{10}{12}$ **11.** $\frac{1}{6}$ of $\frac{4}{5}$ **15.** $\frac{5}{8}$ of 53

4. $\frac{8}{9}$ of 72   **8.** $\frac{7}{9}$ of $\frac{18}{35}$ **12.** $\frac{6}{7}$ of $\frac{6}{7}$ **16.** $\frac{3}{4}$ of 65

B. Multiply. Cancel whenever possible and show the products in lowest terms.

1. $\frac{2}{3} \times \frac{3}{4} \times \frac{1}{5} \times \frac{3}{8}$ **5.** $\frac{5}{12} \times \frac{7}{11} \times \frac{4}{5} \times \frac{22}{25}$ **9.** $\frac{13}{15} \times \frac{7}{8} \times \frac{12}{28} \times \frac{25}{26}$

2. $\frac{1}{2} \times \frac{1}{6} \times \frac{9}{10} \times \frac{2}{3}$ **6.** $\frac{5}{6} \times \frac{18}{19} \times \frac{1}{9} \times \frac{4}{5}$ **10.** $\frac{1}{8} \times \frac{11}{15} \times \frac{40}{41} \times \frac{7}{10}$

3. $\frac{2}{4} \times \frac{1}{8} \times \frac{5}{6} \times \frac{3}{10}$ **7.** $\frac{5}{6} \times \frac{10}{11} \times \frac{6}{7} \times \frac{17}{20}$ **11.** $\frac{19}{21} \times \frac{12}{5} \times \frac{49}{24} \times \frac{10}{3}$

4. $\frac{7}{9} \times \frac{7}{14} \times \frac{2}{7} \times \frac{21}{28}$ **8.** $\frac{11}{12} \times \frac{38}{39} \times \frac{5}{4} \times \frac{16}{19}$ **12.** $\frac{9}{20} \times \frac{13}{15} \times \frac{24}{25} \times \frac{17}{36}$

C. Multiply and show each product in lowest terms.

1. $18\frac{2}{3}$ **2.** $72\frac{3}{4}$ **3.** $21\frac{2}{3}$ **4.** $17\frac{3}{4}$
   $\underline{6}$ $\underline{8}$ $\underline{12}$ $\underline{5}$

5. $42\frac{1}{3}$ **6.** $87\frac{5}{6}$ **7.** $112\frac{1}{2}$ **8.** $113\frac{2}{3}$
   $\underline{4}$ $\underline{9}$ $\underline{21}$ $\underline{7}$

9. 27   **10.** 33   **11.** 18   **12.** 15
   $\underline{3\frac{4}{9}}$ $\underline{3\frac{3}{11}}$ $\underline{2\frac{3}{4}}$ $\underline{5\frac{3}{4}}$

13. $7\frac{5}{6}$ **14.** $4\frac{1}{6}$ **15.** $8\frac{8}{9}$ **16.** $6\frac{3}{20}$
   $\underline{4\frac{1}{5}}$ $\underline{20\frac{3}{10}}$ $\underline{6\frac{3}{4}}$ $\underline{7\frac{5}{9}}$

17. $62\frac{11}{12}$ **18.** $75\frac{1}{6}$ **19.** $36\frac{4}{7}$ **20.** $64\frac{1}{2}$
   $\underline{12\frac{1}{7}}$ $\underline{18\frac{1}{10}}$ $\underline{19\frac{5}{9}}$ $\underline{13\frac{1}{4}}$

Division of Common Fractions and Mixed Numbers

There are several methods of dividing common fractions and mixed numbers. Two of these are (1) the common-multiple method and (2) the reciprocal method.

Division by the Common-Multiple Method. Both terms of a common fraction may be multiplied by the same number, other than zero, without changing the value of the fraction. The common fraction form is merely another means of expressing division. If both terms of a division problem are multiplied by the same number, except zero, the relative values of the terms remain unchanged. Generally in the division of fractions, the lowest common denominator is the best multiple to use because it facilitates canceling and saves time in reducing to lowest terms.

Example A: Divide $\frac{5}{6}$ by $\frac{3}{4}$ using the common denominator as a multiple.

Solution: $\frac{5}{6} \div \frac{3}{4} = \left(\frac{5}{6} \times 12 \right) \div \left(\frac{3}{4} \times 12 \right) = 10 \div 9 = 1\frac{1}{9}$

Division is the arithmetic operation of determining how many times one number is contained in another number. Dividing by a fraction simply determines how many times (or fractional times) the divisor is contained in the dividend, whether the dividend is another fraction or a whole number. Example A shows that the fraction $\frac{5}{6}$ is $1\frac{1}{9}$ as large as the fraction $\frac{3}{4}$. Example B shows that the whole number 5 is $7\frac{1}{2}$ times as large as the fraction $\frac{2}{3}$.

Example B: Divide 5 by $\frac{2}{3}$.

Solution: $5 \div \frac{2}{3} = (5 \times 3) \div \left(\frac{2}{3} \times 3 \right) = 15 \div 2 = 7\frac{1}{2}$

Dividing a common fraction by a whole number always gives a fraction for the quotient.

Example C: Divide $\frac{7}{8}$ by 6.

Solution: $\frac{7}{8} \div 6 = \left(8 \times \frac{7}{8} \right) \div (8 \times 6) = 7 \div 48 = \frac{7}{48}$

Example D illustrates that the common-multiple method may also be used to divide mixed numbers. Observe that changing the fractional parts of the mixed numbers to fractions with a common denominator can help one avoid making errors when the common denominator is used as the multiple.

Example D: Divide $7\frac{1}{3}$ by $3\frac{1}{2}$ using the common denominator as a multiple.

Solution: $7\frac{1}{3} \div 3\frac{1}{2} = (6 \times 7\frac{2}{6}) \div (6 \times 3\frac{3}{6}) = 44 \div 21 = 2\frac{2}{21}$

74

Division by the Reciprocal Method. A **reciprocal** is one of a pair of numbers whose product is 1. The reciprocal of any number may be found by turning the number upside down. Thus, $\frac{2}{3}$ becomes $\frac{3}{2}$, $\frac{1}{2}$ becomes $\frac{2}{1}$, and 5, which is $\frac{5}{1}$, becomes $\frac{1}{5}$. Notice that $\frac{2}{3} \times \frac{3}{2} = 1$, $\frac{1}{2} \times \frac{2}{1} = 1$, and $\frac{5}{1} \times \frac{1}{5} = 1$.

When the reciprocal method of dividing common fractions is applied, the rule is this:

> Invert the divisor and multiply.

Example A: Divide $\frac{5}{6}$ by $\frac{3}{4}$ using the reciprocal of the divisor.

Solution:
$$\frac{5}{6} \div \frac{3}{4} = \frac{5}{\cancel{6}_{3}} \times \frac{\overset{2}{\cancel{4}}}{3} = \frac{10}{9} = 1\frac{1}{9}$$

Example B: Divide 5 by $\frac{2}{3}$ using the reciprocal of the divisor.

Solution:
$$5 \div \frac{2}{3} = \frac{5}{1} \times \frac{3}{2} = \frac{15}{2} = 7\frac{1}{2}$$

Example C: Divide $\frac{7}{8}$ by 6 using the reciprocal of the divisor.

Solution:
$$\frac{7}{8} \div 6 = \frac{7}{8} \times \frac{1}{6} = \frac{7}{48}$$

When the reciprocal method is used to divide mixed numbers, they are usually changed to improper fractions before the divisor is inverted.

Example D: Divide $7\frac{1}{3}$ by $3\frac{1}{2}$ using the reciprocal of the divisor.

Solution:
$$7\frac{1}{3} \div 3\frac{1}{2} = \frac{22}{3} \div \frac{7}{2} = \frac{22}{3} \times \frac{2}{7} = \frac{44}{21} = 2\frac{2}{21}$$

● **Exercise 3-9**

A. Divide by using the common-multiple method. Show all quotients in lowest terms.

1. $\frac{3}{4} \div \frac{5}{4}$ 2. $\frac{7}{8} \div \frac{5}{8}$ 3. $\frac{9}{14} \div \frac{6}{7}$ 4. $\frac{5}{6} \div \frac{3}{4}$

5. $\frac{6}{7} \div 6$ 6. $\frac{7}{12} \div 5$ 7. $\frac{4}{9} \div 8$ 8. $\frac{5}{12} \div 12$

9. $14 \div \frac{4}{5}$ 10. $21 \div \frac{5}{6}$ 11. $37 \div \frac{7}{10}$ 12. $58 \div \frac{8}{9}$

13. $3\frac{2}{3} \div \frac{1}{2}$ **14.** $10\frac{1}{2} \div \frac{3}{4}$ **15.** $5\frac{7}{9} \div \frac{8}{9}$ **16.** $18\frac{1}{3} \div \frac{7}{12}$

17. $16\frac{7}{8} \div 8$ **18.** $18\frac{1}{3} \div 9$ **19.** $27\frac{3}{5} \div 5$ **20.** $36\frac{3}{4} \div 12$

21. $8\frac{2}{3} \div 4\frac{1}{2}$ **22.** $14\frac{1}{6} \div 6\frac{1}{3}$ **23.** $7\frac{1}{2} \div 4\frac{5}{8}$ **24.** $81\frac{7}{9} \div 11$

B. Divide by using the reciprocal method. Show all quotients in lowest terms.

1. $\frac{3}{4} \div \frac{1}{3}$ **2.** $\frac{2}{3} \div \frac{1}{4}$ **3.** $\frac{7}{8} \div \frac{2}{3}$ **4.** $\frac{4}{5} \div \frac{8}{9}$

5. $\frac{9}{10} \div 3$ **6.** $\frac{8}{9} \div 4$ **7.** $\frac{11}{15} \div 7$ **8.** $\frac{23}{24} \div 9$

9. $24 \div \frac{3}{8}$ **10.** $15 \div \frac{2}{3}$ **11.** $36 \div \frac{6}{7}$ **12.** $23 \div \frac{4}{5}$

13. $24\frac{7}{12} \div \frac{5}{6}$ **14.** $27\frac{2}{7} \div \frac{7}{8}$ **15.** $29\frac{5}{6} \div \frac{11}{12}$ **16.** $36\frac{6}{7} \div \frac{5}{21}$

17. $9\frac{11}{12} \div 8$ **18.** $8\frac{4}{6} \div 5\frac{4}{5}$ **19.** $80\frac{3}{5} \div 13$ **20.** $97\frac{1}{7} \div 17$

21. $7\frac{4}{5} \div 9\frac{1}{4}$ **22.** $13\frac{5}{8} \div 9\frac{3}{4}$ **23.** $4\frac{4}{7} \div 5\frac{11}{21}$ **24.** $40\frac{25}{36} \div 9\frac{7}{12}$

Simplification of Complex Fractions

A **complex fraction** contains a fraction or mixed number in its numerator or denominator or both. The following are examples of complex fractions.

$$\frac{\frac{1}{2}}{3} \qquad \frac{\frac{1}{4}}{\frac{1}{2}} \qquad \frac{5}{\frac{1}{4}} \qquad \frac{4\frac{1}{2}}{6} \qquad \frac{6\frac{3}{4}}{4\frac{1}{2}}$$

The line that separates the numerator and denominator of a fraction may be interpreted to mean division. A complex fraction may be simplified by carrying out the indicated division; that is, the numerator is divided by the denominator. Either the common-multiple method or the reciprocal method of dividing common fractions may be employed.

Example A: Simplify $\dfrac{4\frac{1}{2}}{6}$.

Solution:

Common-multiple method:

$$\frac{4\frac{1}{2}}{6} = \frac{4\frac{1}{2} \times 2}{6 \times 2} = \frac{9}{12} = \frac{3}{4}$$

Reciprocal method:

$$\frac{4\frac{1}{2}}{6} = \frac{9}{2} \div \frac{6}{1} = \frac{\overset{3}{\cancel{9}}}{2} \times \frac{1}{\underset{2}{\cancel{6}}} = \frac{3}{4}$$

     Part 1.   Mathematics Applications in Preparing a Basic Foundation

Example B: Simplify $\dfrac{6\frac{3}{4}}{4\frac{1}{2}}$.

Solution:

Common-multiple method:

$$\frac{6\frac{3}{4}}{4\frac{1}{2}} = \frac{6\frac{3}{4} \times 4}{4\frac{1}{2} \times 4} = \frac{27}{18} = \frac{3}{2} = 1\frac{1}{2}$$

Reciprocal method:

$$\frac{6\frac{3}{4}}{4\frac{1}{2}} = \frac{27}{4} \div \frac{9}{2} = \frac{\overset{3}{\cancel{27}}}{\underset{2}{\cancel{4}}} \times \frac{\overset{1}{\cancel{2}}}{\underset{1}{\cancel{9}}} = \frac{3}{2} = 1\frac{1}{2}$$

● **Exercise 3–10**

A. Use the common-multiple method to simplify these complex fractions. Answers should be given in lowest terms.

1. $\dfrac{14}{\frac{2}{3}}$ 3. $\dfrac{12\frac{1}{2}}{4}$ 5. $\dfrac{8\frac{1}{3}}{16\frac{2}{3}}$ 7. $\dfrac{14\frac{1}{9}}{\frac{2}{3}}$ 9. $\dfrac{2\frac{1}{2}}{7\frac{2}{3}}$

2. $\dfrac{8\frac{1}{6}}{\frac{2}{3}}$ 4. $\dfrac{3\frac{1}{3}}{\frac{5}{6}}$ 6. $\dfrac{\frac{1}{2}}{\frac{5}{6}}$ 8. $\dfrac{4\frac{1}{3}}{8\frac{11}{12}}$ 10. $\dfrac{37\frac{1}{2}}{100}$

B. Use the reciprocal method to simplify these complex fractions. Answers should be given in lowest terms.

1. $\dfrac{\frac{5}{6}}{2\frac{3}{4}}$ 3. $\dfrac{\frac{3}{4}}{5\frac{9}{10}}$ 5. $\dfrac{3\frac{1}{2}}{17}$ 7. $\dfrac{\frac{11}{12}}{7\frac{5}{6}}$ 9. $\dfrac{56\frac{1}{4}}{100}$

2. $\dfrac{\frac{7}{8}}{\frac{4}{5}}$ 4. $\dfrac{\frac{7}{9}}{11}$ 6. $\dfrac{\frac{8}{9}}{\frac{3}{4}}$ 8. $\dfrac{8\frac{1}{3}}{9\frac{7}{8}}$ 10. $\dfrac{13\frac{1}{2}}{12\frac{5}{8}}$

EQUATIONS, RATIOS, AND PROPORTIONS

Common Fractions in Equations

Equations that contain common fractions may be slightly more difficult to solve than those in which all the terms are whole numbers. The correct solutions to equations that contain common fractions, however, rest on a knowledge of the basic operations with common fractions presented in this chapter and an understanding of the mathematical rules for solving equations that are presented in Chapter 2. The problems in Exercise 3–11 are designed to give you practice in applying these operations and rules.

Solve for the unknown in each equation. Check each answer.

1. $N + 7\frac{3}{4} = 24\frac{7}{8}$

2. $\frac{5}{8}X = 240$

3. $D \div \frac{7}{9} = 630$

4. $\frac{x}{8} = 58$

5. $\frac{y}{57} = \frac{15}{57}$

6. $\frac{5}{6}N = 420$

7. $\frac{\frac{3}{8}}{Y} = 24$

8. $87\frac{1}{2} - Z = 47\frac{3}{4}$

9. $\frac{66\frac{2}{3}}{D} = 45$

10. $\frac{X}{\frac{3}{5}} = 56\frac{2}{3}$

11. $120 = Y - \frac{1}{5}Y$

12. $\frac{36\frac{2}{3}}{N} = 11\frac{3}{4}$

13. $1\frac{1}{2}X + \frac{5}{12}X = 253$

14. $6\left(Y - 7\frac{3}{10}\right) = 32\frac{2}{5}$

15. $X - 13\frac{1}{12} = \frac{2\frac{1}{2}(X + 8)}{20\frac{4}{7}}$

16. $136 = Z - \frac{1}{6}\left(Z - \frac{1}{6}\right)$

17. $6\left(N + 16\frac{2}{3}\right) = 250$

18. $\frac{4(X - 3)}{\frac{1}{2}} = X + 71\frac{2}{3}$

19. $R = \frac{24}{900 \times \frac{7}{12}}$

20. $\frac{6\frac{1}{2}}{100} \times \frac{3}{2} = \frac{48}{P}$

Ratios

A **ratio** is the indicated quotient of two mathematical expressions. A common fraction, because it may be interpreted to mean a division that will give a quotient, is a ratio. Like common fractions, ratios are usually reduced to lowest terms. The fraction $\frac{4}{12}$ may be reduced to the lowest terms of $\frac{1}{3}$. In ratio form the notation would be 4:12 (read as 4 to 12), which equals 1:3.

Example A: Partners Freese and Lopez invested $24,000 and $36,000, respectively, in a business. Find the ratio of (a) Freese's investment to Lopez', (b) Lopez' investment to Freese's, (c) Freese's investment to the total, and (d) Lopez' investment to the total.

Solution: (a) 24,000:36,000 = 24:36 = 2:3
(b) 36,000:24,000 = 36:24 = 3:2
(c) 24,000 + 36,000 = 60,000 Total
    24,000:60,000 = 24:60 = 2:5
(d) 36,000:60,000 = 36:60 = 3:5

Ratios should be expressed in like terms before being reduced. Notice that the ratio of 28 days to 12 weeks is *not* the ratio of 28 to 12. To obtain a correct ratio the terms must be converted to like terms expressed as days or weeks.

Example B:	What is the ratio of 28 days to 12 weeks?

Solution:	28 days ÷ 7 days = 4 weeks	**Or**	12 weeks × 7 days = 84 days
	4 weeks to 12 weeks = 4:12 = 1:3		28 days to 84 days = 28:84 = 1:3

Ratios appear in a great variety of business computations. Among these are the analysis of financial statements, the allocation of costs and expenses, and the distribution of earnings and losses. As with other kinds of mathematical problems, there is generally more than one way to obtain the correct answer.

Example C: Allocate overhead costs of $32,000 in the ratio of 3:5.

Solution:

Let $3n$ = first number and $5n$ = second number. Then:

$$3n + 5n = \$32,000$$
$$8n = \$32,000$$
$$n = \$4,000$$
$$3n = \$12,000$$
$$5n = \$20,000$$

Or $3 + 5 = 8$

$$\frac{3}{8} \times \$32,000 = \$12,000$$

$$\frac{5}{8} \times \$32,000 = \$20,000$$

When a ratio contains a set of two or more fractions, convert the fractions to fractions with a common denominator and then use the ratio of their numerators.

Example D: Allen, Barnham, and Clayton were partners who shared gains and losses in the ratio of $\frac{1}{2}$, $\frac{3}{8}$, and $\frac{1}{8}$, respectively. After Clayton retired, Allen and Barnham agreed to continue using the ratio of $\frac{1}{2}$ to $\frac{3}{8}$, respectively. Distribute a gain of $42,000 to (a) Allen and (b) Barnham.

Solution:

$$\frac{1}{2} + \frac{3}{8} = \frac{4}{8} + \frac{3}{8} = \frac{7}{8}$$

As the sum of the numerators is different from 8, the common denominator, use the ratio of the numerators 4 and 3.

(a) $4 + 3 = 7$

$$\frac{4}{7} \times \$42,000 = \$24,000$$

(b) $\frac{3}{7} \times \$42,000 = \$18,000$

● **Exercise 3–12**

Solve the following problems. Show ratio answers in lowest terms.

1. A college with 12,000 students has 4,800 students who are majoring in business. What is the ratio of the business students to the total?

2. In a business mathematics class there are 20 men and 15 women. What is the ratio of the men to the women?

3. Sylvia earns $375 a week and saves $25 of it. What is the ratio of her savings to her earnings?

Chapter 3.   Common Fractions

4. The total sales in a market amounted to $3,240 yesterday. Of this total, sales of bakery items accounted for $432. What is the ratio of bakery sales to total sales?

5. A baseball team won 15 games and lost 5. What is the ratio of the games won to the games played?

6. What is the ratio of 72 hours to 2 days?

7. What is the ratio of 4 weeks to 63 days?

8. If $7n$ represents the first of two numbers that are in the ratio of 7:6, how should you write the second number?

9. Allocate 216 in the ratio of 7:5.

10. Allocate 884 in the ratio of 4:13.

11. Rusher, Seymour, and Taylor invested $24,000, $42,000, and $36,000, respectively, in a business. They agreed to share gains and losses based on the ratios of each partner's original investment to the total investment. If their gain amounted to $44,880, how much should go to **(a)** Rusher, **(b)** Seymour, and **(c)** Taylor?

12. In an alloy, 11 parts of tin are combined with 19 parts of copper. This alloy would combine how many pounds of tin with 2,090 pounds of copper?

13. Partners Kern, Lemons, and Mundell are to share a loss of $20,700 in the ratios of $\frac{4}{5}$, $\frac{5}{6}$, and $\frac{2}{3}$, respectively. How much of the loss should be distributed to **(a)** Kern, **(b)** Lemons, and **(c)** Mundell?

14. Partners Drake, Edwards, Fletcher, and Gimmell share gains and losses in the ratios of $\frac{1}{3}$, $\frac{1}{4}$, $\frac{1}{6}$, and $\frac{1}{8}$, respectively. A partnership gain of $84,000 is to be distributed. How much of the gain should be allocated to **(a)** Drake, **(b)** Edwards, **(c)** Fletcher, and **(d)** Gimmell?

Proportion

An expression of the equality of two ratios is a **proportion.** Thus, a proportion is an equation, such as $\frac{8}{12} = \frac{2}{3}$, which states that one ratio (fraction) is equal to another ratio. Of course, the preceding proportion may be written as 8:12 = 2:3. In either case, it is read as "8 divided by 12 equals 2 divided by 3" or in the more common proportion expression of "8 is to 12 as 2 is to 3."

In the proportion 8:12 = 2:3, the numbers 8 and 3 are the **extremes,** and the 12 and 2 are the **means.** In any proportion, *the product of the means equals the product of the extremes.* Notice that 8 × 3 = 24 and 12 × 2 = 24.

Proportion problems usually require you to find the value of one of the missing terms. To solve such problems, the rule of cross multiplying the means and extremes may be used or the customary rules for solving for the value of an unknown in an equation may be used. The second method is preferable.

Example A: Find the value of n in the proportion $\frac{n}{39} = \frac{5}{13}$.

Solution: Multiplying the means and extremes gives:

$$\frac{n}{39} = \frac{5}{13}$$
$$13n = 5 \cdot 39$$
$$13n = 195$$
$$n = 15$$

Using the rule that a divisor becomes a factor on the opposite side of the equals sign gives:

$$\frac{n}{39} = \frac{5}{13}$$
$$n = \frac{5}{13} \times 39$$
$$n = 15$$

There are numerous techniques for solving proportion word problems. An easy method, however, is simply to consider every proportion problem as one in which a fraction equals another fraction. Naturally, the proportion equation is composed of two numerators and two denominators. In this method of solution, *the denominators are always expressed in like terms,* such as hours and hours, workers and workers, miles and miles. A letter for the unknown quantity is used as the numerator on the left side of the equals sign. The remaining known term becomes the numerator on the right side. The most important consideration in this technique is whether the answer should be larger or smaller than the given quantity. If a larger answer is to be expected, the larger of the two like terms is used as the *denominator* on the *left* side.

Example B: Fred is 5 feet tall and casts a shadow that is 8 feet long. A nearby post casts a shadow of 32 feet. How high is the post?

Solution: Notice that the like terms are *shadows,* not feet. As the post casts a longer shadow, the post should be taller (larger) than Fred. Therefore, the larger of the like terms becomes the denominator on the left side.

$$\frac{n}{32} = \frac{5}{8}$$
$$n = \frac{5}{8} \times 32$$
$$n = 20 \text{ feet}$$

When a smaller answer is to be expected, the smaller of the two like terms becomes the denominator on the left.

Chapter 3.   Common Fractions

Example C:	The windows of a building can be cleaned in 18 hours by 4 workers. At the same rate, how long should it take 10 workers to clean the windows?
Solution:	The like terms are *workers*. Because 10 workers should require less time than 4 workers, the 4 becomes the denominator on the left side.

$$\frac{n}{4} = \frac{18}{10}$$
$$n = \frac{18}{10} \times 4$$
$$n = 7\frac{1}{5} \text{ hours}$$

● Exercise 3–13

Solve the following problems, showing fractions in lowest terms.

1. If 48 workers can complete a production job in 27 days, how long should it take 60 workers to complete the job?

2. James is 6 feet tall and casts a shadow of 5 feet. A nearby tree casts a 40-foot shadow. How tall is the tree?

3. If 12 workers are needed to operate 4 machines, how many workers are needed to operate 20 machines?

4. Ten workers are needed to operate 5 machines. How many workers are needed to operate 32 machines?

5. If 320 operators are needed for 80 machines, how many operators are needed for 12 machines?

6. To operate and supervise 250 machines, 450 workers are needed. How many workers are needed for 10 machines?

7. An automobile used 33 gallons of gasoline to travel 924 miles. How far can this automobile travel if the 12-gallon tank is full?

8. If 350 feet of fencing cost $2,800, how much will 85 feet of this fencing cost?

9. An investor earned $1,920 on an investment of $24,000. At the same rate of return, how much would be received on an investment of $17,000?

10. A return of $240 is obtained from an investment of $1,600. At the same rate of return, how much would be obtained on an investment of $4,500?

11. If 1 inch on a map represents 45 miles, how many inches represent 675 miles?

12. A worker who earns $138 in three days would earn how much for working 17 days at the same rate of pay?

13. An automobile can travel 126 miles on 6 gallons of gasoline. How many miles can it travel on 32 gallons of gasoline?

14. If an automobile can travel 182 miles on 7 gallons of gasoline, how many gallons of gasoline will be needed for it to travel 1,040 miles?

15. The owner paid $8,505 in taxes on a property valued at $315,000. At the same rate, how much should be paid on another property valued at $468,000?

16. If $33\frac{1}{3}$ pounds of raw material cost $27, how much will 13,500 pounds cost?

17. A pilot flew from one city to another in 5 hours and 20 minutes at an average speed of 480 mph. How long should the return flight take at an average speed of 512 mph?

18. Water flows from a tank at the rate of 9,600 gallons in 120 minutes. How many minutes will it take for 14,250 gallons to flow from the tank?

19. During November of last year, the manager of a store ordered $144,000 of merchandise. Of this amount, $9,000 was for shoes. During November of this year, the manager plans to order $162,000 of merchandise. At the same rate how much should the shoe order be?

20. The site preparation for a building requires the labor of 32 workers for 54 days. How many workers would be needed to complete the preparation in 6 days less time?

COMMON FRACTIONS IN WORD PROBLEMS

In order to find the correct answers to many word problems, determining which of the basic operations should be performed is quite easy. For some word problems, deciding on the proper operations is not so easy. In the latter case, equations can help in selecting the appropriate operations. The use of equations can facilitate finding the correct answers to both short-statement and long-statement problems.

Short-Statement Problems

Most word problems that consist of short statements can be easily converted from word statements to more precise mathematical statements in the form of equations. Most such word problems that pertain to fractions can be categorized under one of the following three basic kinds of problems: (1) to find a part of a number (Example A), (2) to find what part one number is of another (Example B), and (3) to find a number when a fractional part of it is given (Example C).

Example A: How much is $\frac{5}{6}$ of 36?

Solution: $N = \frac{5}{6} \times 36$ **Check:** $30 = \frac{5}{6} \times 36$

$N = 30$ $30 = 30$

Example B: What part of 21 is 14?

Solution: $P \times 21 = 14$

$P = \frac{14}{21}$ **Check:** $\frac{2}{3} \times 21 = 14$

$P = \frac{2}{3}$ $14 = 14$

Example C: Three-fifths of what number is 24?

Solution: $\frac{3}{5} \times N = 24$

$N = 24 \div \frac{3}{5}$

$N = 24 \times \frac{5}{3}$ **Check:** $\frac{3}{5} \times 40 = 24$

$N = 40$ $24 = 24$

Notice in the preceding examples that the word *of* means multiply and the word *is* means equals. Certain words in statement problems can provide clues to the correct solution of the problems. Words such as *increase* and *more than* may indicate addition; *decrease* and *less than* may mean subtraction; and *goes into* may denote division. The way in which these words are used in the sentence indicates when they should be changed to the appropriate mathematical symbols.

● Exercise 3–14

Use an equation to solve each of the following problems.

1. How much larger than $50\frac{1}{7}$ is $65\frac{1}{3}$?

2. How much less than $83\frac{1}{3}$ is $30\frac{3}{5}$?

3. To what number must $\frac{3}{4}$ be added to get $\frac{23}{24}$?

4. How much is $\frac{5}{6}$ of 99?

5. What fractional part of 69 is 39?

6. The sum of $69\frac{1}{2}$ and $29\frac{1}{4}$ is how much less than $191\frac{3}{8}$ deducted from $434\frac{5}{16}$?

7. Add $79\frac{3}{10}$ to the quotient of $325\frac{12}{25}$ divided by $20\frac{3}{5}$.

8. What number is one-third of $8\frac{3}{4} \times 6\frac{7}{10}$?

9. How much is $\frac{7}{8}$ of 840?

10. What amount is $3\frac{1}{3}$ of 78?

11. How much is 84 increased by $\frac{1}{8}$ of itself?

12. What number equals 252 decreased by $\frac{2}{7}$ of the number?

13. What fractional part of $91\frac{2}{3}$ is $58\frac{1}{3}$?

14. Find $\frac{4}{9}$ of 639.

15. What part of 98 is 54?

16. Forty-two is what part of 72?

17. Fifty is $\frac{4}{5}$ of what number?

18. Five-sevenths of a number is 70; what is the number?

19. How much is $\frac{3}{16}$ of 256?

20. 680 is $\frac{5}{8}$ of what number?

21. $\frac{7}{16}$ is $\frac{3}{4}$ of what number?

22. What part of $\frac{5}{12}$ is $\frac{1}{3}$?

23. What part of 172 is 28?

24. What part of 37 is $12\frac{1}{3}$?

25. $42\frac{1}{2}$ pounds is what part of $56\frac{1}{2}$ pounds?

26. The decrease from 64 to 42 is what part of 64?

27. Thirty-six hundredths of what number is 296?

28. Fourteen and seven-eighths is what number divided by $\frac{5}{7}$?

29. 192 is what number plus one-fourth of that number?

30. What number increased by $\frac{3}{16}$ of itself is 570?

Long-Statement Problems

Careful reading of word problems is always advisable to find which operations are to be performed. Some long-statement problems contain key sentences that can be converted into equations. The content of even the most difficult word-statement problems can be restated to ask a question. This question can then be written in mathematical terms as an equation.

● Exercise 3–15

Solve these problems. Some contain key sentences; others should be restated to ask a question that can be written as an equation.

1. Stardust Electronics Company manufactures a device that costs $54 to produce. The device is sold for $90. What fractional part of the selling price is the cost?

2. An automobile traveled 48 miles in 45 minutes. At this speed, how many miles would it travel in $6\frac{1}{2}$ hours?

3. Atteberry contributed $58,000 in a partnership; Bailey, $78,000; Conners, $96,000; and Duncan, $56,000. What part of the whole did each contribute?

4. On a tract consisting of $49\frac{5}{7}$ usable acres of land, how many lots of $\frac{3}{7}$ acre each can be planned?

5. If 240 pounds of wheat will produce 180 pounds of flour, how many pounds of flour will 8,000 pounds of wheat produce?

6. A field of $29\frac{1}{2}$ acres produced 4,350 bushels of potatoes. What was the average number of bushels per acre?

7. In their partnership, Evans provided $\frac{1}{3}$ of the investment; Finney, $\frac{1}{4}$; and Garson provided the remainder. What part of the investment did Garson provide?

8. From a tract of land containing $723\frac{3}{4}$ acres, $116\frac{2}{3}$ acres and $62\frac{7}{8}$ acres were sold. How many acres were not sold?

9. A manufacturing company used its factory space as follows: $\frac{2}{49}$ for administration, $\frac{3}{7}$ for assembling, and $\frac{1}{7}$ for crating. What part of the factory space was available for other uses?

10. An estate consisting of $600,000 is invested by the trustees in marketable securities and real estate. Investments in real estate total $264,000. What fractional part of the value of the estate is invested in securities?

11. A certain room is $24\frac{3}{4}$ feet long and $16\frac{1}{2}$ feet wide. The width of this room is what part of the length of the room?

12. A house and lot are appraised at $199,800. If the lot is worth $\frac{2}{7}$ as much as the house, what is the value of (a) the house and (b) the lot?

13. Divide $90,000 between partners Hardy and Ivins so that Hardy will have (a) $\frac{2}{3}$ as much as Ivins, (b) $\frac{2}{3}$ less than Ivins, and (c) $\frac{2}{3}$ more than Ivins.

14. LuAnn Jennings spent $\frac{1}{5}$ of her net pay for rent, $\frac{1}{4}$ for food, $\frac{1}{8}$ for clothing, $\frac{1}{6}$ for travel, $\frac{1}{12}$ for entertainment, and saved the balance of $252. How much was her net pay?

15. Kelly and Logan are business partners. Their partnership contract provides that Kelly is to receive $\frac{5}{9}$ and Logan $\frac{4}{9}$ of the gains and losses of the partnership business. If Kelly received $38,400 last year as his share of the profits, how much did Logan receive?

16. A matching necklace and bracelet cost $7,040. The value of the necklace was $4\frac{1}{2}$ times the value of the bracelet. Determine (a) the value of the bracelet and (b) the value of the necklace.

17. A store's sales for two years totaled $1,257,320. Determine the sales for

(a) the first year and (b) the second year if the second year's sales amounted to $\frac{1}{8}$ more than the first year's sales.

18. Depreciation on its plant and equipment last year represented $\frac{1}{4}$ of National Carton Company's total manufacturing costs. Materials represented $\frac{1}{3}$ of the manufacturing costs, and labor costs represented another $\frac{1}{3}$. All other manufacturing costs were listed as Miscellaneous Overhead Costs. If the manufacturing costs last year totaled $9,735,000, how much was the total in Miscellaneous Overhead Costs?

19. During the first five months of the year, Northcrest Furniture Store spent $8,400 for advertising. This amount represents $\frac{3}{8}$ of the store's advertising budget for the year. On an average, how much can Northcrest Furniture Store spend each month for advertising during the remainder of the year?

20. A business building and its contents were valued at $793,000. The value of the contents was $3\frac{1}{3}$ times the value of the building. Find (a) the value of the building and (b) the value of the contents.

21. A table cost $594, which was $\frac{9}{11}$ of the cost of a desk. How much did the desk cost?

22. When Miller's Wholesale Company went bankrupt, it owed Harris Company $8,400. In settlement, Harris Company received $\frac{3}{7}$ of the claim. How much did the company receive?

REVIEW PROBLEMS

Solve these problems. If you have difficulty solving any problem, restudy the appropriate section in this chapter. The problems under a specific number are related to those contained in the exercise with the same last number.

1. Change these fractions to the higher or lower terms indicated.

   a. $\frac{2}{7} = \frac{}{224}$　　b. $\frac{80}{128} = \frac{}{8}$　　c. $\frac{144}{396} = \frac{}{11}$　　d. $\frac{7}{12} = \frac{}{252}$

2. Find the GCD and reduce the fraction to lowest terms.

   a. GCD _____　$\frac{65}{156} = $ _____　　c. GCD _____　$\frac{105}{112} = $ _____

   b. GCD _____　$\frac{57}{95} = $ _____　　d. GCD _____　$\frac{213}{356} = $ _____

3. Determine which of the following numbers are exactly divisible by 2, 3, 4, 5, 6, 8, 9, and 10.
   a. 64,079　　c. 92,000　　e. 74,622　　g. 47,268　　i. 28,285
   b. 63,491　　d. 52,360　　f. 84,157　　h. 31,331　　j. 72,456

4. a. Change each improper fraction to a whole or mixed number in lowest terms.

   (1) $\frac{235}{8}$　　　(2) $\frac{88}{5}$　　　(3) $\frac{341}{4}$　　　(4) $\frac{274}{7}$

   b. Change these mixed numbers to improper fractions.

   (1) $23\frac{7}{8}$　　　(2) $19\frac{2}{3}$　　　(3) $70\frac{7}{9}$　　　(4) $52\frac{5}{8}$

5. Find the lowest common denominator for each set of fractions.

a. $\dfrac{5}{9}, \dfrac{7}{12}, \dfrac{2}{3}, \dfrac{1}{6}$ c. $\dfrac{31}{65}, \dfrac{6}{13}, \dfrac{2}{5}, \dfrac{7}{10}$

b. $\dfrac{3}{7}, \dfrac{2}{3}, \dfrac{4}{9}, \dfrac{5}{6}$ d. $\dfrac{11}{24}, \dfrac{5}{9}, \dfrac{7}{16}, \dfrac{3}{8}$

6. Add and show each sum in lowest terms as a common fraction or mixed number.

a. $\dfrac{3}{15} + \dfrac{4}{5} + \dfrac{2}{3}$ c. $1\dfrac{2}{3} + 3\dfrac{1}{8} + 6\dfrac{1}{4}$ e. $98\dfrac{7}{24} + 85\dfrac{3}{8} + 74\dfrac{17}{36}$

b. $\dfrac{5}{12} + \dfrac{3}{8} + \dfrac{3}{4}$ d. $11\dfrac{1}{9} + 12\dfrac{1}{2} + 14\dfrac{5}{18}$ f. $76\dfrac{11}{63} + 83\dfrac{3}{11} + 47\dfrac{8}{9}$

7. Subtract and show the differences in lowest terms.

a. $\dfrac{8}{9} - \dfrac{3}{4}$ c. $39\dfrac{3}{16} - 17\dfrac{3}{4}$ e. $92\dfrac{1}{15} - 62\dfrac{9}{10}$

b. $\dfrac{11}{15} - \dfrac{3}{8}$ d. $31\dfrac{1}{2} - 16\dfrac{1}{9}$ f. $121\dfrac{1}{2} - 66\dfrac{9}{11}$

8. Multiply and show each product in lowest terms.

a. $\dfrac{9}{10} \times \dfrac{2}{3} \times \dfrac{3}{5} \times \dfrac{5}{7}$ c. $21 \times 4\dfrac{2}{3}$ e. $81\dfrac{7}{12} \times 29\dfrac{2}{7}$

b. $\dfrac{7}{8} \times \dfrac{2}{4} \times \dfrac{5}{6} \times \dfrac{12}{14}$ d. $16\dfrac{5}{7} \times 56$ f. $80\dfrac{5}{8} \times 21\dfrac{11}{12}$

9. a. Divide by using the common-multiple method. Show all quotients in lowest terms.

(1) $\dfrac{5}{6} \div \dfrac{2}{3}$ (3) $42 \div 4\dfrac{2}{3}$ (5) $46\dfrac{1}{3} \div 15$

(2) $\dfrac{11}{12} \div 7$ (4) $3\dfrac{1}{3} \div \dfrac{5}{6}$ (6) $42\dfrac{1}{2} \div 12\dfrac{2}{3}$

b. Divide by using the reciprocal method. Show all quotients in lowest terms.

(1) $\dfrac{3}{8} \div \dfrac{2}{5}$ (3) $14 \div \dfrac{2}{7}$ (5) $12\dfrac{3}{8} \div 18$

(2) $\dfrac{9}{11} \div 12$ (4) $14\dfrac{4}{9} \div \dfrac{5}{6}$ (6) $54\dfrac{5}{12} \div 25\dfrac{5}{6}$

10. Simplify these complex fractions. Answers should be given in lowest terms.

a. $\dfrac{\frac{2}{3}}{17}$ b. $\dfrac{21}{\frac{3}{4}}$ c. $\dfrac{\frac{3}{8}}{\frac{7}{12}}$ d. $\dfrac{\frac{5}{6}}{6\frac{1}{2}}$ e. $\dfrac{9\frac{6}{7}}{\frac{3}{5}}$ f. $\dfrac{8\frac{1}{6}}{12\frac{1}{3}}$

11. Solve for the unknown in each equation. Check each answer.

a. $\dfrac{6}{7}X = 210$ e. $X - 7\dfrac{1}{2} = \dfrac{3\frac{1}{3}(X + 9)}{5\frac{1}{6}}$

b. $\dfrac{9\frac{5}{6}}{N} = 18$ f. $\dfrac{3}{50} \times \dfrac{5}{4} = \dfrac{187\frac{1}{2}}{P}$

c. $85 = Y + \dfrac{1}{4}Y$

d. $7\left(Z + 5\dfrac{2}{7}\right) = 191$

Part 1.   Mathematics Applications in Preparing a Basic Foundation

12. The ratio of direct labor to raw materials on a production job is 5:3. How much did the raw materials cost if the direct labor cost $16,800?

13. George Hill earned $12,000 on an investment of $15,000. At the same rate, how much should be the return on an investment of $10,500?

14. Use an equation in good form to solve each of the following problems.
   a. Four-fifths is what part of $\frac{5}{8}$?
   b. How much is $\frac{7}{12}$ of 32?
   c. Eighteen is what part of 40?
   d. Find the cost of 750 feet of lumber at 84 dollars a thousand board feet.
   e. Fifty-two is $\frac{4}{9}$ of what number?
   f. What part of 86 is 64?
   g. Thirty-nine is three-fourths of what number?
   h. At 45 bushels to an acre, what is the yield of $1\frac{1}{4}$ acres?
   i. If a saddle horse eats $\frac{3}{8}$ bushel of oats each day, how many days will he take to eat 30 bushels of oats?
   j. A diamond ring was valued at $4,875. If the diamond was valued at $7\frac{1}{3}$ times the value of the setting, determine **(1)** the value of the setting and **(2)** the value of the diamond.

15. Solve these word problems.
   a. Karen Wilson received $9,540 as full settlement of her claim against a bankrupt company. In this settlement she received $\frac{5}{6}$ of her total claim against the company. How much was her total claim?
   b. David Bowman bought $267\frac{1}{2}$ acres of farmland. He later bought the adjoining farm consisting of $146\frac{5}{8}$ acres and then sold $187\frac{3}{4}$ acres from the two properties. How many acres of this land did he have left?
   c. The executor collected $630,700 and paid out expenses of $87,700 for an estate. In accordance with the will, the executor then paid the balance to the widow and her four children as follows: one-third to the widow and an equal portion of the remainder to each child. **(1)** How much did the widow receive? **(2)** How much did each child receive?
   d. A special blend of coffee was prepared that contained the following kinds and amounts: $14\frac{1}{2}$ pounds, Arabic; 29 pounds, Brazilian; and $21\frac{3}{4}$ pounds, Colombian. Each kind of coffee was what part of the whole blend?
   e. The owner of a building received $9,960 as the net rental for the year after her agent had charged $105 a month commission, paid $4,140 for repairs, and paid $1,800 for taxes. How much monthly rent did the owner charge the tenant?
   f. A furniture upholsterer uses $3\frac{1}{3}$ yards of fabric to cover a certain chair. There are in stock five bolts of this fabric in various patterns. Each bolt contains 40 yards. How many such chairs can be covered with this fabric?
   g. Production costs of an electric motor manufactured by Western Products Company are $132. In order to reduce these costs by $\frac{2}{11}$, the company plans to install new manufacturing equipment. The company also

plans to reduce the selling price by an amount that will equal $\frac{2}{3}$ of the savings in production costs. If the motor now sells for $212, what will be the new selling price?

You are the manager of Van Leer's Clothing Store, which is one of six such stores in your county. During the first week in January you and the owner, John Van Leer, discussed the company's sales plans for the current year. Your store has five departments. These are shown in this incomplete income statement for the past year:

Van Leer's Clothing Store
(Hometown Store)
Departmental Income Statement
for the Year Ended December 31, 19X1
(in thousands)

| | Clothing Department | | | | | |
	Boys'	Girls'	Men's	Women's	Shoes	Totals
Sales	$85	$135	$387	$390	$155	
Cost of Goods Sold	47	75	244	229	99	
Gross Profit						
Operating Expenses	27	65	131	142	57	
Net Income (or Loss)						

Mr. Van Leer has been researching economic forecasts, reading business magazines and newspapers, and discussing the new year's prospects with other business people. He has reached the following conclusions:

a. Sales, cost of goods, and operating expenses for men's and boys' clothing will remain stable.

b. The cost of girls' clothing is expected to increase $\frac{1}{5}$. Sales in this department should also increase by the same fraction, but operating expenses must increase no more than $\frac{1}{10}$.

c. Sales are likely to decrease by $\frac{1}{20}$ in the women's department and increase by $\frac{1}{10}$ in the shoe department. Total costs and expenses in these departments will not change.

d. Your bonus, which is $\frac{1}{5}$ of the net income after net income is reduced by $\frac{1}{5}$, will remain unchanged.

1. Gross profit is the difference between sales and cost of goods sold. Net income (or loss) is the difference between gross profit and operating expenses. Complete the income statement including the totals. Show any loss in parentheses.

2. The budget for the current year was prepared several weeks ago. Prepare a new departmental budget in thousands based on Van Leer's conclusions. Show common fractions.

3. How much is your bonus for the past year?

4. How much will your bonus be for the current year if the new budget is correct?

Chapter 4

Decimal Fractions

Objectives

After mastering the material in Chapter 4, you will be able to:

- Change decimal fractions to common fractions and vice versa.
- Add, subtract, multiply, and divide decimal fractions.
- Divide quickly by 10 and by multiples of 10.
- Compute quantity prices on an invoice.
- Perform constant operations in addition, subtraction, multiplication, and division with a pocket calculator.
- Calculate checking account balances in a check register.
- Reconcile a statement from a financial institution.
- Recognize aliquot parts and their fractional equivalents.
- Solve word problems that contain decimal fractions.

Although computing with common fractions sometimes gives greater precision than computing with decimal fractions, computing with a common fraction that has a large numerator or denominator may be too cumbersome unless the denominator is a power of ten. If the denominator is a power of ten, such as 10, 100, 1,000, the fraction can be written as a **decimal fraction**—commonly known as a **decimal**—by writing the numerator to the right of a dot that is called the **decimal point.** The denominator of the fraction is not written, but its value is indicated by the number of digits appearing to the right of the decimal point. Thus, $\frac{3}{10}$ may be written as 0.3, $\frac{3}{100}$ as 0.03, and $\frac{3}{1,000}$ as 0.003.

Few calculators have a special key that automatically converts a common fraction to a decimal fraction. Most calculators require that operations with fractions be performed in decimal form only, so common fractions in computations must be changed to decimal form. For example, to compute the cost of $49\frac{1}{2}$ yards of cloth at $17 a yard, the common fraction $\frac{1}{2}$ is changed to 0.5, which is an equivalent decimal fraction. The computation then becomes 49.5 times $17.

Example A: What is the cost of $49\frac{1}{2}$ yards of cloth at $17 a yard?

Solution: 49.5 $\boxed{\times}$ 17 $\boxed{=}$ $\rightarrow$ 841.5

Cost = $841.50

In some problems, however, a calculation should be shortened by changing a decimal fraction to a common fraction. For example, to mentally determine the cost of 36 pounds at $16\frac{2}{3}$¢ a pound, the $16\frac{2}{3}$¢ (that is, $0.16\frac{2}{3}$) can be changed to $\frac{1}{6}$ of a dollar. Multiplying by the common fraction $\frac{1}{6}$ is easier and more precise than multiplying by the decimal fraction 0.1667.

Example B: What is the cost of 36 pounds of fruit at $16\frac{2}{3}$¢ a pound?

Solution: $36 \times \dfrac{1}{6} = 6$

Cost = $6

In Example A, the computation is facilitated through the use of a decimal fraction. In Example B, it is facilitated through the use of the fractional equivalent of an aliquot part, which is defined in a later section of this chapter. Competent business employees should be adept at using both decimal fractions and aliquot parts. They should also be able to mentally convert commonly-used fractions from one form to the other. This facilitates both calculator input and read out.

PROPERTIES OF DECIMAL FRACTIONS

Credit for the basic idea of decimal notation is usually divided between Simon Stevin of Belgium and John Napier of Scotland. In 1585 Stevin published *La Disme* in which he recognized the importance of decimal fractions. Unfortunately his notation was poor. As a result of this, mathematicians were slow to adopt the new concept. In 1603 *La Disme* was translated into English, and in 1617 Napier used decimal fractions in his *Rabdologia*. In this treatise he suggested the use of the dot or the comma as a separator. Because Napier could not decide between the dot and the comma, mathematicians have vacillated between the two. In France, Germany, Italy, and the Scandinavian countries, a comma is used for this purpose; while in England the dot is placed above the line of writing, midway between the top and bottom of the number.

Although mathematicians have not agreed on the use of the dot and comma, they have agreed on the validity of Stevin's concept because in many instances decimal fractions are more meaningful than common fractions. If the cost of producing 43,800 bolts is $628.53, the cost of each bolt may be expressed as $\frac{\$628.53}{43,800}$. But this is too awkward for many computations. After this common fraction is converted to a decimal fraction by dividing the numerator by the denominator, the cost per bolt is found to be $0.01435 and the cost per 1,000 bolts, $14.35. In a similar manner, a cost accountant would determine how much of the $628.53 total production cost had been spent for material, labor, and overhead and then find the per-unit or per-thousand cost of each of these.

The results of such computations are of great value to management in reaching decisions regarding, among others, manufacturing standards, departmental efficiency, the control of expenditures, and the setting of competitive prices. Such calculations, like most of those that are made in commercial, financial, and industrial businesses, must be performed accurately. Computing accurately can be done only when one thoroughly understands the meaning of decimal fractions.

The decimal system of notation is a place-value system based on ten. In a whole number, the first place has a value equal to 1, and each place to the left has a value ten times that of the place to its right. Therefore, each place to the right has a value which is $\frac{1}{10}$ of that to its left.

The places to the right of the ones position follow the same rule. The first place to the right of the decimal point has a value equal to $\frac{1}{10}$ of 1; the second place, $\frac{1}{10}$ of $\frac{1}{10}$, which is $\frac{1}{100}$ or 0.01. Figure 4-1 illustrates this.

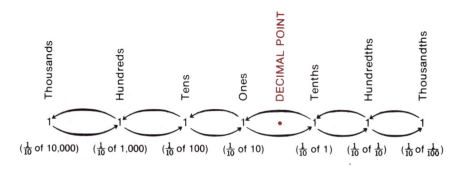

Figure 4-1 Decimal Value

A **mixed decimal fraction** is composed of both a decimal fraction and a whole number (247.3). In a **pure decimal fraction** there is no whole-number portion (0.169). A **complex decimal** is a decimal fraction that contains a common fraction (0.462$\frac{1}{4}$).

		Hundreds	Tens	Ones	DECIMAL POINT	Tenths	Hundredths	Thousandths	Ten Thousandths	Hundred Thousandths
Mixed Decimal Fractions	A.	2	4	7	.	3				
	B.		3	8	.	2	5			
Pure Decimal Fractions	C.			0	.	1	6	9		
	D.			0	.	0	0	0	5	4
Complex Decimal Fractions	E.			0	.	4	6	$2\frac{1}{4}$		
	F.			0	.	0	$7\frac{1}{2}$			

When a numeral contains a decimal point, the point is read as the word "and." As in the reading of mixed numbers and mixed decimals, the word "and" is also used to indicate the common-fraction portion of a complex decimal. The name applied to a decimal numeral is determined by the place occupied by the last whole digit to the right of the decimal point. The numbers in the preceding chart are read as follows:

A. Two hundred forty-seven *and* three *tenths.*
B. Thirty-eight *and* twenty-five *hundredths.*
C. One hundred sixty-nine *thousandths.*
D. Fifty-four *hundred thousandths.*
E. Four hundred sixty-two *and* one-fourth *thousandths.*
F. Seven *and* one-half *hundredths.*

Notice that $0.000\frac{1}{4}$ means $\frac{1}{4}$ of $\frac{1}{1,000}$ and that $0.00\frac{1}{2}$ means $\frac{1}{2}$ of $\frac{1}{100}$.

Equivalent Decimal and Common Fractions

In order to be adept at using common fractions and decimal fractions, you should know how to change a decimal fraction to an equivalent common fraction and how to change a common fraction to an equivalent decimal fraction.

Changing a Decimal Fraction to an Equivalent Common Fraction. To change a decimal fraction to a common fraction, express the decimal in common-fraction form in lowest terms. Whether the numeral is a pure decimal (Example A), a mixed decimal (Example B), or a complex decimal (Example C), the procedure consists of these two steps: (1) write the decimal fraction in common-fraction form and (2) reduce the common fraction to lowest terms.

| Example A: | Change 0.375 to a common fraction in lowest terms. |
| Solution: | When read as "three hundred seventy-five thousandths," the decimal may be easily written as a common fraction and reduced. |

$$0.375 = \frac{375}{1,000} = \frac{75}{200} = \frac{3}{8}$$

| Example B: | Change 38.25 to a mixed number in lowest terms. |
| Solution: | $38.25 = 38\frac{25}{100} = 38\frac{1}{4}$ |

| Example C: | Change $0.12\frac{1}{2}$ to a common fraction in lowest terms. |
| Solution: | $0.12\frac{1}{2} = \frac{12\frac{1}{2}}{100} = \frac{25}{200} = \frac{1}{8}$ |

Changing a Common Fraction to an Equivalent Decimal Fraction. The common fraction $\frac{5}{8}$ may be interpreted to mean division and may be rewritten as $5 \div 8$. Even though it is not shown, the decimal point is understood to fall just to the right of a whole number. Thus, $5 \div 8$ is understood to mean $5. \div 8.$, which shows where the decimal points fall.

To change a common fraction to an equivalent decimal fraction, the numerator is divided by the denominator after the appropriate number of zeros are appended to the right of the decimal point in the dividend. The decimal point is placed in the quotient directly above its location in the dividend. The digits in the quotient are written to the right of the point until the division is complete or until the desired degree of accuracy is reached.

| Example: | Change $\frac{5}{8}$ to an equivalent decimal fraction in thousandths. |
| Solution: | $\frac{5}{8} = 8\overline{)5.000}^{.625}$ **Or** $5 \boxed{\div} 8 \boxed{=} \longrightarrow 0.625$ |

Rounding Decimal Fractions. The rules commonly used to round decimal fractions are:

1. Underline the digit in the place specified. This is the place digit.
2. If the place digit is to the right of the decimal point, drop all digits to the right of the place digit.
3. The first digit in the portion to be dropped is the *test* digit.
4. If the test digit is 5 or larger, add 1 to the place digit.
5. If the test digit is 4 or smaller, do not change the place digit.

     Part 1. Mathematics Applications in Preparing a Basic Foundation

Example A: Round 8.125367 to the nearest ten thousandth.

Solution:

Test digit is 5 or larger.

$$8.125367 = 8.1254$$

Place digit is increased by 1 and digits to right are dropped.

Example B: Round 71.256839 to the nearest ten thousandth.

Solution:

Test digit is 4 or smaller.

$$71.256839 = 71.2568$$

Place digit not increased and digits to right are dropped.

$$\frac{585.}{1000} = .585$$

● Exercise 4–1

A. Change each of the following to an equivalent common fraction or mixed number in lowest terms.

1. 0.6	**7.** 0.000125	**13.** $0.37\frac{1}{2}$	**19.** $14.06\frac{1}{4}$
2. 0.06	**8.** 0.325	**14.** $0.66\frac{2}{3}$	**20.** $18.062\frac{1}{2}$
3. 0.019	**9.** 5.64	**15.** $0.83\frac{1}{3}$	**21.** $21.00\frac{3}{4}$
4. 0.196	**10.** 4.720	**16.** $0.87\frac{1}{2}$	**22.** $8.937\frac{1}{2}$
5. 0.2314	**11.** 7.099	**17.** $7.16\frac{2}{3}$	**23.** $31.08\frac{1}{3}$
6. 0.00816	**12.** 19.105	**18.** $5.91\frac{2}{3}$	**24.** $36.083\frac{1}{3}$

B. Change each of the following to an equivalent in decimal notation. Where applicable, round to the nearest ten thousandth.

1. $\frac{7}{10}$	**7.** $\frac{11}{12}$	**13.** $\frac{88}{9}$	**19.** $6\frac{9}{20}$
2. $\frac{7}{100}$	**8.** $\frac{1}{250}$	**14.** $\frac{5}{325}$	**20.** $5\frac{8}{250}$
3. $\frac{45}{1,000}$	**9.** $\frac{372}{100}$	**15.** $\frac{10}{278}$	**21.** $51\frac{3}{400}$
4. $\frac{75}{10,000}$	**10.** $\frac{295}{1,000}$	**16.** $\frac{83}{12}$	**22.** $46\frac{15}{16}$
5. $\frac{5}{7}$	**11.** $\frac{875}{1,000}$	**17.** $\frac{7}{16}$	**23.** $62\frac{7}{12}$
6. $\frac{5}{16}$	**12.** $\frac{31}{1,000}$	**18.** $3\frac{8}{15}$	**24.** $39\frac{3}{16}$

Chapter 4. Decimal Fractions

OPERATIONS WITH DECIMAL FRACTIONS

As with whole numbers, the basic operations of addition, subtraction, multiplication, and division of decimals must be computed accurately. Such computations must be accurate whether the operations are performed by a computer, a calculator, with pencil and paper, or mentally.

Addition and Subtraction of Decimal Fractions

The procedures for adding and subtracting whole numbers and decimal fractions are basically the same; like denominations should be added to or subtracted from each other. In the case of decimals, whether pure or mixed, this means that when one writes numerals to be added or subtracted the digits should be aligned properly, with the decimal points arranged in a straight vertical line. Proper alignment causes the digits to fall in place so that tenths, hundredths, thousandths, and any other decimal digits will be added to or subtracted from like denominations. When the numerals represent dollars and cents, proper alignment is easy because each amount includes two decimal places. As each dollar is worth one hundred cents, one cent is one hundredth of a dollar and may be written as $0.01 or 1¢.

Example A: Add $30.48 and $9.31.   **Example B:**   Subtract $3.12 from $5.67.

Solution:
$$\begin{array}{r} \$30.48 \\ \underline{9.31} \\ \$39.79 \end{array}$$

Solution:
$$\begin{array}{r} \$5.67 \\ \underline{3.12} \\ \$2.55 \end{array}$$

Of course, a calculator with a floating decimal will place the point properly.

When pencil and paper are being used to solve a problem that contains numerals which end in different place values to the right of the decimal point, the numerals may be rewritten so that each has the same number of places to the right of the point. To do this, zeros may be appended and common fractions may be changed to decimal fractions. This will align the problem and facilitate addition or subtraction.

Example C: Add $3.7\frac{1}{2}$, 0.604, 5.38, and 42.9.

Solution:

$$\begin{array}{l} 3.7\frac{1}{2} \\ 0.604 \\ 5.38 \\ \underline{42.9} \end{array} \quad \text{becomes} \quad \begin{array}{r} 3.750 \\ 0.604 \\ 5.380 \\ \underline{42.900} \\ 52.634 \end{array}$$

If a calculator is being used, common fractions must be changed to decimal notation.

Example D: Subtract $23.213\frac{1}{4}$ from $45.67\frac{1}{2}$.

Solution: $45.67\frac{1}{2}$ becomes 45.675
             $23.213\frac{1}{4}$ becomes 23.21325

45.675 $\boxed{-}$ 23.21325 $\boxed{=}$ $\rightarrow 22.46175$

● Exercise 4–2

A. Find the sum of each problem. Remember to place a decimal point in each answer.

1. $2.14, $1.67, $0.79, $3.16, $0.58   7. 2.17, 0.23, 0.071, 12.4, 0.272

2. $1.65, $1.83, $0.49, $2.18, $0.64   8. 1.69, 0.092, 0.047, 28.5, 0.84

3. $1.75, $0.53, $3.57, $2.76, $0.78   9. 3.174, 0.1362, 0.0875, 1.59, 5.36

4. $3.42, $0.89, $1.53, $1.19, $0.95   10. 1.869, 4.96, 0.0719, 29.73, 4.16

5. $3.21, 75¢, $23.70, $3.14, $2.48   11. 35, 3.55, 7.76, 0.625, 0.375

6. $2.15, $1.59, 87¢, $8.50, 35¢   12. 78.604, 0.7002, 238.7, 7.008, 8.501

13. 0.075, 4.357, 97.58, 37.09, 80.0709

14. 31.21, 5.991, 0.0076, 7.8, 9.59

15. 8.004, 0.07, 8.236, 7.687, $476.8\frac{1}{2}$

16. 87.78, $45\frac{2}{5}$, 23.8478, 0.0043, 0.487

17. 7.84, $43.34\frac{4}{5}$, 81.35, $87\frac{1}{2}$

18. 3.64, $0.87\frac{1}{2}$, $27.48\frac{9}{10}$, $7.35\frac{3}{5}$

19. $10.27\frac{1}{2}$, $0.84\frac{3}{4}$, $19.3\frac{1}{2}$, 12.36, $7.9\frac{1}{2}$

20. $6.083\frac{1}{2}$, $0.37\frac{1}{2}$, $0.00\frac{3}{8}$, $205.06\frac{1}{4}$, $67\frac{7}{8}$

B. To solve each problem, perform the indicated subtraction. Remember to place a decimal point in each answer.

1. $78.90 − $19.28   8. $3.54 − 78¢   15. $98 − 32.9\frac{1}{4}$

2. $61.17 − $35.40   9. $4.38 − 89¢   16. $217.12\frac{1}{2} − 126.18\frac{3}{4}$

3. $50.05 − $23.31   10. 123.25 − 76.8975   17. $37\frac{1}{2} − 3.2\frac{1}{2}$

4. $54.23 − $49.07   11. 726.01 − 243.6   18. $100.379 − 26\frac{3}{8}$

5. $89.09 − $27.54   12. 84.001 − 56.395   19. $107.87\frac{1}{2} − 58\frac{5}{8}$

6. $7.54 − $4.88   13. 2.879 − 2.0086   20. $86.7\frac{1}{4} − 18.268$

7. $5.67 − $1.23   14. 405.05 − 276.7816

Multiplication of Decimal Fractions

Tens times tens equals hundreds: $30 \times 20 = 600$. Likewise, tenths times tenths equals hundredths: $\frac{3}{10} \times \frac{2}{10} = \frac{6}{100}$, which may be written as $0.3 \times 0.2 = 0.06$. In $0.3 \times 0.2 = 0.06$, the number of places to the right of the decimal point in the decimal product equals the sum of the places located to the right of the decimal points in the factors.

The procedure for the multiplication of decimals is:

1. Multiply the numerals as if they represent whole numbers.
2. Place a decimal point in the product so that there are as many places to its right as there are to the right of the decimal points in *both* factors.

Example A: Multiply 6.423×2.

Solution:
```
  6.423    (3 decimal places)
      2    (0 decimal places)
 12.846    (3 decimal places)
```

In pencil and paper solutions to some problems, zeros must be inserted in the product to provide the appropriate number of decimal places.

Example B: Multiply 1.38×0.004.

Solution:
```
   1.38     (2 decimal places)
  0.004     (3 decimal places)
0.00552     (5 decimal places)
```

A floating-decimal calculator will place the decimal point automatically.

Solution: 1.38 $\boxed{\times}$ 0.004 $\boxed{=}$ $\rightarrow$ 0.00552

● Exercise 4–3

Multiply.

1. $53.07
    8
	2. $8.33
	    13
		3. $19.76
		    9
			4. $93.44
			    7
				5. $182.89
				    5

6. 9.998
    12
	7. 973.3
	    15
		8. 0.6652
		    14
			9. 49.15
			    16
				10. 0.052
				    23

11. 4,916
    0.9
	12. 7,990
	    0.13
		13. 55.34
		    1.7
			14. 40.20
			    0.034
				15. 2,633
				    0.0046

16. 527.6
    0.0207
	17. 68.47
	    0.046
		18. 7.46
		    0.0073
			19. 290.1
			    0.00082
				20. 0.0042
				    0.604

21. 492
    $1.4\frac{1}{2}$
	22. $37.27\frac{1}{2}$
	    4.85
		23. $248\frac{3}{4}$
		    0.52
			24. $86.40\frac{1}{8}$
			    76
				25. 76
				    $0.32\frac{1}{2}$

26. 75.86	**27.** $4.4\frac{3}{8}$	**28.** 3.56	**29.** 3.20	**30.** 1.76
$0.43\frac{3}{4}$	6.8	0.0035	$49\frac{1}{4}$	$1\frac{5}{8}$

Division of Decimal Fractions

To divide a decimal by a whole number on paper:

1. Divide the numerals as if they represent whole numbers.
2. Place a decimal point in the quotient directly above the decimal point in the dividend.

As Example A below illustrates, zeros may be needed in the quotient to serve as place holders.

Example A: Divide 0.032 by 8.

Solution:

$$\begin{array}{r} 0.004 \\ 8\overline{)0.032} \\ \underline{32} \end{array}$$

When both the dividend and divisor are multiplied by the same number (except 0), the quotient remains unchanged. As proof of this principle, notice the following:

$$32 \div 16 = 2 \qquad\qquad 30 \div 5 = 6$$
$$320 \div 160 = 2 \qquad\qquad 300 \div 50 = 6$$
$$3,200 \div 1,600 = 2 \qquad\qquad 3,000 \div 500 = 6$$

In division by a decimal fraction, multiplying both the divisor and the dividend by 10 or by a power of 10 facilitates proper placement of the decimal point in the quotient. Multiplying by 10 or by a power of 10 may be accomplished by moving the decimal point to the right.

To divide by a decimal fraction on paper:

1. Eliminate the decimal point in the divisor by moving it the appropriate number of places to the right.
2. Move the decimal point in the dividend the same number of places to the right.
3. Divide as by a whole number.

Example B: Divide 2.842 by 1.4

Solution:

$$\begin{array}{r} 2.03 \\ 1.4\overline{)2.8\,42} \\ \underline{2\,8} \\ 42 \\ \underline{42} \end{array}$$

Both the divisor and dividend have been multiplied by 10, which is accomplished by moving the decimal point one place to the right.

In order to move the decimal point a sufficient number of places in the dividend, zeros may need to be appended on the right.

Example C: Divide 27.9 by 0.062.

Solution:

$$0.062_\wedge \overline{)2\ 7.9\ 0\ 0_\wedge} \quad \begin{array}{r} 4\ 5\ 0. \end{array}$$

$$\begin{array}{r} 2\ 4\ 8 \\ \hline 3\ 1\ 0 \\ 3\ 1\ 0 \\ \hline \end{array}$$

Both the divisor and dividend have been multiplied by 1,000, which is accomplished by moving the decimal point three places to the right.

Or   27.9 $\boxed{\div}$ 0.062 $\boxed{=}$ $\longrightarrow$ 450

●   Exercise 4–4

Divide. Where applicable, round to the nearest ten thousandth.

1. $23\overline{)67.049}$
2. $45\overline{)328.07}$
3. $68\overline{)4.4668}$
4. $0.216\overline{)12.0684}$
5. $3.7\overline{)328.51}$
6. $0.025\overline{)75.875}$
7. $0.56\overline{)5,239.6}$
8. $2.34\overline{)826.408}$
9. $0.413\overline{)932.28}$
10. $8.672\overline{)748.826}$

11. $82.05\overline{)5,076.234}$
12. $78.21\overline{)80.042}$
13. $4.68\overline{)48.748}$
14. $0.3825\overline{)26.654}$
15. $0.07482\overline{)92.817}$
16. $48.216 \div 28.7$
17. $216.875 \div 375$
18. $0.08672 \div 63.28$
19. $758.30 \div 0.0482$
20. $356.82 \div 125$

21. $428 \div 4.125$
22. $74\frac{3}{4} \div 4.5$
23. $827 \div 3\frac{3}{5}$
24. $19.38 \div 4.1\frac{7}{10}$
25. $57.54 \div 21\frac{3}{4}$
26. $0.93\frac{1}{4} \div 0.37\frac{1}{2}$
27. $18.4\frac{5}{8} \div 20\frac{1}{8}$
28. $97\frac{3}{4} \div 3.3\frac{2}{5}$
29. $0.618 \div 0.06\frac{1}{4}$
30. $10.9\frac{7}{8} \div 764$

Division by 10 and Multiples of 10

Dividing by 10 or by a power of 10 may be accomplished by moving the decimal point to the left as many places as there are zeros in the divisor.

$$263 \div 10 = 26.3$$
$$263 \div 100 = 2.63$$
$$263 \div 1,000 = 0.263$$
$$263 \div 10,000 = 0.0263$$

Dividing both the divisor and the dividend by the same number (except 0) will not change the value of the quotient. Dividing both terms by the power of 10 that is sufficient to eliminate the zeros in the divisor can simplify division by numbers ending with zeros.

To divide by a divisor that ends in one or more zeros:

1. Cancel the zeros in the divisor by moving the decimal point the appropriate number of places to the left.
2. Move the decimal point in the dividend the same number of places to the left.
3. Divide as by a whole number.

Example: Divide 40,216 by 8,000.

Solution:
$$
\begin{array}{r}
5.0\ 2\ 7 \\
8{,}0\ 0\ 0\ )\overline{4\ 0{,}2\ 1\ 6} \\
\underline{4\ 0} \\
2\ 1 \\
\underline{1\ 6} \\
5\ 6 \\
\underline{5\ 6}
\end{array}
$$

Both the divisor and dividend have been divided by 1,000, which is accomplished by moving the decimal point three places to the left.

Steps 1 and 2 of the foregoing may be accomplished mentally. The calculator solution to the Example, then, is:

$$40.216 \boxed{\div} \; 8 \; \boxed{=} \longrightarrow 5.027$$

● Exercise 4–5

Divide. Where applicable, round to the nearest ten thousandth.

1. 93 ÷ 10	**17.** 9,842 ÷ 700	**33.** 659.1 ÷ 3,000
2. 65 ÷ 100	**18.** 603 ÷ 8,000	**34.** 816.2 ÷ 8,000
3. 80 ÷ 1,000	**19.** 851 ÷ 70	**35.** 37.2 ÷ 6,000
4. 560 ÷ 20	**20.** 2,332 ÷ 800	**36.** 3.22 ÷ 700
5. 940 ÷ 200	**21.** 3,222 ÷ 9,000	**37.** 857.4 ÷ 600
6. 720 ÷ 2,000	**22.** 544 ÷ 80	**38.** 638.1 ÷ 9,000
7. 810 ÷ 30	**23.** 709 ÷ 900	**39.** 130.7 ÷ 20,000
8. 870 ÷ 300	**24.** 304 ÷ 10,000	**40.** 76.07 ÷ 10.00
9. 780 ÷ 3,000	**25.** 8.34 ÷ 300	**41.** 698.5 ÷ 200.00
10. 28 ÷ 40	**26.** 27.18 ÷ 70	**42.** 271.8 ÷ 3,000.00
11. 370 ÷ 500	**27.** 71.65 ÷ 500	**43.** 88.48 ÷ 40.00
12. 890 ÷ 6,000	**28.** 7.08 ÷ 80	**44.** 17.53 ÷ 500.00
13. 78 ÷ 50	**29.** 5.73 ÷ 50	**45.** 789.6 ÷ 6,000.00
14. 59 ÷ 600	**30.** 45.91 ÷ 90	**46.** 7.049 ÷ 70.00
15. 688 ÷ 7,000	**31.** 9.5 ÷ 5,000	**47.** 3,123.94 ÷ 800.00
16. 486 ÷ 60	**32.** 6.88 ÷ 400	**48.** 420.3 ÷ 9,000.00

Quantity Prices

Multiplying the price of an article by the quantity of that article is known as making an **extension.** Computing extensions on sales tickets and on sales invoices, such as those illustrated in Figures 4–2 and 4–3, is an important activity that must be performed in business countless times each day.

Figure 4–2 A Sales Ticket

A **sales ticket** is prepared by a salesperson in a retail store at the time of the sale. The sales ticket generally shows the date, the customer's name and address, the quantity of each commodity, the price, and the total amount. In some stores, a sales ticket is prepared for each sales transaction. In others, sales tickets are prepared for only certain kinds of transactions, such as credit sales. When used, at least two copies are prepared of each sales ticket. One copy is given to the customer, and one copy is sent to the accounting department for the company's records, retained by the salesperson as a personal record, or used for other purposes as the company requires.

Part 1.   Mathematics Applications in Preparing a Basic Foundation

Date	Invoice No.	Customer No.	Salesman	How Shipped	Terms
Oct. 10, 19__	31047	5171	Higgins	Truck	Net 30 days

PACIFIC PRODUCTS COMPANY

5140 Westwood Boulevard
Los Angeles, CA 90024
Telephone: (213) 878-3265

Sold to: Grant Electric
962 Park Ave.
Pomona, CA 91766

Quantity	Product No.	Description	Price	Amount
18	R–4596	Radio, pocket	$ 37.50	$ 675.00
16	R–0572	Radio, clock	87.50	1,400.00
6	M–1381	Processor, food	98.75	592.50
6	TR–295	Recorder, tape	187.50	1,125.00
3	TR–327	Recorder, video	1,250.00	3,750.00
24	7–600	Cassette, tape	3.75	90.00
48	3–250	Cassette, video	11.25	540.00
		TOTAL		$ 8,172.50

Figure 4-3 A Sales Invoice

An **invoice** is generally used by manufacturers and wholesalers to show the details of a sales transaction. The invoice shows information similar to that which appears on a sales ticket, except that the invoice is more likely to show specific information related to shipping instructions and credit terms. Any number of copies of an invoice may be prepared by the billing department of the seller, depending on company needs. The original is sent to the customer, one carbon copy is sent to the accounting department, and sometimes additional copies are used in other departments. For example, the credit department may use a copy in following up the collection for the goods, or the shipping department may need a copy as authorization to pack and ship the goods.

A great many different kinds of goods are bought and sold in large quantities. Prices on such goods are quoted by the hundred, by the thousand, and by the ton. For example, rope, cable, and fencing are bought and sold by the hundred feet; potatoes, flour, and sugar by the hundred pounds; printed matter, bricks, and building supplies by the thousand; and hay, coal, and ore by the ton.

To save the time of workers and the space on forms, abbreviations and symbols are commonly used in business. Many of the abbreviations and symbols that are used in business are shown in Appendix A.

To determine the total cost when prices are quoted on a quantity basis, convert the quantities into the same terms as those in which the prices are quoted. This principle is illustrated in each of the following examples. Notice that the shortcut method of dividing by 10 and by multiples of 10 is used in each example.

When determining the price of commodities bought or sold by the hundred (C) or hundredweight (cwt), divide the quantity by 100 and multiply by the price per C or per cwt.

Example A: Find the total cost of 3,462 feet of cable at $8.50 per C.

Solution:

$$
\begin{array}{r}
3\,4.6\,2 \quad (3{,}462 \div 100) \\
\times\ \$8.50 \quad (\text{price per C}) \\
\hline
1\,7\,3\,1\,0\,0 \\
2\,7\,6\,9\,6 \\
\hline
\$2\,9\,4.2\,7\,\cancel{0}\,\cancel{0} \quad (\text{total cost})
\end{array}
$$

Or 34.62 $\boxed{\times}$ 8.5 $\boxed{=}$ $\longrightarrow$ 294.27

To determine the total amount for commodities that are bought and sold by the thousand (M), divide the quantity by 1,000 and multiply by the price per M.

Example B: Find the total cost of 6,350 printed forms at $9.23 per M.

Solution:

$$
\begin{array}{r}
6.3\,5 \quad (6{,}350 \div 1{,}000) \\
\times\ \$9.2\,3 \quad (\text{price per M}) \\
\hline
1\,9\,0\,5 \\
1\,2\,7\,0 \\
5\,7\,1\,5 \\
\hline
\$5\,8.6\,1\,\cancel{0}\,\cancel{5} = \$58.61 \quad (\text{total cost})
\end{array}
$$

Or 6.35 $\boxed{\times}$ 9.23 $\boxed{=}$ $\longrightarrow$ 58.61$\cancel{05}$; cost = $58.61

To determine the total amount for commodities that are bought and sold by the ton (T), divide the quantity by 2,000 and multiply by the price per T.

Example C: Find the total cost of 8,460 pounds of ore at $84 per T.

Solution:

$$
\frac{8{,}460}{2{,}000} \times \$84 = \$355.32
$$

Or 8.46 $\boxed{\div}$ 2 $\boxed{\times}$ 84 $\boxed{=}$ $\longrightarrow$ 355.32

When computing amounts of money, the final answer to a problem is rounded to the nearest cent.

Example D: Round the following numbers to the nearest cent.

Solution: $9.3756 = $9.38 $9.3746 = $9.37

Generally, rounding is not done with intermediate amounts; that is, amounts that are found before the final answer is computed. Round to the nearest cent only in answers.

A different rule is followed in determining the price of one article when the price is quoted on a quantity basis. For example, if ten articles are priced to sell for $2.43, the exact price for one article is $0.243. The price charged by the seller for one would be 25 cents.

• Exercise 4–6

Find the total amount for each of the following purchases.

hundred

Thousand

1. 860 ft @ $7.10 per C
2. 1,650 ft @ $31.59 per C
3. 730 ft @ $14.60 per C
4. 974 ft @ $7.28 per C
5. 12,250 @ $8.32 per M
6. 6,700 @ $19.50 per M
7. 12,400 @ $62.50 per M
8. 8,250 @ $28.90 per M
9. 16,980 lb @ $28 per T
10. 19,500 lb @ $17.65 per T
11. 30,140 lb @ $35.12 per T
12. 975 lb @ $32 per T
13. 835 lb @ $25.90 per cwt
14. 1,570 lb @ $16.37 per cwt
15. 980 lb @ $12.50 per cwt
16. 2,550 lb @ $8.75 per cwt
17. 7,500 @ $9.20 per M
18. 940 ft @ $42.25 per C
19. 31,420 lb @ $36 per T
20. 975 @ $67.50 per M
21. 350 lb @ $11.75 per cwt
22. 14,850 lb @ $21.25 per T
23. 2,100 ft @ $44.50 per C
24. 1,260 lb @ $10.20 per cwt

CALCULATOR CONSTANT [K] OPERATIONS

Many calculators are programmed to repeatedly add, subtract, multiply by, or divide by an entered number. The number that is repeated is the **constant.** Some calculators have a constant key [**K**] that must be pressed to cause the machine to perform the repeat operation. If your calculator has a constant key, remember to press it for the following calculations. (See the manual for your calculator.)

Constant Addition. For some calculators, the first addend entered is the repeat addend. For others, the second addend entered is the repeat addend. Try the following by entering: 4 [**+**] 5 [**=**]; now enter 10 [**=**]. If the answer you get is 15, the second addend (5) entered in your calculator is the repeat addend. But if your answer is 14, the first addend (4) is the repeat addend. Any other answer (assuming the correct keys are pressed) indicates that your calculator is not programmed for constant addition.

Chapter 4. Decimal Fractions

Example A: Add 45 to each of the following numbers: 57, 98, 8.06.

Solution: If the first addend entered is the constant:

45 [+] 57 [=] $\longrightarrow$ 102   98 [=] $\longrightarrow$ 143   8.06 [=] $\longrightarrow$ 53.06

If the second addend entered is the constant:

57 [+] 45 [=] $\longrightarrow$ 102   98 [=] $\longrightarrow$ 143   8.06 [=] $\longrightarrow$ 53.06

Another possibility in constant addition is to repeatedly add the constant to whatever number is shown in display by pressing the [=] key. In Example B, the constant is the second number entered.

Example B: Find the sum: 64 + 25 + 25 + 25.

Solution: 64 [+] 25 [=] [=] [=] $\longrightarrow$ 139

Constant Subtraction. In subtraction the second number entered is the constant; that is, the number that may be subtracted repeatedly.

Example A: Subtract 56.87 from each of these: 223, 138, 95.06.

Solution: 223 [−] 56.87 [=] $\longrightarrow$ 166.13

138 [=] $\longrightarrow$ 81.13

95.06 [=] $\longrightarrow$ 38.19

Also the constant may be subtracted repeatedly from the decreasing number in display by pressing the equals key.

Example B: Subtract: 350 − 35 − 35 − 35.

Solution: 350 [−] 35 [=] [=] [=] $\longrightarrow$ 245

Constant Multiplication. Depending on the program in the calculator, the constant multiplier may be either the first or second number entered. Use your calculator to try 6 [×] 7 [=]. Then enter 10 [=]. An answer of 60 indicates that the first number entered (6) is the constant. The answer 70 shows that the second number entered (7) is the constant.

Example A: Multiply each of these numbers by 27: 85, 3.75, 0.09.

Solution: If the first factor entered is the constant:

27 [×] 85 [=] $\longrightarrow$ 2295   3.75 [=] $\longrightarrow$ 101.25   .09 [=] $\longrightarrow$ 2.43

If the second factor entered is the constant:

85 [×] 27 [=] $\longrightarrow$ 2295   3.75 [=] $\longrightarrow$ 101.25   .09 [=] $\longrightarrow$ 2.43

Pressing the equals key will repeatedly multiply the number in display by the constant multiplier. Example B illustrates the sequence for calculators that repeat the first multiplier entered.

Example B: Multiply: $57 \times 5 \times 5 \times 5 \times 5$.

Solution: 5 ⌑ × ⌑ 57 ⌑ = ⌑ ⌑ = ⌑ ⌑ = ⌑ ⌑ = ⌑ → 35625

Constant Division. As in subtraction, the constant is the second number (the divisor) entered in division.

Example A: Divide each of these numbers by 7: 140, 245, 367, 8.75.

Solution: 140 ⌑ ÷ ⌑   7 ⌑ = ⌑ → 20

               245 ⌑ = ⌑ → 35

               367 ⌑ = ⌑ → 52.428571

               8.75 ⌑ = ⌑ → 1.25

The constant also may be repeatedly divided into the decreasing number in display.

Example B: Divide: $55,223 \div 7 \div 7 \div 7 \div 7$.

Solution: 55223 ⌑ ÷ ⌑ 7 ⌑ = ⌑ ⌑ = ⌑ ⌑ = ⌑ ⌑ = ⌑ → 23

● Exercise 4–7

A. Find the sum for each problem.

1. Add 94 to each number:
   a. 173   **b.** 436   **c.** 629   **d.** 17.6   **e.** 25.3

2. Add 475 to each number:
   a. 3,798   **b.** 964   **c.** 8,360   **d.** 24.27   **e.** 534.92

3. Add 82.31 to each number:
   a. 22,117   **b.** 5,941   **c.** 23.35   **d.** 50.993   **e.** 21.895

4. Add 69.57 to each number:
   a. 14,177   **b.** 419   **c.** 87.59   **d.** 43.232   **e.** 2.027

5. $72 + 85 + 85 + 85 + 85$

6. $450 + 68 + 68 + 68 + 68 + 68 + 68$

7. $924 + 5.7 + 5.7 + 5.7 + 5.7 + 5.7$

8. $2,684 + 3.75 + 3.75 + 3.75 + 3.75$

B. Subtract as specified.

1. Subtract 95 from each number:
   a. 272   **b.** 7,839   **c.** 572   **d.** 382.05   **e.** 217.45

2. Subtract 78 from each number:
    a. 134   **b.** 14,120   **c.** 266.9   **d.** 712.77   **e.** 906.34

3. Subtract 31.5 from each number:
    a. 680   **b.** 312   **c.** 393.63   **d.** 4,079.07   **e.** 487.635

4. Subtract 9.247 from each number:
    a. 94   **b.** 954   **c.** 278.55   **d.** 21.9   **e.** 46.682

5. $718 - 31 - 31 - 31 - 31$

6. $842 - 75 - 75 - 75 - 75 - 75$

7. $98.75 - 8.94 - 8.94 - 8.94$

8. $742.19 - 63.7 - 63.7 - 63.7 - 63.7 - 63.7 - 63.7$

C. Multiply as specified.

1. Multiply each number by 34:
    a. 216   **b.** 879   **c.** 16,715   **d.** 27.57   **e.** 45.333

2. Multiply each number by 56:
    a. 67   **b.** 952   **c.** 52,786   **d.** 62.25   **e.** 21.7825

3. Multiply each number by 3.79:
    a. 878   **b.** 2,321   **c.** 87.97   **d.** 8.577   **e.** 5.5242

4. Multiply each number by 0.06:
    a. 71.16   **b.** 6,354   **c.** 9.78   **d.** 622.11   **e.** 0.75

5. $427 \times 6 \times 6 \times 6 \times 6 \times 6 \times 6$

6. $65 \times 15 \times 15 \times 15 \times 15 \times 15$

7. $2.8 \times 1.7 \times 1.7 \times 1.7 \times 1.7 \times 1.7$

8. $7.5 \times 0.75 \times 0.75 \times 0.75$

D. Divide as specified.

1. Divide each number by 6:
    a. 519   **b.** 9,930   **c.** 20,274   **d.** 316.125   **e.** 83.979

2. Divide each number by 14:
    a. 63,386.05 **b.** 6,804   **c.** 28.84   **d.** 95.41   **e.** 18.8545

3. Divide each number by 7.25:
    a. 129.05   **b.** 496.00005 **c.** 21,286   **d.** 21.9849   **e.** 0.29

4. Divide each number by 82.9:
    a. 125.99709 **b.** 791.695   **c.** 6,953.2375 **d.** 17,326.1   **e.** 12,435

5. $87,687,168 \div 16 \div 16 \div 16 \div 16$

6. 82,848,906 ÷ 21 ÷ 21 ÷ 21

7. 36.70016 ÷ 1.6 ÷ 1.6 ÷ 1.6 ÷ 1.6 ÷ 1.6

8. 9,492.1875 ÷ 7.5 ÷ 7.5 ÷ 7.5 ÷ 7.5

CHECKING ACCOUNTS

Those who deposit funds in checking accounts are called **depositors.** The depositors have the right to write checks against their accounts ordering the financial institution to make specific payments. The depositor who writes (draws) the check against his or her account is the **drawer.** The bank that is ordered to make payment is the **drawee.** The person or company to whose order the certain sum of money is payable is the **payee.**

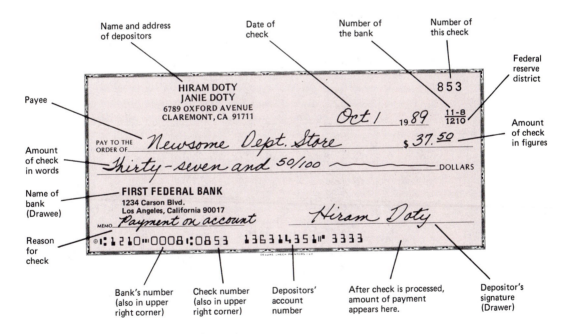

Figure 4-4 A Check

Funds being deposited are usually accompanied by a printed form called a **deposit slip.** (See Figure 4-5.) A deposit slip classifies the funds being deposited into currency, coins, and checks.

Chapter 4. Decimal Fractions

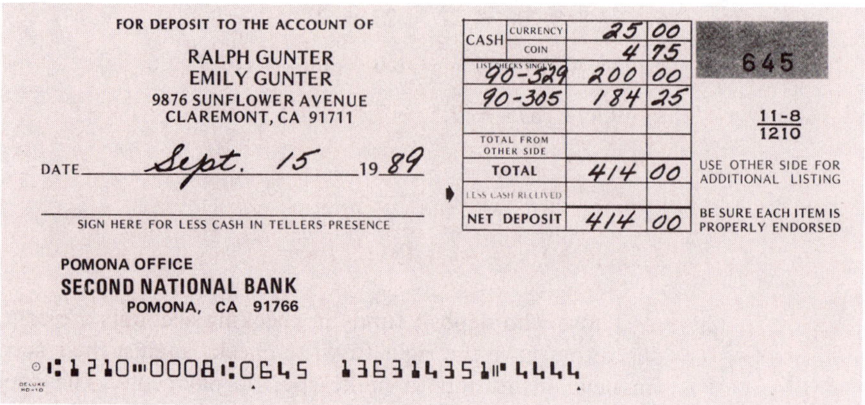

Figure 4–5 A Deposit Slip

Recording Checks and Deposits

An accurate record of all deposits and checks must be kept to insure that the checks written do not total more than the deposits. A record that shows the beginning balance, all deposits, and all checks written is called a **check register.** A personal check register is shown in Figure 4–6.

NUMBER	DATE	DESCRIPTION OF TRANSACTION	PAYMENT/DEBIT (−)	√ T	FEE (IF ANY) (−)	DEPOSIT/CREDIT (+)	BALANCE	
		RECORD ALL CHARGES OR CREDITS THAT AFFECT YOUR ACCOUNT					$ 1480	90
101	9/4	National Insur. Co. Auto Insur.	$ 650 00		$	$	−650	00
							830	90
102	9/6	Green's Garage Repairs	225 60				−225	60
							605	30
	9/7	Deposit				1200 00	+1200	00
							1805	30
103	9/10	Lane Drug Store	31 25				−31	25
							1774	05
104	9/12	Fred Hunter tickets	45 00				−45	00
							1729	05

Figure 4–6 A Personal Check Register

The **balance** is the amount of funds available in the checking account. The amount for which a check is written is subtracted from the balance because it decreases the funds available in the account. A deposit increases the funds available and is added to the balance to obtain a new balance.

Part 1.   Mathematics Applications in Preparing a Basic Foundation

- Exercise 4–8

In each problem, determine the balance after each check or deposit.

1.

Balance	466	81
Check No. 11	70	00
Balance		
Check No. 12	10	98
Balance		
Deposit	819	82
Balance		
Check No. 13	23	79
Balance		
Check No. 14	15	30
Balance		
Deposit	200	00
Balance		
Check No. 15	83	84
Balance		

2.

Deposit	443	93
Check No. 21	16	82
Balance		
Check No. 22	106	00
Balance		
Check No. 23	100	00
Balance		
Deposit	420	02
Balance		
Check No. 24	23	17
Balance		
Check No. 25	26	25
Balance		
Deposit	116	10
Balance		

3.

Balance	469	27
Deposit	933	29
Balance		
Check No. 31	24	30
Balance		
Check No. 32	113	62
Balance		
Check No. 33	70	00
Balance		
Deposit	455	97
Balance		
Check No. 34	38	17
Balance		
Check No. 35	9	30
Balance		

4.

Balance	1,660	12
Check No. 41	84	16
Balance		
Check No. 42	147	79
Balance		
Deposit	5,997	13
Balance		
Check No. 43	392	49
Balance		
Check No. 44	75	74
Balance		
Check No. 45	3,031	39
Balance		
Deposit	154	80
Balance		

Chapter 4. Decimal Fractions

5.

Balance	549	40
Check No. 51	76	75
Balance		
Deposit	634	16
Balance		
Check No. 52	140	00
Balance		
Check No. 53	112	00
Balance		
Deposit	469	34
Balance		
Check No. 54	36	97
Balance		
Check No. 55	24	22
Balance		
Check No. 56	45	35
Balance		
Check No. 57	267	00
Balance		
Deposit	1,685	00
Balance		
Check No. 58	806	25
Balance		
Check No. 59	45	26
Balance		

6.

Balance	1,849	26
Check No. 61	1,545	80
Balance		
Check No. 62	98	31
Balance		
Deposit	2,100	00
Balance		
Check No. 63	100	74
Balance		
Check No. 64	63	44
Balance		
Deposit	991	26
Balance		
Check No. 65	74	30
Balance		
Check No. 66	150	90
Balance		
Deposit	550	00
Balance		
Check No. 67	277	50
Balance		
Check No. 68	263	96
Balance		
Deposit	500	85
Balance		

Statement Reconciliation

Periodically the financial institution sends to the depositors of each checking account a statement showing past activity in the account. This statement, which is usually sent once a month, shows the balance in the account at the beginning of the period, the amount of the individual deposits, the amount of each check charged to the account, any other deductions from or additions to the account, and the balance in the account at the end of the period. (See Figure 4–7.)

FIRST FEDERAL
BANK

DATE	CHECKS AND OTHER DEBITS						DEPOSITS/OTHER CREDITS		BALANCE
	AMOUNT	*	AMOUNT	*	AMOUNT	*	AMOUNT	*	600.81
4/10							100.00	DP	700.81
4/14	339.00	CK							361.81
4/17	23.96	CK							337.85
4/25	19.36	CK					50.00	DP	368.49
4/28	8.47	CK	18.39	CK	55.00	CK			286.63
5/05	15.23	CK							271.40
5/06	170.00	CK	339.00	CK			507.00	DP	269.40
5/08	20.70	CK							248.70
5/10	4.40	SC							244.30

DATE OF LAST STATEMENT	PREVIOUS BALANCE	TOTAL DEBITS	TOTAL CREDITS	SERVICE CHARGES	ENDING BALANCE	CHECKS	DEP	DEBIT MEMOS	ENCLOSURES
4/08	600|81	1,013|51	657|00	4|40	244|30	10	3		10

LEGEND (CODE USED IN * COLUMN)					
DP	DEPOSITS	DM	DEBIT MEMOS	SC	SERVICE CHARGE
RD	DEPOSIT REVERSALS	CK	CHECKS	CI	CHECK IMPRINT CHARGE
CM	CREDIT MEMOS	RC	CHECK REVERSALS		
CA	CASH ADVANCE	CP	CASH RESERVE PAYMENT		

Figure 4–7 A Bank Statement

Chapter 4.   Decimal Fractions

The amount shown on the statement as the balance will seldom agree with the balance shown in the checkbook of the depositor. There are many reasons why these two balances, that is, the checkbook balance and the statement balance, will not be equal. The five most basic reasons are as follows:

1. *Outstanding Checks.* At the time a check is written, the amount of its value is deducted in the checkbook record. Many checks, however, spend days or even weeks flowing through business channels before arriving at the bank to be honored. Those checks that were written and deducted from the checkbook balance but did not arrive at the bank in time to be honored and charged to the account prior to the preparation of the statement are **outstanding checks.** These checks will cause the statement balance to be larger than the checkbook balance because the bank has not yet paid them and deducted their amounts from the depositor's account. The sum of the outstanding checks, therefore, is deducted from the statement balance.

2. *Unrecorded Deposits.* Many deposits are sent through the mail, and many are made after hours through the night depository. On occasion, one of these or some other late deposit will not reach the bank in time to be credited to the account and appear on the current statement but will appear on the next statement. Those deposits that have been recorded in the checkbook, but that are unrecorded on the current statement, cause the statement balance to appear smaller. Late deposits that are unrecorded on the statement are added to the statement balance.

3. *Unrecorded Charges.* Sometimes charges are deducted from a depositor's account for services rendered. In addition to service charges and collection fees, the bank may also deduct for other items, such as checks written for **insufficient,** or **not sufficient, funds.** These are checks that were deposited in the account and that the bank was unable to collect. If the deduction is for a relatively large amount, the depositor is notified by mail on the day of the deduction. When the amounts are small, as for service charges, the depositor is customarily notified on the statement. These unrecorded charges will cause the checkbook balance to appear larger, because they have not been deducted from that balance. Unrecorded charges must be deducted from the checkbook balance.

4. *Unrecorded Credits.* For fees, banks will act as collecting agents on promissory notes and other items. When an item such as a promissory note is collected for a depositor, the proceeds are credited to the account and a memorandum of the transaction is sent. Occasionally items collected near the end of the period will appear on the statement and be unrecorded in the checkbook because official notification of the collection had not been received previously. Such unrecorded credits cause the checkbook balance to appear smaller. Unrecorded credits should be added to the checkbook balance.

5. *Errors.* No matter how elaborate the system of internal control for the automatic detection of errors and no matter how careful the parties are, errors do occur. Both the depositor and the bank make errors that affect the accuracy of the bank balance. Sometimes errors are not discovered until

the bank balance is reconciled. The nature of the error determines whether the statement balance or the checkbook balance should be adjusted.

In order to verify the correctness of the balance in the check record, a statement reconciliation is prepared. (See Figure 4–8.) The preliminary steps in preparing the reconciliation are as follows:

1. Each deposit listed on the statement is compared with the deposits shown in the check record for the same period of time. Any errors or unrecorded items are listed.
2. When canceled checks are returned, they may be in the order in which they were paid. While the checks are in this order, each is compared with its listing on the statement. Any discrepancies or errors are listed.
3. The returned checks are rearranged in numerical order, with any memoranda inserted according to their dates. Each check and memorandum is compared with its entry in the check record. Any unpaid checks, any unrecorded memoranda, and any discrepancies are listed.

After the data have been examined in the preceding manner, the statement reconciliation is prepared. The reconciliation may be prepared in a variety of ways, but the procedure preferred in business is to determine the adjusted checkbook balance and the adjusted bank balance. The adjusted checkbook balance should equal the adjusted bank balance. This method is preferred because it shows the balance that should appear in the check record after the appropriate adjustments have been made. The two basic kinds of adjustments are as follows:

1. *Do that which would have been done if the appropriate information had been available.* Assume that a check for $25 had been deposited by an account holder and that later the check was found to be worthless because it was drawn on an account with insufficient funds. The depositor, however, did not learn of this bad check until the bank statement arrived. If the depositor had been notified earlier that the check had not been honored, the $25 would have been deducted in the check register, for the account is really worth $25 less. As another example, if the depositor knew the amount of the service charges on the day the account is charged, the same amount could be deducted from the checkbook balance. In most cases, however, one must wait until the statement arrives in order to learn how much the account was charged.
2. *Do that which will be done eventually.* Outstanding checks eventually will reach the bank and be subtracted in the record of the account. The sum of the outstanding checks, therefore, is deducted from the statement balance. Late deposits will be recorded by the bank when they are received. For this reason, late deposits that are unrecorded on the bank statement are added to the bank balance.

The two following examples show that even errors can be categorized under the preceding kinds of adjustments. (a) Assume that a bookkeeper erroneously recorded a check for $75 in the check record as a check for $57. Since $18 more would have been subtracted if the bookkeeper had been aware of the mistake, $18 should be subtracted from the checkbook balance to reconcile it with the bank balance. (b) Suppose that the depositor's account is charged with a check for $50 that should have been charged to another depositor's account. The depositor who received the canceled check in error should notify the bank and add the $50 to the statement balance. The bank eventually will add it to the depositor's account in order to correct the record.

In the example below, the balance as shown by the statement was $458.67 on September 30. Mr. Evans' checkbook showed a balance of $627.95 on the same date. Check No. 860 for $19.50 and Check No. 872 for $96.84 had not reached the bank in time to be paid before the statement was prepared. A deposit of $523.87, placed in the depository after closing on September 30, was not recorded on the statement. Returned with the statement was a credit memorandum showing that the bank had collected a note for Mr. Evans. The fee for collecting the maturity value of $250 for this note was $6.50. In addition, the regular service charge was $5.25. When these amounts are properly arranged, added, and subtracted, the correct cash balance on September 30 is shown to be $866.20.

			Richard Evans		
			Bank Statement Reconciliation		
			September 30, 19--		
Checkbook Balance		$627.95	Bank Statement Balance		$458.67
Add:			Add:		
Note Maturity Value		250.00	Deposit September 30		523.87
		$877.95			$982.54
Deduct:			Deduct:		
			Outstanding checks:		
Service charge	$5.25		No. 860	$19.50	
Collection fee	6.50	11.75	No. 872	96.84	116.34
Adjusted Balance		$866.20	Adjusted Balance		$866.20

Exercise 4–9

Prepare a statement reconciliation similar to Figure 4–8 for each of the following problems. Use your name and the date of September 30 in problems 1 through 6.

Part 1. Mathematics Applications in Preparing a Basic Foundation

	Checkbook Balance	Bank Statement Balance	Service Charge	Outstanding Checks	Other Adjustments
1.	$863.97	$546.78	$7.45	$80.10; $61.25; $31.20; $47	Deposit of $529.29 not entered on statement.
2.	$1,053.80	$1,483.68	$8.23	$12.51; $51.50; $8.40; $67.70	$2 charge for collecting a $300 note.
3.	$2,792.32	$3,257.72	$7.50	$115.20; $51; $76.70; $480	Deposit of $250 entered twice in check record.
4.	$602.03	$628.49	$6.65	$101.24; $46.17; $56.80; $11.50	Deposit of $182.60 was not shown on statement.
5.	$6,549.43	$8,320.55	none	$421.80; $46.20; $120.75; $311	Deposit of $871.37 not entered in check record.
6.	$5,733.14	$8,493.63	none	$274.23; $965.74; $1,430.52	Check for $450 entered in checkbook as $540.

7. On May 3, the Green Supply Company received a statement showing a balance of $790.41 on April 30. An examination of the statement revealed that two checks—one for $56.77 and one for $45.13—had not yet reached the bank. The bank had deducted a service charge of $6.85 from the account. The check record balance on April 30 was $695.36.

8. While reconciling her statement on May 31, Joan Howard discovered that she had not recorded in her checkbook a deposit of $735. A check for $84.82 and a check for $79.52 that had been recently mailed to pay two bills had not yet been paid. Her service charges amounted to $5.15. The statement showed a balance of $1,447.86; her checkbook, a balance of $553.67.

9. On November 30, Janet Kemp's checkbook balance was $1,359.13, and her statement showed a balance of $991.80. The following checks were outstanding: $27.42, $46.89, and $71.65. A deposit of $508.54 had been mailed to the bank, but it had not arrived in time to be recorded on the statement. A service charge of $8.50 was shown on the statement. Interest income of $3.75 was shown on the statement.

10. On October 31, the Hall and Roe Company statement showed a balance of $20,589.53. The company's checkbook balance was $17,161.88. Checks for $874.44, $522.33, and $154.38 that the company had written had not yet reached the bank. A bookkeeper for the company had failed to record a late deposit of $1,800. Interest income of $76.50 was recorded on the statement.

11. The balance in Jose Moreno's checkbook on June 30 was $1,448.29. His statement showed a balance of $1,470.24 for that date. Only one check for $12.50 was outstanding. The service charge was $7.16. While reconciling

the two balances, Mr. Moreno discovered that he had made two subtraction errors in his checkbook. The two errors totaled $16.61.

12. On September 30, Cy Bartlett's checkbook balance was $1,137.54. While comparing the canceled checks with the check stubs, he noticed that he had deducted $435 in his checkbook for a check correctly written for $345. Checks for $24.22, $27.19, $12.79, $62.79, $4.75, and $36.97 were outstanding. The statement balance of $1,147.90 did not include a deposit of $220 mailed on September 30. The service charges for September were $7. A $21.35 check marked "Insufficient Funds" that had been deposited by Mr. Bartlett was returned with the statement.

13. The October statement of Jane Wagner's account showed a balance of $1,774.34. Her checkbook balance on the same date was $1,082.30. The bank had charged $5.30 for service and $6.88 for collecting the maturity value of $685.45 on a note for Ms. Wagner. Four checks (No. 451 for $57.61, No. 454 for $11.48, No. 456 for $46.26, and No. 459 for $135) that had been written in October were not returned. A deposit of $231.58 that had been mailed on October 31 was not shown on the statement.

14. During the month of January, Betty Polanski's bank collected $693.44 and $135.27, the maturity values of two notes, for her. The fees for these two collections were $6.50 and $5.25. The statement showed a balance of $1,811.39 on January 31. The checkbook balance on the same date was $1,470.50. Checks for $90, $13.05, and $39 were outstanding. A late deposit of $614.36 did not appear on the statement. The charge for regular services was $3.76.

15. On October 1, Lawrence Packard received his statement showing his September 30 balance to be $511.35. His checkbook balance on the same date was $403.19. The bank had charged his account $4.35 for service and $5.50 for collecting a $375 note. None of these were recorded in Mr. Packard's checkbook. When he compared the canceled checks with the check stubs, he found these checks to be outstanding: $4, $89.27, $101.08, and $43. A deposit of $469.34 that was mailed on September 30 was not recorded on the statement. A check from Jim Teague for $25 that Mr. Packard deposited earlier was returned with the statement. It was stamped NSF (Not Sufficient Funds).

16. The balance in the check register of Stone's Garage on July 31 was $1,034.75. The statement of that date showed a balance of $787.45. These checks were outstanding: No. 227 for $62, No. 228 for $53.06, No. 231 for $89.10, No. 236 for $62.69, and No. 237 for $236. The bookkeeper, in error, had entered a deposit of $200 in the check register twice. A late deposit of $545 was not recorded on the statement. The regular service charge was $5.15.

ALIQUOT PARTS

A number that divides without remainder into a given number is an **aliquot part** of that number. In other words, the factors of a number are also the aliquot parts of that number. For example, notice that 5 and 2 (as well as other factors) are aliquot parts of 10; 25 and 4 are aliquot parts of 100; $12\frac{1}{2}$ and 8 are aliquot parts of 100; 4 and 3 are aliquot parts of 12.

In Example A, dividing by 25 is easy because 25 is an aliquot part of 100. The procedure is to first divide by 100 and then multiply by 4 because 25 is $\frac{1}{4}$ of 100. For the same reason, multiplying by 25 (Example B) is also easy. The procedure is to first multiply by 100 and then divide by 4 because 25 is $\frac{1}{4}$ of 100. When such processes are used, many problems that pertain to fractions, percents, discounts, and similar calculations can be solved mentally.

Example A: Divide 950 by 25.   Example B: Multiply 92 by 25.

Solution: $950 \div 25 = 9.5 \times 4 = 38$ Solution: $92 \times 25 = 9,200 \times \frac{1}{4} = 2,300$

In the two preceding examples, 100 is the **base,** 25 is the **aliquot part,** and $\frac{1}{4}$ is the **fractional equivalent.** The aliquot part of a base may be considered in terms of its fractional equivalent; that is, 25 may be considered as $\frac{1}{4}$ of the base 100.

Numbers that are convenient multiples of aliquot parts are also commonly called aliquot parts. For example, the aliquot part $33\frac{1}{3}$, which is $\frac{1}{3}$ of 100, and its multiple $66\frac{2}{3}$, which is $\frac{2}{3}$ of 100, are both conveniently referred to as aliquot parts.

Aliquot Parts of 100 and $1

Because of the ease with which multiplication and division can be performed by moving the decimal point, aliquot parts of 1, 10, 100, and 1,000 are used most frequently. A knowledge of the aliquot parts of 100 may be extended to include a knowledge of the aliquot parts of 1, 10, and 1,000 through an understanding of the placement of the decimal point. For example, just as the aliquot part 25 is $\frac{1}{4}$ of 100, 0.25 is $\frac{1}{4}$ of 1, 2.5 is $\frac{1}{4}$ of 10, and 250 is $\frac{1}{4}$ of 1,000. As each dollar contains 100 cents, the fractional equivalent of any aliquot part of 100 remains the same when that aliquot part is expressed in cents and based on $1.

An equation can be used to determine the fractional equivalent of an aliquot part in relation to the base. The equation can be translated into mathematical terms from this question: *What fractional part of the base is this aliquot part?* The following examples illustrate that the fractional equivalent is found by placing the aliquot part over the base and reducing the common or complex fraction to lowest terms.

Chapter 4.   Decimal Fractions

Example A: What fractional part of 100 is the aliquot part 25?

Solution: $W \times 100 = 25$

$$W = \frac{25}{100} = \frac{1}{4}$$

Example B: What fractional part of \$1 is $12\frac{1}{2}$¢?

Solution: $W \times \$1 = 12\frac{1}{2}$¢

$$W = \frac{12\frac{1}{2}¢}{100¢} = \frac{(2 \times 12) + 1}{2 \times 100} = \frac{25}{200} = \frac{1}{8}$$

● Exercise 4–10

A. Find the fractional equivalent for each of the following aliquot parts of 100 by asking what fractional part of the base is the aliquot part.

1. ____ × 100 = 50   9. ____ × 100 = $33\frac{1}{3}$ 17. ____ × 100 = $58\frac{1}{3}$

2. ____ × 100 = 25   10. ____ × 100 = $66\frac{2}{3}$ 18. ____ × 100 = $91\frac{2}{3}$

3. ____ × 100 = 75   11. ____ × 100 = $16\frac{2}{3}$ 19. ____ × 100 = $18\frac{3}{4}$

4. ____ × 100 = 20   12. ____ × 100 = $83\frac{1}{3}$ 20. ____ × 100 = 60

5. ____ × 100 = $12\frac{1}{2}$ 13. ____ × 100 = $8\frac{1}{3}$ 21. ____ × 100 = $11\frac{1}{9}$

6. ____ × 100 = $37\frac{1}{2}$ 14. ____ × 100 = 40   22. ____ × 100 = $14\frac{2}{7}$

7. ____ × 100 = $62\frac{1}{2}$ 15. ____ × 100 = $6\frac{1}{4}$ 23. ____ × 100 = 80

8. ____ × 100 = $87\frac{1}{2}$ 16. ____ × 100 = $41\frac{2}{3}$ 24. ____ × 100 = $9\frac{1}{11}$

B. Find the fractional equivalent for each of the following aliquot parts of \$1.

1. $12\frac{1}{2}$¢ =   7. $33\frac{1}{3}$¢ =   13. $58\frac{1}{3}$¢ =   19. $9\frac{1}{11}$¢ =

2. 40¢ =   8. 60¢ =   14. $66\frac{2}{3}$¢ =   20. $87\frac{1}{2}$¢ =

3. 50¢ =   9. 75¢ =   15. $16\frac{2}{3}$¢ =   21. $6\frac{1}{4}$¢ =

4. 20¢ =   10. $41\frac{2}{3}$¢ =   16. $91\frac{2}{3}$¢ =   22. 80¢ =

5. $8\frac{1}{3}$¢ =   11. $62\frac{1}{2}$¢ =   17. $18\frac{3}{4}$¢ =   23. $83\frac{1}{3}$¢ =

6. 25¢ =   12. $37\frac{1}{2}$¢ =   18. $11\frac{1}{9}$¢ =   24. $14\frac{2}{7}$¢ =

Aliquot Parts and Fractional Equivalents

Business students and employees should be able to recognize commonly used aliquot parts and their fractional equivalents without hesitation. These people should be able to see $83\frac{1}{3}$ ¢ and recognize it as \$$\frac{5}{6}$ as easily as they recognize 50¢ to be \$$\frac{1}{2}$. Conversely, they should know that \$$\frac{3}{8}$ is $37\frac{1}{2}$¢. Knowledge of many such aliquot parts and their fractional equivalents enables one not only to make quick, accurate mental computations, but also to enter decimal equivalents of common fractions into calculators and to read decimal fractions in calculator displays as common fractions.

An equation can be used to find what aliquot part of a base is represented by a fractional equivalent. The equation rests on this question: *What aliquot part is this fractional part of the base?* The equation reduces into a division problem in which the numerator or a multiple of the numerator is divided by the denominator. As the following examples illustrate, when the base is $1 or 100, the division is usually carried two places, and any remainder is shown over the divisor as a common fraction in lowest terms. If the base is $1, the aliquot part is shown in cents.

Example A: What aliquot part is $\frac{1}{6}$ of 100?

Solution:

$$W = \frac{1}{6} \times 100 = \frac{100}{6} = 6\overline{)100}^{\,16\frac{2}{3}}$$

Or $100\ \boxed{\div}\ 6\ \boxed{=}\ \longrightarrow 16.666666 = 16\frac{2}{3}$

Example B: What aliquot part is $\frac{3}{8}$ of $1?

Solution:

$$W = \frac{3}{8} \times \$1 = \frac{\$3}{8} = 8\overline{)\$3.00}^{\,\$0.37\frac{1}{2}} = 37\frac{1}{2}¢$$

Or $3\ \boxed{\div}\ 8\ \boxed{=}\ \longrightarrow 0.375;\ \$0.375 = 37.5¢ = 37\frac{1}{2}¢$

Changing $\frac{3}{8}$ to a decimal by dividing 3 by 8 gives the quotient 0.375, which stops (terminates) with the 5. The quotient 0.375 is, therefore, said to be a **terminating decimal.**

Example C: Change $\frac{3}{8}$ to decimal notation.

Solution: $3\ \boxed{\div}\ 8\ \boxed{=}\ \longrightarrow 0.375$ a terminating decimal

When the common fraction $\frac{5}{6}$ is changed to the decimal quotient 0.8333333. . ., the quotient could continue forever with 3s. A number such as 0.8333333. . ., in which the numeral does not stop, is called a **nonterminating** or **repeating decimal.**

Example D: Change $\frac{5}{6}$ to decimal notation.

Solution: $5\ \boxed{\div}\ 6\ \boxed{=}\ \longrightarrow 0.8333333. . .$ a nonterminating decimal

The three dots ". . ." with the preceding decimal indicate that there is no ending digit. A dot or short bar placed over the repeating digit or digits also may be used to show that a numeral is nonterminating: $\frac{5}{6} = 0.833\dot{3}$ or $\frac{1}{11} = 0.09\overline{09}$.

Thus, $\frac{3}{8}$ and $\frac{5}{6}$ may be entered in a calculator as 0.375 and 0.8333333, respectively; and a calculator display of 0.375 may be written on paper as 0.375 or $0.37\frac{1}{2}$ or $0.3\frac{3}{4}$ or $\frac{3}{8}$. Similarly, a calculator display of 0.8333333 may be written as 0.8333. . . or $0.8\overline{3}$ or $0.83\frac{1}{3}$ or $0.8\frac{1}{3}$ or $\frac{5}{6}$, depending on the type of answer desired.

● Exercise 4–11

In cents, show the aliquot part of $1 represented by each of the following fractional equivalents. Show any remainder as a fractional part of a cent.

1. $\frac{1}{10}$	5. $\frac{3}{5}$	9. $\frac{1}{6}$	13. $\frac{3}{8}$	17. $\frac{5}{12}$	21. $\frac{1}{7}$
2. $\frac{1}{2}$	6. $\frac{1}{3}$	10. $\frac{1}{16}$	14. $\frac{1}{12}$	18. $\frac{3}{16}$	22. $\frac{7}{8}$
3. $\frac{1}{5}$	7. $\frac{3}{4}$	11. $\frac{1}{8}$	15. $\frac{2}{3}$	19. $\frac{5}{8}$	23. $\frac{11}{12}$
4. $\frac{1}{4}$	8. $\frac{2}{5}$	12. $\frac{5}{6}$	16. $\frac{1}{11}$	20. $\frac{7}{12}$	24. $\frac{1}{9}$

DECIMALS IN WORD PROBLEMS

Many of the problems that appear in business, professional, and civil service examinations contain decimal fractions and aliquot parts. You can solve such problems quickly and correctly by applying the principles presented in this chapter and by performing accurately the fundamental operations of addition, subtraction, multiplication, and division.

● Exercise 4–12

1. Add 35 ones, 46 tenths, 57 hundredths, 68 thousandths, and 79 ten thousandths.

2. Subtract $28\frac{1}{4}$ hundredths from 579 thousandths.

3. Divide 8 and 435 thousandths by 35 thousandths.

4. Divide 645 thousandths by 15 ten thousandths.

5. How much is the cost of 4,500 pounds at $33\frac{1}{3}$ cents a pound?

6. Two brothers together have $12.79. The older brother has $2.97 more than the younger one. How much money does the younger one have?

7. Rose bought two manila envelopes at 69¢ each and some paper. She paid a total of $4 for these items. How much did the paper cost?

8. If your car averages $33\frac{1}{3}$ miles to a gallon of gasoline, how many gallons will you need to drive the automobile 450 miles?

9. Mid-West Mining Corporation chartered a plane to take a group of its executives and attorneys to New York to investigate the possibility of merging with National Products Company. The plane averaged 520 miles an hour while flying the distance of 1,278 miles. To the nearest tenth, how many hours did the flight take?

10. A realtor had an apartment house of 8 apartments constructed at a cost of $480,000. During the past year, each apartment was rented for the same amount of money. The annual income from rent was 0.104 of the cost of each apartment. How much rent did the realtor collect each month for each apartment?

11. A manufacturer accepted a return of 270 articles and credited a merchant's account with the cost price of $16\frac{2}{3}$¢ each. How much was the account credited?

12. Lots in a housing development were priced at $250 a front foot. Mr. and Mrs. Fisher bought a lot that has a frontage of $89\frac{1}{2}$ feet. At this price, how much did the lot cost them?

13. Carson Company agreed to ship an order of merchandise to a customer with freight charges prepaid. The merchandise weighed 2,640 pounds. The freight charges were $2.91\frac{2}{3}$ per hundred pounds. How much were the freight charges that the Carson Company paid?

14. At $14\frac{2}{7}$¢ an ounce, how many ounces can you buy for $8?

15. A house and lot that cost $164,800 were assessed at $0.37\frac{1}{2}$ of the cost. The combined county, city, and school tax rate was $10.87\frac{1}{2}$ for each $100 of assessed value. At this rate, how much was the tax on this property?

16. At a price of 36¢ a pound, how much will 125 pounds cost?

17. The sum of three numbers is 9.3. The first number is 1.7 and the second number is 4.85. What is the third number?

18. A farmer put 6,120 pounds of chemical fertilizer on a 40-acre field. The fertilizer mixture had an average cost of $18.75 for a hundred pounds. How much was the average cost per acre?

19. A shop owner bought 15 dozen colored pencils at $3.75 a dozen. Each pencil was sold for 45¢. How much difference is there between the total cost and the total selling price?

20. A thin sheet of metal weighs $0.56\frac{1}{4}$ pounds per square foot of area. How many square feet are in a piece of this metal that weighs 72 pounds?

Solve these problems. If you have difficulty solving any problem, restudy the appropriate section in this chapter. The problems under a specific number are related to those contained in the exercise with the same last number.

1. a. Change each of the following to an equivalent common fraction or mixed number and reduce to lowest terms.

(1) 0.08　　　　**(3)** 0.048　　　　**(5)** $0.41\frac{2}{3}$　　　　**(7)** $41.083\frac{1}{3}$

(2) 0.1692　　　**(4)** 6.35　　　　**(6)** $3.18\frac{3}{4}$　　　　**(8)** $90.06\frac{1}{4}$

b. Change each of the following to an equivalent in decimal notation. Where applicable, round to the nearest ten thousandth.

(1) $\frac{21}{100}$　　　**(3)** $\frac{1}{125}$　　　**(5)** $\frac{6}{456}$　　　**(7)** $6\frac{3}{8}$

(2) $\frac{5}{8}$　　　**(4)** $\frac{9,375}{10,000}$　　　**(6)** $\frac{95}{7}$　　　**(8)** $48\frac{2}{7}$

2. a. Add.

(1) $3.14, $8.45, $0.45, $8.74
(2) $89.61, $95.08, $52.13, $32.23
(3) 2.022, 1.291, 6.71, $3.94\frac{1}{2}$
(4) 85.02, 3.476, 0.9949, $3.42\frac{1}{4}$

b. Subtract.

(1) $99.94 − $34.29　　**(3)** 0.0456 − 0.0153　　**(5)** $26.8\frac{1}{2}$ − 8.004

(2) $22.63 − $14.98　　**(4)** 8.002 − 2.46　　　**(6)** 5.905 − $1.8\frac{3}{8}$

3. Multiply.

a. 40.59 $\times$ 7　　**b.** 51.80 $\times$ 32　　**c.** 836.3 $\times$ 9　　**d.** 1.028 $\times$ 7.3　　**e.** 24.7 $\times$ 0.0034

f. 0.092 $\times$ 5.7　　**g.** $384\frac{5}{8}$ $\times$ 0.46　　**h.** 45.12 $\times$ $0.8\frac{1}{8}$　　**i.** 3.01 $\times$ 0.014　　**j.** $31\frac{3}{4}$ $\times$ $5.7\frac{1}{2}$

4. Divide. Where applicable, round to the nearest ten thousandth.

a. $67\overline{)76.829}$　　　**c.** $0.02321\overline{)3.3364}$　　　**e.** 161.04 ÷ $8\frac{4}{5}$

b. $4.14\overline{)81.6201}$　　**d.** 58,867 ÷ 46.9　　　　**f.** 0.5465 ÷ $0.07\frac{1}{2}$

5. Divide. Where applicable, round to the nearest ten thousandth.

a. 91 ÷ 20　　　　**e.** 56.10 ÷ 3,000　　　**i.** 81.6 ÷ 4,000
b. 368 ÷ 50　　　　**f.** 274.8 ÷ 600　　　　**j.** 853.1 ÷ 600
c. 5,145 ÷ 700　　　**g.** 40.25 ÷ 70　　　　**k.** 383.4 ÷ 8,000
d. 0.605 ÷ 50　　　**h.** 725.4 ÷ 900　　　　**l.** 587.7 ÷ 30,000

6. Find the total amount for each of the following purchases.

a. 570 ft @ $9.50 per C　　　**c.** 760 lb @ $4.32 per cwt
b. 9,230 lb @ $13.25 per T　　**d.** 24,250 forms @ $7.85 per M

e. 12,300 lb @ $32 per T   *hundred*   **g.** 950 units @ $7.70 per M *Thousand*

f. 2,425 ft @ $5.50 per C   *hundred*   **h.** 350 lb @ $13.75 per cwt

7. a. Find the sum for each problem.
  (1) Add 378.68 to each number: **(a)** 33,475, **(b)** 593, **(c)** 45.68, **(d)** 73.084, and **(e)** 4.2769
  (2) 847 + 65.92 + 65.92 + 65.92 + 65.92 + 65.92 + 65.92

  b. Subtract as specified.
  (1) Subtract 85.49 from each number: **(a)** 760, **(b)** 4,312, **(c)** 342.64, **(d)** 78.3, and **(e)** 528.86
  (2) 669.79 − 72.8 − 72.8 − 72.8 − 72.8 − 72.8 − 72.8

  c. Multiply as specified.
  (1) Multiply each number by 4.68: **(a)** 967, **(b)** 25,439, **(c)** 78.78, **(d)** 7.655, and **(e)** 8.0605
  (2) 46 × 1.4 × 1.4 × 1.4 × 1.4 × 1.4

  d. Divide as specified.
  (1) Divide each number by 17: **(a)** 72,474.995, **(b)** 7,599.935, **(c)** 95.2, **(d)** 62.169, and **(e)** 0.0119
  (2) 195.3125 ÷ 2.5 ÷ 2.5 ÷ 2.5 ÷ 2.5

8. Determine the balance after each check or deposit.

Balance	886	39
Check No. 71	132	76
Balance		
Check No. 72	62	57
Balance		
Deposit	327	50
Balance		
Check No. 73	98	40
Balance		
Check No. 74	106	19
Balance		

9. a. On November 30 Judy Master's checkbook balance was $808.10. On the same date her statement showed a balance of $396.77. A late deposit of $489.89 was not shown on the statement. Checks for $15, $41.91, and $27.10 were outstanding. The service charge amounted to $5.45. Prepare a bank reconciliation.

  b. Ed Long's October statement showed a balance of $673.30. His checkbook balance was $456.50. The bank had charged $6 for collecting the maturity value of $600 on a note for him and $4.95 for regular service. The following checks were outstanding: $129.10, $216.50, and $26.65. A late deposit of $744.50 was not recorded on the statement. Prepare a bank reconciliation.

10. a. Find the fractional equivalent for each of the following aliquot parts of 100.

(1) ___ $\times$ 100 = $8\frac{1}{3}$ **(4)** ___ $\times$ 100 = $41\frac{2}{3}$

(2) ___ $\times$ 100 = $12\frac{1}{2}$ **(5)** ___ $\times$ 100 = $11\frac{1}{9}$

(3) ___ $\times$ 100 = $83\frac{1}{3}$ **(6)** ___ $\times$ 100 = $87\frac{1}{2}$

b. Find the fractional equivalent for each of the following aliquot parts of $1.

(1) $66\frac{2}{3}$¢   **(3)** $58\frac{1}{3}$¢   **(5)** $16\frac{2}{3}$¢   **(7)** $62\frac{1}{2}$¢

(2) $37\frac{1}{2}$¢   **(4)** $6\frac{1}{4}$¢   **(6)** $91\frac{2}{3}$¢   **(8)** $9\frac{1}{11}$¢

11. In cents, show the aliquot part of $1 represented by each of the following fractional equivalents.

a. $\dfrac{1}{4}$ **c.** $\dfrac{1}{5}$ **e.** $\dfrac{5}{6}$ **g.** $\dfrac{11}{12}$

b. $\dfrac{1}{2}$ **d.** $\dfrac{1}{3}$ **f.** $\dfrac{7}{8}$ **h.** $\dfrac{1}{9}$

12. Solve these problems.

a. Add 87 ones, 76 tenths, 65 hundredths, 54 thousandths, and 43 ten thousandths.

b. From 86 hundredths deduct 473 thousandths.

c. Divide 65 hundredths by 13 thousandths.

d. A farmer sold 160.25 acres of land for $592,925. How much was received for each acre?

e. A purchase was made of $987\frac{1}{2}$ yards of heavy plastic material at $56\frac{1}{4}$ cents a yard and of $1,436\frac{1}{4}$ yards of medium-weight plastic at $41\frac{2}{3}$ cents a yard. How much was the total cost of these two grades of plastic?

f. A manager of a hardware store bought 30 dozen wrenches at $36 a dozen. The manager sold 150 of these at $4.95 each prior to a sale, 200 during the sale at $3.95 each, and the remainder at $2.95 each. How much is the difference between the total cost and the total selling price?

CHALLENGE PROBLEM

    Mark Hopkins and Richard Kaster each had 60 widgets for sale. Hopkins' price was 2 for $1, and Kaster's price was 3 for $1. When told that his friend Kaster thought he could sell all of the widgets at those prices, Hopkins agreed to let him do so. As he was taking Hopkins' widgets, Kaster muttered, "Two widgets for $1 and three widgets for $1 is five widgets for $2! I'll sell them that way." After he sold the widgets, Kaster gave Hopkins $30 owed to him and had $18 left. Kaster's wife thought he had spent $2 because he should have $20. How should he explain?

Chapter 5

Measurements

Objectives

After mastering the material in Chapter 5, you will be able to:

- Change U.S. measurements to larger or smaller units.
- Add, subtract, multiply, and divide U.S. or metric measurements.
- Calculate the perimeter and area of a square, rectangle, triangle, and circle.
- Find the volume of a prism and a right circular cylinder.
- Change metric measurements to larger or smaller units.
- Convert U.S. measurements to metric measurements and vice versa.

Weights and measures may be ranked among the necessaries of life to every individual of human society. They enter into the economical arrangements and daily concerns of every family. They are necessary to every occupation of human industry; to the distribution and security of every species of property; to every transaction of trade and commerce; to the labors of the husbandman; to the ingenuity of the artificer; to the studies of the philosopher; to the researches of the antiquarian; to the navigation of the mariner, and the marches of the soldier; to all the exchanges of peace, and all the operations of war. The knowledge of them, as in established use, is among the first elements of education, and is often learned by those who learn nothing else, not even to read and write. This knowledge is riveted in the memory by the habitual application of it to the employments of men throughout life.

John Quincy Adams
Report to the Congress, 1821

The word *measurement* is interpreted to mean a system of measuring the extent, quantity, or size of something. Numbers used in showing units of measurement are denominate numbers. The word *denominate* is derived from the Latin word *nomen,* meaning "name." A denominate number, then, is one in which the quantity is named. The following are denominate numbers because in each case the measure of quantity is named: 8 feet, 5 dozen, 7 liters, 3 hours, 25 grams, 6 square meters.

U.S. UNITS OF MEASUREMENT

The United States is the only major industrialized country that still uses the old English system of weights and measures as an official system. Even Great Britain has adopted the metric system. Therefore, the old English system is referred to as the United States system. Table 5–1 shows some of the standard units of measure used in the United States.

Reduction of U.S. Measurements

The facts contained in tables of standard units of measure are used as multipliers or divisors to change U.S. measurements to smaller or larger units of measure. Follow these rules:

---

1. To express a U.S. measurement in a smaller unit of measure, multiply the measurement by the number of units contained in one of the larger units.

Example A: Change 8 weeks to days.

Solution: 8 × 7 = 56 days

---

2. To express a U.S. measurement in a larger unit of measure, divide the measurement by the number of units needed to make one of the larger units.

Example B: Change 192 minutes to hours and minutes.

Solution: 192 min ÷ 60 = 3 hours and 12 minutes

Counting

12 units = 1 dozen (doz)
12 dozen = 1 gross (gr)
1 ream (rm) = 500 sheets

Time

60 seconds (sec) = 1 minute (min)
60 minutes = 1 hour (hr)
24 hours = 1 day (da)
7 days = 1 week (wk)
30 days = 1 month (mo) average
$4\frac{1}{3}$ weeks = 1 month
13 weeks = 1 quarter (of a year)
52 weeks = 1 year (yr)
12 months = 1 year
360 days = 1 business year
365 days = 1 year
366 days = 1 leap year
100 years = 1 century (C)

Weight

16 ounces (oz) = 1 pound (lb)
7,000 grains = 1 pound
100 pounds = 1 hundredweight (cwt)
20 hundredweights = 1 ton (T)
2,000 pounds = 1 ton
2,240 pounds = 1 long ton

Dry Measure

2 pints (pt) = 1 quart (qt)
8 quarts = 1 peck (pk)
4 pecks = 1 bushel (bu)
1 bushel = 2,150.42 cubic inches

Liquid Measure

16 fluid ounces (fl oz) = 1 pint
4 gills (gi) = 1 pint
2 pints = 1 quart
4 quarts = 1 gallon (gal)
231 cubic inches = 1 gallon
$31\frac{1}{2}$ gallons = 1 barrel (bbl)
63 gallons = 1 hogshead (hhd)
$7\frac{1}{2}$ gallons = 1 cubic foot (approx.)

Linear Measure

12 inches (in) = 1 foot (ft)
3 feet = 1 yard (yd)
$5\frac{1}{2}$ yards = 1 rod (rd)
$16\frac{1}{2}$ feet = 1 rod
66 feet = 1 chain (surveyor's)
320 rods = 1 mile (mi)
1,760 yards = 1 mile
5,280 feet = 1 mile

Surface or Square Measure

144 square inches (sq in) = 1 square foot (sq ft)
9 square feet = 1 square yard (sq yd)
$30\frac{1}{4}$ square yards = 1 square rod (sq rd)
160 square rods = 1 acre (A)
640 acres = 1 square mile (sq mi) or section
36 sections (or sq mi) = 1 township (twp)

Cubic or Volume Measure

1,728 cubic inches (cu in) = 1 cubic foot (cu ft)
27 cubic feet = 1 cubic yard (cu yd)
128 cubic feet = 1 cord (cd) of wood

Table 5-1 Units of Measure Commonly Used in the United States

Change each of the following. Show any remainder as a common fraction in lowest terms.

1. 27 yards to feet

2. 573 feet to yards

3. 638 pecks to bushels

4. 72 articles to dozens

5. 936 articles to gross

6. 130 pints to quarts

7. 3 long tons to pounds

8. 258 feet to yards

9. 33,550 feet to miles and feet

10. 25,000 sheets to reams

11. 583 quarts to gallons and quarts

12. 769 quarts to bushels and quarts

13. 34 gross to dozens

14. 2,160 fluid ounces to quarts and pints

15. 367 weeks to years and weeks

16. 72,384 seconds to minutes and seconds

17. 853 ounces to pounds and ounces

18. 682 pints to gallons and quarts

19. 87,126 minutes to hours and minutes

20. 7 bushels, 2 pecks, and 3 quarts to pints

21. 8,640 fluid ounces to gallons and quarts

22. 325 minutes to hours and minutes

23. 3 reams to sheets of paper

24. 845 weeks to years and weeks

25. 28 rods 3 yards to feet

Arithmetic Operations With U.S. Measurements

The principles that pertain to the addition, subtraction, multiplication, and division of abstract numbers also apply to the basic operations with denominate numbers. The procedures, therefore, are very similar. The smallest unit of measure is placed to the right, with the successively larger units of measure being arranged in order to the left of that place.

Example A:	Add 3 yards 2 feet 9 inches and 8 yards 1 foot 10 inches.

Solution:

$$\begin{array}{l} 3 \text{ yd } 2 \text{ ft } 9 \text{ in} \\ 8 \text{ yd } 1 \text{ ft } 10 \text{ in} \\ \hline 11 \text{ yd } 3 \text{ ft } 19 \text{ in} = 12 \text{ yd } 1 \text{ ft } 7 \text{ in} \end{array}$$

Explanation: Since 19 inches equals 1 foot 7 inches, the sum becomes 11 yd 4 ft 7 in. Since 4 feet equals 1 yard 1 foot, the sum becomes 12 yd 1 ft 7 in.

Example B: Subtract: 39 gal 1 qt
$$\phantom{\text{Subtract: }} 32 \text{ gal } 2 \text{ qt}$$

Solution:

$$\begin{array}{l} 38 \text{ gal } 5 \text{ qt} \\ 32 \text{ gal } 2 \text{ qt} \\ \hline 6 \text{ gal } 3 \text{ qt} \end{array}$$

Explanation: As 2 quarts is larger than 1 quart, 1 gallon is borrowed from the 39 gallons. The 4 quarts (1 gallon) are added to the 1 quart, giving a total of 38 gal 5 qt.

In one kind of problem requiring multiplication of denominate numbers, the multiplier is an abstract number.

Example C: In hours and minutes, what is the total time worked by a man in 5 days if he worked 6 hours 30 minutes daily?

Solution:

$$\begin{array}{ll} 6 \text{ hr} & 30 \text{ min} \\ & \times\, 5 \\ \hline 30 \text{ hr} & 150 \text{ min} \\ +\, 2 \text{ hr} - & 120 \text{ min} \\ \hline 32 \text{ hr} & 30 \text{ min} \end{array}$$

In another kind of multiplication problem, both factors are denominate numbers. This kind of problem is explained in a subsequent section.

In the division of denominate numbers, there are also two kinds of problems: those requiring division by an abstract number, as in Example D, and those requiring division of one denominate number by another denominate number, as in Example E.

Example D: Divide 34 gallons 2 quarts into 4 equal quantities.

Solution:

$$\begin{array}{lll} 8 \text{ gal} & 2 \text{ qt} & 1 \text{ pt} \\ 4\,)34 \text{ gal} & 2 \text{ qt} & \\ \underline{32 \text{ gal}} & & \\ 2 \text{ gal} = & \underline{8 \text{ qt}} & \\ & 10 \text{ qt} & \\ & \underline{8 \text{ qt}} & \\ & 2 \text{ qt} = & 4 \text{ pt} \\ & & \underline{4 \text{ pt}} \end{array}$$

The division of one denominate number by another denominate number is facilitated if both numbers are expressed in the same unit of measure.

Example E: Divide 31 pounds 2 ounces by 5 pounds 3 ounces.

Solution: If both numbers are expressed in pounds:

$$31\tfrac{2}{16} \div 5\tfrac{3}{16} = 6$$

If both numbers are expressed in ounces:

$$31 \text{ lb } 2 \text{ oz} = 498 \text{ oz}; \; 5 \text{ lb } 3 \text{ oz} = 83 \text{ oz}$$
$$498 \div 83 = 6$$

● Exercise 5–2

1. Add 23 yards 2 feet 9 inches, 35 yards 1 foot 10 inches, and 57 yards 2 feet 8 inches.

2. Add 8 years 30 weeks 4 days, 9 years 43 weeks 5 days, and 12 years 26 weeks 3 days.

3. Subtract 58 hours 38 minutes 37 seconds from 87 hours 25 minutes 49 seconds.

4. Subtract 29 gallons 3 quarts 1 pint from 64 gallons 1 quart.

5. Multiply 42 gallons 3 quarts 1 pint by 8.

6. Multiply 24 yards 2 feet by 6.

7. Divide 29 bushels 3 pecks 3 quarts by 5.

8. Divide 61 yards by 9.

9. Divide 53 pounds 4 ounces by 4 pounds 7 ounces.

10. What is the total number of inches in four steel bars that measure $3\tfrac{1}{2}$ feet, 41 inches, $\tfrac{3}{4}$ yard, and $2\tfrac{1}{2}$ yards?

11. The train travels from Pittsburgh to Denton in 7 hours 15 minutes. The bus makes fewer stops and takes only 5 hours 25 minutes to make the trip between the two towns. How much time can a passenger save by taking the bus?

12. Golden Canning Company puts 12 ounces net weight of corn in cans that weigh 1 ounce each. Two dozen cans are packed in a carton. Each carton weighs 8 ounces. The company shipped 75 cartons to a customer. How many pounds did this shipment weigh?

13. Add 2 years 32 weeks 3 days 12 hours 40 minutes, 3 years 47 weeks 5 days 30 minutes, and 29 weeks 6 days 17 hours 48 minutes.

14. From 16 days 18 hours 45 minutes and 17 seconds subtract 12 days 20 hours and 35 seconds.

15. Subtract 3 years 27 weeks 19 days 22 hours from 5 years 18 weeks 19 hours.

16. There are 8 gallons 2 quarts and 1 pint of milk in one container and 5 gallons 1 quart and 1 pint in another container. How many quart cartons can be filled from these two containers?

17. Find the cost of 28 gallons 3 quarts and 1 pint of vinegar at 72 cents a quart.

18. At birth, a baby weighed 7 pounds 6 ounces. Later the baby weighed 13 pounds 5 ounces. How many pounds and ounces did the baby gain?

19. Boards that are 18 feet 8 inches long are to be cut into four pieces each for use in constructing a picket fence. Each picket will be how long in feet and inches?

20. If 46 quarts 1 pint of milk weigh 104 pounds 10 ounces, what is the weight of 1 gallon of milk in pounds and ounces?

Geometric Figures

Geometry is a branch of mathematics that deals with the measurement, properties, and relationships of points, lines, angles, surfaces, and solids. A **line** in geometry is considered to have length but no width or depth. Lines may extend in vertical, horizontal, or slanting (oblique) positions. Figures composed of lines are **geometric figures.** A **plane figure** is any real or imagined flat surface.

Perimeters of Plane Figures

The length of the boundary of any closed figure is its **perimeter.** The perimeter of a rectangle can be determined by adding twice the length to twice the width. When P is used for the perimeter, l for length, and w for width, the formula may be written:

$$P = 2l + 2w$$

Example A: Find the perimeter of a rectangle that is 7 feet long and 5 feet wide.

Solution: $P = (2 \times 7) + (2 \times 5)$
$P = 14 + 10$
$P = 24$ feet

The perimeter of a square is equal to four times the length of one of its sides (s):

$$P = 4s$$

Chapter 5. Measurements   135

Example B: Find the perimeter of a square that is 9 feet long on each side.

Solution: $P = 4 \times 9 = 36$ feet

The perimeter of a triangle equals the sum of the lengths of the three sides. If the sides are represented by the letters a, b, and c, the formula is:

$$P = a + b + c$$

Example C: What is the perimeter of a triangle whose sides measure 2 inches, $4\frac{3}{8}$ inches, and 3 inches?

Solution: $P = 2 + 4\frac{3}{8} + 3 = 9\frac{3}{8}$ inches

A **circle,** shown in Figure 5–1, is a closed curved line, every point of which is an equal distance from a point within called the **center.** The **circumference** is the curved line that encompasses the circle. The **radius** is a straight line from the center to the circumference of a circle. The **diameter** is a straight line that passes through the center of a circle and connects two opposite points on the circumference. The diameter of a circle, therefore, is twice as long as its radius. An **arc** is any part of the circumference of a circle.

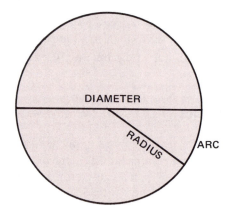

Figure 5–1 A Circle

The circumference of a circle is its perimeter. The ratio of the circumference of a circle to its diameter is constant for all circles. This ratio is usually designated by the Greek letter π (pi).

$$\frac{\text{Circumference}}{\text{diameter}} = \pi$$
$$\text{Circumference} = \pi \times \text{diameter}$$
$$\text{or } C = \pi d$$

The numeric value of π in the foregoing formula cannot be determined precisely. Its value to eight decimal places is 3.14159265, which is usually rounded to 3.14 or 3.1416.

Example D: Find the circumference of a circle that has a diameter of 4 feet.

Solution: $C = \pi d = 3.1416 \times 4 = 12.5664$ feet

As the diameter of a circle is twice its radius, the formula for finding the circumference of a circle is often expressed as:

$$C = 2\pi r$$

Example E: What is the circumference of a circle whose radius is 15 inches?

Solution: $C = 2\pi r = 2 \times 3.1416 \times 15 = 94.248$ inches

● Exercise 5-3

Where applicable in solving these problems, let $\pi = 3.1416$.

1. A sheet of typing paper is about $8\frac{1}{2}$ inches by 11 inches. What is its perimeter?

2. The longer sides of a rectangle are 21 inches each. The shorter sides are 12 inches each. Find the perimeter.

3. Find the perimeter in feet and inches of a rectangle with measurements of 10 feet $4\frac{1}{2}$ inches and 6 feet.

4. Find the perimeter in inches of a rectangle that is 2 feet 8 inches long. Its width is $\frac{5}{8}$ of its length.

5. The perimeter of a square area is 34 yards 2 feet. What is the length of one side?

6. A triangular area is measured to be 15 feet by 22 feet 6 inches by 18 feet. What is the perimeter of the triangle in feet and inches?

7. A 30-inch sidewalk surrounds a building and is 3 feet from its foundation. The building is 60 feet wide and 90 feet long. What is the outer perimeter of the walk?

8. What is the circumference in feet of a pipe with a radius of 27 inches?

9. A farm silo is constructed of reinforced concrete that is 9 inches thick. The circular structure has an inside diameter of 15 feet. To the nearest inch, what is the circumference in feet and inches of (a) the interior and (b) the exterior of the silo?

10. A farmer plans to fence a field that measures 700 yards long and 300 yards wide. How much will the fencing cost at $1.79 per foot?

11. A room that is 19 feet 6 inches long and 16 feet wide has two 36-inch doors. How many feet of baseboard are needed for the room?

12. Ward Hunter is planning to make a rectangular picture frame. He wants the frame to have measurements of 30 inches by 22 inches. Allowing $2\frac{1}{2}$ inches for each corner, how many feet of molding does he need?

13. Carol Simpson plans to weatherstrip the following: 6 windows, each $28\frac{1}{2}$ inches by 4 feet; 5 windows, each 126 inches by 6 feet 6 inches; 3 windows, each 4 feet 3 inches by $40\frac{1}{2}$ inches; and 3 doorways, each 3 feet 6 inches by 6 feet 6 inches. How much will the total cost be at 9¢ a foot?

14. A rancher plans to construct a fence of three strands of barbed wire around a rectangular grazing area that is $1\frac{1}{2}$ miles long and 1 mile wide. (a) How many 80-rod spools of barbed wire should he buy? (b) How much will he pay if each spool is priced at $41.99?

15. How long is the radius if the diameter is (a) 12.7 miles? (b) $15\frac{3}{4}$ feet? (c) 24 feet? (d) 11 yards 1 foot (e) 9 inches?

16. Find the circumference of a circle with a radius of: (a) 600 yards, (b) 465 feet, (c) 5 inches, (d) 7 miles, and (e) 0.9 inch.

17. Find the circumference of a circle having a diameter of: (a) 25 miles, (b) 8 inches, (c) 24 yards, (d) $7\frac{1}{2}$ feet, and (e) $\frac{3}{4}$ foot.

18. If the diameter of a bicycle wheel is 27 inches, (a) how far does it travel in one revolution? (b) To the nearest ten-thousandth, how many revolutions will the wheel make in 1 mile?

19. The circumference of a tree is 4 feet 8 inches. What is its diameter to the nearest inch?

20. Find the perimeter of the area shown in the figure below. The arc is one half of a circle.

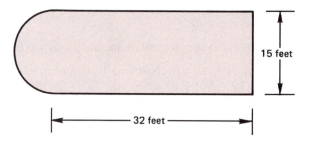

15 feet

32 feet

Areas of Plane Figures

In a preceding section of this chapter, arithmetic operations with denominate numbers is presented. One kind of arithmetic-denominate problem, the multiplication of a denominate number by another denominate number, is presented in this section.

Area of a Square. When a linear measure is multiplied by the same kind of linear measure, area is obtained. **Area** is the measure of the plane surface included within a set of lines. Area is usually stated in terms of square units (such as square feet or square inches) even though the plane surface may be that of a triangle, circle, or any other plane figure. The number of square units found in a given surface is found by multiplication. Notice in Figure 5–2 that 1 square yard contains 9 square feet. The analysis is as follows: 1 yard = 3 feet; 1 square yard = 3 ft × 3 ft = 9 sq ft. Furthermore, 3 × 3 may be written as 3^2; that is, 3 squared. In the following formula for finding the area of a square, *b* is the length of the base.

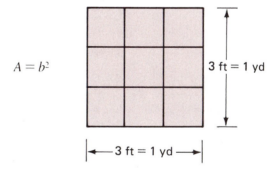

$$A = b^2$$

3 ft = 1 yd

3 ft = 1 yd

Figure 5–2 Area of One Square Yard Equals Nine Square Feet

Area of a Rectangle. The area of the rectangle illustrated in Figure 5–3 contains 3 × 5 or 15 squares. If each square represents 1 foot, the area represented is said to be 15 square feet. Thus, **the area of a rectangle is equal to the product of its length (*l*) and width (*w*).** Length and width should be expressed in the same unit of measure.

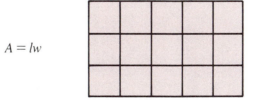

$$A = lw$$

Figure 5–3 Area of a Rectangle

The **acre** is a common United States measurement for area of land. The area of an acre is 160 square rods, which is 4,840 square yards or 43,560 square feet.

Area of a Triangle. Let *ABC* equal any triangle. As Figure 5–4 illustrates, if a second triangle *BCD* that is equal to triangle *ABC* is placed adjacent to the first triangle, a parallelogram is formed. This reveals that the area of a triangle equals one-half the area of a parallelogram having the same base and height. Therefore, **the area of a triangle is equal to one-half the product of its base (*b*) and height (*h*).**

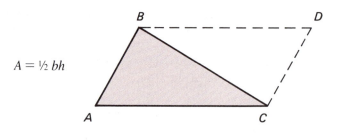

A = ½ *bh*

Figure 5–4 Area of a Triangle

Example: Find the area of a triangle that is 6 inches wide and 8 inches high.

Solution: $A = \frac{1}{2} bh = \frac{1}{2} \times 6 \text{ in} \times 8 \text{ in} = 24 \text{ sq in}$

Area of a Circle. Proving the validity of the formula for finding the area of a circle is beyond the scope of this book. Interested students should refer to geometry textbooks. It can be proved that the area of a circle can be written:

$$A = \pi r^2$$

Example A: Using 3.1416 for π, find the area of a circle with a radius of 4.75 inches.

Solution: $A = \pi r^2 = 3.1416 \times 4.75 \times 4.75 = 70.88235 \text{ sq in}$

Example B: Using 3.1416 for π, find the area of a circle with a diameter of 16 feet.

Solution: radius $= \frac{1}{2} \times 16 \text{ ft} = 8 \text{ ft}$
$A = \pi r^2 = 3.1416 \times 8 \times 8 = 201.0624 \text{ sq ft}$

● Exercise 5–4

Where applicable in solving these problems, let $\pi = 3.1416$.

1. Multiply 5 feet 6 inches by 3 feet 4 inches to obtain square feet.

2. Find the number of acres in a rectangular ranch that is 3 miles wide and 5 miles long.

3. A rectangular field is 40 rods wide and 56 rods long. How many acres are in this field?

4. How many acres are in a plot of ground that measures 900 feet by 1,210 feet?

5. What is the area in square feet of a triangular sail that has a base of 12 feet and a height of 15 feet?

6. A triangle that is 15 feet high has a base of 20 feet. Find its area in square feet.

7. The surface of a rectangular painting contains 5,742 square inches. One dimension is 7 feet 3 inches. What is the length of the other dimension in feet and inches?

8. A room is 18 feet wide and 24 feet long. The owner installed new carpeting at a cost of $22 a square yard. How much did the owner spend for the carpeting?

9. A room is 21 feet long and 15 feet wide. The owner had the floor covered with tiles that each measure 9 inches square. How many tiles were needed to cover the floor?

10. What is the cost per square yard of fabric that is 45 inches wide and costs $3.50 a linear yard?

11. How many square feet are in a circular area that has a radius of 26 feet?

12. The diameter of a certain engine piston is 3 inches. To the nearest ten-thousandth, what is the area of the piston head?

13. Which is larger: (a) the area of a circle that is 9 inches in diameter or (b) the area of a square whose side is 9 inches? How much larger?

14. The directions on the label of a bottle of lawn spray state that the contents mixed with water will cover 450 square feet of lawn. How many bottles of spray are needed to cover a lawn that measures 120 feet by 100 feet, in the middle of which is a house that is 40 feet wide and 50 feet long?

15. The State Highway Department bought 3,630 linear feet of right-of-way through Clyde Bailey's ranch. The right-of-way is 84 feet wide. How much did Bailey receive for the land at $16,350 an acre?

16. A room is 20 feet long, 16 feet wide, and $8\frac{1}{2}$ feet high. How many gallons of paint are needed to cover the walls and ceiling after deducting 84 square feet for doors and windows? Directions on the paint container indicate that one gallon should cover 450 square feet.

17. A circular floor is 60 feet in diameter. How much will it cost to carpet this area at $14.95 per yard or fraction thereof?

18. A sidewalk that is 3 feet wide encloses a circular garden which has a diameter of 68 feet. To the nearest square foot, what is the area of the walk?

19. A rectangular front lawn is 85 feet long and 41 feet wide. Find the cost of lawn seed for this area if one pound covers 125 square feet and costs $1.75 a pound.

20. How many bricks $3\frac{7}{8}$ inches by $7\frac{7}{8}$ inches are needed to construct a walk that is 4 feet wide and 60 feet long? The bricks are to be spaced $\frac{1}{4}$ inch apart to allow for mortar.

21. A packing case has dimensions of 4 feet by 3 feet by 2 feet 6 inches. How many square feet of plywood are needed to manufacture each case?

22. To the nearest ten-thousandth, find the area of the figure at the right. The curved area is a half circle.

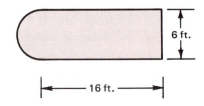

Volumes of Solids

A **solid** is a body or magnitude that has length, width, and height. Solids are of many different shapes. The shape of a solid determines its name, such as rectangular, triangular, cylindrical, etc. Some of the most common solids are considered in this section.

Volume, also called **capacity** or **cubic contents,** is the space occupied as measured in cubic units. When computing the volume of a geometric solid, all linear units of measure should be expressed in the same denomination, such as in inches, or in feet, or in yards. **The volume of any prism equals the area of its base (B) times its height (h).**

$$\text{Prism Volume} = Bh$$

Since the area of a rectangle equals its length times its width, **the volume of a rectangular prism is equal to the product of its length (l), width (w), and height (h).** See Figure 5–5.

$V = lwh$

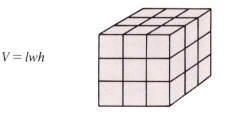

Figure 5–5 Volume of a Rectangular Prism

Example:	Find the capacity in cubic feet of a rectangular solid that is 36 inches long, 2 feet wide, and 4 feet high.
Solution:	36 in ÷ 12 in = 3 ft long $V = lwh = 3$ ft $\times$ 2 ft $\times$ 4 ft = 24 cu ft

Volume of a Right Circular Cylinder. A solid having two equal parallel circles for its bases and a uniformly curved surface for its side is a **cylinder.** An illustration appears in Figure 5–6. A cylinder may be defined in terms of rotation. When a rectangle is rotated about one side as an axis, the resulting geometric solid is a **right circular cylinder.** Each element of the curved surface of a cylinder is perpendicular to its bases. Like that of a prism, **the volume of a right circular cylinder equals the area of its base times its height.** Of course, the area of the circular base of a cylinder equals πr^2.

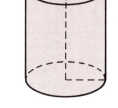

Cylinder Volume $= Bh$
or $V = \pi r^2 h$

Example:	Find the volume of a cylinder that is 7 feet high and has a diameter of 6 feet.
Solution:	radius = 6 ft ÷ 2 = 3 ft $V = \pi r^2 h = 3.1416 \times 3 \times 3 \times 7 = 197.9208$ cu ft

● Exercise 5–5

Where applicable in solving these problems, use 3.1416 for π.

1. A square prism has a base with measurements of 12 inches by 12 inches and an altitude of 20 inches. Find its volume in cubic inches.

2. A rectangular prism has a base with measurements of 8 inches by 10 inches and a height of 15 inches. Find its volume in cubic inches.

3. Bricks were placed in a rectangular stack that is 24 feet wide, 15 feet high, and 40 feet long. What is the cubic content of this stack **(a)** in cubic feet and **(b)** in cubic yards?

4. A classroom is 25 feet wide, 40 feet long, and 9 feet high. Allowing 300 cubic feet of air space per student, what is the maximum number of students that should be assigned to this room?

5. What is the capacity in cubic feet of a truck with inside cargo dimensions of 24 feet by 8 feet 6 inches by 9 feet 3 inches?

6. The volume of a 9-inch cube is how many times larger than the volume of a 3-inch cube?

7. Elaine Harris plans to have a 4-inch thick concrete driveway laid from the street to her garage. The driveway is to be 20 feet wide and 45 feet long. How many cubic yards of concrete are needed?

8. Steel weighs 490 pounds per cubic foot. To the nearest pound, what is the weight of a steel bar that is 18 feet long, 3 inches wide, and $\frac{3}{4}$ inch thick?

9. The concrete foundation for a building is to be 2 feet thick and 9 feet deep. The interior measurements of the foundation are to be 48 feet by 28 feet. Find the number of cubic yards of concrete that are needed.

10. Hanson Masonry Company uses 120 pounds of crushed rock in each cubic foot of concrete mix for sidewalks. How many tons of crushed rock should the company deliver to a house where a sidewalk 80 feet long, $3\frac{1}{2}$ feet wide, and 4 inches deep is to be constructed?

11. A gasoline storage tank with a diameter of 40 feet is 50 feet tall. Find the cubic feet of capacity.

12. The silo on Gail Summers' farm has inside measurements of 60 feet in height and 20 feet in diameter. What is its volume in cubic feet?

13. Malkovich's Grain Storage Company is adding 12 cylindrical bins. The inside of each new bin will measure 28 feet in diameter and 50 feet in height. How many cubic feet of new storage space is being added?

14. A new cylindrical tank is to be installed at a gasoline service station. Its interior dimensions are 8 feet 6 inches in diameter and 20 feet 6 inches in length. If $7\frac{1}{2}$ gallons equal one cubic foot, what is the capacity of the tank to the nearest gallon?

15. How many cubic yards of earth must be removed to make a well 7 feet 6 inches in diameter and 30 feet deep?

16. A cylindrical water tunnel is to be cut through a mountain. The diameter of the tunnel is to be 24 feet and its length is to be $\frac{3}{4}$ of a mile. How many cubic yards of earth must be removed?

17. Water flows through a certain pipe at the rate of 72 feet per minute. If the pipe is 12 inches in diameter, how many gallons of water will flow past a given point in the pipe in one hour?

18. Williams Company wants a cylindrical tank that will hold 1,000 cubic feet of liquid. The tank is to be 10 feet in diameter. To the nearest foot, how long should the tank be?

19. A right cylindrical piece of wood is 20 inches high and has a diameter of 24 inches. (a) How many cubic inches of wood are in this piece? (b) If a

right circular cone with the same base and height as this cylinder is constructed from it, how many cubic inches of wood must be removed?

20. A swimming pool 30 feet wide and 60 feet long is 3 feet deep at one end and slopes evenly to a depth of $9\frac{1}{2}$ feet at the other. **(a)** If the pool is filled to within one foot of the top, how many cubic feet of water will it contain? **(b)** How many gallons of water will it contain?

METRIC UNITS OF MEASUREMENT

An ideal standard of measure is one that is so rigidly defined in relation to some invariable element of nature that it can be determined at any time independently of prototypes. The French government, through decisions made by the National Assembly of France in 1791 and 1795, sponsored an attempt to devise an ideal unit of length in terms of a particular distance on the surface of the earth. An attempt to determine the distance from the North Pole to the equator was made, and the fundamental unit of length, the **meter** (m), was defined as $\frac{1}{10,000,000}$ of that distance. The meter was used as the basis for other elements in the metric system. Larger and smaller measures of a given unit were related by decimal ratios.

Errors were made in the original calculations, so the meter is not exactly $\frac{1}{10,000,000}$ of the earth's quadrant. Today the basic metric unit of length, the **meter,** is defined officially as 1,650,763.73 wave lengths in vacuum of the orange-red spectral light given off by krypton 86, a rare gas that is found in the atmosphere. This definition may seem quite complicated; but with modern instruments of measurement, it does provide an easy method of redetermining the exact length of a meter.

The metric system has gradually displaced other national systems and is in general use in all major industrialized countries except the United States. It is used in the United States, however, in many industries and professions. More and more American companies are adopting it as their system of measurement. In recent decades, Great Britain, Canada, and Australia have adopted the metric system as their official system. On December 23, 1975, President Ford signed the Metric Conversion Act of 1975. Although the act does not make use of the metric system compulsory, the system is expected to become predominant eventually. Business people who work in science or engineering or have trade relations with foreign countries must now know and use the metric system.

Metric Terms and Rules

The International Bureau of Weights and Measures, located at Sevres, France, serves as the permanent secretariat for the Meter Convention. The international bureau coordinates the exchange of information about the use and refinement of the metric system. The General Conference on Weights and Measures, which is the diplomatic organization made of members of the Convention, meets periodically to ratify improvements in the system and the standards.

In 1960, the General Conference adopted an extensive revision and simplification of the metric system. The name *Le Systeme International d'Unites* (International System of Units, which is abbreviated SI) was adopted. Further improvements in and additions to SI standards have been made by the General Conference at subsequent meetings.

Metric Terms. The seven base units adopted by the General Conference in 1960 are shown in Table 5–2. We shall focus attention on only three of these and some derived therefrom, as well as on a few non-SI units that are important and widely used as part of the metric system.

Name	Symbol	Definition
meter	m	unit of length
kilogram	kg	unit of mass (weight)
kelvin*	K	unit of temperature
second	s	unit of time
ampere	A	unit of electrical current
mole	mol	unit of amount of substance
candela	cd	unit of luminous intensity

*Temperature in general is expressed in degrees Celsius (°C), which formerly was called centigrade.

Table 5–2 Metric Base Units of Measurement

The seven base units were designed deliberately to meet the needs of engineers and scientists. Most people need be concerned about only the meter, kilogram, and degrees Celsius (instead of kelvin). The second as a measure of time is already well known, and the other units are seldom used by most people.

A distinct advantage of the metric system is that it is a decimal system composed of multiples so that each unit of measure is exactly ten times as large as the unit just smaller. Thus, it eliminates the awkward conversion of inches to feet, ounces to pounds, feet to miles, etc. Furthermore, the name of each unit indicates how many units as well as what kind of unit. For example (see Table 5–3), **deka** means 10, **hecto** means 100, and **kilo** means 1000. Therefore, a **dekameter** is 10 meters, a **hectometer** is 100 meters, and a **kilometer** is 1000 meters. The metric system also has prefixes for measures smaller than the basic unit. For example, one **decimeter** is 0.1 of a meter, one **centimeter** is 0.01 of a meter, and one **millimeter** is 0.001 of a meter.

The six prefixes (kilo, hecto, deka, deci, centi, and milli) presented in the preceding paragraph are the ones that deserve the greatest attention because they are used most frequently. Furthermore, in conjunction with using the meter as a measure of length, the kilometer, centimeter, and millimeter are

Multiples and Submultiples	Prefix	Symbol	USA Pronunciation	USA Meaning
1 000 000 000 000 000 000 = 10^{18}	exa	E	ex a	One quintillion times
1 000 000 000 000 000 = 10^{15}	peta	P	pet a	One quadrillion times
1 000 000 000 000 = 10^{12}	tera	T	ter a	One trillion times
1 000 000 000 = 10^9	giga	G	jig a	One billion times
1 000 000 = 10^6	mega	M	meg a	One million times
1 000 = 10^3	kilo	k	kill oh	One thousand times
100 = 10^2	hecto	h	heck toe	One hundred times
10 = 10^1	deka	da	deck a	Ten times
Base Unit 1 = 10^0				
0.1 = 10^{-1}	deci	d	des a	One tenth of
0.01 = 10^{-2}	centi	c	sent a	One hundredth of
0.001 = 10^{-3}	milli	m	mil a	One thousandth of
0.000 001 = 10^{-6}	micro	μ	my kro	One millionth of
0.000 000 001 = 10^{-9}	nano	n	nan oh	One billionth of
0.000 000 000 001 = 10^{-12}	pico	p	peek oh	One trillionth of
0.000 000 000 000 001 = 10^{-15}	femto	f	fem toe	One quadrillionth of
0.000 000 000 000 000 001 = 10^{-18}	atto	a	at oh	One quintillionth of

Table 5-3 Value and Meaning of SI Unit Prefixes

most common. Nevertheless, you should remember the meanings, numerical values, and symbols of these six prefixes. One means of helping you to do so is to remember a place-value table similar to Figure 5-7.

kilometer (km) 1000	hectometer (hm) 100	dekameter (dam) 10	meter (m) 1	decimeter (dm) 0.1	centimeter (cm) 0.01	millimeter (mm) 0.001

Figure 5-7 Decimal Value of Common Metric Prefixes

The prefixes shown in Table 5-3 may be used with basic SI units and with certain non-SI units of metric measurement. Consider the kilogram (kg), which is the basic SI unit of mass (commonly thought of as weight). Kilo means 1000, so a kilogram equals 1000 grams. The **gram** (g) was defined in terms of the meter as being the weight of one cubic centimeter (a cube that is 0.01 m per side) of distilled water at its greatest density, or at a temperature of 39.2 degrees Fahrenheit (4 degrees Celsius) and at sea level. One standard-sized paper clip weighs about 1 gram; a nickel, about 5 grams. Because the gram is such a very small unit of measure, the kilogram is now the basic unit of weight. This is the only base unit that contains a prefix as part of its name.

When used to express weight, the milligram, gram, kilogram, and metric ton (t) or tonne are used most frequently. Medicine tablets are labeled by the milligram and canned foods by the gram. Grain is sold to foreign countries by the metric ton, which is one million grams; that is, one thousand kilograms. Meat, butter, and similarly packaged foods will soon be sold in the United States by the kilogram (about 2.2 pounds), 0.5 kilogram (500 g), and 0.25 kilogram (250 g). The microgram is a very small measurement that is used in science and medicine.

The cubic decimeter (a cube 0.1 m per side) was defined as a unit of capacity and given the name **liter** (L), which is pronounced "leeter." Since 10^3 equals 1000, one liter equals 1000 cubic centimeters of capacity. A liter is a non-SI unit that is slightly larger than one U.S. liquid quart. Any prefix shown in Table 5–3 may be attached to the word *liter*. Thus, a *centi*liter (cL) means 0.01 liter and a *kilo*liter means 1000 liters. Certain U.S. soft drink companies are now selling their products in liter-sized bottles. While gasoline and milk are sold by the liter at some places, cough medicine and the like are sold in smaller capacities that are stated in milliliters.

Rules for Writing Metric Terms. An examination of the foregoing paragraphs and tables reveals the following recommended rules for writing metric terms.

> 1. Except for Celsius, unit names are not capitalized unless used at the beginning of a sentence.

Example: 5 meters, *not* 5 Meters

> 2. The appropriate lower case and capital letters are used for the symbols.

Example: 7 mm for 7 millimeters; 7 Mm for 7 megameters

> 3. All symbols are shown in the singular for both singular and plural forms. (The letter *s* should not be appended to the symbols.)

Example: 4 mm, *not* 4 mms

> 4. Exponents rather than abbreviations are used to show square and cubic symbols.

Example: 3 m^2, *not* 3 sq m; 6 cm^3, *not* 6 cu cm (Notice that cm^3 is preferred to cc.)

> 5. A period is not used after a symbol except when the symbol falls at the end of a sentence.

Example:

8 mg, *not* 8 mg.

> 6. A single space is left between a numeral and a symbol.

Example:

20 km, *not* 20km

> 7. A single space instead of the comma is used to separate a numeral into groups of three digits. (Four-digit numerals may be written without the space.)

Example:

25 000 km, *not* 25,000 km

> 8. A zero is used before the decimal point for quantities smaller than 1.

Example:

0.9 mL, *not* .9 mL

> 9. Decimal notation rather than common fraction notation is used to show quantities smaller than 1.

Example:

0.5 g, *not* $\frac{1}{2}$ g

● Exercise 5–6

For each of the following, write on a separate sheet of paper **(a)** the numerical value of the prefix or unit and **(b)** the symbol for the measurement named. Example: hectoliter: **(a)** 100, **(b)** hL.

1. hectometer

2. kilometer

3. dekameter

4. meter

5. decimeter

6. centimeter

7. millimeter

8. decigram

9. centigram

10. milliliter

Chapter 5. Measurements

11. kiloliter

12. dekagram

13. liter

14. kilogram

15. gram

16. centiliter

17. hectogram

18. milligram

19. hectoliter

20. deciliter

21. dekaliter

22. tonne (Show number of grams.)

23. square meter

24. cubic meter

Reduction of Metric Measurements

As the metric system is a decimal system that is based on multiples of 10, changing from one metric unit of measurement to a larger or smaller unit is accomplished simply by moving the decimal point to the left or right the appropriate number of places. As you recall, multiplying and dividing by 10 and by multiples of 10 may be accomplished by moving the decimal point to the right or to the left.

To change a metric value to a smaller metric unit, the decimal point is moved to the right. Figure 5–8 is helpful to understanding the procedure. Notice that the decimal point is moved to the right 1, 2, 3, or more places depending on how far *down* the scale the desired unit lies from the given unit. For example, 1 decimeter is 0.1 of a meter, but it is also equal to 10 centimeters. Therefore, to change from decimeters to centimeters, multiply by 10; that is, move the decimal point one place to the right.

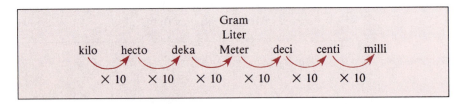

Figure 5–8 Changing to Smaller Metric Units

Example A: Change each of the following as indicated: **(a)** 253 decimeters (dm) to centimeters (cm); **(b)** 184 kilograms (kg) to grams (g); **(c)** 907 dekaliters (daL) to deciliters (dL).

Solution: **(a)** To move *down* the scale 1 place, *multiply* by 10.

$$253 \times 10 = 2530 \text{ cm}$$

(b) To move 3 places *down* the scale, *multiply* by 1000.

$$184 \times 1000 = 184\,000 \text{ g}$$

(c) To move 2 places *down, multiply* by 100.

$$907 \times 100 = 90\ 700 \text{ dL}$$

To change a metric value to a larger metric unit, the decimal point is moved to the left the appropriate number of places. Figure 5–9 illustrates the procedure. In this case the decimal point is moved to the left 1, 2, 3, or more places depending on how far *up* the scale the desired unit is from the given unit. For example, a gram is two places (100 times) larger than a centigram, so the decimal point is moved two places to the left; that is, $1 \div 100 = 0.01$ gram.

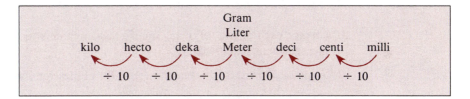

Figure 5–9 Changing to Larger Metric Units

Example B: Change each of the following as indicated: **(a)** 351 centigrams (cg) to grams (g); **(b)** 430 deciliter (dL) to hectoliters (hL); **(c)** 717 meters (m) to dekameters (dam).

Solution: **(a)** To move 2 places *up* the scale, *divide* by 100.

$$351 \div 100 = 3.51 \text{ g}$$

(b) To move *up* the scale 3 places, *divide* by 1000.

$$430 \div 1000 = 0.43 \text{ hL}$$

(c) To move 1 place up, *divide* by 10.

$$717 \div 10 = 71.7 \text{ dam}$$

In summary, notice that the smaller units lie to the right, the larger units to the left; and the decimal point is moved to the right for smaller units, to the left for larger units.

● Exercise 5–7

A. Change each of the following to the larger or smaller units indicated.

1. 85 meters to decimeters

2. 72 683 millimeters to meters

3. 600 meters to centimeters

4. 371 milliliters to liters

5. 8534 liters to kiloliters

6. 497 kilograms to grams

7. 574 meters to millimeters

8. 5.2 kilometers to meters

9. 89 077 hectometers to meters

10. 71 690 dekagrams to grams

11. 76 grams to milligrams

12. 150 deciliters to centiliters

13. 23 557 centigrams to dekagrams

14. 36 619 kilometers to dekameters

15. 51 479 milliliters to dekaliters

16. 76 428 dekagrams to decigrams

17. 34 240 millimeters to decimeters

18. 74 420 grams to tonnes

19. 18 580 dekameters to hectometers

20. 14 megagrams to grams

21. 19 404 deciliters to centiliters

22. 20 858 micrograms to grams

23. 968 tonnes to kilograms

24. 23 281 micrograms to decigrams

B. Change each of the following metric measurements to the units of metric measurement requested.

1. Express 20 meters in **(a)** centimeters, **(b)** millimeters, and **(c)** kilometers.

2. Express 750 meters in **(a)** centimeters, **(b)** millimeters, and **(c)** kilometers.

3. Express 250 centimeters in **(a)** millimeters, **(b)** meters, and **(c)** kilometers.

4. Express 3840 millimeters in **(a)** centimeters, **(b)** meters, and **(c)** kilometers.

5. Express 25 kilometers in **(a)** meters, **(b)** centimeters, and **(c)** millimeters.

6. Express 600 grams in **(a)** kilograms, **(b)** milligrams, and **(c)** dekagrams.

7. Express 6523 liters in **(a)** dekaliters, **(b)** hectoliters, and **(c)** deciliters.

8. Express 9350 milligrams in **(a)** grams, **(b)** decigrams, and **(c)** centigrams.

9. Express 8 kiloliters in **(a)** liters, **(b)** deciliters, and **(c)** hectoliters.

10. Express 145 tonnes in **(a)** grams, **(b)** kilograms, and **(c)** hectograms.

Arithmetic Operations With Metric Measurements

Being denominate numbers, metric measurements are added, subtracted, multiplied, and divided in the same manner as U.S. measurements. However, as metric measurements are based on 10, the processes of "carrying" and "borrowing" are simplified because metric measurements can be shown in decimal notation. Each measurement in a given problem should be changed to equivalents in the desired unit of measure; that is, changed to centimeters, meters, or kilometers depending on what the problem requires.

Example A: Susan Stanton has pieces of lamp chain of the following lengths: 2 meters 25 centimeters, 3 meters 3 decimeters, 1 meter 75 centimeters, and 2.85 meters. In meters, what is the total length of the chains?

Solution:

2 meters 25 centimeters = 2.25 m
3 meters 3 decimeters = 3.3 m
1 meter 75 centimeters = 1.75 m

$$2.25 + 3.3 + 1.75 + 2.85 = 10.15 \text{ m}$$

Example B: At a track meet, Porter threw the javelin 78 meters 64 centimeters. If the winning throw was 87 meters 2 decimeters, by how many meters did Porter miss first place?

Solution: 78 meters 64 centimeters = 78.64 m
87 meters 2 decimeters = 87.2 m

$$87.2 - 78.64 = 8.56 \text{ m}$$

In the multiplication of metric measurements, there are two possibilities: multiplication by an abstract number (Example C) and multiplication of a measurement by a measurement (Example D).

Example C: If a coin weighs 5 grams, how many kilograms will 500 coins weigh?

Solution: 5 g $\times$ 500 = 2500 g = 2.5 kg

Example D: What is the area in square centimeters of a rectangle that is 24 centimeters long and 15 centimeters wide?

Solution: $A = lw = 24 \text{ cm} \times 15 \text{ cm} = 360 \text{ cm}^2$

In division, the problem may require that a metric measurement be divided by an abstract number (Example E) or by another measurement (Example F).

Example E: Don Robertson cut a rope that was 3 meters 65 centimeters long into 5 equal sections. Each section should be how many decimeters long?

Solution: 3 meters 65 centimeters = 3.65 m = 36.5 dm

$$36.5 \text{ dm} \div 5 = 7.3 \text{ dm}$$

Example F: If a nickel weighs 5 grams, a kilogram of nickels should contain how many nickels?

Solution: 1 kilogram = 1000 g

$$1000 \text{ g} \div 5 \text{ g} = 200 \text{ (nickels)}$$

● Exercise 5–8

1. An electrician used the following lengths of electric cable on a job: 2 lengths each 2.5 meters, 1 length 95 centimeters, 3 lengths each 2 dekameters, and 4 lengths each 1.75 meters. How many meters of cable were used?

Chapter 5.   Measurements

2. When a cafeteria opened on Monday, it had 4.5 liters of milk. During the week, the following quantities of milk were received: 45 liters, 60 liters, 50 liters, 65 liters, and 55 liters. When the cafeteria closed on Friday, there were 7 liters of milk left. How many liters of milk had the cafeteria used during this time?

3. A private airplane recently flew from New Orleans to New York in 2 hours at an average speed of 940 kilometers per hour. How many kilometers did the plane fly?

4. A case contains 40 cans of soup that weigh 539 grams each. In kilograms, what is the total weight of the cans of soup?

5. If a nickel weighs 5 grams, how many grams does $3.50 of nickels weigh?

6. The distance from an airport near Chicago to one near San Francisco is 2968 kilometers. If a plane flew from one airport to the other in 3 hours 30 minutes, what was the average speed in kilometers per hour (km/h)?

7. If an airplane climbed 1.2 kilometers in 50 seconds, how many meters per second did it climb?

8. The width of a square is 24 dam. What is its perimeter in meters?

9. If a baseball diamond has measurements of 27 meters 432 millimeters per side, what is the perimeter of the diamond to the nearest thousandth of a meter?

10. A pasture is to be enclosed with three strands of barbed wire. The area to be fenced is 137.16 meters long and 106.68 meters wide. How many meters of barbed wire are needed?

11. If the distance from Denver to New York is 2600 kilometers, how many hours and minutes will a plane flight require at an average speed of 1200 kilometers per hour?

12. Find the circumference in millimeters of a circle that has a diameter of 17 millimeters.

13. Jack True purchased one each of the following lengths of pipe at $1.80 per meter: 7 meters 5 decimeters, 4 meters, 6 meters 4 decimeters, 3 meters 75 centimeters, 2.35 meters, and 0.88 meter. (a) To the nearest meter, how many meters of pipe did he purchase? (b) How much did he pay for it?

14. Which is the better buy: (a) a 1.4 kg box of detergent that sells for $2.38 or (b) a 2.25 kg box of detergent that sells for $3.60? How much better per kilogram?

15. A store purchased 6 crates of berries at $25.36 a crate. Each crate contained twenty 0.5-liter boxes of berries. Before all the berries could be sold, 4 liters were discarded as spoiled. The remaining boxes were sold at $2.15 each. How much is the store's gross profit on the berries?

16. What is the area of a rectangle that is 27 meters long and 18 meters wide?

17. Find the area of a rectangle that is 69 centimeters long and 38 centimeters wide.

18. Find the area of a triangle that has a base of 27 centimeters and a height of 34 centimeters.

19. Find the area of a circle with a diameter of 64 centimeters.

20. The dimensions of a shipping crate are 6 meters by 4 meters by 3 meters. In cubic meters, what is the capacity of the crate?

21. Concrete is to be laid 12 centimeters thick in a driveway that is 12.6 meters long and 6.5 meters wide. How many cubic meters of concrete are needed?

22. The basement of a house is to be 16.6 meters long, 14.4 meters wide, and 1.5 meters deep. How much will be the excavating cost at $8.50 per cubic meter or fractional part thereof?

23. A rectangular swimming pool that is 10 meters wide and 20 meters long is 0.6 meter deep at one end and slopes evenly to a depth of 3 meters at the other end. To the nearest cubic meter, what is the volume of this pool?

24. A cylindrical container is 15 centimeters in diameter and 21 centimeters high. How many cubic centimeters of water will the container hold?

Conversion of U.S. and Metric Measurements

Changing from a metric unit of measure to a standard U.S. unit of measure requires that approximate equivalents be used. To facilitate the conversion, tables of approximate U.S. equivalents may be used. Notice that Table 5–4 is used in the solution to Example A. The table shows that 10 meters equal 32.8084 feet; 1 meter, therefore, must equal 3.28084 feet.

Example A: How many feet equal 7 meters? Round to the nearest hundredth.

Solution: 1 meter = 3.28084 feet (Table 5–4)
Therefore, 7 m = 3.28084 ft × 7 = 22.96588 ft = 22.97 feet

Tables of approximate metric equivalents may be used to change from U.S. units to metric units. (See Table 5–5.)

Example B: How many kilograms equal 5 pounds (U.S. avoirdupois)? Round to the nearest ten-thousandth.

Solution: 1 pound = 453.5924 grams = 0.4535924 kilogram (Table 5–5)
Therefore, 5 lb = 0.4535924 kg × 5 = 2.267962 kg = 2.2680 kilograms

Linear

1 millimeter (mm) = 0.001 meter (m) = 0.0394 inch

10 millimeters (mm) = 1 centimeter (cm) = 0.01 meter = 0.3937 inch

10 centimeters (cm) = 1 decimeter (dm) = 0.1 meter = 3.9370 inches

10 decimeters (dm) = 1 meter (m) = 39.3701 inches

10 meters (m) = 1 dekameter (dam) = 10 meters = 32.8084 feet

10 dekameters (dam) = 1 hectometer (hm) = 100 meters = 328.0840 feet

10 hectometers (hm) = 1 kilometer (km) = 1000 meters = 0.6214 mile

Area

100 square millimeters (mm^2) = 1 square centimeter (cm^2) = 0.0001 m^2 = 0.1550 sq in

100 square centimeters (cm^2) = 1 square decimeter (dm^2) = 0.01 m^2 = 0.1076 sq ft

100 square decimeters (dm^2) = 1 centare* (ca) = 1 m^2 = 10.7639 sq ft

100 square meters (m^2) = 1 are* (a) = 100 m^2 = 119.5990 sq yd

100 ares (a) = 1 hectare* (ha) = 10 000 m^2 = 2.4711 acres

100 hectares (ha) = 1 square kilometer (km^2) = 1 000 000 m^2 = 0.3861 sq mi

*Used in measuring land

Capacity

	Cubic	Dry	Liquid
1 milliliter (mL) =	0.0610 cu in		=0.2705 fluidram
10 milliliters (mL) = 1 centiliter (cL) =	0.6102 cu in		=0.3381 fl oz
10 centiliters (cL) = 1 deciliter (dL) =	6.1025 cu in =	0.1816 pint	= 0.2113 pint
10 deciliters (dL) = 1 liter (L) =	61.0255 cu in =	0.9081 quart	= 1.0567 quarts
10 liters (L) = 1 dekaliter (daL) =	0.3532 cu ft =	1.1351 pecks	= 2.6417 gallons
10 dekaliters (daL) = 1 hectoliter (hL) =	3.5315 cu ft =	2.8378 bushels	
10 hectoliters (hL) = 1 kiloliter (kL) =	1.3079 cu yd		

Weight

1 milligram (mg) = 0.001 gram (g) = 0.0154 grain

10 milligrams (mg) = 1 centigram (cg) = 0.01 gram = 0.1543 grain

10 centigrams (cg) = 1 decigram (dg) = 0.1 gram = 1.5432 grains

10 decigrams (dg) = 1 gram (g) = 0.0353 ounce

10 grams (g) = 1 dekagram (dag) = 10 grams = 0.3527 ounce

10 dekagrams (dag) = 1 hectogram (hg) = 100 grams = 3.5274 ounces

10 hectograms (hg) = 1 kilogram (kg) = 1000 grams = 2.2046 pounds

1000 kilograms (kg) = 1 metric tonne (t) = 1 000 000 grams = 1.1023 tons

Table 5-4 Metric Units of Measure and Their Approximate U.S. Equivalents

Linear

1 inch (in) = 2.540 centimeters (cm)
1 foot (ft) = 0.3048 meter (m)
1 yard (yd) = 0.9144 meter
1 rod (rd) = 5.0292 meters
1 mile (mi) = 1.6093 kilometers (km)

Square or Surface

1 square inch (sq in or in^2) = 6.4516 square centimeters (cm^2)
1 square foot (sq ft or ft^2) = 0.0929 square meters (m^2)
1 square yard (sq yd or yd^2) = 0.8361 square meters
1 square rod (sq rd or rd^2) = 25.2928 square meters
1 acre (A) = 0.4047 hectare (ha) = 4046.8564 square meters
1 square mile (sq mi or mi^2) = 2.5900 square kilometers (km^2)

Cubic

1 cubic inch (cu in or in^3) = 16.3871 cubic centimeters (cm^3)
1 cubic foot (cu ft or ft^3) = 0.0283 cubic meter (m^3) = 28.316 liters (L)
1 cubic yard (cu yd or yd^3) = 0.7646 cubic meter

Dry

1 pint (pt) = 33.6003 cubic inches (cu in) = 0.5506 liter (L)
1 quart (qt) = 67.2006 cubic inches = 1.1012 liters
1 peck (pk) = 537.605 cubic inches = 8.8097 liters
1 bushel (bu) = 2150.42 cubic inches = 35.2391 liters

Liquid

1 fluidram (fl dr) = 0.2256 cubic inches (cu in) = 3.6967 milliliters (mL)
1 fluidounce (fl oz) = 1.8047 cubic inches = 29.5735 milliliters
1 gill (gi) = 7.2188 cubic inches = 118.2908 milliliters
1 pint (pt) = 28.8750 cubic inches = 0.4732 liter (L)
1 quart (qt) = 57.7500 cubic inches = 0.9464 liter
1 gallon (gal) = 231 cubic inches = 3.7854 liters

Weight (Avoirdupois)

1 grain (gr) = 0.0648 gram (g)
1 dram (dr) = 1.7718 grams
1 ounce (oz) = 28.3495 grams
1 pound (lb) = 453.5924 grams
1 short ton (T) = 0.9072 metric ton (MT or t)
1 long ton (lt) = 1.01605 metric tons

Table 5–5 U.S. Units of Measure and Their Approximate Metric Equivalents

Chapter 5.   Measurements

Land Area. The square centimeter takes the place of the square inch, and the square meter takes the place of the square foot and square yard. For larger area measurements of land, a non-SI unit of measure, the **hectare** (pronounced *hect air*) is used in the metric system. A hectare (ha), which replaces the acre, is defined as an area 100 meters long and 100 meters wide; that is, 10 000 square meters.

Temperature Scales. The **kelvin** (K) is the SI base unit for temperature. On the Kelvin scale, the point at which an object would have absolutely no heat— that is, no molecular action—is labeled **absolute zero.** The Kelvin temperature at which water freezes is 273.15, and the boiling point of water is 373.15. Notice there is a difference of 100 K between the freezing and boiling points of water. The **Celsius** (C) scale, formerly called **centigrade,** is based on this range of 100 degrees, with the freezing point equaling zero and the boiling point equaling 100. Celsius is the name of the Swedish astronomer who devised this scale, and Fahrenheit is the name of the German physicist who devised the scale that bears his name. Degrees Celsius (°C) and degrees Fahrenheit (°F) are commonly used to measure temperature. The Kelvin scale is used principally by scientists to make precise measurements.

As Figure 5–10 illustrates, the spread from 0 to the freezing point of water on the Fahrenheit scale is 32 degrees; from the freezing point (32°F) to the boiling point (212°F), the difference is 180°. The ratio of the degrees between freezing and boiling on the Fahrenheit scale to the Celsius scale is 180° to 100°, which is a ratio of 9 to 5. Therefore, a Celsius reading may be converted to the Fahrenheit scale by multiplying the Celsius degrees by $\frac{9}{5}$ and adding 32°.

$$°F = \tfrac{9}{5}°C + 32°$$

Example A:

This morning the radio announcer said the outside temperature was 15° Celsius. What was the equivalent Fahrenheit temperature at that time?

Solution:

$°F = \tfrac{9}{5}°C + 32°$
$°F = \tfrac{9}{5}(15°) + 32°$
$°F = 27° + 32°$
$°F = 59°$

To convert from Fahrenheit degrees to Celsius, the ratio, of course, is reversed and becomes 100 to 180, which is 5:9. A Fahrenheit reading, therefore, may be converted to Celsius by subtracting 32° from the Fahrenheit reading and multiplying the result by $\frac{5}{9}$.

$$°C = \tfrac{5}{9}(°F - 32°)$$

Example B:

The outside temperature is expected to reach 86° Fahrenheit this afternoon. What temperature is expected on the Celsius scale?

Solution:

$°C = \tfrac{5}{9}(°F - 32°)$
$°C = \tfrac{5}{9}(86° - 32°)$
$°C = \tfrac{5}{9} \times 54°$
$°C = 30°$

Figures 5–11, 5–12, and 5–13 are presented to help you to better understand Celsius temperature readings. In Figure 5–13 the Celsius temperatures have been rounded to the nearest ten degrees.

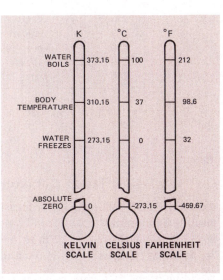

Figure 5-10 Temperature Scales

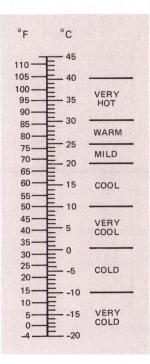

Figure 5-11 Air Temperatures

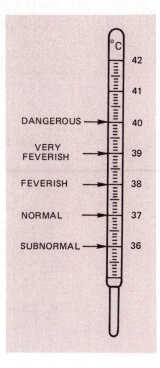

Figure 5-12 Body Temperatures

°C		°F
290	Broil	550
260	Very Hot	500
220	Hot	425
180	Moderate	350
150	Very Warm	300
120	Warm	250
100	Water Boils	212

Figure 5–13 Cooking Temperatures

● Exercise 5–9

A. Use Table 5–4 and Table 5–5 as needed to solve these problems.

1. For each of the following linear measurements, find the equivalent to the nearest hundredth.
   a. 12 ft to meters
   b. 66 yards to meters
   c. 7 m to feet
   d. 84.6 cm to inches
   e. 90 m to yards
   f. 25 in to centimeters

2. For each of the following weight measurements, find the equivalent to the nearest hundredth.
   a. 68 g to ounces
   b. 18 oz to grams
   c. 42 lb to kilograms
   d. 36 kg to pounds
   e. 14 U.S. tons to tonnes
   f. 16 tonnes to U.S. tons

3. For each of the following capacity measurements, find the equivalent to the nearest hundredth.
   a. 9 L to liquid quarts
   b. 35 lq pt to liters
   c. 27 lq qt to liters
   d. 6.6 L to gallons
   e. 18 fl oz to milliliters
   f. 28 cL to fluid ounces

4. For each of the following area measurements, find the equivalent to the nearest hundredth.
   a. 90 sq yd to square meters
   b. 7.25 sq in to square centimeters
   c. 160 A to hectares
   d. 48 ha to acres
   e. 60 m² to square feet
   f. 21.5 sq ft to square meters

5. For each of the following temperature measurements, find the equivalent to the nearest hundredth.
   a. 35°C to °F
   b. 165°C to °F
   c. 75°F to °C
   d. 350°F to °C
   e. 92°F to °C
   f. 90°C to °F

B. Change each of the following to the metric or U.S. equivalent requested. Where applicable, round the final answer to the nearest ten-thousandth.

1. How many miles equal 150 kilometers?

2. How many kilometers equal 80 miles?

3. How many inches equal 12 centimeters?

4. How many centimeters equal 16 inches?

5. How many ounces equal 0.6 kilogram?

6. How many liters equal 5 liquid quarts?

7. How many feet equal 6 meters?

8. How many gallons equal 35 kiloliters?

9. How many kilograms equal 24 pounds?

10. How many hectares equal 480 acres?

C. Solve these problems.

1. A small European car has a maximum speed of 130 kilometers per hour. What is the equivalent speed expressed to the nearest mile per hour?

2. The Greenfield Canning Company, which packs peas in cans that contain 14 ounces (avoir.), plans to sell its foods internationally. What equivalent metric weight, to the nearest gram, should be printed on the label of the peas?

3. The Evansville Company markets its brand of salad oil to distributors throughout the world. Each bottle in which the oil is packed contains $1\frac{1}{2}$ quarts. What metric capacity, expressed to the nearest tenth of a liter, should be placed on the label of each bottle?

4. The Empire State building in New York is 1,248 feet high. The Eiffel tower in Paris is 300 meters high. To the nearest hundredth, the Empire State building is how many meters taller or shorter than the Eiffel tower?

5. Fairmont Company, Inc., plans to build a new plant in France. If the company needs a storage tank that has a capacity of 50,000 U.S. gallons, what size tank, expressed in kiloliters, should be ordered from a supplier in Paris?

6. The Glendale Drug Company sells a new medicine at 35¢ for each capsule containing 8 milligrams of the drug. At this price, what is the value of one gram of the drug?

7. The distance between two cities is 1,042 miles. Convert this distance to the nearest kilometer.

8. Instead of 68°F, what would be the setting on a degree Celsius thermostat that controls the temperature in a home?

9. A grower had 8,000 bags of coffee beans stored in a barn during a coffee shortage. If each bag weighed 60.5 kilograms, how many tons of coffee beans did the grower have stored?

10. The dimensions of a bulletin board are 1.25 meter by 4 meters. To the nearest hundredth of a square foot, what is the area of the board?

11. A recipe suggests that a certain food be fried at a temperature of 365 °F. Under the metric system the instructions should suggest how many degrees Celsius?

12. The outside temperature reading was 25 °C. What was the equivalent reading on the Fahrenheit scale?

REVIEW PROBLEMS

Solve these problems. If you have difficulty solving any problem restudy the appropriate section in this chapter. The problems under a specific number are related to those contained in the exercise with the same last number.

1. Change each of the following as indicated.
- **a.** 224 ounces to pounds
- **b.** 9 hours to minutes
- **c.** 114 feet to yards
- **d.** 569 quarts to gallons and quarts
- **e.** 86 gross to dozens
- **f.** 979 fluid ounces to quarts and pints

2. a. Add 7 years 5 months 16 days, 12 years 8 months 26 days, and 4 years 3 months 9 days.
- **b.** Which is the longest linear measurement: 18.25 feet, $6\frac{1}{2}$ yards, or 257 inches?
- **c.** Multiply 12 pounds 12 ounces by 23. Show the answer in pounds and ounces.
- **d.** A wall that is to be papered has no doors or windows and is 8 feet high and 19 feet 8 inches long. How many 8-foot long pieces of wallpaper that are $20\frac{1}{2}$ inches wide are needed?

3. a. While remodeling a home, the owner decided to add molding around the walls just below the ceiling in the bedroom. How many feet of molding are needed if the room measures 19 feet 10 inches long and 14 feet 6 inches wide?
- **b.** A field is 600 yards long and 200 yards wide. How much would it cost to fence this field at $4.50 per linear foot?
- **c.** A triangle has measurements of 17 feet, 48 feet, and 40 feet 10 inches. In feet, what is the perimeter of the triangle?
- **d.** Find the circumference of a pipe that has a diameter of $4\frac{1}{2}$ inches.

4. a. Find the cost of paving a walk that is $3\frac{1}{2}$ feet wide and 60 feet long at $1.60 a square foot.
- **b.** If the dimensions of a kitchen floor are 14 feet by 16 feet, what would be the cost of new floor covering at $18.95 a square yard or fractional part thereof?
- **c.** Find the area of a triangle with a base of 12 inches and a height of 6 inches.
- **d.** From a certain fire lookout tower, a ranger can see the surrounding forest for a distance of 40 miles in all directions. To the nearest hundredth, how many square miles can be observed from the tower?

5. a. How many cubic yards of earth must be removed for the basement of a building if the excavation is to be 80 feet long, 45 feet wide, and 9 feet deep?

b. A farmer plans to build a storage bin 15 feet long and 12 feet wide. If 1,200 cubic feet of storage capacity is needed, the bin must be how many feet high?

c. Find the volume of a cylinder with a diameter of 16 feet and a height of 24 feet.

6. For each of the following, show **(1)** the numerical value of the prefix and **(2)** the symbol of the measurement named.
   a. kilogram   **c.** hectoliter   **e.** centigram
   b. millimeter   **d.** deciliter   **f.** dekameter

7. Change each of the following as indicated.
   a. 47 350 liters to milliliters   **d.** 96 485 dekaliters to kiloliters
   b. 77 451 hectoliters to kiloliters   **e.** 22 121 decigrams to milligrams
   c. 61 715 milligrams to grams   **f.** 78 004 centimeters to meters

8. a. Jessica Willis plans to fence part of her lawn. Each side of the area to be fenced is 12 meters long. One end is 9.6 meters and the other is 7.75 meters. If she buys a 50-meter roll of fencing, how many extra meters will she have, assuming no waste?

b. What is the area of a square that has a side of 12 cm?

c. The basement of a building is to be 18 meters long, 12 meters wide, and 3 meters deep. How many cubic meters of earth must be excavated?

d. The pattern for a certain size gown requires 4.25 meters of fabric that is 1 meter wide. **(1)** How many such gowns can be made from 26 meters of this fabric? **(2)** How many meters of the fabric would be left?

9. a. To the nearest inch, how many inches are there in 688.34 centimeters?

b. To the nearest gallon, how many gallons are in 60 liters?

c. To the nearest hundredth, how many liters are there in 6 gallons 3 quarts?

d. To the nearest foot, 100 meters is how much longer than 100 yards?

e. A new thermostat shows temperature settings in degrees Celsius only. If a temperature of 86°F is desired, what should be the setting on this thermostat?

f. What should be the Fahrenheit cooking temperature if a recipe suggests a cooking temperature of 210° Celsius?

CHALLENGE PROBLEM

     Mary Whitehurst took a plane to England. While there, she bought a new Jaguar automobile. The money exchange rate was $1.375 for one English pound. On her first trip, before having the car shipped to the United States, she drove it 452 kilometers, averaging 50 miles per hour. On that trip, the car averaged 17.9 miles per gallon, and she paid 44 pence (0.44 pound) per liter of gasoline.

a. To the nearest tenth, how many hours did she drive on her first trip?

b. To the nearest tenth, how many liters of gasoline did the trip require?

c. How much in dollars and cents did she spend for that gasoline?

d. When she arrived in England the temperature was 28 °C. To the nearest tenth, this is how many degrees Fahrenheit?

Chapter 6

Selected Notation Systems

Objectives

After mastering the material in Chapter 6, you will be able to:

- Understand factors, powers, exponents, scientific notation, expanded notation, and the binary system.
- Show products and quotients of powers of 10 as a single power of 10.
- Perform the operations of multiplication and division with powers of 10.
- Change numbers from decimal form to scientific notation and vice versa.
- Use scientific notation to solve problems containing numbers that are too large or too small for multiplying and dividing in an eight-digit calculator.
- Change a binary numeral to a decimal numeral and vice versa.
- Write binary-coded numerals.
- Add, subtract, multiply, and divide with binary numerals.

A thorough understanding of the mathematical topics presented in this chapter will enhance mathematical competence. The learning of one concept often serves as a sound basis for the better comprehension of another concept. For example, an understanding of factors, powers, exponents, scientific notation, and expanded notation will facilitate comprehension of the binary number system or, indeed, of any number system. The more known about number relationships and systems and the more clearly these concepts are organized, the greater will be the ability to solve mathematical problems.

EXPONENTIAL NOTATION

A **factor** is any of two or more numbers which when multiplied together form a product. When a number such as 1,000 is expressed as (10)(10)(10), it is said to be in **factor notation.**

A **power** of a number is the product obtained when a given number is multiplied by itself. Expressions such as 5×5, $3 \times 3 \times 3 \times 3$, and $2 \times 2 \times 2$ may be written as 5^2, 3^4, and 2^3. The expression 5^2 is read as "five squared" or "five to the second power." The expression 3^4 is read as "three to the fourth power," and 2^3 is "two to the third power" or "two cubed." The superior digit above the factor is called an **exponent;** it tells the degree of the power, that is, the number of times the factor is multiplied by itself. An expression such as 3^4 is said to be in **exponential notation.**

The number that is the factor in an exponential expression is the **base.** Thus, in 5^2 the base is 5 and the exponent is 2. The base of a power can be any counting or natural number, even zero if the exponent is not zero. Thus, the third power of 4 is $4^3 = 4 \times 4 \times 4 = 64$. The expression 4^3 is an exponential form for 64.

When the exponent is one, the power is defined to be the base.

$$2^1 = 2$$
$$5^1 = 5$$
$$10^1 = 10$$

For this reason, when the exponent is 1, it is frequently omitted. When the exponent is zero and the base is not zero, the power is defined to be one.

$$2^0 = 1$$
$$5^0 = 1$$
$$10^0 = 1$$

The numbers 10^1, 10^2, 10^3, 10^4, etc., are the **powers of ten.** As the Hindu-Arabic system is a decimal system, these powers of ten play a very important role. Consider these numbers:

$$10^0 = 1$$
$$10^1 = 10$$
$$10^2 = 10 \times 10 = 100$$
$$10^3 = 10 \times 10 \times 10 = 1,000$$
$$10^4 = 10 \times 10 \times 10 \times 10 = 10,000$$
$$10^5 = 10 \times 10 \times 10 \times 10 \times 10 = 100,000$$

The notation 10^4 is another means of writing 10,000; this number consists of "1" followed by four zeros. In a like manner, 10^5 may be written as a number that consists of "1" followed by five zeros. In base ten, if an exponent n is any counting number, then the number 10^n may be written as a numeral consisting of "1" followed by n zeros.

Constant multiplication may be utilized to compute powers with a calculator.

Example: Find the product of (a) 7^2 and (b) 8^3.

Solution: With constant ☐ K

(a) 7 ☐× ☐= $\to$ 49   (b) 8 ☐× ☐= ☐= $\to$ 512

Without constant:

(a) 7 ☐× 7 ☐= $\to$ 49   (b) 8 ☐× 8 ☐× 8 ☐= $\to$ 512

Notice that with constant multiplication for (a) above, the exponent is 2 and the ☐= key is pressed 1 time (2 − 1); likewise, in (b) the exponent is 3 and the ☐= key is pressed 2 times (3 − 1). Thus, when the exponent is any number n, the ☐= key is pressed $n − 1$ times to find the product of the power through constant multiplication on a calculator.

● Exercise 6–1

A. Use exponents to express each of the following.

1. $3 \times 3 \times 3 \times 3$
2. 12×12
3. $5 \times 5 \times 5$
4. $10 \times 10 \times 10 \times 10 \times 10$
5. $(2)(2)(2)(2)(2)(2)(2)$

6. $(100)(100)(100)(100)$
7. $(-1,000)(-1,000)(-1,000)$
8. $-n \times -n \times -n \times -n \times -n$
9. $(-4)(-4)(-4)(-4)(-4)(-4)$
10. $(-6)(-6)(-6)(-6)(-6)(-6)(-6)(-6)(-6)$

B. Use factor notation to express each of the following.

1. 2^8 3. 11^6 5. 4^5 7. N^7 9. 10^8

2. 5^4 4. 10^3 6. 50^9 8. a^2 10. 10^{13}

C. Show the product of each of the following.

1. 3^5 3. 10^4 5. 25^1 7. 27^0 9. 167^2

2. 2^7 4. 10^8 6. 12^3 8. 10^{11} 10. 432^0

Operations With Powers

The size of numbers that can be entered in a calculator is limited by the capacity of the calculator being used. For example, the largest positive number that can be entered in an eight-digit calculator is 99,999,999; and the smallest positive number is .00000001 or 0.0000001 if the calculator shows the zero to the left of the decimal point. Larger and smaller numbers than these cannot be entered in an eight-digit calculator. However, larger and smaller numbers can be changed to scientific notation and easily multiplied and divided. Aiding in such operations is the primary objective of this section. Multiplication and division with scientific numbers are emphasized in the next section. Now, consider negative bases, negative exponents, and powers of 10.

Negative Bases. Some calculators automatically show the correct sign when a negative base is raised by a positive exponent. If your calculator will not accept negative bases, simply remember the rule for multiplying negative numbers. That is, an odd number of negative factors gives a negative product; an even number of negative factors, a positive product. Therefore, when the base is negative, an odd numbered exponent gives a negative product; an even exponent, a positive product.

Example: Find the product of **(a)** -6^3 and **(b)** -7^4.

Solution:

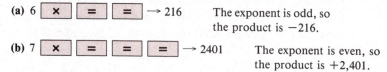

(a) 6 $\boxed{\times}$ $\boxed{=}$ $\boxed{=}$ → 216   The exponent is odd, so
the product is −216.

(b) 7 $\boxed{\times}$ $\boxed{=}$ $\boxed{=}$ $\boxed{=}$ → 2401   The exponent is even, so
the product is +2,401.

Negative Exponents. When the base is any number except zero and the exponent is negative, the exponent may be shown as a positive exponent in the reciprocal of the exponential statement. If b represents the base and n the exponent, then:

$$b^{-n} = \frac{1}{b^n} \qquad \text{and} \qquad \frac{1}{b^{-n}} = b^n.$$

Therefore, raising a number by a negative exponent is interpreted to mean division. Any number divided by itself equals 1; that is, $b \div b = 1$. To use constant division in a calculator to raise a base by a negative exponent, enter the base, press the $\boxed{\div}$ key, and press the $\boxed{=}$ key *one time more* $(n + 1)$ than the exponent (n).

Example A: Raise the base by the negative exponent shown: 8^{-3}.

Solution: $8^{-3} = \frac{1}{8^3} = 1 \div 8^3$

Without constant division:

$8^{-3} = 1$ $\boxed{\div}$ 8 $\boxed{\div}$ 8 $\boxed{\div}$ 8 $\boxed{=}$ → 0.0019531

With constant division:

$8^{-3} = 1$ $\boxed{\div}$ 8 $\boxed{=}$ $\boxed{=}$ $\boxed{=}$ → 0.0019531

Or: $8^{-3} = 8$ $\boxed{\div}$ $\boxed{=}$ $\boxed{=}$ $\boxed{=}$ $\boxed{=}$ → 0.0019531

If the negative exponent is shown in a denominator, it becomes positive when the exponential expression is inverted to obtain its reciprocal. As you recall, to divide by a common fraction, invert the divisor and multiply.

Example B:	Raise this expression by the exponent shown: $\dfrac{1}{9^{-5}}$
Solution:	$\dfrac{1}{9^{-5}} = 9^5 = 9$ ☐× ☐= ☐= ☐= ☐= $\rightarrow$ 59049

Powers of 10. When 10,000 is written as 10^4, it is said to be expressed as a power of 10. If the exponents are integers, the product of powers of 10 may be obtained by adding the exponents of the factors.

Example A: Find the product of $10^3 \times 10^2$.

Solution: $10^3 \times 10^2 = 10^{3+2} = 10^5$

Explanation: $10^3 \times 10^2 = (10)(10)(10) \times (10)(10) = 10^5$

The principle, of course, remains unchanged when negative exponents are involved in the multiplication.

Example B: Find the product of $10^5 \times 10^{-2}$.

Solution: $10^5 \times 10^{-2} = 10^{5-2} = 10^3$

Explanation: $10^5 \times 10^{-2} = (10)(10)(10)(10)(10) \times \dfrac{1}{10^2}$

$$= \dfrac{(10)(10)(10)(10)(10)}{10^2}$$

$$= \dfrac{(10)(10)(10)(10)(10)}{(10)(10)} = 10^3$$

A power of 10 expressed as a denominator may be expressed as a product by changing the sign of the exponent and inverting the denominator of which the exponent is a part.

Example C: Rewrite each of the following as a single power of 10:

(a) $\dfrac{10^3 \times 10^2}{10^4 \times 10^{-5}}$ (b) $\dfrac{10^5 \times 10^4 \times 10^{-3}}{10^2 \times 10^{-3} \times 10^4}$

Solution: (a) $\dfrac{10^3 \times 10^2}{10^4 \times 10^{-5}} = 10^3 \times 10^2 \times 10^{-4} \times 10^5 = 10^6$

(b) $\dfrac{10^5 \times 10^4 \times 10^{-3}}{10^2 \times 10^{-3} \times 10^4} = 10^5 \times 10^4 \times 10^{-3} \times 10^{-2} \times 10^3 \times 10^{-4} = 10^3$

● Exercise 6-2

A. Rewrite each of the following as an equivalent expression with a positive exponent.

1. 7^{-1} 3. 9^{-3} 5. 10^{-2} 7. 6^{-4} 9. $\dfrac{1}{8^{-6}}$ 11. $\dfrac{1}{10^{-3}}$

2. 8^{-2} 4. 10^{-1} 6. 10^{-3} 8. 7^{-5} 10. $\dfrac{1}{10^{-2}}$ 12. $\dfrac{1}{9^{-4}}$

Chapter 6. Selected Notation Systems

B. Calculate each power.

1. 7^2	**8.** 0.5^7	**15.** 7^{-1}
2. 8^3	**9.** -7^6	**16.** 6^{-1}
3. 9^4	**10.** -8^5	**17.** 5.3^{-4}
4. 6^5	**11.** -0.25^3	**18.** 4.6^{-5}
5. 5^6	**12.** -2.5^4	**19.** 0.35^2
6. 4^7	**13.** 9^{-2}	**20.** -42^3
7. 3.6^4	**14.** 8^{-3}	**21.** 3.4^{-4}

C. Show each of the following as a power of 10 with a single positive or negative exponent or as 1.

1. $10^4 \times 10^2$

2. $10^5 \times 10^6$

3. $10^2 \times 10^3 \times 10^4$

4. $10^6 \times 10^2 \times 10^7$

5. $10^6 \times 10^{-4} \times 10^3$

6. $10^{-3} \times 10^{-4} \times 10^5$

7. $10^2 \times 10^{-5} \times 10^1$

8. $10^{-2} \times 10^4 \times 10^{-1}$

9. $\dfrac{10^5 \times 10^{-3}}{10^4 \times 10^{-2}}$

10. $\dfrac{10^{-4} \times 10^3}{10^3 \times 10^{-2}}$

11. $\dfrac{10^{-3} \times 10^2 \times 10^{-1}}{10^2 \times 10^{-3}}$

12. $\dfrac{10^{-2} \times 10^{-4} \times 10^{-3}}{10^{-2} \times 10^{-7}}$

SCIENTIFIC NOTATION

Most pocket calculators will accept no more than eight digits in length. Entering large numbers in such calculators will sometimes cause them to cut off digits in the displayed answer or to indicate an overflow.

Cut Off

Enter these factors in your calculator: 9.8765 $\boxed{\times}$ 4.3201 $\boxed{=}$. The product shown in the calculator display is probably 42.667467, which shows only six places to the right of the decimal point. The exact answer, 42.66746765 shows eight places to the right of the decimal point. The calculator **cut off** the least significant digits—the digits 6 and 5 that are farthest to the right of the decimal point. The calculator, therefore, shows the eight most important digits.

Example: Find **(a)** the exact product and **(b)** the eight-digit calculator product of 9.8765×4.3201.

Solution:

(a)
```
        9.8 7 6 5
      × 4.3 2 0 1
        9 8 7 6 5
    1 9 7 5 3 0 0
    2 9 6 2 9 5
    3 9 5 0 6 0
    4 2.6 6 7 4 6 7 6 5
```

— Cut off —

(b) 9.8765 ⎡×⎤ 4.3201 ⎡=⎤ → 42.667467

If your calculator shows 42.667468, instead of 42.667467, it rounds the last digit in a decimal. Most calculators do not round.

Overflow

Enter this multiplication in your calculator: 56,789 ⎡×⎤ 4,321 ⎡=⎤ . The display shown is probably 2.4538526E or E2.4538526 or 2.4.5.3.8.5.2.6*. An E in the display indicates exponential notation. When the product of the numbers being multiplied is too large to fit the display, an **overflow** is indicated by one of the above methods, among others, or by a flashing display. An overflow usually locks the calculator so that no further operations can be performed until the ⎡CE⎤ or ⎡C⎤ key is pressed.

How accurate is the product E2.4538526? Notice in the example below that the product of the rounded numbers is 240,000,000, which has nine digits. If the decimal point in E2.4538526 is moved *eight* places to the right, the calculator answer will also have nine digits. When overflow is shown on an eight-digit calculator, the decimal point is understood to fall **eight** places to the right of the position shown in the display. For a ten-digit calculator, the decimal point falls ten places to the right. In an eight-digit calculator, then, E2.4538526 in display means 2.4538526×10^8. The product of 245,385,260 is as accurate as most eight-digit calculators can display.

Example: Find **(a)** the estimated product and **(b)** the calculator product of $56,789 \times 4,321$.

Solution:

(a)

56,789	rounds to	60,000
× 4,321	rounds to	× 4,000
		240,000,000 estimate

(b) 56,789 ⎡×⎤ 4,321 ⎡=⎤ → E2.4538526

$E2.4538526 = 2.4538526 \times 10^8 = 245,385,260$

Numbers in Scientific Notation

Recall that positive exponents indicate multiplication and negative exponents indicate division. With a power of 10, a positive exponent may be interpreted as an instruction to multiply by moving the decimal point the appropriate number of places to the right; a negative exponent, to divide by moving the decimal point to the left. In the following example, observe that the positive exponent in 10^3 caused the decimal point to shift *three* places to the *right;* and the negative exponent in 10^{-3} caused the decimal point to shift *three* places to the *left*.

Example A: Show the decimal form of **(a)** 2.34×10^3 and **(b)** 5.67×10^{-3}.

Solution: **(a)** $2.34 \times 10^3 = 2.34 \times 1,000 = 2,340$

(b) $5.67 \times 10^{-3} = 5.67 \times \dfrac{1}{10^3}$

$$= 5.67 \times \dfrac{1}{1,000}$$

$$= 5.67 \div 1,000$$
$$= 0.00567$$

The shifting of the decimal point may be accomplished mentally in accordance with this rule:

To multiply a number by 10^n,
(a) move the decimal point n places to the right if n is positive;
(b) move the decimal point n places to the left if n is negative.

Example B: Show the decimal form of **(a)** 1.23×10^4 and **(b)** 4.56×10^{-4}.

Solution: **(a)** $1.23 \times 10^4 = 1.2300_\wedge = 12,300$
(b) $4.56 \times 10^{-4} = {}_\wedge 0004.56 = 0.000456$

Any given number may be written in many different ways, even in different factored forms using powers of 10. Notice that 9,876 and 0.5432 may be written with many different powers of 10:

$$
\begin{array}{ll}
9,876 = 987.6 \times 10^1 & \qquad 0.5432 = 5.432 \times 10^{-1} \\
 = 98.76 \times 10^2 & \qquad = 54.32 \times 10^{-2} \\
 = 9.876 \times 10^3 & \qquad = 543.2 \times 10^{-3} \\
 = 0.9876 \times 10^4 & \qquad = 5,432 \times 10^{-4} \\
 = 0.09876 \times 10^5 & \qquad = 54,320 \times 10^{-5}
\end{array}
$$

Numbers such as 9.876×10^3 and 5.432×10^{-1} are in **scientific notation.** Such numbers are written with a base (*b*) times a power of 10 (i.e., $b \times 10^n$) in which the base is at least 1 but less than 10 and the exponent (*n*) is a positive or negative whole number.

Part 1.   Mathematics Applications in Preparing a Basic Foundation

Example C:	Write each number in scientific notation: **(a)** 1,234.5 and **(b)** 0.006789.

Solution:	

(a) $1{,}234.5 = 1.2345 \times 10^3$ Exponent 3 shows that decimal point would be moved 3 places to right to get decimal form.

(b) $0.006789 = 6.789 \times 10^{-3}$ Exponent -3 shows that decimal point would be moved 3 places to left to get decimal form.

Computing in Scientific Notation

Numbers that are too large or too small to enter in a calculator may be easily multiplied and divided through the use of scientific notation. The procedure is to change the numbers to scientific notation, multiply and divide, and then convert the answer to decimal form. Study the following example.

Example: Use scientific notation to compute each problem. Show each answer in decimal form.

(a) $123{,}000{,}000 \times 4{,}560{,}000{,}000$

(b) $1{,}234{,}000{,}000 \times 0.000000056$

(c) $\dfrac{7{,}800{,}000{,}000 \times 0.000009}{0.75}$

Solution:

$$
\begin{aligned}
\textbf{(a)}\ 123{,}000{,}000 \times 4{,}560{,}000{,}000 &= 1.23 \times 10^8 \times 4.56 \times 10^9 \\
&= 1.23 \times 4.56 \times 10^{17} \\
&= 5.6088 \times 10^{17} \\
&= 560{,}880{,}000{,}000{,}000{,}000
\end{aligned}
$$

$$
\begin{aligned}
\textbf{(b)}\ 1{,}234{,}000{,}000 \times 0.000000056 &= 1.234 \times 10^9 \times 5.6 \times 10^{-8} \\
&= 1.234 \times 5.6 \times 10^1 \\
&= 6.9104 \times 10^1 \\
&= 69.104
\end{aligned}
$$

$$
\begin{aligned}
\textbf{(c)}\ \frac{7{,}800{,}000{,}000 \times 0.000009}{0.75} &= \frac{7.8 \times 10^9 \times 9 \times 10^{-6}}{7.5 \times 10^{-1}} \\
&= \frac{7.8 \times 9 \times 10^3 \times 10^1}{7.5} \\
&= 9.36 \times 10^4 \\
&= 93{,}600
\end{aligned}
$$

● Exercise 6–3

A. Use an eight-digit calculator to compute each problem. Show each answer in decimal form.

1. 86.7142×12.803

2. 71.0147×15.2434

3. 32.5185×75.3494

4. 59.584×73.6276

5. $69{,}640 \times 5{,}752$

6. $32{,}219 \times 9{,}123$

7. $47{,}647 \times 26{,}362$

8. $61{,}219 \times 38{,}263$

9. $173{,}618 \times 81{,}014$

10. $687{,}250 \times 498{,}203$

11. 95.4761×98.503

12. $954{,}761 \times 98{,}503$

13. $\dfrac{462{,}000}{0.0084}$

14. $\dfrac{8{,}720{,}000}{0.00075}$

15. $\dfrac{5{,}139{,}000}{0.000625}$

16. $\dfrac{97{,}450}{0.00008}$

B. Find the product of each without using a calculator. Show the answers in decimal form.

1. 78.12×10^2

2. 15.62×10^2

3. 50.31×10^{-2}

4. 25.92×10^{-2}

5. 1.296×10^4

6. 4.321×10^4

7. 0.216×10^{-3}

8. 0.181×10^3

9. 442×10^5

10. 162×10^{-5}

11. 0.0124×10^{-4}

12. 0.982×10^6

13. 7.13101×10^3

14. 6.13218×10^4

C. Write each number in scientific notation.

1. 713.1

2. 161.3

3. 21.86

4. 54.18

5. 3,102.45

6. 5,264.83

7. 0.3714

8. 0.40715

9. 0.00434

10. 0.00025

11. 0.05

12. 0.009

13. 788

14. 3,768

15. 8.17

16. 4.678

17. 0.00058

18. 75,358.32

D. Use scientific notation to calculate each problem. Show the answers in decimal form.

1. $576,000,000 \times 648,000,000$

2. $3,245,000,000 \times 251,000,000$

3. $12,441,600,000 \times 4,140,000,000$

4. $600,000,000 \times 165,250,000$

5. $765,000,000 \times 0.000000086$

6. $2,500,000,000 \times 0.000000057$

7. $34,270,000,000 \times 0.0000002143$

8. $564,000,000,000 \times 0.0000000925$

9. $\dfrac{874,000,000,000 \times 450,000,000}{3,750,000,000}$

10. $\dfrac{2,250,000,000 \times 30,375,000}{56,250,000,000,000}$

11. $\dfrac{635,000,000 \times 0.00000275}{31,750,000}$

12. $\dfrac{0.000000452 \times 6,195,000,000}{8,260,000}$

13. $\dfrac{765,225,000}{0.000005625}$

14. $\dfrac{7,031,250,000}{0.0000009375}$

15. $\dfrac{0.05052 \times 0.005271 \times 0.00005}{842 \times 3.765}$

16. $\dfrac{0.00168 \times 0.000126 \times 0.021}{0.0084}$

EXPANDED NOTATION

We have seen that ten $= 10 = 10^1$; that one hundred $= 100 = 10 \times 10 = 10^2$; that one thousand $= 1,000 = 10 \times 10 \times 10 = 10^3$; and that ten thousand $= 10,000 = 10 \times 10 \times 10 \times 10 = 10^4$. Any whole number can be written as an exponential expression. Consider the base-ten number represented by 457.

$$\begin{aligned} 457 &= 400 + 50 + 7 \\ &= (4 \times 100) + (5 \times 10) + (7 \times 1) \\ &= (4 \times 10 \times 10) + (5 \times 10) + (7 \times 1) \\ &= (4 \times 10^2) + (5 \times 10^1) + (7 \times 10^0) \end{aligned}$$

In a similar manner,

$$\begin{aligned} 23,106 &= 20,000 + 3,000 + 100 + 0 + 6 \\ &= (2 \times 10,000) + (3 \times 1,000) + (1 \times 100) + (0 \times 10) + (6 \times 1) \\ &= (2 \times 10^4) + (3 \times 10^3) + (1 \times 10^2) + (0 \times 10^1) + (6 \times 10^0) \end{aligned}$$

A number in this form is in **expanded notation.** This form facilitates the understanding of the relationship of one number system to another, as in the comparison of the decimal system to the binary system.

Notice that when a numeral representing a whole number has five digits, the highest power of ten in the expanded notation is four $(5 - 1)$; when the numeral has four digits, the highest power of ten is three $(4 - 1)$; when the numeral has three digits, the highest power of ten is two $(3 - 1)$. Generally when a numeral representing a whole number has n digits, the highest power of ten is $n - 1$.

- ## Exercise 6–4

A. Write each of the following in expanded notation.

1. 435
2. 947
3. 3,600
4. 3,971
5. 37,172

6. 3,144,000
7. 10,000
8. 49,019
9. 400,546
10. 9,000,234

B. Write each of the following as an ordinary base-ten number.

1. $(6 \times 10^2) + (9 \times 10^1) + (3 \times 10^0)$

2. $(2 \times 10^4) + (4 \times 10^3) + (5 \times 10^2) + (1 \times 10^1) + (7 \times 10^0)$

3. $(4 \times 10^6) + (3 \times 10^5) + (0 \times 10^4) + (6 \times 10^3) + (4 \times 10^2) + (6 \times 10^1) + (1 \times 10^0)$

4. $(5 \times 10^3) + (1 \times 10^2) + (2 \times 10^1) + (3 \times 10^0)$

5. $(2 \times 10^5) + (5 \times 10^4) + (5 \times 10^3) + (5 \times 10^2) + (1 \times 10^1) + (9 \times 10^0)$

6. $(6 \times 10^8) + (0 \times 10^7) + (6 \times 10^6) + (1 \times 10^5) + (6 \times 10^4) + (6 \times 10^3) +$ $(2 \times 10^2) + (6 \times 10^1) + (4 \times 10^0)$

7. $(1 \times 10^{10}) + (3 \times 10^9) + (0 \times 10^8) + (0 \times 10^7) + (1 \times 10^6) + (6 \times 10^5) +$ $(6 \times 10^4) + (8 \times 10^3) + (8 \times 10^2) + (3 \times 10^1) + (7 \times 10^0)$

8. $(2 \times 10^5) + (7 \times 10^4) + (5 \times 10^3) + (0 \times 10^2) + (0 \times 10^1) + (0 \times 10^0)$

BINARY NOTATION

From a practical standpoint, the second most important place-value system of numeration is the base-two system. As *bi* means two, it is called the **binary system.** Because the work of modern electronic computers is based on binary notation, only the decimal system is of greater importance. Special attention, therefore, should be given to this system.

The reason for using the base-two system in electronic computers is that numbers are represented by electronic switches. Just as light switches in a home can be turned on and off, these switches have two possible positions, "on" or "off." By using "off" for 0, and "on" for 1, and a place-value scheme, various numbers can be expressed. The binary number system with symbols 0 and 1 is ideally suited to this scheme.

The binary system, like the decimal system, is a place-value system. Any place-value system has the following four characteristics:

1. A place-value system uses the same number of different symbols as the size of the basic group. For example, in base ten there are ten symbols, 0, 1, 2, 3, 4, 5, 6, 7, 8, 9. In base two there are two symbols, 0 and 1.
2. Place value eliminates the need for the development of new symbols to represent values beyond one less than the basic group. The basic group for the base-ten system is 10. Therefore, $10 - 1 = 9$, the highest value expressed by a single digit in the system.
3. The total value of a number symbol in any one place is determined by multiplying the face value of the symbol by the value assigned to the place. In base ten, 132 equals $(1 \times 10^2) + (3 \times 10^1) + (2 \times 10^0)$.
4. The value represented by a numeral is determined by adding the total value of all the symbols in that numeral. For example, in base ten:

632

means $2 \times 10^0 =$	$2 \times 1 =$	2
means $3 \times 10^1 =$	$3 \times 10 =$	30
means $6 \times 10^2 = 6 \times 10 \times 10 =$		600
	Value	632

In any place-value system of notation, a symbol in the first place on the right represents the number of ones indicated by its face value; a symbol in the second place represents the number of base groups. The essence of place value, as a matter of fact, is the naming of places in consecutive powers of the base group. In other words, in base ten the first place on the right equals 10^0; the second place, 10^1; the third place, 10^2; and so on. In base two the first place equals 2^0; the second place, 2^1; the third place, 2^2; and so on.

The binary system is based on groups of two, just as the decimal system is based on groups of ten. The comparison in Table 6–1 shows how decimal and binary numerals are related. In order to acquire a sound understanding of this relationship, carefully study the three forms of notation.

Decimal Notation	Expanded Binary Notation	Binary Notation
0		0
1	$(1 \times 2^0) =$	1
2	$(1 \times 2^1) + (0 \times 2^0) =$	10
3	$(1 \times 2^1) + (1 \times 2^0) =$	11
4	$(1 \times 2^2) + (0 \times 2^1) + (0 \times 2^0) =$	100
5	$(1 \times 2^2) + (0 \times 2^1) + (1 \times 2^0) =$	101
6	$(1 \times 2^2) + (1 \times 2^1) + (0 \times 2^0) =$	110
7	$(1 \times 2^2) + (1 \times 2^1) + (1 \times 2^0) =$	111
8	$(1 \times 2^3) + (0 \times 2^2) + (0 \times 2^1) + (0 \times 2^0) =$	1000
9	$(1 \times 2^3) + (0 \times 2^2) + (0 \times 2^1) + (1 \times 2^0) =$	1001
10	$(1 \times 2^3) + (0 \times 2^2) + (1 \times 2^1) + (0 \times 2^0) =$	1010
11	$(1 \times 2^3) + (0 \times 2^2) + (1 \times 2^1) + (1 \times 2^0) =$	1011
12	$(1 \times 2^3) + (1 \times 2^2) + (0 \times 2^1) + (0 \times 2^0) =$	1100
13	$(1 \times 2^3) + (1 \times 2^2) + (0 \times 2^1) + (1 \times 2^0) =$	1101
14	$(1 \times 2^3) + (1 \times 2^2) + (1 \times 2^1) + (0 \times 2^0) =$	1110
15	$(1 \times 2^3) + (1 \times 2^2) + (1 \times 2^1) + (1 \times 2^0) =$	1111

Table 6–1 Binary Notation Compared to Decimal Notation

Tables 6–1 and 6–2 show that as the digit 1 is moved one place to the left in a binary numeral, its value increases by a power of two. Note that the power of two always equals the number of digits in the numeral minus one.

Place in Numeral	11	10	9	8	7	6	5	4	3	2	1
Power	2^{10}	2^9	2^8	2^7	2^6	2^5	2^4	2^3	2^2	2^1	2^0
Base-Ten Value	1,024	512	256	128	64	32	16	8	4	2	1

Table 6–2 Binary Place Value-Chart

Changing a Binary Numeral to a Decimal Numeral

Anyone who works in a modern office where computers are used should be able to change a binary numeral to a decimal numeral and a decimal numeral to a binary numeral. This is not difficult when a binary place-value chart is available. Such a chart can be prepared by writing the successive powers of two from right to left as in Table 6–2.

The value of a binary numeral may be determined in relation to a decimal numeral in the following manner:

1. Determine the decimal value of the digits in the binary numeral by referring to a binary place-value chart.
2. Add the decimal values.

Example: Change the binary numeral 11010 to a decimal numeral.

Solution:

Binary System		**Decimal System**
1 1 0 1 0		

means $0 \times 2^0 = 0 \times 1 = 0$
means $1 \times 2^1 = 1 \times 2 = 2$
means $0 \times 2^2 = 0 \times 4 = 0$
means $1 \times 2^3 = 1 \times 8 = 8$
means $1 \times 2^4 = 1 \times 16 = \underline{16}$

26 Decimal Value

● Exercise 6–5

Change the following binary numerals to decimal numerals.

1. 10000	**6.** 100111	**11.** 1001011	**16.** 10010001001
2. 100000	**7.** 100011	**12.** 1101101	**17.** 1001001011
3. 10110	**8.** 11011	**13.** 10110011	**18.** 1010010111
4. 10101	**9.** 10111	**14.** 11001100	**19.** 101101101
5. 11101	**10.** 1011010	**15.** 11010101	**20.** 11001100101

Changing a Decimal Numeral to a Binary Numeral

Use this method to determine the binary value of a decimal numeral:

1. Refer to a binary place-value chart to find the largest power of two that is contained in the decimal numeral. Subtract the base-ten value of this power of two from the decimal numeral and write its equivalent binary numeral.
2. Subtract the base-ten value of the largest power of two contained in the remainder of the decimal numeral therefrom and write the binary numeral, properly aligned from the right, below the binary numeral obtained in Step 1.

3. Continue the above procedures until the decimal numeral has zero remainder.
4. Add the binary values.

Example: Change the decimal numeral 39 to binary notation.

Solution:

Decimal System	Binary System	
39	Refer to Table 6–2	
$-\ 32\ =\ 2^5\ =$	100000	(Notice power 5 and 5 zeros)
7		
$-\ 4\ =\ 2^2\ =$	100	(Two zeros)
3		
$-\ 2\ =\ 2^1\ =$	10	(One zero)
1		
$-\ 1\ =\ 2^0\ =$	1	(No zero)
0	100111	Binary Value

● Exercise 6–6

Change the following decimal numerals to binary numerals.

1. 18	**5.** 51	**9.** 29	**13.** 214	**17.** 912
2. 30	**6.** 62	**10.** 87	**14.** 436	**18.** 1,563
3. 63	**7.** 43	**11.** 101	**15.** 798	**19.** 1,156
4. 47	**8.** 75	**12.** 117	**16.** 1,010	**20.** 1,792

Binary-Coded Decimal System

Binary numerals take up a lot of space whether they are written on paper or placed in a computer. For this reason, many electronic computers do not use the pure binary system alone but use a combination of binary and decimal numerals. For example, the decimal numeral 259 may be expressed as 0010-0101-1001, which is called a **binary-coded decimal.** The 0010 represents the decimal digit 2; the 0101 represents the decimal digit 5; and the 1001 represents 9. Each of the foregoing binary numerals is called a **binary-coded decimal digit.** Notice that each coded digit contains four places and that zeros are appended, when needed, to fill in the four places. The procedure may be analyzed as follows:

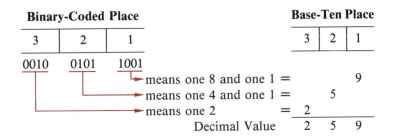

A. Write the decimal numeral expressed by each binary-coded decimal.

1. 0110-0100	**11.** 0011-0101-0010-0110
2. 0001-1000	**12.** 0100-0010-0111-0101
3. 0011-0010	**13.** 1000-0000-0110-1001
4. 1001-0110	**14.** 0001-0011-0100-0011
5. 0111-0101	**15.** 0110-1000-0000-1000
6. 0001-0001-0011	**16.** 0101-0001-0111-0100-0111
7. 0010-0000-1000	**17.** 1001-1000-0101-0001-0010
8. 0110-0101-0111	**18.** 0001-0011-1000-0010-0100
9. 1000-0100-0010	**19.** 0110-0000-0010-0101-0011
10. 0100-1001-0000	**20.** 1000-0111-0011-0100-0010-0101

B. Write each of the following as a binary-coded decimal.

1. 42	**5.** 80	**9.** 945	**13.** 5,371	**17.** 61,173
2. 63	**6.** 214	**10.** 378	**14.** 4,650	**18.** 4,127
3. 19	**7.** 537	**11.** 3,401	**15.** 7,809	**19.** 34,530
4. 57	**8.** 600	**12.** 2,842	**16.** 97,421	**20.** 203,804

Binary Arithmetic

Through practice one can learn to perform the arithmetic operations with binary numerals as easily as with decimal numerals. The same basic rules of addition, subtraction, multiplication, and division are followed.

Addition With Binary Numerals. The procedure for adding binary numerals is similar to that used for adding decimal numerals. First the ones column is added. Then the successive columns on the left (twos, fours, eights, etc.) are added. Addition of binary numerals, however, results in more frequent "carries." In the decimal system, there is a carry to the column on the left when a columnar total exceeds nine. Whereas, in the binary system, there is a carry to the next column when a columnar total exceeds the binary one.

The four possible combinations of binary addition facts are shown below. Observe that the binary sum 10 means 0 and carry 1.

$$
\begin{array}{cccc}
0 & 0 & 1 & 1 \\
+\,0 & +\,1 & +\,0 & +\,1 \\
\hline
0 & 1 & 1 & 10 \\
\end{array}
$$

The binary numeral 100 represents a number (4 in the decimal system) that is 1 more than the binary numeral 11 (3 in decimal form). This means that in the binary system $11 + 1 = 100$. This fact is used occasionally in binary addition.

The accuracy of binary addition may be checked by adding the equivalent decimal numbers. The decimal sum should represent the same number as the binary sum.

Example:

Find the sum of the numbers represented by the binary numerals in the problem below.

Solution:

```
  1 1
    1 1 1   Ones column: 1 + 1 = 10. Write 0, carry 1.
10  1 0 1   Twos column: Carried 1 + 1 = 10; 10 + 1 = 11. Write 1, carry 1.
    1 1 1 0 Fours column: Carried 1 + 1 = 10; 10 + 1 = 11; 11 + 1 = 100.
  1 1 0 1 0            Write 0, carry 10.
            Eights column: Carried 10 + 1 = 11. Write 11.
```

Check:

Binary		Decimal
111	=	7
101	=	5
1110	=	14
11010		26

$$16 + 8 + 2 = 26 \leftarrow \text{equal}$$

- ## Exercise 6–8

Add the following binary problems.

1. 1	2. 10	3. 101	4. 101	5. 10	6. 100
1	1	10	101	11	110

7. 11	8. 11	9. 101	10. 111	11. 1111	12. 11011
1	11	11	101	1110	10101

13. 1	14. 1	15. 11	16. 10	17. 101	18. 1101
1	1	10	11	110	1011
1	1	11	10	111	1001
	1		11		100

19. 100	20. 1001	21. 1111	22. 11011	23. 10101	24. 10010
10	1000	101	1100	1010	11000
101	1100	1010	110	101	10101
111	1101	1001	10111	1101	11001

Subtraction With Binary Numerals. Before considering subtraction with binary numerals, look at Example A, which illustrates subtraction with decimal numerals. Notice that the ten-thousands place is occupied by a zero after the 1 is borrowed and that the intervening zeros in the thousands, hundreds, and tens places all become nines. The borrowed 1 is placed to the left of the 8.

Chapter 6. Selected Notation Systems

Example A: Subtract using these decimal numerals: 10,008
                                                         7,969

Solution:
$$\overset{0\ 9\ 9\ 9\ 1}{\cancel{1}\ \cancel{0},\cancel{0}\ \cancel{0}\ 8}$$
$$\underline{7,9\ 6\ 9}$$
$$2,0\ 3\ 9$$

The following basic facts are used in subtraction of binary numerals:

$$\begin{array}{cccc} 0 & 1 & 1 & 10 \\ -\ 0 & -\ 0 & -\ 1 & -\ 1 \\ \hline 0 & 1 & 0 & 1 \end{array}$$

The last of the subtraction facts $(10 - 1 = 1)$ deserves special attention. The principles used in binary subtraction are the same as those used in decimal subtraction. In binary arithmetic, as in decimal arithmetic, 1 cannot be subtracted from 0 unless a 1 can be borrowed from a place on the left. Any intervening zero, however, becomes 1 instead of 9. Notice in the following illustration that the symbols used in each case have the same numerical value (4). Just as the value of a decimal symbol varies by a power of 10 according to the place it occupies in a numeral, we can assume that the value of the binary symbol varies by a power of 2 according to its position within a numeral.

Binary Place Value

2^2	2^1	2^0	**Expanded Decimal Notation**
1	0	0	$= (1 \times 2^2) + (0 \times 2^1) + (0 \times 2^0)$
			$\ \ 4\ \ \ +\ \ \ 0\ \ \ +\ \ \ 0\ \ = 4$
0	1	10	$= (0 \times 2^2) + (1 \times 2^1) + (2 \times 2^0)$
			$\ \ 0\ \ \ +\ \ \ 2\ \ \ +\ \ \ 2\ \ = 4$

Example B: Find the difference with these binary numerals: 1001000
                                                                       10101

Solution:
$$\overset{0\ 1\ 1\ 1}{1\ 0\ 0\ \cancel{1}\ \cancel{0}\ \cancel{0}\ 0}$$
$$\underline{1\ 0\ 1\ 0\ 1}$$

Step 1. As the 1 in the ones column cannot be subtracted from 0, "borrow" the first 1 found on the left. Write 0 in place of the borrowed 1. Change any intervening 0 to 1. Change the 0 at the point of subtraction to 10.

$$\overset{0\ 1\ 1\ 0\ 1\ 1\ 1}{\cancel{1}\ \cancel{0}\ 0\ \cancel{1}\ \cancel{0}\ \cancel{0}\ 0}$$
$$\underline{1\ 0\ 1\ 0\ 1}$$
$$1\ 1\ 0\ 0\ 1\ 1$$

Step 2. Moving from right to left and "borrowing" when necessary in the manner described in Step 1, subtract each column until the problem is solved.

Check:

	Binary	Decimal
	1001000 =	72
	10101 =	21
	110011	51

$$32 + 16 + 2 + 1 = 51 \longleftarrow \text{equal}$$

Part 1.   Mathematics Applications in Preparing a Basic Foundation

Find the differences for the binary numerals given below.

1. 11
  10
	5. 1111
	   101
		9. 1101
		   111
			13. 11011
			   1101
				17. 101101
				    1011

2. 110
   10
	6. 10
	   1
		10. 1000
		    11
			14. 11101
			   1011
				18. 100100100
				    1011001

3. 101
   10
	7. 100
	   11
		11. 10101
		  1010
			15. 100001
			    100
				19. 101010010
				    1101101

4. 111
   11
	8. 1000
	   101
		12. 10000
		   101
			16. 11101
			  1001
				20. 1001100110
				   10011101

Multiplication With Binary Numerals. There are four basic facts in binary multiplication. These are:

$$
\begin{array}{cccc}
0 & 0 & 1 & 1 \\
\times\,0 & \times\,1 & \times\,0 & \times\,1 \\
\hline
0 & 0 & 0 & 1
\end{array}
$$

The procedures for multiplying with binary numerals are the same as those with decimal numerals. Starting with the digit on the right, partial products are obtained by multiplying the multiplicand by each digit in the multiplier. The sum of the partial products is then computed. The following example illustrates multiplication with binary numerals.

Example: Multiply with these binary numerals: 111 by 101.

Solution:

      111      $1 \times 111 = 111$ the first partial product.
      101      $0 \times 111 = 0$. Write 0 in the twos column of the second partial
      111   product.
    1110 $1 \times 111 = 111$. Write 111 to the left of the 0 in the second partial
100011   product.
              Add the partial products.

Check: **Binary**   **Decimal**

$$
\begin{array}{rcr}
111 & = & 7 \\
101 & = & 5 \\
\hline
111 & & 35 \\
1110 & & \\
\hline
100011 & &
\end{array}
$$

$32 + 2 + 1 = 35 \leftarrow$ equal

Chapter 6.   Selected Notation Systems

Multiply the binary problems given below.

1. 111
   10
	5. 1101
	   101
		9. 10111
		   1011
			13. 110101
			   1011
				17. 1100111
				   11001

2. 111
   11
	6. 1111
	   11
		10. 10100
		   1011
			14. 101111
			   11010
				18. 1001001
				   10111

3. 101
   11
	7. 1101
	   110
		11. 1111
		   111
			15. 101011
			   1011
				19. 10101100
				   11011

4. 111
   101
	8. 1110
	   111
		12. 10111
		   1010
			16. 100111
			   1111
				20. 10011011
				   11111

Division With Binary Numerals. To divide one binary numeral by another, follow the same procedures as in division with decimal numerals. Remember, however, to think in binary terms when performing the steps of multiplying and subtracting.

Observe in the example below that the division is not complete until the 0 is placed in the ones column of the quotient.

Example:

Solution:

Solve this binary problem: $101010 \div 111$.

```
        110
111) 101010
     111
     111
     111
```

Check:

	Binary	Decimal
Dividend:	101010 =	42
Divisor:	111 =	7
	$42 \div 7 = 6$	

Quotient: $110 = 4 + 2 = 6$ ◄— equal

● Exercise 6–11

Divide the binary problems shown below.

1. 101)1111

2. 10)1110

3. 100)11000

4. 11)10101

5. 11)11011

6. 11)100001

7. 110)110110

8. 110)11000

9. 111)100011

10. 111)110001

11. 1110)101010

12. 1011)1101110

13. 1011)1001101

14. 1101)10101001

REVIEW PROBLEMS

Solve these problems. If you have difficulty solving any problem, restudy the appropriate section in this chapter. The problems under a specific number are related to those contained in the exercise with the same last number.

1. Write each of the following in the form specified.

    a. Use an exponent to express $4 \times 4 \times 4$.

    b. Use an exponent to express $(5)(5)(5)(5)(5)(5)$.

    c. Use factor notation to express 7^4.

    d. Show the product of 10^6.

2. a. Rewrite each of the following as an equivalent expression with a positive exponent.

      (1) 8^{-3} (2) 9^{-4} (3) $\dfrac{1}{10^{-2}}$

    b. Calculate each power.

      (1) 5^8 (2) -1.2^5 (3) 4^{-3}

    c. Show each of the following as a power of 10 with a single positive or negative exponent.

      (1) $10^{-4} \times 10^7 \times 10^{-2}$ (2) $\dfrac{10^3 \times 10^7}{10^{-4} \times 10^6}$

3. a. Use an eight-digit calculator to compute each problem. Show each answer in decimal form.

      (1) $162{,}507 \times 35{,}473$ (2) $\dfrac{97{,}255{,}000}{0.0005}$

    b. Find the product of each without using a calculator. Show the answers in decimal form.

      (1) 2.85×10^4 (2) 3.96×10^{-5}

    c. Write each number in scientific notation.

      (1) $4{,}976$ (2) 345.809 (3) 0.00021

    d. Use scientific notation to calculate each problem. Show the answers in decimal form.

      (1) $53{,}460{,}000{,}000 \times 0.000000346$ (2) $\dfrac{13{,}200{,}000 \times 640{,}000{,}000}{0.004125}$

4. a. Write each of the following in expanded notation.

      (1) 576 (2) $4{,}700$ (3) $25{,}380$ (4) $900{,}682$

    b. Write each of the following as an ordinary base-ten number.

      (1) $(9 \times 10^2) + (3 \times 10^1) + (1 \times 10^0)$

      (2) $(4 \times 10^3) + (2 \times 10^2) + (6 \times 10^1) + (8 \times 10^0)$

      (3) $(5 \times 10^5) + (7 \times 10^4) + (0 \times 10^3) + (4 \times 10^2) + (0 \times 10^1) +$
          (8×10^0)

      (4) $(6 \times 10^7) + (4 \times 10^6) + (0 \times 10^5) + (7 \times 10^4) + (3 \times 10^3) +$
          $(0 \times 10^2) + (0 \times 10^1) + (0 \times 10^0)$

5. Change the following binary numerals to decimal numerals.

    a. 1000   c. 110111   e. 1101100   g. 111011011

    b. 10010   d. 111011   f. 1011101   h. 1101101011

6. Change the following decimal numerals to binary numerals.

a. 17	**c.** 69	**e.** 238	**g.** 870
b. 45	**d.** 83	**f.** 564	**h.** 1,321

7. a. Write the decimal numeral expressed by each binary-coded decimal.

(1) 0001-0100   **(4)** 0100-0010-0000
(2) 0110-0100   **(5)** 0101-0111-0001
(3) 1000-0010   **(6)** 1001-0000-0100-0011

b. Write each of the following as a binary-coded decimal.

(1) 26   **(2)** 48   **(3)** 81   **(4)** 460   **(5)** 3,572   **(6)** 9,305

8. Add the following binary problems.

a. 101	**b.** 1001	**c.** 1011
1	11	111

d. 10	**e.** 101	**f.** 10101
1	111	1101
11	100	110

9. Find the differences for the binary numerals given below.

a. 1001	**c.** 11011	**e.** 1001001
101	1101	101101

b. 10010	**d.** 101101	**f.** 110110011
1110	1001	11001110

10. Multiply these binary problems.

a. 101	**c.** 1101	**e.** 110101
10	111	1010

b. 101	**d.** 10101	**f.** 1011001
101	1010	10110

11. Divide these binary problems.

a. 111)‾10101‾   **c.** 1000)‾101000‾   **e.** 1011)‾1001101‾
b. 101)‾11110‾   **d.** 1110)‾101010‾   **f.** 100)‾110100‾

CHALLENGE PROBLEM

Solve this equation. Show the answer in decimal notation.

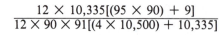

$$\frac{12 \times 10,335[(95 \times 90) + 9]}{12 \times 90 \times 91[(4 \times 10,500) + 10,335]}$$

Part Two
Mathematics Applications in Starting a Business

Most business accounting, even in small firms, is done on computers. Yet, to be effective, business accountants, managers, and owners must know not only how to put data into computers, but also how the principles of accounting apply.

The study of accounting should begin with the study of business mathematics. Indeed, the study of business mathematics is where any career in business should begin. Most business workers deal with money in one way or another. Dealing with money is dealing with numbers, whether it's done directly or indirectly. Even if the business person is not a "numbers cruncher," he or she should understand certain business principles and be able to compute solutions to the types of business problems that appear in this book. Business people who make calculations they don't understand are inviting disaster. Blind faith in calculations without understanding can lead to extremely costly blunders.

Chapter 7

Percentage

Objectives

After mastering the material in Chapter 7, you will be able to:

- Change a percent to a decimal or common fraction.
- Change a decimal or common fraction to a percent.
- Use the percentage equation to find the percentage, the rate, or the base.
- Compute sales, excise, and property taxes.

Citizens Loan Company charges 18 percent interest for certain kinds of loans. The state sales tax rate is 6 percent. Northern Counties Power and Water Company raised 45 percent of its organizing capital by borrowing. Last year, Jeff Hinton earned a 10 percent return on his stock investment. Diane Hodges is paid 8 percent commission for selling merchandise. Martin Corporation budgets $\frac{1}{2}$ percent of each sales dollar for advertising. Bill McDaniel has 25 percent of his salary withheld for federal income tax. McKay Company receives a discount of 2 percent for paying Arrow Products Company promptly. Anne Schneider correctly answered 95 percent of the questions on the test. During its second year, Big Pine Lumber Company had a 200 percent increase in sales. The weather forecaster predicts a 60 percent probability of rain.

The preceding examples illustrate only a few of the many ways in which percents occur in our business and private lives. That part of mathematics that deals with percents is called **percentage.** In business there is probably no mathematical concept that is used more frequently or more extensively than percentage.

As recently as the beginning of the twentieth century, the form "per cent." (two words with a period) was considered to be the correct abbreviation for *per centum*. Later in the century the period was dropped, and then "per" and "cent" were joined to form one word.

Percent, which may be represented by the symbol %, means "in the hundred" or "of each hundred" or simply "hundredth." For example, a person who gets 5% commission for selling earns $5 for each $100 worth of merchandise that he or she sells. As percent means hundredth, 5% means 5 hundredths, which is 0.05 in decimal form.

PERCENT EQUIVALENTS

When a problem contains percents that are to be used for computational purposes, the percents may be changed to common or decimal fractions before the computations are performed. This procedure helps to place the decimal point properly. The following section shows how to perform the conversions of percents to decimals or common fractions and vice versa.

Changing a Percent to a Decimal Fraction

The percent sign represents hundredths. When the sign is removed, the numeral it accompanies is divided by 100. To convert a percent to a decimal fraction:

1. Delete the percent sign.
2. Move the decimal point two places to the left.

Example A: Change **(a)** 6%, **(b)** $7\frac{1}{2}$%, and **(c)** 50% to decimal fractions.

Solution: **(a)** 6% = 0.06   **(b)** $7\frac{1}{2}$% = 7.5% = 0.075   **(c)** 50% = 0.5

Care must be taken when **fractional percents,** such as $\frac{1}{2}$%, $\frac{1}{4}$%, and $\frac{1}{3}$%, are converted to decimal form. Remember that $\frac{1}{2}$% means one-half of 1% and $\frac{1}{4}$% means one-fourth of 1%. The basic rule for converting to decimal form remains unchanged.

Example B: Change **(a)** $\frac{1}{2}$%, **(b)** $\frac{1}{4}$%, and **(c)** $\frac{1}{3}$% to decimal fractions.

Solution: **(a)** $\frac{1}{2}$% = 0.5% = 0.005   **(c)** $\frac{1}{3}$% = 0.333 . . . % = 0.00333 . . .

(b) $\frac{1}{4}$% = 0.25% = 0.0025

Dropping the percent sign from a number may result in a whole number or in a mixed decimal.

Example C: Write **(a)** 200% and **(b)** 325% in decimal notation.

Solution: **(a)** 200% = 2   **(b)** 325% = 3.25

Change each of the following percents to decimal notation.

1. 8%	**6.** $37\frac{1}{2}$%	**11.** $\frac{1}{2}$%	**16.** $\frac{3}{4}$%	**21.** $\frac{1}{3}$%
2. 80%	**7.** 375%	**12.** 25%	**17.** 750%	**22.** $\frac{1}{5}$%
3. 800%	**8.** 3.75%	**13.** $\frac{1}{4}$%	**18.** $6\frac{1}{4}$%	**23.** $\frac{1}{8}$%
4. 35%	**9.** 50%	**14.** 75%	**19.** $4\frac{1}{2}$%	**24.** $\frac{1}{6}$%
5. 7%	**10.** 0.5%	**15.** 7.5%	**20.** 0.25%	**25.** $\frac{2}{3}$%

Changing a Percent to a Common Fraction

To convert a percent to a common fraction:

1. Delete the percent sign.
2. Move the decimal point two places to the left.
3. Change the decimal fraction to a common fraction in lowest terms.

Example: Change **(a)** 6%, **(b)** $7\frac{1}{2}$%, **(c)** 50%, **(d)** $\frac{1}{2}$%, and **(e)** 325% to common fractions or mixed numbers in lowest terms.

Solution:

(a) $6\% = 0.06 = \frac{6}{100} = \frac{3}{50}$

(b) $7\frac{1}{2}\% = 7.5\% = 0.075 = \frac{75}{1,000} = \frac{3}{40}$

(c) $50\% = 0.5 = \frac{5}{10} = \frac{1}{2}$

(d) $\frac{1}{2}\% = 0.5\% = 0.005 = \frac{5}{1,000} = \frac{1}{200}$

(e) $325\% = 3.25 = 3\frac{25}{100} = 3\frac{1}{4}$

● Exercise 7–2

Change each of the following percents to a common fraction or mixed number in lowest terms.

1. 20%	**6.** $12\frac{1}{2}$%	**11.** 8%	**16.** 625%	**21.** $8\frac{1}{3}$%
2. 2%	**7.** 125%	**12.** $14\frac{2}{7}$%	**17.** $56\frac{1}{4}$%	**22.** $16\frac{2}{3}$%
3. 25%	**8.** $37\frac{1}{2}$%	**13.** 0.5%	**18.** $83\frac{1}{3}$%	**23.** $66\frac{2}{3}$%
4. $2\frac{1}{2}$%	**9.** 375%	**14.** $\frac{1}{2}$%	**19.** $\frac{1}{4}$%	**24.** $333\frac{1}{3}$%
5. 10%	**10.** $33\frac{1}{3}$%	**15.** 2.5%	**20.** $6\frac{1}{4}$%	

Changing a Decimal to a Percent

To convert a decimal fraction to a percent:

1. Move the decimal point two places to the right.
2. Append the percent sign to the right of the numeral.

Example: Change (a) 0.07, (b) 0.0625, (c) 0.6, (d) 2.2, and (e) 4 to percents.

Solution:
(a) $0.07 = 7\%$

(b) $0.0625 = 6.25\%$ or $6\frac{1}{4}\%$

(c) $0.6 = 50\%$

(d) $2.2 = 220\%$

(e) $4 = 400\%$

● **Exercise 7–3**

Change each of the following to a percent.

1. 0.4	**6.** 0.605	**11.** 0.9	**16.** $1.62\frac{1}{2}$	**21.** 0.00333. . .
2. 0.04	**7.** 5.25	**12.** $0.0\frac{1}{2}$	**17.** $0.12\frac{1}{2}$	**22.** 0.00666. . .
3. 0.004	**8.** 0.005	**13.** $0.00\frac{1}{4}$	**18.** 0.035	**23.** 0.0333. . .
4. 5	**9.** 2.1	**14.** $0.06\frac{3}{4}$	**19.** 6	**24.** 0.0166. . .
5. 3.5	**10.** 0.8	**15.** $0.00\frac{1}{5}$	**20.** $0.56\frac{1}{4}$	

Changing a Common Fraction to a Percent

To convert a common fraction to a percent:

1. Divide the numerator by the denominator.
2. Move the decimal point in the quotient two places to the right.
3. Append the percent sign to the right of the numeral.

A calculator may be used for the division. If the calculator has a $\boxed{\%}$ key, pressing the $\boxed{\%}$ key will place the decimal point correctly. If the calculator has no $\boxed{\%}$ key, you must remember to move the decimal point two places to the right when appending the percent sign.

Example A: Change (a) $\frac{3}{4}$ and (b) $\frac{1}{3}$ to percents.

Solution: *Without* $\boxed{\%}$ key:

(a) $\frac{3}{4} = 3 \boxed{\div} 4 \boxed{=} \rightarrow 0.75 = 75\%$

(b) $\frac{1}{3} = 1 \boxed{\div} 3 \boxed{=} \rightarrow 0.3333333$

0.3333333 means 0.3333. . . which equals 33.33 . . . % or $33\frac{1}{3}\%$

With $\boxed{\%}$ key:

(a) $\frac{3}{4} = 3 \boxed{\div} 4 \boxed{\%} \rightarrow 75$, which means 75%

(b) $\frac{1}{3} = 1 \boxed{\div} 3 \boxed{\%} \rightarrow 33.333333$, which means 33.333. . . % or $33\frac{1}{3}\%$

To convert a mixed number to a percent follow the above procedure for the common fraction portion and append the result to the whole number portion.

Example B: Change **(a)** $7\frac{1}{2}$ and **(b)** $5\frac{1}{6}$ to percents.

Solution: *Without* ☐**%** key:

(a) $\frac{1}{2} = 1$ ☐**÷** 2 ☐**=** $\rightarrow 0.5; 7\frac{1}{2} = 7 + 0.5 = 7.5 = 750\%$

(b) $\frac{1}{6} = 1$ ☐**÷** 6 ☐**=** $\rightarrow 0.1666666$

$5\frac{1}{6} = 5.1666\ldots = 516.66\ldots\% \text{ or } 516\frac{2}{3}\%$

With ☐**%** key:

(a) $\frac{1}{2} = 1$ ☐**÷** 2 ☐**%** $\rightarrow 50$, which means 50%

$7 = 700\%$, so $700\% + 50\% = 750\%$

(b) $\frac{1}{6} = 1$ ☐**÷** 6 ☐**%** $\rightarrow 16.666666$, which means $16.666\ldots\%$

$5 = 500\%$, so $500\% + 16.666\ldots\% = 516.666\ldots\% \text{ or } 516\frac{2}{3}\%$

● **Exercise 7–4**

Change each of the following to a percent.

1. $\frac{1}{2}$	5. $\frac{1}{25}$	9. $5\frac{3}{4}$	13. $\frac{7}{12}$	17. $4\frac{4}{5}$	21. $\frac{1}{3}$
2. $\frac{3}{8}$	6. $\frac{1}{6}$	10. $\frac{5}{6}$	14. $\frac{3}{20}$	18. $\frac{1}{160}$	22. $\frac{3}{16}$
3. $4\frac{1}{4}$	7. $\frac{5}{8}$	11. $\frac{3}{5}$	15. $\frac{1}{16}$	19. $\frac{15}{16}$	23. $7\frac{9}{16}$
4. $\frac{2}{5}$	8. $3\frac{2}{3}$	12. $\frac{7}{8}$	16. $\frac{11}{12}$	20. $\frac{1}{7}$	24. $6\frac{5}{12}$

THE PERCENTAGE EQUATION

As the word *percent* means hundredths, the phrase *percent of* means hundredths of. We find a percent of a number by computing a specific number of hundredths of that number. For example, to find 6 percent of 160 means to find 6 hundredths (0.06) of 160. A fractional part of a number is found through multiplication. The solution, then, rests on multiplying 160 by 0.06.

Example: Find 6% of 160. (means 0.06×160)

Solution:

Rate   Base   Percentage
$0.06 \times 160 = 9.60$

The word *percentage* has at least a dual meaning. It is used in mathematics to refer to those problems that pertain to percents. It is also used as the name of the product obtained when a percent of a number is found. Percentage is the result of multiplying a particular number, which is the base, by a percent, which is the rate. In the previous example, 160 is the base, 6% is the rate, and 9.60 is the percentage. In summary, the **base** is the number of which a certain number of hundredths is taken; the **rate** is the number of hundredths taken (that is, the number percent); and **percentage** is the product that results when the base is multiplied by the percent.

The relationship of these three quantities is shown in equation form as Percentage = Rate × Base, or more simply as:

$$P = RB$$

This equation is the basic formula for solving many percentage problems. There are three kinds of problems in which this formula can be used: (1) to find the percentage when the base and rate are given, (2) to find the rate when the base and percentage are given, and (3) to find the base when the rate and percentage are given. In such problems, two of the three quantities will be given or will be easily determinable. The third quantity, the unknown quantity, can then be found by inserting the known quantities in the equation and solving for the unknown.

Some people like to place the symbols P, R, and B in a triangle to help them remember how to find any one of the unknown values. Notice the triangle. The P is placed at the top; the R and B, at the bottom in the triangle. The formula for finding each is revealed by covering the letter representing the unknown. Covering the P with your thumb, for example, shows RB, which means $R \times B$. Covering the R shows P over B, which means $P \div B$. Covering the B shows P over R, which means $P \div R$.

Finding the Percentage

The equation $P = RB$ is used to find the percentage. The basic rule for computing percentage is:

> To find percentage, convert the percent to a decimal fraction and multiply.

Example:	Find 34% of $720.
Solution:	As 34% = 0.34, then $720 × 0.34 = $244.80.

Calculator [%] **Key.** If the [%] key on a calculator is used, there is no need to shift the decimal point. Pressing the [%] key shifts the decimal point in the answer automatically. Further, on most calculators there is no need to press the [=] key after the [%] key is pressed.

Example A:	Find 25% of $96.80.
Solution:	*With* [%] key:

$$96.8 \;[×]\; 25 \;[\%]\; \rightarrow 24.2, \text{ means } \$24.20$$

Without [%] key:

$$96.8 \;[×]\; .25 \;[=]\; \rightarrow 24.2, \text{ means } \$24.20$$

When a percent or decimal is nonterminating, enter as many of the repeating decimal digits as the calculator will accept and round to the nearest cent. For example, enter as many 3s as the calculator will accept for $33\frac{1}{3}$%.

Example B:	Find $33\frac{1}{3}$% of $720.
Solution:	*With* [%] key:

$$720 \;[×]\; 33.333333 \;[\%]\; \rightarrow 239.99999, \text{ rounds to } \$240$$

Without [%] key:

$$720 \;[×]\; .33333333 \;[=]\; \rightarrow 239.99999, \text{ rounds to } \$240$$

Percent More Than. To find a percent, such as 8%, *more than* a given number means to *increase* the base by the additional percentage. Some calculators will show the increased number when the [+] and [%] keys are pressed. Others will show the percentage, which is then added to the base automatically when the [=] key is pressed. As the base equals 1 or 100%, the increase rate may be added to 100% to obtain the rate to use if the [%] key is *not* used. For example, 8% more than a number means 108% of that number.

Example:	Find 8% more than 250.
Solution:	*With* [%] key:

$$250 \;[+]\; 8 \;[\%]\; \rightarrow 270 \quad \textbf{or} \quad 250 \;[+]\; 8 \;[\%]\; \rightarrow 20 \;[=]\; \rightarrow 270$$

Without [%] key:

$$250 \;[×]\; 1.08 \;[=]\; \rightarrow 270$$

Percent Less Than. To find a percent, say $7\frac{1}{2}$%, *less than* a given number means to *decrease* the base by the percentage. The procedure is to press the [−] key before the [%] key if the [%] key is used. Otherwise, deduct

Part 2. Mathematics Applications in Starting a Business

the given rate from 100% and use the result as the rate times the base. For example, $7\frac{1}{2}\%$ less than a number means $100\% - 7\frac{1}{2}\%$ or $92\frac{1}{2}\%$ of that number.

Example: Find $7\frac{1}{2}\%$ less than $39.95.

Solution: *With* $\boxed{\%}$ key:

$$39.95 \boxed{-} 7.5 \boxed{\%} \rightarrow 36.95375, \text{means } \$36.95$$

or

$$39.95 \boxed{-} 7.5 \boxed{\%} \rightarrow 2.99625 \boxed{=} \rightarrow 36.95375, \text{means } \$36.95$$

Without $\boxed{\%}$ key ($100\% - 7.5\% = 92.5\%$):

$$39.95 \boxed{\times} .925 \boxed{=} \rightarrow 36.95375, \text{means } \$36.95.$$

Exercise 7–5

Where applicable in each of the following problems, round to the nearest cent.

A. Find the percentage: *part*

1. 8% of $353   *28.24*
2. 26% of $31.50
3. $87\frac{1}{2}\%$ of $560
4. 125% of $512

5. 7.2% of $34.46
6. $3\frac{1}{2}\%$ of $181
7. $\frac{1}{2}\%$ of $630.20
8. $\frac{7}{8}\%$ of $501.20

9. $83\frac{1}{3}\%$ of $582
10. $56\frac{1}{4}\%$ of $88
11. 400% of $25.58
12. $93\frac{3}{4}\%$ of $480

B. Find the amount of commission for each of these.

	Rate of Commission	Amount of Sale
1.	5%	$42
2.	20%	$485
3.	$7\frac{1}{2}\%$	$848
4.	$6\frac{1}{4}\%$	$64
5.	3%	$265.92
6.	$8\frac{1}{3}\%$	$1,098.50

.08333

C. Find the amount that is:

1. 35% more than $140
2. 7% more than $310
3. 9% less than $450   *$409.50*
4. 20% less than $360
5. $12\frac{1}{2}\%$ more than $832

6. $\frac{3}{4}\%$ more than $725
7. $18\frac{3}{4}\%$ less than $49.95
8. $\frac{1}{2}\%$ less than $575
9. $16\frac{2}{3}\%$ less than $864
10. $83\frac{1}{3}\%$ more than $426

Chapter 7. Percentage

195

D. Find the new price for each of the following.

	Price Change	Former Price
1.	10% Increase	$49.50
2.	15% Increase	$65.25
3.	25% Decrease	$164.00
4.	$18\frac{3}{4}$% Decrease	$112.32 91.26 not 90.12
5.	$33\frac{1}{3}$% Increase	$3.90
6.	30% Decrease	$45.20
7.	$6\frac{1}{4}$% Increase	$1,200
8.	$12\frac{1}{2}$% Increase	$850
9.	$16\frac{2}{3}$% Decrease	$2,500
10.	50% Decrease	$3,750

E. Solve these problems.

1. Robert Brooks bought a television set that was priced at $335. He made a down payment of 20% of the price. How much was the down payment?

2. A retail store sold a power saw at 25% more than it cost. How much was the selling price if the saw cost the store $84?

3. A hardware merchant sold a power drill at $37\frac{1}{2}$% more than it cost. If this model cost $76, how much was the selling price?

4. A business increases its advertising expenditures $33\frac{1}{3}$% each year. If the advertising expenses during the base year amounted to $2,700, how much were the expenses for the fourth year?

5. The Continental Insurance Company is allowed to invest 25% of its capital in corporate stock. The company has a total capital of $559,706,600, of which $132,232,950 is now invested in corporate stocks. What is the maximum additional amount that the company may invest in corporate stocks?

6. Paula Pittman owns 125 shares of stock for which she paid $34.50 a share. The dividends that she received during the past year represent a 6.2% return on her investment. What is the total amount of the dividends she received during the year?

Finding the Rate

Finding the rate means to determine what percent one number is of another. The unknown quantity in the basic percentage formula is the rate, the number percent. Shifting the symbols in the formula reveals that the rate can be found by dividing the percentage by the base.

Part 2. Mathematics Applications in Starting a Business

Basic Formula: $RB = P$

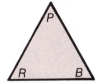

To find the rate: $R = \dfrac{P}{B}$

Example A: What percent of 750 is 60?

Solution:

$R \times 750 = 60$
$\qquad R = 60 \div 750$
$\qquad R = 0.08$
$\qquad R = 8\%$

Or, on a calculator *with* | % | key:

$\qquad\qquad$ 60 | ÷ | 750 | % | → 8, means 8%

Or, on a calculator *without* | % | key:

$\qquad\qquad$ 60 | ÷ | 750 | = | → 0.08 = 8%

Check: 750 | × | 8 | % | → 60 $\qquad$ **or** $\qquad$ 750 | × | .08 | = | → 60

Percents are often used to determine the significance of changes either up or down from base figures. To find the percent of increase or decrease, first find the amount of increase or decrease. Then use that amount, which is always the percentage, in the formula to find the rate.

Example B: A store's sales during October a year ago were $32,000. The store's sales during October this year amounted to $38,000. What is the percent of increase in the October sales this year compared to last year?

Solution: 1. Find the amount of increase.

$$\$38,000 - \$32,000 = \$6,000 \text{ increase (percentage)}$$

2. Use the formula.

$$\$6,000 = R \times \$32,000$$
$$6,000 \div 32,000 = R$$
$$0.1875 = R$$
$$18.75\% = R$$

Check: 32000 | × | 18.75 | % | → 6000

● **Exercise 7-6**

A. Find the rate. The percentage and base are given.

1. _____% of $510 = $102 $\qquad$ **3.** __58 3__% of $840 = $490

2. _____% of $219 = $146 $\qquad$ **4.** _____% of $248 = $93

5. _75_% of $660 = $495

6. _____% of $960 = $180

7. $41 = _____% of $328

8. $230 = _____% of $1,380

9. $156 = _____% of $1,872

10. $228 = _____% of $684

11. $1,085 = _____% of $875

12. $669.90 = _____% of $462

B. Solve these problems.

1. What percent of $240 is $19.20?

2. What percent of $87.50 is $31.50?

3. $16.50 is what percent of $49.50? $33\frac{1}{3}$

4. $31.50 is what percent of $168?

5. $26 is what percent more than $20? 30

6. $56 is what percent more than $48?

7. $120 is what percent less than $150?

8. $136 is what percent less than $160?

9. A fraternal club received $2,124 in dues and paid $302.67 for sick benefits. What percent of the dues was spent for sick benefits?

10. Prior to introducing a new line, a dealer sold a copying machine for 90 percent of its cost. **(a)** What percent of the cost did the dealer lose? **(b)** If the machine cost $498, how much did the dealer lose?

11. An agent received $90.72 as commission for selling $864 worth of goods. What was the rate of commission?

12. In a small town that has a population of 6,800 people, there are 238 persons who are 70 years of age or older. The people who are at least 70 years old are what percent of the population in the town?

13. Tom Freeman had a total income of $19,624 and paid $2,551.24 in taxes during the year. What percent of his total income did he pay in taxes?

14. In a midwestern community college there were 2,400 sophomores enrolled last year and 2,700 this year. By what percent did the enrollment of sophomores increase?

15. The price of an item increased from 72¢ each to 84¢ each. What percent did the price increase?

16. A retailer has $60,000 invested in her store which she has owned for two years. The first year, her net income amounted to $26,400. The next year, her net income amounted to 55% of her original investment. By what percent did her store earnings increase or decrease during the second year?

Part 2. Mathematics Applications in Starting a Business

Finding the Base

Finding the base means to find the number that will yield the percentage (P) when that number is multiplied by the given percent (R). The rate and the percentage will be given or will be easily determinable. The base can be found by placing the known quantities in the formula and solving for the unknown (B). Rearranging the symbols in the basic percentage formula reveals that the base can be found by dividing the percentage by the rate.

Basic Formula: $BR = P$

To find the base: $B = \dfrac{P}{R}$

Example A: Fifty is 8% of what number?

Solution:

$$50 = 8\% \times B$$
$$50 \div 0.08 = B$$
$$625 = B$$

Or, on a calculator *with* $\boxed{\%}$ key:

$$50 \boxed{\div} 8 \boxed{\%} \rightarrow 625$$

Or, on a calculator *without* $\boxed{\%}$ key:

$$50 \boxed{\div} .08 \boxed{=} \rightarrow 625$$

Check: $625 \boxed{\times} 8 \boxed{\%} \rightarrow 50$ **or** $625 \boxed{\times} .08 \boxed{=} \rightarrow 50$

In some problems the base will have been either decreased or increased by a known percent. The base is always equal to 100% of itself. When the base has been decreased by a certain percent, subtract the given percent from 100% to find the rate (R). When the base has been increased by a certain percent, add the given percent to 100% to find R. After finding the rate, use the formula to solve for the base.

Example B: What amount decreased by 12% becomes $378.40?

Solution:

1. The amount is the base (100%) from which 12% has been deducted. Therefore, the rate = 100% − 12% = 88%.
2. Use the formula.

$$\$378.40 = 88\% \times B$$
$$\$378.40 \div 88\% = B$$

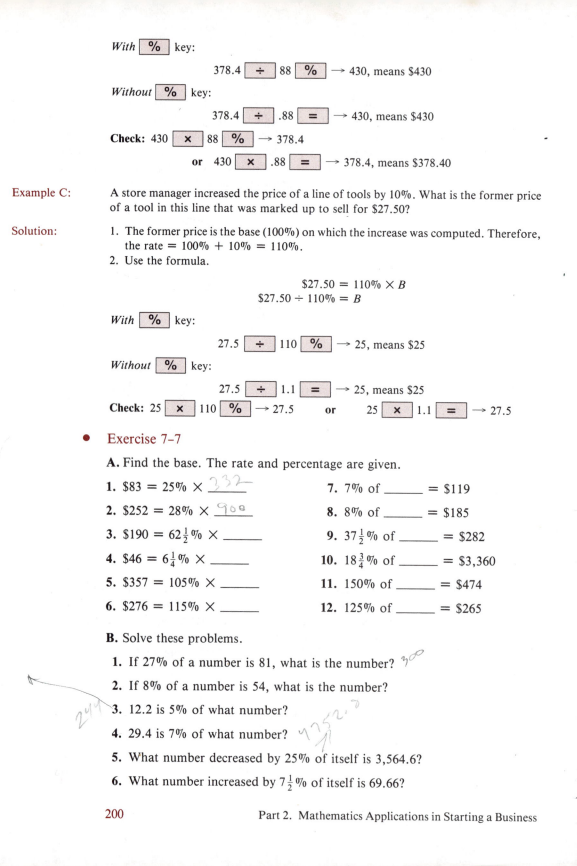

With $\boxed{\%}$ key:

$$378.4 \boxed{\div} 88 \boxed{\%} \rightarrow 430, \text{ means } \$430$$

Without $\boxed{\%}$ key:

$$378.4 \boxed{\div} .88 \boxed{=} \rightarrow 430, \text{ means } \$430$$

Check: $430 \boxed{\times} 88 \boxed{\%} \rightarrow 378.4$

or $430 \boxed{\times} .88 \boxed{=} \rightarrow 378.4, \text{ means } \$378.40$

Example C: A store manager increased the price of a line of tools by 10%. What is the former price of a tool in this line that was marked up to sell for $27.50?

Solution:

1. The former price is the base (100%) on which the increase was computed. Therefore, the rate = 100% + 10% = 110%.
2. Use the formula.

$$\$27.50 = 110\% \times B$$
$$\$27.50 \div 110\% = B$$

With $\boxed{\%}$ key:

$$27.5 \boxed{\div} 110 \boxed{\%} \rightarrow 25, \text{ means } \$25$$

Without $\boxed{\%}$ key:

$$27.5 \boxed{\div} 1.1 \boxed{=} \rightarrow 25, \text{ means } \$25$$

Check: $25 \boxed{\times} 110 \boxed{\%} \rightarrow 27.5$ or $25 \boxed{\times} 1.1 \boxed{=} \rightarrow 27.5$

● **Exercise 7–7**

A. Find the base. The rate and percentage are given.

1. $\$83 = 25\% \times$ _332_
2. $\$252 = 28\% \times$ _900_
3. $\$190 = 62\frac{1}{2}\% \times$ _____
4. $\$46 = 6\frac{1}{4}\% \times$ _____
5. $\$357 = 105\% \times$ _____
6. $\$276 = 115\% \times$ _____

7. 7% of _____ = $119
8. 8% of _____ = $185
9. $37\frac{1}{2}\%$ of _____ = $282
10. $18\frac{3}{4}\%$ of _____ = $3,360
11. 150% of _____ = $474
12. 125% of _____ = $265

B. Solve these problems.

1. If 27% of a number is 81, what is the number? _300_
2. If 8% of a number is 54, what is the number?
3. 12.2 is 5% of what number? _244_
4. 29.4 is 7% of what number? _4752.0_
5. What number decreased by 25% of itself is 3,564.6?
6. What number increased by $7\frac{1}{2}\%$ of itself is 69.66?

       Part 2. Mathematics Applications in Starting a Business

7. How many dollars plus 16% is $620.60?

8. How many dollars less 23% is $288.75?

9. Wilma Metzger has 28% of her capital invested in corporate securities, 45% invested in her merchandising business, and the remainder of $93,528 invested in real estate. What is the total value of her capital?

10. An agent earned $27 at 6% commission for selling an article. What was the selling price of the article?

11. David Rosenberg received a dividend of $256, which is 8% of his investment in Norton Corporation stock. How much is his investment in this company?

12. A stockholder invested $101 million to acquire 41.5% of the outstanding shares of Alvarez Corporation stock. To the nearest $100, what is the value of the company's total outstanding shares of stock?

13. Judy Shorr made a down payment of $760 on a used car. After this payment, she owed 80% of the purchase price. At what price did she buy the car?

14. A store sold an item for $14.49, which includes a federal tax of 10% and a state tax of 5%. Excluding the taxes, the item was sold for how much?

PERCENTAGE APPLICATIONS

The principles of percentage apply to many different kinds of business mathematics problems. Many of the applications that are relatively complicated are presented in subsequent sections of this book. Three of the less complicated uses of percentage, namely those pertaining to sales, excise, and property taxes, are presented in this section.

Sales and Excise Taxes

Many municipal, county, state, and federal taxes, such as sales and excise, are paid directly or indirectly by the ultimate consumer of the goods and services. These taxes are usually collected by the retailer and forwarded to the proper governmental agency.

Sales Tax. A tax levied on the sale of goods and services that is usually calculated as a percent of the selling price and collected by the seller is a **sales tax.** The ordinances and laws regarding which sales are taxable and which are exempt from taxation vary from one governmental agency to another. For example, food sold to individual consumers is exempt from sales tax in some states but not in others. The sales tax rates also vary from state to state and from city to city. The seller, therefore, must know the sales tax laws of each taxing agency that are applicable to the business.

The following formula may be used to calculate the amount of sales tax:

$$Sales\ Tax = Sales \times Sales\ Tax\ Rate$$

The tax rate is normally applied to the total amount of a sale rather than to the individual articles in the sale unless the sale is composed of different kinds of merchandise that are taxed at different rates. When the sale is for less than one dollar, the sales tax may be based on a published schedule that shows the tax on various fractional parts of a dollar. Below are three such schedules based on sales tax rates of 4%, 5%, and 6%.

4% Sales Tax Rate		5% Sales Tax Rate		6% Sales Tax Rate	
Transaction	**Tax**	**Transaction**	**Tax**	**Transaction**	**Tax**
1¢ to 14¢	none	1¢ to 10¢	none	1¢ to 10¢	none
15¢ to 28¢	1¢	11¢ to 27¢	1¢	11¢ to 22¢	1¢
29¢ to 54¢	2¢	28¢ to 47¢	2¢	23¢ to 39¢	2¢
55¢ to 80¢	3¢	48¢ to 68¢	3¢	40¢ to 56¢	3¢
81¢ to $1	4¢	69¢ to 89¢	4¢	57¢ to 73¢	4¢
Plus 4¢ on each additional dollar in the transaction.		90¢ to $1	5¢	74¢ to 90¢	5¢
		Plus 5¢ on each additional dollar in the transaction.		91¢ to $1.08	6¢
				Plus 6¢ on each additional dollar in the transaction.	

Table 7-1 Sales Taxes

Example: Using the preceding 5% sales tax schedule, find the sales tax on each of these sales: (a) 45¢, (b) $25, (c) $83.60.

Solution: **(a)** Tax on 45¢ = 2¢   (per schedule, 28¢ to 47¢)

(b) Tax on $25 = $1.25   ($25 × 0.05)

(c) Tax on $83.60 = $4.18   ($83.60 × 0.05)

> **Or**   Tax on $83.00 = $4.15   ($83 × 0.05)
> Tax on   0.60 =   0.03   (schedule, 48¢ to 68¢)
> Tax on $83.60 = $4.18

Some companies do not keep separate records of the sales tax collected. Such companies record sales and sales taxes together. The sales tax liability is computed, reported, and paid to the appropriate governmental agency periodically (usually monthly or quarterly) as stipulated by law.

Part 2. Mathematics Applications in Starting a Business

Example: During the month of November, a retailer recorded sales and sales taxes totaling $31,638.60. If the sales tax rate is 5%, find **(a)** the amount of the sales and **(b)** the amount of the sales tax.

Solution: **(a)** As it includes the sales (100%) and the sales tax (5%), the amount recorded ($31,638.60) equals 105% of the sales. Therefore,

$$105\% \text{ of Sales} = \$31,638.60$$
$$\text{Sales} = \$31,638.60 \div 1.05$$
$$\text{Sales} = \$30,132$$

(b) Sales Tax = Sales × Sales Tax Rate
Sales Tax = $30,132 × 0.05
Sales Tax = $1,506.60

Check: $30,132.00 sales
    1,506.60 tax
  $31,638.60 amount recorded

Excise Tax. A tax levied within a country on the manufacture, sale, or consumption of goods or on any of various privileges often assessed in the form of a license or other fee is an **excise tax.** Excise taxes began in the United States in 1792 with a federal tax on alcohol. City and state governments, however, also levy excise taxes. Among the excise taxes being levied by these governmental agencies are those on theater tickets, telephone service, transportation tickets, gasoline, tires, luggage, jewelry, cosmetics, and furs. Some excise taxes are based on stipulated percents of the manufacturer's or retailer's selling price. Others are based on quantity sold, such as 9¢ per gallon of gasoline.

● **Exercise 7–8**

1. Use Table 7–1 as needed to find the sales tax at 4% on each of these transactions: **(a)** 25¢, **(b)** 90¢, **(c)** $5.75, **(d)** 14¢, **(e)** 45¢, and **(f)** $2.15.

2. Use Table 7–1 as needed for a state that has a sales tax rate of 5% to find the sales tax on each of these transactions: **(a)** 14¢, **(b)** 89¢, **(c)** $4.10, **(d)** 35¢, **(e)** $9.95, and **(f)** 49¢.

3. A variety store that operates in a state having a sales tax of 6% collected tax on the following sales under one dollar: 346 sales at 10¢ each; 834 at 39¢ each; 679 at 69¢ each; 943 at 79¢ each; and 938 at 98¢ each. **(a)** Use Table 7–1 as needed to find the total amount of sales tax collected on these transactions. **(b)** How much tax does the store owe on these transactions?

4. A service station owner sold 8,376 gallons of gasoline at $1.429 a gallon. The price included a state tax of 14¢ a gallon and a federal tax of 9¢ a gallon. How much total tax must be paid on this gasoline?

5. Find the sales tax at 4%, the excise tax at 10%, and the total amount of money received in each of these transactions: **(a)** $7.69, **(b)** $12.69, **(c)** $78.98, **(d)** $143.12, **(e)** $630.40, and **(f)** $2,795.

6. Find the sales tax at 5%, the excise tax at 7%, and the total amount of money received in each of these transactions: **(a)** $2.98, **(b)** $18.25, **(c)** $75.83, **(d)** $165.43, **(e)** $784.11, and **(f)** $1,604.59.

7. A clerk in a retail store received $25.48 in cash for a sale that included 4% sales tax. Find **(a)** the price of the article sold and **(b)** the amount of the sales tax.

8. A clerk in a clothing store received $72.35 in cash, which included a sales tax of 5%, as payment in full for a coat. Find **(a)** the price of the coat and **(b)** the amount of the sales tax.

9. Yale Company records its sales and sales tax together in an account entitled "Sales." During a recent month $254,862.40 was recorded in the Sales account. The sales tax rate is 6%. Find **(a)** the amount of the taxable sales and **(b)** the sales tax.

10. In recording sales during its first three months of operations, Butler Furniture Company did not differentiate between the amount of its sales and the amount of its 5% sales tax charged on all sales. The records of the company reveal sales of $145,025.03, including sales tax as well as sales returns and allowances of $1,380.20. Find **(a)** the amount of taxable sales and **(b)** the amount of the sales tax.

Property Taxes

Property, whether tangible or intangible, movable or immovable, is that which is subject to ownership; and **ownership** is the right to possess and use a thing to the exclusion of others. Property may be classified in terms of its nature as real or personal. **Real property,** also called **realty** or **real estate,** includes land and anything permanently attached to the land, such as buildings, trees, fences, sidewalks, and other improvements. All property other than realty is **personal property.** It includes inventories, equipment, and intangibles, such as stocks, bonds, receivables, and bank deposits.

Cities, counties, and practically all independent taxing districts (e.g., public schools, parks, and utilities) derive much of their revenue from property taxes. These are usually levied against real property and often against personal property as well. With few exceptions, business enterprises are subject to taxes on both real property and personal property.

Finding the Tax Rate. The taxable value of real property is usually determined by an employee of the governmental taxing unit who is a **tax assessor.** The value assigned to the property by the tax assessor is the **assessed valuation,** which may or may not be related to the fair market value or the cost value of the property. The assessed valuation, however, is usually less than either of these values. For psychological reasons, the assessed valuation is frequently a fixed proportion (for example, 25%) of the fair market value. Although in some cases the owner of taxable personal property may be required to declare its value, it also may be appraised by an assessor.

Some governmental units customarily express real property taxes as so many cents, or dollars and cents, on each $100 of assessed valuation. Others express taxes as so many mills per dollar. A **mill** is 0.1 of a cent; i.e., 0.001 of a dollar.

The **tax rate,** which varies from year to year depending on the financial needs of the government, is found by dividing the total revenue to be raised from the tax by the total assessed value of the property within the jurisdiction of the taxing unit. To assure no shortage of revenue, the tax rate is always rounded up to the next highest digit when rounding is necessary. Notice in the example below that the tax is $4.53 to the nearest cent (not $4.52) per $100 of assessed value.

Example: The town of Pineville has a total assessed valuation of $5,400,000. The town revenue to be raised by property taxation amounts to $244,242. Find the tax rate **(a)** in mills per dollar and **(b)** in dollars and cents per $100 of assessed valuation.

Solution: **(a)** Tax rate = $\dfrac{\text{Revenue to be collected}}{\text{Total assessed valuation}}$

Tax rate = $\dfrac{244{,}242}{5{,}400{,}000}$ = $0.04523 × 1,000 = 45.23 mills per $1

If expressed to the nearest tenth of a mill, the rate is 45.3 mills (4.53¢) per $1.

(b) 0.04523 = $4.523 per $100

If expressed to the nearest cent, the rate is $4.53 per $100 of assessed valuation.

Finding the Property Owner's Tax. Once or twice a year the owner of the property being taxed receives a tax bill from the tax collector. The bill shows the assessed valuation of the property, the tax rate, and the amount of the tax. The taxing unit applies the principles of percentage to compute the amount of the tax. When the assessed valuation of the property and the tax rate are known, the amount of the tax can be found with the following formula:

$$Tax = Assessed\ Valuation \times Tax\ Rate$$

Example: Using the rates found in the preceding example, find the amount of tax on property with an assessed valuation of $24,000 if the tax rate is expressed **(a)** to the nearest tenth of a mill per $1 and **(b)** to the nearest cent per $100.

Solution: **(a)** 45.3 mills = $0.0453
$24,000 × 0.0453 = $1,087.20

(b) $24,000 = 240 hundreds
240 × $4.53 = $1,087.20

Chapter 7. Percentage

1. Find the property tax rate to the correct cent per $100 of assessed valuation for each of the following.

	Revenue to be Collected	Total Assessed Valuation
a.	$ 432,900.00	$ 34,632,000
b.	188,034.00	5,372,400
c.	994,992.90	17,204,500
d.	71,328.45	46,842,000
e.	8,317,500.00	107,670,000
f.	993,590,064.00	35,999,640,000

2. Find the property tax rate to the correct tenth of a mill per dollar of assessed valuation for each of the following.

	Revenue to be Collected	Total Assessed Valuation
a.	$ 434,010	$ 25,530,000
b.	4,442,222	217,756,000
c.	692,640	13,320,000
d.	11,374,860	179,982,000
e.	285,313	46,842,000
f.	2,828,161	186,648,000

3. Change each of the following tax rate quotations to dollars and cents per $100 of assessed valuation.
   a. 75 mills 7.50   c. 6 mills   .60   e. 27.3 mills
   b. $0.0176 1.76   d. $0.0512   f. $0.143   14.30

4. Find the amount of tax on each of the following assessments at the rate given.

	Assessed Valuation	Tax Rate
a.	$ 8,750	$2.84 per $100
b.	15,000	$6.39 per $100
c.	18,840	56.8 mills per $1
d.	118,755	27.6 mills per $1
e.	894,120	$5.48 per $100
f.	424,860	42.6 mills per $1

5. The taxable real property in a city is assessed at $75,000,000. The amount needed to meet the expenses during the coming fiscal year is $5,250,000. The estimated receipts from other sources is $875,000. To the correct tenth of a mill, what is the tax rate per dollar of assessed valuation?

6. The assessed valuation of the taxable property in a city is $363,297,000. If the city's budget requires that $19,836,000 be obtained through property taxes, find the tax rate to the correct cent per $100 of assessed valuation.

7. The taxable real property in a city was assessed at $34,100,000. The city's budget for the coming fiscal year amounts to $918,000. Find **(a)** the tax in mills per dollar and **(b)** the amount of tax a property owner would have to pay if the realty were assessed at $65,000.

8. Linda Gerrard has a home that is assessed at 25% of its market value of $132,800. If the tax rate is 44.7 mills per dollar of assessed valuation, how much annual property tax must she pay?

9. Property having a fair market value of $150,000 is assessed at 50% of its value for tax purposes. This property is subject to a city tax of $7.18 per $100 of valuation, a county tax of $2.32 per $100 of valuation, and a recreation district tax of 41.2¢ per $100 of valuation. Find the total amount of the taxes on this property.

10. In a certain development, houses that sell for $178,500 each are located on both sides of a street, the center of which is the boundary line between Washington and Adams townships. Washington township assesses at 60% of market value and has a tax rate of $6.70 per $100 of assessed value. Adams assesses at 80% but with a rate of $4.50 per $100 of assessed value. **(a)** In which township would a buyer of one of these houses have lower property taxes? **(b)** How much lower?

REVIEW PROBLEMS

Solve these problems. If you have difficulty solving any problem, restudy the appropriate section in this chapter. The problems under a specific number are related to those contained in the exercise with the same last number.

1. Change each of the following percents to decimal notation.
   a. 9% **c.** 300% **e.** $\frac{1}{5}$% **g.** 0.7%
   b. 60% **d.** $8\frac{1}{2}$% **f.** 6.2% **h.** 45%

2. Change each of the following percents to a common fraction or mixed number in lowest terms.
   a. 30% **c.** 35% **e.** 325% **g.** $62\frac{1}{2}$%
   b. 4% **d.** 140% **f.** 4.25% **h.** $93\frac{1}{3}$%

3. Change each of the following to a percent.
   a. 0.2 **c.** 0.006 **e.** $0.00\frac{1}{2}$ **g.** $0.0\frac{1}{4}$
   b. 0.405 **d.** 4.75 **f.** $0.16\frac{2}{3}$ **h.** $1.33\frac{1}{3}$

4. Change each of the following to a percent.
   a. $\frac{1}{4}$ **b.** $\frac{5}{8}$ **c.** $\frac{1}{24}$ **d.** $3\frac{1}{2}$

5. Solve these problems.
   a. How much is 9% of $650?
   b. How much is 25% of $226?
   c. How much is 160% of $95? 152
   d. Find $16\frac{2}{3}$% of $117.

e. Find the amount that is:
   (1) 45% more than $160.
   (2) 8% more than $3,237.
   (3) 7% less than $480.
   (4) $33\frac{1}{3}$% less than $960.

f. Richard Kalman had $840 in his checking account. He wrote a check to buy a tape recorder for $258 less a 15% discount. How much did he still have in the bank?

g. Approximately $16\frac{2}{3}$% of a line of novelty goods sold by a wholesaler are returned to the wholesaler by customers. During the past year total sales of this line amounted to $557,749.80. **(1)** What is the value of the goods that were returned? **(2)** How much were the wholesaler's actual net sales of this line of goods?

h. Betty Walters earns $2,880 a month. This is 20% more than Lennie Williams earns. How much is Lennie's monthly salary?

6. Solve these problems.
   a. 198 is what percent of 264?
   b. 438 is what percent of 876?
   c. 372 is what percent of 992?
   d. $1,260 is what percent of $840?
   e. $22.80 is what percent of $80?
   f. $2.40 is what percent of $7.50?
   g. What percent of $390 is $198.90?
   h. What percent of $35 is $52.50?
   i. A young man who earns $360 a week gave his sister $99 for her birthday present. What percent of his weekly pay did he give her?
   j. A radio that cost a dealer $48 was sold for $64. The difference between the cost and the selling price is: **(1)** what percent of the cost? **(2)** what percent of the selling price?

7. Solve these problems.
   a. $90 is 18% of what amount?
   b. $567 is 40% of what amount?
   c. $42 is 6% of what amount?
   d. $405 is $12\frac{1}{2}$% of what amount?
   e. $714 is $62\frac{1}{2}$% of what amount?
   f. 25% of how many dollars is $47?
   g. What number increased by 12% of itself is 52.304?
   h. What number decreased by 10% of itself is 280.8?
   i. Peggy Kendell invested 55% of her capital in real estate and had $45,900 left. How much was her total capital?
   j. At the business college, there are 20% more women than men enrolled. How many are there of each if the total enrollment is 1,507?

8. Carol Ledgerwood bought a necklace priced at $98.50 on which the excise tax was 10% and the sales tax 5%. Find **(a)** the total tax and **(b)** the total amount that she had to pay.

9. The taxable real property in a city is assessed at $77,145,000. The city's budget for the coming fiscal year amounts to $3,187,075. Find **(a)** the tax rate per $100 of assessed valuation and **(b)** the amount of property tax on realty assessed at $89,600.

CHALLENGE PROBLEM

Ken Schmidt is considering buying a 15-unit apartment building priced at $825,000. He is thinking of offering $800,000 with a down payment of $200,000 from his 7% savings account. His bank will lend him the balance on a 12% mortgage. Monthly payments of $6,320 will pay off the loan and interest in 25 years.

Monthly rental income will be increased from $600 to $625 per apartment. A vacancy allowance of 4% is typical in that location. Schmidt estimates the following expenditures per year based on total rental income: repairs, insurance, utilities, etc., 8%; management expense, 7%. Property taxes in his area average $1\frac{1}{2}$% of selling price.

Part of the mortgage payment pays the interest and the remainder reduces the loan balance. Thus, the owner's equity (value of the property less the indebtedness) grows each month. The owner's increase in equity is the difference between the annual mortgage payments and the annual interest. Assume interest the first year is 12% of the beginning mortgage balance.

The annual depreciation allowance for the potential decrease in the building's value may cause a "paper loss" that will reduce taxes on other income. State and federal income taxes total 39%. Land does not depreciate. The land is worth 20% of the proposed purchase price. The buildings are to be depreciated at 3.5% per year.

a. Gross cash flow is the difference between annual gross income and expenses except for the mortgage payments and depreciation. The anticipated gross cash flow is what percent of the gross income?

b. The capitalization rate is the rate of gross cash flow based on the selling price. To the nearest tenth, how much is the capitalization rate?

c. Net cash flow is the gross cash flow less the mortgage payments. To the nearest tenth, net cash flow is what percent of gross income?

d. Gross income multiplier is the number of times that the selling price is larger than annual gross income. To the nearest tenth, how much is the gross income multiplier?

e. Complete this schedule:

Gross Cash Flow $_____

Less: Interest Expense   _____

    Depreciation   _____

Taxable Income or (Loss)   _____

Tax Benefit (if any)   _____

Equity Increase (Initial)   _____

Net Cash Flow   _____

    Total Current Return   _____

Rate of Return on Owner's Investment   _____

f. Based on this information, should Schmidt offer to buy the building at a price of $800,000 and a down payment of $200,000? Why?

Chapter 8

Simple Interest

Objectives

After mastering the material in Chapter 8, you will be able to:

- Find the number of days between two dates.
- Calculate exact and ordinary interest on notes and drafts.
- Use the interest formula to find the principal, the rate, or the time on a loan.
- Use tables to find simple interest and time on a loan.
- Find the due dates of promissory notes and time drafts.
- Compute bank discount on interest-bearing and non-interest-bearing negotiable instruments.
- Calculate partial payments on notes in accordance with the United States Rule and the Merchants' Rule.

Ronald Stern borrowed $10,000 at 9% from his mother for a business investment. One year later, he paid off the debt by giving her $10,900. In this manner, he paid his mother $900 for the use of the $10,000 for one year.

The amount paid for the use of borrowed money is called **interest.** The money that is borrowed is the **principal.** The percent that is charged for the use of the principal for one year is the **rate** or **rate of interest.** The length of time for which interest is paid is the **time,** which is expressed in years, months, or days. The date on which the principal and interest are to be paid is the **due date** or **maturity date.** The sum of the principal and interest that are to be paid on the due date is the **maturity value.**

Simple interest is paid on the principal only. It is usually paid on loans that extend for a relatively short period of time. **Compound interest** means that the interest for one period is added to the principal before interest is computed for the next period. Compound interest, in which the interest for one period becomes principal in the next period, is commonly reserved for long-term obligations. Only simple interest is considered in this chapter. Compound interest is considered in the next chapter.

The first paragraph of this chapter illustrates a single-payment loan. Ronald paid his mother with a single payment at the end of the specified term of one year. The maturity value of a single-payment loan may consist of principal plus interest, as in the first paragraph, or it may consist of principal only. The latter occurs when the loan is non-interest-bearing or when the interest is paid in advance.

FIGURING TIME

The amount of interest paid for the use of money depends on the length of time for which the money is borrowed. In other words, if the interest rates are equal, the interest on a $500 loan for 1 year is twice the interest on a $500 loan for 6 months. The length of time for which interest is charged is often computed to the nearest day. Thus, computing the exact number of days between two dates may be necessary in order to calculate interest on a loan.

In computing the number of days for interest calculations, usually the first day is omitted and the last day is counted. Omitting the first day is accomplished by subtracting the number representing the first date from the number of days in the month of origin. This gives the number of days remaining in the month.

Example A: A loan that is dated July 7 falls due on September 5 of the same year. Find the exact number of days between these two dates.

Solution:

31	days in July
7	date of note (July 7)
24	days remaining in July
31	days in August
5	days in September (due date)
60	days from July 7 to September 5

When the exact number of days between two dates is being computed, the exact number of days in each month must be known and leap years recognized. Following is a list of the months and the number of days in each.

January	31 days	July	31 days
February	28 days*	August	31 days
March	31 days	September	30 days
April	30 days	October	31 days
May	31 days	November	30 days
June	30 days	December	31 days

*29 days in a leap year

One year is the length of time required for the earth to make one revolution around the sun. This time has been computed to be 365 days, 5 hours, 48 minutes, and 46 seconds, which is approximately $365\frac{1}{4}$ days. To keep the seasons from changing drastically over the centuries, the fractional part of a day that is lost in most years is made up by adding a day to February every four years. Making February have 29 days in leap years, instead of the usual 28 days, gives slightly too much time. The extra time is partially eliminated by considering only century dates that are divisible by 400 to be leap years. The slight remaining variation causes the Gregorian calendar to be in error by only 1 day in 3,323 years.

As a general rule, leap years are those in which the calendar-year dates are divisible by 4, such as 1988, 1992, and 1996. The exception to this rule is that only those century dates that are divisible by 400 are leap years. Therefore, 1800 and 1900 were not leap years, but the year 2000 will be a leap year.

Example B: Find the exact number of days between January 11 and March 21 if both dates fall within the same leap year.

Solution:

31	days in January
11	beginning date (January 11)
20	days remaining in January
29	days in February of a leap year
21	days in March (ending date)
70	days from January 11 to March 21

Unless February of a leap year falls between the two dates, there are 365 days from any date in one year to the same date in the following year. In a leap year, of course, there are 366 days.

Example C: Find the exact number of days from November 12, 1989 to March 24, 1991.

Solution:

November 12, 1989 to November 12, 1990 = 365 days
November 12, 1990 to November 30, 1990 = 18 days
December, 1990 = 31 days
January, 1991 = 31 days
February, 1991 = 28 days
to March 24, 1991 = 24 days
497 days

● Exercise 8-1

Find the exact number of days in each problem.

1. March 12 to May 12

2. June 22 to August 25

3. October 15, 1990 to March 17, 1991

4. May 14 to August 15

5. August 15 to October 29

Chapter 8. Simple Interest   213

6. April 24 to August 6

7. June 15 to September 4

8. October 18 to December 12

9. January 28 to May 10 of a leap year

10. September 29, 1993 to December 2, 1994

11. May 7 to November 2

12. June 17 to September 7

13. December 9, 1989 to June 1, 1990

14. February 7, 1988 to July 23, 1988

15. July 12, 1991 to November 14, 1991

16. November 14, 1989 to January 20, 1990

SIMPLE INTEREST FORMULA

Simple interest is the product of the principal multiplied by the rate and time. This may be stated as the formula:

$$Interest = Principal \times Rate \times Time$$
or
$$I = PRT$$

The rate may be expressed in the formula as a decimal or as a common fraction. If pencil and paper are used for the computation, canceling is facilitated when the rate is expressed as a common fraction.

Example A: Find **(a)** the interest and **(b)** the maturity value of a $900 loan at 12% for 2 years.

Solution: **(a)** Interest = Principal × Rate × Time

$$I = \$9\cancel{0}\cancel{0} \times \frac{12}{1\cancel{0}\cancel{0}} \times 2 = \$216$$

(b) Maturity Value = Principal + Interest
Maturity Value = $900 + $216
Maturity Value = $1,116

Simple interest rates are commonly quoted on a **per annum** basis. That is, when the rate is said to be 12%, it is understood to mean that the interest charge is 12¢ for the use of one dollar for one year. In the computation of simple interest, therefore, the quantity of time used is expressed as a multiple or a fractional part of one year. If the time is stated in months, that number of months is placed over 12 in the formula. When a calculator is used for the computation, the percent sign may be used.

Part 2. Mathematics Applications in Starting a Business

| Example B: | Find the interest on $900 at 12% for 6 months. |
| Solution: | $I = 900 \boxed{\times} 12 \boxed{\%} \boxed{\times} 6 \boxed{\div} 12 \boxed{=} \longrightarrow 54$, means $54 |

Exact Interest. If the time is stated in days, that number of days is placed over 360 or 365, depending on whether ordinary or exact interest is being computed. The federal government and federal reserve banks make interest computations based on the calendar year of 365 days (366 in a leap year). Interest computed on the basis of the calendar year of 365 days is **exact interest.**

| Example: | Find the exact interest on $900 at 12% for 90 days. |
| Solution: | $I = \$900 \times 0.12 \times \dfrac{90}{365} = \$26.63$ |

Ordinary Interest. Most businesses in the United States compute simple interest on the basis of the **business year,** which is assumed to consist of 12 months of 30 days each. Interest computed on the basis of the business year of 360 days is **ordinary interest.**

| Example: | Find the ordinary interest on $900 at 12% for 90 days. |
| Solution: | $I = \$900 \times 12\% \times \dfrac{90}{360} = \$27.00$ |

As a comparison of the two preceding examples reveals, ordinary interest is higher than exact interest. Exact interest is $\frac{5}{365}$, which is $\frac{1}{73}$, less than ordinary interest.

In this book if exact interest is not specified, assume that ordinary interest is to be calculated.

● Exercise 8–2

A. In each of the following, find the ordinary interest to the nearest cent by using the formula method.

1. $240 at 12% for 2 years

2. $360 at 10% for $1\frac{1}{2}$ years

3. $720 at 14% for 3 years

4. $480 at 8% for $2\frac{1}{4}$ years

5. $5,600 at 14% for $1\frac{3}{4}$ years

6. $18,900 at 16% for 1 year

7. $980 at 12% for 6 months

8. $4,630 at 8% for 9 months

9. $1,261 at 14% for 8 months

10. $307 at 12% for 15 months

11. $419 at 16% for 7 months

12. $2,856 at 10% for 5 months

B. In each of the following, find **(a)** the ordinary interest by using the 360-day year and **(b)** the exact interest by using the 365-day year.

1. $993.00 at 18% for 90 days

2. $612.50 at 14% for 120 days

Chapter 8. Simple Interest

3. $9,442 at 12% for 60 days

4. $6,547 at 10% for 180 days

5. $1,965.80 at $17\frac{1}{2}$% for 30 days

6. $59,240 at $19\frac{1}{2}$% for 240 days

7. $3,809.00 at $16\frac{1}{4}$% for 45 days

8. $1,510.30 at $18\frac{3}{4}$% for 75 days

C. Solve these problems.

1. Ying Chou borrowed $3,785 from a friend and promised to repay him in 9 months plus 12% interest. How much interest will he pay when the loan matures?

2. Karen Cooper borrowed $2,450 and $975 both for 1 year at $15\frac{1}{2}$%. How much interest will she pay for these loans?

3. Fred Day lent his friend $750 for $2\frac{1}{2}$ years at 10% simple interest. What is the maturity value of this loan?

4. Jennifer Donahue borrowed $3,450 for 1 year and 3 months at 18% simple interest. What is the maturity value of this loan?

5. At the beginning of the year, James Ellis had $2,145.50 in an account that earns $10\frac{1}{2}$% interest. How much interest was added to his account at the end of the first quarter (3 months) if he made no additions or withdrawals during this time?

6. Sally Fischer owns 7 bonds with a face value of $1,000 each. How much interest does she receive quarterly (3 months) if the interest rate is $9\frac{1}{4}$% a year?

VARIABLES IN THE SIMPLE INTEREST FORMULA

The simple interest formula may be used to find some variable other than interest. When any three of the variables are given, the fourth may be found by substituting the known quantities in the formula $PRT = I$ and solving for the unknown.

Finding the Principal

In interest problems in which principal is the unknown, the rate, the time, and the interest will be given or can be found.

Example: How much is the principal if the interest is $27, the time 90 days, and the rate 9%?

Solution: Using the symbols in the simple interest formula, P is the unknown, $R = 9\%$, $T = \frac{90}{360}$, and $I = \$27$. Therefore:

$$P \times 9\% \times \frac{90}{360} = \$27$$
$$P \times 0.0225 = 27$$
$$P = 27 \div 0.0225$$
$$P = \$1,200$$

Part 2. Mathematics Applications in Starting a Business

Or

means $1,200

Finding the Rate of Interest

When the rate is the unknown, the principal, the time, and the interest will be given in the problem or can be found.

Example:

What interest rate is paid if the interest is $15, the principal $750, and the time 45 days?

Solution:

Using the symbols in the simple interest formula, $P = \$750$, R is the unknown, $T = \frac{45}{360}$, and $I = \$15$. Therefore:

$$750 \times R \times \frac{45}{360} = 15$$
$$R \times 93.75 = 15$$
$$R = 15 \div 93.75$$
$$R = 0.16 = 16\%$$

Or

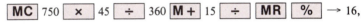

means 16%

Finding the Time

When the time in days, months, or years is the unknown, the principal, the rate, and the interest will be given in the problem or can be found. When computing time in days, use the 360-day year unless the problem specifies that exact interest should be used.

Example A:

What is the time in days if the interest rate is 15%, the principal $1,200, and the interest $37.50?

Solution:

Using the symbols in the simple interest formula $PRT = I$, $P = \$1,200$, $R = 15\%$, T is the unknown, which is $\frac{T}{360}$ days, and $I = \$37.50$. Therefore:

$$1,200 \times 15\% \times \frac{T}{360} = 37.50$$
$$0.5T = 37.50$$
$$T = 37.50 \div 0.5$$
$$T = 75 \text{ days}$$

Or

MC 1200 × 15 % ÷ 360 M+ 37.5 ÷ MR = → 75,

means 75 days

If time is desired in months, use 12 as the denominator under T in the formula.

Example B: What is the time in months if the interest rate is 14%, the principal $1,500, and the interest $52.50?

Solution: Using the symbols in the formula $PRT = I$, $P = \$1,500$, $R = 14\%$, T is the unknown, which is $\frac{T}{12}$ months, and $I = \$52.50$. Therefore:

$$1,500 \times 14\% \times \frac{T}{12} = 52.50$$

$$17.5T = 52.50$$
$$T = 52.50 \div 17.5$$
$$T = 3 \text{ months}$$

Or

means 3 months

● Exercise 8–3

A. Find the principal in each of the following.

	Rate	Time	Interest
1.	18%	90 days	$ 162.00
2.	12%	120 days	43.36
3.	14%	6 months	262.50
4.	$17\frac{1}{2}\%$	8 months	2,447.08

B. Find the interest rate to the nearest 0.1% in each of the following.

	Principal	Time	Interest
1.	$ 900.00	96 days	$ 38.40
2.	1,876.00	150 days	70.35
3.	5,485.00	4 months	237.68
4.	19,237.00	9 months	1,514.92

C. Find the time in days based on the 360-day year in each of the following.

	Principal	Rate	Interest
1.	$ 750.00	12%	$ 16.50
2.	3,245.00	14%	136.29
3.	8,169.00	16%	1,143.66
4.	27,837.00	$19\frac{1}{2}\%$	3,256.93

D. Solve these problems.

1. Interest income of $516 was earned in 8 months on an investment at 12%. How much was invested?

Part 2. Mathematics Applications in Starting a Business

2. What principal will yield $201.60 interest in 3 years at 16% simple interest?

3. What rate must $400 earn for 3 years and 6 months to produce $224 interest?

4. A note for $3,600 was repaid after 135 days with a payment of $3,802.50. What was the rate of interest on the note?

5. How many days are needed for $2,000 to produce $60 interest at 12%?

6. How many months are needed for $390 to yield $13.65 interest at 14%?

7. How many days are needed for $5,700 to amount to $6,080 at 10% simple interest?

8. What principal will accumulate to $4,073.50 in 2 years at 15% simple interest?

FINDING THE TIME AND INTEREST BY USING TABLES

Employees of banks and financial companies who frequently compute interest may do so by using time and interest tables.

Finding the Number of Days by Using a Time Table

Table 8–1 shows the number of each day of the year counting from January 1, which is day number 1, to December 31, which is day number 365. To find the number of days between two dates in the same year, simply subtract the beginning-date number from the ending-date number.

Example: Find the exact number of days from February 17 to July 15 by using Table 8–1.

Solution:
1. Ending-date number: 196   (July 15)
2. Beginning-date number: 48   (February 17)
3. Number of days: 148

Explanation:
1. Find the day-of-the-year number for the ending date (July 15) by finding the number (196) that occupies line 15 in the July column.
2. Find the day-of-the-year number for the beginning date (February 17) by finding the number (48) that occupies line 17 in the February column.
3. Subtract the beginning-date number from the ending-date number.

When the time period includes February 29 during a leap year, 1 day is added to the ending-date number. Thus, for a leap year 48 would be subtracted from 197 to reveal 149 days from February 17 to July 15.

If the time period extends from one year into the following year, find the number of days in each year and add.

Chapter 8. Simple Interest   219

Day of Month	Jan.	Feb.	Mar.	Apr.	May	June	July	Aug.	Sept.	Oct.	Nov.	Dec.	Day of Month
1	1	32	60	91	121	152	182	213	244	274	305	335	1
2	2	33	61	92	122	153	183	214	245	275	306	336	2
3	3	34	62	93	123	154	184	215	246	276	307	337	3
4	4	35	63	94	124	155	185	216	247	277	308	338	4
5	5	36	64	95	125	156	186	217	248	278	309	339	5
6	6	37	65	96	126	157	187	218	249	279	310	340	6
7	7	38	66	97	127	158	188	219	250	280	311	341	7
8	8	39	67	98	128	159	189	220	251	281	312	342	8
9	9	40	68	99	129	160	190	221	252	282	313	343	9
10	10	41	69	100	130	161	191	222	253	283	314	344	10
11	11	42	70	101	131	162	192	223	254	284	315	345	11
12	12	43	71	102	132	163	193	224	255	285	316	346	12
13	13	44	72	103	133	164	194	225	256	286	317	347	13
14	14	45	73	104	134	165	195	226	257	287	318	348	14
15	15	46	74	105	135	166	196	227	258	288	319	349	15
16	16	47	75	106	136	167	197	228	259	289	320	350	16
17	17	48	76	107	137	168	198	229	260	290	321	351	17
18	18	49	77	108	138	169	199	230	261	291	322	352	18
19	19	50	78	109	139	170	200	231	262	292	323	353	19
20	20	51	79	110	140	171	201	232	263	293	324	354	20
21	21	52	80	111	141	172	202	233	264	294	325	355	21
22	22	53	81	112	142	173	203	234	265	295	326	356	22
23	23	54	82	113	143	174	204	235	266	296	327	357	23
24	24	55	83	114	144	175	205	236	267	297	328	358	24
25	25	56	84	115	145	176	206	237	268	298	329	359	25
26	26	57	85	116	146	177	207	238	269	299	330	360	26
27	27	58	86	117	147	178	208	239	270	300	331	361	27
28	28	59	87	118	148	179	209	240	271	301	332	362	28
29	29	*	88	119	149	180	210	241	272	302	333	363	29
30	30	....	89	120	150	181	211	242	273	303	334	364	30
31	31	....	90	....	151	....	212	243	....	304	....	365	31

*For leap years, February has 29 days and the number of each day after February 28 is one greater than the number given in the table.

Table 8–1 The Number of Each Day of the Year

Example:

Find the exact number of days from October 30 to June 24 by using Table 8–1.

Solution:

End-of-year number:	365	(December 31)
Beginning-date number:	303	(October 30)
Days remaining in year:	62	
plus		
Ending-date number:	175	(June 24)
Number of days:	237	

Part 2. Mathematics Applications in Starting a Business

Use Table 8–1 to find the exact number of days in each problem.

1. January 16, 1989 to September 14, 1989

2. August 14, 1987 to December 8, 1987

3. March 23, 1989 to June 20, 1989

4. February 18, 1989 to November 5, 1989

5. December 12, 1989 to October 8, 1990

6. April 7, 1991 to September 11, 1992

7. May 17, 1990 to December 3, 1990

8. September 18, 1992 to April 26, 1993

9. August 13, 1989 to June 12, 1990

10. November 18, 1991 to August 17, 1992 *(273)*

11. June 10, 1990 to April 11, 1991

12. February 9, 1991 to October 14, 1991

13. July 15, 1989 to November 18, 1989

14. October 28, 1989 to March 25, 1990

Finding the Interest by Using a Simple Interest Table

Table 8–2 may be used to compute both ordinary and exact simple interest. It shows the simple interest on $1,000 at 1% for various numbers of days. Many interest computations can be made rapidly and accurately by using the interest table.

By using the interest on $1,000 at 1% as the starting point, interest on any other principal at any rate can be found. The three steps used in the procedure are:

1. Find the ordinary or exact interest on $1,000 at 1% for the *time* desired. (In this step the factors may be added to obtain interest for the correct number of days.)
2. Convert the interest found in Step 1 from 1% to the desired *rate* by using the appropriate multiple. (5 × 1% = 5%)
3. Convert the interest found in Step 2 from interest on $1,000 by multiplying it by the *principal divided by 1,000.*

Days	Ordinary Interest	Exact Interest	Days	Ordinary Interest	Exact Interest
1	0.027 7778	0.027 3973	150	4.166 6667	4.109 5890
2	0.055 5556	0.054 7945	160	4.444 4444	4.383 5616
3	0.083 3333	0.082 1918	170	4.722 2222	4.657 5342
4	0.111 1111	0.109 5890	180	5.000 0000	4.931 5068
5	0.138 8889	0.136 9863	190	5.277 7778	5.205 4795
6	0.166 6667	0.164 3836	200	5.555 5556	5.479 4521
7	0.194 4444	0.191 7808	210	5.833 3333	5.753 4247
8	0.222 2222	0.219 1781	220	6.111 1111	6.027 3973
9	0.250 0000	0.246 5753	230	6.388 8889	6.301 3699
10	0.277 7778	0.273 9726	240	6.666 6667	6.575 3425
20	0.555 5556	0.547 9452	250	6.944 4444	6.849 3151
30	0.833 3333	0.821 9178	260	7.222 2222	7.123 2877
40	1.111 1111	1.095 8904	270	7.500 0000	7.397 2603
50	1.388 8889	1.369 8630	280	7.777 7778	7.671 2329
60	1.666 6667	1.643 8356	290	8.055 5556	7.945 2055
70	1.944 4444	1.917 8082	300	8.333 3333	8.219 1781
80	2.222 2222	2.191 7808	310	8.611 1111	8.493 1507
90	2.500 0000	2.465 7534	320	8.888 8889	8.767 1233
100	2.777 7778	2.739 7260	330	9.166 6667	9.041 0959
110	3.055 5556	3.013 6986	340	9.444 4444	9.315 0685
120	3.333 3333	3.287 6712	350	9.722 2222	9.589 0411
130	3.611 1111	3.561 6438	360	10.000 0000	9.863 0137
140	3.888 8889	3.835 6164	.....	....	....

Table 8-2 Ordinary and Exact Simple Interest on 1000 at 1%

Example A:

Find the ordinary interest on $475 at $16\frac{1}{2}\%$ for 25 days by using Table 8-2.

Solution:

1. Ordinary interest on $1,000 at 1% for 20 days = 0.555 5556
   Ordinary interest on $1,000 at 1% for __5 days = 0.138 8889__
   Ordinary interest on $1,000 at 1% for 25 days = 0.694 4445

2. Ordinary interest on $1,000 for 25 days at 16.5%:

$$16.5 \times 0.694 4445 = 11.458334$$

3. Ordinary interest for 25 days at 16.5% on $475:

$$\$0.475 \times 11.458334 = \$5.442 = \$5.44$$

Subscripts—letters, numerals, or other symbols written slightly below the writing line—are sometimes used in formulas. For example, R_1 and R_2, which are read as "R sub one" and "R sub two," may be used to represent two different rates. The use of R_1 and R_2 rather than letters such as x and y is

Part 2. Mathematics Applications in Starting a Business

preferable because the fact that both quantities are rates is emphasized, and the subscripts 1 and 2 distinguish between the two rates. Generally, the size of the subscript has no relationship to the size of the quantity. That is, a rate represented by R_2 is not necessarily larger than a rate represented by R_1. Subscripts, then, may be used to distinguish one quantity from another. They also may be used as reminders. For instance, in R_{14} the subscript may be a reminder that the rate is 14%. Subscript symbols do not enter into calculations as do exponents, which are **superscripts** written slightly above the line.

Some people believe that solving a problem with a calculator is easier when there is a formula to follow. The procedure of finding simple interest by using Table 8–2 may be summarized in the following formula:

$$I_{o\backslash n} = FR \frac{B}{1000}$$

$I = $ Interest
$o = $ ordinary (reminder only)
$n = $ number of days (reminder only)
$F = $ Factor in table
$R = $ Rate (without % sign)
$B = $ Balance owed (principal)

Using this formula and Table 8–2 gives the following solution to the problem in Example A:

Solution:

$$I_{o\backslash 25} = 0.6944445 \times 16.5 \times \frac{475}{1000}$$

$$I_{o\backslash 25} = \$5.44$$

Finding exact interest may be accomplished in a similar manner.

Example B: Find the exact interest on $6,500 at $9\frac{3}{4}$% for 243 days by using Table 8–2.

Solution:

1. Exact interest on $1,000 at 1% for 240 days = 6.575 3425
   Exact interest on $1,000 at 1% for ___3 days = 0.082 1918
   Exact interest on $1,000 at 1% for 243 days = 6.657 5343

2. Exact interest on $1,000 for 243 days at $9\frac{3}{4}$%:

$$9.75 \times 6.657\ 5343 = 64.910959$$

3. Exact interest for 243 days at $9\frac{3}{4}$% on $6,500:

$$\$6.5 \times 64.910959 = \$421.92$$

Or

$$I_{\overline{x}\backslash n} = FR \frac{B}{1000}$$

$$I_{\overline{x}\backslash 243} = 6.6575343 \times 9.75 \times \frac{6500}{1000}$$

$$I_{\overline{x}\backslash 243} = \$421.92$$

Chapter 8. Simple Interest

223

- Exercise 8–5

A. Use Table 8–2 to find the ordinary interest for each of the following.

1. $435 at 16% for 30 days
2. $2,500 at 18% for 70 days
3. $7,450 at 17% for 65 days
4. $650 at $17\frac{1}{2}$% for 96 days
5. $97,500 at $16\frac{1}{2}$% for 143 days

6. $1,250 at $9\frac{3}{4}$% for 210 days
7. $23,500 at 12% for 187 days
8. $19,750 at 10% for 229 days
9. $342.60 at $18\frac{1}{2}$% for 262 days
10. $850.25 at 12% for 308 days

B. Use Table 8–2 to find the exact interest for each of the following.

1. $3,600 at 12% for 95 days
2. $4,200 at 16% for 130 days
3. $4,350 at 18% for 47 days
4. $7,600 at 14% for 47 days
5. $1,350 at $19\frac{1}{2}$% for 134 days

6. $4,608 at $17\frac{1}{2}$% for 241 days
7. $6,450 at 20% for 166 days
8. $73,500 at $17\frac{1}{2}$% for 347 days
9. $850 at 15% for 239 days
10. $470.80 at $20\frac{1}{4}$% for 236 days

C. Where applicable, use Table 8–1 and Table 8–2 to solve these problems.

1. Find the ordinary interest on $750 at 16% from April 14 to July 18.

2. Find the exact interest on $75,000 at 15% from March 21 to August 23.

3. Sonoma Company charges 18 percent ordinary interest at exact time on overdue bills. Find the amount needed to pay in full a bill for $2,325 that was due on March 27 but not paid until June 13.

4. Chester Miller borrowed $2,850 from Ed Nichols on June 15. He paid the debt with ordinary interest at 14% on October 22. Find the total amount that Miller paid to cancel this debt.

5. A business person borrowed $2,500 on September 18 at $9\frac{1}{2}$% exact interest. If the loan was repaid on the next April 11, how much interest was paid?

6. A business debt of $825 was incurred on March 22 and paid on July 15 with exact interest at $20\frac{1}{2}$%. Find the amount due.

7. If a loan for $3,450 that was borrowed on May 12 at 11% ordinary interest was repaid in full on November 7, how much was the maturity value of the loan?

8. Sharon Mason borrowed $3,750 at $18\frac{3}{4}$% exact interest. How much was the interest charge if she made the loan on April 13 and repaid it on January 19 of the following year?

NEGOTIABLE INSTRUMENTS

Generally whenever a business document of value is readily transferable from one person to another, it is said to be **negotiable. Negotiable instruments** are written promises or orders to pay money that may be transferred by the process of negotiation. To be negotiable legally, an instrument must be:

1. In writing.
2. Signed by the maker or drawer.
3. An unconditional promise or order to pay a certain sum of money.
4. Payable on demand or at a fixed or determinable future date.
5. Payable to a designated person or to that person's order or to bearer.

The common types of negotiable instruments are: (1) checks, including ordinary bank checks, certified checks, bank drafts, cashier's checks, money orders, and travelers' checks; (2) promissory notes, including unsecured notes, as well as mortgage notes and conditional sales notes; and (3) bills of exchange or drafts, including time drafts, sight drafts, and trade acceptances.

A **check** is a negotiable instrument that is drawn on a bank and payable on demand. The depositor who writes the check on his or her account is the **drawer;** the bank that is ordered to pay is the **drawee;** and the person to whom the sum of money is to be paid is the **payee.** As checks ordinarily do not draw interest, they are not discussed further in this chapter.

A **negotiable promissory note** is defined in the Uniform Commercial Code as an unconditional promise in writing made by one person to another, signed by the maker, engaging to pay on demand or at a particular future time a sum certain in money to order or to bearer. The person who makes the promise to pay is the **maker** of the note. The person to whom payment is to be made is the **payee.** The specified sum of money to be paid is the **principal** or **face value** of the note. The length of time that the note runs is its **term.** In Figure 8–1, the maker is Herbert Garner; the payee is Dover Appliance Store; the face value of the note is $800; and the term of the note is 3 months. Promissory notes may be interest-bearing or non-interest-bearing. The note in Figure 8–1 bears interest at 18 percent.

$ 800.00	Urbana, IL 61801	July 23, 19 --
Three months	AFTER DATE __I__ PROMISE TO PAY TO	
THE ORDER OF ___The Dover Appliance Store___		
Eight hundred and no/100 - - - - - - - - - - - - - - - DOLLARS		
PAYABLE AT ___Security National Bank___		
VALUE RECEIVED WITH INTEREST AT 18% per annum		
No. 14 DUE October 23, 19--	*Herbert Garner*	

Figure 8–1 A Promissory Note

Notes are used for a variety of purposes in business. A business may purchase equipment or other assets by giving a note to delay payment in full. A customer who is unable to pay an account on the due date may offer a note to the creditor. Many businesses regularly use notes to borrow money from banks for working capital. Of the many kinds of negotiable instruments in business, the promissory note is used most frequently when interest is charged.

A **bill of exchange** or **draft** is an unconditional order in writing addressed by one person to another. It is signed by the person giving it and requires the person to whom it is addressed to pay on demand or at a fixed or determinable future time a sum certain in money to order or to bearer. It is, in effect, an order by one person on a second person to pay a sum of money to a third person. The person who makes the order is the **drawer,** the person on whom the order to pay is drawn is the **drawee,** and the person to whom payment is to be made is the **payee.** The drawer may designate himself or herself to be the payee. In Figure 8–2, the drawer is Roberta Hawkins, the drawee is John Griffon, and the payee is Juan Garcia.

A drawee who is ordered by a commercial draft to pay money is not legally bound to do so unless the drawee accepts the order. This may be done by writing "Accepted" and signing on the front of the draft. After acceptance the drawee may be identified as the **acceptor.** The commercial draft is treated as a promissory note after the drawee has accepted, for the drawee then has promised to pay the sum of money.

```
$ 400.00                    Bloomington, IN 47401      May 7, 19 --

              Three months after date                         PAY TO

THE ORDER OF ____ Juan Garcia

        Four hundred and no/100 - - - - - - - - - - - - - - DOLLARS

VALUE RECEIVED AND CHARGE TO ACCOUNT OF

To  John Griffon

     4128 Hawthorne Avenue                Roberta Hawkins
```

Figure 8–2 An After-Date Time Draft

Finding the Due Dates of Negotiable Instruments

The **due date** of a promissory note or time draft is the date on which payment is due. Although time is counted forward from a specific date in each case, time is counted forward from the date of origin for a note and from the date of acceptance for an after-sight time draft.

Finding the Due Date of a Note. The term of a note is often expressed in days. When the term of a note is expressed in days, the due date is exactly that number of days after the date of the note. That is, the due date of a 60-day note is exactly 60 days from the date of the note. The exact number of days in each month of the term must be considered.

Example A: Find the due date of a 60-day note dated April 18.

Solution:
$$
\begin{aligned}
\text{April 18 to April 30} &= \ \ 12 \text{ days}\\
\text{May} &= \ \underline{\ 31} \text{ days}\\
\text{Subtotal} &= \ \ 43 \text{ days}\\
60 - 43 &= \ \underline{\ 17} \text{ days in next month}\\
\text{Total} &= \ \ 60 \text{ days}
\end{aligned}
$$

Due Date: June 17

Table 8–1 also may be used to find the due date.

Example B: A 60-day note is dated June 4. Use Table 8–1 to find the due date.

Solution:
1. June 4 is Day No.   155
   Add term of note: _60_
   Day No. of due date   215

2. Due date (Day No. 215) is August 3

When the term of a note is expressed in months or years, the due date falls on the same date in the appropriate number of subsequent months or years. In other words, time is counted forward for the number of months or years given, and the due date falls on the same day of the month. If this date does not appear in the month of maturity, the last date of the month is used. Thus, a one-month note dated August 31 falls due on September 30.

Example C: Find the due date of a two-month note dated June 4.

Solution:
$$
\begin{aligned}
\text{June 4 to July 4} &= 1 \text{ month}\\
\text{July 4 to August 4} &= \underline{1 \text{ month}}\\
&\ \ \ \ 2 \text{ months}
\end{aligned}
$$

Due Date: August 4

Finding the Due Date of a Time Draft. Three drafts commonly used in business transactions are sight drafts, time drafts, and trade acceptances.

A **sight draft** (Figure 8–3) is payable at sight; that is, on presentation of the draft to the drawee. After other methods have failed, a sight draft may be used as a collection device. The creditor draws a sight draft on a debtor and sends it to the debtor's bank for collection. The debtor is notified by the bank that the sight draft has been received, and then must either pay the draft at once or refuse to do so.

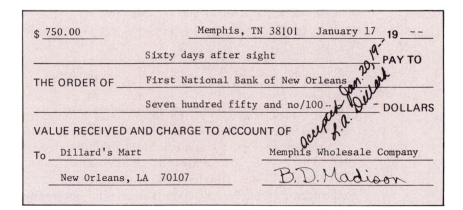

$ 600.00

Chicago, IL 60690   November 2, 19 – –

At Sight   PAY TO

THE ORDER OF   Liberty National Bank

Six hundred and no/100 – – – – – – – – – DOLLARS

VALUE RECEIVED AND CHARGE TO ACCOUNT OF

To   Rosa Martinez   Midwest Wholesale Company

Springfield, IL 62701   *Bruce Clark*

Figure 8–3 A Sight Draft

This procedure is generally more effective than a collection letter because the debtor usually wants to maintain a good credit record with the bank. Sight drafts are also used by sellers for out-of-town shipments of merchandise when they wish to collect before the goods are delivered. For example, an order bill of lading, which leaves title to the merchandise with the seller, is sent to a bank in the buyer's city with a sight draft covering all the charges for the goods. The buyer must pay the amount of the sight draft before the bank will release the bill of lading for the goods. The buyer must obtain the bill of lading in order to get the merchandise from the transportation company. This procedure may be desirable if the buyer has a poor credit rating.

A **time draft** is payable after the lapse of a period of time, such as a certain number of days after sight (Figure 8–4), after date (Figure 8–2), or on a specific date (for example, April 20). Notice that the draft in Figure 8–4 is marked "Accepted" and signed by L. A. Dillard, the drawee. At the time when a draft is drawn, it is simply a written request for payment. As soon as it is accepted by the drawee, it becomes a negotiable instrument.

$ 750.00

Memphis, TN 38101   January 17 19 – –

Sixty days after sight   PAY TO

THE ORDER OF   First National Bank of New Orleans

Seven hundred fifty and no/100 – – – – – – DOLLARS

VALUE RECEIVED AND CHARGE TO ACCOUNT OF

To   Dillard's Mart   Memphis Wholesale Company

New Orleans, LA 70107   *B. D. Madison*

Accepted Jan 20, 19 – –
L. A. Dillard

Figure 8–4 An After-Sight Draft

A time draft may be used as a means of securing a more negotiable form of obligation from a customer who has purchased on credit. It may also be attached to a bill of lading in the manner described for the sight draft. In either case, after the draft is accepted, the seller is protected by a negotiable instrument that may be discounted at a bank if cash is needed at once. **Discounting** negotiable instruments means that the interest is deducted in advance rather than paid at maturity.

A **trade acceptance** (Figure 8–5) is a special form of time draft that arises from a current sale of goods. It always has a statement to this effect printed on its face. Many notes result from the settlement of past-due charge accounts. Because trade acceptances grow out of current sales of goods, most bankers believe they are less likely to be dishonored at maturity.

TRADE ACCEPTANCE

No. ___97___   Houston, TX 77002   August 14, 19 ___--___

TO ___Moore's Department Store___   Tampa, FL 33606

ON ___October 14, 19--___ PAY TO THE ORDER OF ___Ourselves___

___One thousand five hundred and no/100___ DOLLARS ($1,500.00)

The transaction which gives rise to this instrument is the purchase of goods by the acceptor from the drawer. The drawee may accept this bill payable at any bank, banker, or trust company in the United States which he may designate.

ACCEPTED AT ___Tampa, FL___ ON ___Aug. 18___ 19--

PAYABLE AT ___Second National___ BANK

BANK LOCATION ___Tampa, FL 33606___ } Houston Products Co.

BUYER'S SIGNATURE *Moore's Dept. Store*

BY AGENT OR OFFICER *G. G. Moore* / By *J B Lomas*

Figure 8–5 A Trade Acceptance

Like that of a note, the due date of an after-date time draft is found by counting the number of days or months from the date on which the draft is drawn. The due date of an after-sight draft is found by counting the time from the date of acceptance.

Example:

Find the due date of a draft that is payable 90 days after sight. The draft, which was accepted on August 10, is dated August 8.

Solution:

Term of the draft is 90 days after sight, i.e., after the date of acceptance, which is August 10.

$$
\begin{array}{rl}
\text{August 10 to August 31} = & 21 \text{ days} \\
\text{September} = & 30 \text{ days} \\
\text{October} = & \underline{31} \text{ days} \\
\text{Subtotal} = & 82 \text{ days} \\
90 - 82 = & \underline{8} \text{ days in next month} \\
& 90 \text{ days}
\end{array}
$$

Due Date: November 8

- Exercise 8–6

  A. Find the due date of each of the following notes.

Date of Note	Term
1. March 8	60 days
2. August 2	90 days
3. June 17	120 days
4. April 23	145 days
5. May 5	3 months
6. October 31	4 months
7. January 21	6 months
8. February 16 (leap year)	72 days
9. July 12, 1990	2 years
10. November 27, 1991	$1\frac{1}{2}$ years

  B. Find the due date of each of the following drafts.

Date of Draft	Term	Date of Acceptance
1.	June 14	60 days after date	June 21
2.	August 25	45 days after date	September 4
3.	October 12	75 days after sight	October 20
4.	March 20	90 days after sight	April 7
5.	February 8	3 months after date	February 15
6.	May 7	6 months after sight	May 12
7.	July 18	120 days after date	July 16
8.	April 9	4 months after sight	April 21

Discounting Negotiable Instruments

A business person who is in need of funds for two or three months to meet current obligations, such as to pay for merchandise, may borrow from the bank by signing a note promising to repay the bank plus interest at a certain rate at the end of a specific period of time. For example, $2,000 might be borrowed at 12% for 60 days and the bank paid $2,040 (principal plus interest) 60 days later. The policy at many banks, however, is to discount such short-term loans. The discount on $2,000 at 12% for 60 days is $40. Under discounting, the borrower would sign a non-interest-bearing note for $2,000 and receive only $1,960, which is the maturity value of the note less the discount. Interest collected in advance by a bank is called **bank discount** to distinguish it from simple interest paid at maturity. The actual amount of cash received by the borrower is the **proceeds.**

Example:

Melissa Davis borrowed money at her bank by signing a non-interest-bearing, 60-day note for $2,000. The bank discounted the note by charging 12% interest in advance. Find the amount of **(a)** the bank discount and **(b)** the proceeds.

Solution:

(a) $\$2,000 \times 12\% \times \dfrac{60}{360} = \$40$ bank discount

(b) $\$2,000 - \$40 = \$1,960$ proceeds

Notice in the preceding paragraph that the borrower would have the use of $2,000 for 60 days for the simple interest of $40; whereas, under discounting the borrower would have the use of only $1,960 for 60 days for the same charge of $40. Although the same amount of interest is being paid in each case, the discount rate is slightly higher than the interest rate.

Business people who accept notes, drafts, or trade acceptances from customers may obtain funds by discounting these at a bank rather than holding them to maturity. When the company's credit rating is reasonably good, most banks will discount the negotiable instruments received by the company from its customers. This loan procedure is called **discounting commercial paper.** From the bank's viewpoint when it discounts a negotiable instrument, it is making a loan to the borrower based on the maturity value of the instrument, because that is the amount the bank will collect from the maker on the maturity date.

The discount that the bank deducts is based on the maturity value for the remaining life of the note at the discount rate. The calculations for bank discount are quite similar to those for simple interest except that maturity value rather than face value is used and the remaining life of the instrument is used for the time. The calculations may be stated in equation form:

Bank Discount = Maturity Value × Rate × Time

The **term of discount** or **discount period,** which is the time used in computing bank discount, is the exact number of days from the discount date to the due date of the instrument. Bank discount is computed on the basis of a 360-day year. The proceeds are found by subtracting the amount of the discount from the maturity value. The sequence for calculating the proceeds of a discounted negotiable instrument is:

1. Find the maturity value by adding the interest, if any, to the principal.
2. Find the discount period by determining the exact number of days from the date of discount to the date of maturity.
3. Find the bank discount by applying the discount rate charged by the bank to the maturity value of the instrument for the discount period.
4. Find the proceeds by deducting the bank discount from the maturity value of the instrument.

Discounting Non-Interest-Bearing Negotiable Instruments. The following example gives the procedures for finding the bank discount and proceeds of a non-interest-bearing negotiable instrument. Of course, when the instrument is non-interest-bearing, the maturity value is the same as the face value.

Chapter 8. Simple Interest   231

Example: Alan Prescott owned a 90-day trade acceptance for $800, which had been signed by Donna Brinkman and dated July 18. On August 17, Prescott discounted the acceptance at the bank at 12%. Find **(a)** the maturity value, **(b)** the term of discount, **(c)** the bank discount, and **(d)** the proceeds of the acceptance.

Solution: **(a)** As the acceptance is non-interest-bearing, $800 is the maturity value as well as the face value.

(b) The term of discount runs from the discount date, August 17, to the due date, which is October 16 (90 days from July 18). By using a time table or by using the following procedure, the term of discount is found to be 60 days.

  31 days in August
  17 discount date (days expired in August)
  14 days left in August
  30 days in September
  16 days in October
  60 days in discount period (number of
    days bank holds the trade acceptance)

(c) The bank discount on $800 maturity value at 12% for a discount period of 60 days is $16:

$$\$800 \times 12\% \times \frac{60}{360} = \$16$$

(d) The proceeds equal $784, which is the maturity value of $800 less the bank discount of $16:

$$\$800 - \$16 = \$784$$

Discounting After-Sight Time Drafts. As notes, accepted time drafts, and trade acceptances have similar characteristics, the basic procedures for discounting them at a bank are the same. Remember, however, that the life or term of an after-sight time draft is the time from the date of acceptance to the date of maturity, regardless of when the draft is dated. The due date of such a draft is found by counting forward the appropriate number of days or months from the date of acceptance.

Example: A $900 draft dated January 21 was payable 3 months after sight. The draft was accepted on February 5 and discounted at the bank on March 6 at 12%. Find **(a)** the due date, **(b)** the discount period, **(c)** the bank discount, and **(d)** the proceeds.

Solution: **(a)** The due date is May 5, which is 3 months from February 5, the date of acceptance.

(b) The discount period from the discount date of March 6 to the due date of May 5 is 60 days.

(c) The bank discount on $900 maturity value at 12% for the discount period of 60 days is $18:

$$\$900 \times 12\% \times \frac{60}{360} = \$18$$

(d) The proceeds equal the maturity value of $900 less the bank discount of $18; that is, $882:

$$\$900 - \$18 = \$882$$

A. For each of the following non-interest-bearing negotiable instruments, find **(a)** the due date, **(b)** the maturity value, **(c)** the term of discount, **(d)** the bank discount, and **(e)** the proceeds.

	Date	Face Value	Time	Discount Rate	Date of Discount
1.	March 6	$ 900	60 days	12%	March 16
2.	April 8	1,500	90 days	20%	April 23
3.	February 10	2,000	3 months	18%	March 1
4.	January 19	26,000	4 months	14%	April 15
5.	May 14	1,875	6 months	$17\frac{1}{2}$%	September 9
6.	September 21	4,930	120 days	16%	December 12

B. For each of the following drafts, find **(a)** the due date, **(b)** the term of discount, **(c)** the bank discount, and **(d)** the proceeds.

	Face Value	When Payable	Dated	Accepted	Discounted	Rate of Discount
1.	$ 900	60 days after sight	March 23	March 27	March 30	16%
2.	1,400	90 days after sight	May 4	May 10	May 25	$17\frac{1}{2}$%
3.	4,048	4 months after date	February 8	February 10	March 23	12%
4.	71,250	75 days after date	September 9	September 15	October 19	14%
5.	2,700	3 months after sight	June 14	June 18	July 20	10%
6.	3,685	4 months after sight	July 29	August 1	September 6	18%

C. Solve these problems. Note in each problem whether the negotiable instrument is an *after-sight* draft or an *after-date* draft.

1. Thomas Glover drew a 4-month after-sight draft on the Greenburg Company for $500. The company accepted the draft on April 3. Glover discounted the draft at his bank on May 1 at 12%. What proceeds did he receive?

2. A note for $3,245 that matured 45 days after date was dated March 18 and discounted on April 5 at 16%. What proceeds were received?

3. A note for $3,600 that matured in 60 days was dated September 27 and discounted on October 1 at $16\frac{1}{2}$%. Find the proceeds.

4. How much will a bank pay on a draft for $1,260 that is dated May 14, due 3 months after date, accepted on June 17, and discounted at 15% on July 12?

5. A draft for $6,300 that matured 120 days after sight was dated July 17, accepted July 21, and discounted on August 25 at 14%. Find the proceeds.

6. On June 23, Carol Hardaway accepted a draft that was due 75 days after sight and dated June 18. The draft had been drawn on her for $4,075 by Paterson Products Company. The company discounted the draft at $17\frac{1}{2}$% on July 18. Find the proceeds.

Discounting Interest-Bearing Negotiable Instruments. When the negotiable instrument bears interest, the bank considers the interest rate and period of time specified in the instrument in order to determine the maturity value and the due date. After these considerations, the bank-discount rate is used to compute the bank discount, which is based on the maturity value and the remaining life of the instrument.

Example:

On March 1, Dan Baker received a 10%, 75-day note for $600 from a customer. The note matured on May 15 (75 days from March 1). On March 16, Baker discounted the note at his bank, which charged a discount rate of 12%. What proceeds did Baker receive?

Solution:

Face value of the note	$600.00
Add: Interest at 10% from date of note to maturity	12.50
Maturity value.	$612.50
Less: Bank discount at 12% for discount period of 60 days (March 16 to May 15)	12.25
Proceeds (cash received from bank)	$600.25

● Exercise 8–8

A. For each of the following interest-bearing negotiable instruments, find **(a)** the due date, **(b)** the maturity value, **(c)** the discount period, **(d)** the bank discount, and **(e)** the proceeds.

	Date	Face Value	Interest Rate	Time	Discount Rate	Date of Discount
1.	April 17	$ 600	10%	90 days	12%	June 4
2.	November 10	15,000	12%	60 days	14%	December 11
3.	March 21	2,962	14%	3 months	16%	March 31
4.	October 8	3,480	$14\frac{1}{2}$%	4 months	18%	October 26
5.	June 24	4,640	12%	6 months	$18\frac{1}{2}$%	July 7
6.	August 16	17,640	$16\frac{1}{2}$%	150 days	$17\frac{1}{2}$%	September 18

B. Solve these problems.

1. A 4-month note for $885, dated June 15, was discounted July 25 at 15%. Find the proceeds.

2. A 75-day note for $624, dated August 19, was discounted October 1 at $17\frac{1}{2}$%. Find the proceeds.

3. A 6-month note for $5,000, dated January 21, was discounted March 14 at 12%. Find the proceeds.

4. A 3-month note for $986, dated July 19, was discounted on September 4 at 18%. Find the proceeds.

5. On March 21, Robert Behlman received a 75-day, 12% note with a face value of $1,800 from Stephenie Blaine. Behlman discounted the note on April 11 at $17\frac{1}{2}$%. What proceeds did he receive?

Part 2. Mathematics Applications in Starting a Business

6. Frances Scriveri promised to pay her bank $9,450 at the end of 45 days on a loan. If the bank charged 15% interest in advance, how much were **(a)** the bank discount and **(b)** the proceeds?

7. Find **(a)** the bank discount at 12% and **(b)** the proceeds of a 90-day, 10% interest-bearing note for $5,706 that was dated October 18 and discounted on November 17.

8. On May 6, Wendy Walker received a 90-day, 16% note dated May 4 for $3,700 from W. R. Yates. Walker discounted the note at 14% at her bank on June 14. Find **(a)** the maturity date, **(b)** the maturity value, **(c)** the term of discount, **(d)** the bank discount, and **(e)** the proceeds.

9. A note for $1,500 at 12% for 180 days was discounted at 14% at a bank 90 days before maturity. Find **(a)** the bank discount and **(b)** the proceeds.

10. A 90-day note for $37,500, dated August 15, was discounted on September 12 at $16\frac{1}{2}$%. Find the proceeds.

11. Antonio Apodaca discounted a 60-day, $1,750 note at 18% on October 17. The note matured on December 6 and drew interest at 15%. How much did Apodaca receive for this note?

12. Bonnie Barragan signed a 60-day, non-interest-bearing note for $5,000 and discounted it at 18% at her bank. The bank immediately rediscounted the note at $14\frac{1}{2}$% at a Federal Reserve Bank. Federal Reserve Banks use 365 days as a year in rediscounting notes for member banks. The previous discounts have no effect on the rediscount. How much profit did the bank make?

Making Partial Payments on Notes

The payment made to eliminate part of the debt on a note, draft, or other form of indebtedness is called a **partial payment.** Occasionally the holder of an interest-bearing note will accept partial payments on it from the maker. The advantage to the maker is that the partial payments reduce the total amount of interest that must be paid on the debt. There are two general methods used to find the balance due after partial payments are made. These two methods are based on the United States Rule and on the Merchants' Rule.

The United States Rule. The method based on the United States Rule is so named because it results from a ruling made by the United States Supreme Court. Under this method, the first partial payment is applied to pay the interest due on the principal from the date of the indebtedness to the date of the first partial payment. When the partial payment is more than sufficient to pay the interest, the remaining amount is applied to the reduction of the principal. The second partial payment is applied to pay the interest due on the reduced principal from the date of the first partial payment to the date of the second partial payment. Any remaining amount is used to further reduce the principal and so on for each payment. The final balance is the sum of the unpaid principal and the interest up to the date of final payment.

If a partial payment is less than the interest due at the time of the payment, there is no reduction of principal until this payment and subsequent payments are sufficient to exceed the accumulated interest. See the third and fourth payments in the example which follows.

Following is a summary of the steps to use under the United States Rule:

1. Find the interest on the principal at the given rate from the date of the loan to the date of the first partial payment.
2. Find the reduction in the principal by subtracting the interest from the amount of the partial payment. There is no reduction in principal if the payment is not larger than the interest.
3. Find the new principal balance by subtracting the amount of the reduction from the principal.
4. If there are subsequent partial payments, repeat the operations in the preceding steps, but compute interest on the balance due prior to the current payment from the beginning date of that balance to the date of the current partial payment.

Example: Harold Hensley borrowed $10,000 on April 5 by signing a 12% promissory note as the maker. He paid $1,000 on May 5, $2,000 on June 4, $50 on July 24, and $4,000 on August 23. Use the United States Rule to find the balance due on October 22.

Solution:

Principal on April 5		$10,000.00
First payment (May 5)	$1,000.00	
Deduct: Interest on $10,000 for 30 days (April 5 to May 5)	100.00	
Reduction in principal		900.00
Balance on May 5		$ 9,100.00
Second payment (June 4)	$2,000.00	
Deduct: Interest on $9,100 for 30 days (May 5 to June 4)	91.00	
Reduction in principal		1,909.00
Balance on June 4		$ 7,191.00
Third payment (July 24)	$ 50.00	
Deduct: Interest on $7,191 for 50 days (June 4 to July 24)	119.85	
Reduction in principal		–0–
Balance on July 24		$ 7,191.00
Fourth payment ($4,000) and third payment ($50)	$4,050.00	
Deduct: Interest on $7,191 for 80 days (June 4 to August 23)	191.76	
Reduction in principal		3,858.24
Balance on August 23		$ 3,332.76
Add: Interest on $3,332.76 for 60 days (August 23 to October 22)		66.66
Balance on October 22		$ 3,399.42

The Merchants' Rule. Computing the balance due under the Merchants' Rule is easier and, therefore, preferred by some business people. When this rule is applied, the principal earns ordinary interest from the date of indebtedness to the date of final settlement, and interest is saved by the debtor on each partial payment from the date of the payment to the maturity date. On the due date of the loan, the balance due is the unpaid portion of the maturity value of the original debt. The unpaid portion is found by deducting the total of the partial payments and the interest saved on the payments from the maturity value of the loan.

The following steps may be used to find the amount due at maturity.

1. Find the maturity value by adding the principal and its interest for the time from the date of the loan to the due date.
2. Find the total reduction in the debt by adding the partial payments and the interest saved on each from the date of the payment to the due date.
3. Find the balance due by subtracting the total reduction (found in Step 2) from the maturity value (found in Step 1).

Example: On March 7, Mary Harper borrowed $4,000 by signing a 12%, 180-day note as the maker. She made the following payments on the note: $800 on April 6, $500 on May 21, and $900 on August 4. Use the Merchants' Rule to find the balance due on this note on September 3, the due date.

Solution:

Principal on March 7			$4,000.00
Interest on $4,000 for 180 days (March 7 to September 3)			240.00
Maturity value of note			$4,240.00
Deduct partial payments and interest saved:			
First payment (April 6)	$800.00		
Interest saved on $800 for 150 days (April 6 to September 3)	40.00		
Reduction for first payment		$840.00	
Second payment (May 21)	$500.00		
Interest saved on $500 for 105 days (May 21 to September 3)	17.50		
Reduction for second payment		517.50	
Third payment (August 4)	$900.00		
Interest saved on $900 for 30 days (August 4 to September 3)	9.00		
Reduction for third payment		909.00	
Total reductions			2,266.50
Balance due September 3			$1,973.50

As the interest is slightly higher under the United States Rule, compared to the Merchants' Rule, the United States Rule is advantageous for the lender and the Merchants' Rule, for the borrower.

- Exercise 8–9

1. The following payments have been made on a 9-month, 10% note for $4,500 that is dated March 8: $1,250 on May 7, $1,250 on July 6, and $1,500 on September 14. Find the balance due on the note at maturity by the United States Rule.

2. A 12% note dated April 12 for $5,000 had been paid at $1,000 every 30 days from its date. Use the United States Rule to find the balance due on September 9.

3. Use the Merchants' Rule to find the amount due at maturity on a 6-month, 9% note for $3,700, dated March 4, if payments were endorsed on it as follows: $250 on June 3, $1,050 on July 3, and $1,400 on August 23.

4. A property cost $40,000. The buyer paid $20,000 down and agreed to pay $4,000 at the end of each six months to retire the debt in $2\frac{1}{2}$ years at 13% interest. If he decided to retire the debt at the time of the fourth payment, how much should he pay by the Merchants' Rule?

5. A note for $3,900, dated June 18, with interest at 16% was reduced by the following payments: $900 on July 18, $1,000 on September 16, and $1,200 on October 31. Find the balance due on November 30 by the United States Rule.

6. The following partial payments have been made on a note for $3,000 with interest at 16%, dated May 8: July 7, $1,200; August 6, $800; and October 13, $500. Find the balance due on November 12 by using the Merchants' Rule.

7. Howard Manning gave Hayes and Marshall Company a 1-year note for $7,450 at 12% ordinary interest in payment of an overdue account. The note was dated June 26. He made the following payments on the note: $450 on August 25, $100 on November 23, $2,000 on December 31, and $1,800 on February 17. Find the amount due at maturity **(a)** by the United States Rule and **(b)** by the Merchants' Rule.

8. A debt of $8,500 at 12% dated April 1 was to mature 10 months later. The debtor made two payments at $50 each followed by two payments of $2,000 each. Each payment was made at the end of a 60-day period. How much will retire this debt on the due date using **(a)** the United States Rule and **(b)** the Merchants' Rule?

**REVIEW
PROBLEMS**

Solve these problems. If you have difficulty solving any problem, restudy the appropriate section in this chapter. The problems under a specific number are related to those contained in the exercise with the same last number.

1. Find the exact number of days in each problem.
   a. From September 30 to January 15
   b. From October 13 to June 3 in a leap year

2. Solve these problems.
   a. A note dated August 8 for $1,750 is due in 3 months at $15\frac{1}{2}\%$ ordinary interest. Find the maturity value of the note.
   b. While raising capital to start a business, Tina Todd borrowed $8,750 from her father. She repaid the loan $3\frac{1}{2}$ years later plus 9% simple interest. What is the maturity value of this loan?
   c. Teresa Hill borrowed $3,050 for 1 year and 4 months at 12% simple interest. What is the maturity value of this loan?
   d. Alpine Products Company charges 18% simple interest on overdue bills for the exact number of days that each bill is overdue. How much is needed to pay in full a bill for $450 that was due on June 9 but not paid until September 10 with (1) ordinary interest and (2) exact interest?

3. Solve these problems.
   a. A loan produced $75 interest at 12% for 45 days. Find the principal of the loan.
   b. At what interest rate will $675 yield $13.50 interest in 3 months?
   c. How many days are needed for $480 to yield $6.40 interest at 8%?
   d. How many years will be required for $8,250 to yield $3,300 interest at 16%?

4. Use Table 8–1 to find the exact number of days in each problem.
   a. March 18, 1992 to August 19, 1992
   b. October 25, 1989 to May 12, 1990

5. Use Table 8–2 to find the interest for each of the following.
   a. Principal of $984 ordinary interest at $18\frac{1}{2}\%$ for 23 days
   b. Principal of $2,745.50 exact interest at 14% for 134 days

6. Find the due date of each of the following.

	Date of Instrument	Term	Date of Acceptance
a.	May 9	60 days after date	May 12
b.	July 16	3 months after sight	July 26
c.	September 27	90 days after sight	October 6
d.	February 24	4 months after date	March 1

7. Solve these problems.
   a. Jane Campbell signed a promissory note for $450 due in 90 days to her bank. The bank charged 10% interest in advance. Find (1) the bank discount and (2) the proceeds.
   b. Find the amount that a bank will pay on a draft for $850 dated December 9, due 6 months after date, accepted on December 15, and discounted on March 1 at 12%.

Chapter 8. Simple Interest

c. Find the proceeds on a draft for $2,600 that matured 90 days after sight, was dated April 19, accepted on April 22, and discounted May 14 at 15%.

8. Solve these problems.
   a. Marjorie Bassett discounted a 60-day $2,650 note at $18\frac{1}{2}\%$ on October 7. The note was dated September 17 and drew interest at 7%. Find the proceeds.
   b. A 4-month, 12% interest-bearing note with a face value of $2,250 was discounted 60 days before maturity at 14%. What are **(1)** the maturity value, **(2)** the discount, and **(3)** the proceeds?

9. On March 17, Frank Morales borrowed $4,500 at 12% for 8 months. He made the following partial payments: $400 on April 16, $50 on July 15, $1,250 on August 29, and $1,750 on October 18. Find the balance due on November 17 **(a)** by the United States Rule and **(b)** by the Merchants' Rule.

CHALLENGE PROBLEM

Lasell Corporation grants its customers 30 days from date of purchase to pay. However, it also gives a 2% discount on goods purchased if the customer pays within 10 days. Customers who do not pay within 30 days must pay a late fee of 1.5% of the amount owed.

On September 15 Lasell Corporation sold Paul Wood $1,500 worth of merchandise. On October 17 it accepted from Wood $300 in cash and a note for the balance due. The 12%, 60-day note was dated that day. On October 20 Lasell Corporation discounted the note at 15%. The corporation received notice from its bank on December 18 that the note had been dishonored. It paid the bank the maturity value of the note plus a $10 protest fee. On January 15 Wood took possession of the note and paid the maturity value and the protest fee plus 12% interest on both from the due date to the date of payment.

a. How much net proceeds did the company receive on October 20?

b. How much was the total amount received by the company from Wood on January 15?

Part 2. Mathematics Applications in Starting a Business

Chapter 9

Compound Interest
and Annuities

Objectives

After mastering the material in Chapter 9, you will be able to:

- Calculate compound amount and compound interest by using the compound-interest formula.
- Use compound interest, present value, and annuity tables.
- Compute the effective rate of interest.
- Calculate present value at compound interest.
- Find the amount of an ordinary annuity and of an annuity due.
- Compute present value of ordinary annuities and of annuities due.
- Find the periodic payment to a sinking fund.
- Find the periodic payment in amortization.

The Hadley family is considering various investment possibilities to help their young children to finance their college educations. They are thinking of depositing money in a savings fund that pays 8% interest compounded quarterly, and they want to select a long-term plan that is within their financial ability. With this in mind, they asked a friend who works at a bank to answer these four questions: (1) If $20,000 is deposited in the fund today and the principal and interest are allowed to accumulate, how much will they have in fifteen years? (2) If they want to have $50,000 in the bank at the end of fifteen years, how much deposited now will grow to that amount? (3) If they deposit $450 each quarter, how much principal and interest will have accumulated in fifteen years? (4) Finally, if they want to have $50,000 in the bank at the end of fifteen years, how much should they deposit each quarter? The procedures for obtaining answers to questions such as these are presented in this chapter.

COMPOUND INTEREST

Simple interest is computed on a fixed principal for a specific period of time. **Compound interest** is computed on the sum of an original principal plus the accrued interest. When interest is compounded, the interest of one period becomes principal in the next. Thus, the principal does not remain constant but continues to grow as long as the interest is allowed to accumulate, and there are no withdrawals.

Compound interest is commonly applied to long-term loans. Banks and savings and loan companies usually pay compound interest on deposits in savings accounts to encourage their depositors to allow the funds to accumulate for a long period of time.

Computing Compound Interest

The sum of the original principal and its compound interest is the **compound amount. Future value** is the same as compound amount. The difference between the compound amount and the original principal is the compound interest.

Example A: Anna Foster deposited $500 in a fund that pays 12% interest compounded annually. Find **(a)** the amount in the fund and **(b)** the compound interest at the end of 3 years.

Solution:
(a) Original principal $500.00
     Interest for first year ($500 × 0.12) 60.00
Principal for second year....................................... $560.00
     Interest for second year ($560 × 0.12) 67.20
Principal for third year $627.20
     Interest for third year ($627.20 × 0.12) 75.26
Amount in fund at the end of 3 years........................... $702.46

(b) $702.46 − $500 = $202.46   compound interest

The process is summarized in the following compound-interest formula:

$$S = P(1 + i)^n$$

S = Sum of principal and interest—compound amount
P = Principal
i = Interest rate *per period* in decimal form
n = Total number of interest periods

Substituting the appropriate numbers from Example A in the formula gives:

$$S = 500(1 + 0.12)^3$$

Constant multiplication in a calculator may be used to solve this equation. When the number of interest periods (n) is small, the sum of $1 + i$ may be used as the constant multiplier times the principal. In the following solution to Example A, the constant is entered first and the $\boxed{=}$ key is pressed n times.

Solution:

1.12 $\boxed{\times}$ 500 $\boxed{=}$ $\boxed{=}$ $\boxed{=}$ $\rightarrow$ 702.464, means $702.46

Compound interest is given by the following formula:

$$I = S - P$$

I = Compound interest
S = Compound amount
P = Principal

Interest may be compounded (i.e., converted) annually, semiannually, quarterly, monthly, daily, or even more often. The time for which interest is computed is the **interest period** or **conversion period.** If interest is compounded semiannually, the interest period is 6 months, and the interest is computed twice each year. Since interest rates are stated on a per-annum basis, a semiannual rate is one-half of the annual rate. For example, when an investment is made at 12% and compounded semiannually, the investor receives interest at 6% ($\frac{1}{2}$ of 12%) each half year. (Notice: $P \times 12\% \times \frac{1}{2} = P \times 6\%$.) Furthermore, if the investment is allowed to accumulate for 3 years, the interest is computed 6 times; that is, there are 6 conversion periods.

Example B:

Marvin Lyon deposited $500 in a fund that pays 12% interest compounded semiannually. Find the amount in the fund at the end of 3 years.

Solution:

Original principal	$500.00
Interest for first period ($500 × 0.06)	30.00
Principal for second period	$530.00
Interest for second period ($530 × 0.06)	31.80
Principal for third period	$561.80
Interest for third period ($561.80 × 0.06)	33.71
Principal for fourth period	$595.51
Interest for fourth period ($595.51 × 0.06)	35.73
Principal for fifth period	$631.24
Interest for fifth period	37.87
Principal for sixth period	$669.11
Interest for sixth period	40.15
Amount in fund at the end of 3 years	$709.26

In the compound-interest formula, i represents the periodic interest rate and may be computed with this equation:

$$i = \frac{r}{m}$$

i = Interest rate per period in decimal form
r = Nominal interest rate
m = Number of interest periods in 1 year

Using the data in Example B to find i gives:

$$i = \frac{0.12}{2}, \text{ so } i = 0.06.$$

Chapter 9. Compound Interest and Annuities

Another important consideration in the compound-interest formula is the value of *n,* which equals the interest conversion periods in one year times the number of years. Thus, for Example B, $n = 2 \times 3$, which is 6.

Substituting the data from Example B into the compound-interest formula gives:

$$S = 500(1 + 0.06)^6$$

Solution:

means $709.26

The foregoing calculator solution emphasizes using the constant. Another method of solving for the compound amount emphasizes raising $1 + i$ to the power *n* before multiplying by the principal. To raise a number to a power with a pocket calculator, the $\boxed{=}$ key is pressed $n - 1$ times. This second method is recommended in a later exercise. Using the data in Example B and $\frac{r}{m}$ instead of i in the compound-interest formula gives the following alternate solution.

$$S = 500\left(1 + \frac{0.12}{2}\right)^6$$

Solution:

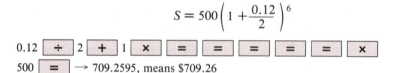

If compounded quarterly, the interest is computed at $\frac{1}{4}$ the annual rate 4 times each year; if monthly, $\frac{1}{12}$ the annual rate 12 times each year.

A comparison of the amount at the end of three years in Example A ($702.46) with the amount in Example B ($709.26) reveals that a given sum grows faster when the interest is compounded more frequently. It also reveals that the APR (annual percentage rate) in Example B is actually higher than the nominal rate of 12%.

- Exercise 9–1

   A. Find **(a)** the compound amount and **(b)** the compound interest for each of the following.

	Principal	Rate	Time	Compounded
1.	$ 800	15%	3 years	Annually
2.	1,600	14%	4 years	Annually
3.	2,000	15%	2 years	Semiannually
4.	6,000	13%	$3\frac{1}{2}$ years	Semiannually
5.	15,000	17%	2 years	Quarterly
6.	50,000	18%	$2\frac{1}{2}$ years	Quarterly

Part 2. Mathematics Applications in Starting a Business

B. Solve these problems.

1. Four years ago a trust fund amounting to $45,000 was invested at 13% compounded annually. Find the amount in the fund now.

2. Sarah Minott inherited $25,000 on the day she became 19 years old. Under the specifications of the will, the money was placed in a trust fund that earned interest at 15% compounded semiannually. What amount was in the fund on Minott's twenty-first birthday?

3. Three years ago, the original amount in a fund was $1,200. The interest rate is 14%. Find **(a)** the simple interest and **(b)** the interest compounded annually.

4. The sum of $15,000 was invested for 3 years at 9% interest compounded semiannually. **(a)** How much was in the fund at the end of three years? **(b)** How much more was earned with compound interest than would have been earned with simple interest?

Using a Compound-Interest Table

Even with a calculator, computing the interest for each period for several years can be tedious. Banks and savings institutions generally use computers to determine compound interest and to automatically adjust depositors' accounts. Individuals may use amount tables to compute compound interest. Tables are available that show the accumulated value of 1 and interest when compounded at various rates for a number of periods.

Finding Compound Interest for Principal Other Than 1. Each dollar in a specific investment earns the same amount of interest at the given rate. The accumulated amount of 1 multiplied by the original principal indicates the accumulated amount in the investment.

To find compound interest by using Table 9–1, follow this procedure:

1. Read down the rate-per-period column of the table to the line that represents the total number of periods. The value found on this line is the *amount of 1.*
2. Multiply the amount of 1 by the principal to find the total amount.
3. Subtract the original principal from the total amount to find the compound interest.

Example:

Kenneth Kilby invested $2,000 in a fund that pays interest at 9% compounded annually. Use Table 9–1 to find **(a)** the amount in the fund and **(b)** the compound interest at the end of 20 years.

Solution:

(a) The value for the twentieth period in the 9% column of the table shows that 1 compounded at 9% amounts to 5.60441077 in 20 years. Therefore:

$$5.6044107 \times \$2,000 = \$11,208.82 \quad \text{amount in fund}$$

(b) $11,208.82 − $2,000 = $9,208.82 \quad compound interest

Chapter 9. Compound Interest and Annuities

n	0.5%	1%	1.5%	2%	3%	4%	5%
1	1.00500000	1.01000000	1.01500000	1.02000000	1.03000000	1.04000000	1.05000000
2	1.01002500	1.02010000	1.03022500	1.04040000	1.06090000	1.08160000	1.10250000
3	1.01507513	1.03030100	1.04567837	1.06120800	1.09272700	1.12486400	1.15762500
4	1.02015050	1.04060401	1.06136355	1.08243216	1.12550881	1.16985856	1.21550625
5	1.02525125	1.05101005	1.07728400	1.10408080	1.15927407	1.21665290	1.27628156
6	1.03037751	1.06152015	1.09344326	1.12616242	1.19405230	1.26531902	1.34009564
7	1.03552940	1.07213535	1.10984491	1.14868567	1.22987387	1.31593178	1.40710042
8	1.04070704	1.08285671	1.12649259	1.17165938	1.26677008	1.36856905	1.47745544
9	1.04591058	1.09368527	1.14338998	1.19509257	1.30477318	1.42331181	1.55132822
10	1.05114013	1.10462213	1.16054083	1.21899442	1.34391638	1.48024428	1.62889463
11	1.05639583	1.11566835	1.17794894	1.24337431	1.38423387	1.53945406	1.71033936
12	1.06167781	1.12682503	1.19561817	1.26824179	1.42576089	1.60103222	1.79585633
13	1.06698620	1.13809328	1.21355244	1.29360663	1.46853371	1.66507351	1.88564914
14	1.07232113	1.14947421	1.23175573	1.31947876	1.51258972	1.73167645	1.97993160
15	1.07768274	1.16096896	1.25023207	1.34586834	1.55796742	1.80094351	2.07892818
16	1.08307115	1.17257864	1.26898555	1.37278571	1.60470644	1.87298125	2.18287459
17	1.08848651	1.18430443	1.28802033	1.40024142	1.65284763	1.94790050	2.29201832
18	1.09392894	1.19614748	1.30734064	1.42824625	1.70243306	2.02581652	2.40661923
19	1.09939858	1.20810895	1.32695075	1.45681117	1.75350605	2.10684918	2.52695020
20	1.10489558	1.22019004	1.34685501	1.48594740	1.80611123	2.19112314	2.65329771
21	1.11042006	1.23239194	1.36705783	1.51566634	1.86029457	2.27876807	2.78596259
22	1.11597216	1.24471586	1.38756370	1.54597967	1.91610341	2.36991879	2.92526072
23	1.12155202	1.25716302	1.40837715	1.57689926	1.97358651	2.46471554	3.07152376
24	1.12715978	1.26973465	1.42950281	1.60843725	2.03279411	2.56330416	3.22509994
25	1.13279558	1.28243200	1.45094535	1.64060599	2.09377793	2.66583633	3.38635494
26	1.13845955	1.29525631	1.47270953	1.67341811	2.15659127	2.77246978	3.55567269
27	1.14415185	1.30820888	1.49480018	1.70688648	2.22128901	2.88336858	3.73345632
28	1.14987261	1.32129097	1.51722218	1.74102421	2.28792768	2.99870332	3.92012914
29	1.15562197	1.33450388	1.53998051	1.77584469	2.35656551	3.11865145	4.11613560
30	1.16140008	1.34784892	1.56308022	1.81136158	2.42726247	3.24339751	4.32194238
31	1.16720708	1.36132740	1.58652642	1.84758882	2.50008035	3.37313341	4.53803949
32	1.17304312	1.37494068	1.61032432	1.88454059	2.57508276	3.50805875	4.76494147
33	1.17890833	1.38869009	1.63447918	1.92223140	2.65233524	3.64838110	5.00318854
34	1.18480288	1.40257699	1.65899637	1.96067603	2.73190530	3.79431634	5.25334797
35	1.19072689	1.41660276	1.68388132	1.99988955	2.81386245	3.94608899	5.51601537
36	1.19668052	1.43076878	1.70913954	2.03988734	2.89827833	4.10393255	5.79181614
37	1.20266393	1.44507647	1.73477663	2.08068509	2.98522668	4.26808986	6.08140694
38	1.20867725	1.45952724	1.76079828	2.12229879	3.07478348	4.43881345	6.38547729
39	1.21472063	1.47412251	1.78721025	2.16474477	3.16702698	4.61636599	6.70475115
40	1.22079424	1.48886373	1.81401841	2.20803966	3.26203779	4.80102063	7.03998871
41	1.22689821	1.50375237	1.84122868	2.25220046	3.35989893	4.99306145	7.39198815
42	1.23303270	1.51878989	1.86884712	2.29724447	3.46069589	5.19278391	7.76158756
43	1.23919786	1.53397779	1.89687982	2.34318936	3.56451677	5.40049527	8.14966693
44	1.24539385	1.54931757	1.92533302	2.39005314	3.67145227	5.61651508	8.55715028
45	1.25162082	1.56481075	1.95421301	2.43785421	3.78159584	5.84117568	8.98500779
46	1.25787892	1.58045885	1.98352621	2.48661129	3.89504372	6.07482271	9.43425818
47	1.26416832	1.59626344	2.01327910	2.53634352	4.01189503	6.31781562	9.90597109
48	1.27048916	1.61222608	2.04347829	2.58707039	4.13225188	6.57052824	10.40126965
49	1.27684161	1.62834834	2.07413046	2.63881179	4.25621944	6.83334937	10.92133313
50	1.28322581	1.64463182	2.10524242	2.69158803	4.38390602	7.10668335	11.46739979

Table 9–1 Amount of 1 at Compound Interest

Part 2. Mathematics Applications in Starting a Business

n	6%	7%	8%	9%	10%	11%	12%
1	1.06000000	1.07000000	1.08000000	1.09000000	1.10000000	1.11000000	1.12000000
2	1.12360000	1.14490000	1.16640000	1.18810000	1.21000000	1.23210000	1.25440000
3	1.19101600	1.22504300	1.25971200	1.29502900	1.33100000	1.36763100	1.40492800
4	1.26247696	1.31079601	1.36048896	1.41158161	1.46410000	1.51807041	1.57351936
5	1.33822558	1.40255173	1.46932808	1.53862395	1.61051000	1.68505816	1.76234168
6	1.41851911	1.50073035	1.58687432	1.67710011	1.77156100	1.87041455	1.97382269
7	1.50363026	1.60578148	1.71382427	1.82803912	1.94871710	2.07616015	2.21068141
8	1.59384807	1.71818618	1.85093021	1.99256264	2.14358881	2.30453777	2.47596318
9	1.68947896	1.83845921	1.99900463	2.17189328	2.35794769	2.55803692	2.77307876
10	1.79084770	1.96715136	2.15892500	2.36736367	2.59374246	2.83942099	3.10584821
11	1.89829856	2.10485195	2.33163900	2.58042641	2.85311671	3.15175729	3.47854999
12	2.01219647	2.25219159	2.51817012	2.81266478	3.13842838	3.49845060	3.89597599
13	2.13292826	2.40984500	2.71962373	3.06580461	3.45227121	3.88328016	4.36349311
14	2.26090396	2.57853415	2.93719362	3.34172703	3.79749834	4.31044098	4.88711229
15	2.39655819	2.75903154	3.17216911	3.64248246	4.17724817	4.78458949	5.47356576
16	2.54035168	2.95216375	3.42594264	3.97030588	4.59497299	5.31089433	6.13039365
17	2.69277279	3.15881521	3.70001805	4.32763341	5.05447028	5.89509271	6.86604089
18	2.85433915	3.37993228	3.99601950	4.71712042	5.55991731	6.54355291	7.68996580
19	3.02559950	3.61652754	4.31570106	5.14166125	6.11590904	7.26334373	8.61276169
20	3.20713547	3.86968446	4.66095714	5.60441077	6.72749995	8.06231154	9.64629309
21	3.39956360	4.14056237	5.03383372	6.10880774	7.40024994	8.94916581	10.80384826
22	3.60353742	4.43040174	5.43654041	6.65860043	8.14027494	9.93357404	12.10031006
23	3.81974966	4.74052986	5.87146365	7.25787447	8.95430243	11.02626719	13.55234726
24	4.04893464	5.07236695	6.34118074	7.91108317	9.84973268	12.23915658	15.17862893
25	4.29187072	5.42743264	6.84847520	8.62308066	10.83470594	13.58546380	17.00006441
26	4.54938296	5.80735292	7.39635321	9.39915792	11.91817654	15.07986482	19.04007214
27	4.82234594	6.21386763	7.98806147	10.24508213	13.10999419	16.73864995	21.32488079
28	5.11168670	6.64883836	8.62710639	11.16713952	14.42099361	18.57990145	23.88386649
29	5.41838790	7.11425705	9.31727490	12.17218208	15.86309297	20.62369061	26.74993047
30	5.74349117	7.61225504	10.06265689	13.26767847	17.44940227	22.89229657	29.95992212
31	6.08810064	8.14511290	10.86766944	14.46176953	19.19434250	25.41044919	33.55511278
32	6.45338668	8.71527080	11.73708300	15.76332879	21.11377675	28.20559861	37.58172631
33	6.84058988	9.32533975	12.67604964	17.18202838	23.22515442	31.30821445	42.09153347
34	7.25102528	9.97811354	13.69013361	18.72841093	25.54766986	34.75211804	47.14251748
35	7.68608679	10.67658148	14.78534429	20.41396792	28.10243685	38.57485103	52.79961958
36	8.14725200	11.42394219	15.96817184	22.25122503	30.91268053	42.81808464	59.13557393
37	8.63608712	12.22361814	17.24562558	24.25383528	34.00394859	47.52807395	66.23184280
38	9.15425235	13.07927141	18.62527563	26.43668046	37.40434344	52.75616209	74.17966394
39	9.70350749	13.99482041	20.11529768	28.81598170	41.14477779	58.55933991	83.08122361
40	10.28571794	14.97445784	21.72452150	31.40942005	45.25925557	65.00086731	93.05097044
41	10.90286101	16.02266989	23.46248322	34.23626786	49.78518112	72.15096271	104.21708689
42	11.55703267	17.14425678	25.33948187	37.31753197	54.76369924	80.08756861	116.72313732
43	12.25045463	18.34435475	27.36664042	40.67610984	60.24006916	88.89720115	130.72991380
44	12.98548191	19.62845959	29.55597166	44.33695973	66.26407608	98.67589328	146.41750346
45	13.76461083	21.00245176	31.92044939	48.32728610	72.89048369	109.53024154	163.98760387
46	14.59048748	22.47262338	34.47408534	52.67674185	80.17953205	121.57856811	183.66611634
47	15.46591673	24.04570702	37.23201217	57.41764862	88.19748526	134.95221060	205.70605030
48	16.39387173	25.72890651	40.21057314	62.58523700	97.01723378	149.79695377	230.39077633
49	17.37750403	27.52992997	43.42741899	68.21790833	106.71895716	166.27461868	258.03766949
50	18.42015427	29.45702506	46.90161251	74.35752008	117.39085288	184.56482674	289.00218983

Table 9–1 Continued

Chapter 9. Compound Interest and Annuities

Finding Compound Interest When Periods Are Other Than One Year. If interest is compounded more frequently than annually, adjustments must be made. The interest rate per period and the number of conversion periods must conform to the more frequent compounding.

Example:

Doris Snyder is thinking of depositing $10,000 in a bank that pays 8% interest compounded quarterly. If she does so and lets the principal and interest accumulate, how much will she have at the end of 10 years? Use Table 9–1.

Solution:

There are 40 conversion periods (4 × 10), and the rate per period is 2% (8% ÷ 4). The amount for the fortieth period in the 2% column is 2.20803966. Therefore:

$$2.2080396 \times \$10,000 = \$22,080.40 \quad \text{amount in fund}$$

Finding Amounts for Periods Not in the Table. Even though Table 9–1 shows only a limited number of periods, it may be used to find the compound amount of 1 for other periods. The amount for an omitted period can be found by multiplying any two or more amounts whose step numbers or periods added together equal the desired number of periods. Notice in the following example that the compound amount of 1 for 50 periods is itself compounded for 10 more periods to find the amount of 1 for 60 periods.

Example:

Janet Burke invested $3,000 in a fund that pays interest at 12% compounded monthly. Use Table 9–1 to find the amount in the fund at the end of 5 years if the principal and interest are allowed to accumulate.

Solution:

There are 60 conversion periods (12 × 5), and the rate per period is 1% (12% ÷ 12). The amount for the fiftieth period in the 1% column of the table is 1.164463182. The amount for the tenth period is 1.10462213. Therefore:

$$1.6446318 \times 1.1046221 = 1.8166966 \quad \text{amount of 1}$$

$$1.8166966 \times \$3,000 = \$5,450.09 \quad \text{amount in fund}$$

Essentially the same amount of 1 for 60 periods (1.8166966) can be found by multiplying together other amounts in the 1% column whose periods total 60. Thus, the amount in the twentieth period (1.22019004) may be multiplied by the amount in the fortieth period (1.48886373) to obtain 1.81669669; the amount in the thirtieth period (1.34784892) multiplied by itself gives 1.81669671. This last method is preferable when a calculator is being used because the factor is easily squared. In these examples, the last digit on the right varies slightly because these amounts and those in the table have been rounded to the eighth place. With an eight-digit calculator the differences will be greater, but these variations are insignificant when the principal is relatively small.

Part 2. Mathematics Applications in Starting a Business

A. Use Table 9–1 to find **(a)** the compound amount and **(b)** the compound interest for each of the following.

	Principal	Rate	Time	Compounded
1.	$ 340	12%	18 years	Annually
2.	1,600	10%	22 years	Annually
3.	7,000	16%	6 years	Semiannually
4.	750	12%	$8\frac{1}{2}$ years	Semiannually
5.	1,820	8%	5 years	Quarterly
6.	2,950	12%	$12\frac{1}{2}$ years	Quarterly
7.	6,300	18%	5 years	Monthly
8.	4,000	12%	$4\frac{1}{2}$ years	Monthly

B. Solve these problems.

1. James Denison invested $2,400 at 11% compounded annually. At the end of 16 years, what are **(a)** the compound amount and **(b)** the compound interest?

2. What will be the amount after two years if $1,000 is invested at 12% interest compounded **(a)** annually? **(b)** semiannually? **(c)** monthly?

3. Find the interest on $2,000 at 8% compounded semiannually for **(a)** 6 years, **(b)** $8\frac{1}{2}$ years, and **(c)** 12 years.

4. A $3,750 note that bears interest at 16% compounded quarterly is due in 3 years. Find the maturity value.

5. Karen Nielson received the amount in a trust fund on the day she became 21 years old. The fund, which earned interest at 12% compounded quarterly, had been established with a deposit of $5,000 on the day she became 5 years old. How much did she receive from the fund?

6. Allen Muchmore invested $18,000. This will amount to $28,989.18 in how many years at 10% compounded annually?

7. A loan of $4,000 was repaid after having been owed for 12 years. The payment totaled $13,993.80. If compounded annually, what rate of interest was paid?

8. Clare Keegan invested $8,000. She let the principal and interest accumulate for 5 years to a total of $17,271.40. What annual rate of interest compounded semiannually did she receive on this investment?

Daily Compounding of Interest

Computers have enabled banks and other financial companies to offer daily compounding of interest to their depositors. Competition has caused some of them to offer continuous (instantaneous) compounding. In continuous compounding, interest is computed many times a second. Tables of factors have been prepared at various interest rates for both daily compounding and continuous compounding. Of course, the compound interest formula may be used.

When the number of conversion periods (n) is large, factoring the exponent and using constant multiplication may be combined to reduce the number of times the $\boxed{=}$ key is pressed. First consider the relatively small exponent of 6.

Example A: Calculate: 1.05^6.

Solution:

$$1.05^6 = 1.05 \times 1.05 \times 1.05 \times 1.05 \times 1.05 \times 1.05$$
$$1.05^6 = (1.05 \times 1.05)(1.05 \times 1.05)(1.05 \times 1.05)$$
$$1.05^6 = 1.05^2 \times 1.05^2 \times 1.05^2$$
$$1.05^6 = (1.05^2)^3$$
$$1.05^6 = 1.05^{2 \times 3}$$

$$1.05 \;\boxed{\times}\;\boxed{=}\quad\boxed{\times}\;\boxed{=}\;\boxed{=}\;\longrightarrow\; 1.3400955$$

$$\underbrace{\qquad\qquad}_{\text{power 2}}\quad\underbrace{\qquad\qquad\qquad}_{\text{power 3}}$$

The expression $1.05^{2 \times 3}$ may be interpreted to mean square 1.05 and then raise the result to the power of 3. Recall that when a number is being raised to a power with a pocket calculator, the $\boxed{=}$ key is pressed $n - 1$ times. Therefore, for each power, the $\boxed{\times}$ key is pressed once and the $\boxed{=}$ key is pressed $n - 1$ times. The first step in this procedure, however, is to break down the exponent into two or more factors.

Example B: Calculate: 1.02^{20}.

Solution:

$$1.02^{20} = 1.02^{2 \times 10}$$
$$1.02^{20} = 1.02^{2 \times 2 \times 5}$$

$$1.02 \;\boxed{\times}\;\boxed{=}\quad\boxed{\times}\;\boxed{=}\quad\boxed{\times}\;\boxed{=}\;\boxed{=}\;\boxed{=}\;\boxed{=}\;\longrightarrow\; 1.4859468$$

Power: 2   2   5

In daily compounding, the value of i is $\frac{r}{365}$ (or 366 for a leap year) unless the problem specifies a 360-day year.

These are the steps to follow to find the compound amount:

1. Factor the exponent completely.
2. Find the value of i.
3. Add 1 to the value of i.
4. Raise $1 + i$ to the power of n by using the factors.
5. Multiply the result by the principal.

     Part 2. Mathematics Applications in Starting a Business

Example C: Rose Asdurian deposited $2,000 in an account that pays 12% interest compounded daily. Find **(a)** the compound amount and **(b)** the compound interest at the end of 30 days.

Solution:

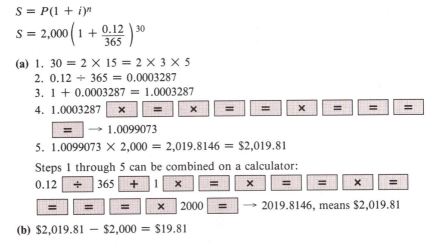

$S = P(1 + i)^n$

$S = 2,000 \left(1 + \dfrac{0.12}{365}\right)^{30}$

(a) 1. $30 = 2 \times 15 = 2 \times 3 \times 5$
2. $0.12 \div 365 = 0.0003287$
3. $1 + 0.0003287 = 1.0003287$
4. 1.0003287 [×] [=] [×] [=] [=] [×] [=] [=] [=]
   [=] $\rightarrow$ 1.0099073
5. $1.0099073 \times 2,000 = 2,019.8146 = \$2,019.81$

Steps 1 through 5 can be combined on a calculator:

0.12 [÷] 365 [+] 1 [×] [=] [×] [=] [=] [×] [=]
[=] [=] [=] [×] 2000 [=] $\rightarrow$ 2019.8146, means $2,019.81

(b) $\$2,019.81 - \$2,000 = \$19.81$

For comparative purposes, notice that the exact interest on $2,000 at 12% for 30 days is $2,000 \times 12\% \times \dfrac{30}{365} = \$19.73$, which is 8¢ smaller than the compound interest of $19.81.

Exercise 9–3

A. Use a pocket calculator to compute each power.

1. 1.02^7	**4.** 1.08^9	**7.** 1.12^{20}	**10.** 1.078^{35}
2. 1.04^{10}	**5.** 1.03^{12}	**8.** 1.18^{28}	**11.** 1.1093^{50}
3. 1.07^8	**6.** 1.05^{15}	**9.** 1.045^{25}	**12.** 1.1064^{70}

B. Use daily compounding based on a 365-day year to find **(a)** the compound amount and **(b)** the compound interest for each of the following.

	Principal	Rate	Days
1.	$ 750	10%	12
2.	3,200	9%	14
3.	4,800	12%	21
4.	1,500	15%	30
5.	29,300	$5\frac{1}{4}\%$	45
6.	63,400	$7\frac{1}{2}\%$	60
7.	250,000	14%	36
8.	375,000	13%	72

Chapter 9. Compound Interest and Annuities

C. Solve these problems.

1. Ron Parker deposited $10,000 in a savings account at the Employees Credit Union, which paid interest at 7% compounded daily. How much was this deposit worth 30 days later?

2. The Second Nationwide Bank pays interest on savings accounts at $5\frac{1}{4}$% compounded daily. If $5,000 is deposited, it will grow to how much in 6 weeks?

3. On October 8, Mark Brosman opened a savings account by depositing $7,500 in an association that pays interest from the first day of the month on deposits made by the tenth day. The interest rate on this account is $6\frac{1}{2}$% compounded daily. With no withdrawals, what would be the compound amount after interest is added through November 12?

4. On January 7, Lillian Ruiz opened a new account with a deposit of $18,000. The savings and loan association paid interest from the first on deposits made by the tenth day of the month. The interest rate was $7\frac{1}{2}$% compounded daily. Ms. Ruiz made another deposit of $2,000 on January 16. How much was in this account after interest was added for January 31?

5. Bank A pays interest at $5\frac{1}{4}$% compounded daily. Bank B pays 5.3% compounded quarterly. Jenny Reed deposited $15,000 on the first day of a 90-day quarter in each bank. After interest has been added for the quarter, the compound amount will be how much **(a)** in Bank A and **(b)** in Bank B? **(c)** Which is better for the depositor, Bank A or Bank B?

6. Credit Union A pays interest at $7\frac{1}{8}$% compounded monthly, and Credit Union B pays 7% compounded daily. Kathy Seidel invested $12,000 in each on the first day of a 30-day month. Find the compound amount of the deposit after interest has been added for the month **(a)** in Credit Union A and **(b)** in Credit Union B. **(c)** Which is better for the depositor, Credit Union A or Credit Union B?

Nominal and Effective Rates of Interest

Customarily, interest rates are quoted on an annual basis regardless of how often the interest is added to the principal. The stated (quoted or published) rate of interest is the **nominal rate.** When a nominal rate is quoted, the number of times per annum that interest is added to the principal should also be given. Thus, if 3% interest is added to the principal every three months, the customary quotation of the nominal rate is "12% compounded quarterly."

The actual or true annual rate of interest is called the **effective rate.** Because an effective rate indicates the true earning power of an investment on an annual basis, converting nominal rates to effective rates is an objective means of comparing various quotations of compound interest.

Compound-interest tables may be used to find effective rates of interest. Each factor in a compound-interest table represents the value of 1 plus compound interest on 1 for n periods. So, if the numeral 1 is subtracted from the factor, the remainder represents interest. For example, if $1.1255088 is the compound amount of $1 at 12% compounded quarterly for one year, then $1 is the principal and $0.1255088 is the interest on that principal for one year. The true annual earning power of $1 invested at 12% compounded quarterly is not 12¢ but actually 12.55¢. Therefore, the true, *effective* rate of interest is 12.55%, not 12%. However, 12% compounded quarterly is essentially the equivalent of 12.55% compounded annually.

To convert a nominal rate to an effective rate by using Table 9–1:

1. Find the factor in the table at the periodic interest rate for the number of conversion periods in one year.
2. Subtract 1 from the factor found in Step 1.
3. Convert the remainder to a percent.

Example A:　Use Table 9–1 to find the effective rate of interest that is equivalent to a nominal rate of 12% compounded quarterly.

Solution:
1. 12% ÷ 4 = 3% column; 4 conversion periods in 1 year.
   The factor on the fourth line in the 3% column of Table 9–1 is 1.12550881.
2. 1.12550881 − 1 = 0.12550881
3. 0.12550881 = 12.55%　effective rate

The following formula may be used:

$$E = (1 + i)^m - 1$$

E = Effective rate of annual interest
i = Interest rate *per period* in decimal form
m = Number of interest periods *per year*

When a calculator is being used, solving the formula is easy. Remember, however, a number is raised to a power by pressing the $\boxed{=}$　key　$n - 1$　times. (For this formula, $m - 1$ times.)

The following example illustrates using the effective-rate formula to solve the same problem that is in the preceding example.

Example B:　Use the preceding formula to find the effective rate of interest that is equivalent to a nominal rate of 12% compounded quarterly.

Solution:
$E = (1 \times i)^m - 1$
$E = (1 + 0.03)^4 - 1$
$E = 1.03^4 - 1$
$E = 1.1255088 - 1$
$E = 0.1255088$
$E = 12.55\%$
Or 1.03 $\boxed{\times}$ $\boxed{=}$ $\boxed{=}$ $\boxed{=}$ $\boxed{-}$ 1 $\boxed{=}$ → 0.1255088, means 12.55%

- Exercise 9–4

A. For each of the following, use Table 9–1 to find the effective rate of interest to the nearest 0.01%.

	Nominal Rate	Compounded
1.	18%	Semiannually
2.	16%	Semiannually
3.	16%	Quarterly
4.	6%	Quarterly
5.	18%	Monthly
6.	12%	Monthly
7.	6%	Monthly
8.	14%	Semiannually

B. For each of the following, use the formula to find the effective rate to the nearest 0.01%.

	Nominal Rate	Compounded
1.	15%	Semiannually
2.	17%	Semiannually
3.	19%	Quarterly
4.	14%	Quarterly
5.	$12\frac{1}{2}\%$	Monthly
6.	$16\frac{3}{4}\%$	Monthly
7.	9%	Monthly
8.	10%	Monthly
9.	8%	Semimonthly
10.	$7\frac{1}{2}\%$	Bimonthly

C. Solve these problems. Show each rate to the nearest 0.01%.

1. Find the true rate of annual interest that is equivalent to 11% compounded monthly.

2. Find the true annual rate of interest that is equivalent to 13.5% compounded bimonthly.

3. Which is better for the depositor: an account that **(a)** yields 14% compounded monthly or **(b)** yields 14.76% compounded annually?

4. Which is better for the investor: an investment that **(a)** earns 16.08% compounded semiannually or **(b)** earns 15.9% compounded quarterly?

5. Find the effective rate of interest for **(a)** a savings account that earns 8% compounded quarterly and **(b)** another that earns $7\frac{3}{4}\%$ compounded monthly. **(c)** Which is better for the depositor, **(a)** or **(b)**?

Part 2. Mathematics Applications in Starting a Business

6. Find the effective rate of interest for **(a)** a checking account that earns 5.3% compounded monthly and **(b)** another that earns $5\frac{1}{4}$% compounded daily based on a 360-day year. **(c)** Which is better for the depositor, **(a)** or **(b)**?

7. A company plans to earn on its investments an average of 11.5% compounded monthly. Would an investment that pays 12% compounded annually provide a yield that is smaller than, equal to, or larger than the desired average?

8. The financial officer of Golden Capital Corporation hopes to average 14% compounded annually on the company's investments. Would an investment that yields 13.5% compounded quarterly be larger than, equal to, or smaller than the desired average?

9. A deposit of $6,000 was placed in a savings account that paid interest at 6% compounded monthly. After three years, the rate was changed to 7% compounded daily based on the 360-day year. **(a)** How much would be in the account 8 weeks after the new rate started? **(b)** What was the effective rate in the beginning? **(c)** What was the effective rate after the rate changed?

10. A $10,000 certificate of deposit earned interest at 12% compounded monthly for 2 years. The certificate proceeds were then placed in a 60-day account that paid 14% interest compounded daily based on the 360-day year. **(a)** What was the compound amount when the 60-day account matured? **(b)** What effective rate did the certificate earn? **(c)** What effective rate did the account pay?

Computing Present Value at Compound Interest

The **present value** of a compound amount that is due sometime in the future is the principal which, invested now at a given rate per period, will grow to the compound amount. If invested at 6% interest compounded semiannually, the value of $1 grows to $1.0609 in one year. From a different perspective, one may say that the present value of $1.0609 is $1. Of course, because money has earning power, its future value is greater than its present value.

Computing present value at compound interest answers this question: What principal invested now (or presently) at a given rate for a certain length of time will yield a specific compound amount?

Compound discount is the difference between a compound amount and its present value. In other words, compound interest on the present value of an investment is the same as the compound discount on the maturity value (compound amount) of that investment. For example, if $9,057.81 (present value) is invested at 8% interest compounded quarterly, it will grow to $20,000 (compound amount) in ten years. In this example, the compound discount is $10,942.19 ($20,000 − $9,057.81).

Using a Present-Value Table. The following example reveals how to find the present value of an amount by multiplying the present value of 1 (found in a table) by the amount. To facilitate finding the present value of amounts, tables that show the present value of 1 at various rates for numerous periods have been prepared.

To find the present value of a compound amount by using Table 9–2, follow this procedure:

1. Find in the table the present value of 1 at the periodic rate for the number of periods to maturity.
2. Find the present value of the amount by multiplying the present value of 1 by the amount.

Example A: Use Table 9–2 to find **(a)** the principal that will amount to $5,000 in 2 years at 12% compounded quarterly and **(b)** the compound discount on the amount.

Solution: **(a)** 8 periods at 3% = 0.78940923   present value of 1
0.78940923 × $5,000 = $3,947.05   present value of $5,000

(b) $5,000 − $3,947.05 = $1,052.95   compound discount

Using a Present-Value Formula. Present value is the principal (P) of a compound amount (S). The compound-amount formula, therefore, may be used to find present value:

$$\text{If } P(1 + i)^n = S$$
$$\text{then } P = \frac{S}{(1 + i)^n}.$$

Of course, the formula can be used for any rate of interest and for any period of time. Recall that $i = \frac{r}{m}$.

Example B: Vicki Dimopoulos owes $12,000, the maturity value of a note that will be due in 2 years. If money is worth 11.5% compounded monthly, what is the present value of this note?

Solution:
$$P = \frac{S}{(1 + i)^n}$$

$$P = \frac{12,000}{\left(1 + \dfrac{0.115}{12}\right)^{24}} \qquad 24 = 2 \times 2 \times 2 \times 3$$

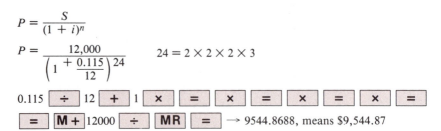

0.115 [÷] 12 [+] 1 [×] [=] [×] [=] [×] [=] [×] [=]
[=] [M+] 12000 [÷] [MR] [=] → 9544.8688, means $9,544.87

n	0.5%	1%	1.5%	2%	3%	4%	5%
1	0.99502488	0.99009901	0.98522167	0.98039216	0.97087379	0.96153846	0.95238095
2	0.99007450	0.98029605	0.97066175	0.96116878	0.94259591	0.92455621	0.90702948
3	0.98514876	0.97059015	0.95631699	0.94232233	0.91514166	0.88899636	0.86383760
4	0.98024752	0.96098034	0.94218423	0.92384543	0.88848705	0.85480419	0.82270247
5	0.97537067	0.95146569	0.92826033	0.90573081	0.86260878	0.82192711	0.78352617
6	0.97051808	0.94204524	0.91454219	0.88797138	0.83748426	0.79031453	0.74621540
7	0.96568963	0.93271805	0.90102679	0.87056018	0.81309151	0.75991781	0.71068133
8	0.96088520	0.92348322	0.88771112	0.85349037	0.78940923	0.73069021	0.67683936
9	0.95610468	0.91433982	0.87459224	0.83675527	0.76641673	0.70258674	0.64460892
10	0.95134794	0.90528695	0.86166723	0.82034830	0.74409391	0.67556417	0.61391325
11	0.94661487	0.89632372	0.84893323	0.80426304	0.72242128	0.64958093	0.58467929
12	0.94190534	0.88744923	0.83638742	0.78849318	0.70137988	0.62459705	0.55683742
13	0.93721924	0.87866260	0.82402702	0.77303253	0.68095134	0.60057409	0.53032135
14	0.93255646	0.86996297	0.81184928	0.75787502	0.66111781	0.57747508	0.50506795
15	0.92791688	0.86134947	0.79985150	0.74301473	0.64186195	0.55526450	0.48101710
16	0.92330037	0.85282126	0.78803104	0.72844581	0.62316694	0.53390818	0.45811152
17	0.91870684	0.84437749	0.77638526	0.71416256	0.60501645	0.51337325	0.43629669
18	0.91413616	0.83601731	0.76491159	0.70015937	0.58739461	0.49362812	0.41552065
19	0.90958822	0.82773992	0.75360747	0.68643076	0.57028603	0.47464242	0.39573396
20	0.90506290	0.81954447	0.74247042	0.67297133	0.55367575	0.45638695	0.37688948
21	0.90056010	0.81143017	0.73149795	0.65977582	0.53754928	0.43883360	0.35894236
22	0.89607971	0.80339621	0.72068763	0.64683904	0.52189250	0.42195539	0.34184987
23	0.89162160	0.79544179	0.71003708	0.63415592	0.50669175	0.40572633	0.32557131
24	0.88718567	0.78756613	0.69954392	0.62172149	0.49193374	0.39012147	0.31006791
25	0.88277181	0.77976844	0.68920583	0.60953087	0.47760557	0.37511680	0.29530277
26	0.87837991	0.77204796	0.67902052	0.59757928	0.46369473	0.36068923	0.28124073
27	0.87400986	0.76440392	0.66898574	0.58586204	0.45018906	0.34681657	0.26784832
28	0.86966155	0.75683557	0.65909925	0.57437455	0.43707675	0.33347747	0.25509364
29	0.86533488	0.74934215	0.64935887	0.56311231	0.42434636	0.32065141	0.24294632
30	0.86102973	0.74192292	0.63976243	0.55207089	0.41198676	0.30831867	0.23137745
31	0.85674600	0.73457715	0.63030781	0.54124597	0.39998715	0.29646026	0.22035947
32	0.85248358	0.72730411	0.62099292	0.53063330	0.38833703	0.28505794	0.20986617
33	0.84824237	0.72010307	0.61181568	0.52022873	0.37702625	0.27409417	0.19987254
34	0.84402226	0.71297334	0.60277407	0.51002817	0.36604490	0.26355209	0.19035480
35	0.83982314	0.70591420	0.59386608	0.50002761	0.35538340	0.25341547	0.18129029
36	0.83564492	0.69892495	0.58508974	0.49022315	0.34503243	0.24366872	0.17265741
37	0.83148748	0.69200490	0.57644309	0.48061093	0.33498294	0.23429685	0.16443563
38	0.82735073	0.68515337	0.56792423	0.47118719	0.32522615	0.22528543	0.15660536
39	0.82323455	0.67836967	0.55953126	0.46194822	0.31575355	0.21662061	0.14914797
40	0.81913886	0.67165314	0.55126232	0.45289042	0.30655684	0.20828904	0.14204568
41	0.81506354	0.66500311	0.54311559	0.44401021	0.29762800	0.20027793	0.13528160
42	0.81100850	0.65841892	0.53508925	0.43530413	0.28895922	0.19257493	0.12883962
43	0.80697363	0.65189992	0.52718153	0.42676875	0.28054294	0.18516820	0.12270440
44	0.80295884	0.64544546	0.51939067	0.41840074	0.27237178	0.17804635	0.11686133
45	0.79896402	0.63905492	0.51171494	0.41019680	0.26443862	0.17119841	0.11129651
46	0.79498907	0.63272764	0.50415265	0.40215373	0.25673653	0.16461386	0.10599668
47	0.79103390	0.62646301	0.49670212	0.39426836	0.24925876	0.15828256	0.10094921
48	0.78709841	0.62026041	0.48936170	0.38653761	0.24199880	0.15219476	0.09614211
49	0.78318250	0.61411921	0.48212975	0.37895844	0.23495029	0.14634112	0.09156391
50	0.77928607	0.60803882	0.47500468	0.37152788	0.22810708	0.14071262	0.08720373

Table 9–2 Present Value of 1 at Compound Interest*

*The factors in this table are the reciprocals of those in Table 9–1.

n	6%	7%	8%	9%	10%	11%	12%
1	0.94339623	0.93457944	0.92592593	0.91743119	0.90909091	0.90090090	0.89285714
2	0.88999644	0.87343873	0.85733882	0.84167999	0.82644628	0.81162243	0.79719388
3	0.83961928	0.81629788	0.79383224	0.77218348	0.75131480	0.73119138	0.71178025
4	0.79209366	0.76289521	0.73502985	0.70842521	0.68301346	0.65873097	0.63551808
5	0.74725817	0.71298618	0.68058320	0.64993139	0.62092132	0.59345133	0.56742686
6	0.70496054	0.66634222	0.63016963	0.59626733	0.56447393	0.53464084	0.50663112
7	0.66505711	0.62274974	0.58349040	0.54703424	0.51315812	0.48165841	0.45234922
8	0.62741237	0.58200910	0.54026888	0.50186628	0.46650738	0.43392650	0.40388323
9	0.59189846	0.54393374	0.50024897	0.46042778	0.42409762	0.39092477	0.36061002
10	0.55839478	0.50834929	0.46319349	0.42241081	0.38554329	0.35218448	0.32197324
11	0.52678753	0.47509280	0.42888286	0.38753285	0.35049390	0.31728331	0.28747610
12	0.49696936	0.44401196	0.39711376	0.35553473	0.31863082	0.28584082	0.25667509
13	0.46883902	0.41496445	0.36769792	0.32617865	0.28966438	0.25751426	0.22917419
14	0.44230096	0.38781724	0.34046104	0.29924647	0.26333125	0.23199482	0.20461981
15	0.41726506	0.36244602	0.31524170	0.27453804	0.23939205	0.20900435	0.18269626
16	0.39364628	0.33873460	0.29189047	0.25186976	0.21762914	0.18829220	0.16312166
17	0.37136442	0.31657439	0.27026895	0.23107318	0.19784467	0.16963262	0.14564434
18	0.35034379	0.29586392	0.25024903	0.21199374	0.17985879	0.15282218	0.13003959
19	0.33051301	0.27650833	0.23171206	0.19448967	0.16350799	0.13767764	0.11610678
20	0.31180473	0.25841900	0.21454821	0.17843089	0.14864363	0.12403391	0.10366677
21	0.29415540	0.24151309	0.19865575	0.16369806	0.13513057	0.11174226	0.09255961
22	0.27750510	0.22571317	0.18394051	0.15018171	0.12284597	0.10066870	0.08264251
23	0.26179726	0.21094688	0.17031528	0.13778139	0.11167816	0.09069252	0.07378796
24	0.24697855	0.19714662	0.15769934	0.12640494	0.10152560	0.08170498	0.06588210
25	0.23299863	0.18424918	0.14601790	0.11596784	0.09229600	0.07360809	0.05882331
26	0.21981003	0.17219549	0.13520176	0.10639251	0.08390545	0.06631359	0.05252081
27	0.20736795	0.16093037	0.12518682	0.09760781	0.07627768	0.05974197	0.04689358
28	0.19563014	0.15040221	0.11591372	0.08954845	0.06934335	0.05382160	0.04186927
29	0.18455674	0.14056282	0.10732752	0.08215454	0.06303941	0.04848793	0.03738327
30	0.17411013	0.13136712	0.09937733	0.07537114	0.05730855	0.04368282	0.03337792
31	0.16425484	0.12277301	0.09201605	0.06914783	0.05209868	0.03935389	0.02980172
32	0.15495740	0.11474113	0.08520005	0.06343838	0.04736244	0.03545395	0.02660868
33	0.14618622	0.10723470	0.07888893	0.05820035	0.04305676	0.03194050	0.02375775
34	0.13791153	0.10021934	0.07304531	0.05339481	0.03914251	0.02877522	0.02121227
35	0.13010522	0.09366294	0.06763454	0.04898607	0.03558410	0.02592363	0.01893953
36	0.12274077	0.08753546	0.06262458	0.04494135	0.03234918	0.02335462	0.01691029
37	0.11579318	0.08180884	0.05798572	0.04123059	0.02940835	0.02104020	0.01509848
38	0.10923885	0.07645686	0.05369048	0.03782623	0.02673486	0.01895513	0.01348078
39	0.10305552	0.07145501	0.04971341	0.03470296	0.02430442	0.01707670	0.01203641
40	0.09722219	0.06678038	0.04603093	0.03183758	0.02209493	0.01538441	0.01074680
41	0.09171905	0.06241157	0.04262123	0.02920879	0.02008630	0.01385983	0.00959536
42	0.08652740	0.05832857	0.03946411	0.02679706	0.01826027	0.01248633	0.00856728
43	0.08162962	0.05451268	0.03654084	0.02458446	0.01660025	0.01124895	0.00764936
44	0.07700908	0.05094643	0.03383411	0.02255455	0.01509113	0.01013419	0.00682978
45	0.07265007	0.04761349	0.03132788	0.02069224	0.01371921	0.00912990	0.00609802
46	0.06853781	0.04449859	0.02900730	0.01898371	0.01247201	0.00822513	0.00544466
47	0.06465831	0.04158747	0.02685861	0.01741625	0.01133819	0.00741003	0.00486131
48	0.06099840	0.03886679	0.02486908	0.01597821	0.01030745	0.00667570	0.00434045
49	0.05754566	0.03632410	0.02302693	0.01465891	0.00937041	0.00601415	0.00387540
50	0.05428836	0.03394776	0.02132123	0.01344854	0.00851855	0.00541815	0.00346018

Table 9–2 Continued

Part 2. Mathematics Applications in Starting a Business

A. Use Table 9–2 to find **(a)** the present value and **(b)** the compound discount for each of the following.

	Amount	Rate	Time	Compounded
1.	$ 2,000	11%	10 years	Annually
2.	3,500	16%	5 years	Quarterly
3.	475	14%	15 years	Semiannually
4.	1,360	12%	2 years	Monthly
5.	980	8%	20 years	Semiannually
6.	4,600	12%	7 years	Quarterly
7.	8,295	10%	25 years	Annually
8.	17,400	6%	4 years	Monthly

B. Solve these problems.

1. If money is worth 9% compounded annually, find **(a)** the present value of $24,000 due in 8 years and **(b)** the compound discount.

2. Find **(a)** the present value and **(b)** the compound discount of $28,500 due 10 years from now if money is worth 12% compounded quarterly.

3. Find the present value that must be deposited now to amount to $24,500 in 5 years at 8% compounded quarterly.

4. The compound amount of 1 is 1.282432 for a certain period of time in a savings account. How much principal must be placed in the account now to amount to $30,000 at the end of that period of time?

5. An investment made $7\frac{1}{2}$ years ago has accumulated to $32,500. How much was invested originally if the 13% interest has been compounded semiannually?

6. Laura Trusler borrowed some money 5 years ago at 15% interest compounded semiannually. She paid $6,700 on the due date to cover the principal and interest. How much did she borrow?

7. Bruce Williams holds a note that calls for the payment of $75,000 plus interest at 11.5% compounded semiannually. He has offered to sell the note, which is due in 15 years, for present value based on 13% interest compounded quarterly. Find the selling price of the note.

8. Roberta Page borrowed $60,000 by promising to repay it in 12 years with interest at 11.25% compounded annually. Four years later she inherited $100,000. How much of her inheritance should she invest at 11.75% compounded semiannually to have just enough to pay off the debt when it falls due?

ANNUITIES

In the preceding part of this chapter, compound interest on a single sum of money is considered. In this part of the chapter, compound interest is applied to a series of equal payments that are made on the interest conversion date.

An **annuity** is a sequence of usually equal payments made at regular intervals of time. Individuals or institutions that want to save money or to eliminate debts may do so by making payments regularly, such as monthly, quarterly, semiannually, or annually. Thus, regular deposits into a savings account, payments of bond interest, installments on a mortgage, and payments from life insurance are but a few examples of annuities.

The time between the successive payments is the **payment interval** or **payment period.** The time from the beginning of the first payment period to the end of the last payment period is the **term** of the annuity.

When classified by term, annuities fall into three categories: contingent annuities, annuities certain, and perpetuities. A **contingent annuity** has an indefinite term. It is an annuity for which the beginning or end of the sequence of payments, or both, happen to be contingent on some specified condition that cannot be predicted accurately. For example, payments made to the beneficiary of a life insurance policy form a contingent annuity because the beginning of the payments depends on the death of the insured. An **annuity certain** is one for which the term begins and ends on definite dates. Thus, payments on a mortgage are an annuity certain. A **perpetuity** is an annuity in which the payments continue forever, such as the interest payments on perpetual bonds.

Two important kinds of annuities certain are ordinary annuities and annuities due. In an **ordinary annuity,** the payments are made at the *end* of each period. Conversely, the payments are made at the *beginning* of each period in an **annuity due.**

Ordinary Annuity

The **amount** of an annuity is its accumulated value at the end of its term. It is an amount that includes the principal and the accumulated compound interest on a series of payments. Notice Figure 9–1 and the example which follows.

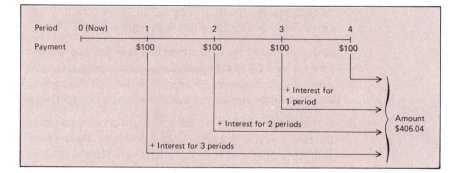

Figure 9–1 Amount of an Ordinary Annuity

Example: For the past year, Zelma Newsome has deposited $100 at the end of each month in a savings account that pays 12% interest compounded monthly. Find **(a)** the amount and **(b)** the compound interest in the account at the end of the fourth month.

Solution: **(a)** Payment at end of first month $100.00
            Interest for second month ($100 × 0.01) 1.00
            Payment at end of second month 100.00
                Amount at end of second month $201.00
            Interest for third month ($201 × 0.01) 2.01
            Payment at end of third month 100.00
                Amount at end of third month $303.01
            Interest for fourth month ($303.01 × 0.01) 3.03
            Payment at end of fourth month 100.00
                Amount at end of fourth month $406.04

(b) $406.04 − (4 × $100) = $6.04   compound interest

Finding the Amount of an Ordinary Annuity by Using an Annuity Table. Tables have been prepared that show the accumulated value (amount) of different series of $1 investments at various rates of interest. To find the amount of an ordinary annuity by using Table 9–3 follow this procedure:

1. Find in the table the accumulated value of a series of $1 deposits compounded at the periodic rate for the number of periods in the annuity.
2. Find the amount of the ordinary annuity by multiplying the amount found in Step 1 by the periodic payment.

Example: David Joplin is thinking of depositing $250 at the end of each calendar quarter in a savings bank that pays 8% interest compounded quarterly. If he does so and allows the deposits and interest to accumulate, how much will be in the account at the end of 10 years? Use Table 9–3.

Solution: 40 periods at 2% = 60.40198318
            60.401983 × $250 = $15,100.50   amount of annuity

● Exercise 9–6

A. For each problem below, use Table 9–3 to find the amount of the ordinary annuity.

	Payment	Payment Interval	Term	Rate	Compounded
1.	$3,000	1 year	20 years	5%	Annually
2.	1,200	3 months	$6\frac{3}{4}$ years	8%	Quarterly
3.	400	1 month	3 years	18%	Monthly
4.	9,700	1 year	17 years	11%	Annually
5.	680	6 months	20 years	16%	Semiannually
6.	750	3 months	$12\frac{1}{2}$ years	12%	Quarterly
7.	3,500	6 months	$13\frac{1}{2}$ years	20%	Semiannually
8.	250	1 month	$2\frac{1}{2}$ years	12%	Monthly

n	0.5%	1%	1.5%	2%	3%	4%	5%
1	1.00000000	1.00000000	1.00000000	1.00000000	1.00000000	1.00000000	1.00000000
2	2.00500000	2.01000000	2.01500000	2.02000000	2.03000000	2.04000000	2.05000000
3	3.01502500	3.03010000	3.04522500	3.06040000	3.09090000	3.12160000	3.15250000
4	4.03010013	4.06040100	4.09090338	4.12160800	4.18362700	4.24646400	4.31012500
5	5.05025063	5.10100501	5.15226693	5.20404016	5.30913581	5.41632256	5.52563125
6	6.07550188	6.15201506	6.22955093	6.30812096	6.46840988	6.63297546	6.80191281
7	7.10587939	7.21353521	7.32299419	7.43428338	7.66246218	7.89829448	8.14200845
8	8.14140879	8.28567056	8.43283911	8.58296905	8.89233605	9.21422626	9.54910888
9	9.18211583	9.36852727	9.55933169	9.75462843	10.15910613	10.58279531	11.02656432
10	10.22802641	10.46221254	10.70272167	10.94972100	11.46387931	12.00610712	12.57789254
11	11.27916654	11.56683467	11.86326249	12.16871542	12.80779569	13.48635141	14.20678716
12	12.33556237	12.68250301	13.04121143	13.41208973	14.19202956	15.02580546	15.91712652
13	13.39724018	13.80932804	14.23682960	14.68033152	15.61779045	16.62683768	17.71298285
14	14.46422639	14.94742132	15.45038205	15.97393815	17.08632416	18.29191119	19.59863199
15	15.53654752	16.09689554	16.68213778	17.29341692	18.59891389	20.02358764	21.57856359
16	16.61423026	17.25786449	17.93236984	18.63928525	20.15688130	21.82453114	23.65749177
17	17.69730141	18.43044314	19.20135539	20.01207096	21.76158774	23.69751239	25.84036636
18	18.78578791	19.61474757	20.48937572	21.41231238	23.41443537	25.64541288	28.13238467
19	19.87971685	20.81089504	21.79671636	22.84055863	25.11686844	27.67122940	30.53900391
20	20.97911544	22.01900399	23.12366710	24.29736980	26.87037449	29.77807858	33.06595410
21	22.08401101	23.23919403	24.47052211	25.78331719	28.67648572	31.96920172	35.71925181
22	23.19443107	24.47158598	25.83757994	27.29898354	30.53678030	34.24796979	38.50521440
23	24.31040322	25.71630183	27.22514364	28.84496321	32.45288370	36.61788858	41.43047512
24	25.43195524	26.97346485	28.63352080	30.42186247	34.42647022	39.08260412	44.50199887
25	26.55911502	28.24319950	30.06302361	32.03029972	36.45926432	41.64590829	47.72709882
26	27.69191059	29.52563150	31.51396896	33.67090572	38.55304225	44.31174462	51.11345376
27	28.83037015	30.82088781	32.98667850	35.34432383	40.70963352	47.08421440	54.66912645
28	29.97452200	32.12909669	34.48147867	37.05121031	42.93092252	49.96758298	58.40258277
29	31.12439461	33.45038766	35.99870085	38.79223451	45.21885020	52.96628630	62.32271191
30	32.28001658	34.78489153	37.53868137	40.56807921	47.57541571	56.08493775	66.43884750
31	33.44141666	36.13274045	39.10176159	42.37944079	50.00267818	59.32833526	70.76078988
32	34.60862375	37.49406785	40.68828801	44.22702961	52.50275852	62.70146867	75.29882937
33	35.78166686	38.86900853	42.29861233	46.11157020	55.07784128	66.20952742	80.06377084
34	36.96057520	40.25769862	43.93309152	48.03380160	57.73017652	69.85790851	85.06695938
35	38.14537807	41.66027560	45.59208789	49.99447763	60.46208181	73.65222486	90.32030735
36	39.33610496	43.07687836	47.27596921	51.99436719	63.27594427	77.59831385	95.83632272
37	40.53278549	44.50764714	48.98510874	54.03425453	66.17422259	81.70224640	101.62813886
38	41.73544942	45.95272361	50.71988538	56.11493962	69.15944927	85.97033626	107.70954580
39	42.94412666	47.41225085	52.48068366	58.23723841	72.23423275	90.40914971	114.09502309
40	44.15884730	48.88637336	54.26789391	60.40198318	75.40125973	95.02551570	120.79977424
41	45.37964153	50.37523709	56.08191232	62.61002284	78.66329753	99.82653633	127.83976295
42	46.60653974	51.87898946	57.92314100	64.86222330	82.02319645	104.81959778	135.23175110
43	47.83957244	53.39777936	59.79198812	67.15946777	85.48389234	110.01238169	142.99333866
44	49.07877030	54.93175715	61.68886794	69.50265712	89.04840911	115.41287696	151.14300559
45	50.32416415	56.48107472	63.61420096	71.89271027	92.71986139	121.02939204	159.70015587
46	51.57578497	58.04588547	65.56841398	74.33056447	96.50145723	126.87056772	168.68516366
47	52.83366390	59.62634432	67.55194018	76.81717576	100.39650095	132.94539043	178.11942185
48	54.09783222	61.22260777	69.56521929	79.35351927	104.40839598	139.26320604	188.02539294
49	55.36832138	62.83483385	71.60869758	81.94058966	108.54064785	145.83373429	198.42666259
50	56.64516299	64.46318218	73.68282804	84.57940145	112.79686729	152.66708366	209.34799572

Table 9–3 Amount of Ordinary Annuity of 1 at Compound Interest

Part 2. Mathematics Applications in Starting a Business

n	6%	7%	8%	9%	10%	11%	12%
1	1.00000000	1.00000000	1.00000000	1.00000000	1.00000000	1.00000000	1.00000000
2	2.06000000	2.07000000	2.08000000	2.09000000	2.10000000	2.11000000	2.12000000
3	3.18360000	3.21490000	3.24640000	3.27810000	3.31000000	3.34210000	3.37440000
4	4.37461600	4.43994300	4.50611200	4.57312900	4.64100000	4.70973100	4.77932800
5	5.63709296	5.75073901	5.86660096	5.98471061	6.10510000	6.22780141	6.35284736
6	6.97531854	7.15329074	7.33592904	7.52333456	7.71561000	7.91285957	8.11518904
7	8.39383765	8.65402109	8.92280336	9.20043468	9.48717100	9.78327412	10.08901173
8	9.89746791	10.25980257	10.63662763	11.02847380	11.43588810	11.85943427	12.29969314
9	11.49131598	11.97798875	12.48755784	13.02103644	13.57947691	14.16397204	14.77565631
10	13.18079494	13.81644796	14.48656247	15.19292972	15.93742460	16.72200896	17.54873507
11	14.97164264	15.78359932	16.64548746	17.56029339	18.53116706	19.56142995	20.65458328
12	16.86994120	17.88845127	18.97712646	20.14071980	21.38428377	22.71318724	24.13313327
13	18.88213767	20.14064286	21.49529658	22.95338458	24.52271214	26.21163784	28.02910926
14	21.01506593	22.55048786	24.21492030	26.01918919	27.97498336	30.09491800	32.39260238
15	23.27596988	25.12902201	27.15211393	29.36091622	31.77248169	34.40535898	37.27971466
16	25.67252808	27.88805355	30.32428304	33.00339868	35.94972986	39.18994847	42.75328042
17	28.21287976	30.84021730	33.75022569	36.97370456	40.54470285	44.50084281	48.88367407
18	30.90565255	33.99903251	37.45024374	41.30133797	45.59917313	50.39593551	55.74971496
19	33.75999170	37.37896479	41.44626324	46.01845839	51.15909045	56.93948842	63.43968075
20	36.78559120	40.99549232	45.76196430	51.16011964	57.27499949	64.20283215	72.05244244
21	39.99272668	44.86517678	50.42292144	56.76453041	64.00249944	72.26514368	81.69873554
22	43.39229028	49.00573916	55.45675516	62.87333815	71.40274939	81.21430949	92.50258380
23	46.99582769	53.43614090	60.89329557	69.53193858	79.54302433	91.14788353	104.60289386
24	50.81557735	58.17667076	66.76475922	76.78981305	88.49732676	102.17415072	118.15524112
25	54.86451200	63.24903772	73.10593995	84.70089623	98.34705943	114.41330730	133.33387006
26	59.15638272	68.67647036	79.95441515	93.32397689	109.18176538	127.99877110	150.33393446
27	63.70576568	74.48382328	87.35076836	102.72313481	121.09994191	143.07863592	169.37400660
28	68.52811162	80.69769091	95.33882983	112.96821694	134.20993611	159.81728587	190.69888739
29	73.63979832	87.34652927	103.96593622	124.13535646	148.63092972	178.39718732	214.58275388
30	79.05818622	94.46078632	113.28321111	136.30753855	164.49402269	199.02087793	241.33268434
31	84.80167739	102.07304137	123.34586800	149.57521702	181.94342496	221.91317450	271.29260646
32	90.88977803	110.21815426	134.21353744	164.03698655	201.13776745	247.32362369	304.84771924
33	97.34316471	118.93342506	145.95062044	179.80031534	222.25154420	275.52922230	342.42944555
34	104.18375460	128.25876481	158.62667007	196.98234372	245.47669862	306.83743675	384.52097901
35	111.43477987	138.23687835	172.31680368	215.71075465	271.02436848	341.58955480	431.66349649
36	119.12086666	148.91345984	187.10214797	236.12472257	299.12680533	380.16440582	484.46311607
37	127.26811866	160.33740202	203.07031981	258.37594760	330.03948586	422.98249046	543.59869000
38	135.90420578	172.56102017	220.31594540	282.62978288	364.04343445	470.51056441	609.83053280
39	145.05845813	185.64029158	238.94122103	309.06646334	401.44777789	523.26672650	684.01019674
40	154.76196562	199.63511199	259.05651871	337.88244504	442.59255568	581.82606641	767.09142034
41	165.04768356	214.60956983	280.78104021	369.29186510	487.85181125	646.82693372	860.14239079
42	175.95054457	230.63223972	304.24352342	403.52813296	537.63699237	718.97789643	964.35947768
43	187.50757724	247.77649650	329.58300530	440.84566492	592.40069161	799.06546504	1081.08261500
44	199.75803188	266.12085125	356.94964572	481.52177477	652.64076077	887.96266619	1211.81252880
45	212.74351379	285.74931084	386.50561738	525.85873450	718.90483685	986.63855947	1358.23003226
46	226.50812462	306.75176260	418.42606677	574.18602060	791.79532054	1096.16880101	1522.21763613
47	241.09861210	329.22438598	452.90015211	626.86276245	871.97485259	1217.74736912	1705.88375247
48	256.56452882	353.27009300	490.13216428	684.28041107	960.17233785	1352.69957973	1911.58980276
49	272.95840055	378.99899951	530.34273742	746.86564807	1057.18957163	1502.49653350	2141.98057909
50	290.33590458	406.52892947	573.77015642	815.08355640	1163.90852880	1668.77115218	2400.01824858

Table 9–3 Continued

Chapter 9. Compound Interest and Annuities

B. Solve these problems.

1. The interest rate on a savings plan is 6% compounded annually. If $600 is deposited in the plan at the end of each year for 10 years, what amount will be in the fund at the end of the 10 years?

2. Find the amount of an annuity of $840 payable at the end of every 6 months for 14 years if the interest rate is 10% compounded semi-annually.

3. If $370 is payable at the end of each quarter for 5 years at 12% interest compounded quarterly, what is the amount of the annuity?

4. At the end of each quarter, Webster Company placed $2,500 in a fund to provide for the replacement of equipment. The fund paid 8% interest compounded quarterly. Find **(a)** the amount in the fund and **(b)** the total interest at the end of 6 years.

5. John Fischer deposited $420 at the end of every 6 months in a fund that earns 12% interest compounded semiannually. How much was in the fund at the end of $7\frac{1}{2}$ years?

6. The Appalachian Power and Water Company sold bonds that were to be redeemed in 20 years. To provide for funds to repay the principal on the bonds, the company invested $54,369.11 at the end of each year at 6% interest compounded annually. To the nearest dollar, what is the face value of the bonds?

7. Paula Ramundo has earned $1,500 a month in net pay for the past year. She deposited 10% of her net pay at the end of each month in a savings account that pays 12% interest compounded monthly. How much was in the fund at the end of the year?

8. At the end of each month for $1\frac{1}{2}$ years, Bill Lehmann deposited $350 into a fund that earns interest at 6% compounded monthly. How much will be in the fund $2\frac{1}{2}$ years after the last deposit was made?

Present Value of an Ordinary Annuity

The **present value** of an annuity is that certain sum of money which, if invested now at a given rate, will provide a sequence of specific payments in the future. As the amount of an annuity may be thought of as the sum of the values in a series of individual compound amounts, the present value of an annuity may also be defined as the sum of the present values of all the payments in the annuity. In short, as Figure 9–2 illustrates, the present value of an annuity may be thought of as a series of compound-discount problems.

Part 2. Mathematics Applications in Starting a Business

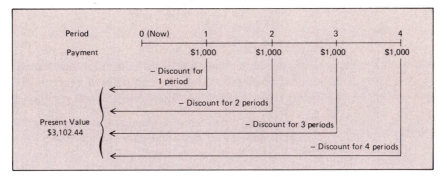

Figure 9-2 Present Value of an Ordinary Annuity

Example A: Carlos Guerra wants to provide for payments of $1,000 at the end of each year for 4 years. The current interest rate is 11% compounded annually. Use Table 9-2 to determine the certain sum of money needed now for this annuity.

Solution:

$1,000 discounted 1 period at 11% ($1,000 × 0.90090090)	$ 900.90
$1,000 discounted 2 periods at 11% ($1,000 × 0.81162243).	811.62
$1,000 discounted 3 periods at 11% ($1,000 × 0.73119138).	731.19
$1,000 discounted 4 periods at 11% ($1,000 × 0.65873097).	658.73
Present value of annuity	$3,102.44

The procedure of finding the present value of an annuity, however, is simplified through the use of annuity tables in which the present values of 1 are shown. When a table such as Table 9-4 is used, the present value of an ordinary annuity is found by multiplying the appropriate factor in the table by the given annuity payment.

Example B: Carl Hoffman wants to receive $1,000 at the end of each month for 4 years from a bank that pays 6% interest compounded monthly. Use Table 9-4 to determine how much must be deposited in the bank now.

Solution: 48 periods at 0.5% = 42.58031778
42.58031778 × $1,000 = $42,580.32   present value of annuity

● **Exercise 9-7**

A. For each problem, use Table 9-4 to find the present value of the ordinary annuity.

	Payment	Payment Interval	Term	Rate	Compounded
1.	$5,000	1 year	25 years	5%	Annually
2.	400	1 month	2 years	6%	Monthly
3.	900	3 months	10 years	8%	Quarterly
4.	1,320	6 months	20 years	10%	Semiannually
5.	650	1 month	$4\frac{1}{6}$ years	12%	Monthly
6.	4,800	1 year	12 years	11%	Annually
7.	710	6 months	$9\frac{1}{2}$ years	14%	Semiannually
8.	6,030	3 months	10 years	16%	Quarterly

Chapter 9. Compound Interest and Annuities

B. Solve these problems.

1. Ellen Burkhart plans to invest a sum of money that will provide her with an income of $18,000 at the end of each year for 20 years. How much money is necessary if the interest rate is 6% compounded annually?

2. A businessperson purchased some store equipment by paying $3,000 in cash and agreeing to pay $800 semiannually for 6 years. With interest at 12%, what is the equivalent cash price?

3. For his son's education, Frank Milhous established an ordinary annuity that would provide monthly payments of $1,000 each for 4 years. If the interest is 12% compounded monthly, how much did he deposit?

4. A certain business is expected to provide an average net income of $30,000 for the next 7 years. Find the present value of the earnings based on an interest rate of 10% compounded annually.

5. Three months before becoming 21 years old, an heir received a gift that provided quarterly payments of $9,600 starting on his twenty-first birthday and continuing for 10 years. What is the equivalent cash value of the gift if money is worth 8% compounded quarterly?

6. The buyer of a residential lot can pay **(a)** $20,000 cash or **(b)** $1,000 at the end of each 3 months for 6 years. If she can invest money at 8% compounded quarterly, which plan is better for her and by how much?

7. A house is offered for sale at $134,000. The buyer has offered to pay $6,250 at the end of each six-month period for 20 years and the balance as a down payment. If he agrees that money is worth 10% compounded semiannually, how much is the down payment?

8. A corporate bond has attached coupons of $20 each, payable at the end of each quarter for 10 years. The bondholder will receive the principal of $1,000 when the bond matures in 10 years. Find the present value of **(a)** the coupons and **(b)** the bond principal for an investor who wants to earn 8% interest compounded quarterly.

Annuities Due

In an annuity due, a payment is made at the beginning of each period. Property rent, subscriptions, and insurance premiums are example of annuities due.

Finding the Amount of an Annuity Due. If two easy adjustments are made, ordinary-annuity tables may be used to find the amount of an annuity due. Both of these adjustments may be accomplished mentally. One adjustment pertains to the number of interest-earning periods in the annuity, and the second pertains to the factor found in the table.

n	0.5%	1%	1.5%	2%	3%	4%	5%
1	0.99502488	0.99009901	0.98522167	0.98039216	0.97087379	0.96153846	0.95238095
2	1.98509938	1.97039506	1.95588342	1.94156094	1.91346970	1.88609467	1.85941043
3	2.97024814	2.94098521	2.91220042	2.88388327	2.82861135	2.77509103	2.72324803
4	3.95049566	3.90196555	3.85438465	3.80772870	3.71709840	3.62989522	3.54595050
5	4.92586633	4.85343124	4.78264497	4.71345951	4.57970719	4.45182233	4.32947667
6	5.89638441	5.79547647	5.69718717	5.60143089	5.41719144	5.24213686	5.07569207
7	6.86207404	6.72819453	6.59821396	6.47199107	6.23028296	6.00205467	5.78637340
8	7.82295924	7.65167775	7.48592508	7.32548144	7.01969219	6.73274487	6.46321276
9	8.77906392	8.56601758	8.36051732	8.16223671	7.78610892	7.43533161	7.10782168
10	9.73041186	9.47130453	9.22218455	8.98258501	8.53020284	8.11089578	7.72173493
11	10.67702673	10.36762825	10.07111779	9.78684805	9.25262411	8.76047671	8.30641422
12	11.61893207	11.25507747	10.90750521	10.57534122	9.95400399	9.38507376	8.86325164
13	12.55615131	12.13374007	11.73153222	11.34837375	10.63495533	9.98564785	9.39357299
14	13.48870777	13.00370304	12.54338150	12.10624877	11.29607314	10.56312293	9.89864094
15	14.41662465	13.86505252	13.34323301	12.84926350	11.93793509	11.11838743	10.37965804
16	15.33992502	14.71787378	14.13126405	13.57770931	12.56110203	11.65229561	10.83776956
17	16.25863186	15.56225127	14.90764931	14.29187188	13.16611847	12.16566885	11.27406625
18	17.17276802	16.39826858	15.67256089	14.99203125	13.75351308	12.65929697	11.68958690
19	18.08235624	17.22600850	16.42616837	15.67846201	14.32379911	13.13393940	12.08532086
20	18.98741915	18.04555297	17.16863879	16.35143334	14.87747486	13.59032634	12.46221034
21	19.88797925	18.85698313	17.90013673	17.01120916	15.41502414	14.02915995	12.82115271
22	20.78405896	19.66037934	18.62082437	17.65804820	15.93691664	14.45111533	13.16300258
23	21.67568055	20.45582113	19.33086145	18.29220412	16.44360839	14.85684167	13.48857388
24	22.56286622	21.24338726	20.03040537	18.91392560	16.93554212	15.24696314	13.79864179
25	23.44563803	22.02315570	20.71961120	19.52345647	17.41314769	15.62207994	14.09394457
26	24.32401794	22.79520366	21.39863172	20.12103576	17.87684242	15.98276918	14.37518530
27	25.19802780	23.55960759	22.06761746	20.70689780	18.32703147	16.32958575	14.64303362
28	26.06768936	24.31644316	22.72671671	21.28127236	18.76410823	16.66306322	14.89812726
29	26.93302423	25.06578530	23.37607558	21.84438466	19.18845459	16.98371463	15.14107358
30	27.79405397	25.80770822	24.01583801	22.39645555	19.60044135	17.29203330	15.37245103
31	28.65079997	26.54228537	24.64614582	22.93770152	20.00042849	17.58849356	15.59281050
32	29.50328355	27.26958947	25.26713874	23.46833482	20.38876553	17.87355150	15.80267667
33	30.35152592	27.98969255	25.87895442	23.98856035	20.76579178	18.14764567	16.00254921
34	31.19554818	28.70266589	26.48172849	24.49859172	21.13183668	18.41119776	16.19290401
35	32.03537132	29.40858009	27.07559458	24.99861933	21.48722007	18.66461323	16.37419429
36	32.87101624	30.10750504	27.66068431	25.48884248	21.83225250	18.90828195	16.54685171
37	33.70250372	30.79950994	28.23712740	25.96945341	22.16723544	19.14257880	16.71128734
38	34.52985445	31.48466330	28.80505163	26.44064060	22.49246159	19.36786423	16.86789271
39	35.35308900	32.16303298	29.36458288	26.90258883	22.80821513	19.58448484	17.01704067
40	36.17222786	32.83468611	29.91584520	27.35547924	23.11477197	19.79277388	17.15908635
41	36.98729141	33.49968922	30.45896079	27.79948945	23.41239997	19.99305181	17.29436796
42	37.79829991	34.15810814	30.99405004	28.23479358	23.70135920	20.18562674	17.42320758
43	38.60527354	34.81000806	31.52123157	28.66156233	23.98190213	20.37079494	17.54591198
44	39.40823238	35.45545352	32.04062223	29.07996307	24.25427392	20.54884129	17.66277331
45	40.20719640	36.09450844	32.55233718	29.49015987	24.51871254	20.72003970	17.77406982
46	41.00218547	36.72723608	33.05648983	29.89231360	24.77544907	20.88465356	17.88006650
47	41.79321937	37.35369909	33.55319195	30.28658196	25.02470783	21.04293612	17.98101571
48	42.58031778	37.97395949	34.04255365	30.67311957	25.26670664	21.19513088	18.07715782
49	43.36350028	38.58807871	34.52468339	31.05207801	25.50165693	21.34147200	18.16872173
50	44.14278635	39.19611753	34.99968807	31.42360589	25.72976401	21.48218462	18.25592546

Table 9–4 Present Value of Ordinary Annuity of 1 at Compound Interest

Chapter 9. Compound Interest and Annuities

n	6%	7%	8%	9%	10%	11%	12%
1	0.94339623	0.93457944	0.92592593	0.91743119	0.90909091	0.90090090	0.89285714
2	1.83339267	1.80801817	1.78326475	1.75911119	1.73553719	1.71252333	1.69005102
3	2.67301195	2.62431604	2.57709699	2.53129467	2.48685199	2.44371472	2.40183127
4	3.46510561	3.38721126	3.31212684	3.23971988	3.16986545	3.10244569	3.03734935
5	4.21236379	4.10019744	3.99271004	3.88965126	3.79078677	3.69589702	3.60477620
6	4.91732433	4.76653966	4.62287966	4.48591859	4.35526070	4.23053785	4.11140732
7	5.58238144	5.38928940	5.20637006	5.03295284	4.86841882	4.71219626	4.56375654
8	6.20979381	5.97129851	5.74663894	5.53481911	5.33492620	5.14612276	4.96763977
9	6.80169227	6.51523225	6.24688791	5.99524689	5.75902382	5.53704753	5.32824979
10	7.36008705	7.02358154	6.71008140	6.41765770	6.14456711	5.88923201	5.65022303
11	7.88687458	7.49867434	7.13896426	6.80519055	6.49506101	6.20651533	5.93769913
12	8.38384394	7.94268630	7.53607802	7.16072528	6.81369182	6.49235615	6.19437423
13	8.85268296	8.35765074	7.90377594	7.48690392	7.10335620	6.74987040	6.42354842
14	9.29498393	8.74546799	8.24423698	7.78615039	7.36668746	6.98186523	6.62816823
15	9.71224899	9.10791401	8.55947869	8.06068843	7.60607951	7.19086958	6.81086449
16	10.10589527	9.44664860	8.85136916	8.31255819	7.82370864	7.37916178	6.97398615
17	10.47725969	9.76322299	9.12163811	8.54363137	8.02155331	7.54879440	7.11963049
18	10.82760348	10.05908691	9.37188714	8.75562511	8.20141210	7.70161657	7.24967008
19	11.15811649	10.33559524	9.60359920	8.95011478	8.36492009	7.83929421	7.36577686
20	11.46992122	10.59401425	9.81814741	9.12854567	8.51356372	7.96332812	7.46944362
21	11.76407662	10.83552733	10.01680316	9.29224373	8.64869429	8.07507038	7.56200324
22	12.04158172	11.06124050	10.20074366	9.44242544	8.77154026	8.17573908	7.64464575
23	12.30337898	11.27218738	10.37105895	9.58020683	8.88321842	8.26643160	7.71843370
24	12.55035753	11.46933400	10.52875828	9.70661177	8.98474402	8.34813658	7.78431581
25	12.78335616	11.65358318	10.67477619	9.82257960	9.07704002	8.42174466	7.84313911
26	13.00316619	11.82577867	10.80997795	9.92897211	9.16094547	8.48805826	7.89565992
27	13.21053414	11.98670904	10.93516477	10.02657992	9.23722316	8.54780023	7.94255350
28	13.40616428	12.13711125	11.05107849	10.11612837	9.30656651	8.60162183	7.98442277
29	13.59072102	12.27767407	11.15840601	10.19828291	9.36960591	8.65010976	8.02180604
30	13.76483115	12.40904118	11.25778334	10.27365404	9.42691447	8.69379257	8.05518397
31	13.92908599	12.53181419	11.34979939	10.34280187	9.47901315	8.73314646	8.08498569
32	14.08404339	12.64655532	11.43499944	10.40624025	9.52637559	8.76860042	8.11159436
33	14.23022961	12.75379002	11.51388837	10.46444060	9.56943236	8.80054092	8.13535211
34	14.36814114	12.85400936	11.58693367	10.51783541	9.60857487	8.82931614	8.15656438
35	14.49824636	12.94767230	11.65456822	10.56682148	9.64415897	8.85523977	8.17550391
36	14.62098713	13.03520776	11.71719279	10.61176282	9.67650816	8.87859438	8.19241421
37	14.73678031	13.11701660	11.77517851	10.65299342	9.70591651	8.89963458	8.20751269
38	14.84601916	13.19347345	11.82886899	10.69081965	9.73265137	8.91858971	8.22099347
39	14.94907468	13.26492846	11.87858240	10.72552261	9.75695579	8.93566641	8.23302988
40	15.04629687	13.33170884	11.92461333	10.75736020	9.77905072	8.95105082	8.24377668
41	15.13801592	13.39412041	11.96723457	10.78656899	9.79913702	8.96491065	8.25337204
42	15.22454332	13.45244898	12.00669867	10.81336604	9.81739729	8.97739698	8.26193932
43	15.30617294	13.50696167	12.04323951	10.83795050	9.83399753	8.98864593	8.26958868
44	15.38318202	13.55790810	12.07707362	10.86050504	9.84908867	8.99878011	8.27641846
45	15.45583209	13.60552159	12.10840150	10.88119729	9.86280788	9.00791001	8.28251648
46	15.52436990	13.65002018	12.13740880	10.90018100	9.87527989	9.01613515	8.28796115
47	15.58902821	13.69160764	12.16426741	10.91759725	9.88661808	9.02354518	8.29282245
48	15.65002661	13.73047443	12.18913649	10.93357546	9.89692553	9.03022088	8.29716290
49	15.70757227	13.76679853	12.21216341	10.94823436	9.90629594	9.03623503	8.30103831
50	15.76186064	13.80074629	12.23348464	10.96168290	9.91481449	9.04165318	8.30449849

Table 9-4 Continued

Part 2. Mathematics Applications in Starting a Business

The first payment in an ordinary annuity begins earning interest at the end of the first period because that is when the payment is made. Notice in Table 9–3 that the factor occupying the first line of each column is 1, which represents the first payment without interest. In an annuity due, however, the first payment starts earning interest at the beginning of the first period. Thus, the first payment in an annuity due earns interest for one period more than the first payment in an ordinary annuity. If n represents the number of interest-earning periods in an ordinary annuity, then $n + 1$ represents the number of interest-earning periods in an annuity due that has the same term. (See Figure 9–3.) Therefore, when an ordinary-annuity table is used to find the amount of an annuity due, 1 is added to the number of periods in the term. For example, to find the amount of an annuity due with 24 payment intervals, the factor on line 25 (24 + 1) of an ordinary-annuity table is selected.

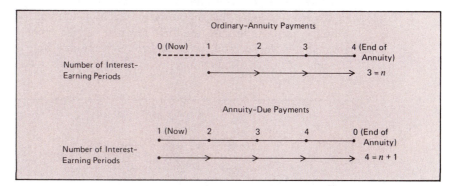

Figure 9–3 Interest-Earning Periods in Annuities

When payment is made with dollars, each factor in an ordinary-annuity table represents all of the $1 payments plus the accrued compound interest on those payments. There is a payment (the last) at the end of an ordinary annuity. Each factor in an ordinary-annuity table includes the last $1 payment without interest. Since there is no payment at the end of an annuity due, the factor found at $n + 1$ in an ordinary-annuity table should be decreased so that it will reflect the correct amount of principal. The principal in an ordinary-annuity table of 1 will be 1 less in any specific step for an annuity due than for an ordinary annuity. Therefore, when an ordinary-annuity table is used to find the amount of an annuity due, 1 is subtracted from the factor found at $n + 1$.

In summary, to find the amount of an annuity due by using Table 9–3, follow these steps:

1. Find in the table the factor at the periodic rate for the number of payment intervals plus 1.
2. Find the accumulated value of each $1 in the annuity-due payment by subtracting 1 from the factor found in Step 1.
3. Find the amount of the annuity due by multiplying the amount found in Step 2 by the periodic payment.

Example:

Use Table 9–3 to find the amount of an annuity if each $100 payment is due at the beginning of each month for 2 years, and the interest at 6% is compounded monthly.

Solution:

$n + 1 = 25$ and $0.5\% =$ rate per month
25 periods at $0.5\% = 26.55911502$
$26.55911502 - 1 = 25.55911502$
$25.5591150 \times \$100 = \$2,555.91$ amount in annuity due

Finding the Present Value of an Annuity Due. The present value of an annuity due is the cash value of the annuity at the beginning of its term. In a manner similar to that of finding the amount of an annuity due by using an ordinary-annuity table, the present value of an annuity due may be found by using an ordinary-annuity table and making two simple adjustments.

As you recall, the present value of an annuity may be thought of as a series of compound-discount problems. In an annuity due, the value "now" of the first payment is worth its full dollar value and, therefore, is not discounted. Figure 9–4 illustrates that an annuity due has 1 discount period less than an ordinary annuity because the first payment of an annuity due is not discounted. For this reason, when an ordinary-annuity table is used to find the present value of an annuity due, the number of periods in the term is decreased by 1.

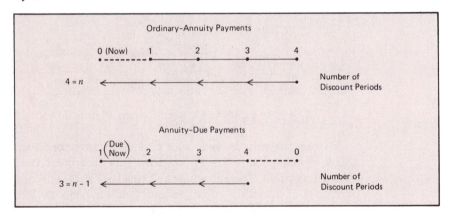

Figure 9–4 Number of Discount Periods in Annuities

Being an ordinary-annuity factor, the factor found at any step in Table 9–4 does not include the first payment of $1 that would be made in an annuity due. To compensate for this, 1 is added to the factor found at $n - 1$.

To find the present value of an annuity due by using Table 9–4, follow these steps:

1. Find in the table the factor at the periodic rate for the number of payment intervals minus 1.
2. Find the present value of each $1 in the annuity-due payment by adding 1 to the factor found in Step 1.
3. Find the present value of the annuity due by multiplying the value found in Step 2 by the periodic payment.

Part 2. Mathematics Applications in Starting a Business

Example:	Use Table 9–4 to find the present value of an annuity if each $1,000 payment is due at the beginning of each quarter for 2 years, and the interest is 8% compounded quarterly.
Solution:	$n - 1 = 7$ and $2\% = $ rate per quarter 7 periods at $2\% = 6.47199107$ $6.47199107 + 1 = 7.47199107$ $7.4719911 \times \$1,000 = \$7,471.99$ present value of annuity due

● Exercise 9–8

A. For each problem, use Table 9–3 to find the amount of the annuity due.

	Payment	Payment Interval	Term	Rate	Compounded
1.	$ 80	1 month	1 year	6%	Monthly
2.	370	6 months	5 years	14%	Semiannually
3.	2,400	3 months	4 years	16%	Quarterly
4.	9,500	1 year	8 years	11%	Annually
5.	5,700	6 months	$7\frac{1}{2}$ years	8%	Semiannually
6.	160	1 month	$1\frac{1}{2}$ years	12%	Monthly

B. For each problem, use Table 9–4 to find the present value of the annuity due.

	Payment	Payment Interval	Term	Rate	Compounded
1.	$8,000	1 year	15 years	9%	Annually
2.	1,200	3 months	5 years	8%	Quarterly
3.	540	1 month	$1\frac{3}{4}$ years	18%	Monthly
4.	3,600	6 months	$12\frac{1}{2}$ years	10%	Semiannually
5.	430	3 months	7 years	12%	Quarterly
6.	6,500	1 year	22 years	10%	Annually

C. Solve these problems.

1. Find the amount of an annuity of $6,000 payable at the beginning of each quarter for 7 years if the interest at 12% is compounded quarterly.

2. If $480 is deposited at the beginning of each month in a fund that pays 6% compounded monthly, what is the amount in the fund at the end of $2\frac{1}{4}$ years?

3. What is the present value of a 20-year lease on a building at $36,000 payable in advance each year if money is worth 11% compounded annually?

4. The owner of a business property is offered $90,000 immediately as the first semiannual payment for a term of 8 years. If money is worth 10% compounded semiannually, what is the cash value of the offer?

5. Six months ago, Edward Phillips paid the last of 20 semiannual life insurance premiums of $290 each. If he had invested each payment at 14% interest compounded semiannually, what would be the total amount now?

6. To claim an inheritance, Eleanor Stowers is to go to the bank today to receive the first quarterly payment of $6,560. If the term of the annuity is 7 years and interest at 12% is compounded quarterly, what is the cash value of the inheritance?

7. A refrigerator may be purchased by paying $42.50 down and 30 monthly payments of $42.50 each. What is the present value if interest is computed at 18% compounded monthly?

8. Sam Bordeaux deposited $100 at the beginning of each month into a fund that pays interest at 12% compounded monthly. After 2 years, he made no further payments but left the fund on deposit for another $3\frac{1}{3}$ years at the same rate of interest. How much was in the fund at the end of that time?

Sinking Funds and Amortization

A fund consisting of equal periodic deposits at compound interest that is allowed to accumulate for the purpose of providing a specific amount of money is a **sinking fund.** For example, to provide the money to pay off the bonds when they mature, the contract between the bondholders and bond issuer may require the issuer to make periodic payments into a fund that accumulates. Thus, the fund is established to provide for the repayment of the original principal on its maturity date. The interest on the original principal is paid as it falls due, but not from the sinking fund. A sinking fund may also be used to provide money for plant expansion, for the replacement of fully depreciated assets, or for other purposes.

The word amortization is often used in accounting as a general term to cover depreciation, depletion, and the writing off (charging to expense) of an intangible asset, as well as to cover the gradual payment of a debt. In this chapter, however, **amortization** is used in a more restricted sense to mean the process of extinguishing the principal and its interest through a series of equal payments at equal intervals of time. For example, the equal monthly payments on real estate loans represent amortization in the restricted sense because each payment covers the interest and a portion of the principal.

In both sinking-fund and amortization problems, the most common objective is to determine the size of the periodic payment. In each case, the problem is one of finding the size of the periodic payment in an annuity. An annuity payment is sometimes called the **rent** even though it may not be a payment for the use of property.

Finding the Periodic Payment to a Sinking Fund. When a debt is repaid by the sinking-fund method, all of the principal remains unpaid until its maturity.

Since the original principal is the amount to be paid at maturity, the final amount of the annuity is known. The problem of finding the size of payment, therefore, is one of finding the rent of an annuity when the amount is known.

The periodic sinking-fund payment that is needed to eliminate an obligation may be determined by referring to an annuity-table and dividing the amount desired at the end of the annuity by the amount of 1 found in the table. However, sinking-fund tables have been prepared and should be used when available because, in this case, multiplying is easier than dividing.

When using Table 9-5 to find the periodic payment needed to accumulate a given amount, proceed as follows:

1. Find in the table the factor at the periodic rate for the number of periods in the annuity.
2. Find the periodic payment (rent) by multiplying the factor found in Step 1 by the amount of the annuity.

Example: Melanie Hersch wants to accumulate $50,000 in 10 years. If she makes regular deposits at the end of each quarter in a bank that pays interest at 8% compounded quarterly, how much should she deposit each time? Use Table 9-5.

Solution: 40 periods at 2% = 0.01655575   rent needed to yield $1
0.0165557 × $50,000 = $827.79   periodic payment

Finding the Periodic Payment in Amortization. In the amortization of a debt, the principal and interest are repaid by a series of installments at regular intervals. Although the size of the payments does not vary, the allocation to principal and to interest does vary. As the principal is reduced by each payment, the interest per period decreases; hence, a larger portion is applied to the principal. The principal diminishes until the last payment eliminates it completely. Thus, the original principal is the present value of an annuity. A present-value table may be used to determine the periodic payment by dividing the original principal of the debt by the value found in the table. Using an amortization table, however, is preferable.

To find the periodic payment by using Table 9-6, follow this procedure:

1. Find in the table the factor at the periodic rate for the number of periods in the annuity.
2. Find the periodic payment by multiplying the factor found in Step 1 by the present value (original principal) of the annuity.

Example: A debt of $1,000 is to be amortized in 3 years by equal payments at the end of each 6-month period. If interest is charged on the debt at 6% compounded semiannually, how much is the periodic payment? Use Table 9-6 to find the periodic payment.

Solution: 6 periods at 3% = 0.18459750
0.1845975 × $1,000 = $184.60   periodic payment

n	0.5%	1%	1.5%	2%	3%	4%	5%
1	1.00000000	1.00000000	1.00000000	1.00000000	1.00000000	1.00000000	1.00000000
2	0.49875312	0.49751244	0.49627792	0.49504950	0.49261084	0.49019608	0.48780488
3	0.33167221	0.33002211	0.32838296	0.32675467	0.32353036	0.32034854	0.31720856
4	0.24813279	0.24628109	0.24444479	0.24262375	0.23902705	0.23549005	0.23201183
5	0.19800997	0.19603980	0.19408932	0.19215839	0.18835457	0.18462711	0.18097480
6	0.16459546	0.16254837	0.16052521	0.15852581	0.15459750	0.15076190	0.14701747
7	0.14072854	0.13862828	0.13655616	0.13451196	0.13050635	0.12660961	0.12281982
8	0.12282886	0.12069029	0.11858402	0.11650980	0.11245639	0.10852783	0.10472181
9	0.10890736	0.10674036	0.10460982	0.10251544	0.09843386	0.09449299	0.09069008
10	0.09777057	0.09558208	0.09343418	0.09132653	0.08723051	0.08329094	0.07950457
11	0.08865903	0.08645408	0.08429384	0.08217794	0.07807745	0.07414904	0.07038889
12	0.08106643	0.07884879	0.07667999	0.07455960	0.07046209	0.06655217	0.06282541
13	0.07464224	0.07241482	0.07024036	0.06811835	0.06402954	0.06014373	0.05645577
14	0.06913609	0.06690117	0.06472332	0.06260197	0.05852634	0.05466897	0.05102397
15	0.06436436	0.06212378	0.05994436	0.05782547	0.05376658	0.04994110	0.04634229
16	0.06018937	0.05794460	0.05576508	0.05365013	0.04961085	0.04582000	0.04226991
17	0.05650579	0.05425806	0.05207966	0.04996984	0.04595253	0.04219852	0.03869914
18	0.05323173	0.05098205	0.04880578	0.04670210	0.04270870	0.03899333	0.03554622
19	0.05030253	0.04805175	0.04587847	0.04378177	0.03981388	0.03613862	0.03274501
20	0.04766645	0.04541531	0.04324574	0.04115672	0.03721571	0.03358175	0.03024259
21	0.04528163	0.04303075	0.04086550	0.03878477	0.03487178	0.03128011	0.02799611
22	0.04311380	0.04086372	0.03870332	0.03663140	0.03274739	0.02919881	0.02597051
23	0.04113465	0.03888584	0.03673075	0.03466810	0.03081390	0.02730906	0.02413682
24	0.03932061	0.03707347	0.03492410	0.03287110	0.02904742	0.02558683	0.02247090
25	0.03765186	0.03540675	0.03326345	0.03122044	0.02742787	0.02401196	0.02095246
26	0.03611163	0.03386888	0.03173196	0.02969923	0.02593829	0.02256738	0.01956432
27	0.03468565	0.03244553	0.03031527	0.02829309	0.02456421	0.02123854	0.01829186
28	0.03336167	0.03112444	0.02900108	0.02698967	0.02329323	0.02001298	0.01712253
29	0.03212914	0.02989502	0.02777878	0.02577836	0.02211467	0.01887993	0.01604551
30	0.03097892	0.02874811	0.02663919	0.02464992	0.02101926	0.01783010	0.01505144
31	0.02990304	0.02767573	0.02557430	0.02359635	0.01999893	0.01685535	0.01413212
32	0.02889453	0.02667089	0.02457710	0.02261061	0.01904662	0.01594859	0.01328042
33	0.02794727	0.02572744	0.02364144	0.02168653	0.01815612	0.01510357	0.01249004
34	0.02705586	0.02483997	0.02276189	0.02081867	0.01732196	0.01431477	0.01175545
35	0.02621550	0.02400368	0.02193363	0.02000221	0.01653929	0.01357732	0.01107171
36	0.02542194	0.02321431	0.02115240	0.01923285	0.01580379	0.01288688	0.01043446
37	0.02467139	0.02246805	0.02041437	0.01850678	0.01511162	0.01223957	0.00983979
38	0.02396045	0.02176150	0.01971613	0.01782057	0.01445934	0.01163192	0.00928423
39	0.02328607	0.02109160	0.01905463	0.01717114	0.01384385	0.01106083	0.00876462
40	0.02264552	0.02045560	0.01842710	0.01655575	0.01326238	0.01052349	0.00827816
41	0.02203631	0.01985102	0.01783106	0.01597188	0.01271241	0.01001738	0.00782229
42	0.02145622	0.01927563	0.01726426	0.01541729	0.01219167	0.00954020	0.00739471
43	0.02090320	0.01872737	0.01672465	0.01488993	0.01169811	0.00908989	0.00699333
44	0.02037541	0.01820441	0.01621038	0.01438794	0.01122985	0.00866454	0.00661625
45	0.01987117	0.01770505	0.01571976	0.01390962	0.01078518	0.00826246	0.00626173
46	0.01938894	0.01722775	0.01525125	0.01345342	0.01036254	0.00788205	0.00592820
47	0.01892733	0.01677111	0.01480342	0.01301792	0.00996051	0.00752189	0.00561421
48	0.01848503	0.01633384	0.01437500	0.01260184	0.00957777	0.00718065	0.00531843
49	0.01806087	0.01591474	0.01396478	0.01220396	0.00921314	0.00685712	0.00503965
50	0.01765376	0.01551273	0.01357168	0.01182321	0.00886549	0.00655020	0.00477674

Table 9–5 Periodic Sinking Fund Payment Which at Compound Interest Amounts to 1

Part 2. Mathematics Applications in Starting a Business

n	6%	7%	8%	9%	10%	11%	12%
1	1.00000000	1.00000000	1.00000000	1.00000000	1.00000000	1.00000000	1.00000000
2	0.48543689	0.48309179	0.48076923	0.47846890	0.47619048	0.47393365	0.47169811
3	0.31410981	0.31105167	0.30803351	0.30505476	0.30211480	0.29921307	0.29634898
4	0.22859149	0.22522812	0.22192080	0.21866866	0.21547080	0.21232635	0.20923444
5	0.17739640	0.17389069	0.17045645	0.16709246	0.16379748	0.16057031	0.15740973
6	0.14336263	0.13979580	0.13631539	0.13291978	0.12960738	0.12637656	0.12322572
7	0.11913502	0.11555322	0.11207240	0.10869052	0.10540550	0.10221527	0.09911774
8	0.10103594	0.09746776	0.09401476	0.09067438	0.08744402	0.08432105	0.08130284
9	0.08702224	0.08348647	0.08007971	0.07679880	0.07364054	0.07060166	0.06767889
10	0.07586796	0.07237750	0.06902949	0.06582009	0.06274539	0.05980143	0.05698416
11	0.06679294	0.06335690	0.06007634	0.05694666	0.05396314	0.05112101	0.04841540
12	0.05927703	0.05590199	0.05269502	0.04965066	0.04676332	0.04402729	0.04143681
13	0.05296011	0.04965085	0.04652181	0.04356656	0.04077852	0.03815099	0.03567720
14	0.04758491	0.04434494	0.04129685	0.03843317	0.03574622	0.03322820	0.03087125
15	0.04296276	0.03979462	0.03682954	0.03405888	0.03147378	0.02906524	0.02682424
16	0.03895214	0.03585765	0.03297687	0.03029991	0.02781662	0.02551675	0.02339002
17	0.03544480	0.03242519	0.02962943	0.02704625	0.02466413	0.02247148	0.02045673
18	0.03235654	0.02941260	0.02670210	0.02421229	0.02193022	0.01984287	0.01793731
19	0.02962086	0.02675301	0.02412763	0.02173041	0.01954687	0.01756250	0.01576300
20	0.02718456	0.02439293	0.02185221	0.01954648	0.01745962	0.01557564	0.01387878
21	0.02500455	0.02228900	0.01983225	0.01761663	0.01562439	0.01383793	0.01224009
22	0.02304557	0.02040577	0.01803207	0.01590499	0.01400506	0.01231310	0.01081051
23	0.02127848	0.01871393	0.01642217	0.01438188	0.01257181	0.01097118	0.00955996
24	0.01967900	0.01718902	0.01497796	0.01302256	0.01129978	0.00978721	0.00846344
25	0.01822672	0.01581052	0.01367878	0.01180625	0.01016807	0.00874024	0.00749997
26	0.01690435	0.01456103	0.01250713	0.01071536	0.00915904	0.00781258	0.00665186
27	0.01569717	0.01342573	0.01144810	0.00973491	0.00825764	0.00698916	0.00590409
28	0.01459255	0.01239193	0.01048891	0.00885205	0.00745101	0.00625715	0.00524387
29	0.01357961	0.01144865	0.00961854	0.00805572	0.00672807	0.00560547	0.00466021
30	0.01264891	0.01058640	0.00882743	0.00733635	0.00607925	0.00502460	0.00414366
31	0.01179222	0.00979691	0.00810728	0.00668560	0.00549621	0.00450627	0.00368606
32	0.01100234	0.00907292	0.00745081	0.00609619	0.00497172	0.00404329	0.00328033
33	0.01027293	0.00840807	0.00685163	0.00556173	0.00449941	0.00362938	0.00292031
34	0.00959843	0.00779674	0.00630411	0.00507660	0.00407371	0.00325905	0.00260064
35	0.00897386	0.00723396	0.00580326	0.00463584	0.00368971	0.00292749	0.00231662
36	0.00839483	0.00671531	0.00534467	0.00423505	0.00334306	0.00263044	0.00206414
37	0.00785743	0.00623685	0.00492440	0.00387033	0.00302994	0.00236416	0.00183959
38	0.00735812	0.00579505	0.00453894	0.00353820	0.00274692	0.00212535	0.00163980
39	0.00689377	0.00538676	0.00418513	0.00323555	0.00249098	0.00191107	0.00146197
40	0.00646154	0.00500914	0.00386016	0.00295961	0.00225941	0.00171873	0.00130363
41	0.00605886	0.00465962	0.00356149	0.00270789	0.00204980	0.00154601	0.00116260
42	0.00568342	0.00433591	0.00328684	0.00247814	0.00185999	0.00139086	0.00103696
43	0.00533312	0.00403590	0.00303414	0.00226837	0.00168805	0.00125146	0.00092500
44	0.00500606	0.00375769	0.00280152	0.00207675	0.00153224	0.00112617	0.00082521
45	0.00470050	0.00349957	0.00258728	0.00190165	0.00139100	0.00101354	0.00073625
46	0.00441485	0.00325996	0.00238991	0.00174160	0.00126295	0.00091227	0.00065694
47	0.00414768	0.00303744	0.00220799	0.00159525	0.00114682	0.00082119	0.00058621
48	0.00389765	0.00283070	0.00204027	0.00146139	0.00104148	0.00073926	0.00052312
49	0.00366356	0.00263853	0.00188557	0.00133893	0.00094590	0.00066556	0.00046686
50	0.00344429	0.00245985	0.00174286	0.00122687	0.00085917	0.00059924	0.00041666

Table 9-5 Continued

Chapter 9. Compound Interest and Annuities

n	0.5%	1%	1.5%	2%	3%	4%	5%
1	1.00500000	1.01000000	1.01500000	1.02000000	1.03000000	1.04000000	1.05000000
2	0.50375312	0.50751244	0.51127792	0.51504950	0.52261084	0.53019608	0.53780488
3	0.33667221	0.34002211	0.34338296	0.34675467	0.35353036	0.36034854	0.36720856
4	0.25313279	0.25628109	0.25944479	0.26262375	0.26902705	0.27549005	0.28201183
5	0.20300997	0.20603980	0.20908932	0.21215839	0.21835457	0.22462711	0.23097480
6	0.16959546	0.17254837	0.17552521	0.17852581	0.18459750	0.19076190	0.19701747
7	0.14572854	0.14862828	0.15155616	0.15451196	0.16050635	0.16660961	0.17281982
8	0.12782886	0.13069029	0.13358402	0.13650980	0.14245639	0.14852783	0.15472181
9	0.11390736	0.11674036	0.11960982	0.12251544	0.12843386	0.13449299	0.14069008
10	0.10277057	0.10558208	0.10843418	0.11132653	0.11723051	0.12329094	0.12950457
11	0.09365903	0.09645408	0.09929384	0.10217794	0.10807745	0.11414904	0.12038889
12	0.08606643	0.08884879	0.09167999	0.09455960	0.10046209	0.10655217	0.11282541
13	0.07964224	0.08241482	0.08524036	0.08811835	0.09402954	0.10014373	0.10645577
14	0.07413609	0.07690117	0.07972332	0.08260197	0.08852634	0.09466897	0.10102397
15	0.06936436	0.07212378	0.07494436	0.07782547	0.08376658	0.08994110	0.09634229
16	0.06518937	0.06794460	0.07076508	0.07365013	0.07961085	0.08582000	0.09226991
17	0.06150579	0.06425806	0.06707966	0.06996984	0.07595253	0.08219852	0.08869914
18	0.05823173	0.06098205	0.06380578	0.06670210	0.07270870	0.07899333	0.08554622
19	0.05530253	0.05805175	0.06087847	0.06378177	0.06981388	0.07613862	0.08274501
20	0.05266645	0.05541531	0.05824574	0.06115672	0.06721571	0.07358175	0.08024259
21	0.05028163	0.05303075	0.05586550	0.05878477	0.06487178	0.07128011	0.07799611
22	0.04811380	0.05086372	0.05370332	0.05663140	0.06274739	0.06919881	0.07597051
23	0.04613465	0.04888584	0.05173075	0.05466810	0.06081390	0.06730906	0.07413682
24	0.04432061	0.04707347	0.04992410	0.05287110	0.05904742	0.06558683	0.07247090
25	0.04265186	0.04540675	0.04826345	0.05122044	0.05742787	0.06401196	0.07095246
26	0.04111163	0.04386888	0.04673196	0.04969923	0.05593829	0.06256738	0.06956432
27	0.03968565	0.04244553	0.04531527	0.04829309	0.05456421	0.06123854	0.06829186
28	0.03836167	0.04112444	0.04400108	0.04698967	0.05329323	0.06001298	0.06712253
29	0.03712914	0.03989502	0.04277878	0.04577836	0.05211467	0.05887993	0.06604551
30	0.03597892	0.03874811	0.04163919	0.04464992	0.05101926	0.05783010	0.06505144
31	0.03490304	0.03767573	0.04057430	0.04359635	0.04999893	0.05685535	0.06413212
32	0.03389453	0.03667089	0.03957710	0.04261061	0.04904662	0.05594859	0.06328042
33	0.03294727	0.03572744	0.03864144	0.04168653	0.04815612	0.05510357	0.06249004
34	0.03205586	0.03483997	0.03776189	0.04081867	0.04732196	0.05431477	0.06175545
35	0.03121550	0.03400368	0.03693363	0.04000221	0.04653929	0.05357732	0.06107171
36	0.03042194	0.03321431	0.03615240	0.03923285	0.04580379	0.05288688	0.06043446
37	0.02967139	0.03246805	0.03541437	0.03850678	0.04511162	0.05223957	0.05983979
38	0.02896045	0.03176150	0.03471613	0.03782057	0.04445934	0.05163192	0.05928423
39	0.02828607	0.03109160	0.03405463	0.03717114	0.04384385	0.05106083	0.05876462
40	0.02764552	0.03045560	0.03342710	0.03655575	0.04326238	0.05052349	0.05827816
41	0.02703631	0.02985102	0.03283106	0.03597188	0.04271241	0.05001738	0.05782229
42	0.02645622	0.02927563	0.03226426	0.03541729	0.04219167	0.04954020	0.05739471
43	0.02590320	0.02872737	0.03172465	0.03488993	0.04169811	0.04908989	0.05699333
44	0.02537541	0.02820441	0.03121038	0.03438794	0.04122985	0.04866454	0.05661625
45	0.02487117	0.02770505	0.03071976	0.03390962	0.04078518	0.04826246.	0.05626173
46	0.02438894	0.02722775	0.03025125	0.03345342	0.04036254	0.04788205	0.05592820
47	0.02392733	0.02677111	0.02980342	0.03301792	0.03996051	0.04752189	0.05561421
48	0.02348503	0.02633384	0.02937500	0.03260184	0.03957777	0.04718065	0.05531843
49	0.02306087	0.02591474	0.02896478	0.03220396	0.03921314	0.04685712	0.05503965
50	0.02265376	0.02551273	0.02857168	0.03182321	0.03886549	0.04655020	0.05477674

Table 9-6 Periodic Payment to Amortize 1

Part 2. Mathematics Applications in Starting a Business

n	6%	7%	8%	9%	10%	11%	12%
1	1.06000000	1.07000000	1.08000000	1.09000000	1.10000000	1.11000000	1.12000000
2	0.54543689	0.55309179	0.56076923	0.56846890	0.57619048	0.58393365	0.59169811
3	0.37410981	0.38105167	0.38803351	0.39505476	0.40211480	0.40921307	0.41634898
4	0.28859149	0.29522812	0.30192080	0.30866866	0.31547080	0.32232635	0.32923444
5	0.23739640	0.24389069	0.25045645	0.25709246	0.26379748	0.27057031	0.27740973
6	0.20336263	0.20979580	0.21631539	0.22291978	0.22960738	0.23637656	0.24322572
7	0.17913502	0.18555322	0.19207240	0.19869052	0.20540550	0.21221527	0.21911774
8	0.16103594	0.16746776	0.17401476	0.18067438	0.18744402	0.19432105	0.20130284
9	0.14702224	0.15348647	0.16007971	0.16679880	0.17364054	0.18060166	0.18767889
10	0.13586796	0.14237750	0.14902949	0.15582009	0.16274539	0.16980143	0.17698416
11	0.12679294	0.13335690	0.14007634	0.14694666	0.15396314	0.16112101	0.16841540
12	0.11927703	0.12590199	0.13269502	0.13965066	0.14676332	0.15402729	0.16143681
13	0.11296011	0.11965085	0.12652181	0.13356656	0.14077852	0.14815099	0.15567720
14	0.10758491	0.11434494	0.12129685	0.12843317	0.13574622	0.14322820	0.15087125
15	0.10296276	0.10979462	0.11682954	0.12405888	0.13147378	0.13906524	0.14682424
16	0.09895214	0.10585765	0.11297687	0.12029991	0.12781662	0.13551675	0.14339002
17	0.09544480	0.10242519	0.10962943	0.11704625	0.12466413	0.13247148	0.14045673
18	0.09235654	0.09941260	0.10670210	0.11421229	0.12193022	0.12984287	0.13793731
19	0.08962086	0.09675301	0.10412763	0.11173041	0.11954687	0.12756250	0.13576300
20	0.08718456	0.09439293	0.10185221	0.10954648	0.11745962	0.12557564	0.13387878
21	0.08500455	0.09228900	0.09983225	0.10761663	0.11562439	0.12383793	0.13224009
22	0.08304557	0.09040577	0.09803207	0.10590499	0.11400506	0.12231310	0.13081051
23	0.08127848	0.08871393	0.09642217	0.10438188	0.11257181	0.12097118	0.12955996
24	0.07967900	0.08718902	0.09497796	0.10302256	0.11129978	0.11978721	0.12846344
25	0.07822672	0.08581052	0.09367878	0.10180625	0.11016807	0.11874024	0.12749997
26	0.07690435	0.08456103	0.09250713	0.10071536	0.10915904	0.11781258	0.12665186
27	0.07569717	0.08342573	0.09144810	0.09973491	0.10825764	0.11698916	0.12590409
28	0.07459255	0.08239193	0.09048891	0.09885205	0.10745101	0.11625715	0.12524387
29	0.07357961	0.08144865	0.08961854	0.09805572	0.10672807	0.11560547	0.12466021
30	0.07264891	0.08058640	0.08882743	0.09733635	0.10607925	0.11502460	0.12414366
31	0.07179222	0.07979691	0.08810728	0.09668560	0.10549621	0.11450627	0.12368606
32	0.07100234	0.07907292	0.08745081	0.09609619	0.10497172	0.11404329	0.12328033
33	0.07027293	0.07840807	0.08685163	0.09556173	0.10449941	0.11362938	0.12292031
34	0.06959843	0.07779674	0.08630411	0.09507660	0.10407371	0.11325905	0.12260064
35	0.06897386	0.07723396	0.08580326	0.09463584	0.10368971	0.11292749	0.12231662
36	0.06839483	0.07671531	0.08534467	0.09423505	0.10334306	0.11263044	0.12206414
37	0.06785743	0.07623685	0.08492440	0.09387033	0.10302994	0.11236416	0.12183959
38	0.06735812	0.07579505	0.08453894	0.09353820	0.10274692	0.11212535	0.12163980
39	0.06689377	0.07538676	0.08418513	0.09323555	0.10249098	0.11191107	0.12146197
40	0.06646154	0.07500914	0.08386016	0.09295961	0.10225941	0.11171873	0.12130363
41	0.06605886	0.07465962	0.08356149	0.09270789	0.10204980	0.11154601	0.12116260
42	0.06568342	0.07433591	0.08328684	0.09247814	0.10185999	0.11139086	0.12103696
43	0.06533312	0.07403590	0.08303414	0.09226837	0.10168805	0.11125146	0.12092500
44	0.06500606	0.07375769	0.08280152	0.09207675	0.10153224	0.11112617	0.12082521
45	0.06470050	0.07349957	0.08258728	0.09190165	0.10139100	0.11101354	0.12073625
46	0.06441485	0.07325996	0.08238991	0.09174160	0.10126295	0.11091227	0.12065694
47	0.06414768	0.07303744	0.08220799	0.09159525	0.10114682	0.11082119	0.12058621
48	0.06389765	0.07283070	0.08204027	0.09146139	0.10104148	0.11073926	0.12052312
49	0.06366356	0.07263853	0.08188557	0.09133893	0.10094590	0.11066556	0.12046686
50	0.06344429	0.07245985	0.08174286	0.09122687	0.10085917	0.11059924	0.12041666

Table 9–6 Continued

Chapter 9. Compound Interest and Annuities

Exercise 9-9

A. For each problem, use Table 9–5 to find the payment that should be made to the sinking fund at the end of each period.

	Amount	Payment Interval	Term	Rate	Compounded
1.	$ 80,000	1 year	14 years	9%	Annually
2.	150,000	3 months	5 years	12%	Quarterly
3.	750,000	6 months	20 years	10%	Semiannually
4.	3,000,000	1 year	30 years	11%	Annually
5.	64,000	1 month	2 years	18%	Monthly
6.	92,000	3 months	6 years	8%	Quarterly

B. For each problem, use Table 9–6 to find the payment that should be made at the end of each period to amortize the debt.

	Present Value	Payment Interval	Term	Rate	Compounded
1.	$ 25,000	6 months	10 years	14%	Semiannually
2.	480,000	1 year	15 years	11%	Annually
3.	36,000	3 months	$4\frac{1}{2}$ years	16%	Quarterly
4.	17,000	1 month	$2\frac{1}{2}$ years	6%	Monthly
5.	248,000	6 months	$8\frac{1}{2}$ years	12%	Semiannually
6.	375,000	3 months	10 years	12%	Quarterly

C. Solve these problems.

1. A special study indicates that the Henderson Company will need a new building in 10 years. If the building cost is estimated to be $750,000 and the interest rate is 10% compounded annually, how much should the company invest in a sinking fund at the end of each year for 10 years?

2. The East Central Company must redeem a $450,000 bond issue in 15 years. How much must it set aside at the end of each 6 months to meet the obligation if interest is paid on the deposits at 6% compounded semiannually?

3. A loan of $27,000, with interest at 8% compounded semiannually, is to be amortized by equal payments at the end of each 6 months for 7 years. Find the periodic payment.

4. To repay a loan of $36,000 that bears interest at 8% compounded quarterly, Dennis Weiberg agreed to amortize the debt in 6 years by making equal payments at the end of each quarter. Find the periodic payment.

5. The Westchester Products Company has recently issued $250,000 of 12%, 20-year bonds. The company treasurer has been instructed to set aside equal deposits at the end of each 6 months so that the accumulated fund, with interest at 10% compounded semiannually, will be sufficient to pay off the bonds at maturity. Find the periodic payment.

Part 2. Mathematics Applications in Starting a Business

6. James and Diane Smolenski borrowed $8,400 to improve their home. The loan bears interest at 12% compounded monthly. If they are to repay the loan with equal installments at the end of each month for 4 years, how much is each payment?

7. Tonkava Products, Inc. borrowed $250,000 at 11% interest compounded annually. This amount and interest are to be paid in 25 equal annual payments. Find the amount of each payment.

8. Virginia Barrow purchased equipment that cost $65,000 and is expected to have a trade-in value of $5,000 in 5 years when fully depreciated. She estimates that the replacement price of the equipment will be 50% higher in 5 years. If she can invest money at 6% compounded semiannually, how much should she invest at the end of each 6 months to accumulate the amount required to replace the equipment?

REVIEW PROBLEMS

Solve these problems. If you have difficulty solving any problem, restudy the appropriate section in this chapter. The problems under a specific number are related to those contained in the exercise with the same last number.

1. Cindy Gillespie invested $2,000 two years ago at 6% interest compounded semiannually. What is the amount in the fund now?

2. On the day Robert became 11 years old, his grandfather placed $7,500 in a savings account that earns 12% compounded quarterly. If the principal and interest were permitted to accumulate, how much was in the fund on Robert's twenty-first birthday?

3. Bank A pays interest at 5.3% compounded daily. Bank B pays 5.35% compounded quarterly. Rosalie Higgins deposited $23,000 on the first day of a 90-day quarter in each bank. After interest has been added for the quarter, the compound amount will be how much **(a)** in Bank A and **(b)** in Bank B? **(c)** Which is better for the depositor, Bank A or Bank B?

4. A deposit of $8,500 was made into a savings account that paid interest at 6.75% compounded monthly. After 2 years, the rate was changed to 6.9% compounded daily based on the 360-day year. **(a)** How much would be in the account 60 days after the new rate started? **(b)** What was the effective rate in the beginning? **(c)** What was the effective rate after the rate changed?

5. A debt of $53,000 will be due at the end of 4 years. If money is worth 6% compounded semiannually, find **(a)** the present value and **(b)** the compound discount.

6. To save for the purchase of a house, Janice and Ralph Coburn deposited $350 at the end of every 3 months in a savings plan that pays 8% interest compounded quarterly. At the end of 63 months, how much had they saved?

7. Olga Simpson, who has just inherited some money, wants to purchase an annuity that will start in one month and pay her $2,000 a month for $3\frac{1}{2}$ years. If the interest rate is 12% compounded monthly, how much does she need to invest?

8. Solve these problems.
   a. To provide for the eventual retirement of outstanding bonds, the Garden City Corporation invests $250,000 in a special fund at the beginning of each year. If interest at 9% is compounded annually, how much will be in the fund at the end of 12 years?
   b. What is the present cash value of a freezer that can be purchased for a down payment of $46 and 24 monthly payments of $46 each, if interest at 18% is compounded monthly?

9. Solve these problems.
   a. The Washington Power Company borrowed $3,750,000 that must be repaid at the end of 25 years. How much should the company invest at the end of each 6 months to accumulate the needed amount if the interest rate is 8% compounded semiannually?
   b. Harold Applebee agreed to lend $12,500 which is to be repaid in equal quarterly installments over a term of $6\frac{1}{2}$ years. If the interest rate is 16% compounded quarterly, how much is the periodic payment?

CHALLENGE PROBLEM

Expected risks involved and rate of return on the investment are two important factors in determining whether or not an investment should be made. Usually a rate of return is demanded that will justify the anticipated risks. The expected return is then discounted at the desired rate to determine whether or not the investment is wise.

Onondaga Corporation is considering investing $30,000 in a project. The officers think the risks involved justify a 12% compound return. Projections indicate that the investment will return $14,000 at the end of the first year, $12,500 at the end of the second year, $12,000 at the end of the third year, and nothing thereafter. Will the investment return the capital invested plus the desired 12%?

Chapter 10

Insurance

Objectives

After mastering the material in Chapter 10, you will be able to:

- Understand the terms *insurance, premium, face value, indemnity, coinsurance, beneficiary, term insurance, endowment policy, nonforfeiture values, settlement options, comprehensive insurance,* and *collision insurance.*
- Calculate premiums for fire, life, and automobile insurance.
- Compute the indemnity of a fire loss under ordinary policies and under coinsurance.
- Determine settlement options and nonforfeiture values in life insurance.

Individuals constantly face the risk of loss—loss of property by fire, storm, theft, or accident and loss of health or life. Businesses also face property losses and the loss of managerial ability through the death or disability of talented officers. A single loss could prove to be ruinous if the resulting financial burden fell entirely on one individual or on one business. When the cost of such losses is shared by many, however, the risk of complete financial disaster is greatly reduced.

Insurance is a system of protection against loss in which a number of individuals agree to pay certain sums for a guarantee that they will be compensated for any specified loss by fire, accident, or death, for instance. The **insured** is the person whose life, property, and personal items are protected by insurance. The **insurer** or **underwriter** is the association or company that sells insurance protection to others. The **premium** is the sum of money that is paid at specified times by the insured to the insurance company for protection. The premiums are used to meet the expenses of the company and to build up funds from which those who suffer losses or their beneficiaries are compensated. An insurance **policy** is a contract whereby, in return for the fixed premium, the insurer guarantees the insured that a certain sum of money will be paid for a specified loss. The **face value** of the policy is the amount of insurance for which the policy is written.

Marine insurance, securing against the loss of a ship and its cargo, and insurance against property loss by fire, water, or theft are considered the earliest forms of insurance protection. Modern developments of insurance encompass the underwriting of policies against almost every conceivable loss by acts of human beings or by acts of nature. Among numerous others, these include marine, life, accident and health, endowment, annuity, fire, rain, burglary, automobile, and social insurance, such as unemployment, industrial, workers' compensation, group health and accident insurance, and old age pensions. Many of the preceding topics are beyond the scope of this book. Some of the social insurance topics are presented in Chapter 11. This chapter is limited to fire, life, and automobile insurance.

FIRE INSURANCE

Fire insurance provides protection against loss by fire and by fire-connected causes, such as smoke and water damage. Different states require standard forms of policy that, although they differ in some details, are all similar in basic provisions. As a rule, these standard policies provide insurance coverage against all direct losses by fire and lightning.

Premiums for Fire Insurance

Insurance is based on the law of averages. With proper statistics pertaining to fire damage to a large number of buildings, for example, an insurance company can forecast with a great degree of accuracy the number of similar buildings that will suffer loss and the extent of the damage to be expected. Knowing the total of the losses and the total value of the buildings to be protected, an insurance company can easily calculate the rate of value to use. Using this rate, they can find the premium to charge each building owner to provide just sufficient funds to meet the expected loss. Actually the rate must be increased to cover the company's expenses and provide a fair profit.

The premium rates for fire insurance vary in accordance with the nature of the property that is insured, its location, the purposes for which it is occupied, and the protection which it has against damage by fire. Thus, the premium rate for fire insurance on a brick building that is located near a fire station and has interior fire-protection sprinklers is lower than that for a frame building which has no protective devices and is located miles from the nearest fire station.

Basic Rates. Premium rates for fire insurance are usually expressed in terms of cents per hundred dollars of insurance for one year. The rules of percentage are applied to compute the amount of the premium. The **rate** is the charge per $100 of protection. The **base** is the number of hundreds in the face of the policy. The **percentage** is the premium that is found when the base is multiplied by the rate.

Example:

Property valued at $80,000 was insured at 60¢ per $100 of protection for one year. Find the amount of the premium.

Solution:

$80,000 ÷ $100 = 800   hundreds
800 × $0.60 = $480   premium for one year

● Exercise 10–1

A. For each of the following, find the premium for one year.

	Face of Policy	Annual Rate
1.	$ 60,000	59¢
2.	90,000	28¢
3.	250,000	37¢
4.	375,000	46¢
5.	125,000	55¢
6.	50,000	40¢
7.	250,000	$37\frac{1}{2}$ ¢
8.	75,000	$33\frac{1}{3}$ ¢
9.	360,000	$56\frac{1}{4}$ ¢
10.	180,000	$83\frac{1}{3}$ ¢

B. Solve these problems.

1. A house valued at $162,000 was insured for 80% of its value at 36¢ per hundred. What is the amount of the premium?

2. The Gordon Company's store building is insured for $370,000 at a rate of 39¢ per $100. The contents are insured for $100,000 at 52¢ per $100. Find the total premium.

3. Find the premium for insurance on property that is insured for $75,000 at an annual rate of $41\frac{2}{3}$ ¢ per $100.

4. A house is insured for $124,000 at the rate of $37\frac{1}{2}$ ¢ per $100. The contents are insured for $44,000 at 31¢ per $100. How much is the total premium?

5. David Maloney insured a rental house for $97,000 at the rate of 48¢ per $100. How much did he pay?

6. The Thorton Department Store building is insured for $460,000 at a rate of $52\frac{1}{2}$ ¢ per $100. The contents are insured for $240,000 at 38¢ per $100 annually. Find the total premium.

Chapter 10. Insurance

Short-Term Rates. An insurance policy with a term of less than one year is a **short-term policy.** The short-term insurance rate is higher than the exact pro rata share of the annual premium. Notice in Table 10–1 that a policy for 180 days, which is slightly less than one-half year, costs 60% of the annual premium. To find the short-term premium, multiply the annual premium by the appropriate percent shown in the table.

Example:

Knowing that title to the property would be transferred in 122 days, the owner insured it during that time for $96,000 at the annual rate of $37\frac{1}{2}$ ¢ per $100. Find the premium.

Solution:

960 × $0.375 = $360   annual premium
From Table 10–1, 122-day premium = 44% of annual premium.
$360 × 0.44 = $158.40   premium for 122 days

Days in Force	Percent Earned	Days in Force	Percent Earned	Days in Force	Percent Earned	Days in Force	Percent Earned
1	5	66–69	29	154–156	53	256–260	77
2	6	70–73	30	157–160	54	261–264	78
3–4	7	74–76	31	161–164	55	265–269	79
5–6	8	77–80	32	165–167	56	270–273	80
7–8	9	81–83	33	168–171	57	274–278	81
9–10	10	84–87	34	172–175	58	279–282	82
11–12	11	88–91	35	176–178	59	283–287	83
13–14	12	92–94	36	179–182	60	288–291	84
15–16	13	95–98	37	183–187	61	292–296	85
17–18	14	99–102	38	188–191	62	297–301	86
19–20	15	103–105	39	192–196	63	302–305	87
21–22	16	106–109	40	197–200	64	306–310	88
23–25	17	110–113	41	201–205	65	311–314	89
26–29	18	114–116	42	206–209	66	315–319	90
30–32	19	117–120	43	210–214	67	320–323	91
33–36	20	121–124	44	215–218	68	324–328	92
37–40	21	125–127	45	219–223	69	329–332	93
41–43	22	128–131	46	224–228	70	333–337	94
44–47	23	132–135	47	229–232	71	338–342	95
48–51	24	136–138	48	233–237	72	343–346	96
52–54	25	139–142	49	238–241	73	347–351	97
55–58	26	143–146	50	242–246	74	352–355	98
59–62	27	147–149	51	247–250	75	356–360	99
63–65	28	150–153	52	251–255	76	361–365	100

Table 10–1 Short-Term or Cancellation Rates for One Year

Cancellation by Insured. A standard fire insurance policy contains a cancellation clause that permits the insured to cancel at any time. If the insured cancels the policy, the short-term rates are used to find the amount of the refund. Of course, the company retains the short-term premium and refunds the balance of the premium to the insured.

Part 2. Mathematics Applications in Starting a Business

Example:	A premium of $720 was paid for fire insurance on a building for one year. The policy was canceled by the insured after having been in force for 270 days. Find **(a)** the premium retained by the company by using Table 10–1 and **(b)** the refund to the insured.	
Solution:	**(a)** $720 × 80% = $576 short-term premium retained by company **(b)** $720 − $576 = $144 refund to insured	

Cancellation by the Insurance Company. The insurance company may cancel a fire insurance policy provided the insured is notified in writing 5 days (10 days to mortgagee) prior to the effective date of the cancellation. This gives the insured time to obtain other insurance. When the insurance company cancels a policy, the company retains only an exact pro rata share of the premium. The ratio is based on the exact number of days the policy was in force in relation to the 365-day year. The balance of the premium is refunded to the insured.

Example:	A premium of $720 was paid for fire insurance on a building for one year. The policy was canceled by the insurance company on an effective date that provided the insured with protection for 270 days. Find **(a)** the premium retained by the company and **(b)** the refund to the insured.
Solution:	**(a)** $720 × $\frac{270}{365}$ = $532.60 retained by company **(b)** $720 − $532.60 = $187.40 refund to insured

A comparison of the two preceding examples reveals that the insured receives a larger refund when the policy is canceled by the company.

● Exercise 10–2

A. Use Table 10–1 to find the premium for each of the following short-term fire insurance policies.

	Face of Policy	Annual Rate	Term of Policy
1.	$ 50,000	61¢	180 days
2.	85,000	43¢	90 days
3.	180,000	$42\frac{1}{2}$¢	240 days
4.	210,000	$58\frac{1}{3}$¢	60 days
5.	450,000	34¢	145 days
6.	175,000	$36\frac{2}{3}$¢	75 days

B. For each of the following one-year policies, find the refund to the insured if the policy was canceled by **(a)** the insured and **(b)** the insurance company.

	Annual Premium	Date of Policy	Date Canceled
1.	$350.00	May 10	September 9
2.	226.00	September 20	March 1
3.	689.00	May 7	November 2
4.	348.00	April 18	June 2
5.	564.00	June 4	August 16
6.	146.00	January 20	October 2

Chapter 10. Insurance

C. Solve these problems.

1. Merchandise was insured for $30,000 for 120 days at the annual rate of 67¢ per $100. Find the premium.

2. Find the premium for $95,000 of insurance on a 90-day policy at the annual rate of 39¢ per $100.

3. A building was insured for $146,000 at an annual rate of 47¢ per $100. After 173 days, the 1-year policy was canceled by the insured. Find the amount of the refund.

4. On April 10, Donald Olson obtained a fire insurance policy for $97,000 on a rental house by paying the rate of 34¢ per $100. He sold the house 241 days later and canceled the policy. How much premium refund should he receive?

5. Sandra Swedersky paid $435 as the premium on a 1-year fire insurance policy. After the policy had been in force for 135 days, it was canceled by the insurance company. How much should the company refund to Swedersky?

6. The premium for a 1-year policy on property insured for $50,000 was $360. Find the premium rate.

Amount of Indemnity on Fire Loss

When a fire loss occurs, the insurance company should be notified immediately so that an adjuster can be sent to determine the extent of the loss by examining the property. The compensation paid by the insurance company to the insured to cover the loss is the **indemnity.**

Settlement Under Ordinary Fire Policy. Most residences are covered by ordinary fire insurance policies. In the event of fire damage under an ordinary policy, the company pays the full amount of the loss up to the face value of the policy. The insurance company, of course, will not pay for any loss in excess of the amount for which the property is insured.

Example:

Property that is valued at $100,000 is insured for $90,000. How much will the insurance company pay under an ordinary fire insurance policy if the loss is **(a)** $80,000, **(b)** $90,000, or **(c)** $100,000?

Solution:

(a) The actual loss of $80,000 will be recovered. An insurance company will never pay more than the actual loss.
(b) The actual loss of $90,000 will be recovered, since it does not exceed the face value of the policy.
(c) The face value of the policy, $90,000, will be recovered because the company will not pay more than the insurance.

Settlement From More Than One Insurance Company. For various reasons, business property is sometimes insured by more than one insurance company. Here are a few of the reasons: the property may be too valuable for one insur-

Part 2. Mathematics Applications in Starting a Business

ance company to carry the whole risk; the owner of the property may wish to do business with two or more insurance agents; the owner may purchase additional insurance from a second company on the recommendation of an agent when the property has increased in value; or the party holding a mortgage on the property may require more than one underwriter.

When fire damage occurs to property that is insured by more than one underwriter, the loss is covered by the companies in proportion to the amount of each policy. As under ordinary policies, the total compensation can exceed neither the amount of loss nor the face value of the policies.

Example:

Property is insured under Globe Insurance Company for $50,000 and under Federal Insurance Company for $30,000. How much should each company pay on a fire loss of $32,000?

Solution:

$50,000   Globe Insurance Company
  30,000   Federal Insurance Company
$80,000   total insurance

$$\frac{50,000}{80,000} \times \$32,000 = \$20,000 \quad \text{Globe's share of loss}$$

$$\frac{30,000}{80,000} \times \$32,000 = \underline{\$12,000} \quad \text{Federal's share of loss}$$
$$\phantom{\frac{30,000}{80,000} \times \$32,000 = } \$32,000 \quad \text{total loss}$$

Settlement Under Coinsurance. Since fire seldom causes the total destruction of the property, the owner may decide to insure the property for only a small part of its value. A smaller premium is paid than if the property were insured for its full value. To encourage owners to buy more coverage, insurance companies offer reduced rates on policies that contain a **coinsurance clause.** Under this clause, the company will pay the full amount of any loss up to the face value of the policy, provided the property is insured for a specified percent of its value. The percent specified varies; it may be 60%, 70%, 80% (the most popular), or 90%. If the clause specifies 80%, it is an **80% coinsurance clause.**

If the insured fails to keep the property insured up to the specified percent, the insurance company will pay only a proportionate share of the loss. When the specified minimum of insurance is not carried, the insured shares with the insurance company in any fire losses that may occur to the property. The ratio of the company's indemnity is based on the relationship of the insurance carried to the insurance required. Generally, the computation of the company's share of each loss may be summarized in the following equation:

$$Indemnity = \frac{Insurance\ Carried}{Insurance\ Required} \times Loss$$

Example:

Property valued at $100,000 is insured for only $70,000. The policy contains an 80% coinsurance clause. A fire caused $40,000 of damage to the property. How much of the loss will the fire insurance company pay?

Solution:

$100,000 × 0.8 = $80,000 insurance required. Therefore:

$$\frac{70,000}{80,000} \times \$40,000 = \$35,000 \quad \text{indemnity}$$

Chapter 10. Insurance

When using the formula, remember that if it yields an amount greater than the face of the policy, the company will pay only the face value. An insurance company will pay neither more than face value nor more than the amount of the loss.

Exercise 10–3

A. For the following ordinary insurance policies, find each company's share of the fire loss.

		Amount of Insurance		
	Amount of Loss	Eastern Insurance Co.	Federal Insurance Co.	Globe Insurance Co.
1.	$ 30,000	$120,000	$180,000	None
2.	75,000	150,000	None	$ 90,000
3.	45,500	100,000	400,000	200,000
4.	184,000	600,000	400,000	200,000
5.	39,000	40,000	60,000	80,000
6.	75,000	18,000	12,000	30,000

B. In each of the following, find the insurance company's indemnity.

	Face of Policy	Amount of Loss	Value of Property	Coinsurance Clause
1.	$ 40,000	$ 33,000	$ 50,000	80%
2.	200,000	161,000	350,000	80%
3.	60,000	65,000	75,000	90%
4.	200,000	80,000	250,000	90%
5.	450,000	480,000	600,000	80%
6.	550,000	840,000	960,000	70%

C. Solve these problems.

1. A warehouse valued at $630,000 was insured for $\frac{6}{7}$ of its value. Find the insurance company's indemnity if the building was completely destroyed by fire.

2. An apartment building was insured by Company A for $700,000 and by Company B for $500,000. How much should each company pay on a fire loss of $300,000?

3. A factory building is insured for $32,000 with Company A, for $96,000 with Company B, and for $128,000 with Company C. A fire loss of $104,000 occurred. What amount should each insurance company pay?

4. A retail store carried $480,000 worth of fire insurance on its merchandise under a policy that contained a 90% coinsurance clause. Fire destroyed $189,000 worth of the merchandise at a time when the inventory records

Part 2. Mathematics Applications in Starting a Business

revealed that the stock on hand had cost $600,000. How much should the insurance company pay?

5. The proprietor of a retail store carried $72,000 worth of insurance on the merchandise under a policy that contained an 80% coinsurance clause. After a fire completely destroyed the property, the records revealed that the merchandise had cost $108,000. How much should the proprietor receive from the insurance company?

6. The merchandise in a department store was completely destroyed by fire. At the time of the fire, the following ordinary insurance was carried on the stock: Company A, $450,000; Company B, $1,300,000; and Company C, $650,000. The value of the stock was $2,800,000. Find the amount paid by each insurance company.

LIFE INSURANCE

Life insurance is a cooperative risk-sharing plan through which people pay portions of their earnings to provide for the time when their earnings cease—because of death, retirement, or poor health. In the United States, the primary use of life insurance is to provide adequate financial protection for the family. Accordingly, life insurance is used by families to fill financial needs that may be created by the loss of the chief wage earner. These are some of the financial needs: money to meet burial expenses, money to meet living expenses while the family readjusts to the new conditions, income for the family while the children are growing up, money for the education of the children, and income for the remaining spouse after the children have grown up.

In addition to these uses, ordinary life insurance is commonly used by businesses to insure the lives of key personnel for the benefit of the business. Often all of the part owners in a partnership are insured on behalf of the business. Therefore, when a partner dies, the partnership is able to pay promptly a predetermined price to the family for the deceased partner's equity in the business. Thus, the surviving partners can avoid delay in the settlement without using their personal or business assets.

The person or organization named in the policy to receive the proceeds of the insurance is the **beneficiary.**

Types of Life Insurance Policies

There are several ways to classify life insurance. One classification depends on the number of people covered in the policy—whether individual or group. **Group life insurance** is a plan whereby a group of people is insured under one policy. Most commonly the group is composed of the employees of a business organization who are insured under a master contract issued to the employer. Group insurance is also issued to unions and other organizations for their members. The group rate is usually smaller than that for a policy of the same amount purchased by one person on an individual policy. Most commonly the coverage is in multiples of $1,000, and the premiums are usually paid annually, semiannually, or quarterly, but may be paid monthly.

Special family policies have also been developed to meet the life insurance needs of families with minor children; however, the following presentation is limited to individual policies. There are three basic types of life insurance policies for individuals. These are term policies, lifetime policies, and endowment policies.

Term Insurance. A **term** policy provides protection only for a given period of time, such as one, five, or ten years. The face of the policy is paid by the company only if the insured dies within the given term. Term insurance may not require payment by the company, usually does not have a cash value, and provides only temporary protection. For these reasons, the premium for term insurance is lower than for any other kind of life insurance. Short-term policies are sold in transportation terminals to provide travelers with low-cost life insurance for the duration of a trip. Term insurance is also used in group policies and for debt management. As an example of the latter, provision for paying off a mortgage can be accomplished through decreasing term insurance.

Lifetime Policies. The two major **lifetime** policies, which provide insurance protection during the lifetime of the insured, differ mainly in the duration of the premium-paying period. The insured may select a policy that calls for (1) payment of premiums during all of his or her remaining life or (2) payment for a definite period of time.

In **straight life** or **whole life** insurance, the policyholder agrees to pay to the insurance company a specified premium periodically until the death of the insured. Of course, the insurance company agrees to pay the face of the policy to the beneficiary at the death of the insured.

The **limited-payment life** policy also provides lifetime insurance, but the payments are limited to a definite period of time, such as 20, 25, or 30 years, or up to a certain age, say to 60 or 65 years of age. The policyholder is thus freed of premium payments during the later years of retirement. However, since the premiums are paid for a shorter period of time, each premium is somewhat larger than under a straight life policy. The face of the limited-payment policy is payable at the death of the insured, whether it occurs before or after all premiums have been paid.

Endowment Policies. An **endowment** life insurance policy contains a savings plan as well as insurance protection. Premiums for this kind of insurance are much higher than for lifetime or term insurance. The larger premiums of an endowment policy build up savings much more rapidly than do those of lifetime policies. The premiums are paid for a specified number of years, such as 20 or 25 years. At the end of the specified time, the cash value equals the face value of the policy and is paid to the insured if alive. Naturally, if the endowment is paid to the insured, the policy is surrendered and the beneficiary collects nothing at the death of the insured. If the insured dies during the specified period, however, the beneficiary receives the face value of the policy.

Premiums for Life Insurance

Life insurance premiums are based primarily on the life expectancy of the insured at the time the policy is taken out. The longer one is likely to live, the lower the premiums. For example, an individual who is 20 years old has a longer life expectancy than someone who is 30 years old. The younger person, therefore, pays the lower premium for a longer period of time.

Life insurance is usually purchased on a **level-premium** basis, which means that the premium does not change from year to year, even though the risk of death grows with age. Under this system, the insured pays more than is needed during the early years to meet the benefit payments. The extra money accumulates in reserve funds to be used for benefit payments in later years. Furthermore, the reserve funds are invested and the earnings resulting therefrom help to pay part of the cost of the insurance.

Though rate tables change to reflect economic fluctuations, Table 10–2 will serve to show the approximate annual premium per $1,000 of life insurance for individuals of various ages who choose one of the basic kinds of policies. For life insurance purposes, the insured's age is based on the nearest birthday. To find the annual premium for a specific policy, the appropriate rate in the table is multiplied by the number of thousands of dollars in the face of the policy. The annual premium is multiplied by one of the factors shown below the table if the semiannual, quarterly, or monthly premium is to be computed.

Age of Insured	5-Year Term	Straight Life	20-Payment Life	20-Year Endowment
20	$ 4.95	$13.30	$22.80	$45.30
21	4.98	13.60	23.20	45.35
22	5.00	14.00	23.70	45.40
23	5.03	14.40	24.20	45.45
24	5.05	14.80	24.70	45.50
25	5.08	15.20	25.20	45.55
30	5.19	17.70	27.60	45.95
35	5.73	21.50	31.50	46.60
40	7.19	25.60	35.40	48.10
45	9.64	31.20	41.30	51.00
50	13.65	38.60	48.70	54.50
55	19.60	48.90	58.10	61.20
60	29.50	61.70	72.40	71.90

Table 10–2 Approximate[1] Annual[2] Premium Per $1,000 of Life Insurance

[1] Premium rates shown are approximate rates per $1,000 of life insurance protection for men. In recognition of somewhat lower mortality rates, premiums for women are approximately those of a male five years younger. Rates of participating policies are slightly higher, but the cost is reduced by annual dividends. Rates of nonparticipating policies are lower than those shown, and no dividends are paid.

[2] Semiannual rate is 52% of the annual rate; quarterly rate, 26.3% of annual rate; monthly rate, 8.9% of annual rate. These factors vary slightly between companies.

Example:　Robert Sumner, who will be 22 years old on May 2, purchased a $25,000 straight life insurance policy on January 20. Use Table 10–2 to find **(a)** the annual premium and **(b)** the quarterly premium.

Solution:
(a) Since his next birthday is less than 6 months away, 22 years is his insurance age. The annual premium per $1,000 in the Straight Life column of the table for age 22 is $14. Therefore:
$14 × 25 = $350 annual premium.

(b) The quarterly rate is 26.3% of the annual rate; therefore:
$350 × .263 = $92.05 quarterly premium.

Life Insurance Dividends

One means of classifying life insurance policies is according to whether they are participating or nonparticipating. For a **participating policy,** the premium rate is somewhat larger than the company expects will be needed under normal conditions. If a portion of the premium is not needed, the policyholder receives a refund that is called a **policy dividend.** Policyholders usually pay premiums for two or three years before becoming eligible for policy dividends, which are normally paid annually. In a **nonparticipating policy,** the premium rate is fixed to represent as closely as possible the amount that is expected to be needed to pay for the cost of providing the insurance. The premium rate is the actual cost to the policyholder, for there are no policy dividends. There is no accurate method of predicting whether a participating or nonparticipating policy will be less expensive over the years.

The policyholder receives notice of the dividend on the policy with the notice that the premium is due. The dividends may be used in one of four ways: (1) taken in cash, (2) used to help pay the premiums, (3) used to purchase additional paid-up insurance, or (4) left with the company to accumulate interest.

● Exercise 10–4

A. For each of the problems below, use Table 10–2 to find the periodic premium.

	Kind of Policy	Age at Issue	Face of Policy	Payment Period
1.	Straight Life	20	$ 70,000	Annually
2.	20-Payment Life	24	90,000	Annually
3.	5-year Term	45	200,000	Monthly
4.	20-year Endowment	23	150,000	Semiannually
5.	20-Payment Life	50	25,000	Quarterly
6.	Straight Life	35	55,000	Semiannually
7.	5-year Term	25	125,000	Monthly
8.	20-year Endowment	40	28,000	Quarterly

Part 2. Mathematics Applications in Starting a Business

B. Solve these problems.

1. At insurable age 20, how much more is the annual premium on a $50,000, 20-year endowment policy than on a 20-payment life policy?

2. How much less will the policyholder pay during the term for a $10,000, 5-year term policy at age 22 than for a straight life policy with the same face value?

3. George Zacher, who was age twenty-one on the preceding October 12, purchased an $80,000, 20-year endowment policy on May 20. How much can he save on premiums each year if he makes quarterly instead of monthly payments?

4. At insurable age 35, Lila Jacoby purchased a $25,000, 20-year endowment policy. How much less would her premiums be annually if she had purchased the policy when she was 25 years of age?

5. Guy Noland, insurable age 23, wants to invest not more than $500 a year in life insurance. In hundred-dollar multiples, what is the largest policy he can purchase in each of the following: **(a)** 20-year endowment, **(b)** 20-payment life, **(c)** straight life, and **(d)** 5-year term?

6. James Travers took out a $70,000, 20-payment life insurance policy at the insurable age of 40. If $7,966.40 in policy dividends were applied to his premiums during the life of the policy, how much was the net cost of the insurance?

7. Carla Rhinehart carries a 20-payment life insurance policy with a face value of $80,000 that was taken out when she was 30 years of age. During the past year, the policy earned a dividend of $253.50 that she plans to use to reduce the next annual premium. What amount should she send to the insurance company for the next premium?

8. When he was exactly 24 years old, Gordon Vasquez purchased a $30,000 straight life policy. At the beginning of the second year and each year thereafter, he received a dividend of 10% of the annual premium. He died at the age of 46 years and 5 months. If he applied each dividend to the next annual premium, how much more did his beneficiary receive than had been paid in premiums?

Nonforfeiture Values

In the early days of life insurance, the policyholder received no further benefits from the insurance company when premium payments were stopped. The insured was said to have "forfeited" the right to further benefits.

Today, however, the individual policies (except most term insurance policies) of all legal reserve life insurance companies provide a choice of values to policyholders who cease paying premiums after a few years. These are **nonforfeiture values** because they are values that are not forfeited by the withdrawing policyholder. The three most common nonforfeiture values are: (1) cash value, (2) reduced paid-up insurance value, and (3) extended term insurance value.

Cash Value. The portion of the premium that is in excess of the cost of the insurance protection accumulates to build up reserves. Each life insurance policy, other than most term policies, accumulates a cash value based on its reserve. The **cash value** is the amount of money that will be paid by the insurance company to the policyholder when the policy is surrendered after premiums have been paid for a specific time, usually one or two years. The size of the cash value depends on the kind of policy, the age of the insured when the insurance was acquired, and the length of time during which premiums were paid. Generally the higher the premium per $1,000 of insurance and the longer the policy has been in force, the higher the cash value will be.

Reduced Paid-up Insurance. The guaranteed cash value of a surrendered policy may be used to obtain a new policy of **reduced paid-up insurance.** The face value of the new policy will be as large as possible, depending on how much insurance the cash value can buy as a single payment at the attained age of the insured.

Extended Term Insurance. If the policyholder stops paying premiums but wants to keep the maximum amount of insurance protection for as long as possible, **extended term insurance,** which will continue the full face value of the policy in force for a specified term, should be selected. The cash value of the policy is used as a single payment to buy the extended term insurance at the attained age of the insured. Of course, the length of the term depends on the size of the cash value. If the insured does not select one of the other nonforfeiture values after defaulting on premium payments, extended term insurance usually is granted automatically by the insurance company.

A table in the policy shows the nonforfeiture values. Table 10–3 shows a portion of such a table from a straight life policy and all of a table from a 20-payment life policy. Of course, the values vary from policy to policy. The values in a straight life policy of one company will vary from those in a straight life policy of another company. As in premium tables, the values shown in nonforfeiture tables are per $1,000 of the policy face.

Example: At the age of 25, Dennis Crawford purchased a $50,000, 20-payment life insurance policy. After making 15 annual premium payments, what are **(a)** the cash value, **(b)** the value of the paid-up insurance and **(c)** the extended term during which he can have $50,000 of insurance protection? (Use Table 10–3.)

Solution: **(a)** $337.29 × 50 = $16,864.50 cash value
(b) $747.76 × 50 = $37,388.00 paid-up insurance
(c) He has been paying premiums on $50,000 of insurance; therefore, he is entitled not to $1,000 but to $50,000 of insurance for the term indicated in the table: 34 years and 102 days.

Part 2. Mathematics Applications in Starting a Business

Straight Life Policy					20-Payment Life Policy				
End of Policy Year	Cash Value	Paid-up Insurance	Extended Term Insurance		End of Policy Year	Cash Value	Paid-up Insurance	Extended Term Insurance	
			Years	Days				Years	Days
1	$ 8.00	$ 26.00	1	219	1	$ 17.45	$ 48.99	2	100
2	19.85	48.72	3	131	2	35.52	98.20	4	275
3	30.14	70.31	5	81	3	54.22	147.57	7	165
4	40.69	91.40	7	299	4	73.57	197.07	10	134
5	51.51	103.09	9	349	5	93.61	246.74	13	166
6	62.60	129.29	11	247	6	114.35	296.52	16	232
7	73.96	156.98	13	40	7	135.82	346.40	19	267
8	85.61	185.69	14	117	8	158.05	396.38	22	197
9	97.55	211.68	15	130	9	181.07	446.45	24	362
10	109.79	240.46	16	87	10	204.89	496.55	27	31
11	122.33	265.72	16	362	11	229.56	546.73	28	320
12	135.19	290.54	17	227	12	255.10	596.92	30	158
13	148.37	314.78	18	54	13	281.55	647.18	31	296
14	161.88	338.57	18	212	14	308.93	697.44	33	25
15	175.73	366.82	18	343	15	337.29	747.76	34	102
16	189.92	387.24	19	45	16	366.66	798.09	35	190
17	204.48	407.15	19	99	17	397.08	848.46	36	331
18	219.38	426.68	19	141	18	428.69	898.89	38	221
19	234.67	445.85	19	176	19	461.25	949.41	41	2
20	250.34	471.00	19	205	20	495.10	1,000.00	—	—

Table 10-3 Approximate Nonforfeiture Values Per $1,000 of Life Insurance Issued at Age 25

Policy Loans

After a life insurance policy has been in force for one or two years, the policyholder can borrow against the cash value. The policy itself serves as collateral for the loan. Since term policies normally have no cash value, they usually have no loan value. The loan value, like the cash value, grows from year to year. The interest on policy loans is charged for the exact number of days. The interest rate is usually low when compared to other personal loans.

Settlement Options

Although practically all ordinary life insurance policies state that the policy benefit will be paid as a single sum of money, the insured, or perhaps the beneficiary, may choose some other payment plan. Most newer policies contain the following five optional plans, called **settlement options.**

Option 1—**Interest.** When the **interest option** is selected, the insurance company holds the proceeds and pays interest at a guaranteed annual rate. The interest rate is generally smaller than that paid by savings institutions.

Option 2—**Time.** Under the **time option,** the insurance company pays regular equal installments for a specified period, such as 10 or 20 years. Interest is paid on remaining money in the fund until it is all paid out.

Option 3—**Amount.** If the **amount option** is chosen, the insurance company pays a selected amount regularly until the proceeds and interest are exhausted.

Option 4—**Life Annuity.** When the **life annuity option** is selected, the insurance company invests the proceeds and then sends a periodic payment to the payee for his or her lifetime. The size of the periodic payment is based on the life expectancy of the payee when the payments begin and on the amount of the proceeds.

Option 5—**Annuity Certain and Lifetime Thereafter.** Because the payee of a life annuity might die soon after the annuity begins, the **annuity certain and lifetime thereafter option** is preferred by some policyholders. Under the latter plan, the insurance company pays regular equal installments for a guaranteed time, such as ten or twenty years, and for as long thereafter as the first beneficiary lives. If the first beneficiary dies before the guaranteed time has lapsed, the payments continue to a second beneficiary for the remainder of the specified time. The size of the payment at any given age is somewhat smaller than that in the straight life annuity.

Tables of settlement options are contained in ordinary life insurance policies. Table 10–4 is representative of such tables.

Example:

Keiko Hayashi, age 55, is the beneficiary of a $50,000 life insurance policy. Rather than take the proceeds in a single payment, she is considering the settlement options. Use Table 10–4 to find the amount of each monthly payment **(a)** for the exact time of 10 years, **(b)** under a life annuity, and **(c)** under an annuity for 10 years certain and life thereafter.

Solution:

(a) $9.40 × 50 = $470 monthly payment for 10 years
(b) $4.61 × 50 = $230.50 monthly payment for life
(c) $4.50 × 50 = $225 monthly payment for 10 years and life

Options 4 & 5

Option 2

Number of Years	Monthly Payment
1	$84.28
2	42.66
3	28.79
4	21.86
5	17.70
6	14.93
7	12.95
8	11.47
9	10.32
10	9.40
11	8.64
12	8.02
13	7.49
14	7.03
15	6.64
16	6.30
17	6.00
18	5.73
19	5.49
20	5.27

Options 4 & 5 — Monthly Payment

Age of Payee When Payments Begin		Life Income Only	10 Years Certain and Life	15 Years Certain and Life	20 Years Certain and Life
Male	Female				
25	30	$3.08	$3.08	$3.07	$3.05
30	35	3.27	3.26	3.24	3.22
31	36	3.31	3.30	3.28	3.25
32	37	3.36	3.34	3.32	3.29
33	38	3.41	3.39	3.36	3.33
34	39	3.45	3.43	3.41	3.37
35	40	3.50	3.48	3.45	3.41
36	41	3.56	3.53	3.50	3.45
37	42	3.61	3.59	3.55	3.50
38	43	3.67	3.64	3.60	3.54
39	44	3.73	3.70	3.65	3.59
40	45	3.79	3.76	3.71	3.64
41	46	3.86	3.82	3.77	3.69
42	47	3.93	3.88	3.82	3.74
43	48	4.00	3.95	3.88	3.79
44	49	4.08	4.02	3.95	3.84
45	50	4.15	4.09	4.01	3.90
46	51	4.24	4.17	4.08	3.95
47	52	4.33	4.25	4.15	4.01
48	53	4.42	4.33	4.22	4.07
49	54	4.51	4.42	4.29	4.12
50	55	4.61	4.50	4.37	4.18
51	56	4.72	4.60	4.44	4.24
52	57	4.83	4.69	4.52	4.30
53	58	4.95	4.79	4.60	4.36
54	59	5.07	4.90	4.69	4.41
55	60	5.20	5.01	4.77	4.47
56	61	5.34	5.12	4.86	4.53
57	62	5.48	5.23	4.94	4.59
58	63	5.64	5.35	5.03	4.64
59	64	5.80	5.48	5.12	4.70
60	65	5.97	5.61	5.21	4.75
61	66	6.15	5.74	5.30	4.80
62	67	6.34	5.87	5.39	4.85
63	68	6.54	6.01	5.48	4.90
64	69	6.75	6.16	5.56	4.94
65	70	6.97	6.30	5.65	4.98
70	75	8.32	7.07	6.05	5.14

Table 10–4 Life Insurance Settlement Options (Monthly Payments for Each $1,000 of Proceeds)

A. For the following, use Table 10–3 to find **(a)** cash value, **(b)** paid-up insurance, and **(c)** time of the extended term insurance. Each policy was purchased when the insured was 25 years old.

No.	Kind of Policy	End of Policy Year	Face of Policy
1.	Straight Life	10	$ 20,000
2.	Straight Life	3	80,000
3.	20-Payment Life	14	30,000
4.	20-Payment Life	8	150,000
5.	Straight Life	20	60,000
6.	20-Payment Life	15	24,000

B. For each of the following, use Table 10–4 to find the monthly payment based on the settlement option listed.

No.	Sex and Age of Payee	Settlement Option	Face of Policy
1.	Male 23	15 years exactly	$ 40,000
2.	Female 30	8 years exactly	25,000
3.	Male 55	Life income	45,000
4.	Male 48	15 years certain and life	200,000
5.	Female 60	10 years certain and life	70,000
6.	Female 55	Life income	45,000
7.	Female 45	20 years certain and life	60,000
8.	Male 63	10 years certain and life	150,000

C. Solve these problems.

1. If purchased at the insurable age of 25, what is the cash surrender value 14 years later of each of the following $34,000 policies: **(a)** 20-payment life and **(b)** straight life?

2. Dan Erickson purchased a $37,500 straight life insurance policy seven years ago when he was 25. Find **(a)** the cash surrender value, **(b)** the paid-

up insurance value, and **(c)** the time for which he may select extended term insurance with the same face value.

3. Emilio Soto, at the insurable age of 25, purchased a $28,000, 20-payment life insurance policy. What is the maximum amount that he can borrow on the policy 16 years later?

4. Luisa Valdez is the beneficiary of a $25,000 life insurance policy. Rather than take the proceeds in a single payment, she has requested equal monthly payments for 15 years. How much will she receive each month?

5. Katherine Kaufman, age 57, is the beneficiary of her deceased husband's $60,000 insurance policy. She has requested a life income. How much will she be paid each month for the rest of her life?

6. On June 4, Brian Gates borrowed $7,500 from the insurance company against the cash value of his life insurance policy. The interest at 6% is due on the premium dates. The annual premium of $252 is due on November 1. What total amount of premium and interest will be due on November 1?

7. Thomas LaRosa took out a $50,000, 20-payment life policy at the age of 25. At the end of six years, he turned in the policy for its cash value. During the six years, he had received policy dividends of $660.90. Find the net cost of the insurance.

8. Floyd Pierce, age 53, is the beneficiary of a $35,000 life insurance policy. He has decided to receive the proceeds for 15 years certain and life. What is the amount of each monthly payment?

9. Edith Sterling chose a settlement option that pays her monthly for 15 years. **(a)** What is the total amount she will receive for the $200,000 policy? **(b)** Is this amount more or less, and by how much, than the face value of the policy?

10. Michael Wirth obtained at age 25 a $60,000 straight life policy on which the premiums are payable annually and a $9,000, 20-payment life policy, premiums payable semiannually. At the end of the twelfth year of both policies, he decided to surrender them for cash value. How much more had he paid in premiums than the total amount received for the policies?

AUTOMOBILE INSURANCE

Automobile insurance provides protection against financial losses from injuries to other people and damage to their property caused by the insured's automobile, as well as losses from injuries to passengers of and damage to the automobile.

Types of Automobile Insurance Coverage

The coverages contained in an automobile insurance policy, which commonly has a term of six months, are selected by the insured to meet specific needs. A person may choose only two types of coverage with minimum benefits, more than five types of coverage with maximum benefits, or a great variety of combinations between these two extremes. Regardless of which type of coverage is selected, the insurance company will pay no more than the amounts specified in the policy. The basic types of coverage that may be combined in one automobile insurance policy are as follows.

Bodily Injury Liability. Coverage that provides the insured with protection against claims arising out of injuries or death to others as a result of the insured's ownership, use, or maintenance of an automobile is **bodily injury liability** insurance. So-called 25-50 coverage provides up to $25,000 protection for each injured person with a maximum of $50,000 payable to two or more persons injured in the same accident.

Property Damage Liability. Protection against claims resulting from damage to another person's car, home, or other property is provided by **property damage liability** insurance. Coverage of $25,000 means that the insurance company will pay up to $25,000 for the total property damage resulting from each accident. Bodily injury and property damage insurance together are frequently called **automobile liability** insurance.

Medical Expenses. Coverage in automobile insurance policies for **medical expenses** provides for the payment of the medical expenses not otherwise covered for the insured, for any relatives residing in the insured's household if accidentally injured while riding in, or struck by, any motor vehicle, and for any passenger injured in the insured's automobile. The coverage, say $25,000, is per person injured in each accident.

Comprehensive Damage. Protection that covers the insured's automobile for loss by fire, theft, windstorm, glass breakage, and from many perils other than collision is provided by **comprehensive** insurance. Comprehensive insurance may be purchased with or without a deductible clause. The premium is lower if the insurance contains a deductible clause, but the insured must carry the deductible portion of the loss. For example, a $100-deductible clause provides that the insured shall pay the first $100 of loss per accident; the insurance company pays the remainder.

Collision Damage. Reimbursement for losses from damage to the insured's car by collision or upset regardless of fault is covered by **collision** insurance, which is most commonly sold with a deductible clause of $100 or more. Since the insured assumes part of the risk, the premium is much lower for insurance with a deductible clause. Comprehensive and collision insurance together are referred to as **physical damage** insurance. In each, the insurance company reimburses the insured for the value of the actual loss, less any deductible amount.

Other Coverages. By paying the appropriate premiums, the insured may acquire protection for other risks, such as emergency road service, uninsured motorists, death, and disability.

No-Fault Automobile Insurance. The present automobile insurance system in most states depends largely on the person at fault paying for damages caused by automobile accidents. Some states provide for **no-fault** automobile insurance that allows the insured driver, passengers in the car, and injured bystanders to receive payment for damages directly from the insured person's own insurance company, without regard as to who was at fault in the accident. Instead of waiting for the insurance company or the courts to decide who was at fault and what the damages should be, the insurance company determines the amount of damage and pays the claim. Those no-fault plans that have been adopted or are under consideration by the individual states allow victims or survivors to sue the party at fault if an automobile accident results in permanent serious disability, permanent disfigurement, or death. Such damages are limited by law in some states.

Premiums for Automobile Insurance

Like life insurance premiums, premiums for automobile insurance are based on laws of probability. In life insurance, the premium depends on the probability of death; in automobile insurance, on the probability of accidents that cause bodily injury (including death), property damage, and physical damage. The probability that such accidents will occur can be predicted rather accurately, depending on where the car is used; the age of the driver; and the car's usage, make, model, and age.

Territory Rates. The greater the number of automobiles in a given area, the greater the likelihood of automobile accidents. For this reason, insurance companies charge much higher rates in heavily populated areas that have a high density of automobiles than in sparsely populated areas that have a low density of automobiles. The area, whether urban or rural, to which a specific set of premium rates is applied is a **territory.** As Table 10–5 shows, the premium rates vary greatly from territory to territory.

Coverage in Thousands of Dollars

Terri-tory Number	Usage Class	Bodily Injury						Property Damage				Medical			
		15 30	20 40	25 50	50 100	100 200	100 300	15	25	50	100	5	25	50	100
62	1A	72	75	78	83	92	98	35	36	38	40	23	25	36	43
	1B	84	87	90	96	107	113	38	40	42	44	24	26	39	47
	1C	92	96	100	105	117	125	43	45	47	49	26	29	41	49
	2A	126	132	138	146	161	171	58	60	62	64	29	31	47	55
	2B	183	191	198	210	233	248	84	87	93	98	36	38	57	68
	2C	150	158	164	174	192	206	68	72	75	80	30	33	50	60
	3	117	122	126	134	149	158	53	56	59	62	27	29	44	52
65	1A	48	50	52	54	60	65	21	23	25	27	20	23	33	39
	1B	54	57	60	63	69	74	24	26	28	30	20	23	33	39
	1C	59	62	65	68	75	80	28	30	32	34	20	23	33	39
	2A	81	84	87	93	102	110	38	40	42	44	24	26	39	47
	2B	117	122	126	134	149	158	53	56	59	62	27	29	44	52
	2C	189	197	204	216	240	255	87	90	96	101	36	38	57	68
	3	74	77	80	84	93	99	35	37	39	41	22	24	36	43
66	1A	84	87	90	96	107	112	38	40	42	44	24	26	39	47
	1B	93	98	102	108	119	128	44	46	48	50	26	28	41	49
	1C	104	108	113	119	132	141	49	51	53	55	26	28	41	49
	2A	143	149	155	164	182	194	65	68	72	75	32	34	50	60
	2B	209	216	225	237	264	281	95	99	105	110	36	38	57	68
	2C	335	347	360	381	423	450	155	162	171	180	41	64	81	97
	3	132	137	143	150	167	177	61	63	66	71	29	32	47	56
69	1A	60	63	66	69	77	83	29	31	33	35	20	22	33	39
	1B	69	72	75	78	89	93	32	34	36	38	22	24	36	43
	1C	77	80	83	87	98	104	35	37	39	40	22	24	36	43
	2A	104	108	112	119	132	141	49	51	53	55	26	28	41	49
	2B	152	158	164	174	192	206	69	74	77	81	32	34	50	60
	2C	246	255	266	281	311	332	111	117	123	129	36	38	57	68
	3	95	99	104	110	122	129	46	48	50	52	26	28	41	49

Table 10–5 Liability and Medical Insurance Semiannual Rates* for Private Automobiles

*15% discount for more than one car; 25% discount for students under 25 who have good grades. Rates have been rounded to the nearest dollar.

Usage Classes. Increasing the number of miles per year that the automobile is driven also increases the probability that more accidents will occur. Thus, the premiums for bodily injury and property damage are higher for cars used in business than for those used to drive a short distance to and from work. Accident statistics of age groups also affect premiums for automobile insurance. For example, premiums charged for drivers under 25 years of age are considerably higher than for those over 25 because young drivers have more serious accidents. Many insurance companies, however, give discounts to students under 25 who maintain good grades and to people who have passed a course in driver training.

When the policy is written, the automobile is classified according to its usage on the basis of the information given to the insurance company. Following is a sample of a system that is used by a large insurance company to classify private, "not-for-hire" passenger automobiles:

Class 1A applies if the automobile is not used in the insured's occupation, not driven to and from work, and not driven by a person under 25 years of age.

Class 1B applies if the automobile is not used in the insured's occupation but is driven up to 10 miles one way to and from work, and there is no driver under 25 years of age.

Class 1C applies if the automobile is not used in the insured's occupation but is driven over 10 miles one way to and from work, and there is no driver under 25 years of age.

Class 2A applies if (1) the automobile is owned or operated by a young married couple (one or both under 25) with children residing in the household or (2) the automobile is the family car that is operated by an unmarried person under 25 who is not the principal driver.

Class 2B applies if the automobile is owned or operated by a young married couple (one or both under 25) without children residing in the household.

Class 2C applies if the automobile is owned or operated by an unmarried person under 25 who is the principal driver.

Class 3 applies if (1) the automobile is used in any person's occupation and does not qualify under Class 2 or (2) the automobile is owned by a corporation, partnership, or association.

Automobile Value. The value of an automobile determines the extent of the loss from theft or from damage to the car resulting from a collision. The insurance company will not pay more than the value of the car for such losses. The age, make, and model are the basic considerations used to find the value of an automobile at a given time. These considerations, in turn, affect the size of the premiums charged for automobile insurance. Premiums for comprehensive and collision insurance, therefore, are much higher for a new, expensive car than for an older, inexpensive car. There are so many different makes and models of automobiles that no itemized list of categories is presented in this section. The categories represented by the letters A, B, C, D, and E in Tables 10–6 and 10–7 are but five examples of the hundreds of categories that are used by insurance companies.

Example: Alvin and Carol Hayes, who are both under 25 years of age and have no children, own a Category C automobile that is used for pleasure only. They live in Territory 65 and want the following automobile insurance coverage: bodily injury with 25-50 coverage; $15,000 property damage; $25,000 medical; comprehensive; and collision with a $100 deductible clause. They purchased the car when it was new a year ago. Find **(a)** the premium for each coverage and **(b)** the total semiannual premium.

Solution: **(a)** Table 10–5; Territory 65; Class 2B.

Bodily Injury (25-50)	$126
Property Damage (15)	53
Medical Expenses (25)	29

Table 10–6; Class 2B; Age 2; Category C.

Comprehensive Damage	69

Table 10–7; Class 2B; Age 2; Category C.

Collision Damage	138

(b) Total Premium $415

Usage Class	Age**	Automobile Make and Model				
		A	B	C	D	E
1A	1	$27	$ 52	$ 82	$125	$169
	2	24	49	77	120	161
	3	20	40	68	97	128
1B	1	35	70	124	170	226
	2	34	67	117	161	215
	3	27	54	94	129	171
1C	1	26	53	91	125	166
	2	25	50	86	119	159
	3	20	40	70	95	126
2A	1	28	54	95	130	174
	2	26	51	90	124	165
	3	21	41	73	100	133
2B	1	20	42	71	99	131
	2	19	39	69	94	125
	3	15	31	55	75	100
2C	1	54	106	188	256	341
	2	51	101	178	244	325
	3	41	81	143	195	260
3	1	35	69	120	165	220
	2	33	65	115	158	210
	3	26	53	91	126	168

Table 10–6 Comprehensive Insurance Semiannual Rates* for Private Automobiles (Territory: 43, 44, 62, 65, 66, 69)

*15% discount for more than one car; 25% discount for students under 25 who have good grades. Rates have been rounded to nearest dollar.
**1 = new to 6 months; 2 = 7-30 months; 3 = over 30 months.

Usage Class	Age**	A Deductible $100	A Deductible $250	B Deductible $100	B Deductible $250	C Deductible $100	C Deductible $250	D Deductible $100	D Deductible $250	E Deductible $100	E Deductible $250
1A	1	$ 71	$ 49	$102	$ 81	$135	$114	$171	$151	$225	$193
	2	67	46	98	77	127	109	162	144	212	181
	3	54	38	73	59	96	82	123	108	160	138
1B	1	84	58	120	96	159	135	201	178	265	226
	2	80	55	115	91	151	128	193	169	251	215
	3	64	44	91	74	121	103	154	135	201	172
1C	1	68	46	98	78	128	109	164	144	214	183
	2	65	45	92	74	122	104	155	138	204	174
	3	51	35	74	59	98	83	125	110	163	139
2A	1	61	49	103	95	135	115	173	153	226	194
	2	59	48	98	79	129	110	164	145	215	184
	3	47	38	79	63	104	88	131	116	173	148
2B	1	76	53	109	88	144	123	183	161	240	205
	2	73	50	104	83	138	116	174	154	229	195
	3	59	40	83	66	110	93	140	119	183	156
2C	1	120	83	171	136	225	191	286	253	375	321
	2	114	78	163	130	215	183	273	240	358	305
	3	91	63	130	104	171	145	219	193	286	245
3	1	94	64	134	108	178	150	225	199	295	253
	2	90	61	128	103	169	143	215	189	281	240
	3	71	49	103	81	135	115	171	151	225	193

Table 10-7 Collision Insurance Semiannual Rates* for Private Automobiles
(Territory: 43, 52, 54, 55, 62, 64, 65, 66, 69, 77)

*15% discount for more than one car; 25% discount for students under 25 who have good grades. Rates have been rounded to nearest dollar.
**1 = new to 6 months; 2 = 7–30 months; 3 = over 30 months.

● Exercise 10–6

A. Use Table 10–5 to find the total semiannual premium for each of these.

	Terri-tory	Usage Class	Coverage Bodily Injury	Coverage Property Damage	Coverage Medical Expenses
1.	65	1A	25-50	$ 15,000	$ 25,000
2.	62	3	50-100	25,000	50,000
3.	66	1C	15-30	50,000	100,000
4.	69	2A	100-200	25,000	50,000
5.	66	2C	20-40	100,000	25,000
6.	62	1B	100-300	50,000	50,000

B. For each of the following, use Tables 10–6 and 10–7 to find the total semi-annual premium for comprehensive insurance and collision insurance with the listed deductible.

	Usage Class	Age of Car	Make and Model	Collision Deductible
1.	2B	1 year	C	$100
2.	1C	2 years	B	250
3.	2A	16 months	A	100
4.	3	New	E	100
5.	1A	3 years	D	250
6.	2C	New	C	250

C. Solve these problems.

1. How much is the annual savings if an unmarried 24-year-old principal driver of a new Category E automobile buys $250-deductible collision insurance instead of $100-deductible?

2. How much more does a 24-year-old driver pay annually for $100-deductible collision insurance on a new Category D pleasure car than a 25-year-old driver if both are unmarried, principal drivers who live in Territory 62?

3. Ronald Corley, 23 years old and unmarried, wants insurance coverage of $250-deductible collision; comprehensive; bodily injury of 50-100, and property damage of $15,000 for his new Category B car. He lives in Territory 66. Find the total semiannual premium.

4. Jean Britten lives in Territory 62 and carries the following insurance on her two-year-old Category E car: 25-50 bodily injury; $25,000 property damage; comprehensive; and $100-deductible collision. She is 24 years old and unmarried. Find the total semiannual premium.

5. Robert Matteson, who is 24 and resides with his wife and child in Territory 65, wants the following insurance for his new Category A car: 50-100 bodily injury; $15,000 property damage; $25,000 medical; $250-deductible collision; and comprehensive damage. Find the total semiannual premium.

6. Diana Salk, who is 27 years old and lives in Territory 62, insures her Category D car with the following coverages: 100-200 bodily injury; $50,000 property damage; $50,000 medical; comprehensive damage; and $100-deductible collision damage. She neither uses the three-year-old car in her occupation nor drives it to work. Find the total semiannual insurance premium.

7. Tim Crowder lost control of his automobile and caused $24,000 damage to Marsha Gilbert's house and $1,735 damage to his own automobile. Luckily nobody was injured. He carried the following insurance: 20-40 bodily injury; $15,000 property damage; comprehensive; and $250-deductible

collision. How much did the insurance company pay for **(a)** the damage to Gilbert's house and **(b)** the damage to Crowder's car?

8. Kristine and Dennis Barrett, who live in Territory 65, kept their three-year-old Category A car instead of trading it in on their new Category D car. Dennis, age 30, still drives the old car 15 miles from home to work and leaves the new car for Kristine, age 27, to drive. They carry the following insurance on both cars in one policy: 25-50 bodily injury; $15,000 property damage; $25,000 medical; comprehensive; and $250-deductible collision. Find the total semiannual premium.

REVIEW PROBLEMS

Solve these problems. If you have difficulty solving any problem, restudy the appropriate unit in this chapter. The problems under a specific number are related to those contained in the exercise with the same last number.

1. Ben Messina insured the contents of his apartment for $15,000 at the rate of $56\frac{1}{4}$ ¢ per $100. Find the premium for the policy.

2. **a.** Merchandise stock valued at $48,000 was insured on June 1 for one year at the rate of 47¢ per $100. The policy was canceled on November 15 by the insured. Find the premium refund.
   b. A building was insured on May 1 for $630,000 at the rate of 41¢ per $100 for one year. Effective on September 23, the policy was canceled by the insurance company. How much premium was returned to the insured?

3. **a.** A building valued at $208,000 is insured for $\frac{5}{8}$ of its value under an ordinary policy. Find the company's indemnity if a fire loss of $75,000 occurred.
   b. Doreen Schneider has an ordinary fire insurance policy for $36,000 on her house with Company A and another for $72,000 with Company B. A fire caused $19,200 damage to the house. How much should she collect from each company?
   c. Property worth $164,000 is insured under an 80% coinsurance clause for $120,000. Fire caused a loss of $24,000. Find the amount of the loss that is covered by insurance.

4. Silas Summers carries a $50,000 straight life policy that he purchased at the insurable age of 35. The dividend, which he will apply to the next annual premium, amounts to $67.50. Find the net amount of the next premium.

5. **a.** Glen Hall, at the age of 25, insured his life for $36,000 with a straight life policy. He has now paid the annual premium 17 times. Find **(1)** the cash value, **(2)** the paid-up insurance value, and **(3)** the extended term during which he may have the full $36,000 of insurance protection.
   b. Carlota Ortiz, who is 63 years old, has decided to receive the proceeds of a $80,000 life insurance policy for 10 years certain and life. How much will she receive each month?

6. Insurance coverages on a new Category A car are as follows: 100-200 bodily injury; $50,000 property damage; comprehensive; and $250-deductible collision. Find the total semiannual premium in Territory 66 if the principal driver is **(a)** a 24-year-old who resides with a spouse and two children, **(b)** a 24-year-old who lives with a spouse and they have no children, and **(c)** a 24-year-old who is unmarried.

CHALLENGE PROBLEM

Richard and Sara Oesterling are a young married couple. They have twin two-year-old daughters, and Sara is expecting their third child. Richard, who is 25 years of age, has recently received a job promotion and wants to purchase their first insurance on his life for family protection. Lisa Walker, an acquaintance who is an insurance agent, has been trying to sell them a $30,000 straight life policy. Richard is considering buying a 20-year endowment policy because he likes its more rapid buildup of cash value. Sara believes they should buy term insurance.

Sara says, "Buy term insurance and invest the difference." She thinks they should buy a 5-year term policy and put the difference in premium payments in their 6% savings account. They are saving for the down payment on a house. Although they have been living within their means, she feels the savings account has not been growing fast enough.

Lisa counters that most young people who buy term policies do not save the difference in premiums. They simply spend the money impulsively. Lisa has also mentioned that straight life insurance has nonforfeiture values, including a buildup of cash value against which one can borrow. Furthermore, term insurance may be extremely expensive when Richard reaches the age of 60 or 65.

a. If they buy the recommended straight life policy rather than the endowment policy, what will be the total 5-year savings in premiums?

b. To what amount will the premium savings in (a) accumulate if deposited annually into their savings account?

c. If they buy the 5-year term policy rather than the endowment policy, what will be the total 5-year savings in premiums?

d. To what amount will the premium savings in (c) accumulate if deposited annually into their savings account?

e. Which type of insurance do you recommend they buy? Why?

(Use the tables in this book for your calculations.)

Part 2. Mathematics Applications in Starting a Business

Chapter 11

Payrolls and Agents' Commissions

Objectives

After mastering the material in Chapter 11, you will be able to:

- Find gross pay by using the conventional method or the overtime-premium method.
- Compute gross pay on the straight piecework basis or a combination of time and piecework.
- Compute employees' and agents' commissions.
- Use social security and federal income tax tables.
- Calculate income tax withholding by the federal percentage method and the annualized method.
- Complete change tally sheets and change memorandums.

In business, the earnings of employees are summarized periodically in forms called **payrolls.** As payrolls represent earnings, government has placed on employers the responsibility to pay not only employers' taxes but also collect and send to the government certain employees' taxes.

The earnings of supervisory and administrative personnel who are paid a fixed amount on a monthly or annual basis are **salaries.** The earnings of skilled and unskilled workers who are paid on an hourly, weekly, or piecework basis are **wages.** Nevertheless, these two terms are often used synonymously and, for expediency, are so used in this chapter.

Any business that has one or more employees must keep adequate payroll records to comply with federal, state, and perhaps local regulations. Two more obvious reasons for keeping payroll records, however, are to determine the amount owed to employees on payday and to compute the company's monthly or annual gains and losses. The exact form of the records is not specified in government regulations, but most employers keep payroll records that show the following basic kinds of information: amounts and dates of earnings that are subject to payroll taxes; the names, addresses, and occupations of employees receiving the earnings; the periods of their employment; the periods for which they are paid by the employer while absent due to sickness or personal injuries and the amount and weekly rate of such payments; their social security numbers; their income tax withholding exemptions; the employer's identification number; and the dates and amounts of payroll tax payments.

Although larger businesses use machines and high-speed electronic equipment to process payroll data, any employee, from a personal as well as business point of view, should understand the mathematical computations pertaining to payrolls and certain payroll taxes.

GROSS PAY

The total amount earned by the employee daily, weekly, monthly, or annually is the **total wages** or **gross pay.** An employees' gross pay is generally based on (1) passage of time, (2) number of units produced, (3) dollar sales, or (4) some combination of these. A specific employer may use any or all of these plans. The kind of plan used depends on the activity in which the employee is engaged and on the nature of the employer's business operations.

Time Basis

The earnings of employees are most frequently based on time worked. When time is the basis, the compensation is usually stated as a specific rate per hour, day, week, month, or year. As most workers are paid on an hourly-wage basis, this is the basis for the problems in this section.

Only certain occupations, such as managerial and administrative, are exempt from the provisions of the Federal Fair Labor Standards Act, which is also called the Wage and Hour Law. Most workers who are paid on an hourly basis are covered by the law. Employees in occupations covered by the law must be paid at a minimum rate of $1\frac{1}{2}$ times the regular rate for all hours over 40 worked per week. For example, when the regular rate is $8 an hour, the minimum "overtime premium" is $4 and the total overtime pay is $12 an hour. Although not required by the law, overtime pay is sometimes based on a shorter workweek of perhaps 35 or 36 hours. Premium rates for working over 8 hours in one day or for working at night or other less desirable times are also fairly common provisions of union contracts. Premium rates may be as much as two or three times the regular rate.

There are two popular methods of computing an employees' overtime earnings. These are the **conventional method** and the **overtime-premium method.** Under either method, the employee's gross pay, which is found by

Part 2. Mathematics Applications in Starting a Business

adding the earnings for his or her regular hours to the earnings for his or her overtime hours, is the same. The significant difference lies only in the method of computation.

Conventional Method of Computing Gross Pay. The conventional method is the older and more common of the two. When this method is used, the employee's regular earnings are found by multiplying only the regular hours by the regular rate of pay. The overtime earnings are found by multiplying the overtime hours by $1\frac{1}{2}$ of the regular rate.

Example: David Drakowski worked 46 hours during the past week. His regular hourly rate of pay is $8.75. Use the conventional method to find his gross pay for the week.

Solution:

Regular earnings = 40 × $8.75 = $350.00
Overtime rate = 1.5 × $8.75 = $13.125
Overtime earnings = 6 × $13.125 = $78.75
Gross pay = $350.00 + $78.75 = $428.75

Overtime-Premium Method of Computing Gross Pay. The overtime-premium method was first used in cost accounting and is becoming increasingly popular. When this method is used, the employee's regular earnings are found by multiplying the total hours worked in the pay period by the regular hourly rate. The overtime earnings are found by multiplying the overtime hours by half of the regular rate. This method emphasizes the "premium" that is paid for overtime.

Example: David Drakowski worked 46 hours during the past week. His regular hourly rate of pay is $8.75. Use the overtime-premium method to find his gross pay for the week.

Solution:

Regular earnings = 46 × $8.75 = $402.50
Overtime rate = 0.5 × $8.75 = $4.375
Overtime earnings = 6 × $4.375 = $26.25
Gross pay = $402.50 + $26.25 = $428.75

Employees are quite sensitive about receiving the correct amount of pay. Proper employee morale cannot be maintained if payroll computations are inaccurate. Payroll computations, therefore, normally are rounded to the nearest cent of gross pay and must be calculated with absolute accuracy.

Exercise 11–1

A. Find the total hours worked and the gross pay for each of the following employees.

		Hours Worked					Total	Rate Per	Gross
	Employee	**M**	**T**	**W**	**T**	**F**	**Hours**	**Hour**	**Pay**
1.	Dolan, D. H.	8	8	7	8	8	______	$10.82	______
2.	Gillespie, S.	8	6	8	7	8	______	7.65	______
3.	Kimmel, C. J.	8	8	8	8	8	______	6.74	______
4.	McLeod, W. B.	8	7	8	$6\frac{1}{2}$	7	______	6.95	______
5.	Romero, D. E.	7	$5\frac{1}{2}$	8	7	8	______	8.25	______
6.	Wilcox, L. L.	8	6	4	8	8	______	9.85	______

B. Use the conventional method of computing overtime to complete the following payroll register. The regular rate is based on a 40-hour workweek. The overtime rate is $1\frac{1}{2}$ times the regular rate.

		Hours Worked						Hours		Rate Per	Wages		Gross
	Employee	M	T	W	T	F	S	Reg.	Ov.	Hour	Reg.	Ov.	Pay
1.	Balboa, R. L.	8	8	$7\frac{1}{2}$	0	8	8	___	___	$ 9.65	___	___	___
2.	Halte, D. E.	8	8	4	8	8	8	___	___	14.74	___	___	___
3.	Lake, J. W.	8	6	7	8	7	$8\frac{1}{2}$	___	___	10.76	___	___	___
4.	Nash, C. C.	8	8	8	8	8	8	___	___	12.92	___	___	___
5.	Sako, K. H.	8	9	0	8	9	8	___	___	15.30	___	___	___
6.	Yeager, W. A.	8	7	8	$4\frac{1}{2}$	8	$7\frac{1}{2}$	___	___	11.90	___	___	___

C. Use the overtime-premium method of computing overtime to complete the following payroll register. The regular rate is based on a 40-hour workweek.

		Hours Worked						Hours		Rate Per	Wages		Gross
	Employee	M	T	W	T	F	S	Reg.	Ov.	Hour	Reg.	Ov.	Pay
1.	Addis, R. T.	4	8	8	7	4	6	___	___	$ 9.87	___	___	___
2.	Helie, W. H.	6	9	4	7	9	8	___	___	12.39	___	___	___
3.	Jordan, R. E.	8	6	6	9	8	8	___	___	13.76	___	___	___
4.	Owens, D. W.	$7\frac{1}{2}$	8	9	0	9	8	___	___	14.18	___	___	___
5.	Tedrow, J. L.	8	0	10	8	9	8	___	___	16.97	___	___	___
6.	Uhlig, M. L.	$8\frac{1}{2}$	8	9	8	6	8	___	___	15.10	___	___	___

D. Use the conventional method of computing overtime to complete the following payroll register. The overtime pay is $1\frac{1}{2}$ times the regular rate for every hour over 8 worked in one day. An asterisk (*) indicates that the employee is paid overtime for those hours because he or she usually does not work that day.

		Hours Worked						Hours		Rate Per	Wages		Gross
	Employee	M	T	W	T	F	S	Reg.	Ov.	Hour	Reg.	Ov.	Pay
1.	Cain, M. L.	8	9	8	9	8	0	___	___	$ 9.80	___	___	___
2.	Esser, T. W.	9	8	10	9	0	8	___	___	14.21	___	___	___
3.	Howell, J. S.	9	0	8	9	9	10	___	___	13.45	___	___	___
4.	Pastor, E. E.	6	10	10	4*	9	10	___	___	16.94	___	___	___
5.	Slavin, J. A.	9	8	9	3*	6	9	___	___	10.50	___	___	___
6.	Zauss, M. E.	8	7	9	8	10	4*	___	___	15.90	___	___	___

Part 2. Mathematics Applications in Starting a Business

Straight Piecework Basis

In piecework wage systems, the employee's pay is based on the number of units produced rather than on the number of hours worked. The primary objective of any piecework system is to provide employees with incentive to increase production. Of course, the employer benefits from the increased production, and the employee benefits from the higher earnings.

The Fair Labor Standards Act provides that covered employees who are paid on a piecework basis also be paid overtime for working in excess of 40 hours a week. Such overtime pay is based essentially on $1\frac{1}{2}$ times the employee's average hourly rate during a 40-hour week. Assume that the piecework quantities shown in the problems which follow were produced within a 40-hour week.

A strong argument in favor of the straight piecework plan is simplicity, for the worker easily understands how gross pay is computed. When this plan is used, the employee is paid a single agreed-on amount (piece rate) for each piece he or she produces. The employee's pay is found by multiplying the number of pieces produced during the period by the piece rate.

Example: Emily Dyson produced 105 articles on Monday, 106 on Tuesday, 103 on Wednesday, 102 on Thursday, and 109 on Friday. Her rate of pay for each article is 75¢. How much did she earn for this production during the week?

Solution: 105 + 106 + 103 + 102 + 109 = 525   articles produced
525 (articles) × $0.75 (rate) = $393.75   gross pay

● Exercise 11–2

Find the gross pay for each of the employees listed. Use the straight piecework plan.

		Pieces Produced						Total	Piece	Gross
	Employee	M	T	W	T	F	S	Pieces	Rate	Pay
1.	Akita, F.	77	66	67	72	0	69	_____	$0.90	_____
2.	Camp, M. D.	83	77	81	79	85	0	_____	0.88	_____
3.	Fleck, E. J.	0	80	84	82	79	78	_____	0.76	_____
4.	Henke, B. E.	55	62	0	57	68	74	_____	0.91	_____
5.	Klein, L. B.	69	0	71	68	70	74	_____	0.99	_____
6.	Randall, K. H.	88	89	93	0	85	90	_____	0.95	_____
7.	Simpson, D. J.	65	68	69	72	73	0	_____	0.82	_____
8.	Tafoya, P. M.	63	65	0	62	64	67	_____	0.94	_____
9.	Vaughn, G. R.	78	79	75	83	82	0	_____	0.85	_____
10.	Vega, G. M.	0	75	73	74	77	72	_____	0.97	_____

Combination Time and Piecework Basis

As means of providing better incentives to production workers, many wage systems that combine both time worked and units produced have been and are currently being used successfully. There are three basic incentive wage systems used in industry: (1) differential piecework plan, (2) bonus for efficient production, and (3) premium for extra production.

Differential Piecework Plan. The purpose of the differential piecework plan is to encourage the worker to produce more pieces by paying more per piece as that individual's production increases. For example, according to the following schedule an employee who produces 36 pieces a day receives $3.00 per piece; whereas, one who produces only 30 pieces a day receives $2.80 per piece.

Example:

Use the following schedule to find the earnings of each of these employees for production today: **(a)** J. Windsor, 36 pieces; **(b)** K. Lane, 30 pieces.

Pieces Produced Daily	Piece Rate
Under 20	$2.20
20–24...............	2.40
25–29...............	2.60
30–34...............	2.80
35–39...............	3.00
40 and more........	3.20

Solution:

(a) 36 × $3.00 = $108
(b) 30 × $2.80 = $84

Efficient Production Bonus. Unlike straight piecework, this bonus plan provides a guaranteed hourly wage. If the employee is only 99% efficient, only the hourly wages are received. A bonus for efficient production is paid to the worker who performs a definite task within the standard time. The bonus usually consists of an agreed-on percent (10% to 50%) of the guaranteed hourly wage. If the task is attained within the time allowed, the earnings are then increased by the bonus percent. Consequently, there is a significant reward given to the employee when 100% efficiency is reached. When performance equals or is better than the standard set for the task, the guaranteed hourly wage is increased by the bonus wage. This amount is then multiplied by the number of hours allowed to find the earnings.

Example:

Frank Griffon is paid $10.50 an hour for an 8-hour day during which the standard task is to produce 32 units. He receives a 20% bonus when his performance is equal to or better than the standard. Find his gross pay for each of three days when he produced **(a)** 31 units, **(b)** 32 units, and **(c)** 33 units.

Solution:

(a) The task (to produce 32 units) was not attained. Therefore:

$10.50   hourly wage
×   8   hours worked
$84.00   earnings

(b) The task was attained. Therefore:

$$
\begin{array}{rl}
\$10.50 & \text{guaranteed hourly wage} \\
+\ \ 2.10 & \text{bonus wage (20\% of \$10.50)} \\
\hline
\$12.60 & \text{hourly wage at or above 100\% efficiency} \\
\times\ \ \ \ \ 8 & \text{hours worked} \\
\hline
\$100.80 & \text{earnings}
\end{array}
$$

(c) The task was attained. Therefore, his pay is $100.80, the same as in **(b)** above.

Extra Production Premium. A disadvantage of the preceding plan is that there is no incentive for extra production. The employee who exceeds the task is paid no more than the employee who just completes the task.

The plan presented in this section, however, does provide incentive for the worker to produce more than the standard quota of units. Under this plan, in addition to being paid the guaranteed hourly wage for producing the standard quota of units, the employee is also paid at the same rate for producing extra units within the standard work period. The standard work period may be an hour, a day, or a week. The employee receives a premium for saving time within the work period, time that is used to produce extra units. If production does not equal or exceed the quota, only the standard hourly or daily wage is paid. When production does exceed the quota, the total work-period wage is, in effect, based on a piece rate because the premium is based on the number of extra units produced in the work period. Premium pay is based on the following formula:

$$
Premium\ Pay = \frac{Extra\ Units}{Quota\ Units} \times Standard\ Pay
$$

Example:

Marian Hampton's daily production quota calls for 96 units during an 8-hour shift for which she is paid $11.25 an hour. She receives a premium for the extra units she produces during a shift. Find her gross pay for **(a)** a shift during which she produced 95 units and **(b)** another shift when she produced 112 units.

Solution:

(a) Units produced do not exceed the quota. Therefore, she receives her standard daily pay of $90 (8 × $11.25).

(b) Units produced do exceed the quota. Therefore:

$$
\frac{16\ \text{(extra)}}{96\ \text{(quota)}} \times \$90\ \text{(standard pay)} = \$15 \quad \text{premium pay}
$$

Total pay for shift: $90 + $15 = $105

Many variations of these basic incentive wage systems have been devised. Such systems carry a variety of names, such as the Bedeaux Point System, the Halsey Plan, the Rowan Plan, the Taylor Differential System, the Merrick Multiple Wage, the Gantt Task and Bonus Plan, and the Emerson Efficiency Wage. Although some are widely used, their specific designs are beyond the scope of this book. The interested student can find detailed explanations of these systems in personnel management books.

A. Use the following schedule and the differential piecework plan to compute the gross pay for each of the employees listed below.

Pieces Produced Daily	Rate Per Piece
Under 30.............	$1.60
30–33..............	$1.67\frac{1}{2}$
34–37..............	1.75
38–41..............	$1.82\frac{1}{2}$
42–45..............	1.90
46–49..............	$1.97\frac{1}{2}$
50–53..............	2.05
54–57..............	$2.12\frac{1}{2}$
58–61..............	2.20
62 and over	$2.27\frac{1}{2}$

	Monday		Tuesday		Wednesday		Thursday		Friday		Gross
	Pcs.	Wages	Pcs.	Wages	Pcs.	Wages	Pcs.	Wages	Pcs.	Wages	Pay
1.	54	___	62	___	68	___	53	___	56	___	___
2.	51	___	58	___	61	___	49	___	32	___	___
3.	54	___	60	___	57	___	30	___	55	___	___
4.	29	___	48	___	59	___	65	___	69	___	___
5.	69	___	57	___	39	___	45	___	66	___	___
6.	52	___	56	___	54	___	44	___	37	___	___

B. Each employee listed in the following schedule worked 8 hours a day to produce the number of units shown.

	Employee	Daily Quota	Hourly Wage	Daily Bonus	Units Produced Daily				
					M	T	W	T	F
1.	Davis, J. W.	40 units	$ 9.50	20%	42	39	40	41	43
2.	Grant, E. L.	50 units	11.25	30%	49	50	47	51	46
3.	Kriege, M. D.	75 units	12.50	25%	77	75	70	71	76
4.	Moran, R. C.	100 units	9.00	15%	89	95	100	100	98
5.	Scheer, D. J.	120 units	12.00	10%	125	130	128	120	123
6.	Vezina, C. A.	80 units	9.75	20%	76	78	80	84	79

Use the data in the preceding schedule and the following columnar headings to prepare a report showing the daily earnings and gross pay of each employee. The employee earns a bonus only when daily production equals or exceeds the daily quota.

| Employee | Daily Wages | | | | | Gross |
Number	Monday	Tuesday	Wednesday	Thursday	Friday	Pay

C. Each employee listed in the following schedule worked 8 hours a day to produce the number of units shown.

| | Employee | Daily Quota | Hourly Wage | Units Produced Daily | | | | |
				M	T	W	T	F
1.	Brady, T. L.	250 units	$11.40	267	283	263	230	261
2.	Frye, N. F.	500 units	11.25	660	483	521	649	700
3.	Jensen, K. A.	350 units	12.75	288	416	350	324	382
4.	Ortiz, O. R.	200 units	13.50	199	278	285	263	210
5.	Roth, A. L.	125 units	14.40	130	143	121	137	144
6.	Vogel, D. E.	50 units	10.50	46	49	50	62	74

Use the data in the preceding schedule and the following columnar headings to prepare a report showing the daily earnings and gross pay of each employee. The employee is paid a premium for extra daily production when it exceeds the daily quota.

| Employee | Daily Wages | | | | | Gross |
Number	Monday	Tuesday	Wednesday	Thursday	Friday	Pay

Commission Basis

Paying earnings on a commission basis to employees who have sales responsibilities is a means of providing them with an incentive to increase sales in a manner similar to that of paying production workers on a piecework basis. As is the case with piecework systems, there are a great variety of plans for paying salespeople on a commission basis. Many of these are simply variations in the three most popular plans, which are: (1) straight commission, (2) salary and commission, and (3) graduated commission.

Straight Commission. When a salesperson works on a **straight commission basis,** the commission is based on the quantity of the sales without a minimum guaranteed salary. Although the commission may be a set amount of money for each item sold, commission on sales is usually a certain percent of the dollar value of the sales. Selling goods that are relatively difficult to sell usually earns a higher rate of commission than selling goods that are sold more easily. Commissions are generally paid on actual sales only; that is, returned goods and canceled orders are not included in the basis used for computing the commission.

To find the amount of the commission when the rate is a percent of sales, multiply the amount of sales (the base) by the percent (the rate).

$$Sales \times Rate\ of\ Commission = Amount\ of\ Commission$$

Example: Diane Mead receives a straight commission of 8% on her monthly sales. During January she sold $24,000 worth of goods. How much commission did she earn in January?

Solution: $24,000 \times 0.08 = $1,920$

Salary and Commission. In many merchandising companies, each salesperson is paid a regular salary plus a percent of his or her total sales or a percent of sales that exceed the quota of sales.

Example: Ned Reinhart, who works in the Wilmington Department Store, is paid $170 a week plus 5% commission on his sales in excess of $3,000. If his sales during the past week amounted to $5,300, how much did he earn?

Solution: $5,300 − $3,000 = $2,300$ sales above quota

Salary:	$170
Commission:	115 (5% of $2,300)
Total earnings:	$285

Graduated Commission: Frequently commissions are paid on a sliding scale. As certain expenses, such as necessary traveling expenses, clerical or paperwork expenses, and packing expenses, do not always increase in direct proportion to increases in the quantity of goods sold, commission rates may become larger as sales volume grows. For example, a graduated commission plan may provide a commission rate of 4% on the first $5,000 of sales, 5% on the next $10,000, and 6% on all sales over $15,000. The total commission under this plan is the sum of the commissions obtained by multiplying the appropriate sales basis by the individual rates.

Example: Anne Travis receives 4% commission on the first $5,000 worth of goods that she sells each month, 5% on the next $10,000, and 6% on sales in excess of $15,000. How much commission did she earn during a month in which she sold $32,000 worth of goods?

Solution:
$5,000 \times 0.04 = $ 200$ commission on first $5,000
$10,000 \times 0.05 = $ 500$ commission on next $10,000
$17,000 \times 0.06 = $ 1,020$ commission on amount over $15,000
$1,720$ total commission

Part 2. Mathematics Applications in Starting a Business

● Exercise 11–4

1. Joe Barham is paid a commission of 7% of his sales. During the past week his sales were $1,095 on Monday, $1,440 on Wednesday, $1,245 on Thursday, $1,434 on Friday, and $1,887 on Saturday. Find his total commission for the week.

2. Freida Sink receives a weekly salary of $225 plus $1\frac{1}{2}$% commission on her sales. During the first week of March, her sales were $5,542.35. How much did she earn during the week?

3. Claudia Davis receives a salary of $150 a week and a commission of 2% on her sales. How much did she earn during a week in which she sold $2,872.11 worth of goods?

4. Lucy Rusher receives a weekly salary of $180 plus a commission of 5% on her sales in excess of $2,000 a week. During a recent week her total sales were $7,125. How much did she earn during the week?

5. Robert Harper receives a salary of $1,200 a month and a commission of 6% on sales in excess of a monthly quota of $12,000. During the past month he sold $37,474.46 worth of goods. How much did he earn?

6. Donald Kemp is paid a monthly salary of $1,500 with 8% commission on his sales over $15,000 a month. His sales in April amounted to $23,697.06. How much did he earn in April?

7. Susan Kirk is paid 6% commission on the first $20,000 of monthly sales and 8% on sales in excess of $20,000. Her sales were $9,750 in February and $34,250 in March. How much were her earnings (a) in February and (b) in March?

8. The salespeople of the Salisbury Company are paid $1,000 a month plus a commission of 2% on sales up to $10,000, 4% on the next $10,000, and 6% on sales over $20,000. Find the earnings of (a) Morton, whose sales were $8,947.80; (b) Navarro, whose sales were $16,235; and (c) Olsen, whose sales were $27,450.

NET PAY

As very few employees are exempt from paying taxes on their earnings, most employees will not receive their full gross pay at the end of the payroll period. Practically all employers are required by law to deduct amounts for social security and income taxes from the earnings of their employees and to send these amounts to the United States Treasury Department through the Internal Revenue Service. The deductions for social security and income taxes are fixed percents of the employee's gross pay. In addition to compulsory

Chapter 11. Payrolls and Agents' Commissions   319 deductions, the employer also may make other deductions, such as for insurance premiums requested by the employees and for union dues. The amount of money received by the employee after these amounts have been deducted from the gross pay is the **take-home pay** or **net pay.**

Employees' Social Security Deductions

The Federal Insurance Contributions Act (FICA), which is also called the Social Security Act, requires employers to withhold a certain percent of the earnings of each employee up to a maximum fixed by law. Both the maximum earnings and the percent are subject to change through legislation by Congress. The examples and problems in this book use 7.15% as the rate and $43,800 as the maximum earnings to which the rate is applied. The procedures for finding the amount of the deduction are the same regardless of the rates used.

The amount that is withheld from the employee's earnings is a tax. The employer is required to pay an equal tax. Thus, the employer pays an additional amount equal to that paid by the employee. The sum of both contributions is forwarded to the Internal Revenue Service through a bank that is an authorized federal depositary.

The major social security benefits to the worker or the worker's survivors are:

1. **Retirement Benefits:** Monthly income payments to the worker beginning at age 65. Reduced payments are payable as early as age 62.
2. **Disability Benefits:** Monthly payments to the worker who is under 65 years of age and unable to work because of disability.
3. **Survivors Benefits:** Payment of burial and monthly benefits to the surviving family of a deceased worker.
4. **Medicare:** Health insurance benefits to those who are over 65 years of age whether or not the insured worker has retired.

More than 90 out of 100 workers in the United States are building protection like this for themselves and their families under the social security program.

The amount to be withheld from the employee's earnings can be found by multiplying the earnings that are subject to the tax by the current social security rate. A social security tax table that is provided by the Internal Revenue Service, however, may be used to save time. Such a table is shown in Table 11–1. To find the amount of the tax by using the table:

1. Read down the wages column until the appropriate wage-bracket line is found.
2. Read to the right on the same line to find the amount listed in the tax-to-be-withheld column that is adjacent to the wages column.

Wages at least	But less than	Tax to be withheld	Wages at least	But less than	Tax to be withheld	Wages at least	But less than	Tax to be withheld	Wages at least	But less than	Tax to be withheld
$0.00	$0.07	$0.00	12.66	12.80	.91	25.39	25.53	1.82	38.12	38.26	2.73
.07	.21	.01	12.80	12.94	.92	25.53	25.67	1.83	38.26	38.40	2.74
.21	.35	.02	12.94	13.08	.93	25.67	25.81	1.84	38.40	38.54	2.75
.35	.49	.03	13.08	13.22	.94	25.81	25.95	1.85	38.54	38.68	2.76
.49	.63	.04	13.22	13.36	.95	25.95	26.09	1.86	38.68	38.82	2.77
.63	.77	.05	13.36	13.50	.96	26.09	26.23	1.87	38.82	38.96	2.78
.77	.91	.06	13.50	13.64	.97	26.23	26.37	1.88	38.96	39.10	2.79
.91	1.05	.07	13.64	13.78	.98	26.37	26.51	1.89	39.10	39.24	2.80
1.05	1.19	.08	13.78	13.92	.99	26.51	26.65	1.90	39.24	39.38	2.81
1.19	1.33	.09	13.92	14.06	1.00	26.65	26.79	1.91	39.38	39.52	2.82
1.33	1.47	.10	14.06	14.20	1.01	26.79	26.93	1.92	39.52	39.66	2.83
1.47	1.61	.11	14.20	14.34	1.02	26.93	27.07	1.93	39.66	39.80	2.84
1.61	1.75	.12	14.34	14.48	1.03	27.07	27.21	1.94	39.80	39.94	2.85
1.75	1.89	.13	14.48	14.62	1.04	27.21	27.35	1.95	39.94	40.07	2.86
1.89	2.03	.14	14.62	14.76	1.05	27.35	27.49	1.96	40.07	40.21	2.87
2.03	2.17	.15	14.76	14.90	1.06	27.49	27.63	1.97	40.21	40.35	2.88
2.17	2.31	.16	14.90	15.04	1.07	27.63	27.77	1.98	40.35	40.49	2.89
2.31	2.45	.17	15.04	15.18	1.08	27.77	27.91	1.99	40.49	40.63	2.90
2.45	2.59	.18	15.18	15.32	1.09	27.91	28.05	2.00	40.63	40.77	2.91
2.59	2.73	.19	15.32	15.46	1.10	28.05	28.19	2.01	40.77	40.91	2.92
2.73	2.87	.20	15.46	15.60	1.11	28.19	28.33	2.02	40.91	41.05	2.93
2.87	3.01	.21	15.60	15.74	1.12	28.33	28.47	2.03	41.05	41.19	2.94
3.01	3.15	.22	15.74	15.88	1.13	28.47	28.61	2.04	41.19	41.33	2.95
3.15	3.29	.23	15.88	16.02	1.14	28.61	28.75	2.05	41.33	41.47	2.96
3.29	3.43	.24	16.02	16.16	1.15	28.75	28.89	2.06	41.47	41.61	2.97
3.43	3.57	.25	16.16	16.30	1.16	28.89	29.03	2.07	41.61	41.75	2.98
3.57	3.71	.26	16.30	16.44	1.17	29.03	29.17	2.08	41.75	41.89	2.99
3.71	3.85	.27	16.44	16.58	1.18	29.17	29.31	2.09	41.89	42.03	3.00
3.85	3.99	.28	16.58	16.72	1.19	29.31	29.45	2.10	42.03	42.17	3.01
3.99	4.13	.29	16.72	16.86	1.20	29.45	29.59	2.11	42.17	42.31	3.02
4.13	4.27	.30	16.86	17.00	1.21	29.59	29.73	2.12	42.31	42.45	3.03
4.27	4.41	.31	17.00	17.14	1.22	29.73	29.87	2.13	42.45	42.59	3.04
4.41	4.55	.32	17.14	17.28	1.23	29.87	30.00	2.14	42.59	42.73	3.05
4.55	4.69	.33	17.28	17.42	1.24	30.00	30.14	2.15	42.73	42.87	3.06
4.69	4.83	.34	17.42	17.56	1.25	30.14	30.28	2.16	42.87	43.01	3.07
4.83	4.97	.35	17.56	17.70	1.26	30.28	30.42	2.17	43.01	43.15	3.08
4.97	5.11	.36	17.70	17.84	1.27	30.42	30.56	2.18	43.15	43.29	3.09
5.11	5.25	.37	17.84	17.98	1.28	30.56	30.70	2.19	43.29	43.43	3.10
5.25	5.39	.38	17.98	18.12	1.29	30.70	30.84	2.20	43.43	43.57	3.11
5.39	5.53	.39	18.12	18.26	1.30	30.84	30.98	2.21	43.57	43.71	3.12
5.53	5.67	.40	18.26	18.40	1.31	30.98	31.12	2.22	43.71	43.85	3.13
5.67	5.81	.41	18.40	18.54	1.32	31.12	31.26	2.23	43.85	43.99	3.14
5.81	5.95	.42	18.54	18.68	1.33	31.26	31.40	2.24	43.99	44.13	3.15
5.95	6.09	.43	18.68	18.82	1.34	31.40	31.54	2.25	44.13	44.27	3.16
6.09	6.23	.44	18.82	18.96	1.35	31.54	31.68	2.26	44.27	44.41	3.17
6.23	6.37	.45	18.96	19.10	1.36	31.68	31.82	2.27	44.41	44.55	3.18
6.37	6.51	.46	19.10	19.24	1.37	31.82	31.96	2.28	44.55	44.69	3.19
6.51	6.65	.47	19.24	19.38	1.38	31.96	32.10	2.29	44.69	44.83	3.20
6.65	6.79	.48	19.38	19.52	1.39	32.10	32.24	2.30	44.83	44.97	3.21
6.79	6.93	.49	19.52	19.66	1.40	32.24	32.38	2.31	44.97	45.11	3.22
6.93	7.07	.50	19.66	19.80	1.41	32.38	32.52	2.32	45.11	45.25	3.23
7.07	7.21	.51	19.80	19.94	1.42	32.52	32.66	2.33	45.25	45.39	3.24
7.21	7.35	.52	19.94	20.07	1.43	32.66	32.80	2.34	45.39	45.53	3.25
7.35	7.49	.53	20.07	20.21	1.44	32.80	32.94	2.35	45.53	45.67	3.26
7.49	7.63	.54	20.21	20.35	1.45	32.94	33.08	2.36	45.67	45.81	3.27
7.63	7.77	.55	20.35	20.49	1.46	33.08	33.22	2.37	45.81	45.95	3.28
7.77	7.91	.56	20.49	20.63	1.47	33.22	33.36	2.38	45.95	46.09	3.29
7.91	8.05	.57	20.63	20.77	1.48	33.36	33.50	2.39	46.09	46.23	3.30
8.05	8.19	.58	20.77	20.91	1.49	33.50	33.64	2.40	46.23	46.37	3.31
8.19	8.33	.59	20.91	21.05	1.50	33.64	33.78	2.41	46.37	46.51	3.32
8.33	8.47	.60	21.05	21.19	1.51	33.78	33.92	2.42	46.51	46.65	3.33
8.47	8.61	.61	21.19	21.33	1.52	33.92	34.06	2.43	46.65	46.79	3.34
8.61	8.75	.62	21.33	21.47	1.53	34.06	34.20	2.44	46.79	46.93	3.35
8.75	8.89	.63	21.47	21.61	1.54	34.20	34.34	2.45	46.93	47.07	3.36
8.89	9.03	.64	21.61	21.75	1.55	34.34	34.48	2.46	47.07	47.21	3.37
9.03	9.17	.65	21.75	21.89	1.56	34.48	34.62	2.47	47.21	47.35	3.38
9.17	9.31	.66	21.89	22.03	1.57	34.62	34.76	2.48	47.35	47.49	3.39
9.31	9.45	.67	22.03	22.17	1.58	34.76	34.90	2.49	47.49	47.63	3.40
9.45	9.59	.68	22.17	22.31	1.59	34.90	35.04	2.50	47.63	47.77	3.41
9.59	9.73	.69	22.31	22.45	1.60	35.04	35.18	2.51	47.77	47.91	3.42
9.73	9.87	.70	22.45	22.59	1.61	35.18	35.32	2.52	47.91	48.05	3.43
9.87	10.00	.71	22.59	22.73	1.62	35.32	35.46	2.53	48.05	48.19	3.44
10.00	10.14	.72	22.73	22.87	1.63	35.46	35.60	2.54	48.19	48.33	3.45
10.14	10.28	.73	22.87	23.01	1.64	35.60	35.74	2.55	48.33	48.47	3.46
10.28	10.42	.74	23.01	23.15	1.65	35.74	35.88	2.56	48.47	48.61	3.47
10.42	10.56	.75	23.15	23.29	1.66	35.88	36.02	2.57	48.61	48.75	3.48
10.56	10.70	.76	23.29	23.43	1.67	36.02	36.16	2.58	48.75	48.89	3.49
10.70	10.84	.77	23.43	23.57	1.68	36.16	36.30	2.59	48.89	49.03	3.50
10.84	10.98	.78	23.57	23.71	1.69	36.30	36.44	2.60	49.03	49.17	3.51
10.98	11.12	.79	23.71	23.85	1.70	36.44	36.58	2.61	49.17	49.31	3.52
11.12	11.26	.80	23.85	23.99	1.71	36.58	36.72	2.62	49.31	49.45	3.53
11.26	11.40	.81	23.99	24.13	1.72	36.72	36.86	2.63	49.45	49.59	3.54
11.40	11.54	.82	24.13	24.27	1.73	36.86	37.00	2.64	49.59	49.73	3.55
11.54	11.68	.83	24.27	24.41	1.74	37.00	37.14	2.65	49.73	49.87	3.56
11.68	11.82	.84	24.41	24.55	1.75	37.14	37.28	2.66	49.87	50.00	3.57
11.82	11.96	.85	24.55	24.69	1.76	37.28	37.42	2.67	50.00	50.14	3.58
11.96	12.10	.86	24.69	24.83	1.77	37.42	37.56	2.68	50.14	50.28	3.59
12.10	12.24	.87	24.83	24.97	1.78	37.56	37.70	2.69	50.28	50.42	3.60
12.24	12.38	.88	24.97	25.11	1.79	37.70	37.84	2.70	50.42	50.56	3.61
12.38	12.52	.89	25.11	25.25	1.80	37.84	37.98	2.71	50.56	50.70	3.62
12.52	12.66	.90	25.25	25.39	1.81	37.98	38.12	2.72	50.70	50.84	3.63

Table 11–1 Social Security Employee Tax Table
(7.15% employee tax deductions)

Chapter 11. Payrolls and Agents' Commissions

Wages at least	But less than	Tax to be withheld
50.84	50.98	3.64
50.98	51.12	3.65
51.12	51.26	3.66
51.26	51.40	3.67
51.40	51.54	3.68
51.54	51.68	3.69
51.68	51.82	3.70
51.82	51.96	3.71
51.96	52.10	3.72
52.10	52.24	3.73
52.24	52.38	3.74
52.38	52.52	3.75
52.52	52.66	3.76
52.66	52.80	3.77
52.80	52.94	3.78
52.94	53.08	3.79
53.08	53.22	3.80
53.22	53.36	3.81
53.36	53.50	3.82
53.50	53.64	3.83
53.64	53.78	3.84
53.78	53.92	3.85
53.92	54.06	3.86
54.06	54.20	3.87
54.20	54.34	3.88
54.34	54.48	3.89
54.48	54.62	3.90
54.62	54.76	3.91
54.76	54.90	3.92
54.90	55.04	3.93
55.04	55.18	3.94
55.18	55.32	3.95
55.32	55.46	3.96
55.46	55.60	3.97
55.60	55.74	3.98
55.74	55.88	3.99
55.88	56.02	4.00
56.02	56.16	4.01
56.16	56.30	4.02
56.30	56.44	4.03
56.44	56.58	4.04
56.58	56.72	4.05
56.72	56.86	4.06
56.86	57.00	4.07
57.00	57.14	4.08
57.14	57.28	4.09
57.28	57.42	4.10
57.42	57.56	4.11
57.56	57.70	4.12
57.70	57.84	4.13
57.84	57.98	4.14
57.98	58.12	4.15
58.12	58.26	4.16
58.26	58.40	4.17
58.40	58.54	4.18
58.54	58.68	4.19
58.68	58.82	4.20
58.82	58.96	4.21
58.96	59.10	4.22
59.10	59.24	4.23
59.24	59.38	4.24
59.38	59.52	4.25
59.52	59.66	4.26
59.66	59.80	4.27
59.80	59.94	4.28
59.94	60.07	4.29
60.07	60.21	4.30
60.21	60.35	4.31
60.35	60.49	4.32
60.49	60.63	4.33
60.63	60.77	4.34
60.77	60.91	4.35
60.91	61.05	4.36
61.05	61.19	4.37
61.19	61.33	4.38
61.33	61.47	4.39
61.47	61.61	4.40
61.61	61.75	4.41
61.75	61.89	4.42
61.89	62.03	4.43
62.03	62.17	4.44
62.17	62.31	4.45
62.31	62.45	4.46
62.45	62.59	4.47
62.59	62.73	4.48
62.73	62.87	4.49
62.87	63.01	4.50
63.01	63.15	4.51
63.15	63.29	4.52
63.29	63.43	4.53
63.43	63.57	4.54

Wages at least	But less than	Tax to be withheld
63.57	63.71	4.55
63.71	63.85	4.56
63.85	63.99	4.57
63.99	64.13	4.58
64.13	64.27	4.59
64.27	64.41	4.60
64.41	64.55	4.61
64.55	64.69	4.62
64.69	64.83	4.63
64.83	64.97	4.64
64.97	65.11	4.65
65.11	65.25	4.66
65.25	65.39	4.67
65.39	65.53	4.68
65.53	65.67	4.69
65.67	65.81	4.70
65.81	65.95	4.71
65.95	66.09	4.72
66.09	66.23	4.73
66.23	66.37	4.74
66.37	66.51	4.75
66.51	66.65	4.76
66.65	66.79	4.77
66.79	66.93	4.78
66.93	67.07	4.79
67.07	67.21	4.80
67.21	67.35	4.81
67.35	67.49	4.82
67.49	67.63	4.83
67.63	67.77	4.84
67.77	67.91	4.85
67.91	68.05	4.86
68.05	68.19	4.87
68.19	68.33	4.88
68.33	68.47	4.89
68.47	68.61	4.90
68.61	68.75	4.91
68.75	68.89	4.92
68.89	69.03	4.93
69.03	69.17	4.94
69.17	69.31	4.95
69.31	69.45	4.96
69.45	69.59	4.97
69.59	69.73	4.98
69.73	69.87	4.99
69.87	70.00	5.00
70.00	70.14	5.01
70.14	70.28	5.02
70.28	70.42	5.03
70.42	70.56	5.04
70.56	70.70	5.05
70.70	70.84	5.06
70.84	70.98	5.07
70.98	71.12	5.08
71.12	71.26	5.09
71.26	71.40	5.10
71.40	71.54	5.11
71.54	71.68	5.12
71.68	71.82	5.13
71.82	71.96	5.14
71.96	72.10	5.15
72.10	72.24	5.16
72.24	72.38	5.17
72.38	72.52	5.18
72.52	72.66	5.19
72.66	72.80	5.20
72.80	72.94	5.21
72.94	73.08	5.22
73.08	73.22	5.23
73.22	73.36	5.24
73.36	73.50	5.25
73.50	73.64	5.26
73.64	73.78	5.27
73.78	73.92	5.28
73.92	74.06	5.29
74.06	74.20	5.30
74.20	74.34	5.31
74.34	74.48	5.32
74.48	74.62	5.33
74.62	74.76	5.34
74.76	74.90	5.35
74.90	75.04	5.36
75.04	75.18	5.37
75.18	75.32	5.38
75.32	75.46	5.39
75.46	75.60	5.40
75.60	75.74	5.41
75.74	75.88	5.42
75.88	76.02	5.43
76.02	76.16	5.44
76.16	76.30	5.45

Wages at least	But less than	Tax to be withheld
76.30	76.44	5.46
76.44	76.58	5.47
76.58	76.72	5.48
76.72	76.86	5.49
76.86	77.00	5.50
77.00	77.14	5.51
77.14	77.28	5.52
77.28	77.42	5.53
77.42	77.56	5.54
77.56	77.70	5.55
77.70	77.84	5.56
77.84	77.98	5.57
77.98	78.12	5.58
78.12	78.26	5.59
78.26	78.40	5.60
78.40	78.54	5.61
78.54	78.68	5.62
78.68	78.82	5.63
78.82	78.96	5.64
78.96	79.10	5.65
79.10	79.24	5.66
79.24	79.38	5.67
79.38	79.52	5.68
79.52	79.66	5.69
79.66	79.80	5.70
79.80	79.94	5.71
79.94	80.07	5.72
80.07	80.21	5.73
80.21	80.35	5.74
80.35	80.49	5.75
80.49	80.63	5.76
80.63	80.77	5.77
80.77	80.91	5.78
80.91	81.05	5.79
81.05	81.19	5.80
81.19	81.33	5.81
81.33	81.47	5.82
81.47	81.61	5.83
81.61	81.75	5.84
81.75	81.89	5.85
81.89	82.03	5.86
82.03	82.17	5.87
82.17	82.31	5.88
82.31	82.45	5.89
82.45	82.59	5.90
82.59	82.73	5.91
82.73	82.87	5.92
82.87	83.01	5.93
83.01	83.15	5.94
83.15	83.29	5.95
83.29	83.43	5.96
83.43	83.57	5.97
83.57	83.71	5.98
83.71	83.85	5.99
83.85	83.99	6.00
83.99	84.13	6.01
84.13	84.27	6.02
84.27	84.41	6.03
84.41	84.55	6.04
84.55	84.69	6.05
84.69	84.83	6.06
84.83	84.97	6.07
84.97	85.11	6.08
85.11	85.25	6.09
85.25	85.39	6.10
85.39	85.53	6.11
85.53	85.67	6.12
85.67	85.81	6.13
85.81	85.95	6.14
85.95	86.09	6.15
86.09	86.23	6.16
86.23	86.37	6.17
86.37	86.51	6.18
86.51	86.65	6.19
86.65	86.79	6.20
86.79	86.93	6.21
86.93	87.07	6.22
87.07	87.21	6.23
87.21	87.35	6.24
87.35	87.49	6.25
87.49	87.63	6.26
87.63	87.77	6.27
87.77	87.91	6.28
87.91	88.05	6.29
88.05	88.19	6.30
88.19	88.33	6.31
88.33	88.47	6.32
88.47	88.61	6.33
88.61	88.75	6.34
88.75	88.89	6.35
88.89	89.03	6.36

Wages at least	But less than	Tax to be withheld
89.03	89.17	6.37
89.17	89.31	6.38
89.31	89.45	6.39
89.45	89.59	6.40
89.59	89.73	6.41
89.73	89.87	6.42
89.87	90.00	6.43
90.00	90.14	6.44
90.14	90.28	6.45
90.28	90.42	6.46
90.42	90.56	6.47
90.56	90.70	6.48
90.70	90.84	6.49
90.84	90.98	6.50
90.98	91.12	6.51
91.12	91.26	6.52
91.26	91.40	6.53
91.40	91.54	6.54
91.54	91.68	6.55
91.68	91.82	6.56
91.82	91.96	6.57
91.96	92.10	6.58
92.10	92.24	6.59
92.24	92.38	6.60
92.38	92.52	6.61
92.52	92.66	6.62
92.66	92.80	6.63
92.80	92.94	6.64
92.94	93.08	6.65
93.08	93.22	6.66
93.22	93.36	6.67
93.36	93.50	6.68
93.50	93.64	6.69
93.64	93.78	6.70
93.78	93.92	6.71
93.92	94.06	6.72
94.06	94.20	6.73
94.20	94.34	6.74
94.34	94.48	6.75
94.48	94.62	6.76
94.62	94.76	6.77
94.76	94.90	6.78
94.90	95.04	6.79
95.04	95.18	6.80
95.18	95.32	6.81
95.32	95.46	6.82
95.46	95.60	6.83
95.60	95.74	6.84
95.74	95.88	6.85
95.88	96.02	6.86
96.02	96.16	6.87
96.16	96.30	6.88
96.30	96.44	6.89
96.44	96.58	6.90
96.58	96.72	6.91
96.72	96.86	6.92
96.86	97.00	6.93
97.00	97.14	6.94
97.14	97.28	6.95
97.28	97.42	6.96
97.42	97.56	6.97
97.56	97.70	6.98
97.70	97.84	6.99
97.84	97.98	7.00
97.98	98.12	7.01
98.12	98.26	7.02
98.26	98.40	7.03
98.40	98.54	7.04
98.54	98.68	7.05
98.68	98.82	7.06
98.82	98.96	7.07
98.96	99.10	7.08
99.10	99.24	7.09
99.24	99.38	7.10
99.38	99.52	7.11
99.52	99.66	7.12
99.66	99.80	7.13
99.80	99.94	7.14
99.94	100.00	7.15

Wages	Taxes
100	$7.15
200	14.30
300	21.45
400	28.60
500	35.75
600	42.90
700	50.05
800	57.20
900	64.35
1,000	71.50

Table 11–1 Continued

Part 2. Mathematics Applications in Starting a Business

Example:	Use Table 11–1 to find the FICA tax on earnings of $177.50.

Solution:	1. Tax on $100 (lower right in table) is $7.15.

2. In the wages column, $77.50 is in the "At least $77.42 but less than $77.56" wage bracket.

3. The social security tax ($5.54) is shown on the same line in the next column to the right.

4. Total tax to be withheld: $7.15 + $5.54 = $12.69

An employee's earnings in excess of $43,800 in 1987 were not subject to social security deductions. When a taxpayer works for more than one employer in a calendar year, social security deductions may be withheld on wages that exceed $43,800. Any excess FICA tax that is withheld may be applied by the employee to pay federal income tax. The employers under these circumstances, however, are not entitled to a refund of FICA taxes.

Employees' Federal Income Tax Withholding

The federal income tax is another payroll tax that the employer is required by law to withhold from the earnings of employees and to forward to the Internal Revenue Service. The amount of tax that must be paid by an employee is based on (1) amount of earnings and (2) number of exemptions claimed. If the worker is single and has no dependents, one exemption may be claimed. If a worker is married and has two dependent children, four exemptions are allowed—one for the worker, one for a spouse who is not claimed on a separate tax return, and one for each child.

Federal Income Tax Withholding Tables. Although their use is not mandatory, income tax withholding tables are provided by the Internal Revenue Service. As many employees are paid weekly, portions of such tables for weekly payroll periods are shown in Tables 11–2 and 11–3. To find the amount of income tax by using a table:

1. Read down the wages column on the left until the appropriate wage-bracket line is reached.
2. Read across on the same line to the column headed by the number of exemptions claimed by the taxpayer.

Example:	Use Table 11–3 to find how much income tax should be deducted from Gregory Johnson's weekly earnings of $275 if he is married and has two dependent children.

Solution:	1. His weekly earnings of $275 are in the "At least $270 but less than $280" wage bracket.

2. The income tax to be withheld ($12.00) is shown on the same line under the exemption column number 4.

| And the wages are- | | And the number of withholding allowances claimed is— | | | | | | | | | | |
At least	But less than	0	1	2	3	4	5	6	7	8	9	10 or more
		The amount of income tax to be withheld shall be—										
$135	$140	$17	$12	$6	$2	$0	$0	$0	$0	$0	$0	$0
140	145	18	13	7	2	0	0	0	0	0	0	0
145	150	19	13	8	3	0	0	0	0	0	0	0
150	160	20	15	9	4	0	0	0	0	0	0	0
160	170	22	16	11	5	1	0	0	0	0	0	0
170	180	23	18	12	7	2	0	0	0	0	0	0
180	190	25	19	14	8	3	0	0	0	0	0	0
190	200	26	21	15	10	4	0	0	0	0	0	0
200	210	28	22	17	11	6	1	0	0	0	0	0
210	220	29	24	18	13	7	2	0	0	0	0	0
220	230	31	25	20	14	9	3	0	0	0	0	0
230	240	32	27	21	16	10	5	0	0	0	0	0
240	250	34	28	23	17	12	6	1	0	0	0	0
250	260	35	30	24	19	13	8	3	0	0	0	0
260	270	37	31	26	20	15	9	4	0	0	0	0
270	280	38	33	27	22	16	11	5	1	0	0	0
280	290	40	34	29	23	18	12	7	2	0	0	0
290	300	41	36	30	25	19	14	8	3	0	0	0
300	310	43	37	32	26	21	15	10	4	0	0	0
310	320	44	39	33	28	22	17	11	6	1	0	0
320	330	46	40	35	29	24	18	13	7	2	0	0
330	340	47	42	36	31	25	20	14	9	3	0	0
340	350	50	43	38	32	27	21	16	10	5	0	0
350	360	53	45	39	34	28	23	17	12	6	2	0
360	370	55	46	41	35	30	24	19	13	8	3	0
370	380	58	48	42	37	31	26	20	15	9	4	0
380	390	61	51	44	38	33	27	22	16	11	5	1
390	400	64	54	45	40	34	29	23	18	12	7	2
400	410	67	56	47	41	36	30	25	19	14	8	3
410	42C	69	59	49	43	37	32	26	21	15	10	4
420	430	72	62	52	44	39	33	28	22	17	11	6
430	440	75	65	55	46	40	35	29	24	18	13	7
440	450	78	68	57	47	42	36	31	25	20	14	9
450	460	81	70	60	50	43	38	32	27	21	16	10
460	470	83	73	63	53	45	39	34	28	23	17	12
470	480	86	76	66	55	46	41	35	30	24	19	13
480	490	89	79	69	58	48	42	37	31	26	20	15
490	500	92	82	71	61	51	44	38	33	27	22	16
500	510	95	84	74	64	54	45	40	34	29	23	18
510	520	97	87	77	67	56	47	41	36	30	25	19
520	530	100	90	80	69	59	49	43	37	32	26	21
530	540	103	93	83	72	62	52	44	39	33	28	22
540	550	107	96	85	75	65	55	46	40	35	29	24
550	560	110	98	88	78	68	57	47	42	36	31	25
560	570	114	101	91	81	70	60	50	43	38	32	27
570	580	117	104	94	83	73	63	53	45	39	34	28
580	590	121	108	97	86	76	66	56	46	41	35	30
590	600	124	111	99	89	79	69	58	48	42	37	31
600	610	128	115	102	92	82	71	61	51	44	38	33
610	620	131	118	106	95	84	74	64	54	45	40	34
620	630	135	122	109	97	87	77	67	57	47	41	36
630	640	138	125	113	100	90	80	70	59	49	43	37
640	650	142	129	116	103	93	83	72	62	52	44	39
650	660	145	132	120	107	96	85	75	65	55	46	40
660	670	149	136	123	110	98	88	78	68	58	47	42
670	680	152	139	127	114	101	91	81	71	60	50	43
680	690	156	143	130	117	105	94	84	73	63	53	45
690	700	159	146	134	121	108	97	86	76	66	56	46
700	710	163	150	137	124	112	99	89	79	69	58	48
710	720	166	153	141	128	115	102	92	82	72	61	51

Table 11–2 Federal Income Tax Witholding
SINGLE Persons—Weekly Payroll Period

Part 2. Mathematics Applications in Starting a Business

And the wages are-		And the number of withholding allowances claimed is—										
At least	But less than	0	1	2	3	4	5	6	7	8	9	10 or more
		The amount of income tax to be withheld shall be—										
$120	$125	$11	$6	$2	$0	$0	$0	$0	$0	$0	$0	$0
125	130	11	6	2	0	0	0	0	0	0	0	0
130	135	12	7	3	0	0	0	0	0	0	0	0
135	140	13	7	3	0	0	0	0	0	0	0	0
140	145	14	8	4	0	0	0	0	0	0	0	0
145	150	14	9	4	0	0	0	0	0	0	0	0
150	160	16	10	5	1	0	0	0	0	0	0	0
160	170	17	12	6	2	0	0	0	0	0	0	0
170	180	19	13	8	3	0	0	0	0	0	0	0
180	190	20	15	9	4	0	0	0	0	0	0	0
190	200	22	16	11	5	1	0	0	0	0	0	0
200	210	23	18	12	7	3	0	0	0	0	0	0
210	220	25	19	14	8	4	0	0	0	0	0	0
220	230	26	21	15	10	5	1	0	0	0	0	0
230	240	28	22	17	11	6	2	0	0	0	0	0
240	250	29	24	18	13	7	3	0	0	0	0	0
250	260	31	25	20	14	9	4	0	0	0	0	0
260	270	32	27	21	16	10	5	1	0	0	0	0
270	280	34	28	23	17	12	6	2	0	0	0	0
280	290	35	30	24	19	13	8	3	0	0	0	0
290	300	37	31	26	20	15	9	4	0	0	0	0
300	310	38	33	27	22	16	11	6	1	0	0	0
310	320	40	34	29	23	18	12	7	3	0	0	0
320	330	41	36	30	25	19	14	8	4	0	0	0
330	340	43	37	32	26	21	15	10	5	1	0	0
340	350	44	39	33	28	22	17	11	6	2	0	0
350	360	46	40	35	29	24	18	13	7	3	0	0
360	370	47	42	36	31	25	20	14	9	4	0	0
370	380	49	43	38	32	27	21	16	10	5	1	0
380	390	50	45	39	34	28	23	17	12	6	2	0
390	400	52	46	41	35	30	24	19	13	8	3	0
400	410	53	48	42	37	31	26	20	15	9	4	0
410	420	55	49	44	38	33	27	22	16	11	6	2
420	430	56	51	45	40	34	29	23	18	12	7	3
430	440	58	52	47	41	36	30	25	19	14	8	4
440	450	59	54	48	43	37	32	26	21	15	10	5
450	460	61	55	50	44	39	33	28	22	17	11	6
460	470	62	57	51	46	40	35	29	24	18	13	7
470	480	64	58	53	47	42	36	31	25	20	14	9
480	490	65	60	54	49	43	38	32	27	21	16	10
490	500	67	61	56	50	45	39	34	28	23	17	12
500	510	68	63	57	52	46	41	35	30	24	19	13
510	520	70	64	59	53	48	42	37	31	26	20	15
520	530	71	66	60	55	49	44	38	33	27	22	16
530	540	73	67	62	56	51	45	40	34	29	23	18
540	550	74	69	63	58	52	47	41	36	30	25	19
550	560	76	70	65	59	54	48	43	37	32	26	21
560	570	77	72	66	61	55	50	44	39	33	28	22
570	580	79	73	68	62	57	51	46	40	35	29	24
580	590	81	75	69	64	58	53	47	42	36	31	25
590	600	84	76	71	65	60	54	49	43	38	32	27
600	610	87	78	72	67	61	56	50	45	39	34	28
610	620	90	80	74	68	63	57	52	46	41	35	30
620	630	93	82	75	70	64	59	53	48	42	37	31
630	640	95	85	77	71	66	60	55	49	44	38	33
640	650	98	88	78	73	67	62	56	51	45	40	34
650	660	101	91	81	74	69	63	58	52	47	41	36
660	670	104	94	83	76	70	65	59	54	48	43	37
670	680	107	96	86	77	72	66	61	55	50	44	39
680	690	109	99	89	79	73	68	62	57	51	46	40

Table 11–3 Federal Income Tax Witholding
MARRIED Persons—Weekly Payroll Period

Chapter 11. Payrolls and Agents' Commissions

Federal Percentage Method of Income Tax Withholding. Some employers prefer not to use the wage-bracket tables in computing the amount of income tax to be deducted and withheld from a payment of wages. They can instead make a percentage computation based on Table 11–4 and the appropriate rate table.

Payroll Period	Amount of One Withholding Exemption
Weekly..	$ 36.54
Biweekly	73.08
Semimonthly....................................	79.17
Monthly..	158.33
Quarterly......................................	475.00
Semiannually	950.00
Annually	1900.00
Daily or miscellaneous (per day of such period) ...	7.31

Table 11–4 Amount of Exemption for Percentage Method Income Tax Withholding

The steps in computing the income tax to be withheld under the percentage method are:

1. Multiply the amount of one withholding exemption (see Table 11–4) by the number of exemptions claimed.
2. Subtract the amount thus determined from the employee's wages.
3. Determine the amount to be withheld by using the appropriate table.

Example:

A married employee has a weekly payroll period for which the pay is $395 and has in effect a withholding exemption certificate claiming three exemptions. Use the percentage method to compute the income tax to be withheld.

Solution:

Total wage payment		$395.00
Amount of one exemption (Table 11–4)	$36.54	
Number of exemptions claimed...........................	3	
Line 2 multiplied by line 3		109.62
Amount subject to withholding............................		$285.38

Tax to be withheld on $285.38 from Table 11–5, *married* person:

Tax on first $93	$ 6.27
Tax on remainder ($192.38 at 15%)	28.86
Total to be withheld	$35.13

In determining the amount of income tax to be deducted and withheld, the last digit of the wage amount may, at the election of the employer, be reduced to zero, or the wage amount may be computed to the nearest dollar. For example, if the weekly wage is $287.43, the employer may eliminate the last digit and determine the income tax on the basis of a wage payment of $287.40, or on the basis of a wage payment of $287.00.

Part 2. Mathematics Applications in Starting a Business

Table 11-5 (Weekly Payroll Period)

(a) SINGLE person—including head of household:

If the amount of wages is: — The amount of income tax to be withheld shall be:

Not over $12 0

Over—	But not over—		of excess over—
$12	—$47	. . . .11%	—$12
$47	—$335	. . . .$3.85 plus 15%	—$47
$335	—$532	. . . .$47.05 plus 28%	—$335
$532	—$1,051	. . .$102.21 plus 35%	—$532
$1,051 .	. . . . . .	. . .$283.86 plus 38.5%	—$1,051

(b) MARRIED person—

If the amount of wages is: — The amount of income tax to be withheld shall be:

Not over $36 0

Over—	But not over—		of excess over—
$36	—$93	. . . .11%	—$36
$93	—$574	. . . .$6.27 plus 15%	—$93
$574	—$901	. . . .$78.42 plus 28%	—$574
$901	—$1,767	. . .$169.98 plus 35%	—$901
$1,767 .	. . . . . .	. . .$473.08 plus 38.5%	—$1,767

Table 11-5 Rates for Percentage Method of Withholding Income Taxes (Weekly Payroll Period)

Table 11-6 (Monthly Payroll Period)

(a) SINGLE person—including head of household:

If the amount of wages is: — The amount of income tax to be withheld shall be:

Not over $53 0

Over—	But not over—		of excess over—
$53	—$203	. . . .11%	—$53
$203	—$1,453	. .$16.50 plus 15%	—$203
$1,453	—$2,303	. .$204.00 plus 28%	—$1,453
$2,303	—$4,553	. .$442.00 plus 35%	—$2,303
$4,553 .	. . . . . .	. .$1,229.50 plus 38.5%	—$4,553

(b) MARRIED person—

If the amount of wages is: — The amount of income tax to be withheld shall be:

Not over $155 0

Over—	But not over—		of excess over—
$155	—$405	. . . .11%	—$155
$405	—$2,488	. . .$27.50 plus 15%	—$405
$2,488	—$3,905	. . .$339.95 plus 28%	—$2,488
$3,905	—$7,655	. . .$736.71 plus 35%	—$3,905
$7,655 .	. . . . . .	. . .$2,049.21 plus 38.5%	—$7,655

Table 11-6 Rates for Percentage Method of Withholding Income Taxes (Monthly Payroll Period)

Table 11-7 (Annual Payroll Period)

(a) SINGLE person—including head of household:

If the amount of wages is: — The amount of income tax to be withheld shall be:

Not over $640 0

Over—	But not over—		of excess over—
$640	—$2,440	. .11%	—$640
$2,440	—$17,440	. . .$198.00 plus 15%	—$2,440
$17,440	—$27,640	. .$2,448.00 plus 28%	—$17,440
$27,640	—$54,640	. .$5,304.00 plus 35%	—$27,640
$54,640	. . . . . .	.$14,754.00 plus 38.5%	—$54,640

(b) MARRIED person—

If the amount of wages is: — The amount of income tax to be withheld shall be:

Not over $1,860 0

Over—	But not over—		of excess over—
$1,860	—$4,860	. . . 11%	—$1,860
$4,860	—$29,860	. . $330.00 plus 15%	—$4,860
$29,860	—$46,860	. . $4,080.00 plus 28%	—$29,860
$46,860	—$91,860	. . $8,840.00 plus 35%	—$46,860
$91,860 .	. . . . . .	. $24,590.00 plus 38.5%	—$91,860

Table 11-7 Rates for Percentage Method of Withholding Income Taxes (Annual Payroll Period)

Annualized Method of Income Tax Withholding. Employers may determine the amount of income tax to be withheld on annualized wages under the percentage method of withholding for an annual payroll period and then prorate the tax back to the payroll period.

This method of determining withholding taxes may be useful to employers who desire to conserve computer memory in that the rates, wage brackets, and exemption values for only an annual payroll period are stored in the machine.

Example:	A single person claiming one exemption is paid $410 a week. Use the annualized-income-tax-withholding method to find the amount of income tax withheld each week.

Solution:

Annual wages ($410 × 52 weeks)	$21,320
Amount of one annual exemption (Table 11–4)	1,900
Amount subject to withholding	$19,420

Annual tax on $19,420 from Table 11–7, *single* person:

Tax on first $17,440	$2,448.00
Tax on remainder ($1,980 at 28%)	554.40
Total tax to be withheld	$3,002.40

Weekly withholding: $3,002.40 ÷ 52 weeks = $57.74

Employees' Earnings and Other Deductions

In addition to withholding amounts for employees' federal income taxes, employers in some cities and states must also withhold employees' city and state income taxes. When this is done, the procedures for handling the deduction are quite similar to those for federal income taxes.

The employer may also make other deductions authorized by the employees either individually or as a group. Following are some of the purposes for which other deductions may be made:

1. To pay the premiums on life, health, hospital, medical, or accident insurance for the employees.
2. To accumulate funds for the purchase of United States Savings Bonds for the employees.
3. To pay the union dues of the employees.
4. For employees' retirement benefits.
5. For contributions to charitable organizations, such as the United Fund.
6. To pay the employer for purchases of company goods or services.
7. To repay loans from the employer, the credit union, or other organizations.

Regardless of the purposes of deductions, the employer must keep accurate records of amounts deducted and allocate the funds as directed.

Employees' Earnings Record

When a payroll sheet such as that illustrated in Figure 11–1 is used, it includes columns to show the deductions as well as gross pay. Several methods of determining gross pay have already been presented. To find net pay, the sum of the deductions is entered in the total deductions column and subtracted from the gross pay. The remainder, the amount due, is entered in the net pay column. In the exemptions column of Figure 11–1, M-3 means the employee is married and claims three exemptions; S-1, that the employee is single and claims only one exemption. The other deductions column is representative of the various deductions that may be made for items other than social security and federal income taxes.

| Employee | Gross Pay | No. of Exemptions | Deductions | | | | Net Pay |
			FICA	Federal Income Tax	Other Deductions	Total Deductions	
Bowers, T. L.	$295.76	M-3	$21.15	$20.00	$ 4.83	$45.98	$249.78
Mathis, J. L.	290.77	S-1	20.79	36.00	36.33	93.12	197.65
Shuler, S. G.	368.53	M-4	26.35	25.00	38.99	90.34	278.19

Figure 11-1 A Payroll Sheet with Deductions

The memory function of a calculator may be used to find net pay.

Example: Use the data shown in Figure 11-1 to find the net pay for T. L. Bowers.

Solution: 295.76 $\boxed{\text{M}+}$ 21.15 $\boxed{+}$ 20 $\boxed{+}$ 4.83 $\boxed{=}$ → 45.98 $\boxed{\text{M}-}$ $\boxed{\text{MR}}$ → 249.78

● Exercise 11-5

A. Copy and complete the following portion of a weekly payroll sheet. To determine the FICA deductions, use Table 11-1. For the income taxes, use Tables 11-2 and 11-3.

| | Employee | Gross Pay | No. of Exemptions | Deductions | | | | Net Pay |
				FICA	Federal Income Tax	Other Deductions	Total Deductions	
1.	Arnold, W. E.	$376.00	M-3	_____	_____	$10.76	_____	_____
2.	Frazier, R.	381.90	M-4	_____	_____	12.90	_____	_____
3.	Gottuso, V. J.	434.79	S-1	_____	_____	14.60	_____	_____
4.	Holcomb, D. M.	298.20	S-3	_____	_____	21.10	_____	_____
5.	Lievan, G. R.	415.86	M-5	_____	_____	23.25	_____	_____
6.	Mendoza, N. R.	390.00	M-2	_____	_____	25.90	_____	_____
7.	Powers, M. J.	403.35	S-1	_____	_____	50.10	_____	_____
8.	Seaver, S. L.	650.40	M-1	_____	_____	0	_____	_____
9.	Travers, W. W.	547.20	M-4	_____	_____	0	_____	_____
10.	Wylie, D. G.	362.82	S-2	_____	_____	19.80	_____	_____

B. Copy and complete this portion of a weekly payroll sheet. The 7.15% deduction for FICA is based on the first $43,800 of earnings. Where applicable, use the social security and income tax withholding tables.

Employee Number	Earnings to End of Previous Week	Gross Pay This Week	No. of Exemptions	Deductions FICA	Federal Income Tax	Other Deductions	Total Deductions	Net Pay
201	$19,247.80	$338.20	M-6	____	____	$11.40	____	____
202	19,310.56	342.75	M-2	____	____	14.50	____	____
203	43,226.42	697.80	S-1	____	____	0	____	____
204	43,440.00	410.70	S-4	____	____	0	____	____
205	46,120.00	664.50	M-7	____	____	25.25	____	____
206	45,050.00	580.60	M-1	____	____	30.50	____	____

C. Solve these problems.

1. In one calendar year, Carl Buckner earned $28,577 from the Nyack Company and $27,092.50 from the Rochester Manufacturing Company. Find the total FICA withheld **(a)** by the Nyack Company and **(b)** by the Rochester Manufacturing Company. **(c)** How much is the FICA overpayment that he could apply to his federal income tax?

2. Peggy Polishuk earned $39,500 last year from Los Angeles Co. and $28,700 from Maine Co. Find the total FICA tax withheld by **(a)** Los Angeles Co. and **(b)** Maine Co. **(c)** How much is the FICA overpayment that she could apply to her federal income tax?

3. James Lamb, who is single, earned $437.50 a week during the past year. Find the amount of his federal income tax that was withheld each week by his employer who used the percentage method.

4. Regina Henderson earns $650 a week. She is married and claims four exemptions. Use the percentage method to find the amount of income tax that is withheld each week.

5. Sally Holifield, who is single, earned $3,268 a month during the past year. Use the percentage method to find how much income tax her employer withheld each month.

6. Steven Hooper, who has a wife and three dependent children, earns $2,850 a month. Find the amount of monthly income tax withheld by his employer by the percentage method.

7. Alan Parker, who earns $750 a week, is married and has five dependent children. How much federal income tax does his employer deduct each week if he uses the annualized-percentage method?

8. Virginia Mullens, who is single, lives with and supports her mother. Ms. Mullens earns $1,960 a month. How much income tax does her employer withhold each month based on an annualized income tax?

Change Tally Sheet and Change Memorandum

Although most companies pay their employees with checks, some pay with cash that has been placed in pay envelopes. When employees are paid with cash, the payroll department must know how many bills and coins are needed for each pay envelope. This information can be found through the use of a change tally sheet. After the net pay for each employee has been determined and entered on a change tally sheet, the number of the various denominations of bills and coins needed to pay each employee is placed in the appropriate change column in line with the employee's name or payroll number. Because each employee should be paid with as few pieces of money as is practicable, the largest common denominations are used. Thus, one $20 bill should be used rather than two $10 bills; one half-dollar, instead of two quarters.

Employee	Net Pay	$20	$10	$5	$1	50¢	25¢	10¢	5¢	1¢
Bowers, T. L.	$249.78	12		1	4	1	1			3
Mathis, J. L.	197.65	9	1	1	2	1		1	1	
Shuler, S. G.	278.19	13	1	1	3			1	1	4
Totals	$725.62	34	2	3	9	2	1	2	2	7

Figure 11-2 A Change Tally Sheet

Denomination	Number	Amount
$20.00	34	$680.00
10.00	2	20.00
5.00	3	15.00
1.00	9	9.00
0.50	2	1.00
0.25	1	0.25
0.10	2	0.20
0.05	2	0.10
0.01	7	0.07
Total		$725.62

The totals of the denominations on the change tally sheet may be transferred to a change memorandum. A payroll clerk can then take the change memorandum and a company check for the total net pay to the bank to obtain the appropriate denominations of money for the payroll. The total on the change memorandum should equal the total net pay shown on the change tally sheet.

Figure 11-3 A Change Memorandum

• Exercise 11-6

1. Prepare a form similar to Figure 11-2 and use the following names and amounts of net pay to complete the change tally sheet: A. L. Adams, net pay $322.78; R. J. Bronson, $347.41; J. A. Desmore, $285.96; R. L. Fuller, $313.25; L. D. Holder, $336.64; K. E. Lindsay, $272.09; M. D. McNeal, $354.33; J. P. Petruk, $298.50; J. S. Schwarz, $210.82; and D. C. Van Hook, $389.17.

2. Prepare a form similar to Figure 11–3 and use the denominational totals found in Problem 1 to complete the change memorandum.

Agents' Commissions

A person or firm that is empowered to transact business for another is an **agent.** The party for whom the agent has power to act is the **principal.** If a house and lot are sold for M. Marshall by a real estate firm that has power to do so, Marshall is the principal for whom the firm acts as agent. The fee paid to an agent is usually a specific percent of the selling price or other accepted basis. The amount received by an agent in payment for services is the **commission.**

Example A:

A house and lot were sold for $156,000 by an agent who charged 6% commission. How much commission was earned?

Solution:

Sales Price × Rate of Commission = Commission

$$156,000 \boxed{\times} 6 \boxed{\%} \rightarrow 9360, \text{ means } \$9,360$$

Depending on their agreement, an agent may be reimbursed for any or all expenditures made in connection with transactions conducted for the principal. The net amount left for the principal, after the agent's commission and authorized expenses have been deducted, is the **net proceeds.**

Example B:

An agent collected a delinquent account of $5,700 for Alta Loma Company. The agent charged 25% for services and was reimbursed $23 for expenses. How much were the net proceeds that Alta Loma Company received?

Solution:

Amount collected		$5,700
Deductions:		
Commission ($5,700 × 25%)	$1,425	
Expenses	23	
Total Deductions		1,448
Net Proceeds		$4,252

Or, on a calculator *with* $\boxed{\%}$ key:

$$5,700 \boxed{-} 25 \boxed{\%} \boxed{-} 23 \boxed{=} \rightarrow 4,252$$

or $\quad 5,700 \boxed{-} 25 \boxed{\%} \boxed{=} \boxed{-} 23 \boxed{=} \rightarrow 4,252, \text{ means } \$4,252$

• Exercise 11–7

1. An agent sold a commodity for $5,750 at $3\frac{1}{2}\%$ commission. How much commission was earned?

2. An agency collected 75% of a $1,500 delinquent account and charged 45% for its services. How much commission did the agency receive?

                    Part 2. Mathematics Applications in Starting a Business

3. A real estate agent sold a house for $154,500 at 5% commission. How much were the net proceeds that the principal received?

4. An agent sold $1,450 worth of merchandise for the principal and deducted commission of 6%. If the agent had no expenses, how much in net proceeds did the principal receive?

5. A real estate agent sold a house for $268,500. How much did the principal receive if the agent charged 5% commission and $97.50 for expenses?

6. A collection agency that charges 35% commission collected in full a debt of $437.50. How much should the agency remit to the principal?

7. A collector succeeded in collecting 80% of $5,435 in doubtful accounts. If the collector's commission rate was 25% of the amount collected, how much did the principal receive?

8. If $90 was charged for selling $3,000 worth of goods, what was the rate of commission?

9. J. Bartolotti gave an agency a delinquent account amounting to $1,250 to collect. The agency collected 70% of the amount and charged 20% for collecting. How much did Bartolotti receive?

10. An agent's commission was $240 for selling $3,200 worth of merchandise. What rate of commission was charged?

11. A realtor's fee for selling a lot was $1,236.90. If the rate of commission was 7%, what was the selling price of the lot?

12. A real estate agent received $7,728, which is 6% of the selling price, for selling a house. How much was the selling price?

Account Sales. Agents who buy and sell goods for their principals are also known as **commission merchants, factors,** or **brokers.** Commission merchants and factors usually have possession of the goods and make sales and purchases in their own names. Brokers usually do not have possession of the goods and generally make contracts in the names of their principals.

These intermediaries operate in the wholesale markets of large cities where they sell goods for farmers and other producers who may be located some distance from marketing centers. They may also buy goods for manufacturers, processors, wholesalers, and retailers. Agricultural products, such as fruits, vegetables, poultry, butter, and eggs, constitute the bulk of the products commonly sold or bought by these agents. Their transactions, however, do include relatively small amounts of manufactured consumer goods. When selling goods for a principal, the commission merchant or factor receives the merchandise, provides storage, finds buyers, negotiates prices, makes deliveries, extends credit, makes collections, and deducts the commission and other charges before remitting the balance to the principal.

Merchandise that is sent to an agent to be sold is a **consignment;** that is, the goods are consigned or entrusted to the agent for sale. The person or firm that sends the goods is the **consignor.** The party to whom goods are sent on consignment, the agent, is the **consignee.**

The commission merchant or factor is expected to get the best price possible for the consignment. Whatever total price the agent does get is the **gross proceeds.** Sometimes the agent guarantees either the payment for goods sold or the quality of the goods bought. The charge made for this service is a **guaranty.** Commission and other expenses of making sales, such as transportation, advertising, storage, guaranty, and insurance, constitute the agent's total charges. When the total charges are deducted from the gross proceeds, the resulting amount, the **net proceeds,** is remitted to the consignor.

The commission and other percentage charges pertaining to a sale of goods by an agent are based on the gross proceeds. The amount of net proceeds is found in the following manner:

1. Find the extension per item by multiplying the quantity of items sold by the price per item.
2. Find the gross proceeds by adding the extensions.
3. Find the total charges, including the commission based on gross proceeds.
4. Find the net proceeds by subtracting the total charges from the gross proceeds.

Example:

Cornucopia Company of St. Louis sold the following quantities of fancy apples for Leslie Russell of Cobden, Illinois: 300 boxes of apples at $7.10 a box; 400 boxes at $6.90 a box; and 320 boxes at $7.60 a box. The company, which charges 4% commission and $\frac{1}{2}$% guaranty, paid $156.80 for freight and cartage of the apples. What is the amount of net proceeds which should be sent to Russell?

Solution:

300 × $7.10 =	$2,130.00	
400 × $6.90 =	2,760.00	
320 × $7.60 =	2,432.00	
Gross Proceeds		$7,322.00
Freight and cartage =	156.80	
Commission, 0.04 × $7,322 =	292.88	
Guaranty, 0.005 × $7,322 =	36.61	
Total Charges		486.29
Net Proceeds		$6,835.71

Or, on a calculator *with* %　key:

MC 300 × 7.1 M+ 400 × 6.9 M+ 320 × 7.6 M+

MR − 4.5 % − 156.8 = → 6835.71, means $6,835.71

After the goods have been sold, the agent sends the consignor a check for the net proceeds and a report that is called an **account sales.** This report shows the gross proceeds, the expenses, the commission, the net proceeds, and other details pertaining to the sale.

An account sales based on the preceding example is illustrated in Figure 11–4.

ACCOUNT SALES

Cornucopia Company

FRESH FRUITS AND VEGETABLES

1431-37 Market Street, St. Louis, MO 63101

Date April 2, 19--

Sales for Account of Leslie Russell

Cobden, IL 62920

March	25	300 boxes Apples	@ $7.10	$2,130	00				
	27	400 boxes Apples	@ $6.90	2,760	00				
	28	320 boxes Apples	@ $7.60	2,432	00				
		Gross Proceeds					$7,322	00	
		Charges:							
		Freight and Cartage		$156	80				
		Commission, 4% of $7,322		292	88				
		Guaranty, ½% of $7,322		36	61		486	29	
		Net Proceeds					$6,835	71	

Figure 11-4 An Account Sales

● Exercise 11-8

A. Find the commission, total charges, and net proceeds for each of the following.

	Gross Proceeds	Commission Rate	Commission Amount	Storage	Freight	Total Charges	Net Proceeds
1.	$ 800.00	7%	_____			_____	_____
2.	480.00	4%	_____	$30.40		_____	_____
3.	1,240.00	5%	_____		$52.97	_____	_____
4.	5,300.00	6%	_____	69.25	73.20	_____	_____
5.	671.50	$7\frac{1}{2}$%	_____	17.33	39.50	_____	_____
6.	2,936.75	$6\frac{1}{4}$%	_____	47.20	48.90	_____	_____

B. Solve these problems.

1. Cunningham sent 750 bags of potatoes to a Boise factor. The factor paid the freight, $342.52, and sold the potatoes at $19.35 a bag. The factor deducted a commission of 5% and the freight charges before sending the net proceeds to Cunningham. How much did Cunningham receive?

2. A poultry grower sent 25 cases of eggs (30 dozen to a case) to a commission merchant to sell. The commission merchant sold the eggs at 84¢ a dozen. Charges were: trucking, $23.50; commission, 8%; and other expenses, $9.79. How much should the grower receive?

3. An apple grower shipped a consignment of 5 carloads of apples to a commission merchant to sell. Each carload contained 1,500 boxes of apples on which the agent paid freight at 35¢ a box and total storage charges of $395.76. The agent then sold the apples at $7 a box, charging 6% commission. Find the net proceeds.

4. A farmer sent a consignment of 4,000 bushels of corn to a factor. The factor paid freight charges of $83.55, cartage of $2\frac{1}{2}$¢ a bushel, storage charges of $21, and insurance of $9. The factor sold 900 bushels of the corn at $4.39 a bushel, 1,500 bushels at $4.45 each, and the remainder at 4.37\frac{1}{2}$ a bushel. The factor charged 5% commission. Find the net proceeds.

5. An orange grower sent a consignment of 3,600 boxes of oranges to an agent. The agent paid freight charges of 65¢ a box, cartage of 12$\frac{1}{2}$¢ a box, and insurance of $36. The agent sold 860 boxes at $6 a box, 940 at $6.75 a box, and the remainder at $6.50 a box. The commission was 4$\frac{1}{2}$%. Find the net proceeds.

6. A commission merchant received from a farmer a consignment consisting of 700 bushels of corn, 500 bushels of oats, and 300 bushels of soybeans. The commission merchant paid $49.60 for freight, $25 for storage, and $8.50 for insurance. The corn was sold at $5.18 a bushel, the oats at 2.62\frac{1}{2}$ a bushel, and the soybeans at $9.85 a bushel. The commission merchant charged 4$\frac{1}{2}$% commission and 1$\frac{1}{2}$% guaranty. Find the net proceeds.

6%

Account Purchase. Although most commission merchants, brokers, and factors specialize in either buying or selling, some perform both functions for their clients. When buying goods, the agent finds the goods requested, negotiates prices, and handles the details of insuring and transporting the goods to the principal.

From the principal's viewpoint, to have the agent's commission based on quantity, such as 2¢ per pound, rather than on price is better. If the commission is based on buying price, the agent may be tempted to buy at the highest rather than the most reasonable price. Naturally, a price the principal is willing to pay can be specified. These intermediaries, however, do rely on repeat orders from their clients and do attempt to buy for them at the most reasonable prices. Even though commission may be based on quantity, it is customarily based on the purchasing price. The total amount paid by the agent for the goods only is the **prime cost.** The agent adds commission and other expenses of the transaction to the prime cost to find the **gross cost,** which is the amount the principal owes the agent for the goods.

When commission is based on price, the amount of commission pertaining to the purchase of goods by an agent for a principal is based on the prime cost. The gross cost is found in this manner:

1. Find the extension per item by multiplying the quantity of items bought by the price per item.
2. Find the prime cost by adding the extensions.
3. Find the total charges, including the commission based on prime cost.
4. Find the gross cost by adding the total charges to the prime cost.

Example:

Hall and Starbuck, commission merchants in New York City, purchased 25 crates of eggs at $27 a crate, 150 pounds of butter at $2.25 a pound, and 500 pounds of cheese at $2.75 a pound for McGregor's Market in Oceanside, New York. If they paid the trucking expenses of $30.80 and charged 5% commission on this purchase, how much is the gross cost?

Solution:

25 × $27 =	$ 675.00	
150 × $2.25 =	337.50	
500 × $2.75 =	1,375.00	
Prime Cost		$2,387.50
Trucking	30.80	
Commission, 5% × $2,387.50 =	119.38	
Total Charges		150.18
Gross Cost		$2,537.68

Or, on a calculator *with* % key:

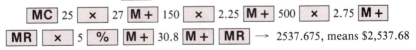

MC 25 × 27 M+ 150 × 2.25 M+ 500 × 2.75 M+
MR × 5 % M+ 30.8 M+ MR → 2537.675, means $2,537.68

After each purchase or periodically, according to their agreement, the agent sends the principal a statement that is called an **account purchase.** This statement shows the prime cost of each item, the charges paid by the agent, the commission, gross cost to the principal, and other details of the purchase. Figure 11-5 illustrates an account purchase.

Chapter 11. Payrolls and Agents' Commissions

ACCOUNT PURCHASE

HALL & STARBUCK

COMMISSION   MERCHANTS   New York, NY   10067

November 9, 19--

Purchased for Account of

McGregor's Market
Oceanside, NY   11572

Nov.	8						
		25 crates Eggs	@ $27	$ 675	00		
		150 lb. Butter	@ $2.25	337	50		
		500 lb. Cheese	@ $2.75	1,375	00		
		Prime Cost				$2,387	50
		Charges:					
		Trucking		30	80		
		Commission, 5%		119	38	150	18
		Total charged to your account				$2,537	68

Figure 11–5 An Account Purchase

● Exercise 11–9

A. Find the commission based on prime cost and the gross cost for each of the following.

	Prime Cost	Commission Rate	Commission Amount	Freight	Storage	Other Charges	Gross Cost
1.	$1,040	7%	___				___
2.	816	8%	___	$48.30			___
3.	9,020	5%	___		$15.42		___
4.	2,300	6%	___	51.40		$ 4.30	___
5.	696	$7\frac{1}{4}$%	___	22.47	6.57		___
6.	5,710	$5\frac{1}{2}$%	___	62.50	11.60	14.35	___

B. Solve these problems.

1. Jeff Frantz bought 350 bushels of oats through a commission merchant. The merchant paid 3.87\frac{1}{2}$ a bushel for the oats and charged 9% commission. Freight and other charges paid by the commission merchant amounted to $84.70. How much gross cost did Frantz pay for the oats?

2. A commission merchant bought 640 boxes of apples for Loretta Flanagan at $9.25 a box. The commission merchant paid freight and other expenses totaling $96 and charged 7% commission. Find the gross cost.

3. A milling company purchased through a factor 4,000 bushels of wheat at $5.85 a bushel. The factor charged 3% commission. The freight charges totaled $768. How much was the gross cost to the milling company?

4. A commission merchant bought 5,800 bushels of corn at $6.25 a bushel. Freight and cartage amounted to $740. Commission of 5% and $\frac{1}{2}$% guaranty were charged. Find the gross cost.

5. Gary Remer bought 2,500 pounds of coffee through a commission merchant who charged 6% commission. The coffee cost $2.75 a pound. Trucking and other expenses totaled $61.80. How much did Remer pay in gross cost?

6. An agent bought 500 pounds of coffee at $2.48 a pound and 320 pounds of cocoa at 96¢ a pound. Trucking was $16.30 and storage was $13.50. The charges were 4% commission and 1% guaranty. Find the gross cost.

REVIEW PROBLEMS

Solve these problems. If you have difficulty solving any problem, restudy the appropriate section in this chapter. The problems under a specific number are related to those contained in the exercise with the same last number.

1. Find the gross pay for each of the following employees who are paid time and a half for all hours over 40 worked in one week: **(a)** Garanci, 44 hours at $9.90 an hour; and **(b)** Vance, 47 hours at $10.15 an hour.

2. Brandeis Company pays its employees in Department E 41$\frac{2}{3}$¢ in wages for each article produced. A worker in this department produced these quantities of articles during the past week: Monday, 152; Tuesday, 167; Wednesday, 161; Thursday, 187; and Friday, 173. Find the worker's gross pay for the week.

3. **a.** On a differential piecework plan, each worker is paid 56 cents each for the first 100 units produced daily. When the worker's daily production exceeds 100 units, he or she is paid 62 cents for each unit produced that day. Find the daily wages of an employee who produced **(1)** 96 units on Monday, **(2)** 119 units on Tuesday, and **(3)** 127 units on Wednesday.

   b. Jackson Manufacturing Company pays each production worker a bonus of 20% when that worker's production equals or exceeds the daily quota of 80 units. If the pay is $8.60 an hour for a 7-hour day, find the daily gross wages of an employee whose production was **(1)** Monday, 78 units; **(2)** Tuesday, 80 units; and **(3)** Wednesday, 83 units.

   c. Nancy Marshall is paid a proportionate premium for any extra daily production that exceeds her quota of 220 units in a 7-hour shift. Her hourly wage is $9.75. Find her daily wages if production was as follows: **(1)** Monday, 232 units; **(2)** Tuesday, 220 units; **(3)** Wednesday, 218 units; and **(4)** Thursday, 236 units.

4. A salesperson earns a commission of 10% on the first $4,000 of monthly sales, 15% on the next $4,000, and 20% on sales over $8,000 a month. What was the salesperson's gross pay for a month during which $10,478 worth of goods was sold?

5. **a.** John Hickman, whose gross pay for the first week in January was $383.77, is married and claims three exemptions for federal income tax withholding. Use Table 11–1 and Table 11–3 to find the amounts withheld for **(1)** social security and **(2)** federal income tax. **(3)** If his pay was not subject to any other deductions, how much was his net pay?

   b. Joan Barnett, who is single and supports herself and her two children, earns $2,975 a month. Find the amount of monthly federal income tax withheld by her employer who uses the annualized-percentage method.

6. Use the following data to prepare a change tally sheet and a change memorandum similar to Figures 11–2 and 11–3: I. D. Atkins, $208.66; W. B. Rivos, $194.45; R. J. Rudolph, $375.09; and R. S. Wasley, $281.64.

7. Solve these commission problems.

   a. A real estate agent sold an apartment building for $1,750,000. How much did the original owner receive if the agent deducted 4% commission and $526 authorized expenses?

   b. If an agent charged $215.10 for selling $4,780 worth of commodities, what rate of commission was charged?

   c. If an agent received $330 for selling goods at $7\frac{1}{2}$% commission, what was the selling price of the goods?

   d. D. Burgess wishes to sell a piece of real property at a price that will bring at least $250,000 after the real estate agent has deducted the 6% commission. What is the lowest price, to the nearest $100, at which Burgess may sell under these circumstances?

8. An egg rancher sent 35 cases of eggs (30 dozen to a case) to a commission merchant. The commission merchant sold the eggs at 89¢ a dozen. The charges were: freight, $15.35; commission, 7%; and other expenses, $12.83. How much should the commission merchant remit to the rancher?

9. A commission merchant received an order for 620 boxes of fruit to be bought on a commission of $3\frac{1}{2}\%$. There were 300 boxes bought at $5.50 a box, 200 at $5.60 a box, and 120 at $5.75 a box. Also, $78.40 was paid for freight and cartage. Find the gross cost.

CHALLENGE PROBLEM

Los Medanos Novelties, Inc. produces small plastic novelties and toys. Its new line of Christmas ornaments is very popular. Even though the company encourages its dealers to buy large quantities before the season starts, many do not do so. Los Medanos has insufficient warehouse space to stock large quantities of the ornaments. Also, predicting which of the new ornaments will be most in demand seems impossible. The past two years the company's 200 production employees have earned a great deal of overtime during the 8 weeks before Christmas.

New production workers earn $6.50 an hour. After six months on the job they earn $7.50 per hour and after one year, $8.75. On average, they earn $8.05 an hour. All are paid time and a half for working more than 40 hours a week, and Los Medanos pays for fringe benefits of $300 a month per employee. Workus Yorway, Inc. has offered to supply extra workers during the rush period for $9.25 per hour per worker. The extra workers would be employees of Workus Yorway, which would pay their wages and all taxes on their wages.

As you are the personnel director, the president of Los Medanos has asked you to recommend one of three choices: (a) No change during the rush season. (b) Contract with Workus Yorway for the use of the needed temporary employees. (c) Hire the new workers on a temporary basis at a wage of $6.50 an hour.

You have checked with the accounting department and learned that during the past two Christmas seasons, the production employees have worked an average of 7 hours a week overtime. As you know, the employer must pay 7.15% FICA tax on the first $43,800 earned by each employee. In addition, Los Medanos pays these other payroll taxes on the first $7,000 of each employ-

ee's earnings: state disability insurance at 1.2%, state unemployment insurance at 1%, and federal unemployment insurance at 0.8%. The state unemployment insurance rate is only 1% because of low employee turnover. However, if each year temporary workers were hired and released two months later, the rate would go to 3.4%.

Justify your recommendation to the president of Los Medanos.

Part Three
Mathematics Applications in Operating a Business

The administrators and managers of a transportation company have business problems and interests considerably different from those who operate a service or manufacturing company. Likewise, the owners of a law firm perform activities different from those performed by the owners of a department store. However, although the interests and activities of the managers in one firm may differ greatly from those in another, there are certain principles involved in operating any business. For example, all sell goods or services, use and/or extend credit, keep business records, and determine whether the enterprise is earning a profit. Furthermore, businesses may be categorized into only three types of ownership. These principles and types of ownership are presented in Part Three.

Chapter 12

Merchandising

Objectives

After mastering the material in Chapter 12, you will be able to:

- Compute trade and cash discounts.
- Compare cash discounts to simple interest.
- Determine credit given for partial payments on invoices.
- Use the markon equation to find the markon, cost, or selling price based on cost.
- Use the markon equation to find the markon, cost, or selling price based on selling price.
- Compute the rate of markon based on cost or selling price.
- Convert a markon rate from a cost base to a selling-price base and vice versa.
- Calculate the list price when a trade discount is given.
- Find the rate of an additional trade discount.

Merchandising may be viewed as including all aspects of buying and selling goods. These include market research, development of new products, and coordination of manufacturing and marketing. This chapter, however, is limited to the basic aspects of purchasing and pricing goods.

PURCHASES DISCOUNTS

To maximize net income, the retailer must buy the desired quality of merchandise at the lowest prices available and sell for more than was paid. Therefore, good business practice requires that buyers take advantage of available discounts.

Trade Discounts

Manufacturers and wholesalers often distribute elaborate catalogs and circulars to their salespeople and customers. A manufacturer of refrigerators and freezers distributes catalogs and promotional materials to dealers who sell such appliances; a manufacturer of furniture, to furniture dealers; a wholesaler of small hand tools, to hardware dealers, to name a few. In short, manufacturers and wholesalers send their catalogs and circulars to the appropriate businesses that are in the trade.

These catalogs and circulars usually show detailed illustrations and descriptions, as well as the prices, of the goods being offered to those in the trade. The price shown is the **list price** and may or may not be the price that is to be paid by the ultimate consumer. The list price, however, is the basis for determining the amount to be paid by the dealer who is in the trade. Quite commonly, a company that issues a catalog will also provide a discount sheet that shows the various rates of discount to the trade. These rates usually vary according to the lines of goods to which they pertain. The rate is expressed as a percent and is based on the list price. A deduction from the list price allowed by the manufacturer or wholesaler to the retailer is a **trade discount.** The price to the dealer, which is the **net price,** is the list price less the trade discount.

To find the net price:

1. Find the amount of the discount by multiplying the list price by the rate of discount.
2. Find the net price by subtracting the amount of the discount from the list price.

Example: Find the net price of merchandise listed at $600 less a discount of 25%.

Solution:

$600   list price (or invoice price)
− 150   discount (25% of $600)
$450   net price (75% of $600)

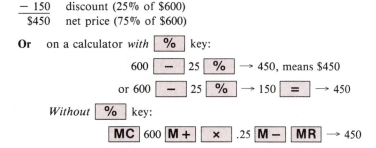

Or on a calculator *with* % key:

600 − 25 % → 450, means $450

or 600 − 25 % → 150 = → 450

Without % key:

MC 600 M+ × .25 M− MR → 450

Series of Discounts. Because of increases or decreases in production costs, or other economic considerations, a manufacturer or wholesaler may need to change actual selling prices. If goods are sold through a catalog, actual prices can be changed by issuing new trade-discount sheets without the necessity of having the catalog reprinted, which is usually quite expensive. The discount sheets may show completely new discount rates, the deletion of some old rates, or the annexing of some new rates. For example, a line of goods that was formerly discounted at 25% may now be discounted at 25% and 10%. Two or more discounts given together may be called a **chain discount** or a **series of discounts.**

The rates in a series of discounts are calculated on decreasing bases. The list price is multiplied by the first discount rate. The amount found in this calculation is subtracted from the list price to obtain a remainder. This remainder is then the base for the second discount rate in the series. The amount obtained by multiplying the remainder by the second discount rate is then subtracted from its base to obtain another remainder. And this remainder may be the base for yet a third discount rate in the series.

Example: Find the net price of merchandise listed at $600 less trade discounts of 25%, 10%, and 10%.

Solution:

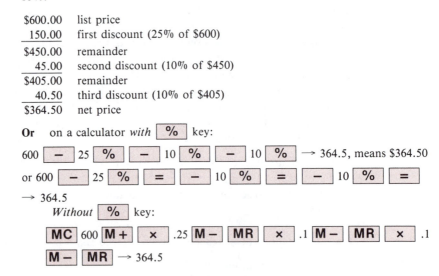

$600.00   list price
 150.00   first discount (25% of $600)
$450.00   remainder
  45.00   second discount (10% of $450)
$405.00   remainder
  40.50   third discount (10% of $405)
$364.50   net price

An alternate method of finding the net price for a problem such as that in the preceding example is recommended because fewer steps are used. The alternate method utilizes the complements of the discount rates. The **complement** of a decimal fraction is the amount that may be added to the decimal to make a sum of 1. Thus, 0.8 is the complement of 0.2 (0.8 + 0.2 = 1.0); 0.25 is the complement of 0.75; and 0.037 is the complement of 0.963. Therefore, the complement of any percent may be found by subtracting the given percent from 100%; that is, the complement of 25% is 75%. Notice how the complements of the discount rates are used to solve the problem in the example above.

Solution:

$600.00   list price
× 0.75   (100% − 25%)
$450.00   remainder
× 0.9   (100% − 10%)
$405.00   remainder
× 0.9   (100% − 10%)
$364.50   net price

Or   on a calculator *with* | % | key:

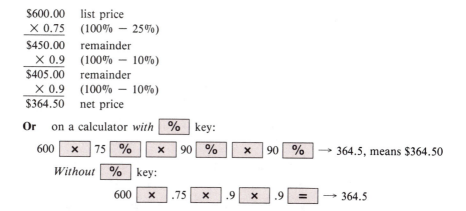

600 | × | 75 | % | × | 90 | % | × | 90 | % | → 364.5, means $364.50

Without | % | key:

600 | × | .75 | × | .9 | × | .9 | = | → 364.5

The rates in a chain discount may be applied in the order given or in a rearranged order because the order in which factors are multiplied does not affect the product of those factors. Usually the discounts are computed in the order given.

● Exercise 12–1

A. Find the net price for each of the following.

1. Invoice amount of $450.30 less trade discounts of $33\frac{1}{3}\%$ and 20%.

2. Invoice amount of $324.32 less trade discounts of 25% and $16\frac{2}{3}\%$.

3. Invoice amount of $80 less trade discounts of $33\frac{1}{3}\%$ and 10%.

4. Invoice amount of $500 less discounts of 20%, $12\frac{1}{2}\%$, and 5%.

5. Invoice amount of $960 less discounts of $16\frac{2}{3}\%$, $12\frac{1}{2}\%$, and 8%.

6. Invoice amount of $266.56 less discounts of $37\frac{1}{2}\%$, 20%, and 10%.

B. For each of the items below, find the amount of discount and net price.

	List Price	Trade Discounts	Amount of Discount	Net Price
1.	$ 240	20%, $16\frac{2}{3}\%$	_____	_____
2.	3,000	$33\frac{1}{3}\%$, 20%	_____	_____
3.	320	25%, 10%	_____	_____
4.	960	$33\frac{1}{3}\%$, 25%	_____	_____
5.	600	20%, 10%	_____	_____
6.	240	$12\frac{1}{2}\%$, 10%, 5%	_____	_____
7.	1,200	30%, 20%, 10%	_____	_____
8.	480	25%, 15%, 5%	_____	_____
9.	840	$33\frac{1}{3}\%$, $12\frac{1}{2}\%$, 5%	_____	_____
10.	680	$37\frac{1}{2}\%$, 20%, 15%	_____	_____

C. Solve these problems.

1. Mullion Appliance Store bought a washing machine at a list price of $720 less trade discounts of 25% and 10%. What net price did the store pay?

2. Globe Electronics sells a video recorder listed for $990 at discounts of 20%, $12\frac{1}{2}$%, and 5%. Find the net price per recorder.

3. A manufacturer of office furniture sells an office chair to dealers in the trade at $150 less discounts of 30% and 20%. How much is the net price?

4. How much does Valley Hardware Company pay for 25 dozen filters listed at $48 a dozen if the discount rates are $18\frac{3}{4}$%, 10%, and 5%?

5. Uniray Company offers to deliver a cassette recorder to a dealer at a list price of $210 less discounts of $33\frac{1}{3}$%, 20%, and 5%. Crest Company offers to deliver a recorder of equal quality for $200 less 25%, 20%, and 10%. **(a)** Which company's offer is better? **(b)** How much can the dealer save on each recorder by taking the better offer?

6. A new salesperson who misunderstood the company's discount terms of 20% and 10% calculated a net price that allowed a discount of 30% to the dealer. If the list price of the merchandise was $750, by how much did the salesperson miscalculate the net price?

Equivalent Discount Rates. A number of different list prices may be subject to the same series of discount rates. Sometimes a person wishes to know the amount of discount on a number of items that are subject to the same series of discounts. In this case, much time may be saved by using the **equivalent discount rate,** which is a rate that is equal to the series. This single rate may be applied to the list price to find the amount of the total discount.

Any list price or the total amount of any invoice that is subject to trade discounts may be considered to be equal to 100%. In short, the **list-price percent** is 100%. From this 100% the rates in any series of discounts may be subtracted in the normal manner. The remainder after all appropriate subtractions have been made is the **net-price percent.** This is the percent that may be applied to the list price to find the net price. Deducting the net-price percent from 100% gives the equivalent discount rate.

To find the equivalent discount rate using pencil and paper:

1. Find the net-price percent by subtracting the discount rates in series from 100%.
2. Find the equivalent discount rate by subtracting the net-price percent from 100%.

Example: Find the single discount rate that is equal to the series of 20%, 10%, and 5%.

Solution:

1. 100.0% list-price percent
  20.0% first discount (20% of 100%)

  80.0%
   8.0% second discount (10% of 80%)

  72.0%
   3.6% third discount (5% of 72%)

  68.4% net-price percent

2. 100.0% list-price percent
  68.4% net-price percent

  31.6% equivalent discount rate

Or on a calculator *with* % key:

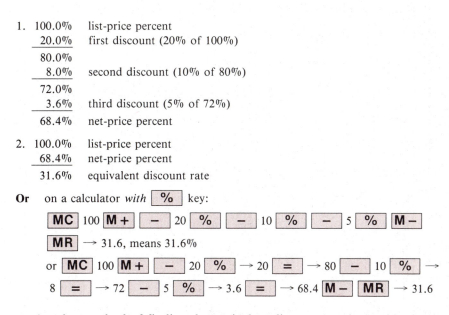

MC 100 M+ − 20 % − 10 % − 5 % M−

MR → 31.6, means 31.6%

or MC 100 M+ − 20 % → 20 = → 80 − 10 % →

8 = → 72 − 5 % → 3.6 = → 68.4 M− MR → 31.6

Another method of finding the equivalent discount rate is to add together the equivalent rates that are subtracted in Step 1. Notice in the example that the sum of 20%, 8%, and 3.6% is 31.6%, which is the equivalent discount rate.

Yet another method is recommended when a calculator is being used. This method utilizes the complements of the discount rates. The solution to the example above using this method is given below. Of course, the sum of the net-price percent and the equivalent discount rate must equal 100%.

Solution:

With % key:

MC 100 M+ × 80 % × 90 % × 95 % → 68.4

M− MR → 31.6, means 31.6%

Without % key:

MC 1 M+ × .8 × .9 × .95 = M− MR → 0.316

● **Exercise 12–2**

A. For each of the following, find the **(a)** net-price percent and **(b)** equivalent discount rate.

1. 25% and 20%

2. 20% and $12\frac{1}{2}$%

3. 20% and $16\frac{2}{3}$%

4. $16\frac{2}{3}$% and 10%

5. $33\frac{1}{3}$%, 20%, and 10%

6. 20%, 10%, and 10%

7. 25%, 20%, and 10%

8. 20%, 20%, and $12\frac{1}{2}$%

9. $33\frac{1}{3}$%, 25%, and 10%

10. 25%, 15%, and 10%

11. 25%, 10%, and 10%

12. $16\frac{2}{3}$%, 10%, and 5%

B. For each of the following, find the equivalent discount rate, the amount of discount, and the net price.

	List Price	Trade Discounts	Equivalent Rate	Amount of Discount	Net Price
1.	$ 714.00	10%, 5%	_____	_____	_____
2.	729.00	20%, 5%	_____	_____	_____
3.	630.00	25%, 5%	_____	_____	_____
4.	750.00	$12\frac{1}{2}$%, 10%	_____	_____	_____
5.	562.50	25%, 20%, 20%	_____	_____	_____
6.	765.25	30%, 20%, $12\frac{1}{2}$%	_____	_____	_____
7.	4,572.00	20%, $16\frac{2}{3}$%, 10%	40	_____	_____
8.	607.50	20%, $12\frac{1}{2}$%, 10%	_____	_____	_____
9.	7,125.00	$33\frac{1}{3}$%, 10%, 10%	_____	_____	_____
10.	573.75	$16\frac{2}{3}$%, 10%, 10%	_____	_____	_____
11.	5,400.00	15%, 10%, 5%	_____	_____	_____
12.	4,800.00	10%, 10%, 5%	_____	_____	_____

C. Solve these problems.

1. A large department store sells watches for $99 each. An importer of fine watches has offered trade discounts of 30%, 20%, and 10%. A second importer has offered to supply watches of equal quality at discount rates of 40%, 10%, and 10%. Other things being equal, is the first or second offer better?

2. A department store buyer purchased the following amounts of merchandise from O'Brien and Riley Products Company: **(a)** $2,375, **(b)** $1,725, **(c)** $1,445, and **(d)** $2,615. The store is allowed discounts of 25%, 20%, and 10%. Use the equivalent discount rate to find the amount of discount allowed on each of these amounts.

3. The series of trade discounts allowed on a number of invoices that should be paid today is 20%, 20%, and 15%. The totals of the invoices are: **(a)** $785, **(b)** $1,262.50, **(c)** $2,575, and **(d)** $847.50. Use the equivalent discount rate to find the total of the discounts allowed on these invoices.

4. Warner Hardware Company received a few shipments of different kinds of small tools from a manufacturer. Each shipment is allowed trade discounts of $33\frac{1}{3}$% and $2\frac{1}{2}$%. The list price may be multiplied by what percent to find the net price of each shipment?

5. The following invoices are subject to trade discounts of 35%, 20%, and 10%: **(a)** $2,500, **(b)** $600, **(c)** $1,875, and **(d)** $2,800. Use the net-price percent to find the net price of each invoice.

6. A merchant plans to pay the following amounts on invoices from Mayer Manufacturing Company, which grants discounts of 20%, $12\frac{1}{2}$%, and

10%. The total amounts of the invoices that are subject to the series of discounts are **(a)** $850, **(b)** $375, **(c)** $550, and **(d)** $1,250. Use the net-price percent to find the total net price that the merchant owes on these invoices.

Cash Discounts

The arrangements agreed to by the buyer and seller regarding when payment for goods is to be made are the **terms** of the sale. Whether the seller expects cash immediately or grants credit to the buyer, the terms should be clear and definite. To help minimize any misunderstanding between the buyer and seller, the terms of sale usually appear on the invoice and are considered to be a part of the sales agreement.

There are many variations in the terms granted by sellers. In some trades the terms are strictly cash. In such trades the terms specified on the invoice may be **COD,** which means cash on delivery, or **terms cash,** which means that payment is expected immediately, say within five days from the date of the invoice. Most manufacturers and wholesalers, however, customarily grant the buyer a longer specified period of time, known as the **credit period,** in which to pay. For example, the words **net 30 days** or simply **n/30** on the invoice mean that a 30-day credit period is being allowed. Credit terms have become traditional in most trades because this practice enables the dealer to carry a larger stock of merchandise and thereby to increase sales. In many cases, the dealer is able to sell the merchandise before the end of the credit period.

A **cash discount** is one that is granted in consideration of immediate payment or payment within a specified time. Cash discounts may be shown on an invoice in a variety of ways.

Ordinary Dating. When cash discounts are granted, they are made part of the credit terms and appear on the invoice. Probably the most popular terms are **2/10, n/30.** These terms mean that the regular credit period is 30 days and that the seller will permit the buyer to deduct 2% of the net amount if the merchandise is paid for within 10 days from the date of the invoice. If the buyer does not pay within 10 days from the date of the invoice, there remains an additional 20 days within which to pay the net amount without being liable for an interest charge or a late fee.

When an invoice shows terms such as 2/10, 1/30, n/60, the number at the left of the diagonal line in each of the first two terms is the discount rate in percent; the number at the right in each term is the number of days allowed in the cash-discount period or the credit period; and the **n** in the last term indicates the net amount (after deducting trade discounts).

Whether or not the buyer earns the cash discount depends on when the payment is made. If the exact number of days from the date of invoice to the date of payment does not exceed the days in the cash discount period, the buyer is entitled to the cash discount. The amount of the cash discount is found by multiplying the net amount of the invoice by the cash-discount percent. If payment is made within the specified cash-discount period, the amount of the cash discount is deducted from the net amount of the invoice.

Example: What amount would be required to pay an invoice for $600 worth of merchandise, terms 2/10, 1/30, n/60, if paid **(a)** within 10 days from the date of the invoice, or **(b)** within 11 to 30 days from the date of the invoice, or **(c)** within 31 to 60 days from the date of the invoice?

Solution: **(a)** Payment within 10 days from date of invoice:

$600   net amount of invoice (after trade discounts)
  12   cash discount (2% of $600)
─────
$588   payment in full

(b) Payment within 11 to 30 days from date of invoice:

$600   net amount of invoice
   6   cash discount (1% of $600)
─────
$594   payment in full

(c) If payment is not made within 30 days from date of invoice, the cash-discount period will have expired. Therefore, the net amount of the invoice, $600, is to be paid.

End-of-Month Dating. The abbreviation **EOM,** meaning end of month, is commonly used in the terms shown on invoices. **EOM** in the terms means that the cash-discount period or the credit period to which it applies begins at the end of the month in which the invoice is dated. Sometimes the abbreviation **prox.** for the Latin *proximo,* meaning next month, is used instead of EOM. When 10/EOM (or 10/prox.) appears on an invoice, it means that the seller is granting the buyer a credit period of 10 days after the end of the month. Similarly, 2/10 EOM means that the buyer is allowed a 2 percent discount if the amount is paid within 10 days after the end of the month. In the following example, the invoice is dated November 12 with terms of 2/10 EOM. The buyer, therefore, is entitled to a cash discount if the goods are paid for by December 10.

Example A: An invoice amounting to $200 with terms of 2/10 EOM is dated November 12. What amount would be required to pay this invoice in full if payment is made on December 10?

Solution:
$200   net amount of invoice
   4   cash discount (2% of $200)
─────
$196   payment in full

Or   on a calculator *with* $\boxed{\%}$ key:

$$200 \boxed{-} 2 \boxed{\%} \rightarrow 196, \text{ means } \$196$$

$$\text{or } 200 \boxed{-} 2 \boxed{\%} \boxed{=} \rightarrow 196$$

Without $\boxed{\%}$ key:

$$200 \boxed{\times} .98 \boxed{=} \rightarrow 196$$

If an invoice with EOM terms is dated on or after the twenty-sixth day of the month, it is treated as if it were dated at the beginning of the next month. Thus, an invoice dated October 26 with terms of 2/10 EOM is subject to a cash discount if paid on or before December 10.

As a general rule, when cash discounts are granted but the end of the credit period (such as n/30) is not specified, an invoice is considered to have a credit period of 20 days beyond the cash-discount period. As with ordinary credit terms, the invoice may be paid during this time without penalty for late payment. An invoice dated October 26 with terms of 2/10 EOM could be paid on December 30 without penalty for late payment.

Example B: An invoice dated October 26, with terms of 3/10 prox., has a net amount of $800. If the seller charges $1\frac{1}{2}\%$ per month for late payment, how much is needed to pay the invoice in full on December 30?

Solution: As the invoice amount is not being paid on or before December 10, there is no cash discount. The amount, however, is being paid within 20 days after the cash-discount period so there is no penalty. The net amount of the invoice, $800, is needed to pay in full.

Receipt-of-Goods Dating. Often a relatively long period of time is required to transport the goods from the seller to the buyer, as via a slow freight train going across the country or a slow ship going to a foreign market. In such cases, basing the terms on the date on which the buyer receives the goods, rather than on the invoice date, is justified. The abbreviation for receipt of goods is **ROG.** Terms such as 2/10, n/30 ROG mean that the cash-discount and credit periods begin when the buyer receives the goods. In other words, the date of receipt, as shown by the bill of lading, is used as the beginning date for determining the last date of the cash-discount period and the last date of the credit period.

Example: An invoice with a net amount of $500 and dated November 15 had terms of 3/10, n/30 ROG. The goods listed on the invoice were received by the buyer on December 1, and payment was made in full on December 11. How much was paid?

Solution: The invoice amount was paid within 10 days from the date on which the goods were received. Therefore, the discount was allowed.

$$
\begin{array}{ll}
\$500 & \text{net amount} \\
\underline{15} & \text{cash discount (3\% of \$500)} \\
\$485 & \text{payment in full}
\end{array}
$$

Or on a calculator *with* ⬚%⬚ key:

$$500\ \boxed{-}\ 3\ \boxed{\%}\ \rightarrow 485,\ \text{means }\$485$$

Without ⬚%⬚ key:

$$500\ \boxed{\times}\ .97\ \boxed{=}\ \rightarrow 485$$

Extra Dating. In order to sell seasonal goods when they are not in season, **extra dating** may be used. Thus, a manufacturer of skis is likely to try to induce sporting goods dealers to buy this product in the summer by offering them extra dating. This permits them to delay paying until the winter season approaches. One advantage to the manufacturer is that by shipping the goods during the off season, less storage space is needed.

Extra dating is shown on an invoice or bill in ways such as these: 4/10–60 extra, or 3/10–90 ex., or 5/10–60x. Thus, 2/10–90x means that a 2 percent discount is allowed if the invoice is paid within 10 days plus 90 extra days, that is, a total of 100 days, from the date of the invoice.

Example:

An invoice for a shipment of umbrellas costing $300 net was dated September 14, terms 5/10–60 ex. **(a)** What is the last date of the cash-discount period? **(b)** How much will pay this invoice in full any time up to the end of the cash-discount period?

Solution:

(a) A 5% cash discount may be taken if the invoice is paid within 70 days (10 days plus 60 extra days) from the date of the invoice. The 70th day from September 14 is November 23.

(b) The amount that will pay this invoice in full on November 23 or an earlier date is $285:

$$\begin{array}{ll} \$300 & \text{net amount of invoice} \\ \underline{15} & \text{cash discount (5\% of \$300)} \\ \$285 & \text{payment in full} \end{array}$$

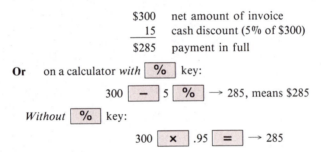

Or   on a calculator *with* $\boxed{\%}$ key:

300 $\boxed{-}$ 5 $\boxed{\%}$ → 285, means $285

Without $\boxed{\%}$ key:

300 $\boxed{\times}$ .95 $\boxed{=}$ → 285

● Exercise 12–3

A. For each of the following, find the cash discount and the net amount.

	Date of Invoice	Amount of Invoice	Terms	Date Paid	Cash Discount	Net Amount
1.	November 14	$ 620.00	2/10, n/30	November 24	_____	_____
2.	October 15	409.00	3/10, 1/30, n/60	October 24	_____	_____
3.	December 18	208.00	2/10, 1/30, n/60	January 11	_____	_____
4.	March 19	700.00	3/15, 2/30, n/60	April 3	_____	_____
5.	June 28	672.00	2/10, 1/40, n/90	August 7	_____	_____
6.	August 27	5,053.00	3/10, 2/45, n/90	September 6	_____	_____
7.	April 11	8,840.00	2/15, 1/45, n/90	May 24	_____	_____
8.	May 14	451.80	3/10, 2/30, n/60	June 14	_____	_____
9.	July 3	256.60	2/10, 1/45, n/90	August 18	_____	_____
10.	January 16	7,983.16	2/10, 1/30, n/60	January 26	_____	_____

Part 3. Mathematics Applications in Operating a Business

B. For each of the following, find the cash discount and the net amount.

	Date of Invoice	Amount of Invoice	Goods Received	Terms	Date Paid	Cash Discount	Net Amount
1.	March 12	$ 720.00	March 15	2/10, n/30 EOM	April 10	_____	_____
2.	November 19	552.00	November 21	3/10 prox.	December 10	_____	_____
3.	June 8	813.00	June 12	4/10 EOM	July 9	_____	_____
4.	October 24	4,084.00	November 3	2/10, n/30 ROG	November 13	_____	_____
5.	July 17	721.40	July 22	2/10-60 extra	September 27	_____	_____
6.	April 25	532.10	May 9	3/10 ROG	May 19	_____	_____
7.	August 16	406.30	August 20	2/10 EOM	September 30	_____	406.30
8.	May 7	4,518.00	May 8	3/10-90 ex.	August 15	_____	_____
9.	November 2	6,658.00	November 27	3/10, 1/20 ROG	December 17	196	_____
10.	April 28	831.60	May 1	4/10 prox.	June 8	_____	_____
11.	June 4	9,501.54	June 7	2/10-60x	August 13	_____	_____
12.	December 23	4,712.23	January 15	3/10, 1/30 ROG	February 14	_____	_____

C. Solve these problems.

1. What is the correct amount of the check sent in payment for $362.50 worth of merchandise, with terms of 3/10, n/30, if the invoice was dated September 12 and paid on September 22?

2. An invoice for $950 worth of goods was issued on November 10 with credit terms of 3/10, 2/20, n/30. How much should the buyer pay on **(a)** November 20? **(b)** November 30? **(c)** December 8?

3. Merchandise totaling $667.50 was bought on August 22, terms 2/10 EOM. **(a)** What is the last date on which the cash discount may be taken? **(b)** If payment were made on September 8, how much would pay the invoice in full?

4. An invoice for $353.40 dated August 16 has terms of 2/10, 1/15, n/30. How much will pay this invoice in full on **(a)** August 24? **(b)** August 31? **(c)** September 15?

5. An invoice for $678.53 worth of goods with terms of 2/15, n/60 is dated August 25. Find **(a)** the last date on which the cash discount may be taken and **(b)** the amount needed to pay this invoice in full on that date.

6. Goods invoiced at $987 were received on May 10. The invoice, dated May 7, listed terms of 2/10 ROG and was paid in full on May 20. The check to pay this invoice was for how much?

7. An invoice for $1,548.90 was dated July 1 and had terms of 3/10 prox. How much should the buyer pay to the seller on August 10?

8. An invoice for $385 was dated July 16 and had terms of 2/20–60 extra. Find **(a)** the final date on which the cash discount may be taken and **(b)** the amount needed to pay the invoice in full on August 17.

Trade and Cash Discounts on the Invoice

An invoice is normally sent to the buyer by the seller through the mail, although occasionally it may be sent with the merchandise. Multiple copies of the invoice are usually prepared, for these may serve as memoranda for the seller's accounting and shipping departments. Furthermore, the packing slips that are enclosed in the cartons or packages in which the goods are sent to the buyer may be duplicate copies of the invoice. The rules pertaining to price changes, methods of payment, provisions for returning goods for credit or refund, and other business policies may be printed on the back side of an invoice if there is insufficient space on the front.

After having been received, one of the first checks on the accuracy of an invoice is made by the buyer's receiving department. This department verifies that the quantity of merchandise listed on the invoice has been received, that the merchandise meets the buyer's specifications, and that it has not been damaged. Merchandise that does not meet the specifications or that is damaged may be returned, or the seller may give the buyer an allowance which reduces the price of the goods. Before any invoice is paid, the accuracy of the computations, the terms agreed on, and other provisions should be checked carefully. Many companies employ office workers whose principal duties include the auditing of invoices. These employees check the accuracy of the arithmetical computations, including the proper handling of freight charges, insurance, discounts, and other provisions that were included in the sales agreement.

Many invoices are subject to both trade and cash discounts. When both kinds of discounts appear on an invoice, the trade discounts are computed first and deducted from the total list price of the merchandise. This gives the net amount of the invoice on which the cash discount is based. The cash discount is always based on the net price of the merchandise whether or not the list price is shown.

Example: An invoice that shows $500 worth of merchandise at list price, less trade discounts of 20% and 10%, with terms of 2/10, n/30 is to be paid within the cash-discount period. How much should the buyer pay?

Solution:

$500.00	list price
100.00	(20% of $500)
$400.00	remainder
40.00	(10% of $400)
$360.00	net amount of invoice
7.20	(2% of $360)
$352.80	payment in full

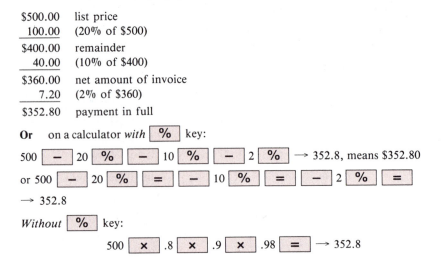

Or on a calculator *with* [%] key:

500 [−] 20 [%] [−] 10 [%] [−] 2 [%] → 352.8, means $352.80

or 500 [−] 20 [%] [=] [−] 10 [%] [=] [−] 2 [%] [=]

→ 352.8

Without [%] key:

500 [×] .8 [×] .9 [×] .98 [=] → 352.8

Part 3. Mathematics Applications in Operating a Business

Returned Goods. Discounts are allowed to the buyer on the basis of the goods actually bought. If part of the merchandise is returned by the buyer, it was not bought and is not subject to trade or cash discounts. When returned goods are listed on the invoice, the buyer must deduct the amount representing their value before computing any discounts that may be allowed.

Example:

An invoice that shows an amount of $400 for merchandise and terms of 2/10, n/30 is to be paid within the cash-discount period. If $50 worth of the merchandise has been returned, how much should the buyer pay?

Solution:

$400	amount of invoice
50	value of returned goods
$350	basis for cash discount
7	cash discount (2% of $350)
$343	payment in full

Or on a calculator *with* % key:

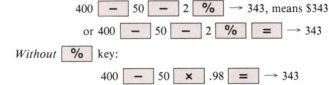

400 $-$ 50 $-$ 2 % $\rightarrow$ 343, means $343

or 400 $-$ 50 $-$ 2 % = $\rightarrow$ 343

Without % key:

400 $-$ 50 $\times$ .98 = $\rightarrow$ 343

Freight Charges. If freight charges have been prepaid by the seller and have been added to the invoice, they must be subtracted from the total to find the basis on which the discount is calculated. The amount of the discount is subtracted from the basis for the discount to find the net value of the merchandise. The freight charges must then be added to the net value of the merchandise to find the amount that is to be paid.

Example:

The total of an invoice with terms of 2/10, n/30 amounts to $1,198.85. Of this amount, $14 is for freight charges that were prepaid by the seller. How much is needed to pay this invoice within the cash-discount period?

Solution:

$1,198.85	total of invoice including freight
$-$ 14.00	freight charges
$1,184.85	basis for cash discount
$-$ 23.70	cash discount (2% of $1,184.85)
$1,161.15	net value of merchandise
$+$ 14.00	freight charges
$1,175.15	payment in full

Or on a calculator *with* % key:

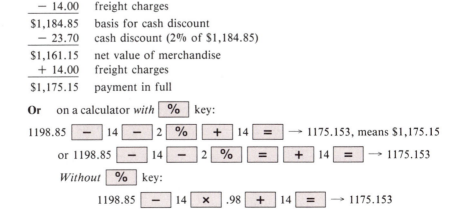

1198.85 $-$ 14 $-$ 2 % $+$ 14 = $\rightarrow$ 1175.153, means $1,175.15

or 1198.85 $-$ 14 $-$ 2 % = $+$ 14 = $\rightarrow$ 1175.153

Without % key:

1198.85 $-$ 14 $\times$ .98 $+$ 14 = $\rightarrow$ 1175.153

Chapter 12. Merchandising

Of course, there is no need to subtract the freight charges when the basis for the cash discount is shown on the invoice, as it is in Figure 12–1 below. After the cash discount has been deducted, however, the freight charges should be added to the net value of the merchandise to find the amount that the buyer pays.

ARMOUR PRODUCTS CO.

5140 Bigelow Boulevard   Pittsburgh, PA 15201

SOLD TO Hamilton Hardware Company

2306 Cedarcroft Avenue

Baltimore, MD 21214

INVOICE NO. H–1632

DATE Jan. 20, 19––

SHIPPED VIA Prepaid Freight

TERMS 2/10, n/30

Quantity	Stock No.	Description	List Price	Total
20	SS–2229	Cookware, 10–pc. Set	61.95	1,239.00
10	SS–4627	Pressure Cooker, 6–qt.	29.95	299.50
6	SS–4428	Pressure Cooker, 4–qt.	24.50	147.00
		TOTAL LIST		1,685.50
		Less 20% and 12½ %		505.65
				1,179.85
		Plus prepaid freight charges		14.00
		Net Total		1,193.85

Figure 12–1 An Invoice

Partial Payment of Invoice. Sometimes a buyer cannot pay the full amount due within the cash-discount period but can make a partial payment on the account to take advantage of the cash discount. When a partial payment is made within the cash-discount period, the buyer is entitled to a discount on the proportionate amount paid.

A 2% discount entitles the buyer to cancel $1 of debt by paying 98 cents. Thus, if the terms are 2/10, n/30, every 98 cents the buyer pays within 10 days entitles the buyer to a $1 reduction in the debt. If the terms are 3/10 EOM, the buyer can reduce $1 of debt for each 97 cents that is paid within 10 days after the end of the month.

To determine how much the buyer is reducing the debt by making a partial payment, divide the amount of the payment by the complement of the cash-discount rate. As you recall, the complement is found by subtracting the cash-discount percent from 100 percent.

Example: An invoice for an amount of $800 was dated December 12, terms 2/10, n/30. On December 15, merchandise listed at $50 was returned. The buyer made a payment of $500 on December 21. Find **(a)** the amount by which the partial payment reduced the debt and **(b)** the balance due.

Solution:

(a) $100\% - 2\% = 98\% = 0.98$ complement

     $\$500 \div 0.98 = \$510.20$ amount credited

(b) $\$800 - \$50 - \$510.20 = \$239.80$ balance due

Or   on a calculator *with* $\boxed{\%}$ key:

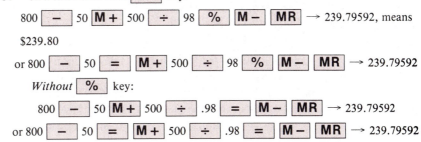

$800 \boxed{-} 50 \boxed{M+} 500 \boxed{\div} 98 \boxed{\%} \boxed{M-} \boxed{MR} \rightarrow 239.79592$, means $239.80

or $800 \boxed{-} 50 \boxed{=} \boxed{M+} 500 \boxed{\div} 98 \boxed{\%} \boxed{M-} \boxed{MR} \rightarrow 239.79592$

Without $\boxed{\%}$ key:

$800 \boxed{-} 50 \boxed{M+} 500 \boxed{\div} .98 \boxed{=} \boxed{M-} \boxed{MR} \rightarrow 239.79592$

or $800 \boxed{-} 50 \boxed{=} \boxed{M+} 500 \boxed{\div} .98 \boxed{=} \boxed{M-} \boxed{MR} \rightarrow 239.79592$

● **Exercise 12–4**

    A. Find the amount credited to the buyer's account for each partial payment and the balance due.

	Date of Invoice	Amount of Invoice	Returned Goods	Terms	Amount Paid	Date of Payment	Amount Credited	Balance Due
1.	June 4	$ 225	$ 25	2/10, n/30	$ 125	June 14	_____	_____
2.	March 12	621	51	3/15, n/60	450	March 26	_____	_____
3.	November 19	400	-0-	3/10 EOM	200	December 9	_____	_____
4.	October 27	185	15	5/10 prox.	100	December 10	_____	_____
5.	June 18	250	-0-	4/20–60 extra	150	September 4	_____	_____
6.	January 14	960	-0-	3/10, 1/20, n/60	560	February 3	_____	_____
7.	August 26	1,400	-0-	5/10–90 ex.	1,200	December 4	_____	_____
8.	April 18	1,600	200	4/20 EOM	1,000	May 18	_____	_____
9.	May 7	2,600	150	6/10 prox.	1,500	June 8	_____	_____
10.	November 2	3,000	300	3/15–60x	1,700	January 16	_____	_____

    B. Solve these problems.

      1. A wholesale company made a sale of merchandise that had a list price of $525 and a trade discount of 20%. The company prepared the sales invoice on April 16 and included a freight charge of $12.50. The credit terms were 2/10, n/30. How much should the buyer pay on **(a)** April 24? **(b)** April 30?

2. A retailer received an invoice that was dated September 16 for the following goods: 2 radios at a list price of $289 each less trade discounts of 20% and 10%, and 12 adapters at a list price of $32 each less trade discounts of 25% and 5%. Freight charges that had been prepaid by the seller and listed on the invoice totaled $15.85. The terms were 2/10 EOM. Find **(a)** the last date on which the cash discount may be taken and **(b)** the total amount needed to pay the invoice in full on that date.

3. A dealer bought merchandise that had a list price of $900 less a trade discount of 25%. The invoice, dated June 12, showed terms of 2/10, n/30. On June 15, the dealer returned merchandise listed at $100 because it had been damaged. How much should the dealer pay on June 21?

4. A total of $31.48 worth of merchandise was returned. The total amount of the invoice was $2,198.23. Find the amount needed to pay this invoice, terms 1/15, n/60, within the cash-discount period.

5. Regular terms of the Hopkins Electric Company are 2/10, 1/30, n/60. On June 6, Aileen Bain bought electric supplies worth $203.64 from the company. On June 27, she purchased supplies totaling $638.45. On July 6, she sent a check in complete payment of both invoices. The check was written for the correct amount. How much was the check?

6. The total amount of an invoice, including freight of $5.84, was $972.21. Terms were 2/10, n/30, and the buyer returned $82.65 worth of merchandise. Find the amount needed to pay this invoice within the cash-discount period.

7. A company whose terms were 2/10, n/30 received a check for $423.36 from a customer for a bill of goods purchased 8 days before. How much discount did the customer deduct?

8. On May 4 a merchant bought goods totaling $267.98 on terms 1/10, n/30. Of this amount, $4.42 was for freight. The next day the merchant returned merchandise and received a credit of $16.50. Five days later a check for $150 was sent to pay part of the bill with the understanding that a discount would be received for the partial payment. How much was due on June 3?

9. Hanson Shoe Company purchased merchandise totaling $2,621.50 from the Adams Shoe Company. The terms of the invoice, which was dated August 1, were 3/10, 2/30, n/60. Hanson Shoe Company could not pay the invoice in full, but on August 9 the company sent a check for $1,200 to apply as a partial payment. On August 30, the company sent another check for $800, and on September 30, a check for the balance. Discounts were granted on the partial payments. Find **(a)** the amount that was credited to the account of Hanson Shoe Company by Adams Shoe Company after receiving the check of August 9, **(b)** the amount of credit granted after receiving the check of August 30, and **(c)** the amount of the check that was sent by Hanson Shoe Company on September 30 to settle the account.

10. A customer saved $62.56 by taking advantage of a 5% cash discount on an invoice. What was the amount of the invoice?

11. On an invoice for $750 with terms of 5/10, 2/20, n/30, dated March 24, two partial payments were made: $300 on April 2 and $350 on April 12. Find the balance due after these payments.

12. On April 12, David Weber purchased $4,250 worth of television sets, terms 4/10, 2/30, n/60. On April 21, he made a payment of $3,000 on account. How much discount did he earn by making this payment?

CASH DISCOUNTS COMPARED TO SIMPLE INTEREST

Businesses do not always have sufficient cash on hand to take advantage of cash discounts offered by companies from which they buy. To enable them to pay invoices within the cash-discount period, many businesses borrow money from banks on short-term loans. As you recall, a cash discount is a given percent of the net amount of the invoice which is saved by paying within a relatively short period of time. Interest, on the other hand, is paid at an annual rate. Cash discounts, even at 1% or 2%, on a given number of dollars, will generally amount to more than the interest on the same number of dollars at a relatively high annual rate. For this reason, businesses often borrow to take advantage of cash discounts.

The amount saved is the cash discount less the interest. The amount necessary to pay the invoice within the cash-discount period is the difference between the amount owed and the discount(s). The length of time for which the money is needed for a specific invoice is the difference between the number of days in the cash-discount period and the credit period. If more than the necessary amount of money is borrowed, the extra amount is considered to be for purposes other than to pay the invoice. Similarly, if the money is borrowed for a period of time that is longer than the difference between the cash-discount terms and the credit terms, the money is being used for additional purposes. Therefore, to find the interest on an invoice for $600 with terms of 2/10, n/30, the principal is $588 ($600 − 2% of $600) and the time is 20 days (30 days − 10 days).

Example:

On June 18, Helen Stowers bought merchandise invoiced at $2,400 with terms of 2/10, n/30. In order to pay the invoice on June 28, she borrowed the money at 12%. How much did she save by borrowing to take advantage of the discount?

Solution:

Discount = 2% × $2,400 = $48
Principal = $2,400 − $48 = $2,352
Time = 30 days − 10 days = 20 days
Interest = $2,352 × 0.12 × $\frac{20}{360}$ = $15.68

Cash Discount − Interest = Amount Saved
$48.00 − $15.68 = $32.32

1. By borrowing $1,008 for 45 days at 18% interest, a business was able to pay cash and obtain a discount of $42 on an invoice. What amount was saved by borrowing the money to take the discount?

2. On August 14, a dealer bought $2,500 worth of merchandise on terms of 3/10, n/60. **(a)** What is the amount necessary to pay for the merchandise on August 24? **(b)** If that amount was borrowed at 15% for 50 days, how much was saved by taking the cash discount?

3. The Bloomfield Furniture Company bought $4,000 worth of merchandise on terms of 2/10, n/30. In order to take advantage of the cash discount, the company borrowed the money at 12% and paid the bill at the end of the cash-discount period. How much did the company save by borrowing the money?

4. How much can a company save in each of the following by borrowing money at interest in order to take each cash discount?

	Amount of Invoice	Terms	Interest Rate
a.	$ 569.70	2/10, n/30	16%
b.	2,083.50	3/10, n/45	14%
c.	5,477.25	2/20, n/60	12%

PRICING GOODS

After marketable goods are obtained through manufacture or purchase, other expenditures are required before the goods are sold to customers. Such expenditures are **operating expenses.** These include sales salaries, office and administrative salaries, advertising, rent, sales taxes, and the like. The amount that is added to the merchandise cost to cover the operating expenses and to provide a profit is the **markon.** The word **markup** is an older term that is still sometimes used to mean markon, but in current accounting terminology and in this book, **markup** means an increase in an original selling price. **Markdown** means a decrease in an original selling price.

Markon Equation

The amount the seller marks onto the merchandise cost to determine the selling price is sometimes computed in relation to the cost of the merchandise and sometimes in relation to the selling price of the merchandise. In other words, markon may be based on cost or on selling price.

Regardless of whether markon is based on cost or on selling price, the markon is always the amount added to cost to find the selling price. The basic relationship of cost, markon, and selling price is summarized in the following equation:

$$Cost + Markon = Selling\ Price$$

Obviously if any two of these quantities are supplied, the third can be found by substituting the given quantities in the equation and solving for the unknown. Thus, if the cost is $75 and the markon is $50, then:

$$\$75 + \$50 = Selling\ Price = \$125$$

and

$$Cost + \$50 = \$125$$

and

$$\$75 + Markon = \$125.$$

Markon Based on Cost

Manufacturers, owners of small retail businesses, and large merchandising concerns that use a wide variety of markon rates to price their merchandise are more likely to use cost as the basis for determining the amount of markon for the goods. Manufacturers use cost accounting systems to find the cost of their products and are more likely to compare markon, selling price, operating expenses, and net income or loss to the cost of the product. Owners of small businesses, perhaps because they actively participate in purchasing the merchandise, are cost conscious and are more likely to think in cost terms. Furthermore, in some retail businesses, such as appliance stores, furniture stores, and jewelry stores, in which the variety of the goods is limited and the cost of each item is relatively expensive, keeping records on a cost basis is preferable.

The **markon rate** is a percent that may be applied to either the cost basis or the selling-price basis to find the amount of the markon. When the rate of markon and the base are given, the amount of the markon can be found easily through the use of the percentage equation; that is, by multiplying the base by the rate. The base, whether cost or selling price, is always equal to 100% or 1.

Finding the Selling Price When Markon is Based on Cost. When the rate of markon is based on cost, the selling price may be found in two steps:

1. Find the amount of the markon. As the rate of markon is based on cost, the amount of the markon is found by multiplying the cost by the rate.

$$Cost \times Rate\ of\ Markon = Markon$$

2. Find the selling price by using the markon equation.

$$Cost + Markon = Selling\ Price$$

A retailer bought a chair for $50. The rate of markon to cover the operating expenses and a reasonable net income is 60% of cost. At this rate of markon, what is the lowest price at which the chair should be sold?

Solution:

1. $50 × 60% = $30   markon

2. cost + markon = selling price

$50 + $30 = $80

Or   50 ☐× ☐ 160 ☐% ☐ → 80, means $80

• ## Exercise 12–6

A. The markon, or gross-profit, rate in each of the following problems is based on cost. Find the selling price.

	Cost	Markon Rate			Cost	Gross Profit Operating Expenses	Net Income
1.	$ 7.50	20%		7.	$ 89.76	15%	10%
2.	9.60	25%		8.	108.60	20%	8%
3.	32.00	$18\frac{3}{4}$%		9.	142.30	25%	7%
4.	53.00	30%		10.	273.69	$33\frac{1}{3}$%	10%
5.	64.50	$33\frac{1}{3}$%		11.	458.20	40%	9%
6.	79.80	50%		12.	836.40	$37\frac{1}{2}$%	$7\frac{1}{2}$%

B. Solve these problems.

1. A jeweler priced a watch that cost $85 at a markon rate of 65% based on cost. How much was the marked selling price?

2. An equipment dealer marks goods at 45% above total cost. At what price should an electric motor be sold that cost $92.50 plus freight of $3.50?

3. A dealer paid $674.50 for a refrigerator and $16.50 for the freight charge. What is the lowest price at which the refrigerator should sell at a markon rate of 55% based on total cost?

4. A travel kit costs a dealer $12.60. The operating expenses are 25% of the cost, and the dealer wants to gain $8\frac{1}{3}$% net income on cost. What should be the selling price of the kit?

5. A washing machine is billed to a dealer at $380, less 25% and 10%, plus a freight charge of $7.50. What should be the selling price of this machine if a markon of 30% on total cost is required?

6. A retail fruit dealer bought 20 crates of strawberries (16 baskets to the crate) at $27 a crate, delivered. The estimate was that 20 baskets would spoil and have to be thrown away. At what price per basket should the remainder be sold for a markon of $33\frac{1}{3}$% on the cost of the 20 crates?

***Finding the Cost When the Selling Price and the Rate of Markon on Cost
are Known.*** To find the cost of an article when the selling price and the rate of
markon based on cost are given:

1. Use the markon equation to express the selling price as a percent of the
   cost.
2. Divide the selling price by that percent.

Example:

The buyer for Jean's Dress Shop wants to buy a line of dresses to sell for $120 each. She
knows that the rate of markon must be 50% of the cost in order for the shop to cover its
costs and expenses and earn a satisfactory net income. What is the highest price she can
afford to pay for each dress?

Solution:

1. Find the selling-price percent.

$$
\begin{array}{r}
100\% \text{ of cost} = \text{Cost} \\
+\ 50\% \text{ of cost} = \text{Markon} \\
\hline
150\% \text{ of cost} = \text{Selling Price} = \$120
\end{array}
$$

2. Find the cost.

$$
\begin{aligned}
150\% \times \text{cost} &= \$120 \\
\text{cost} &= \$120 \div 1.5 \\
\text{cost} &= \$80
\end{aligned}
$$

Or   120 $\boxed{\div}$ 150 $\boxed{\%}$ → 80, means $80

● **Exercise 12–7**

A. The markon, or gross-profit, rate in each of the following problems is
based on cost. Find the cost.

	Selling Price	Markon Rate			Selling Price	Gross Profit Operating Expenses	Gross Profit Net Income
1.	$ 24.18	24%		**7.**	$ 199.65	30%	$7\frac{1}{2}\%$
2.	35.64	32%		**8.**	411.75	26%	9%
3.	136.95	46%		**9.**	900.00	$46\frac{1}{4}\%$	10%
4.	341.16	20%		**10.**	1,223.30	50%	$12\frac{1}{2}\%$
5.	598.25	25%		**11.**	1,429.56	30%	15%
6.	876.70	$37\frac{1}{2}\%$		**12.**	3,114.15	60%	20%

B. Solve these problems.

1. A clothing store sells a line of belts at $29.76 each. What is the highest price
   the store can pay for each belt if the markon for this line is 60% of cost?

2. How much does a retailer pay for an article that sells for $117.95 if the
   markon rate is 75% of cost?

3. What is the maximum amount that a store owner should pay per dozen for
   neckties which sell at $19.80 each if the markon rate is 65% based on cost?

4. The Tempe Dress Shop computes its markon at 45% of cost. How much are **(a)** the cost and **(b)** the markon of a dress that sells for $127.60?

5. The selling price of a watch is $112. Operating expenses are 25% of cost, and the net income is 15% of cost. How much is the cost?

6. The selling price of an air conditioner is $675. The operating expenses are 38% of cost, and the retailer wants a net income of 12%. How much did the air conditioner cost the retailer?

7. How much was the selling price of a machine that was bought for $256 and sold at 25% above cost?

8. A refrigerator cost an appliance store $700. The owner of the store wants to sell the refrigerator at a price that will cover the operating expenses, which are 28% of the cost, and enable the store to earn a net income of 15% on cost. At what price should this refrigerator be marked?

Finding the Rate of Markon or Loss Based on Cost. When merchandise cost is used as the base, the rate (percent) of markon or loss is found by dividing the amount of the markon or of the loss by the cost.

$$Rate\ of\ Markon\ (or\ Loss) = \frac{Markon\ (or\ Loss)}{Cost}$$

Example A shows how the amount of markon and the rate of markon are found when the selling price and the cost are given.

Example A:

The selling price of an article is $180 and the cost is $108. Find **(a)** the markon and **(b)** the rate of markon based on cost.

Solution:

(a) Cost + Markon = Selling Price
$108 + Markon = $180
Markon = $180 − $108
Markon = $72

(b) Rate × Cost = Markon
Rate × $108 = $72
Rate = 72 $\boxed{\div}$ 108 $\boxed{\%}$ $\longrightarrow$ 66.66. . .
Rate = 66.67% or $66\frac{2}{3}$%

Example B shows how the amount of loss and rate of loss based on cost are found when the selling price and cost are given.

Example B:

An article that cost $48 was sold for $40. Find **(a)** the amount of the loss and **(b)** the rate of loss based on cost.

Solution:

(a) Loss = Cost − Selling Price
Loss = $48 − $40
Loss = $8

(b) Rate × Cost = Loss
Rate × $48 = $8
Rate = 8 $\boxed{\div}$ 48 $\boxed{\%}$ $\longrightarrow$ 16.66. . .
Rate = 16.67% or $16\frac{2}{3}$%

Part 3. Mathematics Applications in Operating a Business

- Exercise 12–8

A. In each of the following problems, find **(a)** the amount of the markon or of the loss and **(b)** the rate of markon or loss based on cost. Place an asterisk (*) to the right of each loss amount. Where applicable, round to the nearest 0.1%.

	Selling Price	Cost			Selling Price	Cost
1.	$90.00	$67.50	7.		$132.30	$ 97.65
2.	41.00	30.00	8.		83.10	114.36
3.	60.00	75.00	9.		128.50	172.40
4.	20.00	24.00	10.		118.22	93.00
5.	14.56	10.40	11.		186.00	200.00
6.	12.00	16.00	12.		375.00	300.00

B. Solve these problems.

1. A piano dealer bought a piano for $3,150 and sold it for $5,355. The markon is what percent of the cost?

2. A furniture dealer bought a table for $250 less 40% and sold it for $240. What rate of markon based on cost was used?

3. The list price of a clock is $67.50. A dealer bought one at the list price less $33\frac{1}{3}$% and 10% and sold it at the list price. The markon is what percent of the cost?

4. A store sells bolts for 75 cents each. The store pays $27 per gross, which is 144 bolts. What is the markon rate based on cost?

5. The selling price of an article is $8.70. If the markon rate is 45% of the cost, how much is the cost?

6. A merchant bought a machine for $400 and sold it at a gain of 20% based on cost. Determine the selling price.

7. A jewelry store bought a dozen rings for $5,400 less 25% and sold them at $675 each. What was the markon rate based on cost?

8. Amy Atherton bought a tract of land that she subdivided into eight lots at a total cost of $192,000. She had a house constructed on each lot for a total cost of $729,000. She sold the houses for $160,950 each. Her gross profit was what percent of the cost?

Markon Based on Selling Price

In many retail establishments, selling price is the basis for analyzing markon, expenses, and gains and losses. For example, the earnings of salespeople, the allocations for expenses such as advertising and rent, and various kinds of taxes are frequently based on net sales.

Finding the Selling Price When Markon is Based on Selling Price. The base is always equal to 100% or 1. When the selling price is the base, the selling price must equal 100% of itself. The difference between the selling-price percent (100%) and the markon percent gives the **cost percent.** In other words,

$$Selling\ Price = Cost + Markon$$
$$Selling\ Price - Markon = Cost.$$

Therefore:

$$Selling\text{-}Price\ Percent - Markon\ Percent = Cost\ Percent.$$

To find the selling price when the cost and rate of markon are known:

1. Find the cost percent by subtracting the markon percent from 100%.
2. Find the selling price by dividing the cost by the cost percent.

Example:

A merchant bought a quantity of pots at $31.50 each. The merchant knows that the markon must be 40% of the selling price to cover expenses and provide a satisfactory net income. What is the lowest price at which each pot can be sold to realize the desired markon rate?

Solution:

1. Find the cost percent.

$$Selling\ Price - Markon = Cost$$
$$100\% - 40\% = 60\%$$

2. Find the selling price.

$$60\% \times Selling\ Price = \$31.50$$
$$Selling\ Price = \$31.50 \div 0.6$$
$$Selling\ Price = \$52.50$$

Or   31.5 $\boxed{\div}$ 60 $\boxed{\%}$ $\rightarrow$ 52.5, means $52.50

• Exercise 12–9

A. The markon, or gross-profit, rate in each of these problems is based on selling price. Find the selling price.

	Cost	Markon Rate			Cost	Gross Profit Operating Expenses	Gross Profit Net Income
1.	$ 84.00	20%		**7.**	$ 62.78	20%	8%
2.	33.00	24%		**8.**	544.34	20%	12%
3.	98.00	44%		**9.**	66.69	33%	10%
4.	54.50	25%		**10.**	706.85	30%	$7\frac{1}{2}$%
5.	280.56	30%		**11.**	1,894.75	30%	15%
6.	374.67	40%		**12.**	2,999.70	42%	18%

Part 3. Mathematics Applications in Operating a Business

B. Solve these problems.

1. For how much should a retailer sell an article that cost $23.79 if the desired markon rate is 35% based on selling price?

2. The Montgomery Shoe Store bases its 35% markon rate on selling price. How much are (a) the selling price and (b) the markon for a pair of shoes that cost the store $71.76?

3. John Bolton purchased stationery sets from a wholesaler at $5.22 each. He wants a markon rate of 20% based on the selling price. At what price should he sell each set?

4. How much is the maximum amount that a merchant should pay for an article that is to be sold for $76.68 if the markon rate is 35% of cost?

5. The selling price of a bracelet is $126, which provides a markon of $42. What is the markon rate based on cost?

6. The cost of a dozen brackets is $18. If the markon rate is 40% based on selling price, how much is the selling price of each bracket?

7. A department store bought cloths at $86.40 a dozen. At what price should each cloth be sold for a markon of 40% on the retail price?

8. The New Haven Department Store bought 200 flight bags for $6,000. At what price should the store sell each bag if the markon rate for this merchandise is 45% of selling price?

9. A retailer bought a chair for $262.50. If the markon is to equal 45% of the cost, what should be the selling price?

10. A dealer bought a machine for $900 less trade discounts of 20% and 10%. The dealer sold the machine for $939.60. What was the markon rate based on cost?

Finding the Cost When Markon is Based on Selling Price. A retailer may carry three or four price lines of each kind of merchandise that is stocked. A clothing store, for example, may carry men's ties that sell for $15, $20, and $25. When the buyer wants more merchandise to replenish a specific line, the selling price is already known. The buyer must buy the new goods at a price that will yield a normal markon at the same selling price. In short, the buyer must know the highest per-unit cost that can be paid in order to maintain the selling-price policies.

The highest price that a dealer can pay is the cost, which can be found in two steps:

1. Find the cost percent by subtracting the markon rate from the selling-price percent (100%).
2. Find the cost by multiplying the selling price by the cost percent.

Chapter 12. Merchandising

The owner of the Muncie Dress Shop must buy dresses for a line that sells for $79.80 each. A markon rate of 40% on selling price is necessary in order to meet the operating expenses and earn a reasonable net income. What is the highest price the owner should pay for each dress?

Solution:

1. Find the cost percent.

$$\text{Selling Price} - \text{Markon} = \text{Cost}$$
$$100\% - 40\% = 60\%$$

2. Find the cost.

$$\text{Selling Price} \times \text{Cost Rate} = \text{Cost}$$
$$\$79.80 \times 0.6 = \$47.88$$

Or   79.8 $\boxed{\times}$ 60 $\boxed{\%}$ $\rightarrow$ 47.88, means $47.88

● Exercise 12–10

A. The markon, or gross-profit, rate is based on selling price. Find the cost in each of the following problems.

	Selling Price	Markon Rate			Selling Price	Gross Profit Operating Expenses	Gross Profit Net Income
1.	$ 27.00	40%		7.	$ 72.00	20%	10%
2.	30.00	25%		8.	127.50	25%	$8\frac{1}{3}\%$
3.	57.90	30%		9.	92.50	30%	12%
4.	85.60	27%		10.	116.25	23%	11%
5.	198.32	$37\frac{1}{2}\%$		11.	250.80	$41\frac{1}{3}\%$	$16\frac{2}{3}\%$
6.	382.20	$41\frac{2}{3}\%$		12.	521.56	50%	$12\frac{1}{2}\%$

B. Solve these problems.

1. The owner of a shoe store plans to buy shoes for a line that sells for $98.50 a pair. What is the highest price that should be paid for each pair if the markon must be 38% of the selling price?

2. The owner of a menswear store must buy a quantity of coats for a line that sells for $122.50 each. The operating expenses average 32% of the selling price and the net income 10% of the selling price. What is the highest price that should be paid for a dozen coats in this line?

3. The markon rate used by the Tucson Clothing Store is 45% of the selling price. How much are **(a)** the cost and **(b)** the markon of a sweater that sells for $98.96?

4. What is the most that a store owner should pay per dozen for suncaps which are to sell for $7.50 each if there is to be a 44% markon based on the retail price?

5. A buyer for the Columbia Store wants to buy toys to sell at $12.50 each. What is the highest price that he should pay for each toy if the store's operating expenses average 28% of the selling price and a net income of 8% of the selling price is desired?

6. A clothing store sells a dozen scarves for $155.04. If the operating expenses are 38% of the selling price and the net income is 14% of the selling price, how much does each scarf cost the store?

7. A dealer sells a machine for $1,636.25. If the markon rate is $37\frac{1}{2}$% of cost, how much is the cost?

8. The owner of a garden shop bought 216 plants for $25.92 and paid $5.13 for delivery to the shop. At what price per dozen should the plants be sold if the markon is 60% of the cost?

9. A rack that cost $77.40 has a markon rate of 24% based on selling price. How much is the selling price?

10. The manager of an office equipment store bought some machines at $102 each. The operating expenses are 44% of the selling price and the net income rate is 12% of the selling price. At what selling price should each machine be marked?

Finding the Rate of Markon or Loss Based on Selling Price. When selling price is used as the base, the rate (percent) of markon or loss is found by dividing the amount of the markon or loss by the selling price.

$$Rate\ of\ Markon\ (or\ Loss) = \frac{Markon\ (or\ Loss)}{Selling\ Price}$$

Example A shows how the amount of markon and the rate of markon are found when the selling price and the cost are given.

Example A: An article that cost $24 was sold for $30. Find **(a)** the markon and **(b)** the rate of markon based on selling price.

Solution: **(a)** Cost + Markon = Selling Price
$24 + Markon = $30
Markon = $30 − $24
Markon = $6

(b) Rate × Selling Price = Markon
Rate × $30 = $6
Rate = 6 $\boxed{\div}$ 30 $\boxed{\%}$ → 20
Rate = 20%

Example B shows how the amount of loss and rate of loss based on selling price are found when the selling price and the cost are given.

Example B: An article that cost $90 was sold for $80. Find **(a)** the amount of the loss and **(b)** the rate of loss based on selling price.

Solution: **(a)** Loss = Cost − Selling Price
Loss = $90 − $80
Loss = $10

(b) Rate × Selling Price = Loss
Rate × $80 = $10
Rate = 10 $\boxed{÷}$ 80 $\boxed{\%}$ → 12.5
Rate = 12.5% or $12\frac{1}{2}\%$

● **Exercise 12–11**

A. In each of the following problems, find **(a)** the amount of the markon or of the loss and **(b)** the rate of markon or loss based on selling price. Place an asterisk (*) to the right of each loss amount. Where applicable, round to the nearest 0.1%.

	Selling Price	Cost		Selling Price	Cost
1.	$ 40.00	$ 30.00	**7.**	$ 135.00	$ 75.00
2.	480.00	420.00	**8.**	50.00	57.50
3.	350.00	420.00	**9.**	250.00	125.00
4.	125.00	137.50	**10.**	2,200.00	1,750.00
5.	2,730.00	2,100.00	**11.**	1,300.00	1,700.00
6.	4,500.00	6,000.00	**12.**	312.50	250.00

B. Solve these problems.

1. Bryan's Clothing Store sells a line of coats at $110 each. If each coat costs $71.50, what rate of markon does the store realize on selling price?

2. A clothier bought a coat for $120 and marked it to sell for $200. If the coat was sold at a discount of 10% to the customer, what is the new rate of markon based on actual selling price?

3. A building lot was bought for $18,000. After grading was completed at a cost of $2,544, the lot was sold for $28,000. To the nearest 0.1%, the markon is what percent of the selling price?

4. A clothing store buys men's belts at $180 a dozen and sells them at $29.95 each. To the nearest 0.1%, what is the rate of markon based on selling price?

5. A department store marked some fabric to sell at $9.45 a yard, which was to give a markon rate of $33\frac{1}{3}\%$ of selling price. The material did not sell, so the price was marked down to $7.35 a yard. The goods were sold at this price. What percent of the cost was the store's actual markon?

6. A pet shop buys a pet cage for $31.20 and marks it to sell at $48. The store's overhead is estimated at 25% of net sales. What rate of net income does the store realize on each cage that it sells at the marked price?

7. A fruit dealer bought 10 boxes of oranges (72 to a box) at $18 a box. The dealer had to throw away 36 oranges that had spoiled. The remainder were sold at 2 for 75¢. To the nearest 0.1%, what rate of markon was earned on the selling price?

8. On July 1, a retail store had merchandise on hand worth $21,000 at cost. The selling price of the merchandise was $35,000. Later the store sold part of the merchandise for $15,000. What is the cost value of the remaining merchandise?

9. A used car dealer sold two cars that had cost $4,800 each. The first car was sold at a gain of 20% of the selling price and the second one at a loss of 20% based on cost. Determine the amount of the gain or loss on these two cars.

10. A dealer purchased two machines at a cost of $1,200 each. One machine was sold at a gain of 25% based on cost. The other machine was sold at a different price for a gain of 25% based on selling price. Determine the total gain.

Markon Rate Converted to Another Base

As the preceding sections illustrate, markon may be based on cost or on selling price. Occasionally in business one needs to convert a rate based on cost to a rate based on selling price and vice versa. A manufacturer who marks products on the basis of cost must understand the use of selling price as the base, because many of the company's customers will prefer to think in terms of the selling price as the base. Similarly, retailers who use selling price as the basis for computing markon but buy goods from suppliers who use cost as the basis should be able to convert from a selling-price base to a cost base.

When converting a given rate to the opposite base, remember that the original base is always equal to 100%. To convert a rate based on cost to a rate based on selling price or vice versa, follow these two steps:

1. Find the other-base percent by expressing the given markon, the cost, and the selling price as percents in the markon equation.
2. Find the other-markon rate by dividing the given-markon percent by the other-base percent.

$$Other\text{-}Markon\ Rate = \frac{Given\text{-}Markon\ Percent}{Other\text{-}Base\ Percent}$$

Converting a Rate From a Cost Base to a Selling-Price Base. The following example illustrates how a given rate based on cost is changed to a rate based on selling price. As the given rate is based on cost, the cost is 100% of itself.

Example: The markon rate of an article is 60% of the cost. What is the markon rate based on selling price?

Solution: 1. Find the other-base percent.

$$\text{Cost} + \text{Markon} = \text{Selling Price}$$
$$100\% + 60\% = 160\%$$

2. Find the other-markon rate.

$$\frac{\text{Given-Markon Percent}}{\text{Other-Base Percent}} = \frac{60\%}{160\%}$$

$$\text{Rate} = 60 \boxed{\div} 160 \boxed{\%} \rightarrow 37.5$$
$$\text{Rate} = 37.5\%$$

Check: Let the cost be any amount, such as $200. Then, the markon is $200 × 60% = $120, and the selling price is $200 + $120 = $320. When the markon rate based on the selling price is 37.5%, the markon is $320 × 37.5% = $120.

Converting a Rate From a Selling-Price Base to a Cost Base. The following example shows how a given rate based on selling price may be changed to a rate based on cost. As the given rate is based on selling price, the selling price is 100%.

Example: The markon rate of an article is 20% of the selling price. What is the markon rate based on cost?

Solution: 1. Find the other-base percent.

$$\text{Cost} + \text{Markon} = \text{Selling Price}$$
$$\text{Cost} + 20\% = 100\%$$
$$\text{Cost} = 100\% - 20\%$$
$$\text{Cost} = 80\%$$

2. Find the other-markon rate.

$$\frac{\text{Given-Markon Percent}}{\text{Other-Base Percent}} = \frac{20\%}{80\%}$$

$$\text{Rate} = 2 \boxed{\div} 8 \boxed{\%} \rightarrow 25$$
$$\text{Rate} = 25\%$$

Check: Let the selling price be any amount, such as $300. Then, the markon based on selling price is $300 × 20% = $60, and the cost is $300 − $60 = $240. The markon based on cost is $240 × 25% = $60.

● Exercise 12–12

   A. Convert each of the following markon rates based on cost to the rate based on selling price. Where applicable, round to the nearest 0.1%.

1. 20.5%	**4.** 56.3%	**7.** 42.9%	**10.** $66\frac{2}{3}\%$
2. 39%	**5.** 23.5%	**8.** 80%	**11.** 85.2%
3. 53.8%	**6.** 64%	**9.** $33\frac{1}{3}\%$	**12.** 90%

B. Convert each of the following markon rates based on selling price to the rate based on cost. Where applicable, round to the nearest 0.1%.

1. 13%	**4.** 72%	**7.** 45%	**10.** 39%
2. 26%	**5.** 18%	**8.** 48%	**11.** 50%
3. 55%	**6.** 31%	**9.** 22%	**12.** 60%

C. Solve these problems.

1. What percent of the cost should be used to yield a 25% markon based on the selling price?

2. What rate of markon based on selling price is equal to a markon rate of 40% based on cost?

3. The markon rate on a watch is 26% of the cost. What is the markon rate based on selling price?

4. If the markon rate on a television set is 45% of the selling price, what is the markon rate based on cost?

5. If the markon rate on a typewriter is 36% of the cost, what is the markon rate based on the selling price?

6. The operating expenses to sell a table are 22% of the selling price, and the markon rate is 40% of the selling price. What percent of the cost are the operating expenses?

Markon and Trade Discounts

In addition to determining the markon and the selling price, many businesses that give trade discounts must find the list price to be printed in their catalogs. Furthermore, a business that has decreased its costs may wish to pass the savings on to customers in the form of an additional trade discount. By lowering the actual selling price, the company hopes to increase its volume of sales and its net income.

Finding the List Price When a Trade Discount is Given. The list price of a product that is subject to trade discounts is often called the **marked price** because the seller knows it is not the amount that will be received in payment. The **actual selling price** is the amount the seller expects to receive after the trade discounts have been deducted from the marked price.

To find the marked price that will provide a given rate of markon based on selling price after the customer is allowed a trade discount, follow these two steps:

1. Find the selling price by dividing the cost by the cost percent.
2. Find the marked price by dividing the selling price by the selling-price percent.

Example A illustrates the procedure when the seller wishes to give the customer one discount. Example B illustrates the procedure when more than one discount is given.

Example A:

Aurora Products Company wants to sell an article that cost $120 at a marked price that will earn the company a 40% markon based on selling price and give the customer a 20% discount. Find **(a)** the actual selling price and **(b)** the marked price.

Solution:

(a) Selling Price − Markon = Cost
$$100\% - 40\% = 60\%$$

60% of Selling Price = Cost
60% × Selling Price = $120
Selling Price = $120 ÷ 0.6
Selling Price = $200

(b) Marked Price − Discount = Selling Price
$$100\% - 20\% = 80\%$$

80% of Marked Price = Selling Price
80% × Marked Price = $200
Marked Price = $200 ÷ 0.8
Marked Price = $250

Example B:

What price should a company print in its catalog as the list price of an article that cost $267.75 if the company wants to give the customer trade discounts of 15% and 10% while still realizing a markon of 30% based on the actual selling price?

Solution:

1. Find the selling price.

70% × Selling Price = Cost
70% × Selling Price = $267.75
Selling Price = $267.75 ÷ 0.7
Selling Price = $382.50

2. Find the list price.

15% and 10% = 23.5% equivalent discount rate

List Price − Discount = Selling Price
$$100\% - 23.5\% = 76.5\%$$

76.5% of List Price = Selling Price
76.5% × List Price = $382.50
List Price = $382.50 ÷ 0.765
List Price = $500

Finding the Rate of Additional Discount When Cost is Reduced. When costs are reduced and the savings are passed on to the customer, the reduction in the actual selling price will be proportional to the reduction in the cost. In order to find the additional discount rate, there are only two steps to follow:

1. Find the decrease in the cost by subtracting the new cost from the original cost.
2. Find the rate of additional discount by dividing the cost decrease by the original cost.

Example: An article that cost $90 with a 25% markon based on selling price is listed in a catalog at $150 with a trade discount of 20%. After the catalog was issued, the cost of the article decreased to $81. What additional trade discount may be given to the catalog customer as a result of the cost decrease and still maintain the 25% markon?

Solution:

1. Find the decrease in the cost.

$$\text{Original Cost} - \text{New Cost} = \text{Decrease}$$
$$\$90 - \$81 = \$9$$

2. Find the additional rate of discount.

$$\text{Decrease} \div \text{Original Cost} = \text{Additional Rate}$$
$$\$9 \div \$90 = 10\%$$

Check: New Cost ÷ Cost Percent = Selling Price
$$\$81 \div 0.75 = \$108$$

List Price × Complements of Trade Discounts = New Selling Price
$$\$150 \times 0.8 \times 0.9 = \$108$$

Notice that the additional trade discount of 10% permits the company to sell at a lower price (new selling price) while maintaining its normal margin of 25% of cost. The lower new selling price will help the company to be more competitive and, hopefully, to increase volume and sales.

● **Exercise 12–13**

A. Find the selling price and marked price in each of these problems. The markon is based on the selling price. The discount is based on the marked price.

		Cost	Markon Rate	Selling Price	Discount to Customer	Marked Price
1.	$	36.00	20%	_____	10%	_____
2.		44.80	30%	_____	20%	_____
3.		21.60	40%	_____	25%	_____
4.		480.00	25%	_____	15%, 10%	_____
5.		3,600.00	40%	_____	$16\frac{2}{3}\%$, 10%	_____
6.		800.00	$33\frac{1}{3}\%$	_____	20%, 10%	_____

B. Find the list price and the rate of additional trade discount in each of the following.

	Original Cost	Markon Rate	Original Selling Price	Original Discount Rate	List Price	New Cost	New Selling Price	Additional Discount Rate
1.	$ 48.00	25% on S.P.	_____	20%	_____	$ 43.20	_____	_____
2.	68.00	$33\frac{1}{3}\%$ on S.P.	_____	25%	_____	59.84	_____	_____
3.	315.00	40% on S.P.	_____	30%	_____	292.95	_____	_____
4.	4,800.00	20% on S.P.	_____	40%	_____	4,350.00	_____	_____
5.	1,440.00	25% on Cost	_____	20%	_____	1,317.60	_____	_____
6.	78.40	30% on Cost	_____	30%	_____	66.64	_____	_____

C. Solve these problems.

1. A dealer bought a television set for $442. It was marked to gain 35% on the selling price after allowing the consumer a discount of 15%. What was the marked price?

2. A furniture dealer bought a table for $688.50. The markon is 32% on the selling price after allowing customers a discount of 10% on the marked price. What should be the marked price for the table?

3. A dealer bought a pan for $42 less 25%. It was marked to gain $33\frac{1}{3}$% on the selling price after allowing the consumer a discount of $12\frac{1}{2}$%. How much was the marked price?

4. A retailer buys gadget bags at $186.48 a dozen. What should be the marked price of each bag if the consumer is to be allowed a discount of 20% and a markon of 30% of the selling price is to be realized?

REVIEW PROBLEMS

Solve these problems. If you have difficulty solving any problem, restudy the appropriate section in this chapter. The problems under a specific number are related to those contained in the exercise with the same last number.

1. **a.** A furniture dealer received a bill for $2,132.50 worth of merchandise that is subject to discounts of 20% and 15%. What is the net price to the dealer?
   b. A salesperson mistakenly allowed a trade discount of 35% instead of allowing the correct amount based on the series 25% and 10%. The list price of the goods totaled $600. By how much was the salesperson in error?

2. **a.** Find the single discount rate that is equal to the series of 30%, 15%, and 10%.
   b. Find **(1)** the equivalent discount rate and **(2)** the amount of discount allowed on each of the following invoices: **(a)** $54, **(b)** $37.50, **(c)** $65, and **(d)** $98.75. These invoices are subject to trade discounts of 40%, 20%, and 10%.

3. **a.** An invoice for $632 has terms of 3/15, n/30. The invoice is dated March 23. Find the amount payable on April 5.
   b. An invoice for $2,650 was dated March 15 and had terms of 3/15, 1/30, n/60. Find the amount to pay the invoice in full on April 14.
   c. An invoice for $2,395 is dated April 23 and has terms of 2/10 EOM. Find **(1)** the final date on which the cash discount may be taken and **(2)** the amount needed to pay in full on that date.
   d. A dealer bought merchandise with an invoice total of $2,700. The terms were 3/10, n/30, and the invoice was dated September 7. The dealer paid for the merchandise on September 16. How much was paid?

4. a. How much was paid for merchandise invoiced at a total list price of $2,650 and subject to discounts of 20% and 10% and terms of 2/10, n/30, if bought on August 27 and paid for on September 6?

b. On October 19, the Johnson Hardware Company purchased goods invoiced at $1,726.65 from Brown and Lambert. The terms were 2/30, n/60. On November 10, the Johnson Hardware Company received a credit bill for $284.50 from Brown and Lambert for merchandise returned. On November 18, the cashier of the Johnson Hardware Company issued a check in payment of the amount due Brown and Lambert. The check was written for what correct amount?

c. The total amount of an invoice, including freight of $12.42, was $837.50. Terms were $2\frac{1}{2}$/30, n/60. Find the amount to be paid if the buyer returned $61.87 worth of merchandise and paid the balance within the cash-discount period.

d. An invoice for $350 dated June 12 with terms of 2/10, n/30 was received by the buyer on June 14. The buyer paid $200 on June 21. How much was the balance due after this payment?

5. To be able to take advantage of the cash discount on an invoice of merchandise amounting to $1,800 with terms of 3/10, n/90, Douglas Swanson borrowed enough money to pay the bill by giving his 80-day note at 7%. **(a)** How much money did he need to borrow? **(b)** How much did he save?

6. The gross profit of Garden City Furniture Company is 40% of cost. Based on this information, how much should be **(a)** the markon and **(b)** the selling price of a table that cost the company $467.50?

7. The gross profit of a furniture store last month was $56,000. The markon rate during the month was 40% based on cost. **(a)** What is the value of the cost of goods sold? **(b)** How much were the sales during the month?

8. A furniture store bought a chair for $180 less 20% and sold it for $216. **(a)** How much was the markon? **(b)** What was the rate of markon based on cost?

9. A clothier bought suits at $202.50 each less 20% and 10%. At what price should each suit be sold to make a gross profit of 40% of the retail price?

10. The Photo World Camera Supply Company sells a camera for $147.56. The operating expenses are 43% of the selling price, and the company expects to earn 12% net income. What is the highest price the manager should pay for this camera?

11. Some merchandise that cost $1,767 was sold for $2,325. The overhead expense chargeable to the transaction amounted to $348.75. What is the percent of net income on the selling price?

12. If the markon rate on a radio is 28% of the selling price, what is the markon rate based on cost?

Chapter 12. Merchandising

13. A department store advertised a 10% discount from the marked price of every article in the furniture department. At what price must the tag on a lamp that cost $90 be marked to make the rate of markon 30% of cost after the discount has been deducted?

CHALLENGE PROBLEM

At the time of their marriage, Tim Gendry was the manager of an auto parts store and Arlene was an accountant with a CPA firm that supervised the records of several small businesses. After saving their money for five years, they opened their own auto parts store six months ago. Tim manages the new store and Arlene takes care of the accounting records, but she still works for the accounting firm. They hope that the business will grow so she can work full-time at the store and that eventually they can open other stores. As Tim had become acquainted with many repair-shop owners and do-it-yourselfers while managing the chain store, their store appears to be doing better than expected. The condensed income statement for the six months of operations is as follows:

Sales	$252,000
Cost of goods sold	180,000
Gross profit	$ 72,000
Operating expenses	53,000
Net income	$ 19,000

The markon rate for most of the parts stores in the area is 45%. In order to have a pricing advantage, Tim decided to use 40% based on cost for marking merchandise. He also is permitting customers with whom he is acquainted to charge their purchases on 30-day accounts with no late fee. Sixty percent of the store's sales are on credit.

While reviewing the store's records, Arlene noted that many charge customers are not paying within the 30 days. The average time from date of sale to collection is 43 days, which she considers too high. She further noted that Tim's suppliers grant terms of 2/10, n/30 with a late fee of 1.5%. Cash sales to do-it-yourselfers enable Tim to pay off about 30% of those invoices within the cash-discount period. He pays the remainder within the credit period.

Their bank will lend short-term funds to the firm at the prime rate, which is now $8\frac{1}{2}$%, plus two points. Tim doesn't want to borrow funds to pay for purchases within the cash-discount period. He says, "Paying $10\frac{1}{2}$% to save 2% is foolish."

Arlene is trying to convince Tim to sell to credit customers on the same terms his suppliers give him. Tim believes his 40% markon rate is too low to grant a 2% discount. In reaction to this, she suggests that the markon rate be

increased to 43% which would pay for the lower price to credit customers and still provide a price advantage.

What do you recommend regarding **(a)** the markon rate, **(b)** a cash discount to credit customers, and **(c)** borrowing to pay Tim's suppliers? Use appropriate data to support your recommendations.

Chapter 13

Credit

Objectives

After mastering the material in Chapter 13, you will be able to:

- Find the interest on open-account credit and installment loans.
- Use the Rule of 78ths to determine the unearned finance charge.
- Compute the monthly payment and prepare a loan payment schedule on long-term loans.
- Use APR tables as well as a formula to find the annual percentage rate.

From the viewpoint of the borrower, **credit** is the power to obtain goods or services by giving a promise to pay (money or goods) on demand or at a specified date in the future. From the viewpoint of the lender, **credit** is the present right to future payment. The use of credit as a medium of exchange has served to speed up the production, exchange, and consumption of goods. This, in turn, has caused a higher standard of living. The use of credit, however, is accompanied by some danger. Among the direct dangers of credit is its tendency to encourage overexpansion, overtrading, and speculation which might lead to fraud and embezzlement. It may also induce people to live more extravagantly than their means warrant.

PERSONAL LOANS AND RETAIL CREDIT

Theoretically, to sell for cash is ideal for the retailer. Nevertheless, the retailer can increase sales, and presumably profit, by extending credit to customers. Credit can be a means of increasing not only the number of sales but also the size of the average sale. Credit customers identify with a store and do not shop around as much as do cash customers. The retailer who sells on credit, however, has the additional expenses of record keeping, investigating customers' credit ratings, following up on delinquent accounts, and writing off bad accounts. To cover these expenses and realize an interest return on the money invested in customers' accounts, credit customers may be charged more than the regular cash price of the goods. The extra amount charged for the use of credit is the **finance charge.** When considered as interest on the unpaid balance, the finance charge is sometimes surprisingly high.

Credit Cards

Credit may be extended to consumers prior to their buying goods and services or borrowing money by having them apply for **open-account credit** in the form of charge accounts. After the applicant's credit rating has been checked and approved by the store or bank, a **credit card** is commonly issued. The card enables the consumer to buy or borrow up to a certain **credit limit.** The credit limit may range from $500 to $1,000 initially and be increased later if the consumer establishes a good payment record with the store or bank. Typically, a merchandising or service company issues credit cards that are accepted only in its stores or by its agents. Examples of these are Sears, Roebuck and Company and American Airlines credit cards. The two most popular bank credit cards are VISA and MasterCard. These enable consumers to buy goods and services from thousands of businesses and to borrow money from specific banking companies located all over the world. Other similar international credit cards are those issued by American Express, Diners Club, and Carte Blanche.

The balance shown on a credit-card statement should be paid in full within a specific number of days after the billing date to avoid finance charges and late fees. The number of days for paying the account without causing such fees is commonly 25 or 30 days from the billing date. The due date may be shown on the statement form. If the balance is smaller than a specific amount, often $20, it is to be paid in full. For larger balances a minimum payment (perhaps 5% of the balance rounded up to the next $5 or a minimum of $20, whichever is larger) is to be paid by the due date.

The credit-card companies, such as VISA, American Express, and Carte Blanche, charge an annual fee to the card holder as well as interest charges on amounts not paid by the due date. There is no annual fee for store and service company credit cards, but there are finance charges for amounts not paid by the due date and late fees for past-due amounts. Income from finance charges is often a large portion of the company's net profit, which is why customers are encouraged to buy on credit.

Finance Charge on Previous Balance. The **previous balance** in a charge account is the balance in the account on the billing date of the preceding billing period. Originally, the finance charge on most credit-card accounts was based on the previous balance at the monthly rate of 1% or 1.5%. A monthly rate of 1% is equal to an annual rate of 12% (1% × 12 months), and a monthly rate of 1.5% equals 18% per annum. Currently, most monthly rates range from 1.5% to 2%, which are annual rates of 18% to 24%. The following example illustrates computing finance charges as a percent of the previous balance. This method is still used by some companies.

Example: Debra Allison's charge account shows a beginning unpaid balance of $325.60. She made monthly payments of $50, $60, and $70. The finance charge is computed at $1\frac{1}{2}$% a month on the previous balance. Show **(a)** the finance charge for the third month and **(b)** the unpaid balance after the third payment.

Solution: Month 1: $325.60 × 1.5% = $4.88   finance charge
$4.88 + $325.60 − $50 = $280.48   balance
Month 2: $280.48 × 1.5% = $4.21   finance charge
$4.21 + $280.48 − $60 = $224.69   balance
Month 3: **(a)** $224.69 × 1.5% = $3.37   finance charge
(b) $3.37 + $224.69 − $70 = $158.06   balance

Finance Charge on Average Daily Balance. The **average daily balance** of a charge account is the average of the daily balances in the account during the billing period. The billing date is the same date each month, so the billing period is 28 to 31 days. Most companies now use this method (or a variation) to compute finance charges on credit-card accounts. The average daily balance is found by dividing the sum of the daily balances during the period by the number of days in the billing period.

The sum of like daily balances may be obtained by multiplying the daily balance by the number of days for which there is no change in the balance. The product of days times dollars may be referred to as **day-dollars.** The sum of the day-dollars divided by the number of days in the billing period gives the average daily balance. The finance charge is found by multiplying the average daily balance by the monthly rate. This computation is shown in the following example. Figure 13–1 shows a copy of a fictitious credit statement prepared by a large merchandising company, Sears, Roebuck and Company, that has stores in several countries.

Example: A credit-card statement shows an unpaid balance of $500 on the billing date of November 2. Charges and credits to the account are shown below. The finance charge of 1.5% on the average daily balance is entered on the billing date. Find **(a)** the average daily balance, **(b)** the finance charge, and **(c)** the account balance on the next billing date, which is December 2.

Date	Charge	Credit	Balance
11-02			$500.00
11-07	$ 75.00		575.00
11-17		$175.00	400.00
11-23	200.00		600.00

Part 3. Mathematics Applications in Operating a Business

Sears Charge
Sears, Roebuck and Co.

You may pay by mail or at any Sears store. If you pay by mail using the enclosed pre-addressed envelope, payments received prior to 1 p.m. on a banking day will be credited as of the date received. Payments received after 1 p.m. will be credited on the following banking day. Please send only the top portion of your statement with payment. If you prefer to pay at a Sears store, please bring the entire statement.

If state of residence changes, your account will be transferred, as required, for servicing.
PLEASE MAKE ADDRESS CHANGE OR CORRECTIONS IN ADDRESS AREA BELOW.

OFFICE USE ONLY

8 12345 9876 4

ROBERT HUNTER

567 EL DORADO ST

PLACERVILLE, CA 95667

AMOUNT DUE THIS STATEMENT
$ 20.00

NEW BALANCE
$ 208.11

AMOUNT PAID
$

MAIL ANY BILLING ERROR NOTICE TO Sears Credit Department at address shown below:

YOUR LINE OF CREDIT IS $1760 - AVAILABLE CREDIT $1552

Month	Day	Reference	TRANSACTION DESCRIPTION See reverse for detailed description of department numbers indicated below.	CHARGES	PAYMENTS & CREDITS
11	10		FINANCE CHARGE	1.71	
11	12		CATALOG SALE 06 200	56.65	
11	14		CREDIT - RETURN		9.78
11	20		PAYMENT RECEIVED - THANK YOU		70.00
11	30		HOUSEWARES 11	61.55	
12	05		AUTO ACCESSORIES	50.25	

FINANCE CHARGE RATE(S)	ON AVERAGE DAILY BALANCE OF:	MONTHLY PERIODIC RATE(S)	ANNUAL PERCENTAGE RATE(S)
	$.01 TO $31.00	MIN. FINANCE CHARGE $.50	
	$31.01 TO $3000.00	1.6%	19.2%
	$3000.01 AND ABOVE	1.0%	12.0%

use ACCOUNT NO. on correspondence	BILLING DATE	PREVIOUS BALANCE	NEW BALANCE	MINIMUM PAYMENT
8 12345 9876 4	DEC 10, 19XX	117.73	208.11	20.00

To avoid a FINANCE CHARGE next month, pay the NEW BALANCE shown above within 30 days (28 days for February statements) from BILLING DATE. If you prefer to pay in installments pay the MINIMUM PAYMENT shown above, or more, within 30 days (28 days for February statements) from BILLING DATE. The sooner you pay and the more you pay, the smaller your FINANCE CHARGE.

NOTICE: SEE REVERSE SIDE FOR IMPORTANT INFORMATION.

Source: Courtesy Sears, Roebuck and Co.

1. Billing Date
2. Beginning Balance
3. Charges since last statement
4. Credits since last statement
5. New balance
6. Minimum Payment
7. Line of Credit
8. Interest Rates
9. Date to pay to avoid interest

Figure 13–1 A Credit Account Statement

	Dates	Days		Dollars		Day-Dollars
(a)	**Dates**	**Days**		**Dollars**		**Day-Dollars**
	11-02 to 11-07	5	×	500	=	2,500
	11-07 to 11-17	10	×	575	=	5,750
	11-17 to 11-23	6	×	400	=	2,400
	11-23 to 12-02	9	×	600	=	5,400
		30				16,050

Solution:

16,050 ÷ 30 = $535.00   average daily balance

(b) $535 × 1.5% = $8.025 = $8.03   finance charge

(c) $600 + $8.03 = $608.03   account balance on 12-02

Finance Charge on Adjusted Average Daily Balance. A **cash advance** is money given to a card holder by a participating financial institution on presentation of a credit card. Bank credit-card companies and other companies that provide such services compute the average daily balance by adjusting it for cash advances, check transfers, and other services that are subject to special fees. A good example of this is the cash advance fee, which is commonly 2% of the cash advance.

As the company should not charge twice for a special service, cash advances, special fees, and the like are not included in the computation of the adjusted average daily balance that is used to find the regular finance charge at the specified monthly rate. The basis for the rate is called the **adjusted average daily balance** or something similar. Of course, the card holder must pay for the cash advance and its fee. These and similar charges are included in the balance due. Notice in the following example that the cash advance is not included in the computation of the adjusted average daily balance.

Example: Larry Rost's bank-card account had an unpaid balance of $300 on the billing date of March 8. A purchase of $110 was entered on March 12, a credit of $10 on March 14, a cash advance of $200 on March 25, and a payment of $50 on April 2. Find **(a)** the adjusted average daily balance, **(b)** the finance charge at 1.5% with the cash advance fee of 2%, and **(c)** the unpaid balance on the next billing date (April 8).

Solution:

(a)
3-08 to 3-12	4 × 300 =	1,200
3-12 to 3-14	2 × 410 =	820
3-14 to 4-02	19 × 400 =	7,600
4-02 to 4-08	6 × 350 =	2,100
	31	11,720

11,720 ÷ 31 = $378.06   adjusted average daily balance

(b) $378.06 × 1.5% = $5.67   regular finance charge
$200.00 × 2% = $4.00   cash advance fee
$5.67 + $4.00 = $9.67   total finance charge

(c) $350 + $200 CA + $9.67 FC = $559.67 unpaid balance 4-08

1. Crosier Company charges 1.65% per month on the previous balances of its credit-card accounts. A selected account shows a beginning balance of $474.92 with monthly payments of $80, $95, and $90. Show **(a)** the finance charge and **(b)** the balance due after each payment.

2. There is a beginning balance of $187.45 and monthly payments of $50, $60, and $20 shown in an account that is subject to a monthly finance charge of 1.7% of the previous balance. How much are **(a)** the finance charge and **(b)** the balance due each month?

3. Before three monthly payments of $125, $140, and $97.50 were made, there was an account balance of $1,238.87 in Barbara Castro's account. The finance charge is 1.5% when the previous balance is $1,000 or less with a minimum fee of 50¢. The rate drops to 1% when the previous balance is larger than $1,000. Find **(a)** the finance charge and **(b)** the unpaid balance for each month.

4. An unpaid balance of $1,447.96 was reduced by monthly payments of $250, $230, and $175. The finance charge is 1% on previous monthly balances that exceed $1,000 and 1.6% on balances that are $1,000 or less with a minimum fee of 50¢. Find **(a)** the finance charge and **(b)** the unpaid balance for each month.

5. Three monthly payments of $20 each were applied to an account that had a beginning balance of $65.34. The finance charge is 1.7% on previous balances of $500 or less with a minimum fee of 50¢. The rate is 1.5% on previous balances that exceed $500. Show **(a)** the finance charge and **(b)** the unpaid balance for each month.

6. A finance charge of 1.75% is applied to monthly account balances that are $500 or less with a minimum fee of 50¢. The rate drops to 1.6% on previous balances that exceed $500. An account with a beginning balance of $92.40 had three monthly payments of $35, $35, and $20 applied to it. Show **(a)** the finance charge and **(b)** the balance due for each month.

7. A credit-card statement shows a beginning balance of $278.54 and billing date of November 5. On November 10 a payment of $70 was made. Later two purchases were made: $25.30 on November 20 and $18.37 on November 25. Find the average daily balance on the next billing date.

8. An account with a billing date of September 8 shows a beginning balance of $368.23, charges of $49.64 on September 10, a credit of $15.48 on September 12, and a payment of $150 on September 23. Show the average daily balance as of the next billing date.

9. A credit-card statement shows a beginning balance of $67.98 on the billing date of February 15, a charge of $135.56 on February 20, a payment of $67.98 on March 5, and a charge of $18.45 on March 10. Show the average daily balance on the next billing date.

10. Karen Wallace's charge account is billed on the 20th day of the month. Her current statement shows a beginning unpaid balance of $510.72, a charge of $85.45 on March 5, a payment of $175 on March 12, and another charge of $90.16 on March 18. Find the average daily balance as of the next billing date.

11. A bank-card account shows a billing-date balance of $347.80 on May 7, a charge of $28.49 on May 11, a credit of $6.36 on May 12, a cash advance of $100 on May 23, and a payment of $147.80 on May 25. Find the adjusted average daily balance that is subject to the regular finance charge of 1.75%.

12. Mark Parry's bank-card statement shows a balance of $75.19 on the billing date of April 4, a cash advance of $50 on April 10, a credit of $10.08 on April 11, a payment of $20 on April 29, and a purchase of $51.02 on May 1. Find the adjusted average daily balance that is subject to the finance charge of 1.65%.

13. An account statement shows an unpaid beginning balance of $276.82 on the billing date of December 7, charges of $12.93 on December 10, $74.20 on December 12, $35.05 on December 15, and $247.64 on December 20, and a payment of $35 on December 28. Find (a) the average daily balance and (b) the finance charge at 1.5% of the average daily balance.

14. On the billing date of April 27, an account shows a balance of $806.63 and charges of $260 on May 2, $165.36 on May 4, and $24.38 on May 17. A payment of $146.63 was made on May 22. Find (a) the average daily balance and (b) the finance charge at 1.65% of the average daily balance.

15. A bank-card statement shows a beginning unpaid balance of $524.66 on the statement date of October 5. A payment of $300 was made on October 15. A cash advance of $100 on October 20 and a charge of $47.01 on October 30 were shown also. Find (a) the adjusted average daily balance, (b) the finance charge at 1.55% including a fee of 2% on the cash advance, and (c) the unpaid balance on the next closing date.

16. The billing date for a bank-card account is June 10 and the beginning unpaid balance is $85.29. On June 12 a cash advance of $50 was made. Charges of $50 on June 15, $8.22 on June 16, and $103.18 on June 20 were made to the account. A payment of $20 was entered on June 28 and a purchase of $89.40 was made on July 3. Show (a) the adjusted average daily balance, (b) the finance charge at 1.6% monthly including the fee of 2% for the cash advance, and (c) the unpaid balance on the next closing date.

17. The finance charge by a store is computed at 1.6% monthly on average daily balances up to $1,000 and 1% monthly on average daily balances that exceed $1,000. The beginning unpaid balance of an account with a billing date of July 10 is $1,324.63. A payment of $200 was recorded on July 30 although it was not due until 30 days from the billing date. The

finance charge is entered on the billing date. There were no other entries in the account during July. A charge of $15.82 was made on August 12 and a payment of $400 was made on August 25. Another purchase of $39.56 was recorded on August 30. Find the finance charge for this account on the billing date in **(a)** August and **(b)** September and **(c)** the account balance on September 10.

18. The beginning balance of an account was $1,238.70 on its billing date of October 5. A purchase of $67.84 was recorded on October 10. A payment of $300 was made on October 25. Payments are due 25 days from the billing date, but the finance charge is not entered until the next billing date. A purchase of $24.38 was recorded on November 15 and another payment of $300 was recorded on November 29. The finance charge is 1.65% per month on average daily balances up to $1,000 and 1.25% on average daily balances that exceed $1,000. Find the finance charge on the billing date in **(a)** November and **(b)** December and **(c)** the account balance on December 5.

19. An account that is subject to finance charges of 1.75% on average daily balances up to $1,000 and 1.3% on average daily balances over $1,000 shows a balance of $894.72 on the billing date, May 12. The finance charge is entered in the account on the billing date. Payments are due 25 days from the billing date. A purchase amounting to $12.49 was entered on May 20, and a payment of $200 was entered on May 31. These purchases were entered: $250.63 and $149.85 on June 14, $12.87 on June 16, and $38.59 on July 5. A payment of $175 was entered on July 6. Find the finance charge on the billing date for **(a)** June and **(b)** July and **(c)** the balance owed on July 12.

20. The monthly rate of 1.2% is applied to average daily balances that exceed $1,000 and 1.8% is applied to smaller average daily balances. On the billing date of April 20, an account has a balance of $843.98. Payments are due in 25 days and finance charges are entered on the next billing date. A purchase of $138.43 was entered April 27 and a credit of $24.86 on April 28 for a return of merchandise. A payment of $100 was made on May 11. Purchases of $358.12 and $19.07 were made on May 22. A credit of $19.07 on May 24 and a payment of $100 on June 14 were recorded. Find the finance charge on the billing date for **(a)** May and **(b)** June and **(c)** the amount due on June 20.

Installment Credit

In recent years, the buying of goods on credit has increased rapidly. Many purchases of household appliances, furniture, and automobiles are financed by the sellers or by financial institutions through various installment plans. The consumer as well as the business employee, therefore, should know how to compute the finance charges, the amount of the monthly payment, and the approximate annual percentage rate on installment credit.

Finding the Additional Cost of Installment Buying. When buying on an installment plan, the purchaser usually is required to pay part of the purchase price as a down payment. The buyer signs a contract promising to pay the balance of the purchase price in a series of weekly or monthly payments. The total installment price is the sum of the down payment and all of the installment payments. The additional cost of installment buying is the difference between the cash price and the installment price.

Example:

A student bought a radio on the installment plan for a down payment of $50 and 9 monthly payments of $20 each. The cash price of the set was $200. How much more than the cash price was paid?

Solution:

$ 50.00	down payment
180.00	payments (9 × $20)
$230.00	total installment price
200.00	cash price
$ 30.00	expense of using installment plan

Finding the Monthly Payment. Most retailers who sell on an installment basis add the interest to the initial unpaid balance to find the total amount owed. Under this plan, the purchaser pays interest at a nominal rate on the unpaid balance for the entire life of the installment contract although the amount of the debt is reduced by each payment. A **nominal rate** is a rate that exists in name only. The actual rate may be much higher. The amount of the monthly payment is found by dividing the sum of the unpaid balance and the finance charges by the number of monthly installments.

Example A:

A camera store sells a camera priced at $150 on installment terms of 10% cash as a down payment with the unpaid balance to be paid in 10 equal monthly installments. The store charges 15% nominal interest on the unpaid balance. How much are the monthly installments?

Solution:

$150.00	cash price
15.00	deduct 10% down payment
$135.00	unpaid balance
16.88	interest on $135 at 15% for 10 months
$151.88	total amount to be paid

$151.88 ÷ 10 installments = $15.188   monthly installments

The fraction of a cent (0.2¢) overpayment, which amounts to 2¢ in 10 payments, may be deducted from the last payment. Thus, there are 9 payments of $15.19 and 1 payment of $15.17.

Instead of being computed as nominal interest, the finance charge may be a stated rate of the unpaid balance. This method of computing the finance charge is usually applied to short-term loans of a few months. The term of the loan, whether 6 months or 60 months, does not affect the total finance charge. The base, the unpaid balance, is simply multiplied by the rate to find the finance charge.

Example B: A video camera can be purchased for $1,200 cash or $120 down and 10 monthly payments. The finance charge is 15% of the unpaid balance. Find the amount of the monthly payment.

Solution: $1,200 − $120 = $1,080   unpaid balance
               $1,080 × 15% = $162   finance charge
               ($1,080 + $162) ÷ 10 = $124.20   monthly payment

● Exercise 13–2

1. Tina Yelton borrowed $400 from a consumer finance company and repaid it in 18 monthly installments of $27.52 each. How much was the finance charge on the loan?

2. The cash price of a piano was $2,000. It was bought on the installment plan for a down payment of $100 and 12 monthly installments of $175 each. What is the difference between the installment price and the cash price?

3. You can borrow $1,200 from your bank by agreeing to pay interest at the annual rate of 12% on the face of the loan and to repay the combined total of the principal and interest in 15 equal monthly payments. What will be the amount of each monthly payment?

4. The cash price of a refrigerator is $800. The down payment is $50 and the finance charge is 16% of the unpaid balance. If 12 monthly payments are to be made, find the monthly payments.

5. You can borrow $450 from a consumer finance company and pay it back in 20 monthly payments of $28.20 each. How much is the finance charge on the loan?

6. Bedroom furniture can be bought on the installment plan for a down payment of $50 and 18 monthly installments of $60 each. The cash price is $1,000. What is the difference between the installment price and the cash price?

7. Luis Sanchez borrowed $540 from his bank by agreeing to pay interest at the annual nominal rate of 18% on the principal and to repay the combined total of the principal and interest in 8 equal monthly payments. What was the amount of each monthly payment?

8. Ellen Holmes bought some furniture that had a cash price of $650 by paying $90 down. The finance charge was 14% of the unpaid balance. She paid the total of the balance and the finance charge in 12 equal monthly payments. How much did she pay each month?

9. A living room sofa can be purchased on the installment plan for $83 down and 18 monthly payments that include nominal interest computed at 15% for the total installment period. The cash price of the sofa is $949.25. Find the amount of the monthly payments.

10. The price of an automobile including tax and license was $10,347. The nominal interest was 17.5% for the term of the loan. If the buyer paid $2,347 down and financed the car for 3 years, how much was each monthly payment?

11. The nominal interest for buying an automobile on installments was 18% of the unpaid balance for the term of the loan. Find the monthly payment on an automobile priced at a total of $12,874 with a down payment of $2,500 that was financed for 5 years.

12. You can buy a refrigerator for $895 cash or $85 down and $87.50 a month for 12 months. On the other hand, you have enough money for the down payment and can borrow the remainder of the cash price at 15% interest for 12 months. How much can you save by borrowing in order to buy at the cash price if you repay the loan in one year?

Rule of 78ths

Rebate means to give back part of an amount paid or to deduct from an amount owed. When a purchase or loan is paid by the installment plan, the presumption is that the consumer (debtor) is borrowing the finance charges as well as the principal and, therefore, owes the total of the principal and finance charges. Suppose the consumer decides to pay off the balance of a debt early, rather than continue making payments for the number of months remaining in the contract. Then the lender will not have earned all of the interest that was included in the contract, and the consumer is entitled to a rebate of the unearned finance charge. State laws provide that the consumer be given such a rebate, and the Federal Truth in Lending Law stipulates that the method used to compute any unearned finance charge be revealed to the consumer when the debt is initiated.

Installment payments gradually reduce the amount owed until the debt is eliminated. More is owed in the beginning than at the end. As the debt diminishes, the interest earned on that debt decreases. Therefore, the interest earned is higher in the beginning. Also, opening an installment account is expensive for the lender whether the account is open for two months or for two years. For these reasons many banks and other companies compute interest earned by the **Rule of 78ths,** which is also called the **sum-of-digits** method.

The latter name is probably more descriptive; the sum of the digits for the number of months in the loan is the denominator of a fraction that is used to find the earned (or unearned) interest on the loan. The sum of the digits in the numbers 1 through 12 for a twelve month loan is 78. The **Rule of 78ths** is that the lender earns $\frac{12}{78}$ of the finance charge during the first month of a one-year loan, $\frac{11}{78}$ the second month, $\frac{10}{78}$ the third month, and so on, leaving only $\frac{1}{78}$ for the twelfth month. Figure 13–2 illustrates the concept.

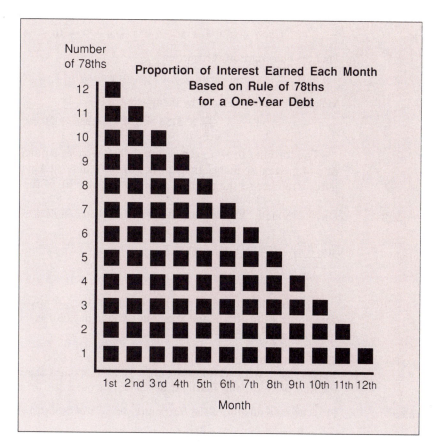

Figure 13-2 Rule of 78ths

A fractional part of the total interest or finance charge is earned by the lender each month. Based on the Rule of 78ths, the denominator of the fraction for a one-year loan is 78, which is the sum of the numbers 1 through 12, the number of months in one year. The numerator for each month is those same numbers in reverse order—12, 11, 10, etc. After three months, the interest earned on a one-year loan equals $\frac{12}{78} + \frac{11}{78} + \frac{10}{78}$ of the finance charge; that is, a total of $\frac{33}{78}$ of the finance charge. If $\frac{33}{78}$ of the finance charge is earned, then $\frac{45}{78}$, which is $\frac{78}{78} - \frac{33}{78}$, is unearned. In a like manner, on a loan that is paid off four months early the **unearned** interest would be $\frac{4}{78} + \frac{3}{78} + \frac{2}{78} + \frac{1}{78}$, which is $\frac{10}{78}$ of the finance charge.

Example A: The finance charge on a 1-year loan was $156. The loan was paid in full 4 months early. Find the interest that was unearned by the lender.

Chapter 13. Credit   393

Solution: Find the denominator of the fraction:

$$1 + 2 + 3 + 4 + 5 + 6 + 7 + 8 + 9 + 10 + 11 + 12 = 78$$

Find the numerator of the fraction:

$$4 + 3 + 2 + 1 = 10$$

Multiply the finance charge by the fraction:

$$\frac{10}{78} \times \$156 = \$20 \quad \text{unearned interest}$$

The formula shown in the example below gives a quick way to find the sum of a numerical sequence that starts with 1. When used in the Rule of 78ths, the letter n represents the number of months in the life of the installment contract.

Example B: Use the formula $\frac{n(n + 1)}{2}$ to find the sum of the numerical sequence 1 through 12.

Solution: $$\frac{n(n + 1)}{2} = \frac{12(12 + 1)}{2} = 6(13) = 78$$

This formula is especially helpful when the life of the installment loan is something other than one year and when the loan is being paid off several months in advance.

Example C: The finance charge for buying some furniture was $600 on an installment plan of 2 years. The buyer decided to pay off the loan 11 months ahead of time. According to the Rule of 78ths, how much rebate should the buyer get for unearned interest?

Solution: Find the denominator of the fraction (2 years = 24 months):

$$\frac{n(n + 1)}{2} = \frac{24(24 + 1)}{2} = 12(25) = 300$$

Find the numerator of the fraction:

$$\frac{n(n + 1)}{2} = \frac{11(11 + 1)}{2} = 11(6) = 66$$

Multiply the finance charge by the fraction:

$$\frac{66}{300} \times \$600 = \$132 \quad \text{unearned interest (rebate)}$$

When the amount of the original loan, the monthly payment, and the number of payments remaining are known, one can determine how much money is needed to pay off a loan that is subject to a rebate in accordance with the Rule of 78ths.

Example D: The price of an automobile including tax and license was $14,798. The buyer paid $4,798 down and signed a contract to pay the balance with 42 monthly payments of $360. After having made 25 payments, the buyer decided to pay off the loan. In accordance with the Rule of 78ths, find (a) the rebate the buyer should get for unearned interest and (b) the amount needed to pay the loan in full.

Solution:

(a) Denominator:

$$\frac{n(n+1)}{2} = \frac{42(42+1)}{2} = 21(43) = 903$$

Numerator ($42 - 25 = 17$ payments remaining):

$$\frac{n(n+1)}{2} = \frac{17(17+1)}{2} = 17(9) = 153$$

Finance charge:

$$\$14{,}798 - \$4{,}798 = \$10{,}000 \quad \text{loan}$$
$$\$360 \times 42 = \$15{,}120 \quad \text{total payments}$$
$$\$15{,}120 - \$10{,}000 = \$5{,}120 \quad \text{finance charge}$$

Rebate:

$$\frac{153}{903} \times \$5{,}120 = \$867.51 \quad \text{unearned interest}$$

(b) $\$360 \times 17 = \$6{,}120 \quad \text{total remaining payments}$
$\$6{,}120 - \$867.51 = \$5{,}252.49 \quad \text{amount of final payment}$

● Exercise 13–3

Solve the following problems. Use the Rule of 78ths where applicable.

1. What is the sum of the digits of the months in a 3-year loan?

2. What is the sum of the digits of the months in a 4-year loan?

3. A 1-year bank loan was paid off at the end of 7 months. What fractional part of the finance charge was earned by the bank?

4. An 18-month bank loan was paid in full at the end of 12 months. What fractional part of the finance charge was earned by the bank?

5. A 1-year bank loan was paid off at the end of 7 months. What fractional part of the finance charge was unearned by the bank?

6. A 1-year bank loan was paid off 6 months early. What fractional part of the finance charge was unearned?

7. A 2-year installment contract was paid in full 8 months early. What fractional part of the finance charge should be rebated to the consumer?

8. A 5-year contract for the purchase of goods was paid off 20 months ahead of schedule. What fractional part of the finance charge should be rebated to the debtor?

9. A 10-month contract was paid off at the end of 6 months. The finance charge was $117. Find the unearned finance charge.

10. An 8-month contract with a finance charge of $180 was paid off at the end of 5 months. Find the unearned finance charge.

11. Ted Morrison bought a microwave oven on a 1-year installment contract that included a finance charge of $135. He paid off the contract 7 months early. Find the unearned finance charge.

12. Annette Mosley signed a 15-month installment contract to buy a refrigerator. Annette paid off the contract, which included a finance charge of $165, 9 months early. Find the unearned finance charge.

13. Mike Hill bought some furniture on a 2-year installment contract that included $640 for finance charges. Mike decided to pay off the contract at the end of 11 months. Find the rebate to which he was entitled.

14. Bonnie Wilson bought some new equipment for her retail shop by borrowing from her bank. She signed a 3-year installment contract. Business was good, so she was able to pay off the loan 14 months early. How much should her rebate be on a finance charge of $2,400?

15. Robert Hurd bought an automobile on an installment plan that required monthly payments of $462.50 after the down payment. The finance charge was $3,875 on the 30-month loan. Robert decided to pay off the contract 12 months early. Find (a) the unearned finance charge and (b) the amount needed for the final payment.

16. A home-improvement loan from a bank included a finance charge of $609 in the 21 monthly payments of $219.48. The loan was paid off 4 months early. Find (a) the interest saved by the borrower and (b) the amount of the final payment.

17. A video camera was purchased for $1,500. The down payment was $300 and the balance was financed for 15 months. The finance charge was 18% of the unpaid balance. The account was paid off 5 months early. Find (a) the finance charge, (b) the monthly payment, (c) the finance charge rebate, and (d) the final payment.

18. Peggy and Adam Rabinowitz bought a new automobile for $11,450 with a down payment of $2,000 and a 3-year installment contract. After making 20 monthly payments of $346.50, they decided to pay off the debt. Find (a) the finance charge, (b) the unearned finance charge, and (c) the amount of the final payment.

19. A buyer signed an installment contract of $12,500 for a 4-year automobile loan. The total finance charge was $6,580. The loan was paid off 19 months early. Find (a) the monthly payment, (b) the unearned finance charge, and (c) the final payment.

20. The owner of a business purchased a delivery vehicle on a 30-month installment plan for the balance of $15,000 at nominal interest of 15% for the term of the loan. Business income increased and the buyer decided to pay off the loan 13 months early. Find (a) the finance charge, (b) the monthly payment, (c) the finance charge rebate, and (d) the final payment.

Long-Term Loans

Most homes are sold today on the basis of a down payment and a mortgage for the balance. The mortgage is normally paid in equal monthly installments. Each installment includes interest on the unpaid balance and a payment on the principal. The amount applied to the principal increases with each successive payment because the amount of interest decreases. When a debt is decreased gradually by payments, it is **amortized.**

Computing the Monthly Payment. Real estate agents and finance company loan officers use payment tables to find quickly the exact amount of the monthly payment on mortgage loans. Such tables show the monthly payment to the nearest cent for loans ranging from hundreds to thousands of dollars at various rates of interest and for differing lengths of time. Other tables, such as Table 9–6, that are somewhat more complicated are also used.

Regarding difficulty of use, Table 13–1 falls between the two kinds of tables just described. The monthly payment for loans varying from hundreds to thousands of dollars at the rates and years shown can be found by multiplying the factor in Table 13–1 by the number of thousands in the loan. The procedure consists of only two steps:

1. Find the monthly payment on $1,000 at the given rate for the term (years) of the loan.
2. Multiply the monthly payment by the number of times 1,000 divides into the loan. (Round up for any fractional part of a cent.)

Example A:

Timothy Aiken bought a lot for $20,000 by paying $5,000 down and securing a 20-year mortgage loan for the balance at $12\frac{1}{2}\%$ interest. Use Table 13–1 to find the uniform monthly payment that will repay the loan with interest by the end of the twentieth year.

Solution:

1. The factor 11.36141 is on the twentieth line in the 12.5% column.
2. $20,000 − $5,000 = $15,000   mortgage loan

$$\frac{\$15,000}{1,000} \times 11.36141 = \$15 \times 11.36141$$
$$= \$170.42115 = \$170.43 \quad \text{monthly payment}$$

The procedure for using Table 13–1 may be summarized in the following formula:

$$P_{\overline{n}|r} = F\frac{B}{1000}$$

P = Payment to be made
n = Number of payments (table line)
r = Annual interest rate (table column)
F = Factor at intersection of n and r in payment table
B = Balance owed (principal)

Using the formula above and Table 13–1 gives the following solution to Example A.

Chapter 13. Credit

$$P_{\overline{n}|}r = F\frac{B}{1000}$$

$$P_{\overline{20}|}12.5 = 11.36141 \times \frac{15,000}{1,000}$$

$$P_{\overline{20}|}12.5 = \$170.43$$

Of course, Table 13-1 may be used for loans that amount to less than $1,000. In such cases the factor representing the principal will be a decimal.

Example B: Lucille Odum borrowed $850 at 18% and promised to repay it by making monthly payments for 2 years. Use Table 13-1 to find the amount of each monthly payment.

Solution: 1. The factor 49.92410 is on the second line in the 18% column.

2. $\dfrac{\$850}{1,000} \times 49.92410 = \$0.85 \times 49.9241$

$$= 42.435485 = \$42.44 \quad \text{monthly payment}$$

Or $\quad P_{\overline{n}|}r = F\dfrac{B}{1000}$

$$P_{\overline{2}|}18 = 49.92410 \times \frac{850}{1000}$$

$$P_{\overline{2}|}18 = \$42.44$$

Preparing a Loan Payment Schedule. After the amount of the monthly payment has been determined, a loan payment schedule may be prepared. A computer can be programmed to compute and print the loan payment schedule in a matter of seconds rather than the hours an individual working with a calculator may need. Figure 13-3 illustrates the first 5 of the 240 monthly payments for the $15,000, $12\frac{1}{2}$%, 20-year loan in Example A. The following example shows how the amounts in the schedule may be calculated when a computer is not available.

Mortgage Loan Payment Schedule

Original Loan, $15,000			Interest, $12\frac{1}{2}$%
Monthly Payments, $170.43			Term, 20 years

Payment Number	Monthly Payment	Payment on Interest	Payment on Principal	Principal Balance
1	$170.43	$156.25	$14.18	$14,985.82
2	170.43	156.10	14.33	14,971.49
3	170.43	155.95	14.48	14,957.01
4	170.43	155.80	14.63	14,942.38
5	170.43	155.65	14.78	14,927.60

Figure 13-3 A Mortgage Payment Schedule

				Interest Rate				
Years	8.5%	9%	9.5%	10%	10.5%	11%	11.5%	12%
1	87.21978	87.45148	87.68351	87.91589	88.1486	88.38166	88.61505	88.84879
2	45.45567	45.68474	45.91449	46.14493	46.37604	46.60784	46.84032	47.07347
3	31.56754	31.79973	32.03295	32.26719	32.50244	32.73872	32.97601	33.21431
4	24.6483	24.88504	25.12314	25.36258	25.60338	25.84552	26.08901	26.33384
5	20.51653	20.75836	21.00186	21.24704	21.4939	21.74242	21.99261	22.24445
6	17.77838	18.02554	18.27469	18.52584	18.77897	19.03408	19.29116	19.55019
7	15.83649	16.08908	16.34398	16.60118	16.86067	17.12244	17.38646	17.65273
8	14.39213	14.6502	14.91089	15.17416	15.44002	15.70843	15.97937	16.25284
9	13.27935	13.54291	13.80936	14.07869	14.35086	14.62586	14.90366	15.18423
10	12.39857	12.66758	12.93976	13.21507	13.4935	13.775	14.05954	14.34709
11	11.68639	11.9608	12.23865	12.51988	12.80446	13.09235	13.3835	13.67788
12	11.10056	11.38031	11.66373	11.95078	12.24141	12.53555	12.83317	13.13419
13	10.61179	10.89681	11.18572	11.47848	11.77502	12.07527	12.37918	12.68666
14	10.19919	10.48938	10.78368	11.08203	11.38434	11.69054	12.00055	12.3143
15	9.84740	10.14267	10.44225	10.74605	11.05399	11.36597	11.6819	12.00168
16	9.54491	9.84516	10.1499	10.45902	10.77242	11.09	11.41165	11.73725
17	9.28292	9.58804	9.89781	10.2121	10.53081	10.85381	11.18096	11.51216
18	9.05457	9.36445	9.67911	9.99844	10.32228	10.6505	10.98295	11.3195
19	8.85446	9.16897	9.4884	9.81259	10.14139	10.47464	10.81218	11.15386
20	8.67823	8.99726	9.32131	9.65022	9.9838	10.32188	10.6643	11.01086
21	8.52239	8.84581	9.17434	9.5078	9.84599	10.18871	10.53578	10.887
22	8.38406	8.71174	9.04461	9.38246	9.72507	10.07223	10.42374	10.77938
23	8.26087	8.59268	8.92974	9.27182	9.61867	9.97008	10.32581	10.68565
24	8.15082	8.48664	8.82775	9.17389	9.52481	9.88027	10.24002	10.60382
25	8.05227	8.39196	8.73697	9.08701	9.44182	9.80113	10.16469	10.53224
26	7.9638	8.30723	8.65599	9.00977	9.36829	9.73127	10.09844	10.46952
27	7.88421	8.23125	8.58361	8.94098	9.30304	9.6695	10.04008	10.41449
28	7.81247	8.163	8.51882	8.8796	9.24504	9.6148	9.98859	10.36613
29	7.7477	8.10158	8.46071	8.82477	9.19341	9.56629	9.94312	10.32359
30	7.68913	8.04623	8.40854	8.77572	9.14739	9.52323	9.90291	10.28613
35	7.46861	7.83993	8.21612	8.59672	8.98134	9.36958	9.76107	10.1555
40	7.33094	7.71361	8.10062	8.49146	8.8857	9.28294	9.68282	10.085

Table 13–1 Monthly Payments Necessary to Amortize a $1,000 Loan

				Interest Rate				
Years	12.5%	13%	13.5%	14%	14.5%	15%	15.5%	16%
1	89.08286	89.31728	89.55203	89.78712	90.02255	90.25831	90.49442	90.73086
2	47.30731	47.54182	47.77701	48.01288	48.24943	48.48665	48.72454	48.96311
3	33.45363	33.69395	33.93529	34.17763	34.42098	34.66533	34.91068	35.15703
4	26.58	26.8275	27.07632	27.32648	27.57795	27.83075	28.08486	28.34028
5	22.49794	22.75307	23.00985	23.26825	23.52828	23.78993	24.05319	24.31806
6	19.81118	20.07411	20.33896	20.60574	20.87443	21.14501	21.41749	21.69184
7	17.92124	18.19196	18.46489	18.74001	19.0173	19.29675	19.57835	19.86206
8	16.52881	16.80726	17.08816	17.3715	17.65726	17.94541	18.23592	18.52879
9	15.46755	15.75359	16.04231	16.3337	16.62772	16.92434	17.22353	17.52525
10	14.63762	14.93107	15.22743	15.52664	15.82868	16.1335	16.44105	16.75131
11	13.97543	14.27611	14.57987	14.88666	15.19644	15.50915	15.82474	16.14317
12	13.43857	13.74625	14.05717	14.37127	14.68849	15.00877	15.33204	15.65825
13	12.99766	13.3121	13.62992	13.95103	14.27538	14.60287	14.93346	15.26704
14	12.63168	12.95264	13.27707	13.6049	13.93603	14.2704	14.6079	14.94845
15	12.32522	12.65242	12.98319	13.31741	13.65501	13.99587	14.3399	14.68701
16	12.0667	12.39988	12.73668	13.07699	13.4207	13.7677	14.11787	14.4711
17	11.84726	12.18614	12.52869	12.87476	13.22424	13.577	13.93292	14.29188
18	11.66001	12.00433	12.35231	12.70383	13.05874	13.41691	13.77819	14.14247
19	11.49951	11.84898	12.20211	12.55876	12.91876	13.28198	13.64826	14.01746
20	11.36141	11.71576	12.07375	12.43521	12.79998	13.1679	13.53881	13.91256
21	11.24218	11.60114	11.9637	12.32967	12.69889	13.07117	13.44636	13.8243
22	11.13896	11.50226	11.86911	12.23929	12.61264	12.98897	13.36812	13.7499
23	11.04937	11.41676	11.78761	12.16173	12.53892	12.91899	13.30176	13.68706
24	10.97144	11.34267	11.71727	12.09504	12.47578	12.85929	13.24539	13.63391
25	10.90354	11.27835	11.65645	12.03761	12.42163	12.80831	13.19745	13.58889
26	10.84427	11.22244	11.60378	11.98808	12.37512	12.7647	13.15663	13.55072
27	10.79247	11.17376	11.55812	11.94532	12.33514	12.72738	13.12183	13.51833
28	10.74713	11.13133	11.51849	11.90836	12.30074	12.6954	13.09215	13.49082
29	10.70741	11.09432	11.48406	11.87639	12.2711	12.66797	13.06681	13.46745
30	10.67258	11.062	11.45412	11.84872	12.24556	12.64444	13.04517	13.44757
35	10.55254	10.95193	11.35341	11.75673	12.16171	12.56813	12.97585	13.38469
40	10.48919	10.89514	11.30261	11.7114	12.12133	12.53224	12.944	13.35648

Table 13–1 Continued

Part 3. Mathematics Applications in Operating a Business

Years	Interest Rate							
	16.5%	17%	17.5%	18%	18.5%	19%	19.5%	20%
1	90.96764	91.20475	91.4422	91.67999	91.91812	92.15658	92.39537	92.63451
2	49.20235	49.44226	49.68285	49.9241	50.16603	50.40862	50.65188	50.8958
3	35.40438	35.65273	35.90207	36.1524	36.40371	36.65602	36.90931	37.16358
4	28.59701	28.85504	29.11437	29.375	29.63692	29.90012	30.1646	30.43036
5	24.58452	24.85258	25.12221	25.39343	25.66621	25.94055	26.21645	26.49388
6	21.96806	22.24613	22.52605	22.80779	23.09135	23.37672	23.66388	23.95283
7	20.14789	20.4358	20.72579	21.01784	21.31192	21.60802	21.90612	22.2062
8	18.82397	19.12145	19.42121	19.72321	20.02744	20.33386	20.64246	20.9532
9	17.82948	18.13619	18.44533	18.75689	19.07082	19.38708	19.70566	20.0265
10	17.06423	17.37977	17.69788	18.01852	18.34165	18.66724	18.99522	19.32557
11	16.46438	16.78832	17.11494	17.44418	17.77599	18.11033	18.44713	18.78634
12	15.98734	16.31923	16.65387	16.9912	17.33114	17.67365	18.01865	18.36609
13	15.60357	15.94295	16.28512	16.63001	16.97753	17.32762	17.68021	18.03522
14	15.29198	15.63838	15.98759	16.3395	16.69405	17.05115	17.41071	17.77265
15	15.03709	15.39004	15.74578	16.10421	16.46523	16.82876	17.1947	17.56297
16	14.8273	15.18634	15.54813	15.91256	16.27952	16.64893	17.02067	17.39466
17	14.65376	15.01843	15.38579	15.75573	16.12812	16.50288	16.87988	17.25903
18	14.50961	14.87947	15.25195	15.62691	16.00425	16.38384	16.76558	17.14936
19	14.38945	14.76409	15.14124	15.52078	15.90259	16.28655	16.67255	17.06046
20	14.28901	14.66801	15.04942	15.43312	15.81897	16.20685	16.59665	16.98825
21	14.20484	14.58782	14.9731	15.36055	15.75003	16.14143	16.53461	16.92948
22	14.13417	14.52077	14.90955	15.30038	15.69312	16.08764	16.48384	16.88158
23	14.07473	14.46461	14.85655	15.25041	15.64606	16.04337	16.44222	16.84251
24	14.02466	14.41751	14.81229	15.20887	15.60711	16.00689	16.40809	16.8106
25	13.98245	14.37797	14.7753	15.1743	15.57484	15.9768	16.38006	16.78452
26	13.94681	14.34473	14.74434	15.14551	15.54809	15.95197	16.35704	16.76319
27	13.9167	14.31678	14.71843	15.12151	15.52589	15.93146	16.33811	16.74574
28	13.89124	14.29326	14.69672	15.10149	15.50746	15.91451	16.32254	16.73146
29	13.86971	14.27344	14.67852	15.08479	15.49216	15.90051	16.30974	16.71977
30	13.85148	14.25675	14.66325	15.07085	15.47945	15.88892	16.2992	16.71019
35	13.79454	14.20526	14.61675	15.02892	15.44168	15.85495	16.26867	16.68278
40	13.76959	14.18324	14.59733	15.01182	15.42664	15.84175	16.25709	16.67264

Table 13-1 Continued

Example: Prepare the first five steps of a mortgage loan payment schedule for a 20-year, $12\frac{1}{2}\%$ loan of $15,000 that is to be paid by monthly installments of $170.43 each.

Solution: Computations for payment number 1 based on original loan:

$$\$15,000 \times 12.5\% \div 12 = \$156.25 \quad \text{interest for 1 month}$$
$$\$170.43 - \$156.25 = \$14.18 \quad \text{payment on principal}$$
$$\$15,000 - \$14.18 = \$14,985.82 \quad \text{principal balance}$$

Computations for payment number 2 based on new balance:

$$\$14,985.82 \times 12.5\% \div 12 = \$156.10 \quad \text{interest for 1 month}$$
$$\$170.43 - \$156.10 = \$14.33 \quad \text{payment on principal}$$
$$\$14,985.82 - \$14.33 = \$14,971.49 \quad \text{principal balance}$$

Computations for payment number 3 based on new balance:

$$\$14,971.49 \times 12.5\% \div 12 = \$155.95 \quad \text{interest for 1 month}$$
$$\$170.43 - \$155.95 = \$14.48 \quad \text{payment on principal}$$
$$\$14,971.49 - \$14.48 = \$14,957.01 \quad \text{principal balance}$$

Computations on succeeding payments follow the same procedure.

The amount of the final payment may be several cents smaller than the regular payment if the regular payment is rounded for a fractional part of a cent.

● Exercise 13-4

A. Find the amount of the monthly payment for each of the following purchases.

	Purchase Price	Down Payment	Rate of Interest	Term of Amortization
1.	$ 7,500	-0-	18%	5 years
2.	12,000	-0-	19%	10 years
3.	950	-0-	$19\frac{1}{2}\%$	15 years
4.	785	-0-	17%	20 years
5.	35,000	$ 7,000	15%	25 years
6.	65,000	15,000	$17\frac{1}{2}\%$	30 years
7.	125,000	20,000	13%	35 years
8.	237,500	25,000	14.5%	28 years
9.	478,000	100,000	12%	23 years
10.	755,875	75,000	9.5%	40 years

B. Solve these problems.

1. Jack Sargent is considering buying a house with a down payment and a $75,000 mortgage amortized over 25 years. Find the monthly payment at these rates of interest: **(a)** 10%, **(b)** 12%, **(c)** 14%, **(d)** 16%, and **(e)** 18%.

2. Geraldine Bridges is buying a house by making a down payment and signing a mortgage for $97,450 to be amortized over 30 years. Find the monthly payment at these rates of interest: **(a)** 11%, **(b)** 13%, **(c)** 15%, **(d)** 17%, and **(e)** 19%.

3. Bill and Betty Kovacik are planning to buy a house. After the down payment their mortgage at 13% will amount to $124,000. Find the monthly payment based on a mortgage amortization term of: **(a)** 30 years, **(b)** 25 years, **(c)** 20 years, **(d)** 15 years, and **(e)** 10 years.

4. Joyce and Harold Chapman are considering buying a business property. Their mortgage will be for $438,000 at 14% interest. Find the monthly payment based on an amortization term of: **(a)** 10 years, **(b)** 15 years, **(c)** 20 years, **(d)** 25 years, and **(e)** 30 years.

5. Vernon Aguire secured a loan of $17,850 through a $9\frac{1}{2}$%, 15-year mortgage on his real property. How much is each monthly payment?

6. Edna Norris bought a lot for $15,000 by making a down payment of $3,000 and securing a loan for the balance at $14\frac{1}{2}$% interest for 8 years. Find the amount of the monthly payment.

7. A lot was purchased for $30,500 on the following terms: $6,000 down, with the balance to be paid in 10 years by monthly installments with interest at 14%. **(a)** Find the amount of each monthly payment. **(b)** Prepare the first five lines of a loan schedule. Show the portion of each payment that applies **(1)** to the interest and **(2)** to the principal; also show **(3)** the principal balance after each payment.

8. Stephen Blume bought a house for $176,000. The terms of the sale were 20% down and payment of the balance monthly over a 25-year amortization at 13.5% interest. **(a)** Find the amount of each payment. **(b)** Prepare the first five lines of a loan schedule. Show the portion of each payment that applies **(1)** to the interest and **(2)** to the principal; also show **(3)** the principal balance after each payment.

THE ANNUAL PERCENTAGE RATE

In most cases, there is a charge for the use of credit. The Federal Truth in Lending Law was enacted to require that consumers be given the exact finance charge and an unbiased method of comparing that charge with the finance charge from a different creditor. The two most important things about the cost of credit are (1) the finance charge and (2) the annual percentage rate (APR). The **finance charge** is the amount of money one pays to obtain credit. The **annual percentage rate** is a percent that enables one to know the expense of using $1 for one whole year. For example, 18% means that the interest expense for using $1 for one year is $0.18, or $18 for the use of $100. When an interest rate is converted to an annual percentage rate, it enables one to compare credit costs regardless of the dollar amount of those costs or the length of time for which the credit is extended.

Regulation Z pertaining to the Truth in Lending Law was issued by the Board of Governors of the Federal Reserve System. All real estate credit transactions and most other credit transactions are covered by Regulation Z. Both the finance charge and the annual percentage rate must be displayed prominently on the forms and statements that are used by a creditor to make the required disclosures. The annual percentage rate shown in the disclosure statements must be accurate to the nearest $\frac{1}{4}\%$.

Finding the annual percentage rate for open-end credit, such as for credit cards and charge accounts, is easy. As the APR is based on one year, the periodic (monthly, weekly, daily) rate is simply multiplied by the number of periods in one year. For example, a monthly rate of 1.5% times 12 months per year gives an annual percentage rate of 18%. A weekly rate of 0.5% times 52 weeks equals an annual percentage rate of 26%.

Finding the annual percentage rate for installment credit is more complicated. The United States Rule is applied; that is, payments on a debt go first to pay the interest on the debt. To simplify the computations, there are tables and various formulas that may be used.

Using APR Tables

Dividing the finance charge by the number of dollars being financed gives a quotient which is the finance charge per dollar borrowed. Multiplying this result by 100 gives the finance charge per $100. The APR tables made available by the Federal Reserve System are basically tables of such quotients. The body of these tables consists of quotients that are each a finance charge per $100. There are tables based on weekly, monthly, and other less common payment plans. Because space is limited, and as monthly payments are most common, the tables in this book are for monthly payment plans only.

These tables are used mainly to find the annual percentage rate and to find the payment needed to amortize a debt by installments.

Finding the Annual Percentage Rate. To use annual percentage rate tables such as Table 13–2, there are essentially only two rules to follow:

1. Multiply the finance charge by 100 and then divide by the total amount being financed. This quotient is the finance charge per $100.
2. Find the number of payments in the first column on the left. Read across on this line until you find the quotient closest to that found in Step 1. The rate found at the top of that column is the annual percentage rate.

Step 1 above is summarized in the following formula:

$$Q_n = \frac{C(100)}{B}$$

Q = Quotient in APR tables
n = Number of payments (table line)
C = Total finance charge
B = Amount borrowed (principal)

Example: A dining table and chairs are on sale for $1,975. The 15-month installment terms provide for a down payment of $250 and a finance charge of $276. Find **(a)** the quotient to look for and **(b)** the annual percentage rate to the nearest $\frac{1}{4}\%$.

Solution: **(a)** $1,975 - $250 = $1,725   amount borrowed (B)

$$Q_n = \frac{C(100)}{B} = \frac{276 \times 100}{1,725}$$
$$Q_{15} = 16.00$$

(b) On line 15 of Table 13–2, the quotient 16.00 falls between 15.83 and 16.01. As 16.01 is closer to 16.00, the rate at the top of that column is the annual percentage rate. Thus, 23.00% is the APR.

Interpolating to Find the APR. If the exact finance charge per $100 (quotient) is found in the table, the rate shown at the top of the column is also exact. When the exact quotient is not found in the table, rather than taking the nearest quotient, a more exact rate may be computed by interpolation. **Interpolation** is a method of prorating amounts. In other words, the distance from the smaller quotient in the table to the actual quotient is considered to be proportionate to the distance from the smaller rate to the actual rate.

For example (see Figure 13–4), the actual quotient for 10 periods is 15.20, which falls between 15.12 and 15.24 in the table. The distance from the smaller rate of 31.75% to the actual APR is considered to be proportionate to the distance from the smaller quotient of 15.12 to the actual quotient of 15.20. A proportion equation may be used to find the amount to add to the smaller rate. These values are used in the example below.

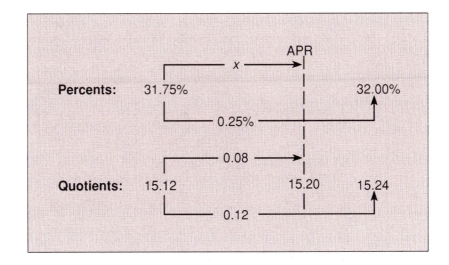

Figure 13–4 Interpolation of Annual Percentage Rate

Chapter 13. Credit

Example:

Kwik Kash Loan Company is offering loans of $1,400 to be repaid with 10 payments of $161.28 each. Find **(a)** the total finance charge, **(b)** the finance charge per $100, and **(c)** the annual percentage rate by interpolation.

Solution:

(a) $(\$161.28 \times 10) - \$1,400 = \$212.80$ finance charge

(b) $Q_n = \dfrac{C(100)}{B} = \dfrac{212.80 \times 100}{1,400}$

$Q_{10} = 15.20$ finance charge per $100

(c) Write a proportion equation using the percents and quotients in Table 13–2.

$$\frac{x}{0.25\%} \qquad \frac{0.08}{0.12}$$

$$x = \frac{8}{12}(0.25\%)$$

$$x = 0.17\%$$

The quotient of 15.12 gives the rate of 31.75%, which is too small for the quotient 15.20 by 0.17%. Therefore, $31.75\% + 0.17\% = 31.92\%$, the annual percentage rate.

Although the annual percentage rate of 31.92% is high, it is well within the legal limits of small loan rates in many states. In some states the maximum legal rate on small loans is much higher.

Finding the Monthly Payment. The annual percentage rate tables may also be used to find the amount of a periodic payment. The quotient formula for finding the finance charge per $100 may be rewritten to find the total finance charge when the quotient is known:

$$\text{If } \frac{C(100)}{B} = Q, \text{ then } C = Q \div \frac{100}{B}, \text{ which becomes } C = \frac{QB}{100}.$$

Of course, the payment (P) is the sum of the amount borrowed (B) and the total finance charge (C) divided by the number of payments (n):

$$P = \frac{B + C}{n}.$$

Example:

A retailer who charges 21% on installment accounts has bedroom furniture for sale at $1,995. A customer wishes to pay $445 down and the balance in 18 monthly payments. Use Table 13–2 to find **(a)** the total finance charge and **(b)** the monthly payment.

Solution:

(a) $\$1,995 - \$445 = \$1,550$ balance
The quotient 17.44 is shown on line 18 of the 21% column of Table 13–2.

$$C_n = \frac{QB}{100} = \frac{17.44 \times 1,550}{100}$$

$$C_{18} = 270.32 \quad \text{total finance charge}$$

(b) $P = \dfrac{B + C}{n} = \dfrac{1,550 + 270.32}{18}$

$P = \$101.13$ monthly payment

NUMBER OF PAYMENTS	ANNUAL PERCENTAGE RATE															
	6.00%	6.25%	6.50%	6.75%	7.00%	7.25%	7.50%	7.75%	8.00%	8.25%	8.50%	8.75%	9.00%	9.25%	9.50%	9.75%
	(FINANCE CHARGE PER $100 OF AMOUNT FINANCED)															
1	0.50	0.52	0.54	0.56	0.58	0.60	0.62	0.65	0.67	0.69	0.71	0.73	0.75	0.77	0.79	0.81
2	0.75	0.78	0.81	0.84	0.88	0.91	0.94	0.97	1.00	1.03	1.06	1.10	1.13	1.16	1.19	1.22
3	1.00	1.04	1.09	1.13	1.17	1.21	1.25	1.29	1.34	1.38	1.42	1.46	1.50	1.55	1.59	1.63
4	1.25	1.31	1.36	1.41	1.46	1.51	1.57	1.62	1.67	1.72	1.78	1.83	1.88	1.93	1.99	2.04
5	1.50	1.57	1.63	1.69	1.76	1.82	1.88	1.95	2.01	2.07	2.13	2.20	2.26	2.32	2.39	2.45
6	1.76	1.83	1.90	1.98	2.05	2.13	2.20	2.27	2.35	2.42	2.49	2.57	2.64	2.72	2.79	2.86
7	2.01	2.09	2.18	2.26	2.35	2.43	2.52	2.60	2.68	2.77	2.85	2.94	3.02	3.11	3.19	3.28
8	2.26	2.36	2.45	2.55	2.64	2.74	2.83	2.93	3.02	3.12	3.21	3.31	3.40	3.50	3.60	3.69
9	2.52	2.62	2.73	2.83	2.94	3.05	3.15	3.26	3.36	3.47	3.57	3.68	3.79	3.89	4.00	4.11
10	2.77	2.89	3.00	3.12	3.24	3.35	3.47	3.59	3.70	3.82	3.94	4.05	4.17	4.29	4.41	4.52
11	3.02	3.15	3.28	3.41	3.53	3.66	3.79	3.92	4.04	4.17	4.30	4.43	4.56	4.68	4.81	4.94
12	3.28	3.42	3.56	3.69	3.83	3.97	4.11	4.25	4.39	4.52	4.66	4.80	4.94	5.08	5.22	5.36
13	3.53	3.68	3.83	3.98	4.13	4.28	4.43	4.58	4.73	4.88	5.03	5.18	5.33	5.48	5.63	5.78
14	3.79	3.95	4.11	4.27	4.43	4.59	4.75	4.91	5.07	5.23	5.39	5.55	5.72	5.88	6.04	6.20
15	4.05	4.22	4.39	4.56	4.73	4.90	5.07	5.24	5.42	5.59	5.76	5.93	6.10	6.28	6.45	6.62
16	4.30	4.48	4.67	4.85	5.03	5.21	5.40	5.58	5.76	5.94	6.13	6.31	6.49	6.68	6.86	7.05
17	4.56	4.75	4.95	5.14	5.33	5.52	5.72	5.91	6.11	6.30	6.49	6.69	6.88	7.08	7.27	7.47
18	4.82	5.02	5.22	5.43	5.63	5.84	6.04	6.25	6.45	6.66	6.86	7.07	7.28	7.48	7.69	7.90
19	5.07	5.29	5.50	5.72	5.94	6.15	6.37	6.58	6.80	7.02	7.23	7.45	7.67	7.89	8.10	8.32
20	5.33	5.56	5.78	6.01	6.24	6.46	6.69	6.92	7.15	7.38	7.60	7.83	8.06	8.29	8.52	8.75
21	5.59	5.83	6.07	6.30	6.54	6.78	7.02	7.26	7.50	7.74	7.97	8.21	8.46	8.70	8.94	9.18
22	5.85	6.10	6.35	6.60	6.84	7.09	7.34	7.59	7.84	8.10	8.35	8.60	8.85	9.10	9.36	9.61
23	6.11	6.37	6.63	6.89	7.15	7.41	7.67	7.93	8.19	8.46	8.72	8.98	9.25	9.51	9.77	10.04
24	6.37	6.64	6.91	7.18	7.45	7.73	8.00	8.27	8.55	8.82	9.09	9.37	9.64	9.92	10.19	10.47
25	6.63	6.91	7.19	7.48	7.76	8.04	8.33	8.61	8.90	9.18	9.47	9.75	10.04	10.33	10.62	10.90
26	6.89	7.18	7.48	7.77	8.07	8.36	8.66	8.95	9.25	9.55	9.84	10.14	10.44	10.74	11.04	11.34
27	7.15	7.46	7.76	8.07	8.37	8.68	8.99	9.29	9.60	9.91	10.22	10.53	10.84	11.15	11.46	11.77
28	7.41	7.73	8.05	8.36	8.68	9.00	9.32	9.64	9.96	10.28	10.60	10.92	11.24	11.56	11.89	12.21
29	7.67	8.00	8.33	8.66	8.99	9.32	9.65	9.98	10.31	10.64	10.97	11.31	11.64	11.98	12.31	12.65
30	7.94	8.28	8.61	8.96	9.30	9.64	9.98	10.32	10.66	11.01	11.35	11.70	12.04	12.39	12.74	13.09
31	8.20	8.55	8.90	9.25	9.60	9.96	10.31	10.67	11.02	11.38	11.73	12.09	12.45	12.81	13.17	13.53
32	8.46	8.82	9.19	9.55	9.91	10.28	10.64	11.01	11.38	11.74	12.11	12.48	12.85	13.22	13.59	13.97
33	8.73	9.10	9.47	9.85	10.22	10.60	10.98	11.36	11.73	12.11	12.49	12.88	13.26	13.64	14.02	14.41
34	8.99	9.37	9.76	10.15	10.53	10.92	11.31	11.70	12.09	12.48	12.88	13.27	13.66	14.06	14.45	14.85
35	9.25	9.65	10.05	10.45	10.85	11.25	11.65	12.05	12.45	12.85	13.26	13.66	14.07	14.48	14.89	15.29
36	9.52	9.93	10.34	10.75	11.16	11.57	11.98	12.40	12.81	13.23	13.64	14.06	14.48	14.90	15.32	15.74
37	9.78	10.20	10.63	11.05	11.47	11.89	12.32	12.74	13.17	13.60	14.03	14.46	14.89	15.32	15.75	16.19
38	10.05	10.48	10.91	11.35	11.78	12.22	12.66	13.09	13.53	13.97	14.41	14.85	15.30	15.74	16.19	16.63
39	10.32	10.76	11.20	11.65	12.10	12.54	12.99	13.44	13.89	14.35	14.80	15.25	15.71	16.17	16.62	17.08
40	10.58	11.04	11.49	11.95	12.41	12.87	13.33	13.79	14.26	14.72	15.19	15.65	16.12	16.59	17.06	17.53
41	10.85	11.32	11.78	12.25	12.72	13.20	13.67	14.14	14.62	15.10	15.57	16.05	16.53	17.01	17.50	17.98
42	11.12	11.60	12.08	12.56	13.04	13.52	14.01	14.50	14.98	15.47	15.96	16.45	16.95	17.44	17.94	18.43
43	11.38	11.87	12.37	12.86	13.36	13.85	14.35	14.85	15.35	15.85	16.35	16.86	17.36	17.87	18.38	18.89
44	11.65	12.15	12.66	13.16	13.67	14.18	14.69	15.20	15.71	16.23	16.74	17.26	17.78	18.30	18.82	19.34
45	11.92	12.44	12.95	13.47	13.99	14.51	15.03	15.55	16.08	16.61	17.13	17.66	18.19	18.73	19.26	19.79
46	12.19	12.72	13.24	13.77	14.31	14.84	15.37	15.91	16.45	16.99	17.53	18.07	18.61	19.16	19.70	20.25
47	12.46	13.00	13.54	14.08	14.62	15.17	15.72	16.26	16.81	17.37	17.92	18.47	19.03	19.59	20.15	20.71
48	12.73	13.28	13.83	14.39	14.94	15.50	16.06	16.62	17.18	17.75	18.31	18.88	19.45	20.02	20.59	21.16
49	13.00	13.56	14.13	14.69	15.26	15.83	16.40	16.98	17.55	18.13	18.71	19.29	19.87	20.45	21.04	21.62
50	13.27	13.84	14.42	15.00	15.58	16.16	16.75	17.33	17.92	18.51	19.10	19.69	20.29	20.89	21.48	22.08
51	13.54	14.13	14.72	15.31	15.90	16.50	17.09	17.69	18.29	18.89	19.50	20.10	20.71	21.32	21.93	22.55
52	13.81	14.41	15.01	15.62	16.22	16.83	17.44	18.05	18.66	19.28	19.89	20.51	21.13	21.76	22.38	23.01
53	14.08	14.69	15.31	15.92	16.54	17.16	17.78	18.41	19.03	19.66	20.29	20.92	21.56	22.19	22.83	23.47
54	14.36	14.98	15.61	16.23	16.86	17.50	18.13	18.77	19.41	20.05	20.69	21.34	21.98	22.63	23.28	23.94
55	14.63	15.26	15.90	16.54	17.19	17.83	18.48	19.13	19.78	20.43	21.09	21.75	22.41	23.07	23.73	24.40
56	14.90	15.55	16.20	16.85	17.51	18.17	18.83	19.49	20.15	20.82	21.49	22.16	22.83	23.51	24.19	24.87
57	15.17	15.84	16.50	17.17	17.83	18.50	19.18	19.85	20.53	21.21	21.89	22.58	23.26	23.95	24.64	25.34
58	15.45	16.12	16.80	17.48	18.16	18.84	19.53	20.21	20.91	21.60	22.29	22.99	23.69	24.39	25.10	25.80
59	15.72	16.41	17.10	17.79	18.48	19.18	19.88	20.58	21.28	21.99	22.70	23.41	24.12	24.84	25.55	26.27
60	16.00	16.70	17.40	18.10	18.81	19.52	20.23	20.94	21.66	22.38	23.10	23.82	24.55	25.28	26.01	26.75

Table 13–2 Annual Percentage Rate Table for Monthly Payment Plans

NUMBER OF PAYMENTS	ANNUAL PERCENTAGE RATE															
	10.00%	10.25%	10.50%	10.75%	11.00%	11.25%	11.50%	11.75%	12.00%	12.25%	12.50%	12.75%	13.00%	13.25%	13.50%	13.75%
	(FINANCE CHARGE PER $100 OF AMOUNT FINANCED)															
1	0.83	0.85	0.87	0.90	0.92	0.94	0.96	0.98	1.00	1.02	1.04	1.06	1.08	1.10	1.12	1.15
2	1.25	1.28	1.31	1.35	1.38	1.41	1.44	1.47	1.50	1.53	1.57	1.60	1.63	1.66	1.69	1.72
3	1.67	1.71	1.76	1.80	1.84	1.88	1.92	1.96	2.01	2.05	2.09	2.13	2.17	2.22	2.26	2.30
4	2.09	2.14	2.20	2.25	2.30	2.35	2.41	2.46	2.51	2.57	2.62	2.67	2.72	2.78	2.83	2.88
5	2.51	2.58	2.64	2.70	2.77	2.83	2.89	2.96	3.02	3.08	3.15	3.21	3.27	3.34	3.40	3.46
6	2.94	3.01	3.08	3.16	3.23	3.31	3.38	3.45	3.53	3.60	3.68	3.75	3.83	3.90	3.97	4.05
7	3.36	3.45	3.53	3.62	3.70	3.78	3.87	3.95	4.04	4.12	4.21	4.29	4.38	4.47	4.55	4.64
8	3.79	3.88	3.98	4.07	4.17	4.26	4.36	4.46	4.55	4.65	4.74	4.84	4.94	5.03	5.13	5.22
9	4.21	4.32	4.43	4.53	4.64	4.75	4.85	4.96	5.07	5.17	5.28	5.39	5.49	5.60	5.71	5.82
10	4.64	4.76	4.88	4.99	5.11	5.23	5.35	5.46	5.58	5.70	5.82	5.94	6.05	6.17	6.29	6.41
11	5.07	5.20	5.33	5.45	5.58	5.71	5.84	5.97	6.10	6.23	6.36	6.49	6.62	6.75	6.88	7.01
12	5.50	5.64	5.78	5.92	6.06	6.20	6.34	6.48	6.62	6.76	6.90	7.04	7.18	7.32	7.46	7.60
13	5.93	6.08	6.23	6.38	6.53	6.68	6.84	6.99	7.14	7.29	7.44	7.59	7.75	7.90	8.05	8.20
14	6.36	6.52	6.69	6.85	7.01	7.17	7.34	7.50	7.66	7.82	7.99	8.15	8.31	8.48	8.64	8.81
15	6.80	6.97	7.14	7.32	7.49	7.66	7.84	8.01	8.19	8.36	8.53	8.71	8.88	9.06	9.23	9.41
16	7.23	7.41	7.60	7.78	7.97	8.15	8.34	8.53	8.71	8.90	9.08	9.27	9.46	9.64	9.83	10.02
17	7.67	7.86	8.06	8.25	8.45	8.65	8.84	9.04	9.24	9.44	9.63	9.83	10.03	10.23	10.43	10.63
18	8.10	8.31	8.52	8.73	8.93	9.14	9.35	9.56	9.77	9.98	10.19	10.40	10.61	10.82	11.03	11.24
19	8.54	8.76	8.98	9.20	9.42	9.64	9.86	10.08	10.30	10.52	10.74	10.96	11.18	11.41	11.63	11.85
20	8.98	9.21	9.44	9.67	9.90	10.13	10.37	10.60	10.83	11.06	11.30	11.53	11.76	12.00	12.23	12.46
21	9.42	9.66	9.90	10.15	10.39	10.63	10.88	11.12	11.36	11.61	11.85	12.10	12.34	12.59	12.84	13.08
22	9.86	10.12	10.37	10.62	10.88	11.13	11.39	11.64	11.90	12.16	12.41	12.67	12.93	13.19	13.44	13.70
23	10.30	10.57	10.84	11.10	11.37	11.63	11.90	12.17	12.44	12.71	12.97	13.24	13.51	13.78	14.05	14.32
24	10.75	11.02	11.30	11.58	11.86	12.14	12.42	12.70	12.98	13.26	13.54	13.82	14.10	14.38	14.66	14.95
25	11.19	11.48	11.77	12.06	12.35	12.64	12.93	13.22	13.52	13.81	14.10	14.40	14.69	14.98	15.28	15.57
26	11.64	11.94	12.24	12.54	12.85	13.15	13.45	13.75	14.06	14.36	14.67	14.97	15.28	15.59	15.89	16.20
27	12.09	12.40	12.71	13.03	13.34	13.66	13.97	14.29	14.60	14.92	15.24	15.56	15.87	16.19	16.51	16.83
28	12.53	12.86	13.18	13.51	13.84	14.16	14.49	14.82	15.15	15.48	15.81	16.14	16.47	16.80	17.13	17.46
29	12.98	13.32	13.66	14.00	14.33	14.67	15.01	15.35	15.70	16.04	16.38	16.72	17.07	17.41	17.75	18.10
30	13.43	13.78	14.13	14.48	14.83	15.19	15.54	15.89	16.24	16.60	16.95	17.31	17.66	18.02	18.38	18.74
31	13.89	14.25	14.61	14.97	15.33	15.70	16.06	16.43	16.79	17.16	17.53	17.90	18.27	18.63	19.00	19.38
32	14.34	14.71	15.09	15.46	15.84	16.21	16.59	16.97	17.35	17.73	18.11	18.49	18.87	19.25	19.63	20.02
33	14.79	15.18	15.57	15.95	16.34	16.73	17.12	17.51	17.90	18.29	18.69	19.08	19.47	19.87	20.49	20.66
34	15.25	15.65	16.05	16.44	16.85	17.25	17.65	18.05	18.46	18.86	19.27	19.67	20.08	20.49	20.90	21.31
35	15.70	16.11	16.53	16.94	17.35	17.77	18.18	18.60	19.01	19.43	19.85	20.27	20.69	21.11	21.53	21.95
36	16.16	16.58	17.01	17.43	17.86	18.29	18.71	19.14	19.57	20.00	20.43	20.87	21.30	21.73	22.17	22.60
37	16.62	17.06	17.49	17.93	18.37	18.81	19.25	19.69	20.13	20.58	21.02	21.46	21.91	22.36	22.81	23.25
38	17.08	17.53	17.98	18.43	18.88	19.33	19.78	20.24	20.69	21.15	21.61	22.07	22.52	22.99	23.45	23.91
39	17.54	18.00	18.46	18.93	19.39	19.86	20.32	20.79	21.26	21.73	22.20	22.67	23.14	23.61	24.09	24.56
40	18.00	18.48	18.95	19.43	19.90	20.38	20.86	21.34	21.82	22.30	22.79	23.27	23.76	24.25	24.73	25.22
41	18.47	18.95	19.44	19.93	20.42	20.91	21.40	21.89	22.39	22.88	23.38	23.88	24.38	24.88	25.38	25.88
42	18.93	19.43	19.93	20.43	20.93	21.44	21.94	22.45	22.96	23.47	23.98	24.49	25.00	25.51	26.03	26.55
43	19.40	19.91	20.42	20.94	21.45	21.97	22.49	23.01	23.53	24.05	24.57	25.10	25.62	26.15	26.68	27.21
44	19.86	20.39	20.91	21.44	21.97	22.50	23.03	23.57	24.10	24.64	25.17	25.71	26.25	26.79	27.33	27.88
45	20.33	20.87	21.41	21.95	22.49	23.03	23.58	24.12	24.67	25.22	25.77	26.32	26.88	27.43	27.99	28.55
46	20.80	21.35	21.90	22.46	23.01	23.57	24.13	24.69	25.25	25.81	26.37	26.94	27.51	28.08	28.65	29.22
47	21.27	21.83	22.40	22.97	23.53	24.10	24.68	25.25	25.82	26.40	26.98	27.56	28.14	28.72	29.31	29.89
48	21.74	22.32	22.90	23.48	24.06	24.64	25.23	25.81	26.40	26.99	27.58	28.18	28.77	29.37	29.97	30.57
49	22.21	22.80	23.39	23.99	24.58	25.18	25.78	26.38	26.98	27.59	28.19	28.80	29.41	30.02	30.63	31.24
50	22.69	23.29	23.89	24.50	25.11	25.72	26.33	26.95	27.56	28.18	28.80	29.42	30.04	30.67	31.29	31.92
51	23.16	23.78	24.40	25.02	25.64	26.26	26.89	27.52	28.15	28.78	29.41	30.05	30.68	31.32	31.96	32.60
52	23.64	24.27	24.90	25.53	26.17	26.81	27.45	28.09	28.73	29.38	30.02	30.67	31.32	31.98	32.63	33.29
53	24.11	24.76	25.40	26.05	26.70	27.35	28.00	28.66	29.32	29.98	30.64	31.30	31.97	32.63	33.30	33.97
54	24.59	25.25	25.91	26.57	27.23	27.90	28.56	29.23	29.91	30.58	31.25	31.93	32.61	33.29	33.98	34.66
55	25.07	25.74	26.41	27.09	27.77	28.44	29.13	29.81	30.50	31.18	31.87	32.56	33.26	33.95	34.65	35.35
56	25.55	26.23	26.92	27.61	28.30	28.99	29.69	30.39	31.09	31.79	32.49	33.20	33.91	34.62	35.33	36.04
57	26.03	26.73	27.43	28.13	28.84	29.54	30.25	30.97	31.68	32.39	33.11	33.83	34.56	35.28	36.01	36.74
58	26.51	27.23	27.94	28.66	29.37	30.10	30.82	31.55	32.27	33.00	33.74	34.47	35.21	35.95	36.69	37.43
59	27.00	27.72	28.45	29.18	29.91	30.65	31.39	32.13	32.87	33.61	34.36	35.11	35.86	36.62	37.37	38.13
60	27.48	28.22	28.96	29.71	30.45	31.20	31.96	32.71	33.47	34.23	34.99	35.75	36.52	37.29	38.06	38.83

Table 13-2 Continued

NUMBER OF PAYMENTS	14.00%	14.25%	14.50%	14.75%	15.00%	15.25%	15.50%	15.75%	16.00%	16.25%	16.50%	16.75%	17.00%	17.25%	17.50%	17.75%
					(FINANCE CHARGE PER $100 OF AMOUNT FINANCED)											
1	1.17	1.19	1.21	1.23	1.25	1.27	1.29	1.31	1.33	1.35	1.37	1.40	1.42	1.44	1.46	1.48
2	1.75	1.78	1.82	1.85	1.88	1.91	1.94	1.97	2.00	2.04	2.07	2.10	2.13	2.16	2.19	2.22
3	2.34	2.38	2.43	2.47	2.51	2.55	2.59	2.64	2.68	2.72	2.76	2.80	2.85	2.89	2.93	2.97
4	2.93	2.99	3.04	3.09	3.14	3.20	3.25	3.30	3.36	3.41	3.46	3.51	3.57	3.62	3.67	3.73
5	3.53	3.59	3.65	3.72	3.78	3.84	3.91	3.97	4.04	4.10	4.16	4.23	4.29	4.35	4.42	4.48
6	4.12	4.20	4.27	4.35	4.42	4.49	4.57	4.64	4.72	4.79	4.87	4.94	5.02	5.09	5.17	5.24
7	4.72	4.81	4.89	4.98	5.06	5.15	5.23	5.32	5.40	5.49	5.58	5.66	5.75	5.83	5.92	6.00
8	5.32	5.42	5.51	5.61	5.80	5.80	5.90	6.00	6.09	6.19	6.29	6.38	6.48	6.58	6.67	6.77
9	5.92	6.03	6.14	6.25	6.35	6.46	6.57	6.68	6.78	6.89	7.00	7.11	7.22	7.32	7.43	7.54
10	6.53	6.65	6.77	6.88	7.00	7.12	7.24	7.36	7.48	7.60	7.72	7.84	7.96	8.08	8.19	8.31
11	7.14	7.27	7.40	7.53	7.66	7.79	7.92	8.05	8.18	8.31	8.44	8.57	8.70	8.83	8.96	9.09
12	7.74	7.89	8.03	8.17	8.31	8.45	8.59	8.74	8.88	9.02	9.16	9.30	9.45	9.59	9.73	9.87
13	8.36	8.51	8.66	8.81	8.97	9.12	9.27	9.43	9.58	9.73	9.89	10.04	10.20	10.35	10.50	10.66
14	8.97	9.13	9.30	9.46	9.63	9.79	9.96	10.12	10.29	10.45	10.62	10.78	10.95	11.11	11.28	11.45
15	9.59	9.76	9.94	10.11	10.29	10.47	10.64	10.82	11.00	11.17	11.35	11.53	11.71	11.88	12.06	12.24
16	10.20	10.39	10.58	10.77	10.95	11.14	11.33	11.52	11.71	11.90	12.09	12.28	12.46	12.65	12.84	13.03
17	10.82	11.02	11.22	11.42	11.62	11.82	12.02	12.22	12.42	12.62	12.83	13.03	13.23	13.43	13.63	13.83
18	11.45	11.66	11.87	12.08	12.29	12.50	12.72	12.93	13.14	13.35	13.57	13.78	13.99	14.21	14.42	14.64
19	12.07	12.30	12.52	12.74	12.97	13.19	13.41	13.64	13.86	14.09	14.31	14.54	14.76	14.99	15.22	15.44
20	12.70	12.93	13.17	13.41	13.64	13.88	14.11	14.35	14.59	14.82	15.06	15.30	15.54	15.77	16.01	16.25
21	13.33	13.58	13.82	14.07	14.32	14.57	14.82	15.06	15.31	15.56	15.81	16.06	16.31	16.56	16.81	17.07
22	13.96	14.22	14.48	14.74	15.00	15.26	15.52	15.78	16.04	16.30	16.57	16.83	17.09	17.36	17.62	17.88
23	14.59	14.87	15.14	15.41	15.68	15.96	16.23	16.50	16.78	17.05	17.32	17.60	17.88	18.15	18.43	18.70
24	15.23	15.51	15.80	16.08	16.37	16.65	16.94	17.22	17.51	17.80	18.09	18.37	18.66	18.95	19.24	19.53
25	15.87	16.17	16.46	16.76	17.06	17.35	17.65	17.95	18.25	18.55	18.85	19.15	19.45	19.75	20.05	20.36
26	16.51	16.82	17.13	17.44	17.75	18.06	18.37	18.68	18.99	19.30	19.62	19.93	20.24	20.56	20.87	21.19
27	17.15	17.47	17.80	18.12	18.44	18.76	19.09	19.41	19.74	20.06	20.39	20.71	21.04	21.37	21.69	22.02
28	17.80	18.13	18.47	18.80	19.14	19.47	19.81	20.15	20.49	20.82	21.16	21.50	21.84	22.18	22.52	22.86
29	18.45	18.79	19.14	19.49	19.83	20.18	20.53	20.88	21.23	21.58	21.94	22.29	22.64	22.99	23.35	23.70
30	19.10	19.45	19.81	20.17	20.54	20.90	21.26	21.62	21.99	22.35	22.72	23.09	23.45	23.81	24.18	24.55
31	19.75	20.12	20.49	20.87	21.24	21.61	21.99	22.37	22.74	23.12	23.50	23.88	24.26	24.64	25.02	25.40
32	20.40	20.79	21.17	21.56	21.95	22.33	22.72	23.11	23.50	23.89	24.28	24.68	25.07	25.46	25.86	26.25
33	21.06	21.46	21.85	22.25	22.65	23.06	23.46	23.86	24.26	24.67	25.07	25.48	25.88	26.29	26.70	27.11
34	21.72	22.13	22.54	22.95	23.37	23.78	24.19	24.61	25.03	25.44	25.86	26.28	26.70	27.12	27.54	27.97
35	22.38	22.80	23.23	23.65	24.08	24.51	24.94	25.36	25.79	26.23	26.66	27.09	27.52	27.96	28.39	28.83
36	23.04	23.48	23.92	24.35	24.80	25.24	25.68	26.12	26.57	27.01	27.46	27.90	28.35	28.80	29.25	29.70
37	23.70	24.16	24.61	25.06	25.51	25.97	26.42	26.88	27.34	27.80	28.26	28.72	29.18	29.64	30.10	30.57
38	24.37	24.84	25.30	25.77	26.24	26.70	27.17	27.64	28.11	28.59	29.06	29.53	30.01	30.49	30.96	31.44
39	25.04	25.52	26.00	26.48	26.96	27.44	27.92	28.41	28.89	29.38	29.87	30.36	30.85	31.34	31.83	32.32
40	25.71	26.20	26.70	27.19	27.69	28.18	28.68	29.18	29.68	30.18	30.69	31.19	31.69	32.19	32.69	33.20
41	26.39	26.89	27.40	27.91	28.41	28.92	29.44	29.95	30.46	30.97	31.49	32.01	32.52	33.04	33.56	34.08
42	27.06	27.58	28.10	28.62	29.15	29.67	30.19	30.72	31.25	31.78	32.31	32.84	33.37	33.90	34.44	34.97
43	27.74	28.27	28.81	29.34	29.88	30.42	30.96	31.50	32.04	32.58	33.13	33.67	34.22	34.76	35.31	35.86
44	28.42	28.97	29.52	30.07	30.62	31.17	31.72	32.28	32.83	33.39	33.95	34.51	35.07	35.63	36.19	36.76
45	29.11	29.67	30.23	30.79	31.36	31.92	32.49	33.06	33.63	34.20	34.77	35.35	35.92	36.50	37.08	37.66
46	29.79	30.36	30.94	31.52	32.10	32.68	33.26	33.84	34.43	35.01	35.60	36.19	36.78	37.37	37.96	38.56
47	30.48	31.07	31.66	32.25	32.84	33.44	34.03	34.63	35.23	35.83	36.43	37.04	37.64	38.25	38.86	39.46
48	31.17	31.77	32.37	32.98	33.59	34.20	34.81	35.42	36.03	36.65	37.27	37.88	38.50	39.13	39.75	40.37
49	31.86	32.48	33.09	33.71	34.34	34.96	35.59	36.21	36.84	37.47	38.10	38.74	39.37	40.01	40.65	41.29
50	32.55	33.18	33.82	34.45	35.09	35.73	36.37	37.01	37.65	38.30	38.94	39.59	40.24	40.89	41.55	42.20
51	33.25	33.89	34.54	35.19	35.84	36.49	37.15	37.81	38.46	39.12	39.79	40.45	41.11	41.78	42.45	43.12
52	33.95	34.61	35.27	35.93	36.60	37.27	37.94	38.61	39.28	39.96	40.63	41.31	41.99	42.67	43.36	44.04
53	34.65	35.32	36.00	36.68	37.36	38.04	38.72	39.41	40.10	40.79	41.48	42.17	42.87	43.57	44.27	44.97
54	35.35	36.04	36.73	37.42	38.12	38.82	39.52	40.22	40.92	41.63	42.33	43.04	43.75	44.47	45.18	45.90
55	36.05	36.76	37.46	38.17	38.88	39.60	40.31	41.03	41.74	42.47	43.19	43.91	44.64	45.37	46.10	46.83
56	36.76	37.48	38.20	38.92	39.65	40.38	41.11	41.84	42.57	43.31	44.05	44.79	45.53	46.27	47.02	47.77
57	37.47	38.20	38.94	39.68	40.42	41.16	41.91	42.65	43.40	44.15	44.91	45.66	46.42	47.18	47.94	48.71
58	38.18	38.93	39.68	40.43	41.19	41.95	42.71	43.47	44.23	45.00	45.77	46.54	47.32	48.09	48.87	49.65
59	38.89	39.66	40.42	41.19	41.96	42.74	43.51	44.29	45.07	45.85	46.64	47.42	48.21	49.01	49.80	50.60
60	39.61	40.39	41.17	41.95	42.74	43.53	44.32	45.11	45.91	46.71	47.51	48.31	49.12	49.92	50.73	51.55

Table 13–2 Continued

NUMBER OF PAYMENTS	ANNUAL PERCENTAGE RATE																
	18.00%	18.25%	18.50%	18.75%	19.00%	19.25%	19.50%	19.75%	20.00%	20.25%	20.50%	20.75%	21.00%	21.25%	21.50%	21.75%
	(FINANCE CHARGE PER $100 OF AMOUNT FINANCED)															
1	1.50	1.52	1.54	1.56	1.58	1.60	1.62	1.65	1.67	1.69	1.71	1.73	1.75	1.77	1.79	1.81
2	2.26	2.29	2.32	2.35	2.38	2.41	2.44	2.48	2.51	2.54	2.57	2.60	2.63	2.66	2.70	2.73
3	3.01	3.06	3.10	3.14	3.18	3.23	3.27	3.31	3.35	3.39	3.44	3.48	3.52	3.56	3.60	3.65
4	3.78	3.83	3.88	3.94	3.99	4.04	4.10	4.15	4.20	4.25	4.31	4.36	4.41	4.47	4.52	4.57
5	4.54	4.61	4.67	4.74	4.80	4.86	4.93	4.99	5.06	5.12	5.18	5.25	5.31	5.37	5.44	5.50
6	5.32	5.39	5.46	5.54	5.61	5.69	5.76	5.84	5.91	5.99	6.06	6.14	6.21	6.29	6.36	6.44
7	6.09	6.18	6.26	6.35	6.43	6.52	6.60	6.69	6.78	6.86	6.95	7.04	7.12	7.21	7.29	7.38
8	6.87	6.96	7.06	7.16	7.26	7.35	7.45	7.55	7.64	7.74	7.84	7.94	8.03	8.13	8.23	8.33
9	7.65	7.76	7.87	7.97	8.08	8.19	8.30	8.41	8.52	8.63	8.73	8.84	8.95	9.06	9.17	9.28
10	8.43	8.55	8.67	8.79	8.91	9.03	9.15	9.27	9.39	9.51	9.63	9.75	9.88	10.00	10.12	10.24
11	9.22	9.35	9.49	9.62	9.75	9.88	10.01	10.14	10.28	10.41	10.54	10.67	10.80	10.94	11.07	11.20
12	10.02	10.16	10.30	10.44	10.59	10.73	10.87	11.02	11.16	11.31	11.45	11.59	11.74	11.88	12.02	12.17
13	10.81	10.97	11.12	11.28	11.43	11.59	11.74	11.90	12.05	12.21	12.36	12.52	12.67	12.83	12.99	13.14
14	11.61	11.78	11.95	12.11	12.28	12.45	12.61	12.78	12.95	13.11	13.28	13.45	13.62	13.79	13.95	14.12
15	12.42	12.59	12.77	12.95	13.13	13.31	13.49	13.67	13.85	14.03	14.21	14.39	14.57	14.75	14.93	15.11
16	13.22	13.41	13.60	13.80	13.99	14.18	14.37	14.56	14.75	14.94	15.13	15.33	15.52	15.71	15.90	16.10
17	14.04	14.24	14.44	14.64	14.85	15.05	15.25	15.46	15.66	15.86	16.07	16.27	16.48	16.68	16.89	17.09
18	14.85	15.07	15.28	15.49	15.71	15.93	16.14	16.36	16.58	16.79	17.01	17.22	17.44	17.66	17.88	18.09
19	15.67	15.90	16.12	16.35	16.58	16.81	17.03	17.26	17.49	17.72	17.95	18.18	18.41	18.64	18.87	19.10
20	16.49	16.73	16.97	17.21	17.45	17.69	17.93	18.17	18.41	18.66	18.90	19.14	19.38	19.63	19.87	20.11
21	17.32	17.57	17.82	18.07	18.33	18.58	18.83	19.09	19.34	19.60	19.85	20.11	20.36	20.62	20.87	21.13
22	18.15	18.41	18.68	18.94	19.21	19.47	19.74	20.01	20.27	20.54	20.81	21.08	21.34	21.61	21.88	22.15
23	18.98	19.26	19.54	19.81	20.09	20.37	20.65	20.93	21.21	21.49	21.77	22.05	22.33	22.61	22.90	23.18
24	19.82	20.11	20.40	20.69	20.98	21.27	21.56	21.86	22.15	22.44	22.74	23.03	23.33	23.62	23.92	24.21
25	20.66	20.96	21.27	21.57	21.87	22.18	22.48	22.79	23.10	23.40	23.71	24.02	24.32	24.63	24.94	25.25
26	21.50	21.82	22.14	22.45	22.77	23.09	23.41	23.73	24.04	24.36	24.68	25.01	25.33	25.65	25.97	26.29
27	22.35	22.68	23.01	23.34	23.67	24.00	24.33	24.67	25.00	25.33	25.67	26.00	26.34	26.67	27.01	27.34
28	23.20	23.55	23.89	24.23	24.58	24.92	25.27	25.61	25.96	26.30	26.65	27.00	27.35	27.70	28.05	28.40
29	24.06	24.41	24.77	25.13	25.49	25.84	26.20	26.56	26.92	27.28	27.64	28.00	28.37	28.73	29.09	29.46
30	24.92	25.29	25.66	26.03	26.40	26.77	27.14	27.52	27.89	28.26	28.64	29.01	29.39	29.77	30.14	30.52
31	25.78	26.16	26.55	26.93	27.32	27.70	28.09	28.47	28.86	29.25	29.64	30.03	30.42	30.81	31.20	31.59
32	26.65	27.04	27.44	27.84	28.24	28.64	29.04	29.44	29.84	30.24	30.64	31.05	31.45	31.85	32.26	32.67
33	27.52	27.93	28.34	28.75	29.16	29.57	29.99	30.40	30.82	31.23	31.65	32.07	32.49	32.91	33.33	33.75
34	28.39	28.81	29.24	29.66	30.09	30.52	30.95	31.37	31.80	32.23	32.67	33.10	33.53	33.96	34.40	34.83
35	29.27	29.71	30.14	30.58	31.02	31.47	31.91	32.35	32.79	33.24	33.68	34.13	34.58	35.03	35.47	35.92
36	30.15	30.60	31.05	31.51	31.96	32.42	32.87	33.33	33.79	34.25	34.71	35.17	35.63	36.09	36.56	37.02
37	31.03	31.50	31.97	32.43	32.90	33.37	33.84	34.32	34.79	35.26	35.74	36.21	36.69	37.16	37.64	38.12
38	31.92	32.40	32.88	33.37	33.85	34.34	34.82	35.30	35.79	36.28	36.77	37.26	37.75	38.24	38.73	39.23
39	32.81	33.31	33.80	34.30	34.80	35.30	35.80	36.30	36.80	37.30	37.81	38.31	38.82	39.32	39.83	40.34
40	33.71	34.22	34.73	35.24	35.75	36.26	36.78	37.29	37.81	38.33	38.85	39.37	39.89	40.41	40.93	41.46
41	34.61	35.13	35.66	36.18	36.71	37.24	37.77	38.30	38.83	39.36	39.89	40.43	40.96	41.50	42.04	42.58
42	35.51	36.05	36.59	37.13	37.67	38.21	38.76	39.30	39.85	40.40	40.95	41.50	42.05	42.60	43.15	43.71
43	36.42	36.97	37.52	38.08	38.63	39.19	39.75	40.31	40.87	41.44	42.00	42.57	43.13	43.70	44.27	44.84
44	37.33	37.89	38.46	39.03	39.60	40.18	40.75	41.33	41.90	42.48	43.06	43.64	44.22	44.81	45.39	45.98
45	38.24	38.82	39.41	39.99	40.58	41.17	41.75	42.35	42.94	43.53	44.13	44.72	45.32	45.92	46.52	47.12
46	39.16	39.75	40.35	40.95	41.55	42.16	42.76	43.37	43.98	44.58	45.20	45.81	46.42	47.03	47.65	48.27
47	40.08	40.69	41.30	41.92	42.54	43.15	43.77	44.40	45.02	45.64	46.27	46.90	47.53	48.16	48.79	49.42
48	41.00	41.63	42.26	42.89	43.52	44.15	44.79	45.43	46.07	46.71	47.35	47.99	48.64	49.28	49.93	50.58
49	41.93	42.57	43.22	43.86	44.51	45.16	45.81	46.46	47.12	47.77	48.43	49.09	49.75	50.41	51.08	51.74
50	42.86	43.52	44.18	44.84	45.50	46.17	46.83	47.50	48.17	48.84	49.52	50.19	50.87	51.55	52.23	52.91
51	43.79	44.47	45.14	45.82	46.50	47.18	47.86	48.55	49.23	49.92	50.61	51.30	51.99	52.69	53.38	54.08
52	44.73	45.42	46.11	46.80	47.50	48.20	48.89	49.59	50.30	51.00	51.71	52.41	53.12	53.83	54.55	55.26
53	45.67	46.38	47.08	47.79	48.50	49.22	49.93	50.65	51.37	52.09	52.81	53.53	54.26	54.98	55.71	56.44
54	46.62	47.34	48.06	48.79	49.51	50.24	50.97	51.70	52.44	53.17	53.91	54.65	55.39	56.14	56.88	57.63
55	47.57	48.30	49.04	49.78	50.52	51.27	52.02	52.76	53.52	54.27	55.02	55.78	56.54	57.30	58.06	58.82
56	48.52	49.27	50.03	50.78	51.54	52.30	53.06	53.83	54.60	55.37	56.14	56.91	57.68	58.46	59.24	60.02
57	49.47	50.24	51.01	51.79	52.56	53.34	54.12	54.90	55.68	56.47	57.25	58.04	58.84	59.63	60.43	61.22
58	50.43	51.22	52.00	52.79	53.58	54.38	55.17	55.97	56.77	57.57	58.38	59.18	59.99	60.80	61.62	62.43
59	51.39	52.20	53.00	53.80	54.61	55.42	56.23	57.05	57.87	58.68	59.51	60.33	61.15	61.98	62.81	63.64
60	52.36	53.18	54.00	54.82	55.64	56.47	57.30	58.13	58.96	59.80	60.64	61.48	62.32	63.17	64.01	64.86

Table 13-2 Continued

ANNUAL PERCENTAGE RATE

(FINANCE CHARGE PER $100 OF AMOUNT FINANCED)

NUMBER OF PAYMENTS	22.00%	22.25%	22.50%	22.75%	23.00%	23.25%	23.50%	23.75%	24.00%	24.25%	24.50%	24.75%	25.00%	25.25%	25.50%	25.75%
1	1.83	1.85	1.87	1.90	1.92	1.94	1.96	1.98	2.00	2.02	2.04	2.06	2.08	2.10	2.12	2.15
2	2.76	2.79	2.82	2.85	2.88	2.92	2.95	2.98	3.01	3.04	3.07	3.10	3.14	3.17	3.20	3.23
3	3.69	3.73	3.77	3.82	3.86	3.90	3.94	3.93	4.03	4.07	4.11	4.15	4.20	4.24	4.28	4.32
4	4.62	4.68	4.73	4.78	4.84	4.89	4.94	5.00	5.05	5.10	5.16	5.21	5.26	5.32	5.37	5.42
5	5.57	5.63	5.69	5.76	5.82	5.89	5.95	6.02	6.08	6.14	6.21	6.27	6.34	6.40	6.46	6.53
6	6.51	6.59	6.66	6.74	6.81	6.89	6.96	7.04	7.12	7.19	7.27	7.34	7.42	7.49	7.57	7.64
7	7.47	7.55	7.64	7.73	7.81	7.90	7.99	8.07	8.16	8.24	8.33	8.42	8.51	8.59	8.68	8.77
8	8.42	8.52	8.62	8.72	8.82	8.91	9.01	9.11	9.21	9.31	9.40	9.50	9.60	9.70	9.80	9.90
9	9.39	9.50	9.61	9.72	9.83	9.94	10.04	10.15	10.26	10.37	10.48	10.59	10.70	10.81	10.92	11.03
10	10.36	10.48	10.60	10.72	10.84	10.96	11.08	11.21	11.33	11.45	11.57	11.69	11.81	11.93	12.06	12.18
11	11.33	11.47	11.60	11.73	11.86	12.00	12.13	12.26	12.40	12.53	12.66	12.80	12.93	13.06	13.20	13.33
12	12.31	12.46	12.60	12.75	12.89	13.04	13.18	13.33	13.47	13.62	13.76	13.91	14.05	14.20	14.34	14.49
13	13.30	13.46	13.61	13.77	13.93	14.08	14.24	14.40	14.55	14.71	14.87	15.03	15.18	15.34	15.50	15.66
14	14.29	14.46	14.63	14.80	14.97	15.13	15.30	15.47	15.64	15.81	15.98	16.15	16.32	16.49	16.66	16.83
15	15.29	15.47	15.65	15.83	16.01	16.19	16.37	16.56	16.74	16.92	17.10	17.28	17.47	17.65	17.83	18.02
16	16.29	16.48	16.68	16.87	17.06	17.26	17.45	17.65	17.84	18.03	18.23	18.42	18.62	18.81	19.01	19.21
17	17.30	17.50	17.71	17.92	18.12	18.33	18.53	18.74	18.95	19.16	19.36	19.57	19.78	19.99	20.20	20.40
18	18.31	18.53	18.75	18.97	19.19	19.41	19.62	19.84	20.06	20.28	20.50	20.72	20.95	21.17	21.39	21.61
19	19.33	19.56	19.79	20.02	20.26	20.49	20.72	20.95	21.19	21.42	21.65	21.89	22.12	22.35	22.59	22.82
20	20.35	20.60	20.84	21.09	21.33	21.58	21.82	22.07	22.31	22.56	22.81	23.05	23.30	23.55	23.79	24.04
21	21.38	21.64	21.90	22.16	22.41	22.67	22.93	23.19	23.45	23.71	23.97	24.23	24.49	24.75	25.01	25.27
22	22.42	22.69	22.96	23.23	23.50	23.77	24.04	24.32	24.59	24.86	25.13	25.41	25.68	25.96	26.23	26.50
23	23.46	23.74	24.03	24.31	24.60	24.88	25.17	25.45	25.74	26.02	26.31	26.60	26.88	27.17	27.46	27.75
24	24.51	24.80	25.10	25.40	25.70	25.99	26.29	26.59	26.89	27.19	27.49	27.79	28.09	28.39	28.69	29.00
25	25.56	25.87	26.18	26.49	26.80	27.11	27.43	27.74	28.05	28.36	28.68	28.99	29.31	29.62	29.94	30.25
26	26.62	26.94	27.26	27.59	27.91	28.24	28.56	28.89	29.22	29.55	29.87	30.20	30.53	30.86	31.19	31.52
27	27.68	28.02	28.35	28.69	29.03	29.37	29.71	30.05	30.39	30.73	31.07	31.42	31.76	32.10	32.45	32.79
28	28.75	29.10	29.45	29.80	30.15	30.51	30.86	31.22	31.57	31.93	32.28	32.64	33.00	33.35	33.71	34.07
29	29.82	30.19	30.55	30.92	31.28	31.65	32.02	32.39	32.76	33.13	33.50	33.87	34.24	34.61	34.98	35.36
30	30.90	31.28	31.66	32.04	32.42	32.80	33.18	33.57	33.95	34.33	34.72	35.10	35.49	35.88	36.26	36.65
31	31.98	32.38	32.77	33.17	33.56	33.96	34.35	34.75	35.15	35.55	35.95	36.35	36.75	37.15	37.55	37.95
32	33.07	33.48	33.89	34.30	34.71	35.12	35.53	35.94	36.35	36.77	37.18	37.60	38.01	38.43	38.84	39.26
33	34.17	34.59	35.01	35.44	35.86	36.29	36.71	37.14	37.57	37.99	38.42	38.85	39.28	39.71	40.14	40.58
34	35.27	35.71	36.14	36.58	37.02	37.46	37.90	38.34	38.78	39.23	39.67	40.11	40.56	41.01	41.45	41.90
35	36.37	36.83	37.28	37.73	38.18	38.64	39.09	39.55	40.01	40.47	40.92	41.38	41.84	42.31	42.77	43.23
36	37.49	37.95	38.42	38.89	39.35	39.82	40.29	40.77	41.24	41.71	42.19	42.66	43.14	43.61	44.09	44.57
37	38.60	39.08	39.56	40.05	40.53	41.02	41.50	41.99	42.48	42.96	43.45	43.94	44.43	44.93	45.42	45.91
38	39.72	40.22	40.72	41.21	41.71	42.21	42.71	43.22	43.72	44.22	44.73	45.23	45.74	46.25	46.75	47.26
39	40.85	41.36	41.87	42.39	42.90	43.42	43.93	44.45	44.97	45.49	46.01	46.53	47.05	47.57	48.10	48.62
40	41.98	42.51	43.04	43.56	44.09	44.62	45.16	45.69	46.22	46.76	47.29	47.83	48.37	48.91	49.45	49.99
41	43.12	43.66	44.20	44.75	45.29	45.84	46.39	46.94	47.48	48.04	48.59	49.14	49.69	50.25	50.80	51.36
42	44.26	44.82	45.38	45.94	46.50	47.06	47.62	48.19	48.75	49.32	49.89	50.46	51.03	51.60	52.17	52.74
43	45.41	45.98	46.56	47.13	47.71	48.29	48.87	49.45	50.03	50.61	51.19	51.78	52.36	52.95	53.54	54.13
44	46.56	47.15	47.74	48.33	48.93	49.52	50.11	50.71	51.31	51.91	52.51	53.11	53.71	54.31	54.92	55.52
45	47.72	48.33	48.93	49.54	50.15	50.76	51.37	51.98	52.59	53.21	53.82	54.44	55.06	55.68	56.30	56.92
46	48.89	49.51	50.13	50.75	51.37	52.00	52.63	53.26	53.89	54.52	55.15	55.78	56.42	57.05	57.69	58.33
47	50.06	50.69	51.33	51.97	52.61	53.25	53.89	54.54	55.18	55.83	56.48	57.13	57.78	58.44	59.09	59.75
48	51.23	51.88	52.54	53.19	53.85	54.51	55.16	55.83	56.49	57.15	57.82	58.49	59.15	59.82	60.50	61.17
49	52.41	53.08	53.75	54.42	55.09	55.77	56.44	57.12	57.80	58.48	59.16	59.85	60.53	61.22	61.91	62.60
50	53.59	54.28	54.96	55.65	56.34	57.03	57.73	58.42	59.12	59.81	60.51	61.21	61.92	62.62	63.33	64.03
51	54.78	55.48	56.19	56.89	57.60	58.30	59.01	59.73	60.44	61.15	61.87	62.59	63.31	64.03	64.75	65.47
52	55.98	56.69	57.41	58.13	58.86	59.58	60.31	61.04	61.77	62.50	63.23	63.97	64.70	65.44	66.18	66.92
53	57.18	57.91	58.65	59.38	60.12	60.87	61.61	62.35	63.10	63.85	64.60	65.35	66.11	66.86	67.62	68.38
54	58.38	59.13	59.88	60.64	61.40	62.16	62.92	63.68	64.44	65.21	65.98	66.75	67.52	68.29	69.07	69.84
55	59.59	60.36	61.13	61.90	62.67	63.45	64.23	65.01	65.79	66.57	67.36	68.14	68.93	69.72	70.52	71.31
56	60.80	61.59	62.38	63.17	63.96	64.75	65.54	66.34	67.14	67.94	68.74	69.55	70.36	71.16	71.97	72.79
57	62.02	62.83	63.63	64.44	65.25	66.06	66.87	67.68	68.50	69.32	70.14	70.96	71.78	72.61	73.44	74.27
58	63.25	64.07	64.89	65.71	66.54	67.37	68.20	69.03	69.86	70.70	71.54	72.38	73.22	74.06	74.91	75.76
59	64.48	65.32	66.15	67.00	67.84	68.68	69.53	70.38	71.23	72.09	72.94	73.80	74.66	75.52	76.39	77.25
60	65.71	66.57	67.42	68.28	69.14	70.01	70.87	71.74	72.61	73.48	74.35	75.23	76.11	76.99	77.87	78.76

Table 13-2 Continued

NUMBER OF PAYMENTS	26.00%	26.25%	26.50%	26.75%	27.00%	27.25%	27.50%	27.75%	28.00%	28.25%	28.50%	28.75%	29.00%	29.25%	29.50%	29.75%
	ANNUAL PERCENTAGE RATE															
	(FINANCE CHARGE PER $100 OF AMOUNT FINANCED)															
1	2.17	2.19	2.21	2.23	2.25	2.27	2.29	2.31	2.33	2.35	2.37	2.40	2.42	2.44	2.46	2.48
2	3.26	3.29	3.32	3.36	3.39	3.42	3.45	3.48	3.51	3.54	3.58	3.61	3.64	3.67	3.70	3.73
3	4.36	4.41	4.45	4.49	4.53	4.58	4.62	4.66	4.70	4.74	4.79	4.83	4.87	4.91	4.96	5.00
4	5.47	5.53	5.58	5.63	5.69	5.74	5.79	5.85	5.90	5.95	6.01	6.06	6.11	6.17	6.22	6.27
5	6.59	6.66	6.72	6.79	6.85	6.91	6.98	7.04	7.11	7.17	7.24	7.30	7.37	7.43	7.49	7.56
6	7.72	7.79	7.87	7.95	8.02	8.10	8.17	8.25	8.32	8.40	8.48	8.55	8.63	8.70	8.78	8.85
7	8.85	8.94	9.03	9.11	9.20	9.29	9.37	9.46	9.55	9.64	9.72	9.81	9.90	9.98	10.07	10.16
8	9.99	10.09	10.19	10.29	10.39	10.49	10.58	10.68	10.78	10.88	10.98	11.08	11.18	11.28	11.38	11.47
9	11.14	11.25	11.36	11.47	11.58	11.69	11.80	11.91	12.03	12.14	12.25	12.36	12.47	12.58	12.69	12.80
10	12.30	12.42	12.54	12.67	12.79	12.91	13.03	13.15	13.28	13.40	13.52	13.64	13.77	13.89	14.01	14.14
11	13.46	13.60	13.73	13.87	14.00	14.13	14.27	14.40	14.54	14.67	14.81	14.94	15.08	15.21	15.35	15.48
12	14.64	14.78	14.93	15.07	15.22	15.37	15.51	15.66	15.81	15.95	16.10	16.25	16.40	16.54	16.69	16.84
13	15.82	15.97	16.13	16.29	16.45	16.61	16.77	16.93	17.09	17.24	17.40	17.56	17.72	17.88	18.04	18.20
14	17.00	17.17	17.35	17.52	17.69	17.86	18.03	18.20	18.37	18.54	18.72	18.89	19.06	19.23	19.41	19.58
15	18.20	18.38	18.57	18.75	18.93	19.12	19.30	19.48	19.67	19.85	20.04	20.22	20.41	20.59	20.78	20.96
16	19.40	19.60	19.79	19.99	20.19	20.38	20.58	20.78	20.97	21.17	21.37	21.57	21.76	21.96	22.16	22.36
17	20.61	20.82	21.03	21.24	21.45	21.66	21.87	22.08	22.29	22.50	22.71	22.92	23.13	23.34	23.55	23.77
18	21.83	22.05	22.27	22.50	22.72	22.94	23.16	23.39	23.61	23.83	24.06	24.28	24.51	24.73	24.96	25.18
19	23.06	23.29	23.53	23.76	24.00	24.23	24.47	24.71	24.94	25.18	25.42	25.65	25.89	26.13	26.37	26.61
20	24.29	24.54	24.79	25.04	25.28	25.53	25.78	26.03	26.28	26.53	26.78	27.04	27.29	27.54	27.79	28.04
21	25.53	25.79	26.05	26.32	26.58	26.84	27.11	27.37	27.63	27.90	28.16	28.43	28.69	28.96	29.22	29.49
22	26.78	27.05	27.33	27.61	27.88	28.16	28.44	28.71	28.99	29.27	29.55	29.82	30.10	30.38	30.66	30.94
23	28.04	28.32	28.61	28.90	29.19	29.48	29.77	30.07	30.36	30.65	30.94	31.23	31.53	31.82	32.11	32.41
24	29.30	29.60	29.90	30.21	30.51	30.82	31.12	31.43	31.73	32.04	32.34	32.65	32.96	33.27	33.57	33.88
25	30.57	30.89	31.20	31.52	31.84	32.16	32.49	32.80	33.12	33.44	33.76	34.08	34.40	34.72	35.04	35.37
26	31.85	32.18	32.51	32.84	33.18	33.51	33.84	34.18	34.51	34.84	35.18	35.51	35.85	36.19	36.52	36.86
27	33.14	33.48	33.83	34.17	34.52	34.87	35.21	35.56	35.91	36.26	36.61	36.96	37.31	37.66	38.01	38.36
28	34.43	34.79	35.15	35.51	35.87	36.23	36.59	36.96	37.32	37.68	38.05	38.41	38.78	39.15	39.51	39.88
29	35.73	36.10	36.48	36.85	37.23	37.61	37.98	38.36	38.74	39.12	39.50	39.88	40.26	40.64	41.02	41.40
30	37.04	37.43	37.82	38.21	38.60	38.99	39.38	39.77	40.17	40.56	40.95	41.35	41.75	42.14	42.54	42.94
31	38.35	38.76	39.16	39.57	39.97	40.38	40.79	41.19	41.60	42.01	42.42	42.83	43.24	43.65	44.06	44.48
32	39.68	40.10	40.52	40.94	41.36	41.78	42.20	42.62	43.05	43.47	43.90	44.32	44.75	45.17	45.60	46.03
33	41.01	41.44	41.88	42.31	42.75	43.19	43.62	44.06	44.50	44.94	45.38	45.82	46.26	46.70	47.15	47.59
34	42.35	42.80	43.25	43.70	44.15	44.60	45.05	45.51	45.96	46.42	46.87	47.33	47.79	48.24	48.70	49.16
35	43.69	44.16	44.62	45.09	45.56	46.02	46.49	46.96	47.43	47.90	48.37	48.85	49.32	49.79	50.27	50.74
36	45.05	45.53	46.01	46.49	46.97	47.45	47.94	48.42	48.91	49.40	49.88	50.37	50.86	51.35	51.84	52.33
37	46.41	46.90	47.40	47.90	48.39	48.89	49.39	49.89	50.40	50.90	51.41	51.91	52.41	52.92	53.42	53.93
38	47.77	48.29	48.80	49.31	49.82	50.34	50.86	51.37	51.89	52.41	52.93	53.45	53.97	54.49	55.02	55.54
39	49.15	49.68	50.20	50.73	51.26	51.79	52.33	52.86	53.39	53.93	54.46	55.00	55.54	56.08	56.62	57.16
40	50.53	51.07	51.62	52.16	52.71	53.26	53.81	54.35	54.90	55.46	56.01	56.56	57.12	57.67	58.23	58.79
41	51.92	52.48	53.04	53.60	54.16	54.73	55.29	55.86	56.42	56.99	57.56	58.13	58.70	59.28	59.85	60.42
42	53.32	53.89	54.47	55.05	55.63	56.21	56.79	57.37	57.95	58.54	59.12	59.71	60.30	60.89	61.48	62.07
43	54.72	55.31	55.90	56.50	57.09	57.69	58.29	58.89	59.49	60.09	60.69	61.30	61.90	62.51	63.11	63.72
44	56.13	56.74	57.35	57.96	58.57	59.19	59.80	60.42	61.03	61.65	62.27	62.89	63.51	64.14	64.76	65.39
45	57.55	58.17	58.80	59.43	60.06	60.69	61.32	61.95	62.59	63.22	63.86	64.50	65.13	65.77	66.42	67.06
46	58.97	59.61	60.26	60.90	61.55	62.20	62.84	63.49	64.15	64.80	65.45	66.11	66.76	67.42	68.08	68.74
47	60.40	61.06	61.72	62.38	63.05	63.71	64.38	65.05	65.71	66.38	67.06	67.73	68.40	69.08	69.75	70.43
48	61.84	62.52	63.20	63.87	64.56	65.24	65.92	66.60	67.29	67.98	68.67	69.36	70.05	70.74	71.44	72.13
49	63.29	63.98	64.68	65.37	66.07	66.77	67.47	68.17	68.87	69.58	70.29	70.99	71.70	72.41	73.13	73.84
50	64.74	65.45	66.16	66.88	67.59	68.31	69.03	69.75	70.47	71.19	71.91	72.64	73.37	74.10	74.83	75.56
51	66.20	66.93	67.66	68.39	69.12	69.86	70.59	71.33	72.07	72.81	73.55	74.29	75.04	75.78	76.53	77.28
52	67.67	68.41	69.16	69.91	70.66	71.41	72.16	72.92	73.67	74.43	75.19	75.95	76.72	77.49	78.25	79.02
53	69.14	69.90	70.67	71.43	72.20	72.97	73.74	74.52	75.29	76.07	76.85	77.62	78.41	79.19	79.97	80.76
54	70.62	71.40	72.18	72.97	73.75	74.54	75.33	76.12	76.91	77.71	78.50	79.30	80.10	80.90	81.71	82.51
55	72.11	72.91	73.71	74.51	75.31	76.12	76.92	77.73	78.55	79.36	80.17	80.99	81.81	82.63	83.45	84.27
56	73.60	74.42	75.24	76.06	76.88	77.70	78.53	79.35	80.18	81.02	81.85	82.68	83.52	84.36	85.20	86.04
57	75.10	75.94	76.77	77.61	78.45	79.29	80.14	80.98	81.83	82.68	83.53	84.39	85.24	86.10	86.96	87.82
58	76.61	77.46	78.32	79.17	80.03	80.89	81.75	82.62	83.48	84.35	85.22	86.10	86.97	87.85	88.72	89.60
59	78.12	78.99	79.87	80.74	81.62	82.50	83.38	84.26	85.15	86.03	86.92	87.81	88.71	89.60	90.50	91.40
60	79.64	80.53	81.42	82.32	83.21	84.11	85.01	85.91	86.81	87.72	88.63	89.54	90.45	91.37	92.29	93.20

Table 13-2 Continued

NUMBER OF PAYMENTS	30.00%	30.25%	30.50%	30.75%	31.00%	31.25%	31.50%	31.75%	32.00%	32.25%	32.50%	32.75%	33.00%	33.25%	33.50%	33.75%
					(FINANCE CHARGE PER $100 OF AMOUNT FINANCED)											
1	2.50	2.52	2.54	2.56	2.58	2.60	2.62	2.65	2.67	2.69	2.71	2.73	2.75	2.77	2.79	2.81
2	3.77	3.80	3.83	3.86	3.89	3.92	3.95	3.99	4.02	4.05	4.08	4.11	4.14	4.18	4.21	4.24
3	5.04	5.08	5.13	5.17	5.21	5.25	5.30	5.34	5.38	5.42	5.46	5.51	5.55	5.59	5.63	5.68
4	6.33	6.38	6.43	6.49	6.54	6.59	6.65	6.70	6.75	6.81	6.86	6.91	6.97	7.02	7.08	7.13
5	7.62	7.69	7.75	7.82	7.88	7.95	8.01	8.08	8.14	8.20	8.27	8.33	8.40	8.46	8.53	8.59
6	8.93	9.01	9.08	9.16	9.23	9.31	9.39	9.46	9.54	9.61	9.69	9.77	9.84	9.92	9.99	10.07
7	10.25	10.33	10.42	10.51	10.60	10.68	10.77	10.86	10.95	11.03	11.12	11.21	11.30	11.39	11.47	11.56
8	11.57	11.67	11.77	11.87	11.97	12.07	12.17	12.27	12.37	12.47	12.57	12.67	12.77	12.87	12.97	13.07
9	12.91	13.02	13.13	13.24	13.36	13.47	13.59	13.69	13.80	13.91	14.02	14.14	14.25	14.36	14.47	14.58
10	14.26	14.38	14.50	14.63	14.75	14.87	15.00	15.12	15.24	15.37	15.49	15.62	15.74	15.86	15.99	16.11
11	15.62	15.75	15.89	16.02	16.16	16.29	16.43	16.56	16.70	16.84	15.97	17.11	17.24	17.38	17.52	17.65
12	16.98	17.13	17.28	17.43	17.58	17.72	17.87	18.02	18.17	18.32	14.47	18.61	18.76	18.91	19.06	19.21
13	18.36	18.52	18.68	18.84	19.00	19.16	19.33	19.49	19.65	19.81	19.97	20.13	20.29	20.45	20.62	20.78
14	19.75	19.92	20.10	20.27	20.44	20.62	20.79	20.96	21.14	21.31	21.49	21.66	21.83	22.01	22.18	22.36
15	21.15	21.34	21.52	21.71	21.89	22.08	22.27	22.45	22.64	22.83	23.01	23.20	23.39	23.58	23.76	23.95
16	22.56	22.76	22.96	23.16	23.35	23.55	23.75	23.95	24.15	24.35	24.55	24.75	24.96	25.16	25.36	25.56
17	23.98	24.19	24.40	24.61	24.83	25.04	25.25	25.47	25.68	25.89	26.11	26.32	26.53	26.75	26.96	27.18
18	25.41	25.63	25.86	26.08	26.31	26.54	26.76	26.99	27.22	27.44	27.67	27.90	28.13	28.35	28.58	28.81
19	26.85	27.08	27.32	27.56	27.80	28.04	28.28	28.52	28.76	29.00	29.25	29.49	29.73	29.97	30.21	30.45
20	28.29	28.55	28.80	29.05	29.31	29.56	29.81	30.07	30.32	30.58	30.83	31.09	31.34	31.60	31.86	32.11
21	29.75	30.02	30.29	30.55	30.82	31.09	31.36	31.62	31.89	32.16	32.43	32.70	32.97	33.24	33.51	33.78
22	31.22	31.50	31.78	32.06	32.35	32.63	32.91	33.19	33.48	33.76	34.04	34.33	34.61	34.89	35.18	35.46
23	32.70	33.00	33.29	33.59	33.88	34.18	34.48	34.77	35.07	35.37	35.66	35.96	36.26	36.56	36.86	37.16
24	34.19	34.50	34.81	35.12	35.43	35.74	36.05	36.36	36.67	36.99	37.30	37.61	37.92	38.24	38.55	38.87
25	35.69	36.01	36.34	36.66	36.99	37.31	37.64	37.96	38.29	38.62	38.94	39.27	39.60	39.93	40.26	40.59
26	37.20	37.54	37.88	38.21	38.55	38.89	39.23	39.58	39.92	40.26	40.60	40.94	41.29	41.63	41.97	42.32
27	38.72	39.07	39.42	39.78	40.13	40.49	40.84	41.20	41.56	41.91	42.27	42.63	42.99	43.34	43.70	44.06
28	40.25	40.61	40.98	41.35	41.72	42.09	42.46	42.83	43.20	43.58	43.95	44.32	44.70	45.07	45.45	45.82
29	41.78	42.17	42.55	42.94	43.32	43.71	44.09	44.48	44.87	45.25	45.64	46.03	46.42	46.81	47.20	47.59
30	43.33	43.73	44.13	44.53	44.93	45.33	45.73	46.13	46.54	46.94	47.34	47.75	48.15	48.56	48.96	49.37
31	44.89	45.30	45.72	46.13	46.55	46.97	47.38	47.80	48.22	48.64	49.06	49.48	49.90	50.32	50.74	51.17
32	46.46	46.89	47.32	47.75	48.18	48.61	49.05	49.48	49.91	50.35	50.78	51.22	51.66	52.09	52.53	52.97
33	48.04	48.48	48.93	49.37	49.82	50.27	50.72	51.17	51.62	52.07	52.52	52.97	53.43	53.88	54.33	54.79
34	49.62	50.08	50.55	51.01	51.47	51.94	52.40	52.87	53.33	53.80	54.27	54.74	55.21	55.68	56.15	56.62
35	51.22	51.70	52.17	52.65	53.13	53.61	54.09	54.58	55.06	55.54	56.03	56.51	57.00	57.48	57.97	58.46
36	52.83	53.32	53.81	54.31	54.80	55.30	55.80	56.30	56.80	57.30	57.80	58.30	58.80	59.30	59.81	60.31
37	54.44	54.95	55.46	55.97	56.49	57.00	57.51	58.03	58.54	59.06	59.58	60.10	60.62	61.14	61.66	62.18
38	56.07	56.59	57.12	57.65	58.18	58.71	59.24	59.77	60.30	60.84	61.37	61.90	62.44	62.98	63.52	64.06
39	57.70	58.24	58.79	59.33	59.88	60.42	60.97	61.52	62.07	62.62	63.17	63.72	64.28	64.83	65.39	65.94
40	59.34	59.90	60.47	61.03	61.59	62.15	62.72	63.28	63.85	64.42	64.99	65.56	66.13	66.70	67.27	67.84
41	61.00	61.57	62.15	62.73	63.31	63.89	64.47	65.06	65.64	66.22	66.81	67.40	67.98	68.57	69.16	69.75
42	62.66	63.25	63.85	64.44	65.04	65.64	66.24	66.84	67.44	68.04	68.65	69.25	69.86	70.46	71.07	71.68
43	64.33	64.94	65.56	66.17	66.78	67.40	68.01	68.63	69.25	69.87	70.49	71.11	71.74	72.36	72.99	73.61
44	66.01	66.64	67.27	67.90	68.53	69.17	69.80	70.43	71.07	71.71	72.35	72.99	73.63	74.27	74.91	75.56
45	67.70	68.35	69.00	69.64	70.29	70.94	71.60	72.25	72.90	73.56	74.21	74.87	75.53	76.19	76.85	77.52
46	69.40	70.07	70.73	71.40	72.06	72.73	73.40	74.07	74.74	75.42	76.09	76.77	77.44	78.12	78.80	79.48
47	71.11	71.79	72.47	73.16	73.84	74.53	75.22	75.90	76.60	77.29	77.98	78.67	79.37	80.07	80.76	81.46
48	72.83	73.53	74.23	74.93	75.63	76.34	77.04	77.75	78.46	79.17	79.88	80.59	81.30	82.02	82.74	83.45
49	74.55	75.27	75.99	76.71	77.43	78.15	78.88	79.60	80.33	81.06	81.79	82.52	83.25	83.98	84.72	85.45
50	76.29	77.02	77.76	78.50	79.24	79.98	80.72	81.46	82.21	82.96	83.70	84.45	85.20	85.96	86.71	87.47
51	78.03	78.79	79.54	80.30	81.06	81.81	82.58	83.34	84.10	84.87	85.63	86.40	87.17	87.94	88.71	89.49
52	79.79	80.56	81.33	82.11	82.88	83.66	84.44	85.22	86.00	86.79	87.57	88.36	89.15	89.94	90.73	91.52
53	81.55	82.34	83.13	83.92	84.72	85.51	86.31	87.11	87.91	88.72	89.52	90.33	91.13	91.94	92.75	93.57
54	83.32	84.13	84.94	85.75	86.56	87.38	88.19	89.01	89.83	90.66	91.48	92.30	93.13	93.96	94.79	95.62
55	85.10	85.93	86.75	87.58	88.42	89.25	90.09	90.92	91.76	92.60	93.45	94.29	95.14	95.99	96.83	97.69
56	86.89	87.73	88.58	89.43	90.28	91.13	91.99	92.84	93.70	94.56	95.43	96.29	97.15	98.02	98.89	99.76
57	88.68	89.55	90.41	91.28	92.15	93.02	93.90	94.77	95.65	96.53	97.41	98.30	99.18	100.07	100.96	101.85
58	90.49	91.37	92.26	93.14	94.03	94.92	95.82	96.71	97.61	98.51	99.58	100.50	101.42	102.34	103.26	104.19	105.12	106.05
59	92.30	93.20	94.11	95.01	95.92	96.83	97.75	98.66	99.58	100.50	101.42	102.34	103.26	104.19	105.12	106.05
60	94.12	95.04	95.97	96.89	97.82	98.75	99.68	100.62	101.56	102.49	103.43	104.38	105.32	106.27	107.21	108.16

Table 13–2 Continued

NUMBER OF PAYMENTS	34.00%	34.25%	34.50%	34.75%	35.00%	35.25%	35.50%	35.75%	36.00%	36.25%	36.50%	36.75%	37.00%	37.25%	37.50%	37.75%
							(FINANCE CHARGE PER $100 OF AMOUNT FINANCED)									
1	2.83	2.85	2.87	2.90	2.92	2.94	2.96	2.98	3.00	3.02	3.04	3.06	3.08	3.10	3.12	3.15
2	4.27	4.30	4.33	4.36	4.40	4.43	4.46	4.49	4.52	4.55	4.59	4.62	4.65	4.68	4.71	4.74
3	5.72	5.76	5.80	5.85	5.89	5.93	5.97	6.02	6.06	6.10	6.14	6.19	6.23	6.27	6.31	6.36
4	7.18	7.24	7.29	7.34	7.40	7.45	7.50	7.56	7.61	7.66	7.72	7.77	7.83	7.88	7.93	7.99
5	8.66	8.72	8.79	8.85	8.92	8.98	9.05	9.11	9.18	9.24	9.31	9.37	9.44	9.50	9.57	9.63
6	10.15	10.22	10.30	10.38	10.45	10.53	10.61	10.68	10.76	10.83	10.91	10.99	11.06	11.14	11.22	11.29
7	11.65	11.74	11.83	11.91	12.00	12.09	12.18	12.27	12.35	12.44	12.53	12.62	12.71	12.80	12.88	12.97
8	13.17	13.27	13.36	13.46	13.56	13.66	13.76	13.86	13.97	14.07	14.17	14.27	14.37	14.47	14.57	14.67
9	14.69	14.81	14.92	15.03	15.14	15.25	15.37	15.48	15.59	15.70	15.82	15.93	16.04	16.15	16.27	16.38
10	16.24	16.36	16.48	16.61	16.73	16.86	16.98	17.11	17.23	17.36	17.48	17.60	17.73	17.85	17.98	18.10
11	17.79	17.93	18.06	18.20	18.34	18.47	18.61	18.75	18.89	19.02	19.16	19.30	19.43	19.57	19.71	19.85
12	19.36	19.51	19.66	19.81	19.96	20.11	20.25	20.40	20.55	20.70	20.85	21.00	21.15	21.31	21.46	21.61
13	20.94	21.10	21.26	21.43	21.59	21.75	21.91	22.08	22.24	22.40	22.56	22.73	22.89	23.05	23.22	23.38
14	22.53	22.71	22.88	23.06	23.23	23.41	23.59	23.76	23.94	24.11	24.29	24.47	24.64	24.82	25.00	25.17
15	24.14	24.33	24.52	24.71	24.89	25.08	25.27	25.46	25.65	25.84	26.03	26.22	26.41	26.60	26.79	26.98
16	25.76	25.96	26.16	26.37	26.57	26.77	26.97	27.17	27.38	27.58	27.78	27.99	28.19	28.39	28.60	28.80
17	27.39	27.61	27.82	28.04	28.25	28.47	28.69	28.90	29.12	29.34	29.55	29.77	29.99	30.20	30.42	30.64
18	29.04	29.27	29.50	29.73	29.96	30.19	30.42	30.65	30.88	31.11	31.34	31.57	31.80	32.03	32.26	32.49
19	30.70	30.94	31.18	31.43	31.67	31.91	32.16	32.40	32.65	32.89	33.14	33.38	33.63	33.87	34.12	34.36
20	32.37	32.63	32.88	33.14	33.40	33.66	33.91	34.17	34.43	34.69	34.95	35.21	35.47	35.73	35.99	36.25
21	34.05	34.32	34.60	34.87	35.14	35.41	35.68	35.96	36.23	36.50	36.78	37.05	37.33	37.60	37.88	38.15
22	35.75	36.04	36.32	36.61	36.89	37.18	37.47	37.76	38.04	38.33	38.62	38.91	39.20	39.49	39.78	40.07
23	37.46	37.76	38.06	38.36	38.66	38.96	39.27	39.57	39.87	40.18	40.48	40.78	41.09	41.39	41.70	42.00
24	39.18	39.50	39.81	40.13	40.44	40.76	41.08	41.40	41.71	42.03	42.35	42.67	42.99	43.31	43.63	43.95
25	40.92	41.25	41.58	41.91	42.24	42.57	42.90	43.24	43.57	43.90	44.24	44.57	44.91	45.24	45.58	45.91
26	42.66	43.01	43.36	43.70	44.05	44.40	44.74	45.09	45.44	45.79	46.14	46.49	46.84	47.19	47.54	47.89
27	44.42	44.78	45.15	45.51	45.87	46.23	46.60	46.96	47.32	47.69	48.05	48.42	48.78	49.15	49.52	49.88
28	46.20	46.57	46.95	47.33	47.70	48.08	48.46	48.84	49.22	49.60	49.98	50.36	50.75	51.13	51.51	51.89
29	47.98	48.37	48.77	49.16	49.55	49.95	50.34	50.74	51.13	51.53	51.93	52.32	52.72	53.12	53.52	53.92
30	49.78	50.19	50.60	51.00	51.41	51.82	52.23	52.65	53.06	53.47	53.88	54.30	54.71	55.13	55.54	55.96
31	51.59	52.01	52.44	52.86	53.29	53.71	54.14	54.57	55.00	55.43	55.85	56.28	56.72	57.15	57.58	58.01
32	53.41	53.85	54.29	54.73	55.17	55.62	56.06	56.50	56.95	57.39	57.84	58.29	58.73	59.18	59.63	60.08
33	55.24	55.70	56.16	56.62	57.07	57.53	57.99	58.45	58.92	59.38	59.84	60.30	60.77	61.23	61.70	62.16
34	57.09	57.56	58.04	58.51	58.99	59.46	59.94	60.42	60.89	61.37	61.85	62.33	62.81	63.30	63.78	64.26
35	58.95	59.44	59.93	60.42	60.91	61.40	61.90	62.39	62.89	63.38	63.88	64.38	64.88	65.37	65.87	66.37
36	60.82	61.33	61.83	62.34	62.85	63.36	63.87	64.38	64.89	65.41	65.92	66.43	66.95	67.47	67.98	68.50
37	62.70	63.22	63.75	64.27	64.80	65.33	65.85	66.38	66.91	67.44	67.97	68.51	69.04	69.57	70.11	70.64
38	64.59	65.14	65.68	66.22	66.76	67.31	67.85	68.40	68.95	69.49	70.04	70.59	71.14	71.69	72.25	72.80
39	66.50	67.06	67.62	68.18	68.74	69.30	69.86	70.43	70.99	71.56	72.12	72.69	73.26	73.83	74.40	74.97
40	68.42	68.99	69.57	70.15	70.73	71.31	71.89	72.47	73.05	73.63	74.22	74.80	75.39	75.98	76.56	77.15
41	70.35	70.94	71.53	72.13	72.73	73.32	73.92	74.52	75.12	75.72	76.32	76.93	77.53	78.14	78.74	79.35
42	72.29	72.90	73.51	74.12	74.74	75.35	75.97	76.59	77.20	77.82	78.44	79.07	79.69	80.31	80.94	81.56
43	74.24	74.87	75.50	76.13	76.76	77.40	78.03	78.67	79.30	79.94	80.58	81.22	81.86	82.50	83.14	83.79
44	76.20	76.85	77.50	78.15	78.80	79.45	80.10	80.76	81.41	82.07	82.72	83.38	84.04	84.70	85.36	86.03
45	78.18	78.84	79.51	80.18	80.85	81.52	82.19	82.86	83.53	84.21	84.88	85.56	86.24	86.92	87.60	88.28
46	80.17	80.85	81.53	82.22	82.91	83.60	84.28	84.98	85.67	86.36	87.06	87.75	88.45	89.15	89.85	90.55
47	82.16	82.87	83.57	84.27	84.98	85.69	86.39	87.10	87.81	88.53	89.24	89.95	90.67	91.39	92.11	92.83
48	84.17	84.89	85.61	86.34	87.06	87.79	88.52	89.24	89.97	90.70	91.44	92.17	92.91	93.64	94.38	95.12
49	86.19	86.93	87.67	88.41	89.16	89.90	90.65	91.40	92.14	92.89	93.65	94.40	55.15	95.91	96.67	97.42
50	88.22	88.98	89.74	90.50	91.26	92.03	92.79	93.56	94.33	95.10	95.87	96.64	97.41	98.19	98.98	99.74
51	90.26	91.04	91.82	92.60	93.38	94.16	94.95	95.74	96.52	97.31	98.10	98.89	99.69	100.48	101.28	102.07
52	92.32	93.11	93.91	94.71	95.51	96.31	97.12	97.92	98.73	99.54	100.35	101.16	101.97	102.79	103.60	104.42
53	94.38	95.20	96.01	96.83	97.65	98.47	99.30	100.12	100.95	101.78	102.61	103.44	104.27	105.10	105.94	106.78
54	96.45	97.29	98.13	98.96	99.80	100.64	101.49	102.33	103.18	104.03	104.87	105.73	106.58	107.43	108.29	109.14
55	98.54	99.39	100.25	101.11	101.97	102.83	103.69	104.55	105.42	106.29	107.16	108.03	108.90	109.77	110.65	111.53
56	100.63	101.51	102.38	103.26	104.14	105.02	105.90	106.79	107.67	108.56	109.45	110.34	111.23	112.13	113.02	113.92
57	102.74	103.63	104.53	105.43	106.32	107.22	108.13	109.03	109.94	110.85	111.75	112.67	113.58	114.49	115.41	116.33
58	104.85	105.77	106.68	107.60	108.52	109.44	110.36	111.29	112.21	113.14	114.07	115.00	115.93	116.87	117.81	118.74
59	106.98	107.91	108.85	109.79	110.73	111.67	112.61	113.55	114.50	115.45	116.40	117.35	118.30	119.26	120.22	121.17
60	109.12	110.07	111.02	111.98	112.94	113.90	114.87	115.83	116.80	117.77	118.74	119.71	120.68	121.66	122.64	123.62

Table 13-2 Continued

Part 3. Mathematics Applications in Operating a Business

Using an APR Formula

The following formula provides a method of finding the exact annual percentage rate that is as fast as, and many think easier than, doing so by interpolation. There are other APR formulas, but the one shown below is the most precise formula currently available. It appears to be complicated, but, with a calculator, it is not very formidable.

$$r = \frac{MC(95n + 9)}{12n(n + 1)(4B + C)}$$

r = Annual Percentage Rate
M = Number of payment periods in one year
C = Finance charges
n = Number of payments in term of loan
B = Amount borrowed (principal)

Example A: Jim Ward borrowed $1,600. The principal and the finance charge of $480 are to be repaid in 30 monthly payments. Use the APR formula to find the annual percentage rate to the nearest 0.01%.

Solution:

$$r = \frac{MC(95n + 9)}{12n(n + 1)(4B + C)}$$

$$r = \frac{12 \times 480[(95 \times 30) + 9]}{12 \times 30 \times 31[(4 \times 1600) + 480]}$$

$$r = 0.2144786$$

$$r = 21.45\%$$

An important consideration when using the formula is that M stands for the number of payment periods in one full year regardless of how many total payments are to be made. Therefore, when the payments are made monthly, 12 is substituted for M; when the payments are made weekly, 52 is substituted for M; and when the payments are made quarterly, 4 is substituted for M. Notice in the example below that M is 52, the number of weeks in one year, and that n is 104, the number of weekly payments in two years.

Example B: Attempting to appeal to workers who are paid on a weekly basis, a personal loan company advertises that a loan of $500 can be repaid by paying only $6.50 a week for two years. What annual percentage rate to the nearest 0.01% does the company charge on such a loan?

Solution: 1. Find the amount of the finance charge.

6.50×104 installments = $676.00
$676 - $500 borrowed = $176.00   finance charge

2. Find the annual percentage rate.

$$r = \frac{MC(95n + 9)}{12n(n + 1)(4B + C)}$$

$$r = \frac{52 \times 176[(95 \times 104) + 9]}{12 \times 104 \times 105[(4 \times 500) + 176]}$$

$$r = \frac{90504128}{2.8514304 \times 10^8} = \frac{0.90504128 \times 10^8}{2.8514304 \times 10^8}$$

$$r = \frac{0.90505128}{2.8514304} = 0.317399$$

$$r = 31.74\%$$

● Exercise 13–5

Use Table 13–2 to solve problems 1–15 and the APR formula for problems 16–20. In problems 1–5, find **(a)** the balance, **(b)** the finance charge at the given rate for the term of the loan, and **(c)** the annual percentage rate.

	Purchase Price	Down Payment	Balance	Number of Payments	Nominal Rate	Finance Charge	APR
1.	$ 500	-0-	_____	12	16%	_____	_____
2.	1,200	$ 200	_____	18	14%	_____	_____
3.	3,700	370	_____	24	13.5%	_____	_____
4.	5,469	540	_____	48	12%	_____	_____
5.	7,850	1,200	_____	60	10%	_____	_____

6. Elaine Sellers bought a television set priced at $600 by paying $100 down and making 12 monthly payments of $50 each. Interpolate to find the annual percentage rate to the nearest 0.01%.

7. Robert Salka borrowed $1,200 from his bank and agreed to pay 12 monthly payments of $112 each. Find **(a)** the finance charge on the loan and **(b)** the annual percentage rate to the nearest 0.01% by interpolating.

8. John Sturdivant bought a camera listed to sell for $395 by paying $45 down and the balance in 15 equal monthly payments of $26.50 each. Interpolate to find the annual percentage rate to the nearest 0.01%.

9. The cash price of a cabinet is $1,600. It can be purchased with no down payment and 10 monthly payments of $180 each. Find the annual percentage rate to the nearest 0.01% by interpolation.

10. An article is listed to sell for $200 cash. The installment plan consists of a $20 down payment and 8 monthly payments of $25 each. Find the annual percentage rate to the nearest 0.01% by interpolation.

11. A used car priced at $4,000 was sold for $500 down and the balance paid in 18 monthly payments including the finance charge at 11.5% APR. Find the amount of each installment.

12. Beverly Reid bought a used car priced at $3,600. She paid $600 down and the balance in 18 monthly payments including a finance charge of 19.25% APR. Find the monthly payment.

13. A dealer has a used car for sale at $4,995. He plans to advertise an APR of 12.75% with a 10% down payment and 33 months to pay. Find the monthly payment.

14. Jim and Jenny Reed want to have a swimming pool installed. The cost of $19,450 can be financed at 15% APR for 54 months. Find the amount of the monthly payment.

15. Dawn Parisi plans to buy a computer with attachments at a total price of $5,247.50. If she can borrow $4,750 at 18.5% for 42 months, how much will her monthly payment be?

16. Tom Atkinson and his wife are considering financing $16,500 for a swimming pool by paying $332 a month for 7 years. Find the annual percentage rate to the nearest 0.01%.

17. A used motor home is advertised for sale at $13,900. The dealer said on the telephone that a down payment of $1,900 and monthly payments of only $213 for $8\frac{1}{2}$ years would buy the vehicle. Find the annual percentage rate to the nearest 0.01%.

18. A boat and trailer priced at $12,725 can be purchased with no down payment and monthly payments of $247.50 for 6 years. Find the annual percentage rate to the nearest 0.01%.

19. Maria Perez bought a radio priced at $190 by paying $15 down and agreeing to pay 40 weekly payments of $5 each. What annual percentage rate to the nearest 0.01% did she pay?

20. David Knepp bought a stereo set priced at $600 by paying $150 down and agreeing to pay the balance plus $24 finance charge in 30 weekly payments. Find **(a)** the amount of each weekly payment and **(b)** the annual percentage rate to the nearest 0.01%.

only no 2

REVIEW PROBLEMS

Solve these problems. If you have difficulty solving any problem, restudy the appropriate section in this chapter. The problems under a specific number are related to those contained in the exercise with the same last number.

1. **a.** The charge account of Carol Boston reveals a beginning unpaid balance of $266.51 and monthly payments of $30, $25, and $44. The finance charge is 1.6% per month of the unpaid balance. Show **(1)** the finance charge for the third month and **(2)** the balance due after the third payment.

   b. An account statement shows an unpaid beginning balance of $468.53 on the billing date of December 8, charges of $21.49 on December 12,

$83.40 on December 16, $53.05 on December 18, and $462.47 on December 21, and a payment of $75 on December 28. Find **(1)** the average daily balance and **(2)** the finance charge at 1.75% of the average daily balance.

c. A bank-card statement shows a beginning unpaid balance of $703.72 on the statement date of June 8. A payment of $400 was made on June 15. A cash advance of $100 on June 22 and a charge of $74.08 on June 30 were shown also. Find **(1)** the adjusted average daily balance, **(2)** the finance charge at 1.65% including a fee of 2% on the cash advance, and **(3)** the unpaid balance on the next closing date.

2. a. Kenneth Gilkey borrowed $360 from his local bank by agreeing to pay interest at the rate of 16% a year on the face of the loan and to repay the combined total of the principal and interest in 12 equal monthly payments. What is the amount of each payment?

b. Martha Crisp can buy a freezer on the installment plan by paying $44 a month for 18 months. She can buy the same freezer by borrowing $600 for 18 months and paying cash. The interest rate on the loan would be 12% per annum. What amount can she save by borrowing the money to pay cash?

3. Alicia Guzman bought an automobile on an installment plan that required monthly payments of $198.74 after the down payment. The finance charge was $3,645 on the 48-month loan. She decided to pay off the contract 15 months early. Find **(a)** the unearned finance charge and **(b)** the amount needed for the final payment.

4. Maxwell Department Store bought a tract of land to use as a parking lot. The store paid $100,000 down and arranged to pay the balance of $400,000 plus $14\frac{1}{2}$% interest over a period of 10 years. Use Table 13–1 to find the amount of each monthly installment.

5. a. Ray Garlo bought a refrigerator-freezer priced at $995 by paying $95 down and the balance in 16 monthly payments of $62.50 each. Use Table 13–2 to find the annual percentage rate to the nearest $\frac{1}{4}$%.

b. Barbara Schaefer borrowed $1,440 for 1 year and gave a mortgage on her automobile as security. She paid the loan in 12 monthly payments of $137 each. Find **(1)** the interest on the loan and **(2)** the annual percentage rate to the nearest 0.01% by interpolation.

c. Karen Beck plans to buy an automobile at a total price of $11,737.50. The dealer is offering a special rate of 12.75% during a sale. If she finances $8,000 for 45 months, how much will her monthly payment be? (Use Table 13–2.)

d. John and Emily Barefoot plan to have a swimming pool installed behind their home. After a down payment of $1,750, they can pay for the $14,750 pool by paying $225 a month for 8 years. Find the annual percentage rate to the nearest 0.01%.

Kathy and Peter Bouazza have owned their home for a few years and plan to live there for three more years. They bought it by making a down payment and signing a variable-rate mortgage. The mortgage rate is now 12.75%, the balance is $85,294, and the monthly payment is $924.70. They have investigated refinancing the mortgage with the current holder, Valley Bank, and with Mountain Bank. Valley Bank offered to refinance the mortgage at a fixed rate of 10.5% for 30 years with a loan fee of $250 plus 2 points (2%). Mountain Bank offered a fixed rate of 10% for 25 years with a loan fee of $150 plus 3 points. In order to keep the mortgage from increasing, the Bouazzas will need to pay the loan fee and points when the loan is approved. Both banks pay 6% interest compounded monthly on savings accounts.

(a) If they refinance with Valley Bank, the lower payment will enable them to recover the loan fee and points in how many months? **(b)** If they refinance with Mountain Bank, how long will it take to recover the loan fee and points? **(c)** Which company's offer is better? **(d)** Should they refinance?

Chapter 14

Selected Accounting Practices

Objectives

After mastering the material in Chapter 14, you will be able to:

- Distribute overhead based on floor space, on sales, on direct labor, or on prime cost.
- Determine the value of an inventory by the specific identification, average cost, fifo, lifo, and cost or market methods.
- Estimate the value of an inventory by the gross profit and retail methods.
- Find the value of goodwill based on a multiple of the average earnings, on a multiple of the extra earnings, or on the capitalized value of the extra earnings.
- Calculate depreciation on fixed assets by the modified accelerated cost recovery system, straight-line, units-of-production, declining-balance, and sum-of-the-years-digits methods.
- Determine the book value of a fixed asset.
- Compute depletion of natural resources through the units-of-production method.

Things of value that are owned by either individuals or businesses are assets. These may be classified in many ways. Two major categories of business assets are current assets and fixed assets. **Current assets** are cash and those items that normally will be converted into cash or consumed within one year.

Examples of current assets include cash, marketable securities, notes receivable, accounts receivable, merchandise inventory, and prepaid expenses. **Accounts receivable** are amounts owed to the firm by its customers. **Fixed assets** are those items of a somewhat fixed or durable nature that are used in the operation of the business. The most common examples of these are land, buildings, and equipment.

Irrespective of its nature or of its classification, one measure of an asset's value is its cost. In other words, the value of any asset, whether it is equipment, building, supplies, or merchandise to be sold, is accounted for on the basis of the number of dollars that have been invested in that asset. The beginning **value** of an asset, therefore, ordinarily means the cost of that asset.

Values do change from day to day. Materials used in manufacturing a product increase in value as they progress through the stages of production and become finished goods. Buildings and equipment age through time and usage and become less valuable, or they are renovated and become more valuable. A company sells merchandise each business day and replenishes its merchandise stock frequently. This causes the value of its merchandise inventory, that is the value of the goods available for sale, to change rapidly. Efficient business management requires that such changes in asset valuations be accounted for periodically.

DISTRIBUTION OF OVERHEAD

In accounting for costs and expenses in manufacturing concerns and department stores, some expenditures may be easily identified with the department benefited. For example, if each salesperson is restricted to a particular sales department, the sales salaries may be assigned to the appropriate departmental salary accounts each time the payroll is prepared. On the other hand, the salaries of company executives and office personnel are not identifiable with a specific sales department and may be allocated to the various departments on some equitable basis.

In any business, those general indirect charges, such as rent, taxes, insurance, and office expenses, that cannot be allocated directly to a particular department or product are **general expenses** or **overhead.**

Allocating overhead to the various departments or products of a company should be based on the proportionate benefits derived by each department or product. Determining an equitable basis requires judgment. Collective judgment may be advisable because two accountants of equal ability may differ in their opinions regarding the proper basis for an allocation. As the cost of collecting and using data in making an allocation must be kept reasonable, information that is readily available may be used although it is not completely satisfactory.

There are various bases for allocating overhead to the respective departments of a business. Among these, the following four are used frequently: floor space, sales, direct labor, and prime cost. Knowledge of these four can be easily transferred to the solution of problems in which another base is used.

Based on Floor Space

Certain costs and expenses are allocated individually to the various departments of a business on the basis of floor space occupied. The total expenditure for rent, for example, is commonly distributed to each department in the ratio of the floor space occupied by that department to the total floor space that is being rented.

Example:

In a small department store, the square feet of floor space occupied by each department is as follows:

Department A	9,000 sq ft
Department B	7,000 sq ft
Office	1,000 sq ft
Storage	3,000 sq ft
Total	20,000 sq ft

The monthly rent for the store is $7,200. Determine how much of the monthly rent should be distributed to each department on the basis of floor space occupied.

Solution:

$$\frac{9,000}{20,000} \times \$7,200 = \$3,240 \quad \text{Department A}$$

$$\frac{7,000}{20,000} \times \$7,200 = \$2,520 \quad \text{Department B}$$

$$\frac{1,000}{20,000} \times \$7,200 = \$\ 360 \quad \text{Office}$$

$$\frac{3,000}{20,000} \times \$7,200 = \frac{\$1,080}{\$7,200} \quad \begin{array}{l}\text{Storage}\\\text{Total}\end{array}$$

Based on Sales

Some expenditures are collectively distributed to the operating departments of a company. To determine departmental net income, the expenses that are charged to service departments must be allocated to the revenue-producing departments. The expenses of operating the office, for example, may be distributed to the revenue-producing departments on an equitable basis, such as departmental sales in relation to total sales.

Example:

The total office expenses of a small department store amounted to $36,000 for the past year. The company's sales during the year were as follows:

Department A	$240,000
Department B	160,000
Total	$400,000

Determine the share of the office expenses that should be allocated to each revenue-producing department on the basis of sales.

Solution:

$$\frac{\$240,000}{\$400,000} \times \$36,000 = \$21,600 \quad \text{Department A}$$

$$\frac{\$160,000}{\$400,000} \times \$36,000 = \frac{\$14,400}{\$36,000} \quad \begin{array}{l}\text{Department B}\\\text{Total}\end{array}$$

Part 3. Mathematics Applications in Operating a Business

Based on Direct Labor

In manufacturing there are three basic costs of converting raw materials into finished products. These are: (1) raw materials, (2) direct labor, and (3) factory overhead. **Raw materials** are the commodities that directly enter into and become a part of the finished product. **Direct labor** is the cost of the labor of the people who work directly on the materials that are converted to finished products. **Factory overhead** includes all manufacturing costs other than those expended for raw materials and direct labor. Factory overhead may include expenditures for factory supplies, repairs to the plant and equipment, depreciation of plant and equipment, heat and power, supervisory labor (indirect labor), payroll taxes on factory wages, and taxes on inventories, plant, and equipment.

The allocation of factory overhead costs to departments or to jobs is based on the same principles as those in the two preceding examples. However, the procedures used may vary. The price charged for an article by a manufacturer may be based on the costs of producing that article. In order to determine as accurately as possible the cost of producing a particular job as soon as it is completed, the factory overhead applicable to that job must be computed. Some degree of accuracy may be sacrificed for time. So that job costs can be available currently, factory overhead may be applied to a specific job when it is completed by the use of a predetermined overhead rate.

The **predetermined overhead rate** is a percent that can be applied to a base, such as direct labor, to find the amount of overhead that should be charged to a specific job or department. It is found by using estimates of the total amount of factory overhead and the total amount of the base (e.g., direct labor). It is the ratio of these estimates expressed as a percent.

Example:

The total factory overhead costs for the year were estimated to be $48,000; the total direct labor costs, $60,000. Based on the relationship of total overhead to total direct labor, find (a) the predetermined overhead rate, (b) the amount of overhead to be applied, and (c) the total cost of a job that has had $500 worth of direct labor and $600 of raw materials applied to it.

Solution:

(a) $\dfrac{\$48,000}{\$60,000} = 0.80 = 80\%$

(b) 500 $\boxed{\times}$ 80 $\boxed{\%}$ →400 or 500 $\boxed{\times}$ .8 $\boxed{=}$ → 400, means $400

(c) $400 + $500 + $600 = $1,500

Based on Prime Cost

Materials and labor are the primary costs incurred to obtain a finished product. Raw materials may be used as the base to compute a predetermined overhead rate. Another basis may be **prime cost,** which is the sum of raw material costs and direct labor costs.

Example:

During the past year, a manufacturing company spent $70,000 for raw materials, $90,000 for direct labor, and $186,400 for factory overhead. Based on the relationship of total overhead to total prime cost, find **(a)** the rate that may be used to allocate overhead costs and **(b)** the amount of overhead that should be allocated to a department that has total prime cost of $27,000.

Solution:

(a) $70,000 + $90,000 = $160,000 prime cost

$$\frac{\$186,400}{\$160,000} = 1.165 = 116.5\%$$

(b) 27000 $\boxed{\times}$ 116.5 $\boxed{\%}$ $\rightarrow$ 31455

or 27000 $\boxed{\times}$ 1.165 $\boxed{=}$ $\rightarrow$ 31455, means $31,455

● Exercise 14–1

1. The total factory overhead of $219,000 is to be distributed on the basis of floor space occupied. The number of square feet occupied by each department is as follows: Assembling, 10,000; Finishing, 3,500; and Office, 1,500. Find the amount of overhead that should be charged to each department.

2. The women's clothing department occupies 2,400 sq ft of the 12,000 sq ft of space on the first floor of Nimbus Department Store. Because it receives more traffic, the first of the two floors is charged with 55% of the store's overhead. During the past year, overhead costs for the store totaled $85,920. On the basis of floor space occupied, how much of the overhead should be charged to this department?

3. The men's department of Beam's Clothing Store sold $49,036 worth of goods during a month in which total sales for the store were $188,600. Administrative expenses for that month amounted to $14,145. How much of the administrative expenses should be allocated to the men's department on the basis of sales?

4. In accordance with its lease agreement, Fairway Market pays 5% of the monthly net sales to the landlord for rent. During a month in which the market's sales totaled $98,788, how much rent expense should be allocated to the meat department which had net sales of $24,294?

5. Factory overhead for the year is estimated to be $540,000, and direct labor cost is estimated at $720,000. What is the predetermined overhead rate based on direct labor?

6. Direct labor cost for the year is estimated to be $810,000, and factory overhead is estimated at $1,080,000. What is the predetermined overhead rate based on direct labor?

7. The total overhead of a factory was estimated to be $567,000 during a year in which direct labor would be $810,000. Each job is charged with its share of overhead based on the relationship of total factory overhead to total direct labor. Find **(a)** the predetermined overhead rate and **(b)** the amount of overhead that should be charged to a job that has had $629 worth of direct labor applied to it.

8. An accountant of Superior Products Company estimated that the company would incur factory overhead in the amount of $4,000,000 and direct labor of $3,200,000 during the year. If these estimates were used to compute the predetermined overhead rate, find **(a)** the overhead rate based on direct labor and **(b)** the amount of overhead charged to Job 1934 that had $3,245 of direct materials and $4,200 worth of direct labor charged to it.

9. Total factory overhead is $95,355; total direct labor, $141,975; and total materials used, $493,725. The distribution of overhead is based on the relationship of total overhead to total prime cost. Find **(a)** the overhead percent of prime cost charged to each department and **(b)** the amount of overhead charged to a department with a prime cost of $101,700.

10. Cucamonga Corporation had a total prime cost of $241,650 and total factory overhead of $217,485. The distribution of overhead is based on the relationship of total overhead to total prime cost. Find **(a)** the overhead rate and **(b)** the share of overhead for a department with a cost of $3,263 for total direct labor and a cost of $8,197 for total materials used.

11. An accountant for Emerson Department Store distributes certain overhead expenses on the basis of floor space occupied by the departments. Complete the following expense-distribution schedule by showing how much of each expense should be allocated to each department.

Department: Floor Space Occupied:	Appliances 17%	Carpeting 15%	Draperies 10%	Furniture 50%	Offices 8%
Expense	**Total**		**Allocation of Expense**		
Depreciation, Building	$37,000.00	_____	_____	_____	_____	_____
Taxes, Property	24,500.00	_____	_____	_____	_____	_____
Heating and Lighting	14,817.20	_____	_____	_____	_____	_____
Insurance, Building	6,938.00	_____	_____	_____	_____	_____

12. Parco Manufacturing Company estimated its factory overhead to be $123,000 and direct labor to be $600,000 during a year. According to company policy, overhead is distributed to each job on the basis of direct labor. **(a)** What is the predetermined overhead rate? **(b)** Complete the summary by showing the amount of overhead applied to each job and the total cost of each job.

Summary of Completed Jobs

Job Number	Date Completed	Materials	Direct Labor	Overhead Applied	Total Cost
721	4-9	$380	$975	————	————
722	4-10	414	717	————	————
724	4-13	324	768	————	————
725	4-15	618	986	————	————
728	4-20	365	698	————	————
731	4-22	532	824	————	————

VALUATION OF INVENTORIES

The value of the merchandise available for sale on a specific date is referred to as the **merchandise inventory.** A company may determine the value of its unsold merchandise by (1) estimating its value, (2) keeping a perpetual record, or (3) taking a physical inventory. Estimating the value of an inventory is usually not recommended unless there are extenuating circumstances, such as when the goods have been destroyed or when there is insufficient time to take a physical inventory. A **perpetual inventory** makes use of records that continuously disclose the quantity of the inventory for each product in stock. The record shows the number of items received, the number of items sold, and, after each receipt or sale, the balance of the item remaining on hand. A perpetual inventory card for one item, an adapter, is shown as Figure 14–1. A **physical inventory** is taken to determine the exact quantity of merchandise on hand by counting, weighing, or measuring each item. Obviously the most accurate method is to take a physical inventory. Because a physical inventory is usually taken periodically, such as monthly, quarterly, or annually, it is often called a **periodic inventory.**

One of the following may be used as the basis of assigning values to either a perpetual or physical inventory of goods.

1. Cost basis
   a. Specific identification
   b. Average cost
   c. First-in, first-out (fifo)
   d. Last-in, first-out (lifo)
2. Cost or market, whichever is lower

Inventory Valuation at Cost

The fact that identical units of a product may have been acquired at different cost prices during the period creates one of the most significant difficulties relative to determining the cost value of an inventory. If the units in the inven-

Item	Adapter		Location	T-38	

Stock No.	H-501	Minimum	20	Maximum	150

Date	Unit Cost	Quantity IN	Quantity OUT	Balance
Jan. 1	$20.00			60
8			20	40
15	20.50	80		120
17			25	95
23			45	50
26	22.00	100		150
31			40	110

Figure 14–1 A Perpetual Inventory Card

tory can be specifically identified, the appropriate cost can be assigned to each unit to obtain the total value of the inventory. If there is a great variety of merchandise carried in stock or if the volume of sales is great, using the specific-identification method of inventory valuation may be too laborious and costly to justify its use. When specific identification is impossible or undesirable, an alternate method may be used. An alternate method may be based on (1) an average of the costs, (2) the order in which the costs were incurred, or (3) the reverse order in which the costs were incurred.

Specific Identification. When each item of an inventory can be identified with a specific purchase, the respective units in the inventory may be valued at their actual cost prices. The computation of the value of 110 units contained in the ending inventory exhibited in Figure 14–1 is shown in the following example.

Example:

The inventory card reveals there were 110 adapters in stock on January 31. Code numbers on the adapters and company records reveal 10 of these cost $20 each, 30 cost $20.50 each, and 70 cost $22 each. Use the specific-identification method to find the value of the January 31 inventory of adapters.

Solution:

70 units $\times$ \$22.00 = \$1,540
30 units $\times$ \$20.50 =   615
10 units $\times$ \$20.00 =   200
110 units $2,355   inventory value

Or 70 [$\times$] 22 [=] [M+] 30 [$\times$] 20.5 [=] [M+] 10 [$\times$]

20 [=] [M+] [MR] $\rightarrow$ 2355, means \$2,355

Average Cost. A weighted average can be used to determine the value of an inventory on the assumption that when prices have varied during a period of time, an average cost should be charged against the revenue of that period. The **weighted-average cost** of an item is found by dividing the total cost of the item by the total number of units of the item that were available for sale during the period. The average cost per unit is then used to compute the total value of the units on hand.

Example:

The inventory card in Figure 14–1 shows that of the adapters available for sale during the January period, 60 cost $20 each, 80 cost $20.50 each, and 100 cost $22 each. The card also shows that on January 31 there were 110 adapters in inventory. Find **(a)** the average per-unit cost of the adapters and **(b)** the value of the ending inventory.

Solution:

(a)

$$\begin{array}{ll} 60 \text{ units} \times \$20.00 = & \$1,200 \\ 80 \text{ units} \times \$20.50 = & 1,640 \\ \underline{100} \text{ units} \times \$22.00 = & \underline{2,200} \\ 240 \text{ units} & \$5,040 \quad \text{total cost} \end{array}$$

$$\$5,040 \div 240 \text{ units} = \$21 \quad \text{average cost per unit}$$

(b) 110 units × $21 = $2,310 inventory value

Or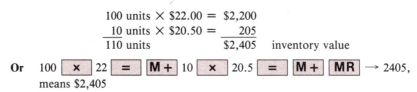

First-In, First-Out. In many businesses the oldest merchandise is sold first. In such businesses, the merchandise flows through the store on a first-in, first-out basis **(fifo).** This method of valuing inventory is based on the assumption that the inventory consists of the last items received because those that were received first have been sold.

Example:

Using the data shown in Figure 14–1, determine the value of the January 31 inventory of 110 items by using the first-in, first-out method of inventory valuation.

Solution:

As the first-in items were first-out, the 110 remaining items consist of the 100 received last (on January 26) and enough of the next preceding delivery to make the inventory total.

$$\begin{array}{ll} 100 \text{ units} \times \$22.00 = & \$2,200 \\ \underline{10} \text{ units} \times \$20.50 = & \underline{205} \\ 110 \text{ units} & \$2,405 \quad \text{inventory value} \end{array}$$

Or 100 ☒ 22 🟰 M+ 10 ☒ 20.5 🟰 M+ MR → 2405, means $2,405

Last-In, First-Out. The assumption that the most recently acquired merchandise is sold first, of course, is not in accord with the actual flow of goods in most businesses. There is, however, a strong theoretical justification for using the last-in, first-out **(lifo)** method of valuing inventories. A going concern must at all times keep a certain quantity of goods in stock. For this reason, as goods are sold, more merchandise must be purchased to replenish the stock on hand. As the making of a sale necessitates a replacement purchase of merchandise, the replacement cost should be charged against the revenue of the sale to determine the income realized.

One interpretation of the lifo method of inventory valuation is that the ending inventory consists of the "old" merchandise that was acquired first.

Example: Using the data shown in Figure 14–1, determine the value of the January 31 inventory of 110 adapters by using the last-in, first-out method of inventory valuation.

Solution: As the last items received are assumed to be the first out, the 110 remaining items consist of the first 60 items plus enough of the next consecutive receipts to make the total.

$$
\begin{array}{rl}
60 \text{ units} \times \$20.00 = & \$1,200 \\
\underline{50} \text{ units} \times \$20.50 = & \underline{1,025} \\
110 \text{ units} & \$2,225 \quad \text{inventory value}
\end{array}
$$

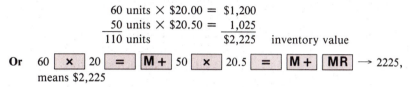

Or   60 ☒ 20 ☐ M+ 50 ☒ 20.5 ☐ M+ MR → 2225, means $2,225

Inventory Valuation at Cost or Market, Whichever Is Lower

In all of the preceding methods, the value of the inventory is computed at cost price. An alternative method is to compare the cost with the market price and to value the inventory at the lower of the two. The word **market** in the phrase "cost or market" means the cost of replacing the item on the date the inventory is taken.

When the lower-of-cost-or-market method is used, the value of the inventory is most commonly computed by finding the cost and the market figures for each item in the inventory and then using the lower of the two amounts in every case. This application of the lower-of-cost-or-market rule is shown in Figure 14–2.

Stock Number	Quantity on Hand	Unit Price		Inventory Value
		Cost	Market	
H-101	10	$20	$18	$ 180
H-102	25	10	12	250
H-103	80	15	16	1,200
H-104	50	9	8	400
Total				$2,030

Figure 14–2 Valuation of Inventory at Cost or Market, Whichever Is Lower

- Exercise 14–2

1. If 300 units were purchased for a total of $900 and later 500 more units were purchased for a total of $1,740, the weighted average cost per unit is how much?

2. A company's beginning inventory of Stock No. 1240 consisted of 400 units at $9.50 each. Purchases during the year were as follows: 300 at $9.60 each, 700 at $9.30 each, 150 at $9.80 each, and 250 at $9.40 each. There were 450 units remaining on hand at the end of the year. Determine the value of the ending inventory by each of the following methods: (a) fifo, (b) lifo, and (c) average cost.

3. Conway Corporation deals in a single product of relatively low cost. The volume of sales during the past year was $540,000 at a sales price of $9 a unit. The inventory at the beginning of the previous year was 8,000 units valued at a cost of $32,300. Purchases for the year were as follows: 18,000 units at $4.25 each, 30,000 units at $4.50 each, and 13,000 units at $4.60 each. Find the value of the ending inventory by using (a) average cost, (b) fifo, and (c) lifo.

4. Using cost or market, whichever is lower, find the total value of the following inventory of items.

| | | Unit Price | |
Stock Number	Quantity on Hand	Cost	Market
511	75	$180	$170
512	140	110	120
513	200	45	50
514	125	62	59
515	12	29	28
516	58	31	29

5. Matthews and Lewis follow the policy of valuing each inventory item at cost or market, whichever is lower. On this basis, find the total value of the following inventory.

| | | Unit Price | |
Stock Number	Quantity on Hand	Cost	Market
811	125	$1.20	$1.10
812	120	0.80	0.75
813	130	0.40	0.45
814	124	1.50	1.60
815	144	0.25	0.30
816	210	0.25	0.20

6. The inventory of V brackets on January 1 of last year consisted of 500 units priced at $5 each. Purchases during the year were as follows: 100 at $5.10

each, 200 at $5.24 each, 160 at $5.20 each, 180 at $5.40 each, and 220 at $5.50 each. At the end of the year on December 31, there were 400 units on hand. Compute the value of the December 31 inventory by **(a)** fifo, **(b)** lifo, and **(c)** average cost.

7. The owner of a specialty store computes the value of each item in inventory at cost or market, whichever is lower. Find the total value of the following items.

		Unit Price	
Stock Number	Quantity on Hand	Cost	Market
1001	58	$3.00	$2.85
1002	62	3.42	3.60
1003	37	5.14	5.40
1004	41	3.98	4.09
1005	39	3.80	3.75
1006	25	6.43	6.18

8. The following data were taken from the records of the Lockwood Corporation:

January 1	On hand	6,000 units @ $12.00 each
February 15	Purchase	9,000 units @ 12.90 each
July 18	Purchase	10,000 units @ 12.57 each
October 9	Purchase	8,000 units @ 12.75 each
December 31	On hand	7,000 units

Compute the value of the ending inventory using **(a)** average cost, **(b)** fifo, and **(c)** lifo.

Estimating Inventory Value

When taking a physical inventory is too costly, too time-consuming, or impossible, the value of the inventory may be estimated. There are two common methods of estimating the value of an inventory, (1) the gross-profit method and (2) the retail method. Both of these methods are based on the calculation of the gross-profit rate. The gross-profit method is based on past experience; the retail method is based on current experience.

Gross-Profit Method. When **purchases** (the value of all merchandise purchased during a given period of time) are added to the value of the merchandise inventory that was on hand at the beginning of the period, the total shows the value of the **goods available for sale** during the period. The value of the inventory at the end of the period represents the goods that were not sold. When the value of the ending inventory is subtracted from the goods available for sale, the **cost of goods sold** is found. The result of subtracting cost of goods sold from net sales is the **gross profit.** This information may be shown on an income statement as follows:

Net Sales		$100,000	(100%)
Beginning inventory.............	$25,000		
Purchases.....................	70,000		
Goods Available for Sale	$95,000		
Less: Ending Inventory	35,000		
Cost of Goods Sold		60,000	(60%)
Gross Profit		$ 40,000	(40%)

Notice the relationship of net sales (100%), cost of goods sold (60%), and gross profit (40%). This may be interpreted to mean that of every sales dollar received, 60 cents were spent for cost of goods and 40 cents remain to cover expenses and earn a profit. This may also be interpreted to mean that the company's average markon rate is 40% of sales.

The cost-of-goods-sold section of the preceding income statement may be summarized in the following equation:

Beginning Inventory + Purchases = Ending Inventory + Cost of Goods Sold

Letting *B* represent beginning inventory, *P,* purchases, *E,* ending inventory, and *C,* cost of goods sold, the equation becomes:

$$B + P = E + C$$

If any three of these terms are known, the fourth can be found easily. On the income statement, ending inventory is normally deducted from goods available for sale to find cost of goods sold. When the gross-profit method is used, however, the value of the ending inventory is found by deducting cost of goods sold from goods available for sale. If cost of goods sold is not known, it can be estimated by applying the gross-profit (markon) rate to its cost or net-sales basis.

Example:

A company that had sales of $200,000 with a markon rate of 40% of sales started the accounting period with a merchandise inventory of $40,000. The company purchased $110,000 worth of goods during the period. Use the gross-profit method to find the value of the ending inventory.

Solution:

As sales were $200,000 and the markon rate is 40%, the gross profit must be $80,000 (40% of $200,000), and the cost of goods sold must be $120,000 (60% of $200,000). Therefore:

$$B + P = E + C$$
$$\$40,000 + \$110,000 = E + \$120,000$$
$$(\$40,000 + \$110,000) - \$120,000 = E$$
$$\$150,000 - \$120,000 = E$$
$$\$30,000 = E$$

                Part 3. Mathematics Applications in Operating a Business

If the sales are $100,000 and the known markon rate is 25% of cost, the cost of goods sold is equal to $100,000 ÷ 1.25 (125%), which is $80,000.

Retail Method. Many chain stores, department stores, and other kinds of retail businesses use the retail method of estimating the value of an ending inventory. Goods for sale in such stores are marked at retail prices. Unless the cost of each item is shown on the price tag, taking an inventory at current retail prices is easier than looking up invoices to find the unit cost. Even if the cost is shown by code on the price tag, recording the retail price is usually easier than converting the code to cost price. This method of approximating an inventory may also be based on the data in the accounting records without taking a physical count of the merchandise on hand.

To use the retail method of inventory valuation, follow these two steps:

1. Find the retail value of the inventory through a physical count or by using sales data.
2. Convert the retail value of the inventory to a cost basis by applying the ratio prevailing between cost and selling price of the goods available for sale during the period.

Example:

The beginning inventory of Barrington Company cost $20,000 and had a retail value of $25,000. Purchases of goods during the year cost $220,000 and were marked to sell for $275,000. Sales during the year amounted to $260,000. Use the retail method to find the estimated value of the ending inventory **(a)** at retail and **(b)** at cost.

Solution:

	Cost	Retail
(a) Beginning Inventory	$ 20,000	$ 25,000
Purchases	220,000	275,000
Goods Available for Sale	$240,000	$300,000
Less: Net Sales		260,000
Ending Inventory at Retail		$ 40,000

(b) Ratio of merchandise available for sale:

$$\frac{\$240,000 \text{ Cost Value}}{\$300,000 \text{ Retail Value}} = 80\%$$

Ending Inventory at estimated cost:

$$\$40,000 \times 80\% = \$32,000$$

● Exercise 14–3

1. By using the formula $B + P = E + C$, find the amount that is missing in each row of data.

	Beginning Inventory	Ending Inventory	Purchases	Cost of Goods Sold
a.	$120,000	_____	$250,000	$272,000
b.	_____	$ 53,000	144,000	134,000
c.	181,000	157,600	208,000	_____
d.	66,600	80,240	_____	136,500

2. A company keeps merchandise records in terms of selling price. On July 1, the books show the following: January 1 inventory, $33,000; purchases to date, $172,400; sales to date, $163,800. What is the estimated retail value of the company's July 1 inventory?

3. A retail company had a January 1 inventory of $200,000 at cost. During the year, merchandise costing $1,300,000 was purchased and sales amounted to $1,740,000. All goods were marked up $33\frac{1}{3}$% on cost to determine selling price. Calculate the estimated cost value of the December 31 inventory by the gross-profit method.

4. The normal gross profit of the Gardner and Moore Company is 30% of selling price. The store was destroyed by fire on the night of December 15, but the records were protected by a fire-proof vault. The records show that the inventory at the beginning of the year cost $80,000, purchases to December 15 were $210,000, and sales to that date were $360,000. What is the estimated cost value of the inventory that was destroyed by fire?

5. Newton Company bought $47,000 worth of goods during December and marked the goods to sell for $72,200. On December 1, the company had an inventory at cost of $18,000. The retail value of the beginning inventory was $27,800. Sales for the month totaled $70,000. Use the retail method to find the cost value of the December 31 inventory.

6. Accountants for Oakland Products, Inc., decided to estimate the company's January 31 inventory for an interim income statement. By examining the records, they discovered that the January 1 inventory had cost $34,420 and had a retail value of $46,650. During January the company had sold $412,000 worth of goods and bought $287,895 worth of goods that had been marked to sell for $413,800. Use the retail method to find the cost value of the January 31 inventory.

7. Bentley Corporation's year-end inventory at marked selling prices totaled $31,800. At the beginning of the year, the goods on hand had cost $19,360 and were marked to sell for $29,420. During the year the company purchased $137,840 worth of merchandise which was marked to sell for $232,580. Use the retail method to find the cost value of the ending inventory.

8. The records of Wheeler Company reveal this information:

	Cost Price	Selling Price
Inventory, January 1	$39,588	65,980
Purchases for the year	94,400	
Net Sales for the year		166,904

Find the estimated value of the ending inventory **(a)** at selling price and **(b)** at cost.

VALUATION OF GOODWILL

Goodwill, an intangible asset, is the present value of the future above-average earnings of a company. Of course, average-earning rates vary from industry to industry. In one industry, normal earnings may average only 5% or 6% on net assets; whereas, in another industry, the average-earning rate may be 15% or even 20% on net assets. A particular business in a given industry may have above-average net income because of its good reputation, favorable location, efficient management, monopoly position, or a variety of other circumstances. Extra earnings of past years are significant only when such extra earnings are expected to continue in the future.

The existence of goodwill is indicated when a business is sold for a price that is in excess of the fair market value of the net assets in the business. For example, assume that a business having net assets valued at $100,000 is sold to a purchaser for $120,000. The premium of $20,000 is paid because of the past earnings of the company and is recorded in the records of the purchaser as goodwill.

The value of goodwill may be determined in many different ways. Only four methods are presented here: (1) an arbitrary agreement, (2) a multiple of the average earnings, (3) the capitalized value of the extra earnings, or (4) a multiple of the extra earnings. **Arbitrary agreement** is the buyer and seller arbitrarily agreeing to the selling price of a business through negotiation. For example, the buyer may offer $115,000 for the business when the seller has offered to take $125,000. After some negotiations, they may arbitrarily agree that the total price will be $120,000. The other three methods of reaching agreement on the value of goodwill are presented on this and subsequent pages.

Goodwill Based on a Multiple of the Average Earnings

four methods are presented here: (1) an arbitrary agreement, (2) a multiple of the average earnings, (3) the capitalized value of the extra earnings, or (4) a multiple of the extra earnings. **Arbitrary agreement** is the buyer and seller arbitrarily agreeing to the selling price of a business through negotiation. For example, the buyer may offer $115,000 for the business when the seller has offered to take $125,000. After some negotiations, they may arbitrarily agree that the total price will be $120,000. The other three methods of reaching agreement on the value of goodwill are presented on this and subsequent pages.

1. Find the average net income by adding together the net income for a given number of past years and dividing the result by the given number of past years.
2. Find the value of goodwill by multiplying the average net income by the number of future years for which the average earnings are projected.

Example:

The amount paid for goodwill by the purchaser of Cambridge Company was equal to three times the average net income of the company for the past four years. The average earnings were expected to continue for three years in the future. Find the value of the goodwill if the amounts of net income for the past four years were $10,000, $12,000, $11,000, and $15,000.

Solution:

1. Find the average net income.

$$\$10,000 + \$12,000 + \$11,000 + \$15,000 = \$48,000$$

$$\frac{\$48,000}{4} = \$12,000 \quad \text{average net income}$$

2. Find the value of goodwill by multiplying.

$$\text{Average Earnings} \times \text{Multiplier} = \text{Goodwill}$$
$$\$12,000 \times 3 = \$36,000$$

This method may be criticized because the concept of extra earnings as the basis for estimating the value of goodwill is ignored.

Goodwill Based on a Multiple of the Extra Earnings

The assumption that extra earnings will continue indefinitely is subject to question because of the competitive pressures and hazards of the free enterprise system. Even if extra earnings do accrue over a long period of time, their presence may not be traceable to a condition that was prevalent at the time of acquisition. Valuing goodwill on the basis of extra earnings, therefore, may be modified in several ways. One method is to assume that any extra earnings will continue only for a specified period of time, such as three, five, eight, or ten years.

Goodwill may be determined as a multiple of the extra earnings. The number of years for which the extra earnings are expected to continue is the multiplier. Depending on the agreement between the buyer and seller, the extra earnings may be based on the normal rate of return or on a fair interest rate. To determine the value of goodwill by this method, multiply the extra earnings by the number of future years (the multiplier).

Example:

The records of Cambridge Company reveal that the average annual net income is $12,000 and the investment in the business is $100,000. The normal rate of return on capital invested in similar businesses is 10%. On the assumption that the extra earnings will continue for five years in the future, find the value of goodwill.

Solution:

1. Find the extra earnings.

Investment in business (net worth)	$100,000
Average annual net income	$12,000
Normal earnings for industry ($100,000 × 10%)	10,000
Extra earnings	$ 2,000

Part 3. Mathematics Applications in Operating a Business

2. Find the value of goodwill by multiplying.

$$\text{Extra Earnings} \times \text{Multiplier} = \text{Goodwill}$$
$$\$2,000 \times 5 = \$10,000$$

Goodwill Based on the Capitalized Value of the Extra Earnings

Goodwill may be considered to be the capitalized value of the extra earning power of a company. The **capitalized value of the extra earning power** of a company is the amount of capital that will yield the extra earnings at the desired rate of return. This method is based on the assumption that extra earnings will continue indefinitely into the future.

To find the value of goodwill by this method, follow these two steps:

1. Find the extra earnings of the company by deducting the normal earnings on the amount invested from the average annual net income of the company.
2. Find the value of goodwill, which is the capitalized value of the extra earnings, by dividing the extra earnings by the desired rate of return.

Example:

The records of Cambridge Company show the average annual net income to be $12,000 and the owner's investment (net worth) in the company to be $100,000. The normal rate of return on capital invested in similar businesses is 10%. Find the value of goodwill by capitalizing the extra earnings at the same rate of return.

Solution:

1. Find the extra earnings.

Investment in business (net worth).............................	$100,000
Average annual net income	$12,000
Normal earnings for industry ($100,000 × 10%)	10,000
Extra earnings	$ 2,000

2. Find the value of goodwill by capitalizing the extra earnings at 10%. (Let C = Capital or Goodwill.)

$$C \times 10\% = \$2,000$$
$$C = \$2,000 \div 0.1$$
$$C = \$20,000$$

● Exercise 14–4

1. The amount of money paid for a business included goodwill valued at 2 years of the company's average earnings for the preceding 3 years. The earnings for the preceding 3 years were as follows: first year, $87,000; sec-

ond year, $101,000; third year, $121,600. Find the value placed on goodwill.

2. The records of a business that is about to be sold show the average net income for the past few years is $20,000. This business has a net worth of $180,000, and 8% is a normal rate of return on an investment in a business of this kind. Find the value to be placed on goodwill if the extra earnings are capitalized at the same rate of return.

3. At the time a business was being sold, the buyer and seller agreed that the average annual net income of $48,000 would continue indefinitely, that the net worth of the business amounted to $178,000, and that a normal rate of return for similar businesses was 15%. Find **(a)** the goodwill cost to the purchaser if the extra earnings are capitalized at the normal rate and **(b)** the total amount the purchaser paid for the business.

4. The amount paid for goodwill by the purchaser of a business was equal to 3 years of the company's average earnings for the past 5 years. Determine the value placed on goodwill if the net income for each of the preceding 5 years was $48,000, $39,000, $63,000, $81,000, and $105,000.

5. Just prior to her retirement, Marilyn Jackson found a buyer who was willing to buy the business at 5 times the average net income for the preceding 4 years, plus the net worth. Net worth of the business was $405,600, and the net income for each of the preceding 4 years was as follows: first year, $94,500; second year, $86,240; third year, $110,520; fourth year, $125,020. Find the price at which the business was sold.

6. Brad Bishop is considering buying Blue Mountain Company. The company has been doing business for 5 years and has had an average annual net income of $32,600 during this time. Goodwill is to be valued at 4 times the average extra earnings over a normal rate of 8% on the net tangible assets that total $188,000. Determine the value of goodwill.

7. Peoria Corporation has net assets having a current fair value of $1,000,000. The company has earned an average of $160,000 during the past few years. If the normal earning rate in this industry is 10%, find the value of the unrecorded goodwill by each of these methods: **(a)** purchase of the average earnings for the next 3 years; **(b)** capitalization of the extra earnings at the normal rate of 10%; and **(c)** purchase of the extra earnings for the next 5 years.

8. Prior to its sale, a company's goodwill was valued at the average annual earnings for 3 years preceding the sale capitalized at 8%, after the following deductions were made from the amount of average earnings: $5,000 earnings from a contract that is expiring; $17,500 for the estimated value of the services rendered by a retiring manager; and 10% interest on the net worth, not including goodwill. Find the value of goodwill if the net worth was $414,760 and the annual earnings for the preceding 3 years were $71,790, $61,640, and $80,170.

VALUATION OF FIXED ASSETS

The cost of a fixed asset includes all expenditures made at the time of acquisition to obtain the asset and prepare it for use. This may include not only the purchase price but also freight charges, installation costs, and other expenditures made to acquire the asset.

The cost of fixed assets, such as buildings, machinery, equipment, trucks, and office furniture, is a capital expenditure, which means the total expenditure may not be deducted as a business expense in the year of purchase. As the value of an asset decreases through wear and tear, age, or obsolescence, the owner may deduct part of the cost as an expense of doing business. **Depreciation** is a recovery of the costs of an asset over a term of years. That is, through depreciating an asset, the owner is enabled to deduct periodically from the revenue a reasonable portion of the cost of the asset. The amount deducted depends on the nature of the asset and how it is used and maintained. Because of its permanent nature, land is not subject to depreciation. Increases or decreases in land value are usually recorded when land is sold or disposed of.

The **service life** of an asset is the estimated period of time during which it may reasonably be expected to be used. The useful service life of an asset depends on its age when acquired and the owner's policies regarding repairs, upkeep, and replacement. The estimated service life of an asset is not necessarily the useful life inherent in the asset, but it is the period over which the asset may reasonably be expected to be used in a specific trade or business.

Salvage value is the **trade-in value** or **scrap value** that is estimated at the time of acquisition to be the amount which will be realized from the asset when it is traded in or sold at the end of its service life. When the owner's policy is to dispose of assets that are still in good operating condition, salvage value may represent a large part of the cost of the asset. On the other hand, if the owner's policy is to use an asset until its useful life is exhausted, salvage value may represent no more than junk value. When salvage value is less than 10 percent of the asset's value, it may be ignored for federal income tax purposes.

The total amount of depreciation that pertains to an asset from the date it is purchased to some later date is referred to as **accumulated depreciation.** The cost of an asset is recorded in the accounting records of the business. As depreciation is charged off against revenue, the accumulated depreciation in the accounting records increases and the book value of the asset decreases. The **book value** of an asset is the difference between the cost of the asset and its accumulated depreciation.

$$Book\ Value = Cost - Accumulated\ Depreciation$$

Property is considered to be **placed in service** when it is in a condition or state of readiness and available for a specific function in a trade or business. Depreciation begins when the asset is first ready for service in a trade or business or for the production of income. The **unadjusted basis** is usually the cost of the asset before any reductions for salvage value or depreciation.

Example A:

Tampa Company purchased a used machine for $12,500 for use in the business. The company then spent an additional $1,500 to recondition the machine. Find the unadjusted basis of this machine.

Solution:

$12,500 + $1,500 = $14,000   unadjusted basis

When a depreciable asset is acquired by obtaining a trade-in allowance, the unadjusted basis is the sum of the book value of the asset being traded in plus the extra amount that is paid in cash or obtained on credit.

Example B:

Temple Company traded in an old copy machine with a value on the company's books of $300 on a new copy machine priced at $5,000. The trade-in allowance was $500. The balance of $4,500 was paid in cash. Find the unadjusted basis for the new machine.

Solution:

$300 + $4,500 = $4,800   unadjusted basis

The five most common methods of computing depreciation are the (1) straight-line method, (2) units-of-production method, (3) sum-of-the-years-digits method, (4) declining-balance method, and (5) modified accelerated cost recovery system (MACRS).

Straight-Line Method

This method may be used for every type of depreciable property. Under the **straight-line method,** the cost of the property less its salvage value is divided by its service life to find the annual depreciation. It lets the owner of the property deduct the same amount each year. Its name is derived from the fact that if the amount to be deducted each year is plotted on graph paper, the result is a straight, horizontal line. Time is the primary criterion for determining annual depreciation by the straight-line method.

The computation is summarized in the following equation:

$$Annual\ Depreciation = \frac{Cost - Salvage\ Value}{Service\ Life}$$

Example A:

At the beginning of the year, Denver Company bought a machine for $6,800 and paid another $600 for a special platform that was installed with the machine. The company estimated that the machine would have a service life of 5 years and that its trade-in value then would be $1,000. Find **(a)** the cost of the machine, **(b)** the annual straight-line depreciation, and **(c)** the machine's book value at the end of three years.

Solution:

(a) $6,800   basic cost of machine
       600   cost of platform
    $7,400   total cost of machine

(b) Annual Depreciation $= \dfrac{Cost - Salvage\ Value}{Service\ Life}$

$\qquad = \dfrac{\$7,400 - \$1,000}{5}$

$\qquad = \dfrac{\$6,400}{5} = \$1,280$

Part 3. Mathematics Applications in Operating a Business

(c) At the end of the third year, accumulated depreciation would be $3 \times \$1,280 = \$3,840$. Therefore:

$$\text{Book Value} = \text{Cost} - \text{Accumulated Depreciation}$$
$$\text{Book Value} = \$7,400 - \$3,840$$
$$\text{Book Value} = \$3,560$$

If monthly depreciation is desired, the annual depreciation may be divided by 12, or the divisor in the equation may be the asset's service life in months rather than in years.

When an asset is not acquired at the beginning of a tax year, the allowable depreciation is prorated for that part of the year that the asset is owned. Depreciation is normally prorated to the nearest month during the first tax year in which the asset is obtained, as well as to the nearest month during the last year in which the asset is depreciated. If an asset is acquired prior to the 15th day of a month, that month is counted; if the asset is disposed of prior to the 15th of a month, that month is not counted. For example, if the tax year coincides with the calendar year, an asset that is acquired on May 14 would usually be depreciated as if it had been acquired on May 1, and depreciation for eight months would be deducted for the first year.

Example B:

On May 14, Detroit Manufacturing Company, which pays its income taxes on a calendar-year basis, bought a machine that cost $2,700. The company estimated that the machine would last 5 years and that it would then have a salvage value of $300. Find the regular straight-line depreciation on the machine for **(a)** the first year and **(b)** the second year.

Solution:

(a) $\text{Monthly Depreciation} = \dfrac{\text{Cost} - \text{Salvage Value}}{\text{Service Life (in Months)}}$

$$= \frac{\$2,700 - \$300}{60}$$

$$= \frac{\$2,400}{60} = \$40$$

Depreciation for 8 months $= 8 \times \$40 = \$320$

(b) Depreciation for 1 year $= 12 \times \$40 = \$480$

● **Exercise 14–5**

A. Compute the annual straight-line depreciation for each of the following.

	Total Cost	Estimated Life in Years	Salvage Value
1.	$ 3,800	7	$ 440
2.	8,100	12	900
3.	19,000	5	2,000
4.	95,000	15	11,000
5.	27,200	20	3,600
6.	145,000	25	15,000

Chapter 14. Selected Accounting Practices

Schedule *add in freight charges as part of cost*

set up

B. On January 7, the Elgin Company bought a machine for $8,000 and paid freight charges of $350 when it was delivered. The company estimated that the machine would have a service life of 6 years and a salvage value of $1,150. Use this information to solve these problems.

Due all of 3

1. How much was the total cost of the machine?

2. How much was the annual straight-line depreciation?

3. Use the following columnar headings to complete a schedule that shows the annual straight-line depreciation, the accumulated depreciation, and the book value of the machine for each year of its service life.

Year	Annual Depreciation	Accumulated Depreciation	Book Value

C. Solve these problems.

1. The Delhi Company purchased equipment by paying $8,000 for it and $150 for its delivery to the company's factory. The company then spent $450 to have the equipment installed. Find the unadjusted basis for depreciating this equipment.

Don't Due

2. In 1989, the Henderson Company bought a 1988 model machine by trading in a 1984 model and paying the balance in cash. The trade-in allowance was $1,200 toward the price of $9,750. The book value of the traded-in machine was $1,500. The company also paid $350 to have the new machine installed. Find the unadjusted basis of the new machine.

3. Find the annual straight-line depreciation on machinery that cost $52,000 and has an estimated life of 10 years and a scrap value of $6,500.

4. An office machine that cost $2,700 is estimated to have a trade-in value of $900 at the end of 5 years of use. How much is the monthly straight-line depreciation on the machine?

5. A firm bought office equipment on July 1 at a cost of $9,800. The service life of the equipment was estimated to be 4 years and the trade-in value to be $1,800. Use the straight-line method of computing depreciation to find (a) depreciation at the end of the first calendar year and (b) depreciation for the second year.

Set up Schedule for

6. Office furniture that cost $7,800 and had a service life of 12 years and an estimated salvage value of $900 was depreciated by the straight-line method. Find the accumulated depreciation at the end of the third year.

7. A machine that cost $8,850 when it was new had an estimated trade-in value of $1,290. If the monthly straight-line depreciation was $70, what was the estimated life of the machine in years?

8. On January 14, Long Beach Farming Company paid $680,000 to construct a warehouse. The company estimated that the building would be

used for 25 years and then have a salvage value of $80,000. The warehouse site was valued at $125,000. Find **(a)** the straight-line depreciation for the first year and **(b)** the book value of the building at the end of the first year.

9. On July 12, Madison Corporation bought a machine for $6,605.40. The freight amounted to $94.60. The cost of installing the machine was $100. The company estimated that the machine would be used for 9 years and then would have a trade-in value of $950. Find **(a)** the straight-line depreciation at the end of the first calendar year and **(b)** the accumulated depreciation after the machine had been owned for 3 years.

10. A building contractor bought a machine for $4,250. The machine was estimated to have a useful life of 8 years and a salvage value of $650 at the end of that time. After the machine had been depreciated on the straight-line basis for 6 years, it was considered to be worn out and was sold for junk for $275. How much difference was there between the book value and the junk value of the machine on the date it was sold?

Units-of-Production Method of Computing Depreciation

Finding depreciation by the units-of-production method is similar to finding it by the straight-line method, except that usage rather than time is the primary criterion on which the computation is based. Units of production may be in hours, miles, or number of operations, for example. Under this method, the life of the asset is estimated in terms of the number of units that may be produced during its useful life. When this method is used for a factory machine, the unit-of-production cost is based on the total number of units that the machine is expected to produce during its useful life. For a delivery truck, the unit-of-production cost is based on the estimated number of miles that the truck is to be driven.

The per-unit depreciation cost is found by dividing the cost of the asset, less its salvage value, by the total number of units that are expected to be produced. The per-unit cost is then multiplied by the number of units produced during a given period of time to find the amount of depreciation.

$$Per\text{-}Unit\ Depreciation = \frac{Cost - Salvage\ Value}{Total\ Units\ to\ Be\ Produced}$$

Example: Emerson Company bought a machine for $5,000. The company estimated that the machine would produce 250,000 units during its useful life and then would have a salvage value of $500. Using the units-of-production method, find **(a)** the per-unit depreciation and **(b)** the depreciation for a year in which the machine produced 26,000 units.

Solution: **(a)** Per-Unit Depreciation $= \dfrac{Cost - Salvage\ Value}{Total\ Units\ to\ Be\ Produced}$

$$= \frac{\$5,000 - \$500}{250,000}$$

$$= \frac{\$4,500}{250,000} = \$0.018$$

(b) Depreciation $= \$0.018 \times 26,000$ units $= \$468$

Exercise 14–6

1. A truck that cost $17,505 and had been driven 87,600 miles was traded in on a new truck. The trade-in allowance was $2,175. How much was the per-mile depreciation expense of operating this truck?

2. Machinery that cost $166,000 has an estimated scrap value of $21,100. It is expected to produce 150,000 units. If it produced 29,200 units during the year, how much depreciation should be allowed on a units-of-production basis?

3. On January 12, the Golden Gate Company purchased a machine for $11,000. Freight charges were $380, and the cost of installation was $120. The company estimated that the machine would be operated 50,000 hours during its useful life and would then have a resale value of $1,500. Use the units-of-production method to find **(a)** the depreciation at the end of the first year if the machine had been used 2,300 hours and **(b)** the book value at the end of the first year.

4. Raleigh Corporation has a machine that cost $11,800 and is expected to have a trade-in value of $1,600 after it has been used to produce 100,000 units. The company used this machine to produce 17,000 units during the first year. Use the units-of-production method to find the depreciation charges for the first year.

5. Dudley Company bought a machine at a cost of $5,900. Its useful life was estimated to be 200,000 units; the trade-in value, $1,100. The company used the machine to produce the following units each year: first year, 38,000 units; second year, 46,000 units; third year, 48,000 units; fourth year, 36,000 units; fifth year, 32,000 units. Use the units-of-production method to compute the depreciation charges for each year.

6. A retailer paid $2,475 for an air conditioner. It was expected to have a salvage value of $275 after being used for 10,000 hours. It was used 14 hours a day, 6 days a week, for 30 weeks in one year. Use the units-of-production method to find the depreciation for the year.

Sum-of-the-Years-Digits Method of Computing Depreciation

Under this method, a common fraction that decreases in size each year is applied to the cost or other basis of the asset less its salvage value. The denominator of the fraction is the total of the digits representing the years of service life of the asset. Thus, if the service life is 5 years, the denominator is 15, which is the sum of the digits $5 + 4 + 3 + 2 + 1$. The numerator of the fraction is the number of years of service life remaining at the beginning of the year for which depreciation is being computed. Thus, if the useful life is 5 years, the common fraction to be applied to the cost less salvage value to find depreciation for the first year is $\frac{5}{15}$. The common fraction for the second year is $\frac{4}{15}$; and for the succeeding years, $\frac{3}{15}$, $\frac{2}{15}$, and $\frac{1}{15}$.

Example:	An asset that was purchased for $6,750 has an estimated service life of 5 years and a trade-in value of $750. Use the sum-of-the-years-digits method to find the depreciation for each year.	
Solution:	The sum of the years digits is:	

$$5 + 4 + 3 + 2 + 1 = 15.$$

The total amount to be depreciated is:

$$\$6,750 \text{ cost} - \$750 \text{ salvage value} = \$6,000.$$

The annual depreciation charges are computed as follows:

$$\text{First year:} \quad \frac{5}{15} \times \$6,000 = \$2,000$$

$$\text{Second year:} \quad \frac{4}{15} \times \$6,000 = 1,600$$

$$\text{Third year:} \quad \frac{3}{15} \times \$6,000 = 1,200$$

$$\text{Fourth year:} \quad \frac{2}{15} \times \$6,000 = 800$$

$$\text{Fifth year:} \quad \frac{1}{15} \times \$6,000 = \underline{\quad 400}$$

$$\text{Total} \qquad\qquad\qquad\qquad \$6,000$$

The sum of the years digits may be found by using the formula

$$\frac{n(n + 1)}{2}$$

in which n represents the number of years of service life. The formula is helpful when the estimated life of the asset is a relatively large number of years. For an asset with a service life of 20 years, the denominator of the fraction is found in the following manner:

$$\frac{n(n + 1)}{2} = \frac{20(20 + 1)}{2} = 210.$$

● Exercise 14–7

A. Use the sum-of-the-years-digits method to find the depreciation for each of the following.

Even

	Article	Cost	Salvage Value	Service Life	Year	Amount
1.	Typewriters	$3,750	$750	5 years	1	_____
2.	Calculators	6,500	650	8 years	3	_____
3.	Chairs	1,800	240	12 years	2	_____
4.	Desks	3,200	400	20 years	4	_____
5.	Filing Cabinets	1,500	200	25 years	10	_____
6.	Tables	900	100	15 years	5	_____

B. Solve these problems.

1. Mt. Vernon Manufacturing Company owns a machine that cost $6,200, has an estimated useful life of 4 years, and has a scrap value of $700. Use the sum-of-the-years-digits method to find the depreciation charges for each year.

2. A machine that cost $9,000 has a probable life of 5 years and an estimated salvage value of $1,500. Show the annual depreciation by the sum-of-the-years-digits method.

3. The salvage value of a machine that cost $2,500 is $300 at the end of 8 years. Find the depreciation for the fourth year under the sum-of-the-years-digits method.

4. A machine that cost $5,500 is expected to have a salvage value of $600 at the end of its useful life of 6 years. Use the following columnar headings to complete a schedule that shows the annual depreciation, the accumulated depreciation, and the book value of the machine for each year of its service life by the sum-of-the-years-digits method.

Year	Annual Depreciation	Accumulated Depreciation	Book Value

Declining-Balance Method of Computing Depreciation

This is an accelerated method that may be used for certain types of property. Under the **declining-balance method,** the depreciation expense for each year is found by multiplying the book value of the property at the beginning of the year by the appropriate fixed rate. The annual rate allowed for some fixed assets is one and a half (150%) or one and a fourth (125%) of the straight-line rate. The allowable rates of 150% and 125%, like the straight-line rate, depend on the type of property being depreciated. Because the appropriate rate is applied to the book value, which decreases each year, it is applied to the "declining balance."

The straight-line depreciation rate may be found by dividing the numeral 1 by the asset's life in years and converting the resulting common fraction to a percent. For example, the straight-line rate for an asset with a service life of 5 years is $\frac{1}{5} = 0.2 = 20\%$. The 150% declining-balance rate for an asset with a service life of 5 years is $20\% \times 1.5 = 30\%$. However, notice that if the service life is 5 years, the following shortcut gives the same rate: $150\% \div 5 = 30\%$. The shortcut is sufficiently accurate for finding the declining-balance rate in most instances.

Example: Find the 150% declining-balance rate for an asset with a service life of 15 years.

Solution: $\frac{1}{15} = 1$ ⟦÷⟧ 15 ⟦%⟧ $\rightarrow 6.66...$ means 6.67%

6.67 ⟦×⟧ 1.5 ⟦=⟧ 10.005 means 10.00%

Or $150\% \div 15 = 10\%$

Salvage value is not deducted from the cost of the property before the rate is applied. Because only a portion of the declining balance is deducted each year, the total cost of the property cannot be depreciated. The value remaining at the end of the property's service life represents its salvage value.

The following is a summary of the procedure for using the declining-balance method:

1. Find the annual rate by dividing 150% or 125% by the number of years of service life.
2. Find the annual depreciation by multiplying the book value at the beginning of the year by the annual rate.

Example:

Bestway, Inc. bought used machinery at a cost of $16,000. The company estimated that it would have a trade-in value of $2,000 after being used for 6 more years. Use the 150% declining-balance method to compute depreciation for the **(a)** first year, **(b)** second year, and **(c)** third year of use.

Solution:

(a) To determine depreciation for the first year, find the 150% rate for this asset:

$$150\% \div 6 = 25\%$$

Find the amount of depreciation:

$$\$16,000 \times 25\% = \$4,000$$

(b) For the second year, find the book value:

$$\$16,000 - \$4,000 = \$12,000$$

Find the amount of depreciation:

$$\$12,000 \times 25\% = \$3,000$$

(c) For the third year, find the book value:

$$\$12,000 - \$3,000 = \$9,000$$

Find the amount of depreciation:

$$\$9,000 \times 25\% = \$2,250$$

● **Exercise 14–8**

Solve these problems.

1. On January 5, the Carbondale Printing Co., Inc. bought a used machine for $96,000. The company believed the machine could be used for 12 more years and would then have a salvage value of $12,000. Compute the depreciation expense for each of the first two years by using the 150% declining-balance method.

2. Previous experience indicates that a certain machine (new) can be operated for 10 years. A used two-year-old machine was purchased for $3,200 and was expected to have a salvage value of $450. Use the 150% declining-balance method to compute depreciation on this machine for the second year of ownership.

3. On January 12 of this year, San Diego Packing Co., Inc. bought a used machine that had a remaining service life of 15 years. The company paid $20,000 and expects the salvage value to be $2,000. Use the 150% declining-balance method to compute depreciation for the second year.

4. A used machine was purchased for $4,800 and is expected to be used for 4 more years and then to have a salvage value of $550. Show the annual depreciation under the 150% declining-balance method for each of the 4 years.

5. A used machine that cost $7,500 has an estimated remaining service life of 5 years and a salvage value of $900. Use the 150% declining-balance method to find the machine's book value at the end of the third year.

6. A used machine was acquired at a cost of $5,600. The purchaser estimated that it has a remaining service life of 6 years and a salvage value of $600. Use the 150% declining-balance method to calculate total depreciation for the first 3 years.

Modified Accelerated Cost Recovery System

The accelerated cost recovery system (ACRS) was considered mandatory for most tangible depreciable assets placed in service from January 1, 1981 through 1986. The Tax Reform Act of 1986, which modified the earlier law, provided a modified accelerated cost recovery system (MACRS) which applies to all tangible property placed in service after December 31, 1986.

Under MACRS, tangible property other than real estate that is placed in service after 1986 is classified into one of the following recovery periods: 3-, 5-, 7-, 10-, 15-, or 20-years. In addition, most real property is classified as residential rental or nonresidential real property.

3-Year Property. This includes property with a life of 4 years or less, such as over-the-road tractors and, as designated, any race horse that is over 2 years old when placed in service and any other horse that is over 12 years old when placed in service.

5-Year Property. This includes property with a class life of more than 4 years but less than 10 years, such as heavy and light general purpose trucks, computers, office machines (typewriters, calculators, etc.), and, as designated, any automobile, and any property used in connection with research and experimentation.

7-Year Property. This class includes property with a class life of 10 years or more but less than 16 years, such as office furniture and fixtures (desks, files, etc.), and, as designated, any single purpose agricultural or horticultural structure. This class also includes any property which does not have a class life and which has not been designated by law as being in any other class.

10-Year Property. This class includes property with a class life of 16 years or more but less than 20 years. It includes vessels, barges, tugs, and similar water transportation equipment.

15-Year Property. This includes property with a class life of 20 years or more but less than 25 years. It includes, as designated, any municipal waste-water treatment plant.

20-Year Property. This class includes property with a class life of 25 years or more, such as farm buildings, and, as designated, any municipal sewer.

Residential Rental Property. This is a rental structure or building for which 80% or more of the gross rental income for the tax year is rental income from dwelling units. If the taxpayer occupies any part of the building or structure, the gross rental income includes the fair rental value of the part so occupied. A unit in a hotel, motel, inn, or other establishment is not treated as a dwelling unit if more than half of the units are used on a transient basis.

Nonresidential Real Property. This includes most real property which is not residential rental property and real property with a class life of 27.5 years or more.

Depreciation Methods. For property in a 3-, 5-, 7-, or 10-year class, use the double (200%) declining-balance method for the appropriate recovery period and the half-year convention. Under MACRS, the **half-year convention** treats covered property that is placed in service, or disposed of, during a tax year as having been placed in service, or disposed of, on the midpoint of that tax year. A half-year of depreciation is allowable for the first year property is placed in service regardless of when the property is placed in service during that year. If the property is held for the entire recovery period, a half-year of depreciation is allowable for the year following the recovery period. During the other years of the recovery period, a full year of depreciation is allowable. If the property is disposed of during the recovery period, a half-year of depreciation is allow-able for the year of disposition.

Example:

DeKalb Products, Inc. purchased a 7-year property for $10,000 and placed it in service on April 18, 1987. To the nearest dollar, compute MACRS depreciation on this property for **(a)** 1987, **(b)** 1988, and **(c)** 1989.

Solution:

(a) To determine depreciation for the first year (1987), find the 200% declining-balance rate for this asset:

$$100\% \div 7 = 14.29\%$$
$$14.29\% \times 2 = 28.58\%$$

Find the amount of depreciation:

$$\$10,000 \times 28.58\% = \$2,858$$

Use the half-year convention:

$$\$2,858 \div 2 = \$1,429$$

(b) For the second year (1988), find the book value:

$$\$10,000 - \$1,429 = \$8,571$$

Find the amount of depreciation:

$$\$8,571 \times 28.58\% = \$2,450$$

(c) For the third year (1989), find the book value:

$$\$8,571 - \$2,450 = \$6,121$$

Find the amount of depreciation:

$$\$6,121 \times 28.58\% = \$1,749$$

For property in either the 15- or 20-year class, use the 150% declining-balance method and the half-year convention.

Example:

Forsythe Services, Inc. purchased 15-year property for $40,000 and placed it in service on March 16, 1987. Compute MACRS depreciation on this property for **(a)** 1987 and **(b)** 1988 to the nearest dollar.

Solution:

(a) To determine depreciation for the first year, find the 150% declining-balance rate for this asset:

$$150\% \div 15 = 10\%$$

Find the amount of depreciation:

$$\$40,000 \times 10\% = \$4,000$$

Use the half-year convention:

$$\$4,000 \div 2 = \$2,000$$

(b) For the second year, find the book value:

$$\$40,000 - \$2,000 = \$38,000$$

Find the amount of depreciation:

$$\$38,000 \times 10\% = \$3,800$$

For all property other than real property, change to the straight-line method for the first tax year for which that method when applied to the book value at the beginning of the year will yield a larger deduction. Notice in the example below that the straight-line deduction of $892 ($2,230 ÷ 2.5 remaining years) is used for 1992 because it is larger than the declining-balance deduction of $637.

Example:

DeKalb Products, Inc. purchased a 7-year property for $10,000 and placed it in service on April 18, 1987. (Same property as that in the example on page 449.) To the nearest dollar, compute MACRS depreciation on this property for each year of its service life.

Solution:

For 1987: $1,429
    1988: $2,450   See page 449 and above.
    1989: $1,749
    1990: $6,121 − $1,749 = $4,372
           $4,372 × 28.58% = $1,250
    1991: $4,372 − $1,250 = $3,122
           $3,122 × 28.58% = $892
    1992: $3,122 − $892 = $2,230
           $2,230 × 28.58% = $637
           But $2,230 ÷ 2.5 = $892
    1993: $2,230 ÷ 2.5 = $892
    1994: $892 ÷ 2 = $446

Part 3. Mathematics Applications in Operating a Business

The taxpayer may elect to use the straight-line method over the recovery period for non-real property. The election to use the straight-line method for a class of property applies to all property placed in service in the year of election. Once made, the election to use the straight-line method over the recovery period is irrevocable.

The straight-line method must be used for residential rental and most non-residential real property. Residential rental property is depreciated over 27.5 years using the straight-line method and the mid-month convention. Under the **mid-month convention** all property placed in service, or disposed of, during any month is treated as placed in service, or disposed of, on the midpoint of that month. Salvage value is ignored. However, depreciation for the first and last year must be prorated and the mid-month convention applied.

Example:

On March 6, 1987, Charles Ligon bought and placed in service an apartment building. The property cost $400,000 including the land valued at $100,000. To the nearest dollar, find the MACRS depreciation on this property for each of these: (a) annually, (b) monthly, (c) March, 1987, and (d) the year of 1987.

Solution:

(a) $400,000 − $100,000 = $300,000   basis
$300,000 ÷ 27.5 = $10,909   annual depreciation
(b) $10,909 ÷ 12 = $909   monthly depreciation
(c) $909 ÷ 2 = $455   depreciation for March
(d) April through December = 9 months
($909 × 9) + $455 = $8,636

Most nonresidential property is depreciated over 31.5 years using the straight-line method and the mid-month convention.

Example:

On December 5 Grant Manufacturing Co., Inc. paid $200,000 to have a warehouse constructed on land for which it had paid $50,000. The building was placed in service on December 7, 1987. To the nearest dollar, find the MACRS depreciation on this property for each of these: (a) 1987, (b) 1988, and (c) the last year of the recovery period.

Solution:

(a) $200,000 ÷ 31.5 = $6,349   annual depreciation
$6,349 ÷ 12 = $529   monthly depreciation
$529 ÷ 2 = $265 depreciation for 1987
(b) $200,000 ÷ 31.5 = $6,349
(c) $6,349 − $265 = $6,084

If during any tax year the aggregate bases of all property, except real property, which is placed in service during the last 3 months of that tax year exceed 40% of the aggregate of all such property placed in service during that tax year, a mid-quarter convention instead of the half-year convention is used. Under the **mid-quarter convention,** all covered property placed in service, or disposed of, during any quarter of a tax year is treated as placed in service, or disposed of, at the mid-point of that quarter. For the problems in this book, assume that the aggregate bases do not exceed 40% of the covered property placed in service that year.

A. In each of the following, the tax year is the calendar year. To the nearest dollar, find the MACRS depreciation for the year the asset was placed in service.

	Basis of Asset	Class of Property	Month Placed in Service
1.	$ 980	3-year	May
2.	4,000	3-year	July
3.	7,500	5-year	June
4.	90,000	5-year	March
5.	125,000	7-year	September
6.	345,000	7-year	December
7.	180,000	10-year	February
8.	475,000	10-year	April
9.	250,000	15-year	January
10.	360,000	20-year	November
11.	1,800,000	residential rental	August
12.	2,400,000	nonresidential real	October

B. In each of the following, the tax year is the calendar year. Round to the nearest dollar.

1. The Columbus Company bought a 5-year property that cost $2,500 on February 28, 1987, and then paid $500 to have the property delivered and installed on March 5, 1987. Find the MACRS depreciation on this property for **(a)** 1987 and **(b)** 1988. **(c)** Find the book value at the end of 1988.

2. A 7-year property was bought and placed in service by the Decatur Corporation on October 3, 1987, at a cost of $14,500. Find the MACRS depreciation on the property for each year of the recovery period.

3. The Tullahoma Service Corporation placed in service on May 2, 1987, a 7-year property that cost $28,000. Find the MACRS depreciation on the property for each year of the recovery period.

4. On March 18, 1987, the Canton Canning Co., Inc., bought and placed in service a 3-year property that cost $4,500. Find the MACRS depreciation on this property for **(a)** 1987, **(b)** 1988, **(c)** 1989, and **(d)** 1990.

5. On August 12, 1987, the Syr Darya Products Co., Inc., bought a 10-year property for $75,000. This property was similar to new property that the company had bought for $112,000 on April 20, 1987. Later, on November 2, 1987, the company bought another 10-year property for $25,000. Find the company's total MACRS depreciation on these properties for **(a)** 1987, **(b)** 1988, and **(c)** 1989.

6. The Acme Company bought a temporary building for use as offices on the company's site. The company paid $187,500 and placed it in service on

June 4, 1987. Find the MACRS depreciation on this property for **(a)** 1987, **(b)** 1988, and **(c)** 1989.

7. Iris Santiago bought and placed in service on September 12, 1987, an apartment building that cost $750,000 excluding the land, which was valued at $200,000. Find the MACRS depreciation for **(a)** 1987 and **(b)** 1988. **(c)** Find the book value at the end of 1988.

8. On December 20, 1987, Joan Sterling placed a house in service as a rental. The basis of the house was $118,000. She had purchased and placed in service on December 2, 1987, another house with a basis of $134,000. Find the MACRS depreciation on these houses for **(a)** 1987 and **(b)** 1988. **(c)** Find the book value at the end of 1988.

9. The Midlands Products Co., Inc. placed in service on July 23, 1987, a new building that had cost $32,750,000 including the land valued at $2,750,000. Find the MACRS depreciation on this property for **(a)** 1987, **(b)** 1988, and **(c)** 1989.

10. On January 21, 1987, the Benton Canning Co., Inc. acquired and placed in service a 20-year property that cost $2,587,000. Find the MACRS depreciation on this property for **(a)** 1987, **(b)** 1988, and **(c)** 1989.

DEPLETION OF NATURAL RESOURCES

Deposits of valuable minerals, gas, oil, and tracts of timber are examples of **natural resources.** Such assets are also called **wasting assets** because their quantity diminishes as they are converted into merchandise and sold.

The cost of a wasting asset includes the expenditures that apply only to the natural resource, not to the buildings, machinery, and other fixed assets that may be used in extracting the resource. Such fixed assets are subject to the usual depreciation charges. Enterprises that engage in extracting natural resources record the cost of the wasting asset in appropriate accounts and allocate such costs against periodic revenues. The periodic allocation of the cost of a natural resource against the revenue derived from the resource is **depletion.**

A percentage method consisting of specific rates, such as 15% of the gross income from a copper mine, may be used for certain wasting assets. However, the periodic depletion expense may be computed on a production basis similar to the units-of-production method of calculating depreciation. The cost of the wasting asset less any salvage value is divided by the estimated total units to be produced, such as tons of ore or thousands of feet of lumber. The annual depletion charge is found by multiplying the number of units sold during the year by the per-unit depletion cost.

$$Per\text{-}Unit\ Depletion = \frac{Cost - Salvage\ Value}{Total\ Units\ to\ Be\ Produced}$$

Example: Sierra Mining Company paid $390,000 for the mineral rights to an estimated 500,000 tons of ore. The company expects the residual value of the property to be $40,000. Find **(a)** the per-unit depletion charge and **(b)** the annual depletion for a year in which 20,000 tons of ore were sold.

Solution:

(a) Per-Unit Depletion $= \dfrac{\$390,000 - \$40,000}{500,000}$

$= \$0.70$ per ton

(b) $20,000 \times \$0.70 = \$14,000$

● **Exercise 14–10**

1. Logan Products Company acquired an ore deposit at a cost of $5,700,000. Estimates by the company's engineers indicated that the deposit contained 1.25 million tons of ore and that the residual value of the property would be $600,000. Find the depletion for a year in which 190,000 tons of ore were sold.

2. The estimated recoverable tonnage in a coal mine was placed at 2,345,000 tons. The value of "Coal Rights" in the company's records was $33,533,500. Compute the depletion expense for a year in which 42,360 tons were sold.

3. The Rolla Products Company paid $1,800,000 for land that contained an estimated 800,000 cubic yards of gravel. The company expects the land to have a residual value of $360,000. Compute the depletion for a year in which 71,250 cubic yards of gravel were sold.

4. The Ozark Lumber Company bought a timber tract for $1,000,000. The land was worth an estimated $200,000 without the timber. The company expected to produce 12.5 million board-feet (12,500 M board-feet) of timber from the tract. How much is the company's depletion allowance for a year in which 250 M board-feet of timber were sold?

5. The Morgantown Coal Company paid $14,000,000 for the coal rights to many acres of land. The company then acquired a building site over the coal for $50,000 and erected buildings at a cost of $200,000. The company estimated that the area covered by the rights would yield 1,600,000 tons of coal. Find **(a)** the per-unit depletion cost and **(b)** the depletion expense for a period in which 20,000 tons of coal were sold.

6. Liberty Monument Company paid $1,900,000 for land that contained an estimated 600,000 cubic yards of granite. The company expects the land to have a residual value of $490,000. A contractor with earthmoving equipment removed the surface earth above the deposit for a total cost of $58,800. Find the depletion for a year in which 35,000 cubic yards of granite were sold.

Solve these problems. If you have difficulty solving any problem, restudy the appropriate section in this chapter. The problems under a specific number are related to those contained in the exercise with the same last number.

1. Solve these overhead problems.
   a. During the past week, sales of the departments of Prim Clothing Store were as follows: Men's Department, $4,200; Women's Department, $8,600; Boys' Department, $8,200; Girls' Department, $8,400; and Shoe Department, $2,400. The overhead for the week totaled $6,360. Overhead is charged to each department on the basis of sales. How much overhead should be charged to each department?
   b. Nimrod Products Company's grinding department occupies 7,500 sq ft of floor space in the company's factory that has a total of 60,000 sq ft. Based on the floor space occupied, how much of the company's $558,000 factory overhead should be allocated to the grinding department?
   c. In December an accountant estimated that the company would incur factory overhead of $6,000,000 during the coming year. It was also estimated that during the same year the company would use $7,500,000 worth of direct labor. If these estimates were used to compute the pre-determined overhead rate based on direct labor cost, (1) what is the overhead rate and (2) how much overhead should be charged to Job 3258 that was completed the following February and charged with $5,250 worth of direct materials and $6,400 worth of direct labor?
   d. Total factory overhead is $600,000; total direct labor, $1,500,000; and total materials used, $3,500,000. The distribution of overhead is based on the relationship of total overhead to total prime cost. Find (1) the overhead percent of prime cost charged to each department and (2) the amount of overhead charged to a department with a prime cost of $750,000.

2. a. A company's beginning inventory of a particular product consisted of 600 units at $8.50 each. Purchases during the year were as follows: 900 at $8.60 each; 1,050 at $8.40 each; 450 at $8.80 each; and 500 at $8.68 each. There were 675 units remaining on hand at the end of the year. Find the value of the ending inventory by (1) average cost, (2) fifo, and (3) lifo.
   b. Find the total value of the following inventory by using the lower-of-cost-or-market rule for each item.

Stock Number	Quantity on Hand	Cost	Market
1201	150	$38	$35
1202	10	12	15
1203	125	40	37
1204	85	50	50
1205	240	20	21
1206	200	45	50

3. The Glendale Company's merchandise stock was completely destroyed by a fire. The company's accounting records show the following: inventory on January 1, $140,000; purchases to date of fire, $1,040,000; and net sales to date of fire, $1,200,000. The company marks up merchandise 20% on sales to find selling price. Calculate the estimated cost value of the inventory that was destroyed by the fire.

4. A buyer is negotiating for the purchase of the Bridgewater Company. A consultant to the buyer states that the net assets have a fair market value of $296,000 and that net income has averaged $36,720 for the past 5 years. The buyer states that a return of 9% on net assets is a normal return for a company in this industry. Find the value of the goodwill based on **(a)** the sum of the estimated extra earnings for the next 5 years, **(b)** the extra earnings capitalized at 9%, and **(c)** the first half of extra earnings capitalized at 9%, the second half at 12%.

5. A company purchased a pump for $2,750. Its estimated life was 6 years with a salvage value of $350. At the end of 3 years and 8 months, the pump was sold for $950. What is the difference between the selling price and the straight-line book value of the pump on the date it was sold?

6. A business purchased a machine that it planned to keep 4 years and use to produce 100,000 units. It cost $12,100 and was expected to have a trade-in value of $2,500. After it produced 80,000 units in 2 years and 8 months, it was traded in on a new one. The trade-in allowance amounted to $3,832. **(a)** How much was the monthly straight-line depreciation? **(b)** What was its book value when traded? **(c)** What was the difference between its trade-in value and the book value when traded? **(d)** On a units-of-production basis, how much was the depreciation for a year in which it produced 26,712 units?

7. A farming company has a building that cost $1,390,000 with a service life of 25 years and a salvage value of $140,000, equipment that cost $380,000 with a service life of 12 years and a salvage value of $50,000, and machinery that cost $27,000 with a service life of 7 years and a salvage value of $3,000. Find **(a)** the annual straight-line depreciation on the building, **(b)** the depreciation on the equipment for the second year using the 150% declining-balance method, and **(c)** the depreciation on the machinery for the third year using the sum-of-the-years-digits method.

8. Hudson Excavating Company bought a used asset for $48,150. It had an expected service life of 7 years and an estimated scrap value of $6,150. **(a)** How much was the book value at the end of the third year using the straight-line method? **(b)** How much depreciation should be charged for 16,240 units on the units-of-production method if the life expectancy is 400,000 units? **(c)** Using the 150% declining-balance method, what would be the book value at the end of the second year?

9. In 1987, Roscommon Company purchased and placed in service the following MACRS depreciable property: April 18, 3-year property with

an unadjusted basis of $4,000; June 4, 3-year property that cost $3,500; November 2, nonresidential real property with an unadjusted basis of $250,000; May 7, 20-year property that cost $23,000; and January 17, 5-year property valued at $12,000. To the nearest dollar, find the MACRS depreciation for 1987 on (a) the 3-year property, (b) the 5-year property, (c) the 20-year property, and (d) the nonresidential real property.

10. An estimated 25,842,000 board-feet of timber had a net value of $969,075 in the company's records at the beginning of the year. During the year, the company sold 5,480,000 board-feet of the timber. Find (a) the depletion cost per thousand feet and (b) the depletion expense for the year.

CHALLENGE PROBLEM

The Leicester Company, which sells a single product, began business on May 1, 1988, with 2,000 units in stock. The purchases and sales for the year are shown below.

Purchases

Date	Number of Units	Cost per Unit
April 20	2,000	$12.00
June 17	4,000	13.00
August 12	4,000	13.50
September 8	3,000	14.80
October 15	3,000	15.20
November 10	5,000	14.90
December 16	1,000	15.70

Sales

May	1,000 units	September	2,500 units
June	2,500 units	October	2,400 units
July	1,800 units	November	2,900 units
August	2,800 units	December	3,300 units

Income from Sales totaled $572,600.

On January 3, 1989, T. C. Janks, president of the company, asked for your advice on accounting for the physical inventory that was taken on December 31, 1988. The inventory records agreed with the inventory count of 2,800 units.

a. In good form show the value of the December 31, 1988, inventory by the (1) average cost method, (2) last-in, first-out method, and (3) first-in, first-out method.

b. Compute the gross profit for 1988 under each of the three methods in **(a)**.

c. Which of the three inventory methods in **(a)** best reflects the true value of the ending inventory?

d. Which of the three inventory methods in **(a)** do you recommend using for income tax purposes?

Chapter 15

Business Earnings and Ownership

Objectives

After mastering the material in Chapter 15, you will be able to:

- Understand the meaning of and computations for *net sales, cost of goods sold, gross profit, operating expenses,* and *net income.*
- Understand the sole proprietorship, partnership, and corporate forms of business ownership.
- Distribute partnership earnings on the basis of equality, an arbitrary ratio, beginning investment, average investment, and after partners' allowances for salaries and interest.
- Calculate dividends per share of common and preferred stock when the preferred is cumulative or noncumulative, participating or nonparticipating.

The right of individuals to own property is the foundation on which our competitive economic system rests. The right to own a legitimate business enterprise is considered to be as valid as the right to own one's home. An individual, of course, may own all of the property invested in a business or may share ownership rights with others.

When a business is conducted successfully, its total ownership increases from the earning of profits. Conversely, an enterprise is considered to be unsuccessful if its operations result in losses. Those who invest in a business enterprise are willing to risk losing all or part of their investment because they

459

expect to receive income from the profits earned by the enterprise. Thus, the primary objective of a business enterprise is to earn a profit. The ability of an enterprise to earn a profit and the manner in which those earnings are shared are essential considerations for its owners, managers, and creditors.

PROFITS

From one point of view, there are two basic kinds of businesses: those that sell services and those that sell goods. Examples of those that sell services are physicians, attorneys, public accountants, cleaners, real estate agents, and utility companies. Examples of those that sell goods are retail, wholesale, and manufacturing firms. In either kind of business, the owners hope to sell their goods or services in order to make profits. **Revenue** is the income derived by these companies through selling their services or goods. In a company that sells services, the revenue may be labeled **fees.** In a company that sells goods, revenue commonly is called **sales.**

Both kinds of businesses make expenditures from revenue for **operating expenses,** such as employees' salaries, rent, advertising, taxes, and the like. In a service business, **net profit** or **net income** is the amount by which revenue exceeds the operating expenses. As this amount is subject to income taxes and other deductions, net income is the preferred term. Of course, if operating expenses exceed revenue, a **net loss** will be the result. Finding net income for a service company may be summarized as follows:

$$R - E = N$$
$R =$ Revenue
$E =$ Expenses of operating the business
$N =$ Net Income

Example A:

During the past year, John Ponsetti, a certified public accountant, received fees totaling $200,000. His operating expenses were: salaries and payroll taxes for accountants and a secretary, $110,000; rent, $12,000; utilities, $4,800; supplies used, $4,000; depreciation of office furniture and equipment, $2,400; miscellaneous expenses, $1,800. Find his net income or loss for the year.

Solution:

Fees		$200,000
Less Operating Expenses:		
Salaries and payroll taxes	$110,000	
Rent	12,000	
Utilities	4,800	
Supplies used	4,000	
Depreciation expense	2,400	
Miscellaneous expenses	1,800	
Total Operating Expenses		135,000
Net Income		$ 65,000

Part 3. Mathematics Applications in Operating a Business

Merchandise consists of goods produced or purchased for sale to customers. Merchandise is an asset that has two values: (1) a cost value and (2) a selling-price value.

Merchandise costs consist of all expenditures made to acquire marketable goods, including the amounts paid to produce or buy the goods, as well as to insure, transport, and store them prior to their arrival in the marketplace.

The **selling price** of merchandise is the amount of money that the seller will accept in exchange for the goods. This value, which is often called the **retail value,** must exceed the seller's costs and expenses in order to clear a profit. **Gross sales** means the selling-price value of all the goods sold during a specific period of time, such as one month or one year. **Sales returns and allowances** include both the selling price of goods returned by customers and allowances given to customers for damaged or defective goods that the customers keep. **Net sales** is the difference between gross sales and sales returns and allowances. When there are no sales returns and allowances, the word **sales** is adequate to represent the selling-price value of the goods sold.

After marketable goods are obtained through manufacture or purchase, certain other expenditures are usually required before the goods are sold to customers. Such expenditures are **operating expenses** and include amounts paid for sales salaries, office and administrative salaries, advertising, rent, sales taxes, and the like.

The amount paid by a business to purchase merchandise that it plans to offer for sale is called **purchases.** The merchandise that is available for sale by a business may be referred to as the **stock in trade** of that business. **Merchandise inventory** is the value of the stock in trade that is in the business at a specific time; that is, at the time when a list or inventory of the merchandise in the business is prepared. A merchandise inventory is usually prepared annually but may be done more frequently, such as monthly or quarterly.

Cost of goods sold is the cost value of the merchandise sold during a specific period of time (month, quarter, or year). The value of the **goods available for sale** during a month may be obtained by adding the cost of the merchandise purchased during the month to that available at the beginning of the month. Of course, a business must keep some goods on display and in the storeroom. Therefore, a company will seldom sell all of the goods it has available for sale. The value of the goods in inventory at the end of the month subtracted from the goods available for sale gives the cost of goods sold. The following equation and the example below illustrate this computation:

$$C = B + P - E$$

C = Cost of goods sold
B = Beginning inventory of merchandise
P = Purchases of merchandise
E = Ending inventory of merchandise

The amount obtained when cost of goods sold is deducted from net sales is the **gross profit,** which is frequently referred to as the **margin.** Naturally, the seller can make a profit only if the markon is large enough to provide a gross profit that exceeds the operating expenses. The seller will experience a loss when sales for a specific period are not sufficient to meet all the costs and expenses for that period. The markon rate is sometimes referred to as the gross-profit rate. The amount by which the gross profit exceeds the operating expenses is the **net income** or **net profit.**

Example B:

During January, Augusta Company had sales of $220,000, sales returns and allowances of $5,000, merchandise inventory on January 1 of $25,000 and on January 31 of $35,000, and operating expenses of $95,000. The company had purchases of $110,000 during January. Find **(a)** the cost of goods sold, **(b)** the gross profit, and **(c)** the net income for the month.

Solution:

Sales		$220,000
Less Sales Returns and Allowances		5,000
Net Sales.....................................		$215,000
Cost of Goods Sold:		
Merchandise Inventory, January 1.................	$ 25,000	
Purchases	110,000	
Goods Available for Sale........................	$135,000	
Less Merchandise Inventory, January 31	35,000	
(a) Cost of Goods Sold............................		100,000
(b) Gross Profit		$115,000
Less Operating Expenses............................		95,000
(c) Net Income		$ 20,000

Based on the foregoing, two simple equations may be formulated:

$$G = S_n - C$$

G = Gross profit from sales
S_n = Sales, net
C = Cost of goods sold

$$N = G - E$$

N = Net income
G = Gross profit
E = Expenses of operating the business

Periodically businesses prepare financial statements. One statement, the **income statement,** summarizes the sales, costs, and expenses for the period and shows the amount of net income or net loss for that period. An income statement is shown as Figure 15–1.

Part 3. Mathematics Applications in Operating a Business

Abilene Mercantile Company
Income Statement
For the Year Ended December 31, 19--

Operating revenue:		
Sales......................................		$300,000
Less sales returns and allowances		4,000
Net sales		$296,000
Cost of goods sold:		
Merchandise inventory, January 1	$ 35,000	
Purchases	160,000	
Goods available for sale.....................	$195,000	
Less merchandise inventory, December 31	30,000	
Cost of goods sold........................		165,000
Gross profit from sales		$131,000
Operating expenses:		
Salaries and commissions expense	$60,000	
Rent expense..................................	18,000	
Advertising expense...........................	7,000	
Depreciation expense, store equipment	5,000	
Payroll taxes expense	6,000	
Utilities expense	2,500	
Store supplies expense........................	1,500	
Insurance expense	1,200	
Miscellaneous expense.........................	800	
Total operating expenses.....................		102,000
Net income before income taxes..................		$ 29,000

Figure 15-1 An Income Statement

Exercise 15-1

A. On a separate sheet of paper, show the amount of each item that is missing from the following table.

	Beginning Inventory	Purchases	Goods Available	Ending Inventory	Cost of Goods Sold
1.	$ 20,000	$ 100,000	$_____	$ 25,000	$_____
2.	30,000	240,000	_____	22,000	_____
3.	175,000	_____	745,000	_____	607,000
4.	362,500	_____	1,289,000	_____	840,700
5.	_____	563,000	735,000	186,200	_____
6.	_____	1,824,000	2,104,000	374,500	_____

Chapter 15. Business Earnings and Ownership

B. On a separate sheet of paper, show the amount of each item that is missing from the following table. Show any loss figure with an asterisk (*) to its right.

	Sales	Sales Returns	Net Sales	Cost of Goods Sold	Gross Profit	Operating Expenses	Net Income or Loss*
1.	$ 250,000	$ 5,000	$_____	$ 110,250	$_____	$ 105,150	$_____
2.	_____	7,500	187,500	_____	84,375	_____	9,280
3.	1,785,000	35,700	_____	_____	656,750	366,650	_____
4.	396,650	_____	390,700	227,580	_____	164,120	_____
5.	_____		10,852,000	4,221,000	_____	5,180,000	_____
6.	_____	4,000	350,000	_____	150,790	_____	25,800

C. Solve these problems.

1. Bethel Company had merchandise in stock on May 1 valued at $37,500. On May 31, there was only $25,400 of merchandise in stock. During the month, the company purchased $97,360 of merchandise. Find **(a)** the goods available for sale and **(b)** the cost of goods sold during the month of May.

2. During the year 19X2, Lewis Company bought $2,345,970 of merchandise. On December 31, 19X1, the company's merchandise inventory was valued at $186,840. On December 31, 19X2, the merchandise inventory value was listed at $250,950. Find **(a)** the goods available for sale and **(b)** the cost of goods sold during 19X2.

3. On November 30, Puerto Rico Company had merchandise in stock valued at $1,425,000. During November the company bought merchandise that cost $15,386,000, which made total goods available for sale of $17,049,000. Find **(a)** the cost of goods sold during November and **(b)** the merchandise inventory on November 1.

4. St. Joseph Company had a merchandise inventory of $486,390 on April 1. The company's income statement for April showed $390,486 as the cost of goods sold and $650,430 for the goods available for sale. Find **(a)** the merchandise inventory on April 30 and **(b)** the purchases during the month.

5. Central Store had sales of $83,700, sales returns of $1,700, cost of goods sold of $45,000, and operating expenses of $30,000. Find the gross profit.

6. The following figures are shown on the income statement of the Centerville Company: sales returns, $16,875; selling expenses, $35,550; administrative expenses, $42,200; general expenses, $8,500; sales, $694,300; and cost of goods sold, $480,000. Find the gross profit.

7. During the past year, Willard Company had operating expenses of $80,000, cost of goods sold of $58,575, and sales of $183,660. Find the net income or loss.

8. Lynette Peck, an attorney, had the following income and expenditures: fees, $92,175; salaries, $26,400; rent, $24,000; depreciation, $3,700; supplies used, $2,250; payroll taxes $1,800; utilities, $2,750; miscellaneous expenses, $1,250. Find the net income or loss.

9. Mary McReynolds, a realtor, had the following business income and expenditures: commissions, $190,000; payments to employees, $110,000; rent, $7,200; advertising, $8,160; depreciation of furniture and equipment, $1,120; utilities, $2,500; supplies used, $1,900; and miscellaneous expenses, $810. Find the net income or loss.

10. Use the following information to find the net income or loss for the following service business: rent expense, $8,400; advertising, $1,080; salaries, $44,000; income from fees, $61,500; insurance expense, $6,400; supplies expense, $7,600; utilities, $1,750; miscellaneous expenses, $410.

BUSINESS OWNERSHIP

Although some enterprises operate under other kinds of organization, the three principal forms of business ownership are the sole proprietorship, the partnership, and the corporation.

A business owned by one person is a **sole proprietorship.** Most small businesses are in this category. Because the owner makes the managerial decisions and receives all the profits, this form of business organization provides a great stimulus to private enterprise. It is easily established and requires fewer governmental reports than the other forms of business ownership. On the other hand, the amount that an individual can invest is limited. Two individuals together can raise more capital than either one of them can alone. A major disadvantage of the sole proprietorship is that the owner is personally responsible for all the debts of the business.

A business owned by two or more persons in a contractual relationship, by which they agree to engage in business, is a **partnership.** In addition to merchandising businesses, this kind of organization is used extensively by those firms that provide professional services. Doctors, attorneys, and accountants, for example, frequently form partnerships within their respective professions. Even though the partners should have a written contract, forming a partnership is almost as easy as forming a sole proprietorship, and the stimulus to individual enterprise is almost as great. The major weakness of the partnership form of ownership is that each partner is liable for all the debts of the business. Thus, the poor judgment of one partner may cause the others to assume a heavy financial burden.

A business created by state or federal law that has a distinct existence as an artificial being, separate and apart from the persons who are responsible for its organization and operation, is a **corporation.** One creates a corporation by filing **articles of incorporation** or a **certificate of incorporation** and paying the appropriate fees to the proper state or federal agency. The state or federal government then issues a **charter of incorporation** or a certified copy of the certificate of incorporation.

The corporate form of business ownership facilitates the accumulation of large sums of capital through the sale of shares to stockholders. Those who buy shares of stock in the corporation are **stockholders** and are its owners. In contrast to the sole proprietorship and partnership forms of ownership, the liability of a stockholder for the debts of the corporation is usually limited to the amount invested in the business. The corporation has a continuous existence until legally dissolved. Its shares owned by stockholders may be sold by them without the consent of the other stockholders. Because of these advantages, the corporation is the principal form of business ownership where large-scale operations predominate, as in manufacturing, mining, transportation, public utilities, banking, insurance, and large-scale marketing. There are three major disadvantages to the corporate form of ownership: it is subjected to stricter control by federal and state governments; it is usually more heavily taxed than the other two forms; and it may be limited to certain kinds of business activities as specified in its charter or certificate of incorporation.

Regardless of the type of business ownership, profit is the major concern. Realizing profit depends upon the managerial ability of the people involved. A wide range of experience and knowledge helps an entrepreneur to be successful. Finances are a basic part of any organization; therefore, it is necessary to know about assets, liabilities, and equity.

Things of value that are owned are **assets. Equities** represent rights in, or claims against, assets. The two principal kinds of equities in the assets of a business are those of the creditors and those of the owners. Debts owed to creditors are called **liabilities.** The claims of the creditors against the assets of a business are represented by the liabilities of the enterprise. Examples of liabilities are notes payable, accounts payable, bonds payable, and mortgages payable. **Accounts payable** are amounts owed to creditors on current accounts. The proprietors', the partners', or the stockholders' claims against the assets of the enterprise are the **owner's equity, proprietorship, capital,** or **net worth.**

As equities represent the total claims against assets, the relationship of assets and equities may be shown in the following equation:

$$Assets = Equities$$

Creditors have a primary claim on the assets of a business, and its owners have a residual claim. This relationship can be shown in the equation by using the term **liabilities** to represent the creditors' equities:

$$Assets = Liabilities + Owners' Equity$$

The foregoing equation, which is the **accounting equation,** may be modified to indicate a particular kind of business ownership simply by using "Partners' Equity" or "Stockholders' Equity" in place of "Owners' Equity." Furthermore, the residual claim of the owners may be emphasized by transposing the liabilities to the opposite side of the equation:

$$Assets - Liabilities = Owners' Equity$$

Example A: Casper Company is a sole proprietorship that has the following assets: cash, $5,000; accounts receivable, $10,500; merchandise, $50,000; furniture and fixtures, $37,500; and building and land, $150,000. The company's liabilities consist of accounts payable, $2,500; notes payable, $1,500; and mortgage on the building and land, $50,000. What is the owner's equity in Casper Company?

Solution:

Assets		Liabilities	
Cash	$ 5,000	Accounts Payable	$ 2,500
Accounts Receivable	10,500	Notes Payable	1,500
Merchandise	50,000	Mortgage Payable	50,000
Furniture and Fixtures	37,500		
Building and Land	150,000		
Total Assets	$253,000	Total Liabilities	$54,000

Assets	−	Liabilities	=	Owner's Equity
$253,000	−	$54,000	=	$199,000

The net worth of a corporation belongs to all of the stockholders of the corporation. Each share of stock represents a fractional part of the ownership. A stockholder's equity is in direct proportion to the number of shares owned by that individual compared to the number of shares owned by all of the stockholders.

Example B: The records of Mansfield Corporation show a net worth of $24,900,000. Roberta Graham owns 500 of the 1,500,000 shares of stock that have been issued by this corporation. What is Graham's equity in the corporation?

Solution: $$\frac{500}{1,500,000} \times \$24,900,000 = \$8,300$$

● Exercise 15–2

A. Find the missing amount in each of the following problems.

	Assets	−	Liabilities	=	Owner's Equity
1.	$21,140	−	$ 8,598	=	$_____
2.	60,203	−	18,260	=	_____
3.	85,113	−	_____	=	72,844
4.	79,974	−	_____	=	54,939
5.	_____	−	52,233	=	62,319
6.	_____	−	15,438	=	99,058

Chapter 15. Business Earnings and Ownership

B. Solve each of the following problems.

1. Howard Bartel, owner of a retail store, has the following assets: cash, $500; merchandise, $7,500; store equipment, $6,000; and store supplies, $150. He owes $750 for merchandise purchased on credit. How much is his equity?

2. Edith Hines has the following assets invested in a business: cash, $7,000; merchandise, $48,000; office supplies, $840; office equipment, $13,500; delivery equipment, $45,000; and land and buildings, $850,000. She owes the following amounts: accounts payable, $29,000; notes payable, $18,650; and mortgage payable, $488,750. What is the amount of her proprietorship?

3. Forbes and Marshall are partners in a furniture store that has the following assets and liabilities: cash, $7,720; merchandise, $175,880; store supplies, $1,390; office supplies, $980; land and building, $670,000; store fixtures, $24,720; delivery equipment, $54,750; debt owed to National Furniture Company, $34,160; and notes payable, $59,780. How much is the owners' equity in this business?

4. Charles Cotter owns a manufacturing company that has buildings and land valued at $1,750,000. There is a mortgage of $350,000 against this property. The machinery and equipment are valued at $172,000. Inventories show $70,000 worth of raw materials at cost and $222,000 worth of finished goods at cost. Accounts receivable total $48,000, and accounts payable total $83,000. Cotter's bank holds the company's note for $37,500. How much is his net worth in the company?

5. The R. A. Best Corporation, which has issued 1,200,000 shares of stock, has a net worth of $10,800,000. Jan Binkley owns 440 shares of stock in the corporation. How much is her equity in the company?

6. The Marquette Corporation, with 24,000 shares of issued stock, has assets of $3,650,000 and liabilities of $1,865,000. Dan Atkins owns 750 shares of the stock. Find **(a)** the net worth of the company and **(b)** Atkins' equity in the company.

DISTRIBUTION OF EARNINGS AND LOSSES

The earnings and losses of any business, whether a sole proprietorship, partnership, or corporation, may be determined on an income statement. (See Figure 15–1.) However, the manner in which the earnings and losses are distributed to the owners is dependent on the ownership form of business.

Sole Proprietorship Earnings

If the business is a sole proprietorship, the sole owner is entitled to all of the earnings, but he or she must also absorb all of the losses. The owner may withdraw all of the earnings for personal use, leave all of the earnings in the business for expansion, or withdraw only part of the earnings and leave the remainder in the business. Of course, a business that has extensive losses is usually dissolved by the owner or creditors.

Partnership Earnings

If the partnership agreement does not specify how the earnings and losses are to be shared, the partners receive equal shares, regardless of the amount invested in the partnership by each or the value of the time and energy devoted to the partnership by each. When the sharing of losses is not specified in the partnership contract, losses are distributed in the same manner as earnings are shared. As there is an infinite variety of ways in which partnership earnings and losses may be shared, the partners should be certain that their contract specifies the manner of distribution to which they have agreed.

The following are some of the most common methods of distributing partnership earnings and losses. Many variations in and combinations of these methods are possible.

Distribution on Basis of Equality. Mathematically the equal distribution of partnership earnings and losses is quite simple. If there are only two partners, each receives half of the earnings or losses; if three, each receives one-third; if four, each receives one-fourth. For example, in the equal distribution of $30,000 of partnership earnings, each of two partners receives $15,000; each of three partners, $10,000; and each of four partners, $7,500.

Distribution on Basis of Arbitrary Ratio. Instead of sharing gains and losses equally, the partners may decide to use an arbitrary ratio, such as 3 to 2, which may be written as $\frac{3}{5}$ to $\frac{2}{5}$ or as 60% to 40%.

Example:

Andrews and Badillo have invested $80,000 and $40,000 in a partnership, with the understanding that Andrews will receive 60% and Badillo will receive 40% of the partnership gains and losses. Distribute the partnership gain of $30,000.

Solution:

$30,000 × 60% = $18,000   Andrews' share
$30,000 × 40% = $12,000   Badillo's share

Distribution on Basis of Beginning Investment Ratio. The partners may decide that the amount originally invested by each or the amount in a partner's capital account at the beginning of a fiscal year should be the basis for allocating partnership gains and losses. To find an individual partner's share when profits are distributed in proportion to investments, follow these two steps:

1. Express each partner's investment, or capital, as a fractional part of the total invested in the partnership.
2. Multiply that fraction by the total gains or losses being distributed.

Chapter 15. Business Earnings and Ownership

Example: Clinton and Doane have invested $45,000 and $25,000, respectively, in a partnership with the understanding that they will share earnings and losses in proportion to their investments. Find each partner's share in the partnership net income of $42,000.

Solution:

$45,000 + $25,000 = $70,000   total investment

$$\frac{\$45,000}{\$70,000} \times \$42,000 = \$27,000 \quad \text{Clinton's share}$$

$$\frac{\$25,000}{\$70,000} \times \$42,000 = \$15,000 \quad \text{Doane's share}$$

Distribution on Basis of Average Investment Ratio. By mutual agreement, partners may withdraw from or add to their partnership investments. To give significance to the length of time a partner's capital is used by the partnership, they may decide to allocate earnings and losses in proportion to each partner's average investment during the fiscal period. To find a partner's share when gains and losses are distributed on this basis, follow these steps:

1. Find the average investment of each partner.
2. Add together the average investments of the partners to find the total average investment in the partnership.
3. Multiply the partner's fractional part of the average investment by the total amount being allocated.

Equated time is used to find each partner's average investment. Generally the investment is multiplied by the number of months during which the amount was in the partnership. The result of this multiplication is called **month-dollars.** When a partner's investment changes, the new balance of the investment is multiplied by the number of months until the next change. This procedure is repeated for each time the investment changes during the year. The month-dollars then may be added together and the total divided by 12, the number of months in a year, to obtain the partner's average investment.

Example: Emory and Franklin agreed in their partnership contract that gains and losses are to be divided in proportion to their average annual investments. Emory, who had $60,000 invested in the partnership on January 1, withdrew $4,000 of her investment on July 1. Franklin, who had $30,000 invested on January 1, withdrew $2,000 on April 1, and then increased his investment in the partnership by $3,000 on August 1. Distribute the partnership net income of $70,200.

Solution:

1. Emory: **Month-Dollars**

    January 1 to July 1: $60,000 × 6 = $360,000

    July 1 to December 31: $56,000 × 6 =   336,000

                      Total month-dollars = $696,000

    $696,000 ÷ 12 = $58,000   Emory's average investment

    Franklin:

    January 1 to April 1: $30,000 × 3 = $ 90,000

    April 1 to August 1: $28,000 × 4 =   112,000

    August 1 to December 31: $31,000 × 5 =   155,000

                      Total month-dollars = $357,000

    $357,000 ÷ 12 = $29,750   Franklin's average investment

2. $58,000 + $29,750 = $87,750$ total average investment

3. $\dfrac{\$58,000}{\$87,750} \times \$70,200 = \$46,400$ Emory's share

$\dfrac{\$29,750}{\$87,750} \times \$70,200 = \$23,800$ Franklin's share

The previous example indicates the rationale on which this method of distribution is based. However, as the ratio of the partners' total month-dollars is the same as the ratio of their average investments, an alternate, shortcut computation gives the same distribution.

Solution:

1. The same as in the preceding example.

2. $696,000 + $357,000 = $1,053,000$ total month-dollars

3. $\dfrac{\$696,000}{\$1,053,000} \times \$70,200 = \$46,400$ Emory's share

$\dfrac{\$357,000}{\$1,053,000} \times \$70,200 = \$23,800$ Franklin's share

Distribution on Basis of Arbitrary Ratio After Interest on Investment. Another means of giving consideration to the size of each partner's investment in the business is to allocate interest at a specific rate of the beginning or average investments. The so-called interest is not an expense of the business. This is just another method of allocating earnings and losses on an equitable basis. After the interest allowances have been distributed, the remainder is distributed equally or in accordance with an arbitrary ratio.

Example:

On January 1, Grinnell had $200,000 and Hernandez $150,000 invested together in a partnership. Their contract specifies that each partner is to be allowed 8% interest on his investment and the remainder divided equally. If the partnership net income is $50,000, how much should each partner receive?

Solution:

Net Income		$50,000
Less Interest Allowances:		
Grinnell ($200,000 × 8%)	$16,000	
Hernandez ($150,000 × 8%)	12,000	28,000
Remainder.		$22,000

$22,000 ÷ 2 = $11,000$ each partner's share of remainder

Distribution	**Grinnell**	**Hernandez**
Interest	$16,000	$12,000
Remainder of net income	11,000	11,000
Total.	$27,000	$23,000

Distribution on Basis of Arbitrary Ratio After Salary Allowances. In consideration of the value of the time spent on partnership business, partners may agree that one or more of them is to receive a specific salary before or during the distribution of the partnership's earnings and losses. Salaries withdrawn from the business by partners are not expenses of the partnership as are sal-

Chapter 15. Business Earnings and Ownership

aries paid to employees. Partners' salaries are simply withdrawals of their earnings or investments. After the salaries have been allocated, the remaining profit or loss may be distributed equally or on the basis of an arbitrary ratio.

Example: Ivins and Jedda are partners with investments of $180,000 and $120,000, respectively. The partners have agreed in their contract to share earnings and losses by (1) distributing annual salary allowances of $12,000 to Ivins and $20,000 to Jedda, and (2) sharing the remainder in the arbitrary ratio of 3:2, respectively. Show each partner's share of the current net income of $60,000.

Solution:

Net Income		$60,000
Less Salaries:		
Ivins	$12,000	
Jedda	20,000	32,000
Remainder..		$28,000

$\frac{3}{5} \times \$28,000 = \$16,800$ Ivins' share of remainder

$\frac{2}{5} \times \$28,000 = \$11,200$ Jedda's share of remainder

Distribution	**Ivins**	**Jedda**
Salary..	$12,000	$20,000
Remainder of net income...............................	16,800	11,200
Total..	$28,800	$31,200

● **Exercise 15–3**

A. In each of the following problems, use the ratio shown to find each partner's share of the gain or loss.

		Investments			
	Partner A	**Partner B**	**Partner C**	**Gain or Loss**	**Respective Ratio**
1.	$ 45,000	$ 27,000		$ 24,000	3:2
2.	25,000	40,000		14,280	3:4
3.	150,000	250,000	$200,000	108,000	5:4:3
4.	240,000	300,000	270,000	83,250	Equally

B. In each of the following problems, the net income is to be divided in proportion to the partners' investments. Find each partner's share.

		Investments		
	Partner A	**Partner B**	**Partner C**	**Net Income**
1.	$ 36,000	$ 60,000		$ 50,400
2.	390,000	210,000		190,000
3.	48,000	96,000	$72,000	48,600
4.	64,000	32,000	48,000	72,144

C. Find each partner's share of the net income in each of the following. Interest at the given rate is allowed on the investments, and the balance is divided in accordance with the given ratio.

	Investments				Interest	
	Partner A	Partner B	Partner C	Net Income	Rate	Balance Ratio
1.	$ 30,000	$ 40,000		$ 26,200	10%	3:1
2.	45,000	30,000		29,700	6%	45%, 55%
3.	75,000	105,000	$ 90,000	102,150	7%	$\frac{1}{4}, \frac{1}{2}, \frac{1}{4}$
4.	200,000	440,000	360,000	197,600	8%	2:1:4

D. Solve these problems.

1. During the past year, the partnership of Walsh and York had total sales of $394,260, cost of goods sold of $315,420, and operating expenses of $52,740. Walsh received 35% of the net income as his share for the year. How much did each partner receive?

2. Richmond, Sheridan, and Thomas invested $140,000, $210,000, and $280,000, respectively, in a partnership. Their gross profit for the year was $452,000 and their expenses were $284,000. If they share earnings and losses in proportion to their investments, how much of the net income should each partner receive?

3. Vennard and Waldorf agreed to share partnership gains and losses in proportion to their average investments. Vennard's investment was $100,000 on January 1 and $80,000 on April 1. Waldorf's investment was $160,000 on January 1 and $120,000 on July 1. Divide a gain of $90,000.

4. Auburn and Baylor had respective investments on January 1 of $72,000 and $100,000. Auburn invested an additional $24,000 on May 1, and Baylor withdrew $16,000 on August 1. Net income for the year was $48,000. Divide the net income in proportion to their average investments.

5. Chan and Dawson are partners with investments on January 1 of $126,000 and $150,000, respectively. On June 1, Chan withdrew $16,000 and then invested $24,000 on August 1. Dawson invested $10,000 on July 1 and again on September 1. Use the ratio of their average investments to divide a net income of $53,400.

6. In the partnership of Essex and Fergus, a net income of $56,600 for one year is to be divided between the partners in the following manner: (1) Essex is to be allowed an annual salary of $25,000, and Fergus, $19,000; (2) the remainder of the net income is to be divided in the ratio of 4:5, respectively. How much is each partner's total share of the net income?

7. Novak invested $105,000, and Olson, $120,000. During the past year, Novak withdrew a salary of $1,800 a month and Olson withdrew a salary of $2,400 a month. The remainder of the net income was divided in the ratio of 4:3, respectively. Find each partner's total share in a net income of $57,120.

8. Gardner and Webb are partners with investments of $171,000 and $189,000, respectively. The interest rate allowed on their investments is 7%, and the remaining net income is divided in the ratio of 3:5, respectively. Show each partner's share in a net income of $56,400.

9. Hampton, Irving, and Juarez formed a partnership in which they invested $30,000, $45,000, and $60,000, respectively. For the first year, their gross profit was $193,140 and their expenses were $125,010. The partners received 8% on their investments, and the remaining net income was shared equally. How much was each partner's total share of the net income?

10. Jefferson invested $180,000 and Kennedy invested $270,000 in a partnership. During the first year, the partnership net income was $60,000 and during the second year it was $144,000. The net income is shared in proportion to the partners' investments at the beginning of each year. **(a)** Find each partner's share of the net income for the first year. **(b)** Find each partner's share of the net income for the second year if Jefferson withdrew his full share each year and Kennedy withdrew only half of her share for the first year.

Corporate Earnings

The total amount of stock that a corporation's charter permits it to issue is its **authorized capital stock.** The stock that a corporation has actually sold and issued to stockholders is its **outstanding capital stock.** A corporation need not issue all of its authorized stock. In fact, many corporations issue only a portion of the authorized stock and save the remainder for future expansion. When a corporation has issued all of its authorized stock, however, it may obtain authorization from the corporation commissioner of its state of incorporation to issue additional stock.

Capital stock is divided into **shares** that are equal, for each class of stock, in the ownership equity which they represent. Ownership in a corporation is evidenced by a certificate, which is called a **stock certificate,** that may represent any number of shares. The value per share that is printed on the stock certificate is the stock's **par value** or **face value.** Shares of stock that do not have a value printed on the certificate are known as **no-par-value stock.** The charter of a corporation that has no-par-value stock specifies the number of shares that may be issued.

Each stockholder owning common stock usually is entitled to one vote for each share of common stock that is owned. The stockholders of a corporation elect a group of persons, known as the **board of directors,** to manage the business. The board of directors determines the general policies of the corporation and elects the officers.

The two principal sources of capital for a corporation are the investments of its owners and the net income that is retained in the business. A distinction is made between these two sources of capital by showing two separate kinds of proprietary accounts in the corporation's accounting records. These accounts may be labeled (1) contributed capital and (2) retained earnings.

A corporation's net income is computed monthly, quarterly, or annually and recorded in the retained earnings account. The balance of the retained earnings account represents earnings that may be distributed to the stockholders. The board of directors decides how much of the earnings is to be distributed to the stockholders and how much is to be retained for future expansion or for distribution in less prosperous years. The amount of the earnings distributed to the stockholders is called a **dividend.** The dividend may be expressed as a percent of the par value of the shares or in dollars and cents per share.

A corporation may issue two classes of capital stock. Stock issued by a corporation that gives the stockholder preferential rights to earnings or other priorities, such as first ownership claim on assets in a dissolution, is **preferred stock.** Stock issued by a corporation that does not give the stockholder special preference is called **common stock.** When a corporation issues only one class of stock, it is generally known as common stock.

Most preferred stock is preferred as to dividends, which means that preferred stockholders are entitled to a specific rate or amount of dividends per share before any dividends are paid to the common stockholders. As a corporation must have earnings before a dividend can be paid, there can be no guarantee of dividends to either preferred or common stockholders. A preference as to dividends, however, does mean that preferred dividends will be allocated before the common dividends are allocated.

Preferred stock is usually cumulative. **Cumulative preferred stock** is a class of stock on which not only the current dividends but also all unpaid dividends of prior years (dividends in **arrears**) must be paid in full before any dividends can be paid on common stock. That is, the unpaid preferred dividends accumulate until paid.

Example A: The Wabash Corporation has outstanding 1,000 shares of $100 par value 6% cumulative preferred stock and 2,000 shares of $100 par value common stock. No dividends were declared during the past two years. The board of directors of the corporation has just declared a cash dividend of $19,000. How much will be distributed **(a)** per share of preferred stock and **(b)** per share of common stock?

Solution: **(a)** $1,000 \times \$100 = \$100,000$ par value of outstanding preferred stock
$\$100,000 \times 6\% = \$6,000$ annual preferred dividends
$\$6,000 \times 3 = \$18,000$ preferred dividends due for current and past two years
$\$18,000 \div 1,000 = \$18$ accumulated dividend per share of preferred stock

(b) $\$19,000 - \$18,000 = \$1,000$ dividends remaining for common stockholders
$\$1,000 \div 2,000 = \$0.50$ dividend per share of common stock

Noncumulative preferred stock is stock on which the preferred right to receive a dividend is lost in any year when dividends are not declared.

Chapter 15. Business Earnings and Ownership

Assume that the preferred stock of Wabash Corporation (preceding Example A) is noncumulative. How much of the $19,000 dividend will be distributed **(a)** per share of preferred stock and **(b)** per share of common stock?

Solution:

(a) As there are no dividends in arrears and the amount declared for dividends is obviously sufficient to pay the preferred dividends, the computation of the dividend per share of preferred stock is simple:

$$\$100 \times 6\% = \$6 \quad \text{dividend per share of preferred stock}$$

(b) $\$6 \times 1,000 = \$6,000 \quad$ preferred dividends
$\$19,000 - \$6,000 = \$13,000 \quad$ dividends remaining for common stockholders
$\$13,000 \div 2,000 = \$6.50 \quad$ dividend per share of common stock

The preferred stock in the preceding examples is nonparticipating. **Nonparticipating preferred stock** receives no more dividends than the stated rate or amount per share specified by the stock certificate, even though the dividends paid per share of common stock may be much greater proportionately. If the stock certificate provides that the owners of preferred are to share in the earnings beyond the stipulated dividend, the stock is said to be **participating preferred.** Such participation generally follows after the common stock is allocated a like percent per share to agree with the percent per share for preferred. Accordingly, preferred and common stock dividends will agree in percent distribution but not necessarily in dollar distribution because of the difference in par value. For example, if participating preferred receives a 6% dividend, then common stock must receive a 6% dividend. If par values were $100 and $50 respectively, preferred would receive $6 per share and common $3 per share.

Often the annual participation is limited so that after the preferred receives a certain dividend, it no longer shares in the dividends of that year. For example, a 6% cumulative preferred stock might have a limited participation feature entitling it to a maximum dividend of 9% if common is paid 9% or more in one year. When provided for, however, the participation is more often unlimited than limited; stock with this unlimited feature is said to be **fully participating.**

Example C:

Daytona Corporation has outstanding 2,000 shares of $100 par value, 6% cumulative, participating preferred stock and 10,000 shares of $50 par value common stock. The board of directors has declared a cash dividend of $56,000. If there are no dividends in arrears, how much is to be distributed **(a)** per share of preferred stock and **(b)** per share of common stock if the preferred stock is fully participating?

Solution:

$2,000 \times \$100 = \$200,000 \quad$ par value of preferred stock
$\$200,000 \times 6\% = \$12,000 \quad$ regular preferred dividend
$10,000 \times \$50 = \$500,000 \quad$ par value of common stock
$\$500,000 \times 6\% = \$30,000 \quad$ regular common dividend
$\$56,000 - \$12,000 - \$30,000 = \$14,000 \quad$ balance for participation
$\$200,000 + \$500,000 = \$700,000 \quad$ par value of capital stock
$\$14,000 \div \$700,000 = 2\% \quad$ rate of participation per $1 of par value
$6\% + 2\% = 8\% \quad$ total dividend rate

(a) $\$100 \times 8\% = \$8 \quad$ dividend per share of preferred stock

(b) $\$50 \times 8\% = \$4 \quad$ dividend per share of common stock

When the declaration of dividends is obviously more than sufficient to meet the stipulated preferred rate and to give the same rate to common stock, the total dividend rate can be found by dividing the declared dividend by the total value of both classes of stock. The solution to the previous example is shown in detail to emphasize the principles of participation. Notice, however, that $56,000 (dividends declared) divided by $700,000 (total par value) gives the total dividend rate of 8%.

● Exercise 15–4

1. The Westminster Corporation has 7,500 shares of stock outstanding. The board of directors has voted a dividend of $4,875. How much is the dividend in cents per share?

2. The Lincoln Corporation, which has $675,000 of common stock outstanding, earned a net income of $56,765.40 after taxes. The directors declared a 6% dividend and voted to leave the remainder of the net income in the retained earnings account. How much of the net income was kept in the retained earnings account?

3. The capital stock of a corporation consists of $150,000 of nonparticipating preferred stock and $450,000 of common stock. The dividend rate on the preferred stock is 6%. If the directors have declared a dividend of $43,650, what is the percent of dividend to be paid per share of common stock?

4. The directors of Eagle Corporation have announced dividends of $42,750. There are outstanding 4,500 shares of $50 par value, 7% nonparticipating preferred stock and 12,000 shares of $25 par value common stock. If there are no dividends in arrears on the preferred stock, how much will the stockholders receive (a) per share of preferred stock and (b) per share of common stock?

5. Armstrong Enterprises, Inc., has outstanding 15,000 shares of no-par-value common stock and 3,000 shares of 5%, $100 par value cumulative preferred stock. During the past four years, no dividends were declared. This year a dividend of $135,000 is to be distributed. How much is to be paid (a) on each share of preferred stock and (b) on each share of common stock?

6. The outstanding stock of the Elmhurst Manufacturing Corporation consists of 2,000 shares of no-par-value common stock and 2,000 shares of 6%, $100 par value cumulative preferred stock. During the past three years, earnings were so low that dividends were not declared. At the end of this year, the directors agreed to distribute a $60,000 dividend out of cur-

rent earnings. Find the amount to be paid (a) on each share of preferred stock and (b) on each share of common stock.

7. The capital stock of Lake Michigan Shipping, Inc., consists of 6,600 shares of $20 par value common stock and 2,100 shares of 7%, $100 par value noncumulative nonparticipating preferred stock. No dividends had been declared for four years, including the current year, when the directors agreed to distribute $24,600 in dividends. How much will be received by the stockholders (a) per share of preferred stock and (b) per share of common stock?

8. The Columbia Industries, Inc., has capital stock outstanding of 4,200 shares of $100 par value common stock and 3,000 shares of $50 par value, $7\frac{1}{2}$% noncumulative nonparticipating preferred stock. Dividends have not been declared for the past two years. If the directors declare a dividend of $45,900, how much will be paid (a) per share of preferred stock and (b) per share of common stock?

9. Cumberland Manufacturing Company, which has been in business for three years, has outstanding 35,000 shares of no-par-value common stock and 50,000 shares of $50 par value, $6\frac{1}{2}$% cumulative preferred stock. For each of the first two years, dividends of $2 per share of preferred stock were paid. The third year dividends of $537,750 were declared. How much of the dividends should be paid (a) on each share of preferred stock and (b) on each share of common stock?

10. The C. J. Howard Corporation has capital stock consisting of 1,800 shares of $50 par value, 5 percent cumulative nonparticipating preferred stock and $180,000 of $10 par value common stock. There were no dividends in arrears prior to the past year when $2,700 of dividends were paid. At year's end, dividends of $17,100 were declared. How much is to be paid (a) per share of preferred stock and (b) per share of common stock?

11. Nassau Corporation has outstanding 1,000 shares of $100 par value, 6 percent cumulative, participating preferred stock and 12,000 shares of $25 par value common stock. There are no dividends in arrears because the company has been prosperous in recent years. An annual dividend of $36,000 has been declared by the board of directors. Find the amount to be distributed (a) per share of preferred stock and (b) per share of common stock if the preferred is fully participating.

12. Citrus Corporation has outstanding 2,000 shares of $100 par value, 5 percent cumulative, participating preferred stock and 100,000 shares of $20 par value common stock. The company has regularly paid full dividends on the preferred stock. This year the board of directors agreed to pay out a total of $165,000 in dividends. Find the amount to be paid (a) per share of preferred stock and (b) per share of common stock. The preferred stock is fully participating.

Solve these problems. If you have difficulty solving any problem, restudy the appropriate section in this chapter. The problems under a specific number are related to those contained in the exercise with the same last number.

1. **a.** On June 1, Fisher Company had merchandise valued on inventory at $231,450. The value of the June 30 merchandise inventory was $301,800. During the month of June the company bought $760,900 of merchandise. Find **(1)** the goods available for sale and **(2)** the cost of goods sold in June.

   b. Florida Sales Company recently recorded the following income and expenditures: sales, $144,400; salaries expense, $19,875; advertising, $2,670; sales returns, $2,850; rent, $9,450; utilities, $1,065; insurance expense, $1,600; cost of goods sold, $49,580; and miscellaneous expenses, $980. Find the net income or loss.

2. **a.** Harold Meyer has the following assets invested in a retail business: building and land, $48,000; fixtures, $7,200; and merchandise stock at cost, $12,600. There is a $15,000 mortgage on the building and land, $4,200 is owed on the fixtures, and $2,750 is owed to suppliers. How much is Meyer's equity in the business?

   b. The Central Products Company has issued 130,000 shares of stock. The company's assets total $5,640,000; its liabilities, $700,000. Theresa Ackard owns 350 shares of the company's stock. Find **(1)** the company's net worth and **(2)** Ackard's equity in the company.

3. **a.** Two business partners, Ulster and Vanderbilt, divide their gains and losses in a ratio of 3 to 2 in favor of Ulster. Find the amount of each partner's share in a loss of $16,250.

   b. In the partnership of Malone and Newton, Malone's investment is $45,000, and Newton's is $36,000. Their net income for the past year was $41,400. If allocated in the ratio of their investments, how much of the net income should each partner receive?

   c. Riva and McMurray, partners, share gains and losses in the ratio of their average investments. Riva's investment in the business on January 1 was $22,500. He invested an additional $7,500 on July 1 and $5,000 on September 1. McMurray's investment on January 1 was $33,000. She withdrew $6,000 on May 1 and invested $9,000 on October 1. Find each partner's share in the net income of $18,460.

   d. Lamar and McCook formed a partnership by investing $54,000 and $78,000, respectively. They agreed that each partner would receive 8% interest on investment. Lamar would receive a salary of $24,000 a year and McCook, a salary of $18,000 a year. The remainder of the net income would be divided equally. The net income for the first year was $57,900. Find each partner's total share of the net income.

4. **a.** Miami Express, Inc., has outstanding 6,500 shares of $100 par value, 5% cumulative preferred stock and 90,000 shares of $10 par value com-

mon stock. No dividends have been paid to the stockholders for the past two years. The board of directors agreed to distribute $205,500 in dividends at the end of this year. Find **(1)** the total amount paid on the preferred stock and **(2)** the amount paid on each share of common stock.

b. The Pacific-Delaware Company, Inc., has capital stock consisting of $350,000 worth of $50 par value, 6% noncumulative preferred stock and $450,000 worth of $12.50 par value common stock. During the past two years, dividends of $1.50 per share of preferred stock were paid annually. At the end of this year, dividends of $58,800 were declared. How much is to be paid **(1)** on each share of preferred stock and **(2)** on each share of common stock?

CHALLENGE PROBLEM

Ginny Galarza opened a computer software store on January 5, 1987, by investing $5,000 in cash, $15,000 in merchandise, and store equipment (7-year property) valued at $8,000. She had purchased the store equipment with a $2,000 down payment on an installment contract. During the year she paid out $70,000 in cash to purchase additional merchandise, $24,500 for operating expenses, and $3,000 on the installment contract. She also withdrew $18,000 during the year for personal use. At the end of the year she prepared the following balance sheet:

Ginny's Software Store
Balance Sheet, December 31, 1987

Assets		Equities	
Cash	$ 4,500	Accounts payable (for	
Accounts receivable	16,000	merchandise)	$27,800
Merchandise inventory	23,400	Contracts payable	3,000
Store equipment	8,000	G. Galarza, Capital	21,100
	$51,900		$51,900

a. In good form compute the total sales for the year.

b. Calculate the cost of goods sold.

c. Compute the MACRS depreciation to the nearest dollar on the store equipment.

d. Prepare an income statement showing the results of the first year of operations including net income.

Part Four
Mathematics Applications in Analyzing a Business

As a business enterprise grows in size and complexity, its managers must be able to analyze financial statements, reports, and statistical data with increasingly greater skill and accuracy. Successful business decisions must be based on accurate analyses of definite facts rather than on snap judgments. Depending on their importance, decisions regarding the proper analyses of data presented in statements, reports, tables, and graphs are often balanced by group judgment rather than the opinion of an individual.

Chapter 16

Analyses of Financial Statements

Objectives

After mastering the material in Chapter 16, you will be able to:

- Make vertical and horizontal analyses of business income statements and balance sheets.
- Determine a company's working capital.
- Compute the current ratio, acid-test ratio, and other important business ratios.
- Find merchandise turnover based on cost or selling price.

The purpose of this chapter is to show how people extract helpful information from financial statements and reports.

ANALYSES OF FINANCIAL STATEMENTS

Not only the managers, but investors, creditors, governmental agencies, and union officials are interested in analyzing a company's financial statements. Investors are interested in a company's earnings record and its potential future growth and prosperity. Creditors are concerned about the debt-paying ability of the company. Governmental agencies may use a company's records for assessing income and property taxes, for regulatory purposes, and for statistical analyses of the economy. Union officials may glean data from a company's records for collective bargaining purposes. The company's managers study the financial records to measure its past success, as well as to formulate company policies for its success in the future.

The two most important financial statements are the income statement and the balance sheet. The **income statement** of a company reveals its revenue, costs, expenses, and net income or loss for a period of time, such as for one month, three months, or one year. The **balance sheet** shows the financial condition of assets, liabilities, and the owners' equity on a specific date. Both the income statement and the balance sheet must be analyzed carefully. A distorted picture may be obtained by reviewing only the income statement. For example, a company with a relatively high net income may not be financially sound if it has borrowed heavily.

The interpretation of the financial statements may be based on vertical analysis and on horizontal analysis. **Vertical analysis** is the analysis of the relationship between items in a single statement, such as the relationship between net sales and cost of goods sold or net sales and operating expenses. These relationships are usually expressed as percents. **Horizontal analysis** is the analysis of the relationship between an individual item in the current statement with the same item in an earlier statement or series of such statements. Increases or decreases shown may be expressed as percents.

Vertical Analysis of Income Statements

In most businesses income from sales is the primary source of revenue. Costs and expenses are paid from the revenue derived from sales. The basis for a vertical analysis of an income statement, therefore, is net sales. As sales returns and allowances are not sources of revenue, these amounts are deducted from total sales to obtain net sales. Being the base, the amount of net sales equals 100%. All other items on the income statement are shown as a percent of net sales. For example, the percent for cost of goods sold in the Brevard Company Income Statement, Figure 16–1, was computed:

$$\frac{\$11,500 \text{ cost of goods sold}}{\$25,000 \text{ net sales}} = 46.0\%$$

Constant operation and the $\boxed{\%}$ key on a calculator may be used to great advantage to find the rates for a vertical analysis of the income statement and the balance sheet. Rates for only the first few lines of the income statement are illustrated in the following example. The remaining rates may be determined in the same manner.

Brevard Company
Income Statement
For Month Ended May 31, 19--

			Percents
Revenue:			
Sales............................		$25,375	101.5
Less sales returns and allowances		375	1.5
Net sales............................		$25,000	100.0
Less cost of goods sold:			
Merchandise inventory, May 1, 19--	$ 2,250		9.0
Purchases	12,000		48.0
Goods available for sale	$14,250		57.0
Less merchandise inventory, May 31, 19-- ..	2,750		11.0
Cost of goods sold		11,500	46.0
Gross profit on sales........................		$13,500	54.0
Operating expenses:			
Selling expenses	$ 6,400		25.6
Delivery expenses........................	3,200		12.8
Office expenses	1,575		6.3
Miscellaneous expenses	225		0.9
Total operating expenses		11,400	45.6
Net income............................		$ 2,100	8.4

Figure 16–1 Income Statement for Brevard Company

Example: Use the data in Figure 16–1 to show the rate of net sales that each of the following is: **(a)** sales, **(b)** sales returns, **(c)** beginning merchandise inventory, and **(d)** purchases. Round to the nearest 0.1%.

Solution:
(a) 25375 $\boxed{\div}$ 25000 $\boxed{\%}$ → 101.5, means 101.5%

(b) 375 $\boxed{\%}$ → 1.5, means 1.5%

(c) 2250 $\boxed{\%}$ → 9, means 9.0%

(d) 12000 $\boxed{\%}$ → 48, means 48.0%

Horizontal Analysis of Income Statements

The figures on financial statements covering a single year are not very meaningful by themselves. Most annual reports to stockholders now include statements for both the current year and the preceding year. Many corporations provide summaries for five- or ten-year periods. Even these comparative

Part 4. Mathematics Applications in Analyzing a Business

statements, however, can be better analyzed when the figures are expressed as percents.

The percents in a comparative income statement may be arranged in two ways. In one form the arrangement is similar to that shown in Figure 16–1, except that information for two or more years is shown. The percent for a single item in a specific year is based on net sales for that year. The percent of an item for the current year is compared to the percent for the same item for one or more preceding years. For example, in the comparative income statement for Cogswell Manufacturing Company, Figure 16–2, notice that the cost of goods sold compared to net sales is 5.2% smaller for 19X2 than for 19X1. Also observe that net income is 2.5% greater for 19X2 than for 19X1.

Cogswell Manufacturing Company
Comparative Income Statement
For Years Ended December 31, 19X2 and 19X1

	19X2		19X1	
	Amount	Percent	Amount	Percent
Sales	$123,420	102.0	$109,080	101.0
Less sales returns and allowances ...	2,420	2.0	1,080	1.0
Net sales	$121,000	100.0	$108,000	100.0
Less cost of goods sold..........	78,890	65.2	76,000	70.4
Gross profit	$ 42,110	34.8	$ 32,000	29.6
Operating expenses:				
Wages and salaries	$ 18,150	15.0	$ 19,120	17.7
Rent........................	2,420	2.0	1,620	1.5
Depreciation	5,200	4.3	4,140	3.8
Other expenses	9,080	7.5	3,340	3.1
Total operating expenses	$ 34,850	28.8	$ 28,220	26.1
Net income	$ 7,260	6.0	$ 3,780	3.5

Figure 16–2 Comparative Income Statement for Cogswell Manufacturing Company

A second form of comparative income statement is designed to show the amounts and percents of increase or decrease for each item in the statement during the current year. The figure for each item in the preceding year serves as the base for determining the amount and percent of increase or decrease. In the comparative income statement for Monterey Trading Company, Figure 16–3, net sales increased from $200,000 in 19X1 to $240,000 in 19X2. This is an increase of $40,000, or 20%. A decrease may be shown in parentheses, with a minus sign, or with an asterisk.

The information shown in Figure 16–2 is sometimes combined in a condensed comparative income statement, as illustrated in Figure 16–3.

Chapter 16. Analyses of Financial Statements

	19X2	19X1	Increase or Decrease* During 19X2	
			Amount	Percent
Net sales.....................	$240,000	$200,000	$40,000	20.0
Cost of goods sold	156,000	120,000	36,000	30.0
Gross profit	$ 84,000	$ 80,000	4,000	5.0
Operating expenses	64,000	68,000	4,000*	5.9*
Net income..................	$ 20,000	$ 12,000	8,000	66.7

Monterey Trading Company
Condensed Comparative Income Statement
For Years Ended December 31, 19X2 and 19X1

Figure 16-3 Condensed Comparative Income Statement for Monterey Trading Company

● Exercise 16-1

1. Find the percent of net sales for each item in the following statement. Where applicable, round to the nearest 0.1%.

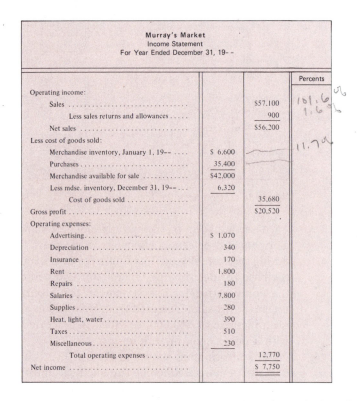

Murray's Market
Income Statement
For Year Ended December 31, 19- -

			Percents
Operating income:			
Sales		$57,100	
Less sales returns and allowances		900	
Net sales		$56,200	
Less cost of goods sold:			
Merchandise inventory, January 1, 19--	$ 6,600		
Purchases............................	35,400		
Merchandise available for sale	$42,000		
Less mdse. inventory, December 31, 19--...	6,320		
Cost of goods sold		35,680	
Gross profit		$20,520	
Operating expenses:			
Advertising.........................	$ 1,070		
Depreciation	340		
Insurance	170		
Rent	1,800		
Repairs	180		
Salaries	7,800		
Supplies	280		
Heat, light, water.................	390		
Taxes.............................	510		
Miscellaneous......................	230		
Total operating expenses		12,770	
Net income		$ 7,750	

Part 4. Mathematics Applications in Analyzing a Business

2. Find the percent of net sales for each item in the following statement. Where applicable, round to the nearest 0.1%.

	19X2		19X1	
Carson and Newman **Comparative Income Statement** **For Years Ended December 31, 19X2 and 19X1**	Amount	Percent	Amount	Percent
Sales......................................	$129,874		$131,645	
Less sales returns and allowances.....	874		1,045	
Net sales...............................	$129,000		$130,600	
Less cost of goods sold:				
Merchandise inventory, January 1	$ 60,000		$ 73,000	
Purchases......................	106,200		101,100	
Merchandise available for sale	$166,200		$174,100	
Less mdse. inventory, December 31 ...	76,240		60,000	
Cost of goods sold	$ 89,960		$114,100	
Gross profit	$ 39,040		$ 16,500	
Operating expenses:				
Selling expenses..................	$ 15,220		$ 11,500	
Delivery expenses	8,500		7,200	
Office expenses	6,500		6,400	
Miscellaneous expenses	720		950	
Total operating expenses	$ 30,940		$ 26,050	
Net income or loss*	$ 8,100		$ 9,550*	

3. In the comparative income statement for Clarion Company, shown on page 488, find the net change and the percent of change in each item from 19X1 to 19X2. Where applicable, round to the nearest 0.1%. Place an asterisk (*) to the right of amounts and percents that represent decreases.

4. Supply the information required to complete the comparative income statement for King's Bookstore, shown on page 488. Where applicable, round to the nearest 0.1%. Place an asterisk (*) to the right of amounts and percents that represent decreases.

5. During the year the sales of Tri-State Company were $270,000. The cost of goods sold totaled $189,000; selling expenses, $29,700; and administrative expenses, $27,000. Use this information to prepare an income statement for the company, showing the amounts and the percents based on sales.

6. The following information was taken from the income statement of a store: net sales, $405,000; cost of goods sold, $283,500; operating expenses, $81,000; net income, $40,500. If the sales increased the following year to $558,000, by how much could the expenses be allowed to increase and still keep the present percentage relationship?

Chapter 16. Analyses of Financial Statements

Clarion Company
Comparative Income Statement
For Years Ended December 31, 19X2 and 19X1

	19X2	19X1	Increase or Decrease* During 19X2 Amount	Percent
Sales...........................	$144,000	$134,160		
Less sales return and allowances....	2,400	1,800		
Net sales........................	$141,600	$132,360		
Less cost of goods sold:				
Merchandise inventory, January 1 ..	$ 92,100	$ 81,000		
Purchases....................	96,500	85,500		
Merchandise available for sale......	$188,600	$166,500		
Less mdse. inventory, December 31 .	86,600	92,100		
Cost of goods sold	$102,000	$ 74,400		
Gross profit	$ 39,600	$ 57,960		
Operating expenses:				
Selling expenses	$ 17,200	$ 15,000		
General expenses	12,700	10,500		
Total operating expense.....	$ 29,900	$ 25,500		
Net income	$ 9,700	$ 32,460		

King's Book Store
Comparative Income Statement
For Years Ended December 31, 19X2 and 19X1

	19X2 Amount	Percent	19X1 Amount	Percent	Increase or Decrease* During 19X2 Amount	Percent
Net sales.............	$96,000		$84,200		11,800	
Cost of goods sold	71,000					
Gross profit			$22,000			
Operating expenses:						
Salary expense	$12,300		$11,800			
Rent expense	2,400		2,000			
Heating and lighting expense ..	220		240			
Depreciation expense	190		170			
Advertising expense	500		750			
Miscellaneous expense	160		90			
Total operating expense						
Net income..........						

Part 4. Mathematics Applications in Analyzing a Business

Vertical Analysis of Balance Sheets

A **balance sheet** is a statement that gives a formal presentation of the nature and value of the assets, liabilities, and proprietorship of a business. In essence, the accounting equation,

$$Assets = Liabilities + Proprietorship,$$

is shown in the balance sheet. Notice in Figure 16–4, below, that the total assets equal the total liabilities and proprietorship. (Instead of proprietorship, owner's equity, capital, or net worth may be used in the accounting equation.)

Scott Drug Company
Balance Sheet
December 31, 19– –

			Percent
ASSETS			
Current assets:			
Cash...........................	$ 1,700		1.0
Notes receivable....................	8,400		4.8
Accounts receivable..................	13,500		7.8
Merchandise inventory.................	18,000		10.3
Total current assets..............		$ 41,600	23.9
Fixed assets:			
Equipment........................	$37,400		21.5
Building..........................	75,000		43.1
Land............................	20,000		11.5
Total fixed assets................		132,400	76.1
Total assets.........................		$174,000	100.0
LIABILITIES			
Current liabilities:			
Notes payable......................	$ 6,420		3.7
Accounts payable....................	13,880		8.0
Total current liabilities.............		$ 20,300	11.7
Long-term liabilities:			
Mortage payable.....................		30,000	17.2
Total liabilities......................		$ 50,300	28.9
PROPRIETORSHIP			
Hiram Scott, proprietorship.................		$123,700	71.1
Total liabilities and proprietorship.............		$174,000	100.0

Figure 16–4 Balance Sheet for Scott Drug Company

The first step in a vertical analysis of a balance sheet is the computation of percents for the various items appearing on the statement. As the percent of each item in relation to the total is desired, the base (100%) on which the percents are computed is either total assets or total liabilities and proprietorship.

Thus, in Figure 16–4, the percentage relationship of merchandise inventory to total assets is determined as follows:

$$\frac{\$18{,}000 \text{ merchandise inventory}}{\$174{,}000 \text{ total assets}} = 10.3\%$$

All of the percents in Figure 16–4 are computed in this manner based on total assets.

Using total assets as the constant divisor in a calculator facilitates finding the rates.

Example: Using the data in Figure 16–4, find the percent that each current asset is of total assets. Round to the nearest 0.1%.

Solution:

1700 $\boxed{\div}$ 174,000 $\boxed{\%}$ → 0.9770114, means 1.0%   cash

8400 $\boxed{\%}$ → 4.8275862, means 4.8%   notes receivable

13500 $\boxed{\%}$ → 7.7586206, means 7.8%   accounts receivable

18000 $\boxed{\%}$ → 10.344827, means 10.3%   merchandise inventory

Horizontal Analysis of Balance Sheets

A horizontal analysis of balance sheet items consists of analyzing the relationship between an individual item or group total in the current balance sheet with the same item or total of one or several preceding balance sheets. For example, current assets on June 30 of the present year may be compared to the current assets on June 30 of the preceding year. The increase or decrease in the item is usually expressed as a percent. A **comparative balance sheet** (Figure 16–5) is one that shows the values of the assets, liabilities, and proprietor-

Centralia Company
Comparative Balance Sheet
June 30, 19X2 and 19X1

	19X2	19X1	Increase or Decrease* Amount	Percent
ASSETS				
Current assets..................	$ 242,500	$ 266,200	$ 23,700*	8.9*
Long-term investments...........	705,500	666,800	38,700	5.8
Fixed assets (net)................	900,000	875,000	25,000	2.9
Total assets	$1,848,000	$1,808,000	$ 40,000	2.2
LIABILITIES				
Current liabilities...............	$ 364,500	$ 315,000	$ 49,500	15.7
Long-term liabilities..............	150,000	250,000	100,000*	40.0*
Total liabilities..................	$ 514,500	$ 565,000	$ 50,500*	8.9*
STOCKHOLDERS' EQUITY				
Preferred stock (6%, $100 par)	$ 300,000	$ 300,000	–0–	–0–
Common stock ($10 par)...........	800,000	750,000	$ 50,000	6.7
Retained earnings	233,500	193,000	40,500	21.0
Total stockholders' equity	$1,333,500	$1,243,000	$ 90,500	7.3
Total liabilities & stockholders' equity......................	$1,848,000	$1,808,000	$ 40,000	2.2

Figure 16–5 Comparative Balance Sheet for Centralia Company

ship on two or more dates, generally the same date of the preceding month or year. Comparative analysis reveals whether the business is in a better or poorer financial condition on the later date than it was on an earlier date.

25%

● Exercise 16–2

Due on monday 12-11

1. During the past year, the Wonsan Corporation had net sales of $3,153,400. The following expenditures were made during the year: **(a)** salaries, $250,000; **(b)** rent, $98,000; **(c)** advertising, $60,000; **(d)** depreciation, $42,310; **(e)** repairs, $146,352. To the nearest 0.1%, find the percent that each expenditure is of net sales.

2. The balance sheet of Yahata Products, Inc. shows total assets of $594,000. Express each of these as a percent of total assets: **(a)** current assets, $150,000; **(b)** equipment, $96,000; **(c)** current liabilities, $43,000; **(d)** common stock, $400,000; **(e)** retained earnings, $210,000. Where applicable, round to the nearest 0.1%.

3. Find the percent of total assets for each item in the following balance sheet. Find the percent of each liability and the proprietorship based on total liabilities and proprietorship (100%). Where applicable, round to the nearest 0.01%.

Peirce Company
Balance Sheet
December 31, 19--

			Percent
ASSETS			
Current assets:			
Cash	$ 7,950		
Notes receivable	6,480		
Accounts receivable	26,970		
Merchandise inventory	31,980		
Total current assets		$ 73,380	
Fixed assets:			
Equipment	$ 10,120		
Building	267,500		
Land	37,500		
Total fixed assets		315,120	
Total assets		$388,500	
LIABILITIES			
Current liabilities:			
Notes payable	$ 5,390		
Accounts payable	22,420		
Total current liabilities		$ 27,810	
Long-term liabilities:			
Mortgage payable		142,000	
Total liabilities		$169,810	
PROPRIETORSHIP			
Janice L. Peirce, proprietorship		218,690	
Total liabilities and proprietorship		$388,500	

Chapter 16. Analyses of Financial Statements

491

4. In the following comparative balance sheet, find the net change and the percent of change in each item from 19X1 to 19X2. Where applicable, round to the nearest 0.1%. Place an asterisk (*) to the right of amounts and percents that represent decreases.

Merritt and Marshall
Comparative Balance Sheet
December 31, 19X2 and 19X1

	19X2	19X1	Increase or Decrease* Amount	Increase or Decrease* Percent
ASSETS				
Current assets:				
Cash	$ 10,890	$ 7,050		
Notes receivable	7,600	4,800		
Accounts receivable	11,100	9,860		
Merchandise inventory	17,050	18,600		
Total current assets	$ 46,640	$ 40,310		
Fixed assets:				
Equipment	$ 52,800	$ 46,740		
Building and land	144,000	144,000		
Total fixed assets	$196,800	$190,740		
Total assets	$243,440	$231,050		
LIABILITIES				
Current liabilities:				
Accounts payable	$ 9,940	$ 8,400		
Notes payable	17,850	16,200		
Total current liabilities	$ 27,790	$ 24,600		
Long–term liabilities:				
Mortgage payable	59,000	62,600		
Total liabilities	$ 86,790	$ 87,200		
PROPRIETORSHIP				
John Merritt, proprietorship	$ 74,400	$ 70,000		
Max Marshall, proprietorship	82,250	73,850		
Total liabilities and proprietorship	$243,440	$231,050		

FINANCIAL STATEMENT RATIOS

Some items on the financial statements are estimated and, therefore, should be interpreted in relation to other factors. Furthermore, the standard interpretations of analyses vary in accordance with the economic characteristics of specific industries. There are general patterns and rules of thumb, however, that apply to most analyses.

Over the years, managers, investors, and security analysts have found that the analysis of financial statements is made easier by examining ratios that focus on significant relationships in the balance sheet and the income statement. Those presented in this section, of course, are not the only ratios that have been developed. Nevertheless, the ratios shown are basic.

Balance Sheet Ratios

A **ratio** is a means of expressing the relationship of one number to another. For example, a common fraction may be interpreted as a ratio and expressed as $\frac{9}{15}$ or as 9:15. Ratios, like common fractions, are usually expressed in lowest terms. The preceding ratio, then, is 3:5, which is read as "3 to 5." The ratios used in the analysis of financial statements are customarily found by dividing the first number by the second. Thus, the ratio of 3:5 means 3 ÷ 5, which is 0.6 and is written as 0.6:1 or in percent notation as 60%. The following computations for balance sheet ratios are based on the balance sheet for the Belknap Company, Figure 16-6.

Belknap Company Balance Sheet December 31, 19- -		
ASSETS		
Current assets:		
Cash......................................	$15,000	
Notes receivable.............................	3,000	
Accounts receivable, net.........................	27,000	
Merchandise inventory.........................	40,000	
Total current assets........................		$ 85,000
Fixed assets:		
Equipment......................................	$54,600	
Less accumulated depreciation....................	6,600	
Total fixed assets...........................		48,000
Total assets		$133,000
LIABILITIES		
Current liabilities:		
Notes payable....................................	$ 7,000	
Accounts payable.................................	10,800	
Accrued interest payable	2,200	
Total current liabilities		$ 20,000
Long-term liabilities:		
Mortgage payable.................................		30,000
Total liabilities....................................		$ 50,000
PROPRIETORSHIP		
Karen Belknap, proprietorship..........................		83,000
Total liabilities and proprietorship.......................		$133,000

Figure 16–6 Balance Sheet for Belknap Company

Working Capital. The difference between the total current assets and the total current liabilities is called the **net current assets** or **working capital.** Current liabilities, debts due within one year, are paid from current assets. Therefore, working capital represents the amount of current assets remaining if all current liabilities are paid immediately. The ability of a company to meet current debts, expand volume, and take advantage of buying opportunities is often determined by the size of its working capital.

$$Current\ Assets - Current\ Liabilities = Working\ Capital$$
$$\$85,000 - \$20,000 = \$65,000$$

Current Ratio. The ratio of total current assets to total current liabilities is called the **current ratio** or **working-capital ratio**. This ratio is probably the most frequently used for industrial companies. Most analysts believe that the current ratio should be at least 2:1. This means that there should be $2 in current assets for every $1 in current liabilities. Of course, this is a rule of thumb that varies because there are so many different kinds of companies. The following calculation illustrates that Belknap Company has $4.25 in current assets for each $1 in current liabilities.

$$Current\ Ratio = \frac{Current\ Assets}{Current\ Liabilities} = \frac{\$85,000}{\$20,000} = 4.25{:}1$$

Acid-Test Ratio. Current assets that may be quickly converted into cash are called **quick assets.** Normally the quick assets on a balance sheet are cash, receivables, and marketable securities. Inventories are omitted because they are more difficult to sell.

The relationship of quick assets to current liabilities is the **acid-test ratio,** which is also known as the **quick ratio.** This is an important supplement to the current ratio because it indicates the company's ability to meet current obligations. When the quick assets are less than current liabilities, the company may experience difficulty in converting the non-quick assets if it must do so to meet current debts. A ratio of 1:1 is considered to be the minimum.

$$Acid\text{-}Test\ Ratio = \frac{Quick\ Assets}{Current\ Liabilities} = \frac{\$45,000}{\$20,000} = 2.25{:}1$$

Owners' Equity to Creditors' Equity Ratio. Funds with which to operate a business are obtained from the owners in the form of invested capital or from creditors in the form of borrowed capital that must be repaid. A comparison of the owners' equity with the liabilities indicates the proportion of funds supplied by the owners to those supplied by outside creditors. Generally, in a merchandising company, creditors' equity should not equal or exceed owners' equity because this may indicate that the company is meeting current operational expenses with borrowed capital. The following calculation illustrates that the owner of Belknap Company has invested $1.66 to each $1 lent to the company by creditors.

$$\frac{Owners'\ Equity}{Total\ Liabilities} = \frac{\$83,000}{\$50,000} = 1.66{:}1$$

Fixed Assets to Long-Term Liabilities Ratio. Long-term debts are often secured by mortgages on specific fixed assets. The ratio of fixed assets to long-term liabilities provides a measure of the margin of safety that the mortgage holder has. It also indicates the potential ability of the company to borrow additional long-term capital.

$$\frac{Fixed\ Assets}{Long\text{-}Term\ Liabilities} = \frac{\$48,000}{\$30,000} = 1.6{:}1$$

- **Exercise 16–3**

1. Blue Ridge Company, Inc. has total current liabilities of $200,000, total long-term liabilities of $650,000, total fixed assets of $478,000, and current assets of $350,000. Find the company's working capital.

2. The balance sheet of the Bucks Distributing Company shows the following:

Accounts payable	$ 15,000
Notes payable	25,000
Mortgage payable	150,000
Frank Bucks, net worth	134,000
Betty Bucks, net worth	89,000

Find **(a)** the creditors' equity and **(b)** the owners' equity in this firm.

3. The balance sheet of the Carl and Albert Company shows the following:

Accounts payable	$ 23,000
Notes payable	16,000
Mortgage payable	145,000
Robert Albert, net worth	76,500
Janet Carl, net worth	112,500

Find **(a)** the creditors' equity and **(b)** the owners' equity in this firm.

4. Desert Products, Inc. has total current assets of $380,000, total fixed assets of $546,000, total long-term liabilities of $540,600, and current liabilities of $162,000. Find the company's working capital.

5. The balance sheet of the Xenia Corporation shows the following:

Machinery	$150,000
Equipment	97,800
Buildings and land	450,000
Accounts payable	32,600
Notes payable	108,500
Mortgage payable	265,000

Find the firm's **(a)** total assets and **(b)** long-term liabilities.

6. The balance sheet of the Yadkin Corporation shows the following:

Machinery	$375,000
Equipment	104,300
Buildings and land	620,000
Accounts payable	53,800
Notes payable	99,600
Mortgage payable	357,000

Find the firm's **(a)** total assets and **(b)** long-term liabilities.

7. These data were taken from the balance sheet of Cowley Corporation: cash, $71,000; marketable securities, $60,000; accounts receivable,

$105,000; merchandise inventory, $264,000; notes payable, $83,000; accounts payable, $52,000. Find the (a) current ratio and (b) acid-test ratio. Where applicable, round to the nearest tenth.

8. An examination of the Davidson Corporation's records revealed these data: current assets, $450,000; fixed assets, $830,000; current liabilities, $128,000; long-term liabilities, $219,000; preferred stock outstanding, $240,000; common stock outstanding, $400,000. Find (a) the ratio of owners' equity to creditors' equity and (b) the ratio of fixed assets to long-term liabilities. Where applicable, round to the nearest tenth.

9. Use the data presented in the 19X2 column of the balance sheet in Figure 16–7 below to compute (a) the working capital, (b) the current ratio, (c) the acid-test ratio, (d) the owner's equity to creditors' equity ratio, and (e) the fixed assets to long-term liabilities ratio. Round to the nearest hundredth.

Olney Distributing Company Comparative Balance Sheet December 31, 19X2 and 19X1		
	19X2	19X1
ASSETS		
Current assets:		
Cash....................................	$ 36,000	$ 44,000
Accounts receivable	178,000	211,000
Merchandise inventory......................	240,000	300,000
Total current assets	$ 454,000	$ 555,000
Fixed assets:		
Equipment.....................................	$ 210,000	$ 175,000
Building and land...............................	870,000	850,000
Total fixed assets	$1,080,000	$1,025,000
Total assets	$1,534,000	$1,580,000
LIABILITIES		
Current liabilities:		
Notes payable.....................................	$ 48,000	$ 65,000
Accounts payable.................................	160,000	198,000
Total current liabilities......................	$ 208,000	$ 263,000
Long–term liabilities:		
Mortgage payable................................	500,000	560,000
Total liabilities	$ 708,000	$ 823,000
PROPRIETORSHIP		
Edward Knight, proprietorship........................	826,000	757,000
Total liabilities and proprietorship......................	$1,534,000	$1,580,000

Figure 16–7 Comparative Balance Sheet for Olney Distributing Company

10. Use the data in the 19X1 column of the balance sheet in Figure 16–7 to find **(a)** the working capital, **(b)** the current ratio, **(c)** the acid-test ratio, **(d)** the owner's equity to creditors' equity ratio, and **(e)** the fixed assets to long-term liabilities ratio. Round to the nearest hundredth.

Merchandise Inventory Ratio

The ratio of the value of the goods sold to the value of the average merchandise inventory is the **merchandise turnover.** The number of times that the average merchandise inventory is converted into sales during the year is an indication of the merchandising efficiency of the business. A low turnover rate may indicate that the goods are not being sold rapidly enough or that too large an inventory of merchandise is being kept. Keeping the investment in merchandise at a minimum is desirable so that more funds will be available to meet current obligations. If the inventory is too large, there is also the danger of loss through price declines and deterioration or obsolescence of the merchandise. A turnover rate that is too high may indicate that the inventory is too low, which in turn may cause the loss of sales because the merchandise is not available to customers.

The **average inventory** is found by dividing the sum of the inventories available for one year by the number of such inventories. If an annual inventory is taken, the inventories taken at the beginning and at the end of the year are added together and divided by 2. If quarterly inventories are taken, the amounts of the beginning, ending, and three intervening quarterly inventories are added and divided by 5. The formula is:

$$Average\ Inventory = \frac{Sum\ of\ the\ Inventories}{Number\ of\ Inventories\ in\ Sum}$$

Merchandise inventory may be valued at cost or at retail. Turnover of merchandise inventory, therefore, may be computed in relation to the cost of goods sold or in relation to the retail or sales price of the goods sold. The value of goods sold and the value of the average inventory must both be computed on the same basis — both at cost or both at selling price.

Finding Merchandise Turnover at Cost Price. Merchandise turnover may be calculated by dividing cost of goods sold by the cost value of the average merchandise inventory. **Cost of goods sold** is the cost value of the merchandise sold during the year. **Average merchandise inventory at cost** is the average cost value of goods that were on hand for sale at any one time during the year. The formula is:

$$Merchandise\ Turnover\ at\ Cost = \frac{Cost\ of\ Goods\ Sold}{Average\ Inventory\ at\ Cost}$$

Example:	Use the data in Figure 16-8 to find **(a)** Belknap Company's average inventory and **(b)** its merchandise turnover to the nearest hundredth.

Solution:

(a) $\dfrac{\$21,000 + \$40,000}{2} = \$30,500$ average inventory

(b) $\dfrac{\$149,000}{\$30,500} = 4.8852459 = 4.89$ merchandise turnover

---

Belknap Company
Income Statement
For Year Ended December 31, 19--

Revenue:		
Sales		$219,240
Less sales returns and allowances		3,240
Net sales.		$216,000
Less cost of goods sold:		
Merchandise inventory, January 1, 19--	$ 21,000	
Purchases of merchandise.	168,000	
Goods available for sale	$189,000	
Less merchandise inventory, December 31, 19--.	40,000	
Cost of goods sold		149,000
Gross profit on sales.		$ 67,000
Operating expenses:		
Selling expenses	$ 24,110	
Delivery expenses.	15,700	
Office expenses	8,200	
Miscellaneous expenses	1,090	
Total operating expenses		49,100
Net operating income.		$ 17,900
Other income and expense:		
Add interest earned	$ 140	
Deduct interest expense.	2,040	
Deduction from income.		1,900
Net income.		$ 16,000

Figure 16-8 Income Statement for Belknap Company

Finding Merchandise Turnover at Sales Price. Merchandise turnover may also be found by dividing the net sales for the year by the retail value of the average inventory. A company's merchandise turnover found at sales price will be the same as that found at cost only if there have been no additional markups, markdowns, or shortages of goods. The formula is:

$$\textit{Merchandise Turnover at Sales Price} = \frac{\textit{Net Sales}}{\textit{Average Inventory at Sales Price}}$$

Example:

What is the rate of merchandise turnover to the nearest tenth if the average inventory based on selling price is $78,000, net sales amount to $244,200, and cost of goods sold is $200,100?

Solution:

$$\frac{\$244,200}{\$78,000} = 3.1307692 = 3.1 \quad \text{merchandise turnover}$$

● **Exercise 16–4**

1. Cost of goods sold amounted to $45,340 and average merchandise inventory at cost was $12,436. Find the merchandise turnover to the nearest hundredth.

2. Net sales totaled $64,648 and average merchandise inventory at retail was $34,730. Find the merchandise turnover to the nearest hundredth.

3. The quarterly inventories at cost were as follows: January 1, $18,304; April 1, $20,617; July 1, $23,506; October 1, $27,810; December 31, $19,233. Find the average inventory.

4. Merchandise inventory at cost at the beginning of the year was $52,500, and at the end of the year, it was $42,000. Goods sold during the year cost $184,000. Find **(a)** the average merchandise inventory and **(b)** the merchandise turnover to the nearest hundredth.

5. Smith's Sportswear Shop takes inventory every six months at sales prices. Its inventory at the beginning of the past year was $59,223; six months later it was $70,034; and at the end of the year it was $60,616. Net sales for the year were $256,390. Find **(a)** the average inventory and **(b)** the merchandise turnover to the nearest tenth.

6. Net sales for the past year totaled $203,830. The periodic merchandise inventories at retail were as follows: January 1, $108,965; May 1, $124,540; September 1, $134,817; December 31, $132,550. Find **(a)** the average merchandise inventory and **(b)** the merchandise turnover to the nearest hundredth.

7. Bowan and Gualdani began the fiscal year with a merchandise inventory of $68,433 at cost. During the year they bought $509,633 worth of goods. Their inventory at the end of the year was $116,281. Find **(a)** the cost of goods sold, **(b)** the average merchandise inventory, and **(c)** the merchandise turnover.

8. The average merchandise inventory based on retail was $140,620. The markon rate was 45% of the sales price. Find the merchandise turnover to the nearest tenth if the cost of goods sold during the year totaled $884,334.

9. During the past year, Oakley Company carried an average merchandise inventory of $225,000 at cost. The markon rate is $33\frac{1}{3}\%$ of cost. If the merchandise turnover rate was 8.1 based on retail, how much were the net sales?

10. During the past year, Belleville Company had sales of $425,000 and an average inventory of $95,000 at retail. By modernizing the building and expanding the advertising program, the owners expect to increase sales by $100,000 and decrease the average inventory by $5,000. If the plan accomplishes the expected results, how many more stock turnovers will the company have this year than it had during the past year? Compute the answer to the nearest hundredth.

Other Financial Ratios

In addition to the turnover of merchandise inventory, there are other significant ratios based on the data contained in the income statement. Still others are based on data contained in both the income statement and the balance sheet. Some of the most important of these ratios are presented in this section.

Net Income to Net Sales. One indication of how satisfactorily the business has been operated during the year is the ratio of net income to net sales. This ratio is normally expressed as a percent. The following example shows that Belknap Company's net income was 7.4% of net sales. This means that for every $1 of net sales, the company's net income was 7.4¢. By comparing the net income ratio from year to year for the company and with other companies carrying the same kinds of goods, the earnings record of the company can be judged. An increase in sales volume does not necessarily mean that the company has improved, for it is possible for sales to increase while earnings per dollar decrease. The formula for this ratio is:

$$Net\ Income\ to\ Net\ Sales = \frac{Net\ Income}{Net\ Sales}$$

Example: Use the data in Figure 16–8 to compute the ratio of net income to net sales to the nearest 0.1%.

Solution: $\dfrac{\$16,000}{\$216,000} = 0.074074 = 7.4\%$ net income to net sales

Net Income to Owners' Equity. Whether the owners are getting a reasonable return on their investment is indicated by the ratio of net income to owners' equity. This is one of the most significant of all the financial ratios. Of course, a large or increasing ratio is preferred, but an extraordinarily high ratio may invite more intense competition or governmental regulations. Many business executives hesitate to invest in new plants and equipment unless they think that the new investment will yield an annual return of at least 10%. The formula for this ratio is:

$$Net\ Income\ to\ Owners'\ Equity = \frac{Net\ Income}{Owners'\ Equity}$$

Example:

Use the data in Figure 16–6 and Figure 16–8 to compute Belknap Company's ratio of net income to owner's equity to the nearest 0.1%.

Solution:

$$\frac{\$16,000}{\$83,000} = 0.192771 = 19.3\%$$

Return on Total Assets. Earnings in relation to the total assets is a measure of the productivity of the assets, without regard to the equity of the owners or of the creditors. This ratio is computed by adding interest expense to net income and dividing the sum by the total assets. As interest is paid for the use of borrowed capital, adding the interest paid to net income shows the total amount earned by the assets without considering whether the assets were acquired with owners' capital or creditors' capital. The following example shows that Belknap Company earned 13.56¢ for each dollar invested in the assets of the company. The formula for this ratio is:

$$Return\ on\ Total\ Assets = \frac{Net\ Income + Interest\ Expense}{Total\ Assets}$$

Example:

Use the data in Figure 16–6 and Figure 16–8 to find the return on the total assets of Belknap Company to the nearest 0.01%.

Solution:

$$\frac{\$16,000 + \$2,040}{\$133,000} = 0.135639 = 13.56\%$$

Turnover of Accounts Receivable. The relationship of accounts receivable and credit sales, which gives an indication of how rapidly accounts receivable are collected, is called the **turnover of accounts receivable.** The following example illustrates that, on the assumption that all sales were on credit, Belknap Company's accounts receivable were collected 8 times during the year. Theoretically only credit sales and average accounts receivable should be used in the computation. This information, however, is seldom available on published financial statements. Therefore, the following formula is often used to compute this ratio:

$$Turnover\ of\ Accounts\ Receivable = \frac{Net\ Sales}{Accounts\ Receivable}$$

Example:

Use the data in Figure 16–6 and Figure 16–8 to find the turnover of accounts receivable of Belknap Company.

Solution:

$$\frac{\$216,000}{\$27,000} = 8\ times$$

Chapter 16. Analyses of Financial Statements

Number of Days' Sales Uncollected. Another measure of a company's collection efficiency is the number of days' sales uncollected or the collection period. This measure gives an approximation of the length of time during the year that accounts receivable remain outstanding. Depending on the selling terms customarily given in the industry, customers may be given 30, 60, or 90 days in which to pay for goods charged to accounts receivable. Many business people believe that the credit period revealed by this computation should not exceed $1\frac{1}{3}$ of the credit terms granted. Knowledge of the credit terms given by the company or similar companies in the same industry helps to evaluate the result of this computation. When available, average accounts receivable and credit sales are used. If these amounts are not available, the following formula may be used.

$$Days' Sales\ Uncollected = \frac{Accounts\ Receivable \times 365}{Net\ Sales}$$

Example:

Use the data in Figure 16–6 and Figure 16–8 to find the number of days' sales uncollected to the nearest tenth.

Solution:

$$\frac{\$27,000 \times 365}{\$216,000} = 45.625 = 45.6 \quad days'\ sales\ uncollected$$

● Exercise 16–5

1. The following data were taken from the current statements of Wilburton Supply Company: accounts receivable, $208,000; Will Burton, Capital, $780,000; net income, $240,000; sales, $2,630,000; sales returns and allowances, $125,000; interest expense, $25,000; total assets, $1,836,000. Find each of the following to the nearest tenth: **(a)** net income to net sales, **(b)** return on total assets, and **(c)** turnover of accounts receivable.

2. The following data were taken from the current statements of Abadan Products Company: accounts receivable, $221,000; Jill Abadan, Capital, $803,000; net income, $160,000; sales, $1,870,000; sales returns and allowances, $238,000; interest expense, $37,000; total assets, $954,000. Find each of the following to the nearest tenth: **(a)** net income to owner's equity, **(b)** turnover of accounts receivable, and **(c)** number of days' sales uncollected.

3. Use the data presented in the 19X2 columns of Figure 16–7 and Figure 16–9 to compute **(a)** net income to net sales, **(b)** net income to owner's equity, **(c)** return on total assets, **(d)** turnover of accounts receivable, and **(e)** number of days' sales uncollected. Round to the nearest tenth.

Part 4. Mathematics Applications in Analyzing a Business

Olney Distributing Company
Comparative Income Statement
For Years Ended December 31, 19X2 and 19X1

	19X2	19X1
Revenue:		
Sales.....	$4,750,000	$3,100,000
Less sales returns and allowances	250,000	100,000
Net sales.....	$4,500,000	$3,000,000
Less cost of goods sold:		
Cost of goods sold	2,925,000	1,800,000
Gross profit on sales.....	$1,575,000	$1,200,000
Operating expenses:		
Selling expense.....	$ 950,000	$ 550,000
General expense	460,000	450,000
Total operating expenses	$1,410,000	$1,000,000
Net operating income.....	$ 165,000	$ 200,000
Other expense:		
Interest expense.....	30,000	36,000
Net income.....	$ 135,000	$ 164,000

Figure 16-9 Comparative Income Statement for Olney Distributing Company

4. Use the data presented in the 19X1 columns of Figure 16–7 and Figure 16–9 to compute **(a)** net income to net sales, **(b)** net income to owner's equity, **(c)** return on total assets, **(d)** turnover of accounts receivable, and **(e)** number of days' sales uncollected. Round to the nearest tenth.

REVIEW PROBLEMS

Solve these problems. If you have difficulty solving any problem, restudy the appropriate section in this chapter. The problems under a specific number are related to those contained in the exercise with the same last number.

1. During a recent year, Highland Distributors, Inc., had sales of $758,000. At the beginning of the year, the goods on hand totaled $48,318, and at the end of the year, they totaled $61,625. Purchases during the year amounted to $598,640. Operating expenses included the following: salaries, $62,418; depreciation, $10,262; advertising, $5,030; and miscellaneous, $4,824. Find the percent of net sales to which each of the following is equal: **(a)** cost of goods sold, **(b)** gross profit, **(c)** total operating expenses, and **(d)** net income.

2. The following data were taken from the balance sheet of Rockford Company: current assets, $253,500; fixed assets, $573,000; current liabilities, $153,000; long-term liabilities, $249,600; and proprietorship, $423,900.

Chapter 16. Analyses of Financial Statements

Find the percent of total assets to which each of the following is equal: **(a)** current assets, **(b)** fixed assets, **(c)** current liabilities, **(d)** long-term liabilities, and **(e)** proprietorship.

3. Use the data shown in Figure 16–4 to compute **(a)** the working capital, **(b)** the current ratio, **(c)** the acid-test ratio, **(d)** the owner's equity to creditors' equity ratio, and **(e)** the fixed assets to long-term liabilities ratio. Round the ratios to the nearest hundredth.

4. Use the following data to compute the merchandise turnover:

Sales		$547,500
Merchandise inventory, January 1, 19--	$ 62,100	
Purchases	388,350	
Goods available for sale	$450,450	
Merchandise inventory, December 31, 19--	58,500	
Cost of goods sold		391,950
Gross profit on sales		$155,550

5. **a.** The data presented below were taken from the financial staetments of Veloz Corporation:

Current assets	$840,000	
Fixed assets	810,000	$1,650,000
Current liabilities	$150,000	
Long-term liabilities	300,000	450,000
Owners' equity		1,200,000
Net sales		2,160,000
Net income		154,800
Interest expense		18,000

Find the following ratios: **(1)** owners' equity to creditors' equity, **(2)** fixed assets to long-term liabilities, **(3)** net income to net sales, **(4)** return on total assets, and **(5)** net income to owners' equity. Round to the nearest hundredth.

b. The following data were taken from the financial statements of a company:

Sales	$480,000
Sales returns and allowances	9,600
Accounts receivable, January 1, 19--	89,000
Accounts receivable, December 31, 19--	71,000

Find **(1)** the turnover of accounts receivable and **(2)** the number of days' sales uncollected. Round to the nearest hundredth.

Amanda Lemon owned two general merchandise super stores. On her death three years ago, the capital stock in the company was inherited by her two sons, Bob and Jim. As the two stores were comparable in capital and earnings, the brothers decided to split the company into two separate corporations. Bob owns 55% of the capital stock in BLM Corporation which operates the store located near St. Louis. Jim owns 55% of the capital stock in JLM Corporation which operates the store located near Tulsa.

At a recent meeting, Jim mentioned that the stockholders in his company were getting a larger rate of return than those in Bob's company. He suggested that Bob should utilize the equity of lenders to finance the expansion of his company. During the past two years, the growth in Bob's company has been financed by issuing common stock; the growth in Jim's, by borrowing.

The income statements for both companies for the past year are shown below followed by the balance sheets at the end of that year.

	JLM Corp.	BLM Corp.
Sales	$1,860,120	$1,775,250
Sales returns and allowances	18,720	17,550
Net sales	$1,841,400	$1,757,700
Cost of goods sold	1,104,840	1,054,620
Gross profit	$ 736,560	$ 703,080
Selling expenses	$ 338,220	$ 306,360
General expenses	182,160	164,970
Total operating expenses	$ 520,380	$ 471,330
Operating income	$ 216,180	$ 231,750
Interest expense	38,720	10,750
Net income before income tax	$ 177,460	$ 221,000

Assets	JLM Corp.	BLM Corp.
Cash	$ 44,520	$ 41,340
Accounts receivable	19,080	5,300
Plant assets	932,800	960,360
Total assets	$ 996,400	$1,007,000
Liabilities		
Current liabilities	$ 19,180	$ 19,610
Long-term liabilities	373,120	80,030
Total liabilities	$ 392,300	$ 99,640
Stockholders' Equity		
Common stock ($10 par value)	$ 106,000	$ 530,000
Retained earnings	498,100	377,360
Total stockholders' equity	$ 604,100	$ 907,360
Total liabilities and stockholders' equity	$ 996,400	$1,007,000

a. Compute the following for both corporations:

    (1) Ratio of plant assets to long-term liabilities

    (2) Ratio of stockholders' equity to creditors' equity

    (3) Ratio of net sales to total assets

    (4) Rate earned on total assets

    (5) Rate earned on owners' equity

    (6) The book value per share of stock

b. Explain why in both companies the rate earned on stockholders' equity is greater than the rate earned on total assets.

c. Explain why the rate of return on stockholders' equity for JLM Corporation is significantly greater than that for BLM Corporation.

d. Comment on Jim's suggestion that Bob should borrow funds for BLM Corporation rather than issue more shares of stock.

Chapter 17

Statistics and Graphs

Objectives

After mastering the material in Chapter 17, you will be able to:

- Organize numerical data.
- Compute measures of central tendency: arithmetic mean, median, and mode.
- Find the square root of a number.
- Calculate measures of dispersion: range, quartile deviation, and standard deviation.
- Prepare line, bar, and circle graphs to illustrate numerical data.

STATISTICS

Statistics is a branch of mathematics that deals with the collection, analysis, interpretation, and presentation of quantities of numerical data. The analyses of the statistical data of a company range from interpreting simple accounting records and reports to solving complex statistical formulas.

Organization of Numerical Data

To facilitate interpretation and analysis, statistical data must be arranged in an orderly manner. There are two principal methods of arranging numerical data. In one method, each of the various values is presented in order of size. This arrangement is an **array.** In the other arrangement, called a **frequency distribution,** the values are grouped to show the frequency with which each size or class occurs. For example, the numbers 60, 50, 54, 60, 47, 56, 60, 54, 50, 67, 60, and 54, which represent the number of articles produced by twelve workers in a plant, have less meaning when presented in this unorganized manner than when presented in an array (Figure 17–1) or in a frequency distribution (Figure 17–2). The difference between the smallest and the largest value in a set of data is the **range.** Notice that the range of 20 (67–47) is more apparent in the array or in the frequency distribution than in the unorganized data. Furthermore, the number of times that each value occurs is more apparent in the frequency distribution than in the array.

Value
67
60
60
60
60
56
54
54
54
50
50
47

Number of
Values: 12

Figure 17–1 An Array

Value	Frequency
67	1
60	4
56	1
54	3
50	2
47	1
Total	12

Figure 17–2 A Frequency Distribution Without Class Intervals

When a large number of varying values are to be presented, they may be grouped to show the number of times sizes occur within size classes. For example, Figure 17–3 shows the number of articles produced by fifty workers in a plant.

Number of Articles (Class)	Number of Workers (Frequency)
76–80	3
71–75	12
66–70	18
61–65	9
56–60	6
51–55	2
Total	(N) 50

Figure 17–3 A Frequency Distribution With Class Intervals

The smallest and the largest values possible within a given class are the **class limits.** The size of each class is the **class interval,** which may be defined as the range between the higher limits of two adjoining classes. The class interval in Figure 17–3 is 5 (60 − 55 = 5).

The point that is halfway between the class limits is the **midpoint.** The lowest class limits in Figure 17–3 are 51–55, and the midpoint of that class is 53. When it is not obvious by inspection, the midpoint can be found by dividing the sum of the limits in the class by 2. For example:

$$\frac{51 + 55}{2} = \frac{106}{2} = 53 \quad \text{midpoint}$$

Measures of Central Tendency (Averages)

An **average** is a single value that is used to represent a group of values. There are several different kinds of averages. Since one kind of average may be more representative of a specific set of values than another kind, one should understand the nature of each kind. The three most commonly used averages are the arithmetic mean, the median, and the mode.

Arithmetic Mean. The most common average is the **arithmetic mean.** This is found by adding the values and dividing the sum by the number of values. (See Chapter 1.) Multiplication is a shortcut method of adding. Therefore, each value shown in a frequency distribution without class intervals is multiplied by the frequency of that value, and the products obtained are added together to find the sum of the values. This sum is then divided by the number of values to find the mean.

Example A: Find the arithmetic mean of the values shown in Figure 17–2.

Solution:

Value (v)	Frequency (f)	Product (vf)
67	1	67
60	4	240
56	1	56
54	3	162
50	2	100
47	1	47
Total	12	672

672 ÷ 12 = 56   mean

When the values are presented in a frequency distribution with class intervals, the midpoint of a class is used as the value of that class. Each midpoint is multiplied by the frequency of the class, and the products are added to find the sum of the values. The mean is found by dividing the sum of the products by the number of values.

Chapter 17. Statistics and Graphs

To the nearest tenth, find the arithmetic mean of the values shown in Figure 17–3.

Solution:

Number of Articles (Class)	Number of Workers (f)	Midpoint of Class (m)	Product (fm)
76–80	3	78	234
71–75	12	73	876
66–70	18	68	1,224
61–65	9	63	567
56–60	6	58	348
51–55	2	53	106
Total	50		3,355

$3{,}355 \div 50 = 67.1$ mean

The arithmetic mean is affected by every item in a set of values. Undue weight, therefore, may be given to extreme items. The arithmetic mean should be used only to represent data that are relatively homogeneous.

Median. The value found at the midpoint of an ordered set of values is the **median.** In other words, it is the value in an array below and above which there are an equal number of values. If the number of values in an array is odd, the median is the middle value. For example, the median of the values 3, 4, 7, 9, and 14 is 7, which is preceded by two values and followed by two values. If the number of values is even, the median is the value midway between the two middle values. The number of values that lie above and below the median may be found by dividing the number of values in the distribution by 2; that is, $\frac{n}{2}$.

Example A:

Find the median of the values shown in Figure 17–1.

Solution:

$\frac{n}{2} = \frac{12}{2} = 6$

Thus, 6 values must lie above and 6 values must lie below the median. The sixth value from the bottom is 54 and the sixth from the top is 56. Therefore,

$$\frac{54 + 56}{2} = 55 \quad \text{median}$$

As with ungrouped data, the median of data that are grouped in classes is considered to be at the point in the distribution below which half (50%) of the data will fall and above which half will be located. On the assumption that the values are spread evenly through the units of the class interval, the median is considered to be located a proportionate distance above the lower limit of the designated class. Because there are 50 values in Figure 17–3 (Example B below), the median is considered to be at the point below which 25 values lie and above which 25 values lie.

Example B:

To the nearest tenth, find the median of the values shown in Figure 17–3.

Solution:

1. Find the number of values that must lie above and below the median.

$$\frac{n}{2} = \frac{50}{2} = 25$$

2. Find the class within which the median falls by counting $\frac{n}{2}$ frequencies from the bottom of the frequency column.

$$2 + 6 + 9 = 17$$

Since 8 more values are needed to make 25, the median lies within the 18 values in the Class 66–70.

3. Find the amount to be added to the lower limit of that class by prorating the class interval. Of the 18 items, 8 (that is, $25 - 17$) must fall below the median, and the class interval is 5. Therefore, the amount to be added to the lower limit of the class is $\frac{8}{18} \times 5$, which is 2.222. . .

4. Find the estimated median by adding the amount found in Step 3 to the lower limit of the class.

$$66 + 2.2 = 68.2 \quad \text{median}$$

The solution to Example B above may be summarized in the following formula in which L is the lower limit of the class that the median must be in, p is the number of values to be counted above L, f is the frequency, and c is the class interval.

$$\text{Median of Distribution} = L + \frac{p}{f} c$$

Thus, the solution to Example B may be written as follows:

$$\text{Median of Distribution} = 66 + \left(\frac{8}{18} \times 5 \right) = 66 + 2.2 = 68.2$$

The accuracy of the median of a distribution may be checked by using an alternate method in which one counts down from the top of the frequency distribution rather than up from the bottom. Notice that there are 15 (3 + 12) values in the two top classes of Figure 17–3. These 15 values subtracted from 25 mean that 10 values must lie below the lower limit in the Class 71–75. Therefore:

$$\text{Median of Distribution} = 71 - \left(\frac{10}{18} \times 5 \right) = 71 - 2.8 = 68.2$$

When the median is used as an average, no more weight is given to an extreme item than to one near the median. Extreme items are not likely to make the median less representative of the data when there are a large number of items in the set. If there are only a few items, however, the median may not be representative.

Mode. The value that occurs the greatest number of times in a given set of data is the **mode.** For example, in the set of 2, 5, 5, 5, 8, 10, 14, and 17, the mode is 5 because it is the most common value. There may be no mode in the set; for example, the set 3, 4, 6, 7 has no mode. On the other hand, a set of data may have more than one mode. In the set 5, 7, 7, 9, 11, 11, 15 there are two modes, 7 and 11, and the set is said to be **bimodal.**

Chapter 17. Statistics and Graphs

In a frequency distribution without class intervals, the mode is the value that occurs most frequently. In Figure 17–2, for example, 60 is the mode. In frequency distributions that have class intervals, the **modal class** is usually considered to be the class with the most frequencies. The midpoint of the modal class serves satisfactorily as the mode. In Figure 17–3, the modal class is 66–70, and the midpoint of 68 may be used as the mode. The mode of data grouped in classes is seldom used unless the modal class is well defined.

Using the mode is desirable when one wishes to eliminate the effects of extreme items. Both the mode and the median are "position" averages. Neither should be considered to be very significant unless there are several values in the set of data.

● Exercise 17–1

1. Find **(a)** the range, **(b)** the mean, **(c)** the median, and **(d)** the mode of the following numbers: 69.4, 79, 67.3, 70.1, 68.8, 79.4, 70.3, 67.7, 68.8.

2. The following data represent the miles traveled by 12 students who commute from home to college: 19, 10, 3, 28, 21, 9, 21, 33, 28, 13, 16, 21. Find **(a)** the range, **(b)** the mean, **(c)** the median, and **(d)** the mode.

3. To the nearest tenth, find **(a)** the mean, **(b)** the median, and **(c)** the mode of the following set of numbers: 412, 499, 412, 499, 388, 499, 412, 388, 499, 388.

4. Find **(a)** the mean, **(b)** the median, and **(c)** the mode of the following set of numbers: 788, 254, 258, 254, 170, 466, 254, 547, 258.

5. To the nearest tenth of a pound, find **(a)** the mean, **(b)** the median, and **(c)** the mode of the weights of the following candidates for a high school track team:

Weight Class	Frequency
211–225	3
196–210	12
181–195	28
166–180	14
151–165	2
Total	59

6. To the nearest cent, find **(a)** the mean, **(b)** the median, and **(c)** the mode of the January sales made by certain employees of Danbury Company. A recent survey reveals the following data:

January Sales	Frequency
$18,000–$19,999	5
16,000– 17,999	39
14,000– 15,999	74
12,000– 13,999	46
10,000– 11,999	9

7. The following numbers represent the articles produced by a group of workers in one day:

21	30	6	27	11	29	30	21	30	15
7	12	21	20	6	8	21	30	24	20
11	26	16	22	19	26	22	26	29	30
26	25	15	21	14	25	24	21	24	

Use the following classes to prepare a frequency distribution: 6–10, 11–15, 16–20, 21–25, and 26–30. To the nearest unit, find **(a)** the mean and **(b)** the median of the frequency distribution.

8. A class of business mathematics students made the following scores on a test:

95	80	95	77	80	74	85	86
81	90	94	55	59	88	67	52
72	66	72	60	67	78	89	96
53	83	58	78	68	81	61	76

Use the following classes to prepare a frequency distribution: 91–100, 81–90, 71–80, 61–70, 51–60. To the nearest tenth, find **(a)** the mean and **(b)** the median of the frequency distribution.

Square Root of a Number

The **root** of a number is an equal factor of that number. In $2^3 = 2 \times 2 \times 2 = 8$, 2 is the **cube root** of 8 and, conversely, 8 is the **cube** of 2. Likewise, in $5^2 = 5 \times 5 = 25$, 5 is the square root of 25 and 25 is the **square** of 5. As 5^2 is exactly 25, 25 is the **perfect square** of 5. The **square root** of any number may be defined as one of the two equal factors of that number. Thus, 5 is one of the two equal factors in 25.

In each of the following, notice the number of digits in the square root and in its square:

(a)	(b)	(c)	(d)
$1^2 = 1$	$10^2 = 100$	$100^2 = 10,000$	$0.1^2 = 0.01$
$3^2 = 9$	$31^2 = 961$	$316^2 = 99,856$	$2.5^2 = 6.25$
$4^2 = 16$	$32^2 = 1,024$	$317^2 = 100,489$	$8.85^2 = 78.3225$
$9^2 = 81$	$99^2 = 9,801$	$999^2 = 998,001$	$41.23^2 = 1,699.9129$

Column (a) shows that the square root of a one- or two-digit number contains one digit, column (b) shows that the square root of a three- or four-digit number contains two digits, and column (c) shows that the square root of a five- or six-digit number contains three digits. Thus, the square root of 46,412 contains three digits. Similarly, column (d) shows that decimals produce squares that contain twice as many digits to the right of the decimal point as there are to the right of the decimal point in the square root. Consequently, the square root of 72.0801 contains one digit to the left and two digits to the right of the decimal point.

Certain statistical computations require that square roots be found. The radical sign ($\sqrt{}$) is used to show that the square root of a number is to be found. For example, $\sqrt{64}$ may be read as "the square root of 64" and interpreted, "find the square root of 64."

Using a Calculator With $\boxed{\sqrt{x}}$ **Key to Find the Square Root.** Many pocket calculators have a $\boxed{\sqrt{x}}$ key. When pressed, this key operation finds the square root of the number in display. The check to the solution in the following example shows that 43.2 is the perfect square root of 1,866.24.

Example:

Find the square root of 1,866.24.

Solution:

1866.24 $\boxed{\sqrt{x}}$ $\rightarrow$ 43.2

Check: 43.2 $\boxed{\times}$ $\boxed{=}$ $\rightarrow$ 1866.24

Finding the Square Root Without $\boxed{\sqrt{x}}$ **Key.** Notice that $4^2 = 16$ and $16 \div 4 = 4$; that $5^2 = 25$ and $25 \div 5 = 5$; and that $6^2 = 36$ and $36 \div 6 = 6$. These illustrate that when a square is divided by its square root the quotient equals the square root. This is the basis for the **quotient-average** method of finding square roots on a calculator without the $\boxed{\sqrt{x}}$ key.

Example A:

Find the square root of 38 by the quotient-average method.

Solution:

1. Because $6^2 = 36$ and $7^2 = 49$, the square root of 38 falls between 6 and 7. As the given number 38 is closer to 36 than to 49, the square root is closer to 6 than to 7. Select an estimate of the square root, such as 6.2.

2. Divide the estimate into the given number.

   38 $\boxed{\div}$ 6.2 $\boxed{=}$ $\rightarrow$ 6.1290322   quotient

3. Average the quotient and the estimate to get a new estimate.

   6.1290322 $\boxed{+}$ 6.2 $\boxed{\div}$ 2 $\boxed{=}$ $\rightarrow$ 6.164516   new estimate

4. Use the new estimate in Steps 2 and 3.

   38 $\boxed{\div}$ 6.164516 $\boxed{=}$ $\rightarrow$ 6.164312   new quotient

   6.164312 $\boxed{+}$ 6.164516 $\boxed{\div}$ 2 $\boxed{=}$ $\rightarrow$ 6.164414   new quotient

5. Repeat the process until desired accuracy is obtained.

   38 $\boxed{\div}$ 6.164414 $\boxed{=}$ $\rightarrow$ 6.164414   same as divisor

   Check: 6.164414 $\boxed{\times}$ $\boxed{=}$ $\rightarrow$ 37.999. . .,   so 6.164414 is not the perfect square root of 38. However, it is as accurate as possible when an eight-digit calculator is used.

Recall that a number containing three or four whole digits has a two-digit square root. Therefore, the first estimate of the square root of 586.9605 (Example B) should be a two-digit number. As $20^2 = 400$ and $25^2 = 625$, the square root of 586.9605 must fall closer to 25 than to 20.

Example B: Find $\sqrt{586.9605}$ to the nearest hundredth.

Solution: 1. Select an estimate of the square root, perhaps 24.

2. Divide the estimate into the given number.

586.9605 ⟦ ÷ ⟧ 24 ⟦ = ⟧ → 24.456687   quotient

3. Average the quotient and the estimate to get a new estimate.

24.456687 ⟦ + ⟧ 24 ⟦ ÷ ⟧ 2 ⟦ = ⟧ → 24.228343   new estimate

4. Repeat the process until desired accuracy is obtained.

586.9605 ⟦ ÷ ⟧ 24.228343 ⟦ = ⟧ → 24.226192   new quotient

Notice that the new estimate (24.228343) and the quotient (24.226192) both round to 24.23 in hundredths.

Check: 24.23 ⟦ × ⟧ ⟦ = ⟧ → 587.0929, so 24.23 is not the perfect square root of 586.9605. However, its accuracy to the nearest hundredth satisfies the problem.

● Exercise 17–2

Find the square root of each of the following. Where applicable, round to the nearest hundredth.

1. 784	**4.** 746,496	**7.** 148.996	**10.** 238
2. 1,849	**5.** 3,398.89	**8.** 646.53433	**11.** 973
3. 18,769	**6.** 87.0489	**9.** 45	**12.** 572

Measures of Dispersion

Obtaining representative values of data other than measures of central tendency is sometimes desirable. **Measures of dispersion** may be computed to measure the spread of the data, to detemine whether the average is representative of the data, or to find the extent to which the data vary from the average. The three most common measures of dispersion are the range, the quartile deviation, and the standard deviation.

Range. In an earlier section of this chapter, the range is defined as the difference between the smallest and the largest values in a set of data. The range is usually most significant when there are no extreme items in the data. For example, a range of 40 is more significant for the numbers 60, 70, 80, 90, 100 than for the numbers 60, 62, 65, 70, 100.

Quartile Deviation. When the values in an array are divided into four equal parts (quarters), the values at the division points are called **quartiles.** Quartiles are numbered from the low end of the values. Thus, the first quartile (Q_1) is the value at the point below which one-fourth of the total number of values lie, the second quartile (Q_2) and the median are identical, and the third quartile (Q_3) is the value that divides the lower three-fourths of the values from the upper one-fourth. Deciles and percentiles are similar to quartiles except that they are found by dividing the number of values into 10 and 100 parts respectively.

Unlike the range, the quartile deviation (QD) is not affected by the size of extreme items, for it measures the spread of the central items only. The **quartile deviation** is the difference between the first quartile and the third quartile divided by two. The formula for this computation is:

$$QD = \frac{Q_3 - Q_1}{2}$$

Example:

Find **(a)** the first quartile, **(b)** the second quartile, **(c)** the third quartile, and **(d)** the quartile deviation for this set of numbers: 8, 4, 3, 7, 6, 12, 10, 27, 19, 16, 14, 23.

Solution:

(a) Prepare an array. Q_1 is the value at the point on the scale of values below which one-fourth of the values lie. Since there are 12 items and $\frac{1}{4}$ of 12 is 3, the first quartile lies between the third and fourth smallest values. Therefore, Q_1 is the midpoint between the values 6 and 7, which is 6.5.

(b) Q_2 is the median, the value above and below which an equal number of the values lie. Since $\frac{1}{2}$ of 12 is 6, the value of Q_2 lies halfway between the central values of 10 and 12. The value is 11.

(c) Q_3 is the value at the point below which $\frac{3}{4}$ of the items lie. As $\frac{3}{4}$ of 12 is 9, the value of Q_3 lies halfway between 16 and 19. The value is 17.5.

$$
\begin{array}{c}
27 \\
23 \\
\rightarrow \quad \dfrac{19}{16} \quad Q_3 = \dfrac{16 + 19}{2} = 17.5 \\
14 \\
\rightarrow \quad \dfrac{12}{10} \quad Q_2 = \dfrac{10 + 12}{2} = 11 \\
8 \\
\rightarrow \quad \dfrac{7}{6} \quad Q_1 = \dfrac{6 + 7}{2} = 6.5 \\
4 \\
3
\end{array}
$$

(d) $QD = \dfrac{Q_3 - Q_1}{2} = \dfrac{17.5 - 6.5}{2} = \dfrac{11}{2} = 5.5$

Standard Deviation. The **deviation** of a value is its distance from the mean of the distribution. The **standard deviation** (s) is a common measurement of the variation or spread of all the values from a central point in a distribution.

The deviations of values above the mean in an array are considered to be positive; those below, negative. The amount of deviation is more important than the direction of deviation because the deviations are squared and the signs eliminated. The square root of the arithmetic mean of the squared deviations is

516

Part 4. Mathematics Applications in Analyzing a Business

the standard deviation. More explicitly, to compute the standard deviation of an array:

1. Find the amount by which each value deviates from the mean by finding the difference between the value and the mean. Deviations above the mean are positive; those below, negative.
2. Square each deviation.
3. Find the mean of the squares by dividing the sum of the squares by the number of values.
4. Find the standard deviation by finding the square root of the mean found in Step 3.

In formula form, the procedure of computing the standard deviation may be written as follows:

$$s = \sqrt{\frac{\Sigma d^2}{n}}$$

In the formula, Σ is the Greek letter sigma and should be read "the sum of." Thus, Σd^2 is the sum of the squared deviations from the mean and n is the number of items in the set of data.

Example A: To the nearest unit, find **(a)** the standard deviation of this set of data: 4, 6, 8, 15, 17 and **(b)** the number of values within plus or minus one standard deviation ($\pm 1s$) of the mean.

Solution: **a.** Mean $= \dfrac{50}{5} = 10$

Item (Value)	Deviation from Mean (d)	Deviation Squared (d^2)
17	+7	49
15	+5	25
8	−2	4
6	−4	16
4	−6	36
50		130

$$s = \sqrt{\frac{130}{5}} = \sqrt{26} = 5.0990195 = 5$$

b. The mean $-1s = 10 - 5 = 5$; the mean $+1s = 10 + 5 = 15$. The number of values within $\pm 1s$ of the mean (from 10 to 15): 3. (The values are 6, 8, 15.)

When the values are shown in a frequency distribution, the formula is

$$s = \sqrt{\frac{\Sigma f d^2}{n}}$$

in which f is the frequency of appearance. If the data appear in a frequency distribution with class intervals, the midpoint of each class interval is used to find the deviation of each class from the mean.

Example B: Find the standard deviation of the following frequency distribution.

Number of Articles (Class)	Number of Workers (f)	Midpoint of Class (m)	mf	Deviation from Mean (d)	Deviation Squared (d²)	fd²
76–80	3	78	234	+13	169	507
71–75	6	73	438	+8	64	384
66–70	12	68	816	+3	9	108
61–65	18	63	1,134	−2	4	72
56–60	9	58	522	−7	49	441
51–55	2	53	106	−12	144	288
Total	50		3,250			1,800

Solution: $\text{Mean} = \dfrac{3,250}{50} = 65; \ s = \sqrt{\dfrac{1,800}{50}} = \sqrt{36} = 6$

In a normal distribution of values, approximately 68.3% of the values fall within plus or minus one (± 1) standard deviation from the mean, and about 95.4% of the values fall within ± 2 standard deviations from the mean. Thus, when the values in a distribution are considered to be similar to a normal distribution, the proportional range of the values can be determined if the mean and the standard deviation are known.

When the standard deviation is small, the values are relatively homogeneous and spaced near the mean. If the standard deviation is large, the values are widely scattered from the mean. Thus, the larger the standard deviation, the greater is the spread or dispersion of the values from the mean.

● **Exercise 17–3**

1. The following numbers represent the number of years that a group of 8 employees have worked for Eagle Grove Company: 14, 10, 20, 6, 25, 30, 23, and 16. Find **(a)** the quartile deviation and **(b)** the standard deviation.

2. The weight in pounds of each of 8 members of the swim team is 140, 164, 174, 150, 178, 176, 185, and 209. To the nearest hundredth, find **(a)** the quartile deviation and **(b)** the standard deviation.

3. The units produced by 12 workers are 190, 210, 200, 215, 183, 225, 192, 218, 220, 237, 194, and 212. To the nearest hundredth, find **(a)** the quartile deviation and **(b)** the standard deviation.

4. Sixteen students made the following scores on a business mathematics test: 61, 75, 68, 64, 70, 85, 84, 88, 83, 95, 90, 97, 92, 100, 82, 62. To the nearest hundredth, find **(a)** the quartile deviation and **(b)** the standard deviation.

5. Use the following frequency distribution to find **(a)** the mean and **(b)** the standard deviation to the nearest hundredth.

Part 4. Mathematics Applications in Analyzing a Business

Class	Frequency
36–40	4
31–35	6
26–30	12
21–25	10
16–20	6
11–15	2

6. The scores made on a test by the students in a business mathematics class were:

96	91	83	80	55	72	74	64
66	63	73	84	65	93	81	77
68	67	58	95	66	86	66	82
84	97	76	78	74	75	79	70

Use the following classes to prepare a frequency distribution: 91–100, 81–90, 71–80, 61–70, 51–60. To the nearest tenth, find **(a)** the mean and **(b)** the standard deviation from the mean of the frequency distribution. **(c)** How many of the actual scores fall within ± 1 standard deviation from the mean? **(d)** How many of the actual scores fall within ± 2 standard deviations from the mean?

GRAPHS

Interpreting the interrelationships of data that have been collected and presented in tables is often quite difficult. Furthermore, after careful study and analysis, even an expert may experience difficulty in conveying to another person that the interpretation is correct. Many sound plans are rejected merely because the facts are not presented clearly. The busy executive appreciates the presentation of statistical data in a form that will permit one to grasp easily and quickly the essential points. In short, to obtain maximum results, the most effective methods of presenting data should be used. Tables of data are usually more precise, but properly prepared graphs can bring out facts that may remain hidden in tables or masses of data. A **graph** is a diagram composed of a series of points, a line, a curve, or an area that represents a variable in comparison with that of one or more other variables. Graphs, therefore, are used for presenting many kinds of statistical data and are recognized as effective supplements to tables of data.

Although a reasonable degree of accuracy is necessary, a graph usually cannot be as exact as a table. The degree of accuracy in a graph, however, must be such that visual comparisons are not impaired. When figures are rounded for practical purposes of graphic presentation, care should be exerted to provide this degree of accuracy.

In planning the construction of a graph, its purpose must be kept clearly in mind. The type of graph chosen should then be the one that will enable the reader to comprehend the essential points most easily and clearly. The types of graphs that are chosen most frequently are line graphs, bar graphs, and circle graphs.

Line Graphs

The graph that is adaptable to a greater variety of uses than any other is the line graph. Probably its most common use is in presenting historical data. In this presentation, equal spaces on the horizontal axis of the graph represent equal time intervals, such as weeks, months, or years. When used, time should read from left to right beneath the horizontal scale.

A fundamental rule in preparing line or bar graphs that show comparison of size is that the scale begin with zero. When this rule is not followed, the values are inaccurately represented. On occasion, however, breaking the scale may be advisable. In this case, the zero should be shown and a pair of wavy lines drawn across the face of the graph at the position where the scale is broken.

After the data have been assembled and checked for accuracy, follow these procedures to construct a line graph:

1. Use graph paper if available. If not, show interval lines on plain paper.
2. Show the time element from left to right beneath the horizontal axis and quantity or value at the left of the vertical axis starting with zero at the bottom.
3. Select a size (such as 2, 5, 10, 25, or their multiples) that is convenient for plotting the data in uniform intervals on the vertical scale.
4. Place a dot on the graph at each point where the time and quantity relationships intersect. To do this, count up from the horizontal scale to the appropriate quantity for each time period.
5. Use a straight edge to connect the dots with a solid or broken line.
6. Give the graph a brief but descriptive title and show the legend if any.

When two or more variables are plotted in one graph, lines of different colors or of dashes or dots may be used.

Example:

Use the data shown in the following condensed comparative income statement of Huron Company to prepare a multiple line graph.

HURON COMPANY
Condensed Comparative Income Statement
for Years 19X0–19X9

Year	Net Sales	Cost of Goods Sold	Expenses	Net Income
19X0	$300,000	$180,000	$ 95,000	$25,000
19X1	295,000	175,000	90,000	30,000
19X2	285,000	175,000	81,000	29,000
19X3	315,000	188,000	100,000	27,000
19X4	380,000	225,000	115,000	40,000
19X5	397,000	243,000	124,000	30,000
19X6	475,000	305,000	145,000	25,000
19X7	455,000	275,000	135,000	45,000
19X8	428,000	263,000	132,000	33,000
19X9	395,000	247,000	120,000	28,000

Solution:

See Figure 17–4.

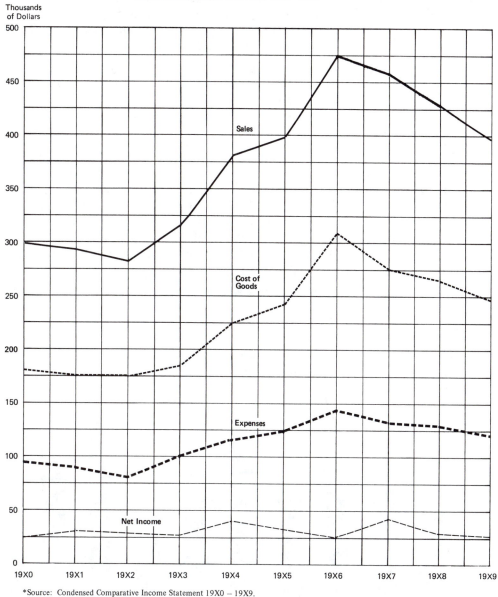

HURON COMPANY
Sales, Costs, Expenses, and Net Income 19X0 — 19X9*

Thousands
of Dollars

Sales

Cost of
Goods

Expenses

Net Income

19X0   19X1   19X2   19X3   19X4   19X5   19X6   19X7   19X8   19X9

*Source: Condensed Comparative Income Statement 19X0 — 19X9.

Figure 17–4 A Multiple Line Graph

Bar Graphs

Although they may be used to represent data in time series, bar graphs are most commonly used to show simple comparisons of size. The bars used in such graphs may be heavy lines or rectangles of equal width. The length of each bar corresponds to the size of the data represented.

Vertical and Horizontal Bar Graphs. There is no particular rule for choosing between vertical or horizontal bars, except that only vertical bars should be used to show a time series.

After the data have been assembled and checked for accuracy, follow the procedures listed below to prepare a bar graph:

1. Use graph paper if available. Otherwise show interval lines on plain paper.
2. Select a scale that will facilitate the interpretation of the graph.
3. If one element is time, locate it on the horizontal axis. If one element is value and the other quantity, place quantity on the horizontal axis.
4. Place the vertical and horizontal scales on the graph and draw the equally spaced bars in proportion to the data being represented.
5. Give the graph a brief but descriptive title and show the legend if any.

Example: Use the data in the Net Income column of the comparative income statement shown in the preceding example to prepare a bar graph.

Solution: See Figure 17–5.

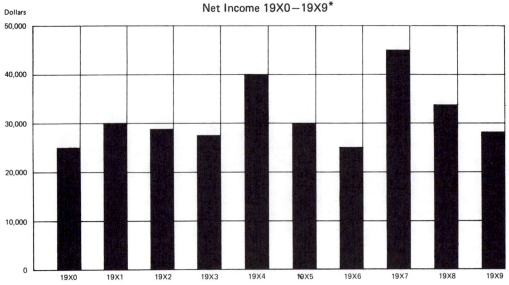

Figure 17–5 A Bar Graph

Part 4. Mathematics Applications in Analyzing a Business

Component Bar Graphs. An excellent means of presenting the component parts of a whole is the component bar graph. Each bar in the graph is divided into proportionate parts to represent the components in the data. Because of the difficulty of comparing one circular area with another, the component bar is better than the circle when the size of a component is to be compared to that of a similar one in another aggregate. Having only a few components in each bar aids interpretation.

Example:
Shelton's Clothing Store had sales as listed below during June. Prepare a component bar graph that shows the cash, credit, and total sales for each department.

Department	Cash Sales	Credit Sales	Total Sales
Men's Wear	$28,000	$20,000	$48,000
Women's Wear	14,000	24,000	38,000
Shoes	16,000	8,000	24,000

Solution:
See Figure 17–6.

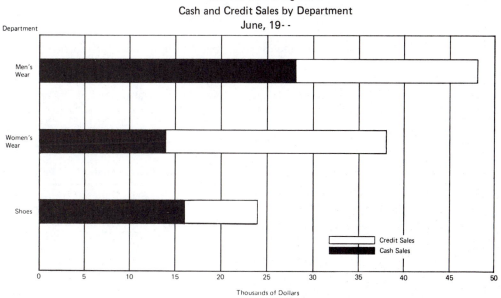

Figure 17–6 A Component Bar Graph

Circle Graphs

In comparing components on the basis of the percentage distribution, the bar graph and circle graph are about equally effective. The circle graph, however, is probably used more frequently to show the percentage comparison of component parts. Circle graphs, which are often called "pie charts," can be made more effective by coloring or shading the sectors. Usually the sectors are arranged in order of size, from large to small. Horizontal wording should be placed within the sectors when there is sufficient space to do so. If several percentages are to be shown in one graph, the circle should be large enough to show each part clearly.

After the data have been assembled and checked for accuracy, follow these steps to construct a circle graph:

1. Draw a circle of appropriate size.

2. Convert each part of the data to a percent of the whole.

3. Since there are 360° in a circle, multiply 360° by the percent of each component. (One percent is the equivalent of 3.6°. If $1 is used as the base, 1¢ = 3.6°.)

4. Use a protractor to divide the circle into sectors so that each arc corresponds to the number of degrees needed to represent the component.

5. Label the sectors and give the graph a short, descriptive title.

Example:

The capital structure of Villanova Power Company at the end of the year is shown below. Prepare a circle graph based on the data.

	Millions of Dollars	Percent
Long-Term Liabilities	$ 66,740	47%
Preferred Stock	21,300	15%
Common Stock and Retained Earnings	53,960	38%
Total	$142,000	100%

Solution:

Long-Term Liabilities	47% × 360° =	169.2°
Preferred Stock	15% × 360° =	54.0°
Common Stock and Retained Earnings	38% × 360° =	136.8°
Total	100%	360.0°

Part 4. Mathematics Applications in Analyzing a Business

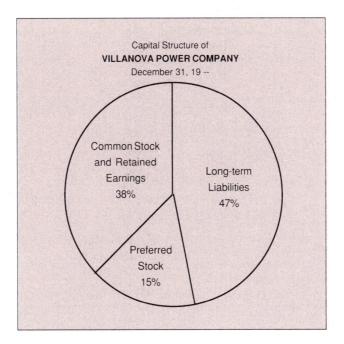

Capital Structure of
VILLANOVA POWER COMPANY
December 31, 19 --

Common Stock
and Retained
Earnings
38%

Long-term
Liabilities
47%

Preferred
Stock
15%

Figure 17–7 A Circle Graph

● Exercise 17–4

1. Use the data below to prepare a line graph. Show a solid line for *Sales* and a broken line for *Costs and Expenses*.

Cherokee Corporation
Sales, Costs and Expenses
for the Years 19X1–19X5

Year	Sales	Costs and Expenses
19X1	$250,000	$175,000
19X2	200,000	300,000
19X3	275,000	225,000
19X4	300,000	250,000
19X5	325,000	300,000

2. Use the data below to prepare a bar graph.

Lees Products Co., Inc.
Units Produced
for the Years 19X1–19X5

Year	Number of Units
19X1	75,000
19X2	100,000
19X3	80,000
19X4	60,000
19X5	85,000

3. Prepare a circle graph to illustrate the distribution of manufacturing costs of Ellsworth Company for the past year.

Raw Materials	45%
Direct Labor	25%
Overhead	30%

4. Use the data below to prepare a component bar graph.

Middlesex Sales Company
Cash and Credit Sales
for the Months January–May 19––

Month	Cash	Credit	Total
January	$30,000	$25,000	$55,000
February	25,000	40,000	65,000
March	20,000	30,000	50,000
April	35,000	35,000	70,000
May	40,000	30,000	70,000

5. Use the following data to prepare a line graph that shows the Berkshire Corporation's earnings and dividends paid for the ten-year period.

Year	Net Income	Dividends Paid
19X0	$42,214,652	$24,476,000
19X1	53,633,721	30,540,000
19X2	52,630,604	24,503,600
19X3	66,773,723	34,606,700
19X4	48,900,480	25,712,000
19X5	45,927,990	26,331,000
19X6	48,135,396	30,945,300
19X7	46,762,900	22,994,200
19X8	42,946,632	31,365,000
19X9	75,244,623	33,912,000

6. Prepare a line graph that shows the Sales, Cost of Goods Sold, and Expenses of Keokuk Distributing Company for the past ten years.

Year	Sales	Cost of Goods Sold	Expenses
19X0	$416,000	$280,000	$107,000
19X1	484,000	310,000	148,000
19X2	520,000	320,000	185,000
19X3	470,000	290,000	160,000
19X4	560,000	340,000	178,000
19X5	600,000	370,000	207,000
19X6	660,000	390,000	214,000
19X7	714,000	440,000	230,000
19X8	897,000	520,000	265,000
19X9	816,000	470,000	252,000

7. Listed below are the sales of the Cascade Company for the first nine months of the year. Prepare a vertical bar graph that shows the sales for each month. Use vertical intervals of $50,000.

January	$105,000
February	75,000
March	135,000
April	210,000
May	165,000
June	120,000
July	90,000
August	130,000
September	180,000

8. Use the following data to prepare a horizontal component bar graph that shows the cash and credit sales of Simpson's Department Store for the past year.

Department	Cash Sales	Credit Sales
Furniture	$210,000	$565,000
Appliance	390,000	330,000
Carpeting	135,000	165,000
Hardware	110,000	40,000

9. The following data were extracted from the balance sheet of the Lima Technical Corporation. Use the data to prepare a circle graph to illustrate how the company was capitalized on December 31, 19--.

Bonds	$56,000,000
Preferred stock	40,000,000
Common stock	64,000,000

10. Use the data in the following condensed income statement to prepare a circle graph that shows the distribution of Ithaca Company's "sales dollar" for the past year.

Sales	$805,850
Cost of Goods Sold	$322,340
Operating Expenses	386,808
Net Income	96,702

REVIEW PROBLEMS

Solve these problems. If you have difficulty solving any problem, restudy the appropriate section in this chapter. The problems under a specific number are related to those contained in the exercise with the same last number.

1. a. Find **(1)** the range, **(2)** the mean, **(3)** the median, and **(4)** the mode of the following numbers: 78, 69, 56, 39, 69, 47, 88, 27, 60, 51, 65.

b. One portion of a marketing survey determined the ages of the respondents based on their birth dates. The respondents' ages were rounded to the nearest birthday at the time of the survey. To the nearest tenth, find **(1)** the mean, **(2)** the median, and **(3)** the mode of the following:

Age Group	Frequency
36–40	191
31–35	256
26–30	765
21–25	428
16–20	160
Total	1,800

2. Find the square root of each of the following numbers: **(a)** 676, **(b)** 168.764, **(c)** 598. Where applicable, round to the nearest hundredth.

3. a. The following numbers represent the number of articles produced by each worker in one department: 52, 66, 60, 53, 59, 64, 64, 70. To the nearest hundredth, find **(1)** the quartile deviation and **(2)** the standard deviation.

b. The test scores of the 500 people who took a recent U.S. Civil Service examination are shown in the following frequency distribution. To the nearest hundredth, find **(1)** the mean and **(2)** the standard deviation.

Test Score	Frequency
91–100	14
81–90	120
71–80	240
61–70	104
51–60	22
Total	500

Part 4. Mathematics Applications in Analyzing a Business

4. a. The number of units distributed by New Haven Trailers, Inc., are shown below. Prepare a line graph based on the data.

Year	Number of Units	Year	Number of Units
19X0	525	19X5	1,200
19X1	660	19X6	1,340
19X2	800	19X7	1,290
19X3	930	19X8	1,230
19X4	1,000	19X9	1,400

b. The total sales during the past year for each of the four branches of Buena Vista Company are listed below. Prepare a horizontal bar graph that illustrates the data.

Branch	Sales
Westwood	$560,000
Lakewood	380,000
Eastland	740,000
Montclair	520,000

c. The Guinn family's monthly budget is as follows: food, $960; housing, $800; clothing, $320; insurance and savings, $480; charity, $224; recreation and miscellaneous, $416. Prepare a circle graph that shows the percent of each expenditure.

CHALLENGE PROBLEM

Below are the scores made on a mathematics test by the applicants for clerk-cashier positions at a new shopping mall that is to open soon.

Test Scores	Number of Applicants
100	1
95	5
90	8
85	12
80	13
75	21
70	13
65	10
60	7
55	5
50	3
	98

a. Compute the standard deviation of the distribution.

b. How many scores should one expect to find in a normal distribution of 98 scores between the following limits:

    1. Between $+1s$ and $-1s$?
    2. Between $+2s$ and $-2s$?
    3. Between $+1s$ and $+2s$?

c. How many scores actually fall within each of the limits in (b)?

d. Is the distribution nearly normal? Explain.

Part Five

Mathematics Applications for Investing in a Corporation

Individuals with extra funds may wish to invest those funds in stocks and bonds. Likewise, the administrators of a successful proprietorship, partnership, or corporation may wish to invest the extra funds of the company in order to maximize the company's return on the invested capital.

Because there is an element of risk in buying and selling securities, not all investors prosper. Nevertheless, over the years, the average investor has earned a reasonable return. Generally, investments have risen in value and have been protected from the risk of inflation. Just as some companies fail, some investors fail. The risk of loss through investing in securities can be lessened, however, by studying the fundamentals of buying and selling stocks and bonds.

Chapter 18

Investments in Securities

Objectives

After mastering the material in Chapter 18, you will be able to:
* Find the total investment when buying stocks and bonds.
* Determine the net proceeds from the sale of stocks and bonds.
* Compute the amount of gain or loss on the sale of stocks and bonds.
* Find the rate of gain or loss on an investment in stocks or bonds.

A broker called urging his client to buy stock in ABC Corporation because it was going to have extraordinary earnings. A few days later, the broker called to report that the client had lost 50 percent of the investment but shouldn't worry because the broker knew the money could be recovered by investing in the stock of another "hot" company — XYZ, Inc. Some weeks later, the broker called to report another loss of 50 percent but the investor should not be concerned because the broker had a "surefire" investment tip this time. The client interjected, "You know, a friend of mine recommends the bonds of Surething Corporation." The broker said, "Bonds! Gee, I don't know <u>anything</u> about *bonds*." — (Old joke told by investors.)

People who have more money than needed for the daily necessities of living can simply put it away in cookie jars or safe deposit boxes. By doing so, however, they are allowing the money to remain idle without being of use to anyone. Money has power — earning power that should be exercised.

A person who does not want extra money to lie dormant can do two things with it: (1) spend it, or (2) invest it. When one invests money, one expects to get it back, usually with income for its use. An investor may lend money to a bank by placing funds in a savings account or to a governmental unit or corporation by buying bonds. An investment is bought with the hope that it will make a profit through its earning power or by being sold later at a higher price. In agreement with others, an investor may buy all or part of the ownership rights in a company, such as a sole proprietorship, partnership, or corporation.

Millions of people have come to regard **securities** (stocks and bonds) as a good form of investment. At the time of this writing, hundreds of millions of shares are purchased and sold daily on the New York Stock Exchange (NYSE). The volume in other markets averages more millions of shares a day. Many American corporations have hundreds of thousands of shareowners. American Telephone and Telegraph Company and General Motors Corporation have millions of shareowners.

Persons who wish to place their funds in investments that yield higher returns than interest paid by savings institutions should first provide for their daily and emergency needs. That is, they should first provide for enough ready cash for adequate food, shelter, and clothing, for insurance to protect the family, and for emergency needs. Among numerous possibilities, such ready cash may be kept in checking accounts, savings accounts, certificate accounts, or money market funds. After these provisions are met, there are, of course, many ways in which an investor can invest money. Very commonly, however, investments are placed in securities.

INVESTING IN STOCK

One who buys shares of stock in a company is buying part of the ownership of that company. The company's board of directors generally sets a specific price on the first stock offered for sale. After the stock has been sold initially, it may be traded in the market. Its value is determined by the amount that a buyer will pay and a seller will take. This value is its **market value,** which is not the same as its par value or book value.

The daily sales and prices of the major securities are published in metropolitan newspapers. The prices are listed as whole and mixed numbers that represent dollars. Through custom, a dollar is called a **point** and is measured in eighths. Therefore, $\frac{1}{8}$ point is equivalent to 12.5 cents. The stocks are listed alphabetically under columnar headings that are almost self-explanatory. For example, an examination of Table 18–1 reveals that on the date covered by the listing, Am Boat was paying an annual dividend of $1.60 on each share of stock and that 43,600 shares of the stock were bought and sold on that date. Furthermore, the first sale of the day was at $72\frac{1}{8}$ ($72.125) a share; the highest price was $72\frac{1}{2}$; the lowest, $72\frac{1}{8}$; and the last sale of the day was at $72\frac{1}{4}$, which is

Stock and Div. in $	Sales in 100s	Open	High	Low	Close	Net Chg.
Am Boat 1.60	436	$72\frac{1}{8}$	$72\frac{1}{2}$	$72\frac{1}{8}$	$72\frac{1}{4}$	$+\frac{1}{4}$
AM Food	3193	$11\frac{3}{8}$	$11\frac{3}{8}$	$11\frac{1}{8}$	$11\frac{1}{8}$	$-\frac{1}{4}$
AMO Air 2.40	1016	$57\frac{1}{8}$	$57\frac{5}{8}$	57	$57\frac{1}{8}$	$-\frac{1}{8}$
AMO Air pf 3.75	z70	63	63	63	63	$+1\frac{1}{2}$
ApexCo	971	7	$7\frac{1}{8}$	$6\frac{7}{8}$	7	...
Atl Tool	1501	38	38	38	38	-1
Ben Coal 1.80	1026	35	$36\frac{3}{8}$	$34\frac{7}{8}$	$36\frac{3}{8}$	$+1\frac{3}{8}$
Cal Fair 2	10228	$51\frac{1}{2}$	52	$51\frac{3}{8}$	$51\frac{3}{8}$	$-\frac{1}{2}$
CB Grain 1.32	5103	$72\frac{1}{2}$	$72\frac{1}{2}$	71	71	-2
Cntrl Corp pf 6	2630	$100\frac{3}{4}$	$100\frac{3}{4}$	$100\frac{1}{2}$	$100\frac{1}{2}$	$-\frac{1}{4}$
Dnvr Met 1.25	4133	$145\frac{1}{4}$	$146\frac{1}{8}$	$145\frac{1}{4}$	$145\frac{7}{8}$	$+\frac{3}{4}$
Dnvr Met pf 4.50	7	$74\frac{7}{8}$	$74\frac{7}{8}$	$74\frac{1}{2}$	$74\frac{7}{8}$	$+\frac{1}{8}$
EZData .88	6251	$78\frac{1}{4}$	$79\frac{7}{8}$	$78\frac{1}{4}$	$79\frac{1}{2}$	$+\frac{7}{8}$
Eltron 2.40	7213	$51\frac{7}{8}$	$52\frac{1}{8}$	$51\frac{5}{8}$	$51\frac{3}{4}$	$-\frac{1}{4}$
Gen Ind 3.40	16407	$81\frac{3}{4}$	$82\frac{3}{8}$	$81\frac{3}{4}$	$82\frac{1}{8}$	...
Gen Ind pf 5	15	$83\frac{3}{4}$	84	$83\frac{1}{2}$	84	$+\frac{1}{2}$
GRT Inc 1.48	9245	$40\frac{1}{8}$	$40\frac{1}{4}$	40	$40\frac{1}{8}$	$+\frac{3}{8}$
Idl Papr 3.20	4151	$326\frac{1}{2}$	$331\frac{1}{2}$	$325\frac{1}{2}$	$331\frac{1}{2}$	$+5$
Kay Mkt 1	12250	29	$29\frac{1}{2}$	25	$28\frac{3}{4}$	$-3\frac{3}{4}$
LDC Util 4.25	z300	$67\frac{1}{2}$	$67\frac{3}{4}$	$67\frac{1}{2}$	$67\frac{3}{4}$	$+\frac{3}{4}$
McMull 1	4235	124	125	$123\frac{1}{2}$	$124\frac{5}{8}$	$+1\frac{3}{8}$
NW Mach 1.20	6984	135	$135\frac{3}{4}$	$134\frac{3}{4}$	$135\frac{1}{4}$	$+\frac{1}{4}$
Nu Val 1	10	$36\frac{3}{4}$	$36\frac{3}{4}$	$36\frac{1}{4}$	$36\frac{3}{8}$	$-\frac{3}{8}$
Nu Val pf 3.75	z100	$58\frac{1}{2}$	$58\frac{1}{2}$	58	58	$-1\frac{1}{2}$
Parke Cp .40	1398	$20\frac{1}{8}$	$20\frac{3}{8}$	20	$20\frac{3}{8}$	$-\frac{1}{8}$
Qual Tex 1	12108	$53\frac{3}{4}$	$54\frac{7}{8}$	$53\frac{3}{4}$	$54\frac{1}{4}$	$+\frac{7}{8}$
Rocky Mt 1	8234	$46\frac{7}{8}$	$47\frac{1}{8}$	$46\frac{3}{4}$	47	...
Sky Pac 1.20	23242	72	$72\frac{3}{8}$	$71\frac{1}{2}$	$71\frac{3}{4}$	...
Sou Mot 1.80	214	40	$40\frac{5}{8}$	$39\frac{3}{4}$	$40\frac{3}{8}$	$+1$
Sun East 1	1379	$15\frac{3}{4}$	$15\frac{7}{8}$	$15\frac{3}{4}$	$15\frac{7}{8}$	$+\frac{1}{8}$
SW Pow 1.80	15444	$84\frac{1}{4}$	$84\frac{5}{8}$	84	$84\frac{1}{2}$	$+\frac{1}{2}$
TranCon	6131	$12\frac{1}{4}$	$12\frac{5}{8}$	$12\frac{1}{4}$	$12\frac{1}{2}$	$+\frac{3}{8}$
UROC 2.40	50689	$47\frac{1}{8}$	$48\frac{1}{8}$	47	$47\frac{7}{8}$	$+1\frac{1}{8}$
US Elec 1.20	8321	$34\frac{5}{8}$	36	$34\frac{5}{8}$	36	$+1\frac{3}{8}$
Wyte Swan 1.80	132	274	274	$274\frac{1}{4}$	$273\frac{3}{8}$	$-\frac{7}{8}$
XLCorp	155	$51\frac{1}{4}$	$51\frac{5}{8}$	$50\frac{1}{4}$	$50\frac{1}{2}$	$-\frac{1}{2}$

How to read the table: Total sales are listed in 100-share lots unless preceded by z, which means the total is for the actual number of shares traded. Dividends are annual disbursements based on the preceding quarterly or semiannual declarations. The abbreviation "pf" means preferred stock. The net change reflects the increase or decrease in the Close column compared to the amount in that column on the preceding business day.

Table 18-1 Quotations of Fictitious Stocks

$\frac{1}{4}$ point, or 25¢ a share, above the closing price on the preceding date that this stock was traded. In addition, some newspapers show the highest price and lowest price recorded in the preceding year or the current year to date for each stock listed. Such figures usually appear to the left of the name of the stock.

Buying Stock

Most stocks listed on the New York Stock Exchange are bought and sold in 100-share **trade units** or **round lots.** For some stocks that are not traded frequently, 10 shares is a round lot. An **odd lot** consists of any number of shares less than a round lot. Thus, any transaction containing from 1 to 99 shares is an odd lot for a stock with a 100-share trading unit; from 1 to 9 shares is an odd lot for a stock with a 10-share trading unit. Stocks may be bought and sold in round lots or in odd lots or in a combination of both.

Large block orders consisting of many round lots are usually made on behalf of pension funds, mutual funds, and insurance companies rather than for individuals.

Total Cost of Round-Lot Orders. An individual who owns stock in a public corporation may sell the shares to whomever he or she chooses. Similarly, the potential purchaser of such stock may buy from whomever she or he chooses. Generally, however, the potential buyer doesn't know who wants to sell. A **stockbroker** helps buyers and sellers of securities by acting as an agent for them. For this service, a commission is charged.

A **single transaction** is an order for a specific stock that is executed, confirmed, and settled for an account in one day. The price per share multiplied by the number of shares in a transaction is the **money value** of the order.

The total cost paid by the purchaser of the stock is the basis for determining the amount of the gain or loss when the stock is sold. The total cost of an order of stock is the sum of the money value and the commission.

Money Value + Commission = Total Cost

Example: An investor bought 300 shares of stock at $51\frac{3}{8}$ a share plus $192.48 commission. Find the total cost of the shares.

Solution: $51.375 \times 300 = $15,412.50   money value of 300 shares
$15,412.50 + $192.48 = $15,604.98   total cost

Total Cost of Odd-Lot Orders. If a broker is given an order for 90 shares of a 100-share trading-unit stock, that stock is bought from an odd-lot dealer who performs a kind of wholesaling function on the exchange by breaking up round lots of securities into smaller quantities. The odd-lot dealer does business only with other brokers on the stock exchange floor, not with the public. For performing this "wholesale" service, the charge is usually one-eighth of a point ($12\frac{1}{2}$¢) for each share of stock bought or sold that is listed on the New York Stock Exchange. This charge, which is referred to as the **odd-lot differential,** is added to the round-lot price of the security at the time of the purchase.

To find the total cost of an odd-lot purchase of stock, follow these steps:

1. Find the odd-lot price per share by adding the odd-lot differential to the round-lot price.

2. Find the money value of the stock by multiplying the odd-lot price per share by the number of shares in the transaction.

3. Find the total cost by adding the commission to the money value of the order.

Example:

An investor bought 90 shares of stock at the round-lot price of $68\frac{1}{4}$ a share and paid the discount broker $77.15 in commission. Find the total cost of this order.

Solution:

1. $68\frac{1}{4} + \frac{1}{8} = 68\frac{3}{8} = \$68.375$ odd-lot price per share

2. $\$68.375 \times 90 = \$6,153.75$ money value of transaction

3. $\$6,153.75 + \$77.15 = \$6,230.90$ total cost of order

Total Cost of Combination Orders. Some orders of stock are combinations of one or more round lots and an odd lot. In computing the money value, such orders are treated as two separate transactions. In other words, the money value of the odd-lot portion of the order is computed as a separate transaction because of the odd-lot differential.

To find the total cost of a combination order:

1. Find the money value of the round-lot portion of the order.

2. Find the money value of the odd-lot portion of the order.

3. Find the total cost of the order by adding the commission to the amounts found in Steps 1 and 2.

Example:

An investor bought 410 shares of stock at $25\frac{1}{2}$ per share plus commissions totaling $152. Find the total cost of this order.

536   Part 5. Mathematics Applications for Investing in a Corporation

Solution:

1. $\$25.50 \times 400 = \$10,200$ money value of 400 shares

2. $25\frac{1}{2} + \frac{1}{8} = 25\frac{5}{8} = \$25.625$ odd-lot price per share
   $\$25.625 \times 10 = \$256.25$ money value of 10 shares

3. $\$10,200 + \$256.25 + \$152 = \$10,608.25$ total cost

● Exercise 18–1

A. Find the total cost of each of the following round-lot orders.

	Number of Shares Purchased	Price per Share	Commission
1.	100	$34\frac{1}{4}$	$ 59.75
2.	300	76	358.16
3.	500	$128\frac{3}{4}$	702.75
4.	6,000	$18\frac{7}{8}$	1,202.74
5.	2,000	$2\frac{1}{2}$	236.75
6.	400	123	667.64
7.	800	$28\frac{5}{8}$	373.14
8.	9,000	$14\frac{3}{8}$	1,153.53
9.	1,000	$32\frac{1}{2}$	523.38
10.	50,000	$6\frac{1}{8}$	3,760.69

B. Find the total cost of each of the following odd-lot orders. The trading unit in each problem is 100 shares.

	Number of Shares Purchased	Round-Lot Price per Share	Commission
1.	90	$15\frac{1}{8}$	$ 39.23
2.	30	$44\frac{1}{4}$	38.81
3.	50	$69\frac{1}{4}$	70.25
4.	25	$7\frac{1}{2}$	27.41
5.	80	$23\frac{3}{8}$	44.30
6.	40	$82\frac{7}{8}$	88.75
7.	15	$127\frac{5}{8}$	54.68
8.	20	$53\frac{5}{8}$	46.25
9.	10	$88\frac{3}{4}$	34.40
10.	30	$321\frac{1}{4}$	111.95

C. Find the total cost of each of the following stock orders. The trading unit in each problem is 100 shares.

	Number of Shares Purchased	Round-Lot Price per Share	Commission
1.	160	$56\frac{7}{8}$	$ 232.16
2.	320	60	363.15
3.	7,850	15	1,072.61
4.	2,500	125	2,255.38
5.	210	$31\frac{3}{8}$	156.40
6.	825	$14\frac{1}{2}$	256.70
7.	538	$37\frac{1}{2}$	368.30
8.	9,400	$3\frac{3}{4}$	677.04
9.	1,750	$39\frac{5}{8}$	738.57
10.	69,200	$8\frac{1}{2}$	3,224.83

D. Find the total cost, including commission, in each of the following problems. Use the stock listings in Table 18-1. The trading unit in each problem is 100 shares.

	Company	Number of Shares Purchased	Price in Table	Commission
1.	Am Boat	100	Open	$ 97.63
2.	AM Food	20	Open	27.80
3.	Ben Coal	200	High	183.65
4.	Cntrl Corp	300	High	393.06
5.	EZData	500	Low	411.85
6.	Gen Ind	150	Low	263.75
7.	Idl Papr	10	Close	78.68
8.	NW Mach	90	Close	337.45
9.	Parke Cp	8,750	Open	1,308.16
10.	Rocky Mt	430	High	369.85
11.	Sun East	4,000	Low	794.45
12.	UROC	600	Close	478.67

Selling Stock

Both conservative and speculative investors like to "buy at the low and sell at the high." People should not speculate in the stock market, however, unless they can afford to lose the investment. No one has yet devised a method of determining exactly when the price of a stock is at its high or low point. On the other hand, one should not buy shares of stock and then forget about them. Successful investing requires the investor to pay attention to the securities, for deciding when to sell can be as important as deciding when to buy. Taking a

Part 5. Mathematics Applications for Investing in a Corporation profit is not the only reason for selling a stock. The investor may decide to sell a stock because it has not performed as well as had been expected or simply because the money is needed for other purposes.

Money Value on Sale of Stock. The market price of an odd lot of a specific stock is set by the immediately preceding sale of a round lot of that stock. As the odd-lot dealer's commission is deducted from the sale price, the seller receives an amount that is $\frac{1}{8}$ point per share less than the preceding market price when selling "at market." For example, if a round lot is selling at $56\frac{1}{8}$, the seller of an odd lot will receive 56, which is the price that will be reported. Of course, the seller can specify the selling price for an odd lot. If $56\frac{1}{4}$ is wanted, the seller can wait until the round-lot price is $56\frac{3}{8}$. In the latter case, the price reported by the broker would be $56\frac{1}{4}$.

Commission rates are applied to sales as well as to purchases of stock. The odd-lot price reported to the client by the broker is the round-lot price increased by the odd-lot differential when stock has been purchased. The round-lot price is decreased by the odd-lot differential when stock has been sold.

An investor sold 250 shares of stock at the round-lot price of $72\frac{1}{2}$. Find the money value of the stock.

$72.50 \times 200 = \$14,500$ money value of 200 shares
$72\frac{1}{2} - \frac{1}{8} = 72\frac{3}{8}$ odd-lot selling price per share
$\$72.375 \times 50 = \$3,618.75$ money value of 50 shares
$\$14,500 + \$3,618.75 = \$18,118.75$ money value of 250 shares

Taxes on Sale of Stock. When stock is sold, certain taxes and fees in addition to the commission charged by the broker must be paid. Some states and cities levy taxes against the sale of stocks through the registered exchanges located within their borders. The broker withholds the taxes and fees and then periodically forwards them to the appropriate authorities.

The Securities and Exchange Commission is a federal regulatory body that has the power to see that complete and accurate information regarding securities offered for sale in interstate commerce and through the mails be made available to prospective purchasers, and that no fraud be practiced in connection with the sale of such securities. To help defray its expenses, a fee is applied to all sales through any registered exchange and to odd-lot sales that would be cleared through such an exchange if 100 shares were being sold.

Net Proceeds From Sale of Stock. When shares of stock are sold through a broker, the seller receives the total selling price less the sum of the broker's commission and the taxes and fees. The amount the seller receives is the **net proceeds.** This computation may be expressed in the following equation:

Net Proceeds = Total Selling Price − (Commission + Taxes + Fees)

Of course, the total selling price of each lot of stock is the product of the number of shares in the lot multiplied by the selling price per share.

Example:

Kimitaka Kato instructed his broker to sell 410 shares of stock at the round-lot price of $52\frac{1}{2}$ per share. He paid the broker's commission of $469.94 and stock-transfer taxes and fees of $20.94. Find the net proceeds.

Solution:

$52.50 \times 400 = \$21,000$ money value of 400 shares
$52\frac{1}{2} - \frac{1}{8} = 52\frac{3}{8}$ odd-lot selling price per share
$\$52.375 \times 10 = \$523.75$ money value of 10 shares

Total selling price ($21,000 + $523.75)		$21,523.75
Less: Broker's commission...........................	$469.94	
Taxes and fees	20.94	490.88
Net proceeds		$21,032.87

- ### Exercise 18–2

In the following problems, find the net proceeds. Use the prices listed in Table 18–1. The trading unit in each problem is 100 shares.

	Company	Number of Shares Sold	Price in Table	Commission and SEC Fee
1.	AMO Air	100	Open	$ 187.75
2.	Apex Co	5,000	Open	406.95
3.	Cal Fair	200	High	212.61
4.	Dnvr Met	50	High	85.39
5.	Eltron	2,500	Low	1,466.76
6.	GRT Inc	600	Low	493.08
7.	McMull	340	Close	709.82
8.	Nu Val	500	Close	452.95
9.	Qual Tex	90	Open	168.36
10.	Sky Pac	1,300	High	1,014.27
11.	TranCon	8,250	Low	855.41
12.	Wyte Swan	400	Close	1,042.46

Return on Stock Investment

As a shareowner, the investor has the right to share in any dividends declared while he or she owns the stock. Furthermore the investor hopes to gain by selling the stock at a price above that which was given. Of course, if one must sell at a price below cost, a loss will result.

Amount of Capital Gain or Loss From Sale of Stock. The capital gain or loss from the sale of stock is the difference between the net proceeds and the total cost of the shares sold. A gain is realized when the net proceeds exceed the total cost. A loss results when the total cost exceeds the net proceeds.

Gain from Sale = Net Proceeds − Total Cost

Loss from Sale = Total Cost − Net Proceeds

Example: Barrows bought 400 shares of common stock at 38 plus $174.84 commission. A few months later, the 400 shares were sold at 45 less commission and SEC fee totaling $196.96. Find **(a)** the total cost, **(b)** the net proceeds, and **(c)** the amount of capital gain or loss from the sale.

Solution: **(a)** $38 \times 400 = \$15,200$ money value of 400 shares when bought
            $\$15,200 + \$174.84 = \$15,374.84$ total cost of 400 shares

            (b) $45 \times 400 = \$18,000$ money value of 400 shares when sold
            $\$18,000 - \$196.96 = \$17,803.04$ net proceeds

            (c) $\$17,803.04 - \$15,374.84 = \$2,428.20$ capital gain from sale

Rate of Yield on Stock. A person who invests in stock may have dividend income as well as capital gains or losses from the sale of stock. Dividends may be paid quarterly, semiannually, or annually. Many large corporations pay dividends quarterly.

Rate of yield refers to the annual income expressed as a percent of an investment. In the case of stock, the annual income is the amount of annual dividends received and the investment is the total cost of the stock. Therefore, the rate of yield on stock is found by dividing the annual dividends by the total cost of the stock "yielding" the dividends.

$$Rate\ of\ Yield = \frac{Annual\ Dividends}{Total\ Cost\ of\ Stock}$$

Example: Hal Marino bought stock at $112 a share including commission. During the past year, he received a quarterly dividend of $1.54. Find the rate of yield.

Solution: $\$1.54 \times 4 = \$6.16$ annual dividends per share
            $\dfrac{\$6.16}{\$112} = 0.055 = 5.5\%$ rate of yield

Rate of Total Gain or Loss on Stock Investment. The sum of the total dividends received during the time a stock is held and the capital gain from the sale of that stock is the **total gain** from that investment. Some investors determine the rate of total gain or loss on an investment by dividing the total gain or loss by the total cost of the investment. This quotient expressed as a percent reflects the rate of return for the whole period of time during which the investment was held.

$$Total\ Dividends\ Received + Capital\ Gain = Total\ Gain\ from\ Investment$$

$$\frac{Total\ Gain\ from\ Investment}{Cost\ of\ Investment} = Rate\ of\ Total\ Gain$$

Chapter 18. Investments in Securities

Jane Bender bought common stock at 36 a share. She received a regular quarterly dividend of 50¢ a share. After owning the stock for $2\frac{1}{2}$ years, she sold it at 43 a share. Assume that the buying and selling prices reflect all commissions and the SEC fee. Find the rate of gain on cost.

Solution:

Gain from dividends (10 quarters × $0.50)	$ 5.00
Capital gain ($43 − $36)	7.00
Total gain per share	$12.00

Rate of Gain on Cost = $\dfrac{\$12}{\$36} = 0.33\frac{1}{3} = 33\frac{1}{3}\%$

● **Exercise 18–3**

A. In each of the following problems, find **(a)** the total cost, **(b)** the net proceeds, and **(c)** the capital gain or loss.

Name of Stock	Number of Shares Traded	Round-Lot Purchase Price	Commission on Purchase	Round-Lot Selling Price	Commission and Taxes on Sale
1. Apex Co	200	$5\frac{1}{4}$	$ 46.30	7	$ 53.43
2. Fair Corp	800	$81\frac{1}{2}$	806.38	$90\frac{3}{8}$	870.20
3. Goodtime	400	$37\frac{3}{4}$	224.42	$33\frac{1}{2}$	237.55
4. Midwest Oil	530	$15\frac{3}{8}$	118.83	$11\frac{5}{8}$	130.89
5. Parke Co	3,200	$14\frac{1}{8}$	878.38	$20\frac{7}{8}$	707.76
6. So Central	640	$60\frac{5}{8}$	444.53	$54\frac{3}{4}$	462.75

B. To the nearest tenth of a percent, find the rate of yield for each of the following investments.

	Total Cost per Share	Par Value per share	Dividend per Share	Frequency of Dividend
1.	$ 80	$100	6%	Annually
2.	40	50	5%	Annually
3.	30	25	7%	Annually
4.	9	10	$6\frac{1}{2}\%$	Annually
5.	72		$1.30	Semiannually
6.	36		0.90	Semiannually
7.	320		3.60	Quarterly
8.	50		0.60	Quarterly

C. Solve these problems.

1. Hennessy bought 80 shares of Consolidated Edison, 5% preferred, $100 par value stock for $6,000 including commission. He received a quarterly dividend of $1.25 during the 3 years and 9 months that he held the stock. At the end of this time, he sold the stock and received net proceeds of

$5,840 from his broker. Find the amount of his gain or loss on this investment.

2. Foley purchased 5% cumulative preferred stock at 86 including commission. She sold the $100 par value stock 4 years later, clearing 93. There were no dividends in arrears. To the nearest 0.1%, find the rate of total gain on the investment.

3. A block of common stock was purchased at $75\frac{1}{4}$ and sold at $89\frac{3}{4}$. These prices reflect all commissions and the SEC fee. Dividends of $0.40 were paid semiannually to the investor during the 3 years he held the stock. To the nearest 0.1%, find the rate of total gain on the investment.

4. An investor bought 100 shares of common stock at $44\frac{1}{4}$. The stock was held for $1\frac{1}{2}$ years and then sold at 42. These prices reflect all commissions and the SEC fee. A quarterly dividend of 60¢ was received regularly. Find **(a)** the gain from dividends, **(b)** the capital loss from the sale, **(c)** the total gain or loss, and **(d)** the rate of gain or loss on the investment.

5. A certain common stock yields a regular quarterly dividend of $0.50 a share. How much must be invested in the stock at 40 to receive annual dividends of $500 if the broker's commission is $203?

6. A 6% preferred, $100 par value stock is selling at 90. Disregarding commission, how much must be invested to receive annual dividends of $1,200?

INVESTING IN BONDS

People who buy bonds lend their money to the issuing institution. A **bond** is a written promise to repay a specific amount of borrowed money and to pay a certain rate of interest to the owner of the bond. It is, in effect, a long-term promissory note that is to fall due some ten, twenty, or more years from the issuance date.

The principal amount that the issuer promises to pay per bond on the maturity date which is printed on the bond certificate is the **face value** or **par value.** Although occasionally bonds are issued in denominations of $100 and $500, most corporate bonds are issued with a face value of $1,000. The interest is usually payable every six months or annually. Sometimes, as with the U.S. Savings Bonds, Series E, interest accumulates and becomes payable only when the bond matures or is cashed.

A **registered bond** is one for which the name of the owner is registered with the issuer. Usually the owner automatically receives a check from the issuer when the interest is due. When registered bonds are sold, the transfer must be recorded on the records of the issuer so that the interest will be sent to the new owner.

A **bearer bond** or **coupon bond** is not registered with the issuer. Whoever holds it is presumed to own it. Such a bond has a number of coupons attached to it. Each coupon calls for the payment, on a certain date, of the interest that is due. The owner of the bond then collects the interest by clipping the coupon and sending it to the issuer's agent or depositing it with a bank for collection. Bearer bonds may be sold and transferred with less formality than that required for registered bonds.

Bonds of the United States Government—backed as they are by the integrity of the nation—are considered to be the most stable of all investments. State and local governments also issue **municipal bonds** to acquire funds for streets, parks, hospitals, and other public improvements. Municipal bonds are attractive to some investors because, with few exceptions, the interest income from such bonds is exempt from federal income tax.

When a corporation issues and sells bonds, it may mortgage its plant or equipment as security for its promise to pay the face value of the bonds. In the event of a company's failure, if the mortgaged property is inadequate to meet the claims of the bondholders, the balance of the debt owed to them must be paid before proceeds from the sale of any remaining assets can be divided among the stockholders.

A company that has a sound credit rating and a good financial reputation may issue **debenture bonds,** which are backed only by its promise to pay rather than by mortgaged property.

Buying Bonds

Corporations usually sell a whole issue of bonds to an investment firm which then tries to sell the bonds at higher prices to the public through stock exchanges or over-the-counter markets.

Bond prices, which fluctuate from day to day in accordance with changing interest rates, are quoted as a percent of face value. A bond quotation of $98\frac{1}{2}$ means that the bond is selling for $98\frac{1}{2}$ % of face value. Thus, a price of $98\frac{1}{2}$ for a bond with a face value of $1,000 means $985 per bond; a price of $102 means its price is $1,020.

The sales of bonds through exchanges are reported in the financial pages of daily newspapers in cities throughout the country. Fictional quotations of corporate bonds are shown in Table 18–2. Notice that in addition to the current prices, each listing shows the name of the issuing corporation, the rate of interest, and the year of maturity. For example, Bantree Corporation bonds that bear $7\frac{1}{2}$ % interest and will be due in 2013 are listed as Bantree $7\frac{1}{2}$ s13. The Net Change column shows whether the current closing price is higher or lower than the closing price on the preceding day that such bonds were traded in the market. The Bantree Corporation net change of "$-\frac{1}{8}$" means that the preceding closing price must have been $90\frac{1}{4} + \frac{1}{8}$, or $90\frac{3}{8}$.

Commission on Bond Transactions. As when stock is bought or sold, the commission on bonds increases the buyer's cost and decreases the seller's proceeds. Most brokers charge a flat minimum commission per bond; for example, $10 per bond.

Name of Bond	Sales in $1,000s	High	Low	Close	Net Chg.
Abco $6\frac{5}{8}$s98	436	87	$86\frac{1}{4}$	$86\frac{1}{4}$	$-\frac{3}{4}$
Amoy Met $5\frac{3}{4}$s19	1	$83\frac{1}{2}$	$83\frac{1}{2}$	$83\frac{1}{2}$	$+\frac{1}{2}$
Bantree $7\frac{1}{2}$s13	194	$90\frac{3}{8}$	$90\frac{1}{8}$	$90\frac{1}{4}$	$-\frac{1}{8}$
Cal Pw $6\frac{7}{8}$s99	10	$101\frac{1}{4}$	$101\frac{1}{4}$	$101\frac{1}{4}$	. . .
Clar Co 4s03	9	$58\frac{1}{4}$	$57\frac{5}{8}$	$58\frac{1}{4}$	$+\frac{5}{8}$
DAL El 13s17	11	$77\frac{1}{8}$	77	$77\frac{1}{8}$	$+\frac{5}{8}$
Dax Min 13s11	10	68	68	68	$+1\frac{1}{2}$
EDEM $9\frac{1}{2}$s07	1027	$80\frac{1}{2}$	$80\frac{1}{2}$	$80\frac{1}{2}$	$-1\frac{1}{2}$
Eri Prod 5s2020	75	$18\frac{1}{2}$	$18\frac{3}{8}$	$18\frac{3}{8}$	. . .
Fen Corp $8\frac{7}{8}$s05	5	$71\frac{1}{2}$	$71\frac{3}{8}$	$71\frac{1}{2}$	$+\frac{1}{8}$
GT Steel $12\frac{1}{2}$s06	130	$83\frac{1}{4}$	$82\frac{1}{2}$	$82\frac{1}{2}$	$-\frac{1}{2}$
Glades $14\frac{1}{8}$s10	35	$101\frac{3}{8}$	$101\frac{3}{8}$	$101\frac{3}{8}$	. . .
Hlth Mkt $12\frac{1}{4}$s21	31	91	$90\frac{3}{4}$	91	. . .
Kal Sea 6s08	224	64	$63\frac{1}{2}$	$63\frac{3}{4}$	$+\frac{1}{4}$
Keswick $10\frac{1}{2}$s13 cv	27	$105\frac{1}{8}$	103	103	$-2\frac{1}{8}$
Lo Med 4s03	25	$50\frac{5}{8}$	49	$50\frac{5}{8}$	$+2\frac{5}{8}$
Mstr Chem 12s14 cv	86	$108\frac{1}{4}$	$107\frac{1}{2}$	$107\frac{7}{8}$	. . .
News Corp $4\frac{1}{4}$s05	336	$58\frac{7}{8}$	$58\frac{1}{2}$	$58\frac{3}{4}$	$-\frac{1}{8}$
NRG Elec 5.60s11	65	$85\frac{1}{2}$	$85\frac{1}{2}$	$85\frac{1}{2}$	. . .
Nys Info 6s18	13	$79\frac{1}{2}$	$79\frac{1}{4}$	$79\frac{1}{2}$	$+\frac{1}{4}$
Ocean Pw $14\frac{3}{4}$s23	5	60	60	60	-3
Parde $14\frac{3}{8}$s09 cv	33	$102\frac{1}{4}$	$101\frac{3}{4}$	$101\frac{3}{4}$	$-\frac{3}{8}$
Rosdata $7\frac{1}{4}$s08	2	100	100	100	. . .
SC Air $13\frac{3}{4}$s18	29	$82\frac{1}{8}$	$81\frac{3}{4}$	$81\frac{3}{4}$	$-\frac{3}{8}$
TNC Papr 15s12 cv	55	$108\frac{1}{8}$	$108\frac{1}{8}$	$108\frac{1}{8}$	$+\frac{1}{8}$
Toyama $14\frac{3}{8}$s20	24	$80\frac{1}{4}$	78	$80\frac{1}{4}$	$+2\frac{1}{4}$
Turku 11s19 cv	4	107	107	107	. . .
ULA Oil 9s08 cv	14	95	$92\frac{1}{2}$	95	$+1\frac{3}{4}$
Val Grain $9\frac{5}{8}$s16	143	$83\frac{5}{8}$	$82\frac{1}{4}$	83	$+\frac{3}{8}$
Wel Co $17\frac{1}{2}$s24	1	$96\frac{1}{2}$	$96\frac{1}{2}$	$96\frac{1}{2}$	$+\frac{1}{2}$

Table 18–2 Quotations of Fictitious Corporate Bonds

Cost of Bonds Bought on the Interest Date. The specific dates on which interest is to be paid each year are printed on the bond certificate. The interest paid on each payment date covers the period of time preceding the payment.

For example, many bond certificates provide for semiannual interest payments to be made on January 1 and July 1. In such cases, the payment on July 1 covers interest on the bond for the six months from January 1 through June 30; the January 1 payment, for the six months from July 1 through December 31 of the preceding year. Notice that the payment made on an interest date does not include interest for that date. The investor who sells bonds on their interest-payment date is entitled to the interest for the preceding period of time. The one who buys bonds on their interest-payment date is entitled to the interest starting on that date. Therefore, the investment in bonds bought on the interest date is the sum of the total market value of the bonds and the total commission on the purchase.

Total Expenditure for Bonds Bought Between Interest Dates. When bonds are traded between interest dates, the seller is entitled to the accrued interest because his or her capital was invested until the settlement date. Customarily, then, the purchaser pays the seller the quoted price plus the interest that has accrued from the preceding interest-payment date to and including the day before the settlement date. The **settlement date** is the date on which the buyer makes payment and acquires title to the bond.

To find the total expenditure when bonds are bought between interest dates, proceed as follows:

1. Find the market value of the bonds by multiplying the price of one bond by the number of the bonds in the purchase.
2. Find the accrued interest on the face value of the bonds at the given rate for the time from the preceding interest date to the settlement date.
3. Find the total commission charges by multiplying the commission per bond by the number of bonds in the purchase.
4. Find the total expenditure for the bond purchase by adding together the total market value, the accrued interest, and the total commission charges.

The preceding steps may be summarized in the following equation:

$$Market\ Value + Accrued\ Interest + Commission = Total\ Expenditure$$

Example:

Eight $1,000 bonds, with 12% interest payable January 1 and July 1, were purchased at $97\frac{5}{8}$ plus accrued interest and commission of $10 per bond. The interest accrual was for 100 days. Find **(a)** the total market value of the bonds, **(b)** the accrued interest, **(c)** the total commission, and **(d)** the total expenditure for the bonds.

Solution:

(a) $97\frac{5}{8}\% = 0.97625$
$0.97625 \times \$1,000 = \$976.25$ market price per bond
$\$976.25 \times 8 = \$7,810$ market value of 8 bonds

(b) $\$1,000 \times 8 = \$8,000$ face value of 8 bonds
$\$8,000 \times 12\% \times \dfrac{100}{360} = \$266.67$ accrued interest

(c) $\$10 \times 8 = \$80$ total commission

(d) $\$7,810 + \$266.67 + \$80 = \$8,156.67$ total expenditure

When accrued interest is paid in a bond purchase, it is recovered on the next interest date. For example, the purchaser of the bonds in the preceding example will receive the next semiannual interest payment of $480 ($8,000 × 12% × $\frac{1}{2}$). In effect, this payment includes the $266.67 accrued interest that was paid, as well as $213.33 interest on the investment from the settlement date to the interest payment date.

• Exercise 18–4

A. Find the total expenditure for each of the following bond purchases if bought on the interest date. Face value of each bond is $1,000, and the commission charge is $10 per bond.

	Number of Bonds	Market Price
1.	2	99
2.	5	$95\frac{3}{4}$
3.	10	102
4.	20	$101\frac{5}{8}$
5.	32	$87\frac{1}{2}$
6.	43	$100\frac{3}{8}$

B. In each of the following problems, assume that the face value of each bond is $1,000 and that interest is payable semiannually. Find **(a)** the total market value, **(b)** the accrued interest, **(c)** the total commission at $5 per bond, and **(d)** the total expenditure for each bond purchase.

	Number of Bonds Purchased	Market Price	Time for Accrued Interest	Bond Interest Rate
1.	5	$98\frac{1}{2}$	2 months	6%
2.	10	96	160 days	8%
3.	18	$101\frac{3}{4}$	105 days	10%
4.	25	$103\frac{7}{8}$	80 days	14%
5.	37	$80\frac{5}{8}$	4 months	$15\frac{1}{2}$%
6.	50	$102\frac{1}{4}$	42 days	$16\frac{1}{2}$%

Chapter 18. Investments in Securities

C. In each of the following problems, assume that the face value of each bond is $1,000 and that interest is payable semiannually. Find **(a)** the total market value, **(b)** the accrued interest, **(c)** the total commission at $10 per bond, and **(d)** the total expenditure for each bond purchase. Use the prices listed in Table 18–2.

Name of Bond	Number of Bonds Purchased	Price in Table	Time for Accrued Interest
1. Cal Pw	10	High	2 months
2. Clar Co	5	High	34 days
3. Eri Prod	3	Low	78 days
4. Glades	35	Low	45 days
5. Mstr Chem	50	Close	None
6. Rosdata	2	Close	None
7. Toyama	12	High	2 months
8. ULA Oil	7	Low	70 days

Selling Bonds

Broker's commission and accrued interest, if any, are computed in exactly the same way for bond sales as for bond purchases. One must remember, however, that the broker deducts the commission for selling.

SEC Fee on Sale of Bonds. There is a Securities and Exchange Commission (SEC) fee when corporate bonds are traded through a recognized exchange. The SEC fee, which is paid by the seller, is the same for bonds as for stock. The SEC charge is not applied to federal, state, or municipal bonds. The broker deducts the SEC fee before sending the net proceeds to the seller.

Net Proceeds From Sale of Bonds. When bonds are sold on the interest date, the broker deducts the commission and the SEC fee from the total market value of the bonds in the transaction and sends the remainder to the seller.

If bonds are sold between interest dates, the seller is entitled to the interest that has accrued from the preceding interest date to and including the day before the settlement date. To find the net proceeds of corporate bonds sold between interest dates, follow these steps:

1. Find the market value by multiplying the price per bond by the number of bonds being sold.
2. Find the accrued interest on the face value of the bonds at the given rate for the time from the preceding interest date to the settlement date.
3. Find the net proceeds by subtracting the sum of the commission and the SEC fee from the sum of the total market value and the accrued interest.

The preceding steps may be summarized in the following equation:

Net Proceeds = Market Value + Accrued Interest − (Commission + SEC Fee)

Example:

Bill Cook sold twenty $1,000 bonds through the New York Stock Exchange at $97\frac{1}{4}$. Interest on the 6% bonds is payable each January 1 and July 1. Cook was entitled to interest for 110 days. Find **(a)** the market value of the bonds, **(b)** the accrued interest, and **(c)** the net proceeds from the sale if the commission and SEC fee totaled $202.

Solution:

(a) $20 \times 0.9725 \times \$1,000 = \$19,450$ market value

(b) $\$20,000 \times 0.06 \times \dfrac{110}{360} = \$366.67$ accrued interest

(c)

Market value of bonds	$19,450.00
Plus accrued interest	366.67
Total	$19,816.67
Less commission and fee	202.00
Net proceeds	$19,614.67

• Exercise 18–5

In each of the following problems, the face value of each bond is $1,000. Find **(a)** the total market value, **(b)** the accrued interest if any, and **(c)** the net proceeds from each sale. Use the prices listed in Table 18–2.

	Name of Bond	Number of Bonds Sold	Price in Table	Time for Accrued Interest	Commission and Fees
1.	Bantree	100	High	None	$509.04
2.	Dax Min	10	High	None	100.68
3.	Fen Corp	5	Low	None	50.36
4.	Kal Sea	124	Low	1 month	627.87
5.	Lo Med	15	Close	135 days	150.76
6.	News Corp	20	Close	None	101.18
7.	NRG Elec	5	High	96 days	50.43
8.	Parde	23	Low	72 days	117.34
9.	TNC Papr	5	Close	128 days	50.54
10.	Val Grain	73	High	81 days	371.10

Return on Bond Investment

Interest income and capital gains from selling at a price above that which was paid are the two primary sources of income from an investment in bonds. Amounts and rates of capital gains and losses on bonds are computed in the same manner as on stocks.

Amount of Annual Income From Bonds. The investor's annual income from bonds is the interest payments received from the issuer of the bonds. To find the annual income from a specific investment in bonds, multiply the annual interest income from one bond by the number of bonds in that investment.

Chapter 18. Investments in Securities

Example: Find the annual income from twelve $1,000 bonds that bear 6% interest.

Solution: $1,000 × 0.06 = $60   annual interest per bond
$60 × 12 = $720   annual income from 12 bonds

Amount of Bond Investment Needed to Yield Given Annual Return. An investor who wants a minimum annual income from bonds can determine the size of the needed investment if the current market price and interest rate of the bonds are known.

To find the investment necessary to produce a given annual income from bonds, follow this procedure:

1. Find the annual interest income from one bond by multiplying the face value of one bond by the interest rate.
2. Find the number of bonds needed by dividing the desired annual income by the annual interest income from one bond. Any fractional part is treated as one whole bond.
3. Find the necessary investment by multiplying the price and commission on one bond by the number of bonds needed.

Example: Sylvia Stevens wants to buy a sufficient number of Excell Corporation 12% bonds to provide her with an annual income of $4,800. The bonds can be purchased at $97\frac{1}{4}$ and have a face value of $1,000. The broker's commission is $10 per bond. Find the amount of money that must be invested in these bonds to obtain the desired return.

Solution:
1. $1,000 × 12% = $120   annual income from 1 bond

2. $4,800 ÷ $120 = 40   number of bonds needed

3. $1,000 × 0.9725 = $972.50   market value of 1 bond
$972.50 + $10 commission = $982.50   cost of 1 bond
$982.50 × 40 = $39,300   necessary investment

Rate of Annual Yield on Bonds. The annual income on investment is frequently referred to as the "yield." The **rate of annual yield** on bonds is the annual interest income expressed as a percent of the bond investment. Hence, the rate of annual yield on bonds equals the annual interest income from bonds divided by the bond investment.

$$Rate\ of\ Annual\ Yield = \frac{Annual\ Bond\ Interest\ Income}{Bond\ Investment}$$

Example: What is the rate of annual yield on a $1,000, 12% bond priced at 74 plus $10 commission?

Solution: $1,000 × 12% = $120   annual interest income
$1,000 × 0.74 = $740   market value
$740 + 10 = $750   investment
$120 ÷ $750 = 16%   rate of yield to nearest hundredth percent

Rate of Yield to Maturity. **Bond premium** is that amount by which the purchase price is more than the face value of a bond investment. **Bond discount** is the amount by which the purchase price is less than the face value. The issuer of bonds promises to repay the face value of the bonds, no more, no less. An investor who has paid a premium on bonds will not receive all of the investment from the issuer when the bonds mature. An investor who paid less than face value will receive at maturity an amount greater than the investment. Consequently, bonds sold at a premium yield less than the rate of interest printed on the bonds; bonds sold at a discount yield more than the printed interest rate.

When an investor plans to keep a bond investment for a long period of time, the bond premium or discount should be written off, i.e., **amortized** over the remaining life of the bonds so that at maturity the amount in the investment will equal the face value of the bonds. For example, the discount on a $1,000 bond purchased at $945 is $55, which is $1,000 − $945. If the bond has a remaining life of ten years, the annual amortization of the discount is $55 ÷ 10, or $5.50.

The rate of annual yield provides an adequate measure of return on bond investments that are to be kept for a short period of time. If the bonds are to be kept for a relatively long period of time, a more precise rate of yield should be calculated. The **rate of yield to maturity** shows the average rate of yield over the remaining life of the bonds, for it includes an adjustment for bond premium or discount.

To compute the rate of yield to maturity on a bond investment that contains a premium, follow these steps:

1. Find the premium by subtracting the face value of the bonds from the amount of the investment.
2. Find the annual premium amortization by dividing the premium by the number of years to maturity.
3. Find the remainder of annual interest by subtracting the premium amortization from the annual interest income.
4. Find the average investment by dividing the sum of the investment and the face value of the investment by 2.
5. Find the rate of yield to maturity by dividing the remainder of annual return by the average principal invested.

The preceding steps may be summarized in the following equation:

$$Rate\ of\ Yield\ to\ Maturity = \frac{Annual\ Interest - Annual\ Premium\ Amortization}{Average\ Investment}$$

Example: Ten years before they matured, five $1,000 bonds were bought at $1,035 each including commission. Find the rate of yield to maturity on these 15% bonds.

Solution:

1. $1,035 − $1,000 = $35   premium per bond

2. $35 ÷ 10 = $3.50   annual premium amortization

3. $1,000 × 0.15 = $150   annual interest per bond
   $150 − $3.50 = $146.50   remainder of annual interest

4. $\dfrac{\$1,035 + \$1,000}{2} = \$1,017.50$ average investment per bond

5. $146.50 ÷ $1,017.50 = 14.40%   rate of yield to maturity

To compute the rate of yield to maturity on a bond investment that was purchased at a discount, follow these steps:

1. Find the discount by subtracting the investment from the face value of the bonds.
2. Find the annual discount amortization by dividing the discount by the number of years to maturity.
3. Find the sum of the annual yield by adding the annual discount amortization to the annual interest.
4. Find the average investment by dividing the sum of the investment and the face value of the investment by 2.
5. Find the rate of yield to maturity by dividing the sum of the annual yield by the average principal invested.

The preceding steps may be summarized in the following equation:

$$Rate\ of\ Yield\ to\ Maturity = \frac{Annual\ Interest + Annual\ Discount\ Amortization}{Average\ Investment}$$

Example: An investor bought fifteen Control Data $5\frac{1}{2}$s07 at 63 including commission 20 years before maturity. Find the rate of yield to maturity.

Solution:

1. $1,000 − $630 = $370   discount per bond

2. $370 ÷ 20 = $18.50   annual discount amortization

3. $1,000 × 0.055 = $55   annual interest per bond
   $55 + $18.50 = $73.50   total annual yield per bond

4. $\dfrac{\$630 + \$1,000}{2} = \$815$ average investment per bond

5. $73.50 ÷ $815 = 9.02%   rate of yield to maturity

As each bond in a specific class will yield the same return as any other bond in that class, the figures pertaining to only one bond may be used to simplify the computation of either rate of annual yield or rate of yield to maturity.

1. How much is the annual income from twenty bonds with a face value of $1,000 each that pay $14\frac{1}{2}\%$ interest?

2. How much is the annual income on fifteen $1,000, $6\frac{1}{4}\%$ bonds?

3. How much interest is received each semiannual payment date on twelve $1,000 bonds that pay 15% interest?

4. How much interest is received on each interest date by a bondholder who owns seven $1,000 bonds that bear 12% interest, payable on January 1 and July 1?

5. A $1,000, $16\frac{1}{2}\%$ bond was purchased at 104 including commission. To the nearest hundredth percent, what is the rate of annual yield on the investment?

6. A $1,000 bond that pays 15% interest was purchased at 85 including commission. To the nearest hundredth percent, what is the rate of annual yield?

7. To the nearest hundredth percent, what is the rate of annual yield on a $1,000, $4\frac{1}{4}\%$ bond purchased at $83\frac{5}{8}$ plus $10 commission?

8. To the nearest hundredth percent, what is the rate of annual yield on a $1,000, 16% bond that was purchased at $102\frac{1}{4}$ plus $10 commission?

9. Elizabeth Summers has decided to purchase a number of Continental Corporation 12% bonds at $92\frac{3}{4}$ including commission. **(a)** How many $1,000 bonds should she purchase to provide an annual interest income of $3,600 from the investment? **(b)** What will be the amount of her total investment in the bonds?

10. Mike Lombard wants to buy a sufficient number of $14\frac{1}{2}\%$ bonds to provide an annual income of $12,325. **(a)** How many $1,000 bonds should he purchase? **(b)** How much will his total investment be if the bonds can be bought at $86\frac{7}{8}$ plus $5 brokerage fee per bond?

11. What amount must be invested in $15\frac{1}{2}\%$ bonds at $101\frac{1}{4}$ including commission to provide an annual income of $17,980?

12. Allied Cement $7\frac{1}{4}\%$ bonds are selling at 105 including commission. What amount of money must be invested in the bonds to yield a minimum annual income of $6,640?

13. Ten $1,000, 12% bonds were bought at $102\frac{1}{2}$ including commission ten years before maturity. Find the rate of yield to maturity to the nearest hundredth percent.

14. Shoreline Corporation issued $600,000 of 12%, 20-year bonds on February 1. Interest is payable semiannually on February 1 and August 1. The investor paid $97\frac{1}{2}$ including commission. Find the rate of yield to maturity.

15. Betty Mandell bought 300 bonds at 84 including commission. The 8%, $1,000 bonds mature eight years from the date of purchase. To the nearest hundredth percent, find the rate of yield to maturity.

16. John Parker purchased thirty Natl Bus 10s95 bonds, maturing 7 years 6 months from the date of purchase. The price was $101\frac{3}{8}$ including commission. To the nearest hundredth percent, find the rate of yield to maturity.

REVIEW PROBLEMS

Solve these problems. If you have difficulty solving any problem, restudy the appropriate section in this chapter. The problems under a specific number are related to those contained in the exercise with the same last number.

1. David Proctor ordered 400 shares of stock listed on the New York Stock Exchange at $86\frac{1}{4}$. What was the total cost of the stock including commission of $705.90?

2. Susan Frier sold through her broker 30 shares of AMO Air at the round-lot price of $57\frac{1}{2}$. How much did she receive after the broker deducted the commission and fee of $34.22?

3. a. An investor bought 200 shares of stock and sold them a few months later. If the shares were bought at 68 plus a commission of $221.60 and sold at 75 less commission and fees of $240.30, how much was the net capital gain?
b. A share of stock that cost $70 yields a quarterly dividend of $1.05. What is the rate of yield?
c. A block of Eltron stock, which pays a quarterly dividend of 60¢, was bought at $49\frac{3}{8}$ including commission. The stock was held for $2\frac{1}{2}$ years and then sold at 54 in net proceeds per share. To the nearest 0.1%, find the rate of total gain on cost.

4. Robert Schultz purchased through the New York Stock Exchange four $1,000 bonds that bear interest at $5\frac{1}{2}$%, payable on January 1 and July 1. The quoted price was $80\frac{3}{8}$ plus commission of $10 per bond. The interest accrued was for 93 days. What is the total expenditure for this investment?

5. Eloise Calvo sold 5 Sky Pac $14\frac{3}{4}$s13 at $81\frac{3}{4}$ on the interest date. Accrued interest was not included. How much net proceeds did she receive if the commission and fees totaled $50.41?

6. a. Paul Kramer owns fifteen $1,000, $12\frac{1}{2}$% bonds. What is the amount of his annual income from these bonds?
b. If twelve $1,000 bonds that bear interest at $15\frac{3}{4}$% are purchased at $86\frac{1}{4}$ including commission, what will be the rate of annual yield?

c. Allegany Corporation issued $600,000 of 12%, 25-year bonds on March 1. Interest is payable semiannually on September 1 and March 1. The investor paid 95 including commission. To the nearest hundredth percent, find the rate of yield to maturity.

CHALLENGE PROBLEM

On January 2, 19X1, Li-ming Shen bought 10,000 shares of Skyview Corporation's outstanding stock at a total cost of $100,000. The following events occurred on the dates shown:

19X1

April 18   Skyview Corporation declared a cash dividend of 60 cents per share, payable on May 1 to stockholders of record April 30.

May   1   Skyview paid the dividend declared on April 18.

19X2

Jan.   2   Skyview Corporation announced that its net income for 19X1 was $50,000.

May   7   Skyview Corporation declared a stock dividend of one share of stock for each two shares already outstanding.

June 1   Skyview issued the stock dividend declared on May 7.

Nov.   2   Skyview Corporation declared a cash dividend of 50 cents per share, payable on December 1 to stockholders of record November 30.

Dec.   1   Skyview paid the cash dividend declared on November 2.

19X3

Jan.   2   Skyview Corporation announced that its net income for the year 19X2 was $72,000.

Jan.   5   Shen sold 5,000 shares of her Skyview Corporation stock, receiving $8 per share after paying the commission and SEC fee.

Show your calculations for each of the following:

a. Compute the cost per share of Shen's investment in Skyview Corporation on January 4, 19X3.

b. How much is her total capital gain (or loss) on the 5,000 shares that she sold?

c. What is the total cost value of the Skyview stock she had remaining after selling the 5,000 shares?

d. To the nearest tenth, compute the rate of yield for **(1)** 19X1 and **(2)** 19X2.

e. To the nearest tenth, calculate the rate of total gain (or loss) on the 5,000 shares that she sold.

Appendix A

Abbreviations Used in Business

A, ampere; acre(s); area
A., a., answer
a, atto
A/C, a/c, ac., account
acct., account; accountant
ACRS, accelerated cost recovery system (a depreciation method)
Agt., agt., agent; agreement
a.m., before noon
amt., amount
ann., (L., *anni*), annual; annuity
APR, annual percentage rate
a/s, account sales
aud., auditor
av., avg., average
B, b, base
bal., balance
bbl, barrel(s)
bd., board; bond; bundle
bg., bag(s)
bk., bank; block; book
bkpg., bookkeeping
bkpr., bookkeeper
bkt., basket; bracket
B/L, bill of lading
B/O, back order

bot., bought
bl, bale; barrel
bldg., building
bu, bureau; bushel(s)
bx., box
C, hundred; circumference; Celsius
cap., capital; capitalize
cat., catalog
C.B.D., cash before delivery
C.C., cc, carbon copy; cashier's check
cd, candela; cord
cg, centigram(s)
chg., charge
C.I.F., c.i.f., cost, insurance, and freight
ck., cask; check
C.L., c.l., carload; carload lot(s)
C.L.U., Chartered Life Underwriter
cL, centiliter(s)
cm, centimeter(s)
cm³, cubic centimeter(s)
cml., coml., commercial
Co., co., Company; county
COD, c.o.d., cash on delivery; collect on delivery
Corp., corporation

CPA, C.P.A., Certified Public
    Accountant
Cr., cr., credit; creditor
crt., crate
ctn., carton
cu, cubic
cv., cvt., convertible (bonds)
cwt, hundredweight
d, dram(s); diameter
D., d., da, date; day(s)
dag, dekagram(s)
daL, dekaliter(s)
dam, dekameter(s)
d.b.a., doing business as
deb., deben., debenture
deg., degree
dept., department
dft., draft
dg, decigram(s)
dis., disc., disct., discount
div., divided; dividend
dL, deciliter(s)
D/L, demand loan
do., ditto
dm, decimeter(s)
doz, dz, dozen(s)
Dr, Dr, debit; debtor; Doctor
dr., dr, debit; debtor; drachma;
    dram(s)
d.s., days after sight
E, exa
ea., each
e. & o.e., errors and omissions
    excepted
e.g., (L., *exempli gratia*), for example
enc., encl., enclosure
EOM, e.o.m., end of month
est., established; estimated
etc., (L., *et cetera*), and so forth
ex., example; exception; executive;
    extra; without
exch., exchange
ex. div., without dividend
exp., expense(s); export; express
F, Fahrenheit
f., folio or page
f, femto
fac., facsim., facsimile
FIFO, fifo, first in, first out
fin., financial
FISH, fish, first in, still here

fl oz, fluid ounce(s)
FOB, f.o.b., free on board
frt., freight
ft, foot; feet
fwd., forward
G, giga
g, gram(s)
gal, gallon(s)
gds., goods
gi, gill(s)
gr, grain(s); gross
G.T.C., g.t.c., good till canceled,
    or countermanded
guar., guarantee
h, hecto; height; hour
hdqrs., headquarters
hg, hectogram(s)
hf., half
hL, hectoliter(s)
hm, hectometer(s)
HP, H.P., hp, h.p., horsepower
hr, h, hour(s)
ht., height; heat
i.e., (L., *id est*), that is
in, inch(es)
Inc., inc., Incorporated; inclosure;
    income; increase
ins., insurance
int., interest
inv., invoice
invt., inventory
IOU, I.O.U., I owe you
j/a, joint account
K, kelvin
K., k., carat
k, kilo (thousand)
kg., keg(s)
kg, kilogram(s)
kL, kiloliter(s)
km, kilometer(s)
kw, kilowatt
kwh, kwhr, kilowatt hour
l, length
L, liter(s)
lb, (L., *libra*), pound(s)
L/C, l/c, letter of credit
L.C.L., l.c.l., less than carload lot
LIFO, lifo, last in, first out
l.p., list price
L.S., (L., *locus sigilli*), the place of the
    seal

Appendix A. Abbreviations Used in Business

lt, long ton(s)
Ltd., ltd., limited
M, thousand; mega
M., m., mile; mill; minute; month
m, meter(s)
MACRS, modified accelerated cost recovery system
max., maximum
mdse., merchandise
mem., memo., memorandum
mfd., manufactured
mg, milligram(s)
Mgr., Mgr, Manager
mi, mile; mill
min., minimum; mining, minor
min, minute(s)
misc., miscellaneous
mL, milliliter(s)
mm, millimeter(s)
MO, m.o., money order
mo, month(s)
mol, mole
mph, m.p.h., miles per hour
mtge., mortgage
N., n., noon
n, nano
N.F., n/f, no funds
No., no., (L., *numero*), number
N.S.F., not sufficient funds
nt wt, net weight
o/c, overcharge; over the counter
OD, O.D., overdraft; overdrawn
o/d, on demand
o.e., omissions excepted
o/s, out of stock
off., offered; officer; official
OK, all correct
oz, ounce(s)
P, perimeter; peta
p, pico
p., page; penny; pint
P.A., P/A, Purchasing Agent; power of attorney; private account
pat., patent; patented
payt., payment
PBX, P.B.X., private branch (telephone) exchange
P/C, p/c, petty cash; prices current
pc., piece; price(s)
P.D., p.d., (L., *per diem*), by the day
pd., paid

pf., pfd., pref., preferred
PIA, primary insurance amount
pk., pack
pk, peck(s)
pkg., package(s)
p.m., after noon
P.P., p.p., parcel post; postpaid
pp., pages; privately printed
ppd., postpaid; prepaid
pr., pair(s); paper; power; present; price
prem., premium
prop., property
propr., proprietor
prox., (L., *proximo*), next month
pt., part; point
pt, pint(s)
pwt, pennyweight
q., qr., quarter; quire
qt., quantity
qt, quart(s)
quot., quotation
r, radius
rd., round
rd, rod
rec., receipt; record; recorded; recorder
recd., received
ref., reference; referred
reg., registered
res., reserve
retd., returned
rev., revenue; reverse; review; revise; revolving
rm, ream (paper)
ROG, r.o.g., receipt of goods
rpt., report
Rts., rights (stocks and bonds)
Ry., railway
s, second(s)
S/D, sight draft
sec, second(s)
sec., secy., secretary
set., settlement
sh., share
ship., shipped
shpt., shipt., shipment
shtg., shortage
SI, International System of Measurements
Sig., sig., signature
sq, square

stge., storage
stk., stock
Supt., supt., superintendent
T, tera; ton(s)
t., tare; time
t, metric ton(s)
tfr., tr., transfer
trans., transactions; transferred
treas., treasurer; treasury
ult., (L, *ultimo*), last month
V, volume
viz. , (L., *videlicet*), namely

vol., volume
vs., (L., *versus*), against
w, width
wk., work
wk, week(s)
wrnt., warrant
wt., weight
x, extra
x-rts., ex-rights
yd, yard(s)
yr, year(s)

Appendix A. Abbreviations Used in Business

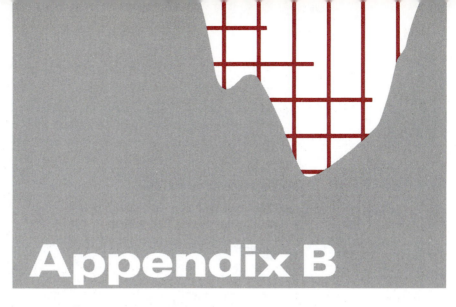

Appendix B

Symbols Used
in Business Mathematics

+	addition, plus; positive
&	and
. . .	and so on
@	at
∵	because; since
¢	cent(s)
✔	check; correct
°	degree(s)
÷	division, divide
$	dollar(s)
=	equals, is equal to; the sign of equality
≠	is not equal to
′	foot; feet; minute(s)
/	fraction (e.g., 3/4); divide
>	greater than
≯	is not greater than

C	hundred
"	inch(es); second(s)
∞	infinity
<	less than
≮	is not less than
×	multiplication, multiply; times
#	number (when written before a figure)
	pound(s) (when written after a figure)
n	any number
π	pi
%	percent; hundredths
£	pounds sterling
$\sqrt{}$	radical sign meaning square root
(), [], {}	signs of aggregation (parentheses, brackets, braces), used to show that the quantities enclosed are to be considered together

:	is to	
		signs of proportion (ratio), e.g., $a:b::c:d$ equals $\dfrac{a}{b} = \dfrac{c}{d}$
::	as	

−	subtraction, minus; negative
Σ	sum of finite quantities
∴	therefore
M	thousand

Appendix C

List of Tables

Answers to Odd-Numbered Problems in Exercises and to all Review Problems

The following answers include answers to odd-numbered problems in the exercises and answers to all problems in the reviews.

CHAPTER 1

Exercise 1–1, page 5

A. 1. Forty-eight
3. Two thousand, four hundred thirteen
5. Nine hundred thirty thousand, nine hundred thirty
7. Eighty million, seventy-eight thousand, six hundred fifty-one
9. Eighty-six billion, twenty-seven million, sixty-five thousand, nine
11. Twenty-two million, three thousand, sixty
13. Seventy-three trillion, twenty-five million, five hundred ninety thousand, fifty-eight
15. Nine billion, thirty-three thousand

17. Seventeen billion, four million, forty-six thousand, sixty-nine
19. Seven trillion, two hundred nine billion, sixty-nine million, nine hundred sixty-one thousand

B. 1. 43
3. 7,383
5. 80,674
7. 1,822,210
9. 7,009,004,003

Exercise 1–2, page 7

1. 6,000
3. 20,000
5. 10,600,000

7. 620,000,000
9. 493,445,576,000,000
11. 4,757,600,000,000,000
13. 73,181,300,000,000
15. 10,000,000,000,000

Exercise 1–3, pages 8–9

1. 1,628
3. 2,197
5. 2,947
7. 18,683
9. 15,915
11. 132,201
13. 424,723
15. 10,481,985

Exercise 1–4, pages 9–10

1. 2,472
    <u>1,697</u>
    4,169

3. 16,718
    <u>19,641</u>
    36,359

5. 3,086
    <u>2,565</u>
    5,651

7. 27,407
    <u>26,269</u>
    53,676

9. 3,274
    3,259
    <u>2,593</u>
    9,126

11. 15,333
    20,548
    <u>17,549</u>
    53,430

Exercise 1–5, pages 10–11

1. 64
3. 68
5. 81
7. 267
9. 3,421

Exercise 1–6, pages 11–12

A. 1. 387
   3. 228
   5. 211
   7. 422
   9. 373
   11. 376
   13. 1,996
B. 1. 221
   3. 398
   5. 230
   7. 197
   9. 315
   11. 411
   13. 2,059
C. 1. 861
   3. 926
   5. 954
   7. 978
   9. 1,050
   11. 1,249
   13. 1,259
   15. 7,238

Exercise 1–7, page 13

1. 128
3. 21,479
5. 2,995,550
7. 2,968
9. 233,436
11. 470
13. 29,901
15. 1,298,695
17. 1,555
19. 220,037

Exercise 1–8, page 14

A. 1. 2,316
   3. 912
   5. 5,619
   7. 4,297
   9. 23,903
B. 1. 2,330
   3. 6,279
   5. 1,546
   7. 5,591
   9. 27,232

C. 1. −492
3. +1,974
5. −920
7. +1,465
9. −595
11. 100,736
13. 7,190

Exercise 1–9, page 15

1. 16,383
3. 49,558
5. 90,143
7. 130,732
9. 70,749,540
11. 918,904
13. 3,305,088
15. 9,175,245

Exercise 1–10, page 16

1. 53,298
3. 22,977
5. 66,066
7. 895,875
9. 3,811,893
11. 37,127,819
13. 498,666,168
15. 719,650,130

Exercise 1–11, pages 16–17

1. 6,390
3. 1,944,000
5. 156,000
7. 33,390,000
9. 39,000,000
11. 810,000
13. 24,150,000
15. 26,684,000
17. 22,720,000
19. 712,800,000

Exercise 1–12, page 18

1. 3,687 R12
3. 5,040 R5
5. 10,747 R16
7. 10,071 R160
9. 10,234 R57

11. 17,230 R89
13. 2,163 R252
15. 61,566 R48

Exercise 1–13, page 19

1. 79
3. $797\frac{4}{7}$
5. $12,693\frac{4}{5}$
7. $263,140.83
9. $14,647\frac{2}{3}$

Review Problems, pages 19–21

1. a. 71,000,400,935
   b. 43,292,000
2. a. 28,000
   b. 93,500,000
3. a. 248,768
   b. 337,784
   c. 1,820,166
   d. 14,451,884
4. a. 3,611
      3,000
      6,611
   b. 3,144
      3,753
      6,897
5. a. 46
   b. 52
   c. 298
   d. 3,558
6. a. 179
   b. 253
   c. 305
   d. 234
   e. 355
   f. 259
   g. 265
   h. 264
   i. 327
   j. 211
   k. 1,326
   l. 337
   m. 142
   n. 310
   o. 220
   p. 139
   q. 228

r. 198
s. 256
t. 182
u. 284
v. 1,148
7. a. 39,662
b. 22,493
c. 34,381
d. 51,581
8. a. 4,194
b. 4,284
c. 2,112
d. 3,702
e. 2,187
f. 9,841
g. 939
h. 61,129
i. 33,870
j. 27,259
9. a. 58,138
b. 22,152
c. 196,980
d. 6,637,950
10. a. 35,136
b. 75,603
c. 146,688
d. 5,272,405
11. a. 12,960
b. 2,580,000
c. 38,560,000
d. 5,670,000
e. 52,020,000
f. 6,314,000
12. a. 10,622 R35
b. 24,302 R194
c. 10,909 R24
d. 40,305
13. a. $87\frac{1}{7}$
b. 901
c. 9,381
d. 24,231

CHAPTER 2

Exercise 2–1, page 27

1. +12
3. −16
5. +4

7. +4
9. +5
11. −1
13. −9
15. −6
17. −2*ab*
19. −13*x*

Exercise 2–2, page 29

1. +56
3. −56
5. −63
7. −44
9. −120
11. +170*a*
13. −216*x*
15. +415*abc*
17. −210
19. +5,184

Exercise 2–3, page 30

1. +4
3. −14
5. −1
7. −10
9. +1
11. −110
13. +58
15. +6
17. −36*ab*
19. −18*xy*

Exercise 2–4, page 31

1. +3
3. −3
5. +3
7. −6
9. +4
11. −9
13. −5
15. −18
17. +18*x*
19. −23

Exercise 2–5, pages 34–35

A. 1. Commutative
3. Associative

568   Answers to Odd-Numbered Problems

5. Commutative
7. Distributive
9. Distributive

B. 1. $(5 \times 70) + (5 \times 30)$
3. $(20 \times 8) + (7 \times 8)$
5. $(6 \times 50) + (6 \times 9)$

C. 1. $9 \times (3 + 5)$
3. $7 \times (10 + 14)$
5. $(15 + 23) \times 10$

D. 1. $(5 \times 10) + (5 \times 2)$
3. $(3 \times 30) + (3 \times 5)$
5. $(7 \times 300) + (7 \times 70) + (7 \times 6)$

E. 1. $(4 \times 5) - (4 \times 2)$
3. $(27 \times 5) - (12 \times 5)$
5. $3 \times (38 - 20)$

11. $Y = 4$
13. $a = 50$
15. $Y = 31$
17. $N = 12$
19. $x = 62$
21. $x = 9$
23. $a = 20$
25. $b = 13$
27. $c = 34$
29. $N = 37$

Exercise 2–6, page 36

1. $x = 70$
3. $z = 11$
5. $X = 20$
7. $Z = 43$
9. $X = 146$
11. $63 = Z$

Exercise 2–7, pages 38–39

1. $x = 42$
3. $z = 1,089$
5. $8 = x$
7. $Y = 15$
9. $N = 5$
11. $x = 4$
13. $x = 16$
15. $N = 54$
17. $N = 29$
19. $81 = x$
21. $74 = z$
23. $x = 5$
25. $Z = 46$
27. $x = 21$
29. $Z = 42$

Exercise 2–8, page 41

1. $x = 7$
3. $N = 97$
5. $x = 64$
7. $Z = 10$
9. $a = 30$

Exercise 2–9, pages 43–44

A. 1. 3,212
3. 19,186
5. 281,087
7. 261,098

B. 1. 239
3. 22,952
5. 4,683
7. $-50,563$

C. 1. 41
3. $-42,958$
5. $-31,549$

D. 1. 3
3. 7
5. 240
7. -372

E. 1. $10,171
3. 3,112
5. 5,628
7. (2,153)

Exercise 2–10, page 45

A. 1. 38,761
3. 143,568
5. 597,584
7. 744,200
9. 36,546,356

B. 1. 87
3. 86
5. 154
7. 927

C. 1. 3,712
3. 4,352
5. 168,495
7. 31,845

Exercise 2–11, page 47

A. 1. Subtract
   3. Add
   5. Multiply
   7. Divide
   9. Add
B. 1. $(15 + 7) \div 11$
   3. $24 \div (6 + 2)$
   5. $(18 + 4) \div (15 - 3)$
   7. $3 \times 7 \times 108 \div 6 \div 9$
      or $(3 \times 7 \times 108) \div (6 \times 9)$
   9. $[8 \times (16 - 4)] \div 24$
   11. $[1600 \div (14 + 6)] \div (36 + 4)$
C. 1. 27
   3. 8
   5. 1,127
   7. 552
   9. 609
   11. 1,731
   13. 199
   15. 18
   17. 134
   19. 49

Exercise 2–12, page 48

1. 3,452
3. 3,987
5. 3,422
7. 1,534
9. 12
11. 6

Exercise 2–13, pages 50–51

1. $n + 5$
3. $n + 7$
5. $y - 8$
7. pr
9. $\dfrac{r}{b}$
11. $\dfrac{t}{2}$
13. $2.5x$
15. $0.25z$
17. $4(x + y)$
19. $x - \dfrac{x}{2}$
21. a. $n + 5$
    b. $n + x$

c. $n - 5$
d. $n - y$
23. a. $x + 3$
    b. $x - 3$
    c. $2x$
    d. $\dfrac{x}{2}$
25. $x - 245$
27. $s - 28$
29. $2n + 1$

Exercise 2–14, pages 53–54

1. $x = 138$
   $x + 7 = 145$
3. $x = 30$
   $x + 24 = 54$
5. $n = 46$
   $n - 13 = 33$
7. $x = 68$
   $x + 2 = 70$
   $x + 4 = 72$
   $x + 6 = 74$
9. $x = 278$
   $x + 39 = 317$
11. $x = 50$
    $2x = 100$
    $x + 6 = 56$
13. $x = 29$
    $2x = 58$
15. $x = 132$
    $x + 2 = 134$
17. $x = 71$
    $x + 2 = 73$
    $x + 4 = 75$
19. $x = 48$
21. a. $x = 8$
    b. $4x = 32$
23. $x = 162$
25. $x = \$89$
    $3x = \$267$
27. $x = 361$
    $x + 75 = 436$
29. a. $x = 8$
    b. $20 - x = 12$

Review Problems, pages 55–57

1. a. $+ 13$
   b. $- 16$
   c. $+2$

Answers to Odd-Numbered Problems

d. $-3x$
e. -101
f. $+83$
g. -20
h. $-21ab$
2. a. $+54$
   b. -54
   c. -54
   d. $+54$
   e. $-4,035ab$
   f. $+378$
   g. $+980$
   h. -768
3. a. $+21$
   b. $+89$
   c. -16
   d. $-103n$
   e. -90
   f. -45
   g. $+219$
   h. $+678xy$
4. a. $+13$
   b. $+18$
   c. -19
   d. -16
   e. $+9$
   f. -17
   g. -39
   h. $+64$
5. a. $(6 \times 20) + (6 \times 9)$
   b. $(40 \times 5) + (7 \times 5)$
   c. $6(7 + 8)$
   d. $4(23 - 15)$
   e. $(8 \times 27) - (8 \times 4)$
   f. $(5 \times 40) + (5 \times 5)$
6. a. 15
   b. 185
   c. 106
   d. 36
7. a. 38
   b. 27
   c. 195
   d. 3
   e. 18
   f. 39
8. a. 2
   b. 20
   c. 9
   d. 5
   e. 15
   f. 12

9. a. $-4,912$
   b. $-58,287$
   c. 250
   d. -654
10. a. 2,070,180
    b. 56,693,952
    c. 125
    d. 2,742
    e. 34,884
    f. 29,382
11. a. (1) $1,288 \times 5 \times 6 \div 8 \div 7$
        or $(1,288 \times 5 \times 6) \div (8 \times 7)$
        (2) $[(34 + 8) \times 4] \div 14$
    b. 150
    c. 89
12. a. 7,385
    b. 1,244
    c. 12
    d. 15
13. a. $3(x + y)$
    b. $x - 7$
    c. $\dfrac{n}{2}$
    d. $y - \dfrac{y}{2}$
14. a. 139, 187
    b. 127, 128, 129
    c. 95, 97, 99
    d. 63, 126, 132
    e. 12, 22
    f. 398, 461
    g. $720
    h. $74,500
    i. (1) 3
       (2) 12
    j. (1) $55,200
       (2) $110,400
       (3) $331,200

CHAPTER 3

Exercise 3–1, page 61

1. 6
3. 8
5. 36
7. 75
9. 112

11. 81
13. 1
15. 2
17. 5
19. 3
21. 9
23. 3

Exercise 3–2, pages 62–63

1. GCD 9; $\frac{17}{20}$

3. GCD 7; $\frac{5}{12}$

5. GCD 1; $\frac{104}{265}$

7. GCD 6; $\frac{54}{65}$

9. GCD 15; $\frac{23}{28}$

11. GCD 12; $\frac{11}{31}$

13. GCD 19; $\frac{11}{14}$

15. GCD 16; $\frac{31}{40}$

17. GCD 23; $\frac{13}{15}$

19. GCD 13; $\frac{125}{132}$

Exercise 3–3, page 64

1. 2, 4, 8
3. None
5. 2, 3, 4, 6, 8
7. 2, 3, 4, 5, 6, 8, 9, 10
9. 2, 3, 4, 5, 6, 8, 9, 10
11. None
13. 2, 3, 4, 5, 6, 9, 10
15. 2, 3, 4, 6, 9
17. 2, 3, 4, 6
19. 2, 4, 8
21. 5
23. None
25. 2, 5, 10
27. 2, 4
29. 3
31. 3
33. 2, 4, 5, 8, 10
35. 3

37. 2
39. 2, 3, 6
41. 3, 5, 9
43. 2
45. 2, 3, 4, 6
47. 2, 4, 8
49. 5

Exercise 3–4, page 65

A. 1. $13\frac{1}{3}$

3. $72\frac{1}{2}$

5. $27\frac{1}{8}$

7. $6\frac{1}{4}$

9. $42\frac{1}{9}$

11. $12\frac{7}{8}$

13. $20\frac{3}{4}$

15. $8\frac{5}{16}$

17. $75\frac{1}{7}$

19. $21\frac{2}{3}$

21. $10\frac{19}{24}$

23. $78\frac{11}{48}$

25. $74\frac{1}{75}$

B. 1. $\frac{71}{5}$

3. $\frac{55}{2}$

5. $\frac{153}{8}$

7. $\frac{2,573}{8}$

9. $\frac{173}{5}$

11. $\frac{356}{9}$

13. $\frac{170}{3}$

15. $\frac{2,164}{9}$

17. $\dfrac{5,419}{10}$

19. $\dfrac{2,411}{20}$

21. $\dfrac{8,963}{10}$

23. $\dfrac{2,201}{16}$

25. $\dfrac{1,667}{48}$

Exercise 3–5, pages 66–67

A. 1. 180
  3. 60
  5. 2,520
  7. 72
  9. 4,410

B. 1. LCD 72; $\dfrac{60}{72}$, $\dfrac{18}{72}$, $\dfrac{27}{72}$, $\dfrac{32}{72}$

  3. LCD 90; $\dfrac{36}{90}$, $\dfrac{75}{90}$, $\dfrac{60}{90}$, $\dfrac{70}{90}$

  5. LCD 60; $\dfrac{52}{60}$, $\dfrac{51}{60}$, $\dfrac{35}{60}$, $\dfrac{54}{60}$

Exercise 3–6, pages 68–69

A. 1. $\dfrac{7}{9}$

  3. $1\dfrac{5}{8}$

  5. $1\dfrac{1}{3}$

  7. $9\dfrac{1}{18}$

  9. $15\dfrac{9}{16}$

11. $1\dfrac{7}{8}$

13. $2\dfrac{5}{36}$

15. $1\dfrac{51}{80}$

17. $74\dfrac{11}{18}$

19. $116\dfrac{35}{36}$

21. $39\dfrac{69}{70}$

23. $53\dfrac{11}{84}$

25. $252\dfrac{79}{144}$

27. $88\dfrac{19}{320}$

29. $2,033\dfrac{11}{18}$

B. 1. $258\dfrac{1}{4}$

  3. $225\dfrac{1}{4}$

Exercise 3–7, pages 70–71

1. $\dfrac{1}{4}$

3. $\dfrac{1}{8}$

5. $\dfrac{13}{24}$

7. $\dfrac{41}{60}$

9. $\dfrac{19}{60}$

11. $19\dfrac{1}{2}$

13. $15\dfrac{1}{3}$

15. $219\dfrac{1}{8}$

17. $11\dfrac{3}{4}$

19. $14\dfrac{5}{6}$

21. $7\dfrac{1}{3}$

23. 12

25. $18\dfrac{3}{10}$

27. $36\dfrac{5}{9}$

29. $43\dfrac{13}{28}$

31. $7\dfrac{11}{18}$

33. $134\dfrac{1}{30}$

35. $29\dfrac{1}{30}$

37. $34\dfrac{3}{4}$

39. $46\dfrac{11}{16}$

41. $25\dfrac{1}{18}$

43. $40\dfrac{2}{3}$

45. $104\dfrac{17}{30}$

47. $478\dfrac{53}{70}$

49. $372\dfrac{23}{24}$

Exercise 3–8, page 73

A. 1. 12
   3. 42
   5. $\frac{1}{2}$
   7. $\frac{1}{2}$
   9. $\frac{8}{15}$
   11. $\frac{2}{15}$
   13. $43\frac{1}{5}$
   15. $33\frac{1}{8}$

B. 1. $\frac{3}{80}$
   3. $\frac{1}{64}$
   5. $\frac{14}{75}$
   7. $\frac{85}{154}$
   9. $\frac{5}{16}$
   11. $14\frac{7}{9}$

C. 1. 112
   3. 260
   5. $169\frac{1}{3}$
   7. $2,362\frac{1}{2}$
   9. 93
   11. $49\frac{1}{2}$
   13. $32\frac{9}{10}$
   15. 60
   17. $763\frac{83}{84}$
   19. $715\frac{11}{63}$

Exercise 3–9, pages 75–76

A. 1. $\frac{3}{5}$
   3. $\frac{3}{4}$
   5. $\frac{1}{7}$
   7. $\frac{1}{18}$

9. $17\frac{1}{2}$
11. $52\frac{6}{7}$
13. $7\frac{1}{3}$
15. $6\frac{1}{2}$
17. $2\frac{7}{64}$
19. $5\frac{13}{25}$
21. $1\frac{25}{27}$
23. $1\frac{23}{37}$

B. 1. $2\frac{1}{4}$
   3. $1\frac{5}{16}$
   5. $\frac{3}{10}$
   7. $\frac{11}{105}$
   9. 64
   11. 42
   13. $29\frac{1}{2}$
   15. $32\frac{6}{11}$
   17. $1\frac{23}{96}$
   19. $6\frac{1}{5}$
   21. $\frac{156}{185}$
   23. $\frac{24}{29}$

Exercise 3–10, page 77

A. 1. 21
   3. $3\frac{1}{8}$
   5. $\frac{1}{2}$
   7. $21\frac{1}{6}$
   9. $\frac{15}{46}$

B. 1. $\frac{10}{33}$
   3. $\frac{15}{118}$

Answers to Odd-Numbered Problems

5. $\dfrac{7}{34}$

7. $\dfrac{11}{94}$

9. $\dfrac{9}{16}$

Exercise 3–11, page 78

1. $N = 17\frac{1}{8}$

3. $D = 490$

5. $y = 15$

7. $Y = \dfrac{1}{64}$

9. $D = 1\frac{13}{27}$

11. $150 = Y$

13. $X = 132$

15. $X = 16$

17. $N = 25$

19. $R = \dfrac{8}{175}$

Exercise 3–12, pages 79–80

1. 2:5

3. 1:15

5. 3:4

7. 4:9

9. $7n = 126$
    $5n = 90$

11. a. \$10,560
  b. \$18,480
  c. \$15,840

13. a. \$7,200
  b. \$7,500
  c. \$6,000

Exercise 3–13, pages 82–83

1. $21\frac{3}{5}$

3. 60

5. 48

7. 336

9. \$1,360

11. 15 inches

13. 672 miles

15. \$12,636

17. 5 hours

19. \$10,125

Exercise 3–14, pages 84–85

1. $L = 15\frac{4}{21}$

3. $N = \dfrac{5}{24}$

5. $N = \dfrac{13}{23}$

7. $N = 95\frac{1}{10}$

9. $N = 735$

11. $N = 94\frac{1}{2}$

13. $W = \dfrac{7}{11}$

15. $N = \dfrac{27}{49}$

17. $N = 62\frac{1}{2}$

19. $N = 48$

21. $N = \dfrac{7}{12}$

23. $N = \dfrac{7}{43}$

25. $N = \dfrac{85}{113}$

27. $N = 822\frac{2}{9}$

29. $N = 153\frac{3}{5}$

Exercise 3–15, pages 85–87

1. $N = \dfrac{3}{5}$

3. Atteberry: $\dfrac{29}{144}$; Bailey: $\dfrac{13}{48}$; Conners: $\dfrac{1}{3}$;
Duncan: $\dfrac{7}{36}$

5. 6,000 lbs.

7. $\dfrac{5}{12}$

9. $X = \dfrac{19}{49}$

11. $\dfrac{2}{3}$

13. a. Ivins, \$54,000; Hardy, \$36,000
  b. Ivins, \$67,500; Hardy, \$22,500
  c. Ivins, \$33,750; Hardy, \$56,250

15. \$30,720

17. a. \$591,680
  b. \$665,640

19. \$2,000

21. \$726

Review Problems, pages 87–89

1. **a.** 64
   b. 5
   c. 4
   d. 147

2. **a.** GCD 13; $\frac{5}{12}$

   b. GCD 19; $\frac{3}{5}$

   c. GCD 7; $\frac{15}{16}$

   d. GCD 1; $\frac{213}{356}$

3. **a.** None
   b. None
   c. 2, 4, 5, 8, 10
   d. 2, 4, 5, 8, 10
   e. 2, 3, 6
   f. None
   g. 2, 3, 4, 6, 9
   h. None
   i. 5
   j. 2, 3, 4, 6, 8

4. **a.** (1) $29\frac{3}{8}$

   (2) $17\frac{3}{5}$

   (3) $85\frac{1}{4}$

   (4) $39\frac{1}{7}$

   b. (1) $\frac{191}{8}$

   (2) $\frac{59}{3}$

   (3) $\frac{637}{9}$

   (4) $\frac{421}{8}$

5. **a.** 36
   b. 126
   c. 130
   d. 144

6. **a.** $1\frac{2}{3}$

   b. $1\frac{13}{24}$

   c. $11\frac{1}{24}$

d. $37\frac{8}{9}$

e. $258\frac{5}{36}$

f. $207\frac{233}{693}$

7. **a.** $\frac{5}{36}$

   b. $\frac{43}{120}$

   c. $21\frac{7}{16}$

   d. $15\frac{7}{18}$

   e. $29\frac{1}{6}$

   f. $54\frac{15}{22}$

8. **a.** $\frac{9}{35}$

   b. $\frac{5}{16}$

   c. 98

   d. 936

   e. $2,389\frac{19}{84}$

   f. $1,767\frac{1}{32}$

9. **a.** (1) $1\frac{1}{4}$

   (2) $\frac{11}{84}$

   (3) 9

   (4) 4

   (5) $3\frac{4}{45}$

   (6) $3\frac{27}{76}$

   b. (1) $\frac{15}{16}$

   (2) $\frac{3}{44}$

   (3) 49

   (4) $17\frac{1}{3}$

   (5) $\frac{11}{16}$

   (6) $2\frac{33}{310}$

Answers to Odd-Numbered Problems

10. **a.** $\frac{2}{51}$

   b. 28

   c. $\frac{9}{14}$

   d. $\frac{5}{39}$

   e. $16\frac{3}{7}$

   f. $\frac{49}{74}$

11. **a.** $X = 245$

   b. $N = \frac{59}{108}$

   c. $Y = 68$

   d. $Z = 22$

   e. $X = 37\frac{1}{2}$

   f. $P = 2,500$

12. $10,080

13. $8,400

14. **a.** $1\frac{7}{25}$

   b. $18\frac{2}{3}$

   c. $\frac{9}{20}$

   d. $63

   e. 117

   f. $\frac{32}{43}$

   g. 52

   h. $56\frac{1}{4}$

   i. 80

   j. (1) $585

     (2) $4,290

15. **a.** $11,448

   b. $226\frac{3}{8}$

   c. (1) $181,000

     (2) $90,500

   d. $\frac{2}{9}$ Arabic, $\frac{4}{9}$ Brazilian, $\frac{1}{3}$ Colombian

   e. $1,430

   f. 60

   g. $196

CHAPTER 4

Exercise 4–1, page 97

A. 1. $\frac{3}{5}$

  3. $\frac{19}{1,000}$

  5. $\frac{1,157}{5,000}$

  7. $\frac{1}{8,000}$

  9. $5\frac{16}{25}$

  11. $7\frac{99}{1,000}$

  13. $\frac{3}{8}$

  15. $\frac{5}{6}$

  17. $7\frac{1}{6}$

  19. $14\frac{1}{16}$

  21. $21\frac{3}{400}$

  23. $31\frac{1}{12}$

B. 1. 0.7

  3. 0.045

  5. 0.7143

  7. 0.9167

  9. 3.72

  11. 0.875

  13. 9.7778

  15. 0.0360

  17. 0.4375

  19. 6.45

  21. 51.0075

  23. 62.5833

Exercise 4–2, page 99

A. 1. $8.34

  3. $9.39

  5. $33.28

  7. 15.143

  9. 10.3477

  11. 47.31

  13. 219.1729

  15. 500.847

  17. 220.038

  19. 50.7825

B. 1. $59.62

  3. $26.74

  5. $61.55

  7. $4.44

  9. $3.49

  11. 482.41

13. 0.8704
15. 65.075
17. 34.25
19. 49.250

Exercise 4–3, pages 100–101

1. $424.56
3. $177.84
5. $914.45
7. 14,599.5
9. 786.40
11. 4,424.4
13. 94.078
15. 12.1118
17. 3.14962
19. 0.237882
21. 713.40
23. 129.3500
25. 24.700
27. 30.17500
29. 157.600

Exercise 4–4, page 102

1. 2.9152
3. 0.0657
5. 88.7865
7. 9,356.4286
9. 2,257.3366
11. 61.8676
13. 10.4162
15. 1,240.5373
17. 0.5783
19. 15,732.3651
21. 103.7576
23. 229.7222
25. 2.6455
27. 0.9174
29. 9.8880

Exercise 4–5, page 103

1. 9.3
3. 0.080
5. 4.7
7. 27
9. 0.26
11. 0.74
13. 1.56
15. 0.0983

17. 14.06
19. 12.1571
21. 0.358
23. 0.7878
25. 0.0278
27. 0.1433
29. 0.1146
31. 0.0019
33. 0.2197
35. 0.0062
37. 1.429
39. 0.0065
41. 3.4925
43. 2.212
45. 0.1316
47. 3.9049

Exercise 4–6, page 107

1. $61.06
3. $106.58
5. $101.92
7. $775.00
9. $237.72
11. $529.26
13. $216.27
15. $122.50
17. $69.00
19. $565.56
21. $41.13
23. $934.50

Exercise 4–7, pages 109–111

A. 1. a. 267
    b. 530
    c. 723
    d. 111.6
    e. 119.3
3. a. 22,199.31
    b. 6,023.31
    c. 105.66
    d. 133.303
    e. 104.205
5. 412
7. 952.5
B. 1. a. 177
    b. 7,744
    c. 477
    d. 287.05
    e. 122.45

Answers to Odd-Numbered Problems

3. a. 648.5
   b. 280.5
   c. 362.13
   d. 4,047.57
   e. 456.135
5. 594
7. 71.93
C. 1. a. 7,344
   b. 29,886
   c. 568,310
   d. 937.38
   e. 1,541.322
3. a. 3,327.62
   b. 8,796.59
   c. 333.4063
   d. 32.50683
   e. 20.936718
5. 19,922,112
7. 39.755996
D. 1. a. 86.5
   b. 1,655
   c. 3,379
   d. 52.6875
   e. 13.9965
3. a. 17.8
   b. 68.4138
   c. 2,936
   d. 3.0324
   e. 0.04
5. 1,338
7. 3.5

Exercise 4–8, pages 113–114

1. $1,282.72
3. $1,603.14
5. $1,784.10

Exercise 4–9, pages 118–120

1. $856.52
3. $2,534.82
5. $7,420.80
7. $688.51
9. $1,354.38
11. $1,457.74
13. $1,755.57
15. $743.34

Exercise 4–10, page 122

A. 1. $\frac{1}{2}$
   3. $\frac{3}{4}$
   5. $\frac{1}{8}$
   7. $\frac{5}{8}$
   9. $\frac{1}{3}$
   11. $\frac{1}{6}$
   13. $\frac{1}{12}$
   15. $\frac{1}{16}$
   17. $\frac{7}{12}$
   19. $\frac{3}{16}$
   21. $\frac{1}{9}$
   23. $\frac{4}{5}$
B. 1. $\frac{1}{8}$
   3. $\frac{1}{2}$
   5. $\frac{1}{12}$
   7. $\frac{1}{3}$
   9. $\frac{3}{4}$
   11. $\frac{5}{8}$
   13. $\frac{7}{12}$
   15. $\frac{1}{6}$
   17. $\frac{3}{16}$
   19. $\frac{1}{11}$
   21. $\frac{1}{16}$
   23. $\frac{5}{6}$

Exercise 4–11, page 124

1. 10¢
3. 20¢
5. 60¢
7. 75¢
9. $16\frac{2}{3}$ ¢
11. $12\frac{1}{2}$ ¢
13. $37\frac{1}{2}$ ¢
15. $66\frac{2}{3}$ ¢
17. $41\frac{2}{3}$ ¢
19. $62\frac{1}{2}$ ¢
21. $14\frac{2}{7}$ ¢
23. $91\frac{2}{3}$ ¢

Exercise 4–12, pages 124–125

1. 40.2459
3. 241
5. $1,500
7. $2.62
9. 2.5 hr
11. $45
13. $77.00
15. $6,720.75
17. 2.75
19. $24.75

Review Problems, pages 126–128

1. a. (1) $\dfrac{2}{25}$

    (2) $\dfrac{423}{2,500}$

    (3) $\dfrac{6}{125}$

    (4) $6\frac{7}{20}$

    (5) $\dfrac{5}{12}$

    (6) $3\frac{3}{16}$

    (7) $41\frac{1}{12}$

    (8) $90\frac{1}{16}$

  b. (1) 0.21
    (2) 0.625
    (3) 0.008
    (4) 0.9375
    (5) 0.0132
    (6) 13.5714
    (7) 6.375
    (8) 48.2857

2. a. (1) $20.78
    (2) $269.05
    (3) 13.968
    (4) 92.9134
  b. (1) $65.65
    (2) $7.65
    (3) 0.0303
    (4) 5.542
    (5) 18.846
    (6) 4.0675

3. a. 284.13
  b. 1,657.60
  c. 7,526.7
  d. 7.5044
  e. 0.08398
  f. 0.5244
  g. 406.9275
  h. 36.66
  i. 0.04214
  j. 182.5625

4. a. 1.1467
  b. 19.715
  c. 143.7484
  d. 1,255.1599
  e. 18.3
  f. 7.2867

5. a. 4.55
  b. 7.36
  c. 7.35
  d. 0.0121
  e. 0.0187
  f. 0.458
  g. 0.575
  h. 0.806
  i. 0.0204
  j. 1.4218
  k. 0.0479
  l. 0.0196

6. a. $54.15
  b. $61.15
  c. $32.83
  d. $190.36

Answers to Odd-Numbered Problems

e. $196.80
f. $133.38
g. $7.32
h. $48.13
7. a. (1) (a) 33,853.68
     (b) 971.68
     (c) 424.36
     (d) 451.764
     (e) 382.9569
   (2) 1,242.52
   b. (1) (a) 647.51
     (b) 4,226.51
     (c) 257.15
     (d) −7.19
     (e) 443.37
   (2) 160.19
   c. (1) (a) 4,525.56
     (b) 119,054.52
     (c) 368.6904
     (d) 35.8254
     (e) 37.72314
   (2) 247.39904
   d. (1) (a) 4,263.235
     (b) 447.055
     (c) 5.6
     (d) 3.657
     (e) 0.0007
   (2) 5
8. $813.97
9. a. $802.65
   b. $1,045.55
10. a. (1) $\frac{1}{12}$
       (2) $\frac{1}{8}$
       (3) $\frac{5}{6}$
       (4) $\frac{5}{12}$
       (5) $\frac{1}{9}$
       (6) $\frac{7}{8}$
    b. (1) $\frac{2}{3}$
       (2) $\frac{3}{8}$
       (3) $\frac{7}{12}$
       (4) $\frac{1}{16}$

(5) $\frac{1}{6}$
(6) $\frac{11}{12}$
(7) $\frac{5}{8}$
(8) $\frac{1}{11}$
11. a. 25¢
    b. 50¢
    c. 20¢
    d. $33\frac{1}{3}$ ¢
    e. $83\frac{1}{3}$ ¢
    f. $87\frac{1}{2}$ ¢
    g. $91\frac{2}{3}$ ¢
    h. $11\frac{1}{9}$ ¢
12. a. 95.3083
    b. 0.387
    c. 50
    d. $3,700
    e. $1,153.91
    f. $482.00 GP

CHAPTER 5

Exercise 5–1, page 132

1. 81 ft
3. $159\frac{1}{2}$ bu
5. $6\frac{1}{2}$ gross
7. 6,720 lb
9. 6 mi 1,870 ft
11. 145 gal 3 qt
13. 408 doz
15. 7 yr 3 wk
17. 53 lb 5 oz
19. 1,452 hr 6 min
21. 67 gal 2 qt
23. 1,500 sheets
25. 471 ft

Exercise 5–2, pages 134–135

1. 117 yd 1 ft 3 in
3. 28 hr 47 min 12 sec
5. 343 gal
7. 5 bu 3 pk 7 qt

9. 12 oz
11. 1 hr 50 min
13. 7 yr 6 wk 1 da 6 hr 58 min
15. 1 yr 40 wk 1 da 21 hr
17. $83.16
19. 4 ft 8 in

Exercise 5–3, pages 137–138

1. 39 in
3. 32 ft 9 in
5. 8 yd 2 ft
7. 344 ft
9. **a.** 47 ft 1 in
   b. 51 ft 10 in
11. 65 ft
13. $30.78
15. **a.** 6.35 mi
    b. 7.875 ft
    c. 12 ft
    d. $5\frac{2}{3}$ yd
    e. $4\frac{1}{2}$ in
17. **a.** 78.54 mi
    b. 25.1328 in
    c. 75.3984 yd
    d. 23.562 ft
    e. 2.3562 ft
19. 18 in

Exercise 5–4, pages 140–142

1. $18\frac{1}{3}$ sq ft
3. 14 acres
5. 90 sq ft
7. 5 ft 6 in
9. 560 tiles
11. 2,124 sq ft
13. **a.** 63.6174 sq in **b.** 81 sq in
    (b) is 17.3826 sq in larger.
15. $114,450
17. $4,709.25
19. $49
21. 59 sq ft

Exercise 5–5, pages 143–145

1. 2,880 cu in
3. **a.** 14,400 cu ft
   b. $533\frac{1}{3}$ cu yd
5. 1,887 cu ft

7. $11\frac{1}{9}$ cu yd
9. $106\frac{2}{3}$ cu yd
11. 62,832 cu ft
13. 369,452.16 cu ft
15. 49.0875 cu yd
17. 25,446.96 gal/hr
19. **a.** 9,047.808 cu in
    b. 6,031.872 cu in

Exercise 5–6, pages 149–150

1. **a.** 100
   b. hm
3. **a.** 10
   b. dam
5. **a.** 0.1
   b. dm
7. **a.** 0.001
   b. mm
9. **a.** 0.01
   b. cg
11. **a.** 1000
    b. kL
13. **a.** 1
    b. L
15. **a.** 1
    b. g
17. **a.** 100
    b. hg
19. **a.** 100
    b. hL
21. **a.** 10
    b. daL
23. **a.** 1
    b. m^2

Exercise 5–7, pages 151–152

A. 1. 850 dm
    3. 60 000 cm
    5. 8.534 kL
    7. 574 000 mm
    9. 8 907 700 m
    11. 76 000 mg
    13. 23.557 dag
    15. 5.1479 daL
    17. 342.4 dm
    19. 1858 hm
    21. 194 040 cL
    23. 968 000 kg

Answers to Odd-Numbered Problems

B. 1. a. 2000 cm
  b. 20 000 mm
  c. 0.02 km
 3. a. 2500 mm
  b. 2.50 m
  c. 0.0025 km
 5. a. 25 000 m
  b. 2 500 000 cm
  c. 25 000 000 mm
 7. a. 652.3 daL
  b. 65.23 hL
  c. 65 230 dL
 9. a. 8000 L
  b. 80 000 dL
  c. 80 hL

Exercise 5–8, pages 153–155

 1. 72.95 m
 3. 1880 km
 5. 350 g
 7. 24 m/s
 9. 109.728 m
 11. 2 hr 10 min
 13. $45
 15. $88.64
 17. 2622 cm²
 19. 3216.9984 cm²
 21. 9.828 m³
 23. 360 m³

Exercise 5–9, pages 160–162

A. 1. a. 3.66 m
  b. 60.35 m
  c. 22.97 ft
  d. 33.31 in
  e. 98.42 yd
  f. 63.5 cm
 3. a. 9.51 qt
  b. 16.56 L
  c. 25.55 L
  d. 1.74 gal
  e. 532.32 mL
  f. 9.47 fl oz
 5. a. 95°
  b. 329°
  c. 23.89°
  d. 176.67°
  e. 33.33°
  f. 194°

B. 1. 93.21 mi
 3. 4.7244 in
 5. 21.18 oz
 7. 19.6850 ft
 9. 10.8862 kg
C. 1. 81 mi
 3. 1.4 L
 5. 190 kL
 7. 1677 km
 9. 533.5132 T
 11. 185°

Review Problems, pages 162–163

 1. a. 14 lb
  b. 540 min
  c. 38 yd
  d. 142 gal 1 qt
  e. 1,032 doz
  f. 30 at $1\frac{3}{16}$ pt
 2. a. 24 yr 5 mo 21 da
  b. 257 in is longest
  c. 293 lb 4 oz
  d. 12 pieces
 3. a. 68 ft 8 in
  b. $21,600
  c. $105\frac{5}{6}$ ft
  d. 14.1372 in
 4. a. $336
  b. $473.75
  c. 36 sq in
  d. 5,026.56 sq mi
 5. a. 1,200 cu yd
  b. $6\frac{2}{3}$ ft
  c. 4,825.4976 cu ft
 6. a. 1000 kg
  b. 0.001 mm
  c. 100 hL
  d. 0.1 dL
  e. 0.01 cg
  f. 10 dam
 7. a. 47 350 000 mL
  b. 7745.1 kL
  c. 61.715 g
  d. 964.85 kL
  e. 2 212 100 mg
  f. 780.04 m
 8. a. 8.65 m
  b. 144 cm²
  c. 648 m³

d. (1) 6
   (2) 0.5 m
9. a. 271 in
   b. 16 gal
   c. 25.55 L
   d. 28 ft
   e. 30°
   f. 410°

CHAPTER 6

Exercise 6–1, page 167

A. 1. 3^4
   3. 5^3
   5. 2^7
   7. $-1,000^3$
   9. -4^6
B. 1. $2 \times 2 \times 2 \times 2 \times 2 \times 2 \times 2 \times 2$
   3. $11 \times 11 \times 11 \times 11 \times 11 \times 11$
   5. $4 \times 4 \times 4 \times 4 \times 4$
   7. $n \times n \times n \times n \times n \times n \times n$
   9. $(10)(10)(10)(10)(10)(10)(10)(10)$
C. 1. 243
   3. 10,000
   5. 25
   7. 1
   9. 27,889

Exercise 6–2, pages 169–170

A. 1. $\dfrac{1}{7^1}$

   3. $\dfrac{1}{9^3}$

   5. $\dfrac{1}{10^2}$

   7. $\dfrac{1}{6^4}$

   9. 8^6
   11. 10^3
B. 1. 49
   3. 6,561
   5. 15,625
   7. 167.9616
   9. 117,649
   11. -0.015625
   13. 0.0123456
   15. 0.1428571
   17. 0.0012673

19. 0.1225
21. 0.0074831
C. 1. 10^6
   3. 10^9
   5. 10^5
   7. 10^{-2}
   9. 1
   11. 10^{-1}

Exercise 6–3, pages 173–174

A. 1. 1,110.2019
   3. 2,450.2494
   5. 400,569,280
   7. 1,256,070,200
   9. 14,065,488,000
   11. 9,404.6822
   13. 55,000,000
   15. 8,222,400,000
B. 1. 7,812
   3. 0.5031
   5. 12,960
   7. 0.000216
   9. 44,200,000
   11. 0.00000124
   13. 7,131.01
C. 1. 7.131×10^2
   3. 2.186×10^1
   5. 3.10245×10^3
   7. 3.714×10^{-1}
   9. 4.34×10^{-3}
   11. 5×10^{-2}
   13. 7.88×10^2
   15. 8.17×10^0
   17. 5.8×10^{-4}
D. 1. 373,248,000,000,000,000
   3. 515,082,240,000,000,000,000
   5. 65.79
   7. 7,344.061
   9. 104,880,000,000
   11. 0.000055
   13. 136,040,000,000,000
   15. 0.0000000000042

Exercise 6–4, pages 175–176

A. 1. $(4 \times 10^2) + (3 \times 10^1) + (5 \times 10^0)$
   3. $(3 \times 10^3) + (6 \times 10^2) + (0 \times 10^1) +$
      (0×10^0)
   5. $(3 \times 10^4) + (7 \times 10^3) + (1 \times 10^2) +$
      $(7 \times 10^1) + (2 \times 10^0)$

Answers to Odd-Numbered Problems

7. $(1 \times 10^4) + (0 \times 10^3) + (0 \times 10^2) +$
   $(0 \times 10^1) + (0 \times 10^0)$
9. $(4 \times 10^5) + (0 \times 10^4) + (0 \times 10^3) +$
   $(5 \times 10^2) + (4 \times 10^1) + (6 \times 10^0)$

B. 1. 693
   3. 4,306,461
   5. 255,519
   7. 13,001,668,837

Exercise 6–5, page 178

1. 16
3. 22
5. 29
7. 35
9. 23
11. 75
13. 179
15. 213
17. 587
19. 365

Exercise 6–6, page 179

1. 10010
3. 111111
5. 110011
7. 101011
9. 11101
11. 1100101
13. 11010110
15. 1100011110
17. 1110010000
19. 10010000100

Exercise 6–7, page 180

A. 1. 64
   3. 32
   5. 75
   7. 208
   9. 842
   11. 3,526
   13. 8,069
   15. 6,808
   17. 98,512
   19. 60,253
B. 1. 0100-0010
   3. 0001-1001
   5. 1000-0000
   7. 0101-0011-0111

9. 1001-0100-0101
11. 0011-0100-0000-0001
13. 0101-0011-0111-0001
15. 0111-1000-0000-1001
17. 0110-0001-0001-0111-0011
19. 0011-0100-0101-0011-0000

Exercise 6–8, page 181

1. 10
3. 111
5. 101
7. 100
9. 1000
11. 11101
13. 11
15. 1000
17. 10010
19. 10010
21. 100111
23. 110001

Exercise 6–9, page 183

1. 1
3. 11
5. 1010
7. 1
9. 110
11. 1011
13. 1110
15. 11101
17. 100010
19. 11100101

Exercise 6–10, page 184

1. 1110
3. 1111
5. 1000001
7. 1001110
9. 11111101
11. 1101001
13. 1001000111
15. 111011001
17. 101000001111
19. 1001000100100

Exercise 6–11, page 184

1. 11
3. 110

5. 1001

7. 1001

9. 101

11. 11

13. 111

Review Problems, pages 184–186

1. a. 4^3
   b. 5^6
   c. $7 \times 7 \times 7 \times 7$
   d. 1,000,000

2. a. (1) $\dfrac{1}{8^3}$

   (2) $\dfrac{1}{9^4}$

   (3) 10^2

   b. (1) 390,625
   (2) -2.48832
   (3) 0.015625
   c. (1) 10^1
   (2) 10^8

3. a. (1) 5,764,610,800
   (2) 194,510,000,000
   b. (1) 28,500
   (2) 0.0000396
   c. (1) 4.976×10^3
   (2) 3.45809×10^2
   (3) 2.1×10^{-4}
   d. (1) 18,497.16
   (2) 2,048,000,000,000,000,000

4. a. (1) $(5 \times 10^2) + (7 \times 10^1) + (6 \times 10^0)$
   (2) $(4 \times 10^3) + (7 \times 10^2) + (0 \times 10^1) +$
       (0×10^0)
   (3) $(2 \times 10^4) + (5 \times 10^3) + (3 \times 10^2) +$
       $(8 \times 10^1) + (0 \times 10^0)$
   (4) $(9 \times 10^5) + (0 \times 10^4) + (0 \times 10^3) +$
       $(6 \times 10^2) + (8 \times 10^1) + (2 \times 10^0)$

   b. (1) 931
   (2) 4,268
   (3) 570,408
   (4) 64,073,000

5. a. 8
   b. 18
   c. 55
   d. 59
   e. 108
   f. 93
   g. 475
   h. 875

6. a. 10001
   b. 101101
   c. 1000101
   d. 1010011
   e. 11101110
   f. 1000110100
   g. 1101100110
   h. 10100101001

7. a. (1) 14
   (2) 64
   (3) 82
   (4) 420
   (5) 571
   (6) 9,043
   b. (1) 0010-0110
   (2) 0100-1000
   (3) 1000-0001
   (4) 0100-0110-0000
   (5) 0011-0101-0111-0010
   (6) 1001-0011-0000-0101

8. a. 110
   b. 1100
   c. 10010
   d. 110
   e. 10000
   f. 101000

9. a. 100
   b. 100
   c. 1110
   d. 100100
   e. 11100
   f. 11100101

10. a. 1010
   b. 11001
   c. 1011011
   d. 11010010
   e. 1000010010
   f. 11110100110

11. a. 11
   b. 110
   c. 101
   d. 11
   e. 111
   f. 1101

CHAPTER 7

Exercise 7-1, page 190

1. 0.08

3. 8

Answers to Odd-Numbered Problems

5. 0.07

7. 3.75

9. 0.5

11. 0.005

13. 0.0025

15. 0.075

17. 7.5

19. 0.045

21. 0.00333. . .

23. 0.00125

25. 0.00666. . .

Exercise 7–2, page 190

1. $\frac{1}{5}$

3. $\frac{1}{4}$

5. $\frac{1}{10}$

7. $1\frac{1}{4}$

9. $3\frac{3}{4}$

11. $\frac{2}{25}$

13. $\frac{1}{200}$

15. $\frac{1}{40}$

17. $\frac{9}{16}$

19. $\frac{1}{400}$

21. $\frac{1}{12}$

23. $\frac{2}{3}$

Exercise 7–3, page 191

1. 40%

3. $\frac{2}{5}$%

5. 350%

7. 525%

9. 210%

11. 90%

13. $\frac{1}{4}$%

15. $\frac{1}{5}$%

17. $12\frac{1}{2}$%

19. 600%

21. $\frac{1}{3}$%

23. $3\frac{1}{3}$%

Exercise 7–4, page 192

1. 50%

3. 425%

5. 4%

7. $62\frac{1}{2}$%

9. 575%

11. 60%

13. $58\frac{1}{3}$%

15. $6\frac{1}{4}$%

17. 480%

19. $93\frac{3}{4}$%

21. $33\frac{1}{3}$%

23. $756\frac{1}{4}$%

Exercise 7–5, pages 195–196

A. 1. $28.24

3. $490

5. $2.48

7. $3.15

9. $485

11. $102.32

B. 1. $2.10

3. $63.60

5. $7.98

C. 1. $189.00

3. $409.50

5. $936.00

7. $40.58

9. $720.00

D. 1. $54.45

3. $123.00

5. $5.20

7. $1,275.00

9. $2,083.33

E. 1. $67

3. $104.50

5. $7,693,700

Exercise 7–6, pages 197–198

A. 1. 20%

3. $58\frac{1}{3}$%

5. 75%

7. $12\frac{1}{2}\%$

9. $8\frac{1}{3}\%$

11. 124%

B. 1. 8%

   3. $33\frac{1}{3}\%$

   5. 30%

   7. 20%

   9. $14\frac{1}{4}\%$

   11. $10\frac{1}{2}\%$

   13. 13%

   15. $16\frac{2}{3}\%$

Exercise 7–7, pages 200–201

A. 1. $332

   3. $304

   5. $340

   7. $1,700

   9. $752

   11. $316

B. 1. 300

   3. 244

   5. 4,752.8

   7. $535

   9. $346,400

   11. $3,200

   13. $3,800

Exercise 7–8, pages 203–204

1. a. 1¢

   b. 4¢

   c. 23¢

   d. 0

   e. 2¢

   f. 9¢

3. a. $147.27

   b. $149.55

5. a. Sales Tax: $0.31; Excise Tax: $0.77
      Total Received: $8.77

   b. Sales Tax: $0.51; Excise Tax: $1.27
      Total Received: $14.47

   c. Sales Tax: $3.16; Excise Tax: $7.90
      Total Received: $90.04

   d. Sales Tax: $5.72; Excise Tax: $14.31
      Total Received: $163.15

   e. Sales Tax: $25.22; Excise Tax: $63.04
      Total Received: $718.66

   f. Sales Tax: $111.80; Excise Tax: $279.50
      Total Received: $3,186.30

7. a. $24.50

   b. $0.98

9. a. $240,436.22

   b. $14,426.17

Exercise 7–9, pages 206–207

1. a. $1.25

   b. $3.50

   c. $5.79

   d. $0.16

   e. $7.73

   f. $2.76

3. a. $7.50

   b. $1.76

   c. $0.60

   d. $5.12

   e. $2.73

   f. $14.30

5. 58.4 mills per $1

7. a. 27 mills per $1

   b. $1,755

9. $7,434

Review Problems, pages 207–209

1. a. 0.09

   b. 0.6

   c. 3

   d. 0.085

   e. 0.002

   f. 0.062

   g. 0.007

   h. 0.45

2. a. $\frac{3}{10}$

   b. $\frac{1}{25}$

   c. $\frac{7}{20}$

   d. $1\frac{2}{5}$

   e. $3\frac{1}{4}$

   f. $\frac{17}{400}$

   g. $\frac{5}{8}$

   h. $\frac{14}{15}$

3. **a.** 20%
   b. 40.5%
   c. 0.6%
   d. 475%
   e. $\frac{1}{2}$%
   f. $16\frac{2}{3}$%
   g. 2.5%
   h. $133\frac{1}{3}$%
4. **a.** 25%
   b. $62\frac{1}{2}$%
   c. $4\frac{1}{6}$%
   d. 350%
5. **a.** $58.50
   b. $56.50
   c. $152.00
   d. $19.50
   e. **(1)** $232.00
      (2) $3,495.96
      (3) $446.40
      (4) $640.00
   f. $620.70
   g. **(1)** $92,958.30
      (2) $464,791.50
   h. $2,400
6. **a.** 75%
   b. 50%
   c. $37\frac{1}{2}$%
   d. 150%
   e. $28\frac{1}{2}$%
   f. 32%
   g. 51%
   h. 150%
   i. $27\frac{1}{2}$%
   j. **(1)** $33\frac{1}{3}$%
      (2) 25%
7. **a.** $500
   b. $1,417.50
   c. $700
   d. $3,240
   e. $1,142.40
   f. $188
   g. 46.7
   h. 312
   i. $102,000
   j. 685 men; 822 women
8. **a.** $14.78
   b. $113.28
9. **a.** $4.14 per $100
   b. $3,709.44

CHAPTER 8

Exercise 8–1, pages 213–214

1. 61
3. 153
5. 75
7. 81
9. 103
11. 179
13. 174
15. 125

Exercise 8–2, pages 215–216

A. 1. $57.60
   3. $302.40
   5. $1,372.00
   7. $58.80
   9. $117.69
   11. $39.11
B. 1. a. $44.69 ordinary interest
      b. $44.07 exact interest
   3. a. $188.84 ordinary interest
      b. $186.25 exact interest
   5. a. $28.67 ordinary interest
      b. $28.28 exact interest
   7. a. $77.37 ordinary interest
      b. $76.31 exact interest
C. 1. $340.65
   3. $937.50
   5. $56.32

Exercise 8–3, pages 218–219

A. 1. $3,600
   3. $3,750
B. 1. 16%
   3. 13%
C. 1. 66 days
   3. 315 days
D. 1. $6,450
   3. 16%
   5. 90 days
   7. 240 days

Exercise 8–4, page 221

1. 241
3. 89
5. 300
7. 200

9. 303

11. 305

13. 126

Exercise 8–5, page 224

A. 1. $5.80
   3. $228.67
   5. $6,390.31
   7. $1,464.83
   9. $46.13

B. 1. $112.44
   3. $100.82
   5. $96.65
   7. $586.68
   9. $83.49

C. 1. $31.67
   3. $2,415.67
   5. $133.39
   7. $3,638.70

Exercise 8–6, page 230

A. 1. May 7
   3. October 15
   5. August 5
   7. July 21
   9. July 12, 1992

B. 1. August 13
   3. January 3
   5. May 8
   7. November 15

Exercise 8–7, page 233

A. 1. a. Due date: May 5
     b. Maturity value: $900
     c. Term of discount: 50 days
     d. Bank discount: $15.00
     e. Proceeds: $885.00
   3. a. Due date: May 10
     b. Maturity value: $2,000
     c. Term of discount: 70 days
     d. Bank discount: $70.00
     e. Proceeds: $1,930.00
   5. a. Due date: November 14
     b. Maturity value: $1,875
     c. Term of discount: 66 days
     d. Bank discount: $60.16
     e. Proceeds: $1,814.84

B. 1. a. Due date: May 26
     b. Discount period: 57 days

c. Bank discount: $22.80
   d. Proceeds: $877.20
3. a. Due date: June 8
   b. Discount period: 77 days
   c. Bank discount: $103.90
   d. Proceeds: $3,944.10
5. a. Due date: September 18
   b. Discount period: 60 days
   c. Bank discount: $45.00
   d. Proceeds $2,655.00

C. 1. $484.33
   3. $3,507.60
   5. $6,091.75

Exercise 8–8, pages 234–235

A. 1. a. Due date: July 16
     b. Maturity value: $615.00
     c. Discount period: 42 days
     d. Bank discount: $8.61
     e. Proceeds: $606.39
   3. a. Due date: June 21
     b. Maturity value: $3,065.67
     c. Discount period: 82 days
     d. Bank discount: $111.73
     e. Proceeds: $2,953.94
   5. a. Due date: December 24
     b. Maturity value: $4,918.40
     c. Discount period: 170 days
     d. Bank discount: $429.68
     e. Proceeds: $4,488.72

B. 1. $854.76
   3. $4,785.00
   5. $1,796.57
   7. a. $116.97
     b. $5,731.68
   9. a. $55.65
     b. $1,534.35
  11. $1,748.91

Exercise 8–9, page 238

1. $687.70
3. $1,139.95
5. $989.07
7. a. $3,796.19
   b. $3,745.68

Review Problems, pages 238–240

1. a. 107 days
   b. 234 days

2. **a.** $1,817.81
   b. $11,506.25
   c. $3,538.00
   d. (1) $470.93
      (2) $470.64
3. **a.** $P = \$5,000$
   b. $R = 8\%$
   c. $T = 60$ days
   d. $T = 2.5$ years
4. **a.** 154 days
   b. 199 days
5. **a.** $11.63
   b. $141.11
6. **a.** July 8
   b. October 26
   c. January 4
   d. June 24
7. **a. (1)** $11.25
      (2) $438.75
   b. $821.67
   c. $2,526.33
8. **a.** $2,625.81
   b. (1) $2,340
      (2) $54.60
      (3) $2,285.40
9. **a.** $1,345.38
   b. $1,328.42

CHAPTER 9

Exercise 9–1, pages 244–245

A. 1. a. $1,216.70 Compound Amount
   b. $416.70 Compound Interest
3. a. $2,670.94 Compound Amount
   b. $670.94 Compound Interest
5. a. $20,926.67 Compound Amount
   b. $5,926.65 Compound Interest
B. 1. $73,371.31
3. a. $504.00
   b. $577.85

Exercise 9–2, page 249

A. 1. a. $2,614.59 Compound Amount
   b. $2,274.59 Compound Interest
3. a. $17,627.19 Compound Amount
   b. $10,627.19 Compound Interest

5. a. $2,704.42 Compound Amount
   b. $884.42 Compound Interest
7. a. $15,392.28 Compound Amount
   b. $9,092.28 Compound Interest
B. 1. a. $12,746.15
   b. $10,346.15
3. a. $1,202.06
   b. $1,895.80
   c. $3,126.61
5. $33,155.26
7. 11%

Exercise 9–3, pages 251–252

A. 1. 1.1486855
3. 1.718186
5. 1.4257607
7. 9.6462911
9. 3.0054325
11. 178.83379
B. 1. a. $752.47
   b. $2.47
3. a. $4,833.24
   b. $33.24
5. a. $29,490.15
   b. $190.15
7. a. $235,474.27
   b. $3,474.27
C. 1. $10,057.66
3. $7,556.26
5. a. $15,195.32
   b. $15,198.75
   c. Bank B

Exercise 9–4, pages 254–255

A. 1. 18.81%
3. 16.99%
5. 19.56%
7. 6.17%
B. 1. 15.56%
3. 20.40%
5. 13.24%
7. 9.38%
9. 8.31%
C. 1. 11.57%
3. a. 14.93%
   b. (a) is better
5. a. 8.24%
   b. 8.03%
   c. (a) is better

7. Smaller than

9. a. $7,258.65
  b. 6.17%
  c. 7.25%

Exercise 9-5, page 259

A. 1. a. $704.37 Present Value
  b. $1,295.63 Compound Discount
  3. a. $62.40 Present Value
  b. $412.60 Compound Discount
  5. a. $204.12 Present Value
  b. $775.88 Compound Discount
  7. a. $765.60 Present Value
  b. $7,529.40 Compound Discount
B. 1. a. $12,044.79
  b. $11,955.21
  3. $16,487.80
  5. $12,636.86
  7. $58,893.76

Exercise 9-6, pages 261–264

A. 1. $99,197.86
  3. $18,910.39
  5. $176,158.42
  7. $423,849.79
B. 1. $7,908.48
  3. $9,942.04
  5. $9,775.91
  7. $1,902.38

Exercise 9-7, pages 265–266

A. 1. $70,469.72
  3. $24,619.93
  5. $25,477.48
  7. $7,338.27
B. 1. $206,458.57
  3. $37,973.96
  5. $262,612.59
  7. $26,755.72

Exercise 9-8, pages 271–272

A. 1. $991.78
  3. $54,474.03
  5. $118,699.82
B. 1. $70,289.20
  3. $9,811.06
  5. $8,310.62

C. 1. $265,313.10
  3. $318,214.59
  5. $13,300.90
  7. $1,063.17

Exercise 9-9, pages 278–279

A. 1. $3,074.65
  3. $6,208.58
  5. $2,235.14
B. 1. $2,359.82
  3. $2,843.76
  5. $23,670.31
C. 1. $47,058.98
  3. $2,556.06
  5. $2,069.53
  7. $29,685.05

Review Problems, pages 279–280

1. $2,251.02
2. $24,465.28
3. a. $23,302.42
  b. $23,307.63
  c. Bank B is better
4. a. $9,837.27
  b. 6.96%
  c. 7.14%
5. a. $41,838.69
  b. $11,161.31
6. $9,024.16
7. $68,316.22
8. a. $5,488,346
  b. $967.40
9. a. $24,563.25
  b. $782.09

CHAPTER 10

Exercise 10-1, page 283

A. 1. $354.00
  3. $925.00
  5. $687.50
  7. $937.50
  9. $2,025.00
B. 1. $466.56
  3. $312.50
  5. $465.60

Exercise 10-2, pages 285–286

A. 1. $183
   3. $558.45
   5. $765.00
B. 1. a. $196.00
     b. $233.01
   3. a. $275.60
     b. $351.11
   5. a. $394.80
     b. $451.20
C. 1. $86.43
   3. $288.20
   5. $274.11

Exercise 10-3, pages 288–289

A. 1. $12,000 Eastern's Share
     $18,000 Federal's Share
   3. $6,500 Eastern's Share
     $26,000 Federal's Share
     $13,000 Globe's Share
   5. $8,666.67 Eastern's Share
     $13,000 Federal's Share
     $17,333.33 Globe's Share
B. 1. $33,000
   3. $57,777.78
   5. $450,000
C. 1. $540,000
   3. $13,000 Company A's Share
     $39,000 Company B's Share
     $52,000 Company C's Share
   5. $72,000

Exercise 10-4, pages 292–293

A. 1. $931.00
   3. $171.59
   5. $320.20
   7. $56.52
B. 1. $1,125.00
   3. $58.14
   5. a. $11,000
     b. $20,600
     c. $34,700
     d. $99,400
   7. $1,762.50

Exercise 10-5, pages 298–299

A. 1. a. $2,195.80
     b. $4,809.20

     c. 16 years 87 days
   3. a. $9,267.90
     b. $20,923.20
     c. 33 years 25 days
   5. a. $15,020.40
     b. $28,260
     c. 19 years 205 days
B. 1. $265.60
   3. $234.00
   5. $350.70
   7. $218.40
C. 1. a. $10,503.62
     b. $5,503.62
   3. $10,266.48
   5. $289.80
   7. $1,181.60
   9. a. $239,040
     b. More: $39,040

Exercise 10-6, pages 305–307

A. 1. $96
   3. $206
   5. $591
B. 1. $207
   3. $85
   5. $205
C. 1. $108
   3. $778
   5. $234
   7. a. $15,000
     b. $1,485

Review Problems, pages 307–308

1. $84.38
2. a. $99.26
   b. $1,556.88
3. a. $130,000
   b. $6,400 Company A's share
     $12,800 Company B's share
   c. $21,951.22
4. $1,007.50
5. a. (1) $7,361.28
     (2) $14,657.40
   b. $428
6. a. $331
   b. $442
   c. $731

CHAPTER 11

Exercise 11–1, pages 311–312

A. 1. Total Hours: 39; Gross Pay, $421.98
  3. Total Hours: 40; Gross Pay: $269.60
  5. Total Hours: $35\frac{1}{2}$; Gross Pay: $292.88

B. 1. Regular Hours: $39\frac{1}{2}$; Overtime Hours: 0
  Regular Wages: $381.18
  Overtime Wages: 0; Gross Pay: $381.18
  3. Regular Hours: 40; Overtime Hours: $4\frac{1}{2}$
  Regular Wages: $430.40
  Overtime Wages: $72.63
  Gross Pay: $503.03
  5. Regular Hours: 40; Overtime Hours: 2
  Regular Wages: $612.00
  Overtime Wages: $45.90
  Gross Pay: $657.90

C. 1. Regular Hours: 37; Overtime Hours: 0
  Regular Wages: $365.19
  Overtime Wages: 0; Gross Pay: $365.19
  3. Regular Hours: 45; Overtime Hours: 5
  Regular Wages: $619.20
  Overtime Wages: $34.40
  Gross Pay: $653.60
  5. Regular Hours: 43; Overtime Hours: 3
  Regular Wages: $729.71
  Overtime Wages: $25.46
  Gross Pay: $755.17

D. 1. Regular Hours: 40; Overtime Hours: 2
  Regular Wages: $392.00
  Overtime Wages: $29.40
  Gross Pay: $421.40
  3. Regular Hours: 40; Overtime Hours: 5
  Regular Wages: $538.00
  Overtime Wages: $100.88
  Gross Pay: $638.88
  5. Regular Hours: 38; Overtime Hours: 6
  Regular Wages: $399.00
  Overtime Wages: $94.50
  Gross Pay: $493.50

Exercise 11–2, page 313

1. Total Pieces: 351; Gross Pay: $315.90
3. Total Pieces: 403; Gross Pay: $306.28
5. Total Pieces: 352; Gross Pay: $348.48
7. Total Pieces: 347; Gross Pay: $284.54
9. Total Pieces: 397; Gross Pay: $337.45

Exercise 11–3, pages 316–317

A. 1. Monday: $114.75; Tuesday: $141.05
  Wednesday: $154.70; Thursday: $108.65
  Friday: $119.00; Gross Pay: $638.15
  3. Monday: $114.75; Tuesday: $132.00
  Wednesday: $121.13; Thursday: $50.25
  Friday: $116.88; Gross Pay: $535.01
  5. Monday: $156.98; Tuesday: $121.13
  Wednesday: $71.18; Thursday: $85.50
  Friday: $150.15; Gross Pay: $584.94

B. 1. Monday: $91.20; Tuesday: $76.00
  Wednesday: $91.20; Thursday: $91.20
  Friday: $91.20; Gross Pay: $440.80
  3. Monday: $125.00; Tuesday: $125.00
  Wednesday: $100.00; Thursday: $100.00
  Friday: $125.00; Gross Pay: $575.00
  5. Monday: $105.60; Tuesday: $105.60
  Wednesday: $105.60; Thursday: $105.60
  Friday: $105.60; Gross Pay: $528.00

C. 1. Monday: $97.40; Tuesday: $103.24
  Wednesday: $95.94; Thursday: $91.20
  Friday: $95.21; Gross Pay: $482.99
  3. Monday: $102.00; Tuesday: $121.23
  Wednesday: $102.00; Thursday: $102.00
  Friday: $111.33; Gross Pay: $538.56
  5. Monday: $119.81; Tuesday: $131.79
  Wednesday: $115.20; Thursday: $126.26
  Friday: $132.71; Gross Pay: $625.77

Exercise 11–4, page 319

1. $497.07
3. $207.44
5. $2,728.47
7. a. February: $585
  b. March: $2,340

Exercise 11–5, pages 329–330

A. 1. FICA: $26.88
  Federal Income Tax: $32.00
  Total Deductions: $69.64
  Net Pay: $306.36
  3. FICA: $31.09
  Federal Income Tax: $65.00
  Total Deductions: $110.69
  Net Pay: $324.10
  5. FICA: $29.73
  Federal Income Tax: $27.00
  Total Deductions: $79.98
  Net Pay: $335.88

7. FICA: $28.84
   Federal Income Tax: $56.00
   Total Deductions: $134.94
   Net Pay: $268.41
9. FICA: $39.12
   Federal Income Tax: $52.00
   Total Deductions: $91.12
   Net Pay: $456.08
B. 201. FICA: $24.18
   Federal Income Tax: $10.00
   Total Deductions: $45.58
   Net Pay: $292.62
203. FICA: $41.01
   Federal Income Tax: $146.00
   Total Deductions: $187.01
   Net Pay: $510.79
205. FICA: 0
   Federal Income Tax: $54.00
   Total Deductions: $79.25
   Net Pay: $585.25
C. 1. a. $2,043.26
      b. $1,937.11
      c. $848.67
   3. $65.52
   5. $724.33
   7. $66.46

Exercise 11–6, pages 331–332

1. | | Net Pay | $20 | $10 | $5 | $1 |
    |---|---|---|---|---|---|
    | Totals: | $3,130.95 | 151 | 6 | 5 | 21 |

	50¢	25¢	10¢	5¢	1¢
Totals:	5	6	5	5	20

Exercise 11–7, pages 332–333

1. $201.25
3. $146,775
5. $254,977.50
7. $3,261.00
9. $700
11. $17,670

Exercise 11–8, pages 335–336

A.	Commission Amount	Total Charges	Net Proceeds
1.	$56.00	$ 56.00	$ 744.00
3.	62.00	114.97	1,125.03
5.	50.36	107.19	564.31

B. 1. $13,444.35
   3. $46,329.24
   5. $19,334.77

Exercise 11–9, pages 338–339

A.	Commission Amount	Gross Cost
1.	$ 72.80	$1,112.80
3.	451.00	9,486.42
5.	50.46	775.50

B. 1. $1,563.01
   3. $24,870
   5. $7,349.30

Review Problems, pages 339–341

1. a. $455.40
   b. $512.58
2. $350
3. a. (1) $53.76
      (2) $73.78
      (3) $78.74
   b. (1) $60.20
      (2) $72.24
      (3) $72.24
   c. (1) $71.97
      (2) $68.25
      (3) $68.25
      (4) $73.21
4. $1,495.60
5. a. (1) $27.44
      (2) $34.00
      (3) $322.33
   b. $510.83
6. | | Net Pay | $20 | $10 | $5 | $1 |
    |---|---|---|---|---|---|
    | Totals: | $1,059.84 | 51 | 2 | 2 | 8 |

	50¢	25¢	10¢	5¢	1¢
Totals:	2	1	4	2	9
7. a. $1,679,474
   b. 4.5%
   c. $4,400
   d. $266,000
8. $840.90
9. $3,659.50

CHAPTER 12

Exercise 12–1, pages 347–348

A. 1. $240.16
3. $48.00
5. $644.00

B.
	Amount of Discount	Net Price
1.	$ 80.00	$160.00
3.	104.00	216.00
5.	168.00	432.00
7.	595.20	604.80
9.	374.50	465.50

C. 1. $486
3. $84.00
5. a. Uniray Company
   b. $1.60

Exercise 12–2, pages 349–351

A. 1. a. 60%
   b. 40%
3. a. $66\frac{2}{3}\%$
   b. $33\frac{1}{3}\%$
5. a. 48%
   b. 52%
7. a. 54%
   b. 46%
9. a. 45%
   b. 55%
11. a. $60\frac{3}{4}\%$
    b. $39\frac{1}{4}\%$

B.
	Equivalent Rate	Amount of Discount	Net Price
1.	$14\frac{1}{2}\%$	$ 103.53	$ 610.47
3.	$28\frac{3}{4}\%$	181.13	448.87
5.	52%	292.50	270.00
7.	40%	1,828.80	2,743.20
9.	46%	3,277.50	3,847.50
11.	27.325%	1,475.55	3,924.45

C. 1. Second offer is better.
3. $2,494.32
5. a. $1,170.00
   b. $280.80
   c. $877.50
   d. $1,310.40

Exercise 12–3, pages 354–355

A.
	Cash Discount	Net Amount
1.	$12.40	$ 607.60
3.	2.08	205.92
5.	6.72	665.28
7.	88.40	8,751.60
9.	0	256.60

B.
	Cash Discount	Net Amount
1.	$ 14.40	$ 705.60
3.	32.52	780.48
5.	0	721.40
7.	0	406.30
9.	66.58	6,591.42
11.	190.03	9,311.51

C. 1. $351.62
3. a. September 10
   b. $654.15
5. a. September 9
   b. $664.96
7. $1,502.43

Exercise 12–4, pages 359–361

A.
	Amount Credited	Balance Due
1.	$ 127.55	$ 72.45
3.	206.19	193.81
5.	156.25	93.75
7.	1,263.16	136.84
9.	1,595.74	854.26

B. 1. a. $424.10
   b. $432.50
3. $588.00
5. $827.28
7. $8.64
9. a. $1,237.11
   b. $816.33
   c. $568.06
11. $77.07

Exercise 12–5, page 362

1. $19.32
3. $53.87

Exercise 12–6, page 364

A. 1. $9.00
   3. $38.00
   5. $86.00
   7. $112.20
   9. $187.84
  11. $682.72
B. 1. $140.25
   3. $1,071.05
   5. $343.20

Exercise 12–7, pages 365–366

A. 1. $19.50
   3. $93.80
   5. $478.60
   7. $145.20
   9. $576.00
  11. $985.90
B. 1. $18.60
   3. $144
   5. $80
   7. $320

Exercise 12–8, page 367

A. 1. a. Markon: $22.50
     b. Rate: $33\frac{1}{3}\%$
   3. a. Loss: $15.00
     b. Rate: 20%
   5. a. Markon: $4.16
     b. Rate: 40%
   7. a. Markon: $34.65
     b. Rate: 35.5%
   9. a. Loss: $43.90
     b. Rate: 25.5%
  11. a. Loss: $14.00
     b. Rate: 7%
B. 1. 70%
   3. $66\frac{2}{3}\%$
   5. $6.00
   7. 100%

Exercise 12–9, pages 368–369

A. 1. $105
   3. $175
   5. $400.80
   7. $87.19
   9. $117.00
  11. $3,445

B. 1. $36.60
   3. $6.53
   5. 50%
   7. $12
   9. $380.63

Exercise 12–10, pages 370–371

A. 1. $16.20
   3. $40.53
   5. $123.95
   7. $50.40
   9. $53.65
  11. $104.50
B. 1. $61.07
   3. a. $54.43
     b. $44.53
   5. $8
   7. $1,190
   9. $101.84

Exercise 12–11, pages 372–373

A. 1. a. Markon: $10
     b. Rate: 25%
   3. a. Loss: $70
     b. Rate: 20%
   5. a. Markon: $630
     b. Rate: 23.1%
   7. a. Markon: $60
     b. Rate: 44.4%
   9. a. Markon: $125
     b. Rate: 50%
  11. a. Loss: $400
     b. Rate: 30.8%
B. 1. 35%
   3. 26.6%
   5. $16\frac{2}{3}\%$
   7. 29.8%
   9. $240

Exercise 12–12, pages 374–375

A. 1. 17%
   3. 35%
   5. 19%
   7. 30%
   9. 25%
  11. 46%
B. 1. 14.9%
   3. 122.2%
   5. 22%

7. 81.8%

9. 28.2%

11. 100%

C. 1. $33\frac{1}{3}$%

3. 20.6%

5. 26.5%

Exercise 12–13, pages 377–378

A. 1. Selling Price: $45; Marked Price: $50

3. Selling Price: $36; Marked Price: $48

5. Selling Price: $6,000; Marked Price: $8,000

B. 1. Original Selling Price: $64
List Price: $80
New Selling Price: $57.60
Additional Discount Rate: 10%

3. Original Selling Price: $525
List Price: $750
New Selling Price: $488.25
Additional Discount Rate: 7%

5. Original Selling Price: $1,800
List Price: $2,250
New Selling Price: $1,647
Additional Discount Rate: 8.5%

C. 1. $800

3. $54

Review Problems, pages 378–380

1. a. $1,450.10

b. $15

2. a. 46.45%

b. (1) 56.8%

(2) (a) $30.67

(b) $21.30

(c) $36.92

(d) $56.09

3. a. $613.04

b. $2,623.50

c. (1) May 10

(2) $2,347.10

d. $2,619

4. a. $1,869.84

b. $1,413.31

c. $756.55

d. $145.92

5. a. $1,746

b. $26.84

6. a. $187

b. $654.50

7. a. $140,000

b. $196,000

8. a. $72

b. 50%

9. $243

10. $66.40

11. 9%

12. 38.9%

13. $130

CHAPTER 13

Exercise 13–1, pages 387–389

1. a. $5.19

b. $229.60

3. a. $14.96

b. $914.98

5. a. $0.50

b. $7.74

7. $238.98

9. $158.35

11. $305.30

13. a. $509.24

b. $7.64

15. a. $330.53

b. $7.12

c. $378.79

17. a. $12.54

b. $15.35

c. $807.90

19. a. $14.46

b. $14.05

c. $1,012.66

Exercise 13–2, pages 391–392

1. $95.36

3. 92.00

5. $114.00

7. $75.60

9. $58.95 (first 17 payments), $59.01 (last payment)

11. $328.51

Exercise 13–3, pages 395–396

1. 666

3. $\frac{63}{78}$

5. $\frac{15}{78}$

7. $\frac{36}{300}$

9. $21.27

11. $48.46

13. $194.13

15. **a.** $650
    b. $4,900

17. **a.** $216
    b. $94.40
    c. $27
    d. $445

19. **a.** $397.50
    b. $1,063.10
    c. $6,489.40

Exercise 13-4, pages 402–403

A. **1.** $190.46
    3. $16.34
    5. $358.64
    7. $1,149.96
    9. $4,039.18

B. **1.** **a.** $681.53
        b. $789.92
        c. $902.83
        d. $1,019.17
        e. $1,138.08

    3. **a.** $1,371.69
        b. $1,398.52
        c. $1,452.76
        d. $1,568.90
        e. $1,851.46

    5. $186.40

    7. **a.** $380.41
        b. Payment Number 1:
        Monthly Payment: $380.41
        Payment on Interest: $285.83
        Payment on Principal: $94.58
        Principal Balance: $24,405.42
        Payment Number 2:
        Monthly Payment $380.41
        Payment on Interest: $284.73
        Payment on Principal: $95.68
        Principal Balance: $24,309.74
        Payment Number 3:
        Monthly Payment: $380.41
        Payment on Interest: $283.61
        Payment on Principal: $96.80
        Principal Balance: $24,212.94

Payment Number 4:
  Monthly Payment: $380.41
  Payment on Interest: $282.48
  Payment on Principal: $97.93
  Principal Balance: $24,115.01
Payment Number 5:
  Monthly Payment: $380.41
  Payment on Interest: $281.34
  Payment on Principal: $99.07
  Principal Balance: $24,015.94

Exercise 13-5, pages 416–417

1. **a.** $500
   b. $80
   c. 28.25%

3. **a.** $3,330
   b. $899.10
   c. 24%

5. **a.** $6,650
   b. $3,325
   c. 17.25%

7. **a.** $144
   b. 21.46%

9. 26.42%

11. $212.63

13. $162.22

15. $154.48

17. 15.55%

19. 34.70%

Review Problems, pages 417–418

1. **a.** **(1)** $3.51
       (2) $179.13
   b. **(1)** $826.98
       (2) $14.47
   c. **(1)** $416.81
       (2) $8.88
       (3) $486.68

2. **a.** $34.80
   b. $84.00

3. **a.** $371.94
   b. $2,609.16

4. $6,331.48

5. **a.** 15.25%
   b. 25.20%
   c. $224.57
   d. 13.91%

CHAPTER 14

Exercise 14–1, pages 424–426

1. Assembling: $146,000
   Finishing: $51,100
   Office: $21,900
3. $3,677.70
5. 75%
7. a. 70%
   b. $440.30
9. a. 15%
   b. $15,255
11. Appliances, 17%: $6,290.00, $4,165.00, $2,518.92, $1,179.46
    Carpeting, 15%: $5,550.00, $3,675.00, $2,222.58, $1,040.70
    Draperies, 10%: $3,700.00, $2,450.00, $1,481.72, $693.80
    Furniture, 50%: $18,500.00, $12,250.00, $7,408.60, $3,469.00
    Offices, 8%: $2,960.00, $1,960.00, $1,185.38, $555.04

Exercise 14–2, pages 430–431

1. $3.30
3. a. $39,600
   b. $41,400
   c. $36,550
5. $543.50
7. $1,031.45

Exercise 14–3, pages 433–434

1. a. $98,000
   b. $43,000
   c. $231,400
   d. $150,140
3. $195,000
5. $19,500
7. $19,080

Exercise 14–4, pages 437–438

1. $206,400
3. a. $142,000
   b. $320,000
5. $925,950
7. a. $480,000
   b. $600,000
   c. $300,000

Exercise 14–5, pages 441–443

A. 1. $480
   3. $3,400
   5. $1,180
B. 1. $8,350
   3. First Year:
        Annual Depreciation: $1,200
        Accumulated Depreciation: $1,200
        Book Value: $7,150
      Second Year:
        Annual Depreciation: $1,200
        Accumulated Depreciation: $2,400
        Book Value: $5,950
      Third Year:
        Annual Depreciation: $1,200
        Accumulated Depreciation: $3,600
        Book Value: $4,750
      Fourth Year:
        Annual Depreciation: $1,200
        Accumulated Depreciation: $4,800
        Book Value: $3,550
      Fifth Year:
        Annual Depreciation: $1,200
        Accumulated Depreciation: $6,000
        Book Value: $2,350
      Sixth Year:
        Annual Depreciation: $1,200
        Accumulated Depreciation: $7,200
        Book Value: $1,150
C. 1. $8,600
   3. $4,550
   5. a. $1,000
      b. $2,000
   7. 9 years
   9. a. $325
      b. $1,950

Exercise 14–6, page 444

1. $0.175
3. a. $460
   b. $11,040
5. First Year: $912
   Second Year: $1,104
   Third Year: $1,152
   Fourth Year: $864
   Fifth Year: $768

Exercise 14–7, pages 445–446

A. 1. $1,000
   3. $220

Answers to Odd-Numbered Problems

5. $64

B. 1. First Year: $2,200
Second Year: $1,650
Third Year: $1,100
Fourth Year: $550

3. $305.56

Exercise 14–8, pages 447–448

1. First Year: $12,000
Second Year: $10,500

3. $1,800

5. $2,572.50

Exercise 14–9, pages 452–453

A. 1. $327
3. $1,500
5. $17,863
7. $18,000
9. $12,500
11. $24,548

B. 1. a. $600
b. $960
c. $1,440
3. $1,249
5. a. $21,200
b. $38,160
c. $30,528
7. a. $7,956
b. $27,273
c. $714,771
9. a. $436,508
b. $952,381
c. $952,381

Exercise 14–10, page 454

1. $775,200

3. $128,250

5. a. $8.75
b. $175,000

Review Problems, pages 455–457

1. a. $840 $1,720 $1,640 $1,680 $480
b. $69,750
c. (1) 80%
(2) $5,120
d. (1) 12%
(2) $90,000

2. a. (1) $5,778
(2) $5,880
(3) $5,745
b. $28,045

3. $220,000

4. a. $50,400
b. $112,000
c. $98,000

5. $333.33

6. a. $200
b. $5,700
c. $1,868
d. $2,564.35

7. a. $50,000
b. $41,562.50
c. $4,285.71

8. a. $30,150
b. $1,705.20
c. $29,724.17

9. a. $2,500
b. $2,400
c. $862.50
d. $992

10. a. $37.50 per M
b. $205,500

CHAPTER 15

Exercise 15–1, pages 463–465

A. 1. $120,000 Goods Available
$95,000 Cost of Goods Sold
3. $570,000 Purchases
$138,000 Ending Inventory
5. $172,000 Beginning Inventory
$548,800 Cost of Goods Sold

B. 1. $245,000 Net Sales
$134,750 Gross Profit
$29,600 Net Income
3. $1,749,300 Net Sales
$1,092,550 Cost of Goods Sold
$290,100 Net Income
5. -0- Sales Returns
$6,631,000 Gross Profit
$1,451,000 Net Income

C. 1. a. $134,860 Goods Available for Sale
b. $109,460 Cost of Goods Sold

3. **a.** $15,624,000 Cost of Goods Sold
   b. $1,663,000 Merchandise Inventory 11-1
5. $37,000
7. $45,085
9. $58,310

Exercise 15–2, pages 467–468

A. 1. $12,542
   3. $12,269
   5. $114,552
B. 1. $13,400
   3. $841,500
   5. $3,960

Exercise 15–3, pages 472–474

A. 1. $14,400 Partner A's Share of Gain
   $9,600 Partner B's Share of Gain
   3. $45,000 Partner A's Share of Gain
   $36,000 Partner B's Share of Gain
   $27,000 Partner C's Share of Gain
B. 1. $18,900 Partner A's Share of Net Income
   $31,500 Partner B's Share of Net Income
   3. $10,800 Partner A's Share of Net Income
   $21,600 Partner B's Share of Net Income
   $16,200 Partner C's Share of Net Income
C. 1. Partner A: $ 3,000 Interest
                    14,400 Remainder
                    $17,400 Total

   Partner B: $4,000 Interest
                    4,800 Remainder
                    $8,800 Total

   3. Partner A: $ 5,250.00 Interest
                    20,812.50 Remainder
                    $26,062.50 Total

   Partner B: $ 7,350.00 Interest
                    41,625.00 Remainder
                    $48,975.00 Total

   Partner C: $ 6,300.00 Interest
                    20,812.50 Remainder
                    $27,112.50 Total

D. 1. Walsh: $9,135; York: $16,965
   3. Vennard: $34,000; Waldorf: $56,000
   5. Chan: $23,733.33; Dawson: $29,666.67
   7. Novak: $25,440; Olson: $31,680
   9. Hampton: $21,510; Irving: $22,710;
      Juaraz: $23,910

Exercise 15–4, pages 477–478

1. $0.65
3. 7.7%
5. **a.** Preferred: $25
   b. Common: $4
7. **a.** Preferred: $7
   b. Common: $1.50
9. **a.** Preferred: $5.75
   b. Common: $7.15
11. **a.** Preferred: $9
   b. Common: $2.25

Review Problems, pages 479–480

1. **a.** **(1)** $992,350 Goods Available for Sale
      (2) $690,550 Cost of Goods Sold
   b. $56,330 Net Income
2. **a.** $45,850 Owner's Equity
   b. **(1)** $4,940,000
      (2) $13,300
3. **a.** $9,750 Ulster's share
      $6,500 Vanderbilt's share
   b. $23,000 Malone's share
      $18,400 Newton's share
   c. $8,710 Riva's share
      $9,750 McMurray's share
   d. $30,990 Lamar's share
      $26,910 McCook's share
4. **a.** **(1)** $97,500
      (2) $1.20
   b. **(1)** $3
      (2) $1.05

CHAPTER 16

Exercise 16–1, pages 486–488

1.	Percent
Sales	101.6
Less sales returns and allowances .	1.6
Net sales........................	100.0
Cost of goods sold	63.5
Gross profit.....................	36.5
Total operating expenses	22.7
Net income	13.8

3. Increase or Decrease*

Amount	Percent
$ 9,840	7.3
600	33.3
9,240	7.0
11,100	13.7
11,000	12.9
22,100	13.3
5,500*	6.0*
27,600	37.1
18,360*	31.7*
2,200	14.7
2,200	21.0
4,400	17.3
22,760*	70.1*

5.

Amount	Percent
$270,000	100.0
189,000	70.0
$ 81,000	30.0
56,700	21.0
$ 24,300	9.0

Exercise 16–2, pages 491–492

1. **a.** 7.9%
   b. 3.1%
   c. 1.9%
   d. 1.3%
   e. 4.6%
3.   Percent
       2.05
       1.67
       6.94
       8.23
              18.89
       2.60
       68.85
       9.65
              81.11
              100.00
       1.39
       5.77
              7.16
              36.55
              43.71
              56.29
              100.00

Exercise 16–3, pages 495–497

1. $150,000
3. **a.** $184,000
   b. $189,000
5. **a.** $697,800
   b. $265,000
7. **a.** 3.7:1
   b. 1.7:1
9. **a.** $246,000
   b. 2.18 to 1
   c. 1.03 to 1
   d. 1.17 to 1
   e. 2.16 to 1

Exercise 16–4, pages 499–500

1. 3.65
3. $21,894
5. **a.** $63,291
   b. 4.1
7. **a.** $461,785
   b. $92,357
   c. 5
9. $2,430,000

Exercise 16–5, pages 502–503

1. **a.** 9.6%
   b. 14.4%
   c. 12.0 times
3. **a.** 3%
   b. 16.3%
   c. 10.8%
   d. 25.3
   e. 14.4

Review Problems, pages 503–504

1. **a.** 77.2%
   b. 22.8%
   c. 10.9%
   d. 11.9%
2. **a.** 30.7%
   b. 69.3%
   c. 18.5%
   d. 30.2%
   e. 51.3%
3. **a.** $21,300
   b. 2.05:1
   c. 1.16:1

d. 2.46:1
e. 4.41:1
4. 6.5
5. a. (1) 2.67 to 1
   (2) 2.7 to 1
   (3) 7.17%
   (4) 10.47%
   (5) 12.9%
  b. (1) 5.88
   (2) 62.07

CHAPTER 17

Exercise 17–1, pages 512–513

1. a. 12.1
 b. 71.2
 c. 69.4
 d. 68.8
3. a. 439.6
 b. 412
 c. 499
5. a. 188
 b. 188.2
 c. 188
7.

Class	f	m	fm
26–30	12	28	336
21–25	13	23	299
16–20	4	18	72
11–15	6	13	78
6–10	4	8	32
Totals	39		817

 a. 21
 b. 23

Exercise 17–2, page 515

1. 28
3. 137
5. 58.3
7. 12.21
9. 6.71
11. 31.19

Exercise 17–3, pages 518–519

1. a. 6
 b. 7.5
3. a. 13
 b. 15.57
5. a. 26.25
 b. 6.57

Exercise 17–4, pages 525–528

1.

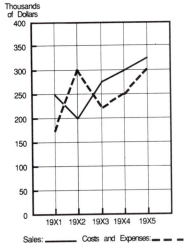

CHEROKEE CORPORATION
Sales, Costs and Expenses
for the Years 19X1–19X5

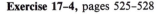

Sales: _____ Costs and Expenses: _ _ _

3.

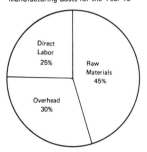

ELLSWORTH COMPANY
Manufacturing Costs for the Year 19--

Answers to Odd-Numbered Problems

5.

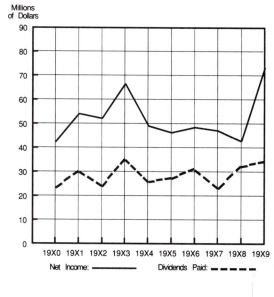

BERKSHIRE CORPORATION
Earnings and Dividends Paid 19X0–19X9

Net Income: ——————   Dividends Paid: ▬ ▬ ▬ ▬ ▬

7.

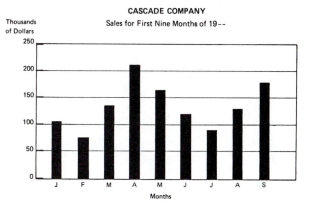

CASCADE COMPANY
Sales for First Nine Months of 19--

Months

9.

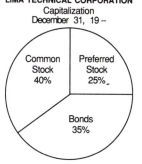

LIMA TECHNICAL CORPORATION
Capitalization
December 31, 19--

Common Stock 40%   Preferred Stock 25%   Bonds 35%

Answers to Odd-Numbered Problems

Review Problems, pages 528–529

1. **a. (1)** 61
   (2) 59
   (3) 60
   (4) 69
   b. (1) 27.7
   (2) 28
   (3) 28
2. **a.** 26
   b. 12.99
   c. 24.45
3. **a. (1)** 4.5
   (2) 5.85
   b. (1) 75.5
   (2) 8.58
4. **a.**

NEW HAVEN TRAVEL TRAILERS, INC.
Number of Units Sold, 19X0-19X9

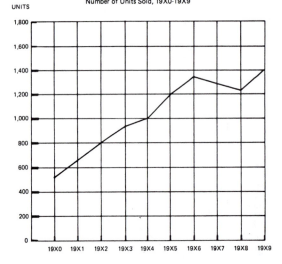

b.

BUENA VISTA COMPANY
Sales by Branch, 19--

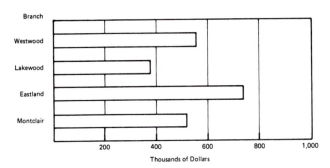

Answers to Odd-Numbered Problems

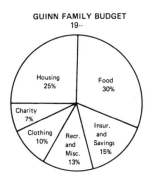

GUINN FAMILY BUDGET
19--

Housing 25%
Food 30%
Charity 7%
Clothing 10%
Recr. and Misc. 13%
Insur. and Savings 15%

CHAPTER 18

Exercise 18-1, pages 537-538

A. 1. $3,484.75
3. $65,077.75
5. $5,236.75
7. $23,273.14
9. $33,023.38
B. 1. $1,411.73
3. $3,539.00
5. $1,924.30
7. $1,970.93
9. $923.15
C. 1. $9,339.66
3. $118,828.86
5. $6,746.40
7. $20,548.05
9. $70,088.57
D. 1. $7,310.13
3. $7,458.65
5. $39,536.85
7. $3,394.93
9. $177,408.16
11. $63,794.45

Exercise 18-2, page 540

1. $5,524.75
3. $10,187.39
5. $127,595.74
7. $41,657.68
9. $4,657.89
11. $100,200.84

Exercise 18-3, pages 542-543

A. 1. **a.** $1,096.30
b. $1,346.57
c. Gain: $250.27
3. **a.** $15,324.42
b. $13,162.45
c. Loss: $2,161.97
5. **a.** $46,078.38
b. $66,092.24
c. $20,013.86
B. 1. 7.5%
3. 5.8%
5. 3.6%
7. 4.5%
C. 1. Gain: $1,340
3. Gain: 22.5%
5. $10,203

Exercise 18-4, pages 547-548

A. 1. $2,000
3. $10,300
5. $28,320
B. 1. **a.** $4,925
b. $50
c. $25
d. $5,000
3. **a.** $18,315
b. $525
c. $90
d. $18,930
5. **a.** $29,831.25
b. $1,911.67
c. $185
d. $31,927.92
C. 1. **a.** $10,125
b. $114.58
c. $100
d. $10,339.58
3. **a.** $551.25
b. $32.50
c. $30
d. $613.75
5. **a.** $53,937.50
b. No Accrued Interest
c. $500
d. $54,437.50
7. **a.** $9,630
b. $287.50
c. $120
d. $10,037.50

Exercise 18–5, page 549

1. **a.** $90,375
   b. No Accrued Interest
   c. $89,865.96
3. **a.** $3,568.75
   b. No Accrued Interest
   c. $3,518.39
5. **a.** $7,593.75
   b. $225
   c. $7,667.99
7. **a.** $4,275
   b. $74.67
   c. $4,299.24
9. **a.** $5,406.25
   b. $266.67
   c. $5,622.38

Exercise 18–6, pages 553–554

1. $2,900
3. $900

5. 15.87%
7. 5.02%
9. **a.** 30
   b. $27,825
11. $117,450
13. 11.60%
15. 10.87%

Review Problems, pages 554–555

1. $35,205.90 Total Cost
2. $1,687.03 Net Proceeds
3. **a.** $938.10 Capital Gain on Sale
   b. 6% Rate of Yield
   c. 21.5% Rate of Yield
4. $3,311.83 Total Expenditure
5. $4,037.09 Net Proceeds
6. **a.** $1,875 Annual Interest Income
   b. 18.26% Rate of Yield
   c. 12.51% Rate of Yield to Maturity

Answers to Odd-Numbered Problems

Index

I

identification, specific inventory valuation, 427
identity element, 65
improper fraction, 59
  converting, 64
income, net, 460, 462
income statement, 462, 463, 483, 484, 498
  comparative, 485, 503
  condensed comparative, 486
  horizontal analysis of, 484–486
  vertical analysis of, 483–484
incorporation:
  articles of, 465
  certificate of, 465
  charter of, 466
indemnity, 286
  amount of on fire loss, 286–289
installment buying, finding the additional cost of, 390
installment credit, 389–392
instrument, negotiable, 225
insurance, 281
  automobile, 299–307
  automobile liability, 300
  collision, 301
  fire, 282
  life, 289–299
  physical damage, 301
insurance policy, 282
  face value of, 282
insured, 281
insurer, 281
interest, 211
  compound, 212, 242–259
  compounding daily, 250-252
  computing compound, 242–245
  exact, 215
  finding
    by using a simple interest table, 221–224
    by using tables, 219–224
  formula for simple, 214–216
  nominal and effective rates of, 252–255
  ordinary, 215
  period, 243
  rate of, 211
    finding, 217
  simple, 212
  variables in formula, 216–219
interest-bearing negotiable instrument, discounting, 234

interest-earning periods in annuities, 269
interest settlement option, life insurance, 296
interpolation, 405
  of annual percentage rate, 405–406
  using to find annual percentage rate, 405–406
interval, class, 509
inventory
  average, 497
  merchandise, 421, 462
  periodic, 426
  perpetual, 426
  physical, 426
  valuation of, 426–434
inventory valuation
  at cost, 426–429
  at cost or market, whichever is lower, 429–431
  average cost, 428
  estimating, 431–434
  fifo, 428
  gross-profit method of, 431–434
  lifo, 428–429
  retail method of, 433
  specific identification, 427
investing
  in bonds, 543–554
  in stock, 533–543
invoice, 105, 358
  partial payment of, 358–359
  sales, 105

K

kelvin, 158

L

labor, direct, 423
land area, in metric terms, 158
last-in, first-out, 428–429
level-premium life insurance, 291
liability, 466
liability and medical insurance semiannual rates
  for private automobiles, 302
life, service, 439
life annuity settlement option, life insurance, 296
life insurance, 289–299
  amount settlement option, 296
  annuity certain and lifetime thereafter option, 296

Index

617

S